YEARBOOK OF AMERICAN & CANADIAN CHURCHES 2001

Previous Issues

Sixty-Ninth Issue   Annual

YEARBOOK OF AMERICAN & CANADIAN CHURCHES 2001

Edited by Eileen W. Lindner

Prepared and edited for the
National Council of the Churches of Christ in the U.S.A.
475 Riverside Drive, New York, NY 10115-0050

Published and Distributed
by Abingdon Press
Nashville

YEARBOOK OF AMERICAN & CANADIAN CHURCHES
2001

Telephone: (212) 870-2031

Fax: (212) 870-2817

E-mail: yearbook@ncccusa.org

Printed in the United States of America
ISBN 0-687-04914-8
ISSN 0195-9034
Library of Congress catalog card number
16-5726

Preparation of this *Yearbook* is an annual project of the National Council of the Churches of Christ in the United States of America.

This is the sixty-ninth edition of a yearbook that was first published in 1916. Previous editions have been entitled: *Federal Council Yearbook* (1916-1917), *Yearbook of the Churches* (1918-1925), The *Handbook of the Churches* (1927), *The New* *Handbook of the Churches* (1928), *Yearbook of American Churches* (1933-1972), and *Yearbook of American & Canadian Churches* (1973-2000).

Eileen W. Lindner	*Editor*
Marcel A. Welty	*Redevelopment & Technical Director*
Derek J. Mancini-Lander	*Assistant Editor*
Nathan Hanson	*Assistant Editor*

Editor's Preface

The *2001 Yearbook of American & Canadian Churches* is distinct in many ways from the sixty-eight editions that have preceded it, and ironically, has much in common with each of them. Foremost among the common elements throughout the nearly seventy years of publication has been the constancy of help offered with generosity of spirit from the hundreds of individuals who make the *Yearbook* possible annually. Many, but by no means all, of the persons who contribute to the accuracy of the *Yearbook* are known to its staff. At local congregations across the country tens of thousands of individuals record and report attendance, membership, and financial data to regional and/or national agencies. Those agencies, in turn, compile the data and ultimately share it with us. Ordinarily we have contact only with national level staff yet all are colleagues and are due our thanks, for without their efforts the *Yearbook* would not be possible.

As we move toward completion of the *Yearbook* each year we rely especially upon our colleagues of long-standing, Sylvia and John Ronsvalle of the empty tomb, inc. Giving generously of their time, they help us secure data that is lacking and assist in the analysis of the giving trends. Nancy Merrill of the Association of Theological Schools; Mark Duffy, Episcopal Church Archivist; and Ric Justice of Wylie, Texas have each contributed to specific sections of the *Yearbook* and deserve the thanks of both ourselves and our readers.

As we go to print with the 2001 edition Derek Mancini-Lander concludes his service as Assistant Editor of the *Yearbook*. Derek has brought uncommon skill and professionalism to his work and doubles in length his initial commitment to his tenure on the *Yearbook* staff. As he departs to new professional challenges he does so with our deepest respect, appreciation, and affection.

Features of the 2001 Yearbook

- Our special theme treatment this year explores the implications of the flow of government dollars into church sponsored programs through the "Charitable Choice" provisions of federal laws. Identifying the early trends and research related to Charitable Choice is in keeping with the *Yearbook*'s long tradition of seeking to provide careful observation of the American religious landscape and share it with our readers along with the most accurate and complete data we can obtain.
- In the "Trends and Developments, 2001" chapter, the reader will find that **Table 2** has been reintroduced. This table conveniently ranks the largest 25 churches in the U.S. by membership.
- The chapter "Emerging Electronic Church" lists in once place the Internet address of listed U.S. Religious Bodies, as well as a sampling of search resources and church data and research repositories.
- The "Directory of Selected Faith Traditions" has been updated and relocated to Directory 6, "Sources of Religion-Related Research," where it will permanently remain as a valuable research tool. This directory,

which features 'points and places of contact' for Buddhists, Hindus, Jews, and Muslims, was originally developed for the 2000 edition of the *Yearbook* as part of the theme chapter on religious pluralism.

- As a part of the *Yearbook of American and Canadian Churches* redevelopment program, we have preserved all the data from *Yearbook* editions since 1916 on a single CD-ROM. While this has been a time consuming task this new product makes available data from the entire corpus of the 68 years of the *Yearbook*. To obtain information on cost and how to order, visit our website at www.ncccusa.org/yearbook.

We hope and trust the *2001 Yearbook* will distinguish itself for the reader through the presentation of data and through careful analysis.

Eileen W. Lindner
Editor

Contents

I

PERSPECTIVES ON AMERICA'S RELIGIOUS LANDSCAPE

Trends & Developments, 2001

The long delayed conclusion of the 2000 U.S. Presidential election has served as a national object lesson in the many difficulties inherent in numerical record keeping. Moreover, our protracted national election process, with its numerous counts and recounts, particularly in Florida, remind us that few "counting" processes are devoid of broader meaning and significance. Whether it is presidential ballots or church membership at stake, perceptions and intent help shape the outcomes. Error is easily introduced and only with great persistence removed from final tabulations, especially in so vast a nation as this one. Happily the outcomes of church membership counts do not bring with them the magnitude of consequence represented by a presidential election. Nonetheless, for students of the American religious scene, such data are of significance. The tables that follow have been developed with care, albeit with data collected by innumerable sources, some quite skilled and others less so.

Longitudinal Membership

Table 1 offers a longitudinal view of the aggregate growth in membership of the churches reporting through the *Yearbook of American & Canadian Churches*. The continuation of this data in 1999 shows no remarkable change. Indeed it is continued stable church membership figures that makes the U.S. affiliation patterns unique. While religious pluralism continues to grow at the close of the millenium, the Christian membership patterns continue to account for a majority of those living in the United States.

Church Membership Ranking

Table 2 provides a schedule of the ranking of the 25 largest churches in the U.S. This table helps address one of the most frequently asked questions by the press and by sociologists and other researchers. In earlier years this table was a regular feature of the *Yearbook* and is reintroduced for the convenience of readers, saving them from the task of compiling this ranking from individual data reported elsewhere.

Patterns of Membership Gains and Losses

Table 3 provides a four-year glimpse of the membership patterns of selected large churches at century end. These ten churches were selected in order to permit the reader to view the short term membership patterns of churches from across the theological spectrum. The raw numbers of membership gain or loss are reported here as well as the percentage change for each church in each year. The short term of four years should signal the need for real caution in drawing

Table 1
INCLUSIVE MEMBERSHIP 1890–1999

Year	Membership	Source	Year	Membership	Source
1890	41,699,342	CRB	1965	124,682,422	YBAC
1906	35,068,058	CRB	1966	125,778,656	YBAC
1916	41,926,852	CRB	1967	126,445,110	YBAC
1926	54,576,346	CRB	1968	128,469,636	YBAC
1931	59,268,764	CH	1969	128,505,084	YBAC
1932	60,157,392	CH	1970	131,045,053	YBAC
1933	60,812,624	CH	1971	131,389,642	YBAC
1934	62,007,376	CH	1972	131,424,564	YBAC
1935	62,678,177	CH	1973	131,245,139	YBAC
1936	55,807,366	CRB	1974	131,871,743	YBACC
1936	63,221,996	CH	1975	131,012,953	YBACC
1937	63,848,094	CH	1976	131,897,539	YBACC
1938	64,156,895	YBAC	1977	131,812,470	YBACC
1940	64,501,594	YBAC	1978	133,388,776	YBACC
1942	68,501,186	YBAC	1979	133,469,690	YBACC
1944	72,492,699	YBAC	1980	134,816,943	YBACC
1945	71,700,142	CH	1981	138,452,614	YBACC
1946	73,673,182	CH	1982	139,603,059	YBACC
1947	77,386,188	CH	1983	140,816,385	YBACC
1948	79,435,605	CH	1984	142,172,138	YBACC
1949	81,862,328	CH	1985	142,926,363	YBACC
1950	86,830,490	YBAC	1986	142,799,662	YBACC
1951	88,673,005	YBAC	1987	143,830,806	YBACC
1952	92,277,129	YBAC	1988	145,383,739	YBACC
1953	94,842,845	YBAC	1989	147,607,394	YBACC
1954	97,482,611	YBAC	1990	156,331,704	YBACC
1955	100,162,529	YBAC	1991	156,629,918	YBACC
1956	103,224,954	YBAC	1992	156,557,746	YBACC
1957	104,189,678	YBAC	1993	153,127,045	YBACC
1958	109,557,741	YBAC	1994	158,218,427	YBACC
1959	112,226,905	YBAC	1995	157,984,194	YBACC
1960	114,449,217	YBAC	1996	159,471,758	YBACC
1961	116,109,929	YBAC	1997	157,503,033	YBACC
1962	117,946,002	YBAC	1998*	150,105,525	YBACC
1963	120,965,238	YBAC	1999*	151,161,906	YBACC
1964	123,307,499	YBAC			

*Note: The total membership figure for this year excludes the membership of the National Baptist Convention, U.S.A., Inc., which has been included in the total membership figure of previous years.

CRB—Census of Religious Bodies, Bureau of the Census, Washington
CH—*The Christian Herald*, New York
YBAC—*Yearbook of American Churches*, New York
YBACC—*Yearbook of American and Canadian Churches*, New York

any implications from these numbers. Cautiously, however, some general findings can be considered. The decline of membership of the old "mainline" churches appears to have slowed in the case of The United Methodist Church and the Presbyterian Church (U.S.A.), while accelerating somewhat for the Evangelical Lutheran Church in America. The membership of these churches, often seen as theologically and socially progressive, had been declining at a faster rate a decade earlier. Over the same period the *rate* of growth of churches that are generally considered to be theologically and/or socially conservative seems generally to have slowed, as can be seen in the case of the first three years data for the Assemblies of God and the Southern Baptist Convention, and the four year cycle of the Church of Jesus Christ of Latter Day Saints. The inclusion of the 1999 data indicates a modest return to accelerated growth for the Assemblies of God and the Southern Baptist Convention. While the Roman

Table 2
US MEMBERSHIP DENOMINATIONAL RANKING: Largest 25 Churches*

Denomination Name	Inclusive Membership	Percent of Total Reported	Cumulative Percentage
The Catholic Church	62,391,484	41.29%	41.29%
Southern Baptist Convention	15,851,756	10.49%	51.78%
The United Methodist Church	8,377,662	5.54%	57.33%
The Church of God in Christ	5,499,875	3.64%	60.97%
Evangelical Lutheran Church in America	5,149,668	3.41%	64.38%
The Church of Jesus Christ of Latter-day Saints	5,113,409	3.38%	67.76%
Presbyterian Church (U.S.A.)	3,561,184	2.36%	70.12%
National Baptist Convention of America, Inc.	3,500,000	2.32%	72.43%
The Lutheran Church—Missouri Synod (LCMS)	2,582,440	1.71%	74.14%
Assemblies of God	2,574,531	1.70%	75.85%
Progressive National Baptist Convention, Inc.	2,500,000	1.65%	77.50%
African Methodist Episcopal Church	2,500,000	1.65%	77.50%
National Missionary Baptist Convention of America	2,500,000	1.65%	77.50%
Episcopal Church	2,317,794	1.53%	82.34%
Greek Orthodox Archdiocese of America	1,954,500	1.29%	83.64%
Pentecostal Assemblies of the World, Inc.	1,500,000	0.99%	84.63%
Churches of Christ	1,500,000	0.99%	84.63%
American Baptist Churches in the U.S.A.	1,454,388	0.96%	86.59%
United Church of Christ	1,401,682	0.93%	87.51%
African Methodist Episcopal Zion Church	1,276,662	0.84%	88.36%
Baptist Bible Fellowship International	1,200,000	0.79%	89.15%
Christian Churches and Churches of Christ	1,071,616	0.71%	89.86%
The Orthodox Church in America	1,000,000	0.66%	90.52%
Jehovah's Witnesses	990,340	0.66%	91.18%
Church of God (Cleveland, Tennessee)	870,039	0.58%	91.75%

*Although recent data from the National Baptist Convention, U.S.A. is unavailable at this time, it is thought to be one of the largest 25 churches in the U.S.

Catholic Church continues to grow in membership, over this four-year period it shows an overall downward trend in the *rate* of growth.

Financial Trends

Table 4 reports on U.S. financial data for 1999. The table reports an encouraging upturn in church giving in 1999. In the midst of the longest and strongest economic recovery in U.S. history, a jump in total giving as well as in per capita giving and benevolence giving can be observed. While the total membership for the churches reporting financial data actually declined slightly in 1999, the contributions per capita increased by approximately $20.00 per person. While this is surely a modest sum in such a booming economy, its consequence is substantial when calculated in total receipts, which grew by more than $750 million dollars (or 2.88 percent) to reach nearly $27 billion dollars. Similarly, while benevolences (that is, those funds utilized for the well-being of others) accounted for 15 percent of the total giving in 1998, in 1999 benevolences accounted for 16 percent of the total, an increase of 1 percentage point or some $150 million. All this financial news is positive and encouraging.

11

Table 3
PATTERNS OF US MEMBERSHIP CHANGE OF SELECTED LARGE CHURCHES 1996–1999

Denomination	1996 Membership Change	Percentage Change	1997 Membership Change	Percentage Change	1998 Membership Change	Percentage Change	1999 Membership Change	Percentage Change
The Catholic Church	927,460	1.54	355,855	0.58	810,522	1.30	373,048	0.60
Southern Baptist Convention	28,668	0.18	199,550	1.25	-162,158	-1.03	122,400	0.77
The United Methodist Church	-43,284	-0.51	-44,005	-0.52	-40,539	-0.48	-33,841	-0.40
Evangelical Lutheran Church in America	-9,579	-0.18	4,145	0.08	-6,830	-0.13	-28,557	-0.55
The Church of Jesus Christ of Latter-Day Saints	88,500	1.88	123,100	2.50	99,951	1.99	90,358	1.78
Presbyterian Church (U.S.A.)	-32,114	-0.88	-26,622	-0.74	-35,794	-0.99	-13,775	-0.39
The Lutheran Church—Missouri Synod	6,589	0.25	1,892	0.07	-8,632	-0.33	-11,964	-0.46
Assemblies of God	79,606	3.33	26,986	1.08	31,238	1.25	48,719	1.90
American Baptist Churches in the U.S.A.	-14,133	-0.93	2,066	0.14	2,067	0.14	-53,012	-3.64

Table 4
US FINANCIAL SUMMARIES 1993-1999

Year	Number Reporting	Full or Confirmed Members	Inclusive Members	Total Contributions	Per Capita Full or Confirmed Members	Per Capita Inclusive Members	Total Congregational Contributions
1993	52	41,842,642	46,667,687	$19,631,560,798	$469.18	$420.67	$16,152,245,431
1994	47	40,997,058	44,886,207	$15,308,625,032	$373.41	$341.05	$15,308,625,032
1995	55	43,104,555	48,115,704	$21,433,517,908	$497.24	$445.46	$17,743,597,668
1996	55	43,321,039	50,047,599	$24,970,133,464	$576.40	$498.93	$20,422,403,297
1997	58	44,804,383	49,936,836	$25,181,416,276	$562.03	$504.27	$21,212,711,615
1998	62	44,574,101	49,679,497	$26,242,626,313	$588.74	$528.24	$22,202,379,038
1999	62	44,288,906	49,196,965	$26,997,610,588	$609.58	$548.77	$22,801,548,715

Year	Per Capita Full or Confirmed Members	Per Capita Inclusive Members	Total Benevolences	Per Capita Full or Confirmed Members	Per Capita Inclusive Members	Benevolences as a Percentage of Total Contributions
1993	$386.02	$346.11	$3,481,455,047	$83.20	$74.60	18%
1994	$373.41	$341.05	$3,259,090,326	$79.50	$72.61	21%
1995	$411.64	$368.77	$3,689,920,239	$85.60	$76.69	17%
1996	$471.42	$408.06	$3,739,584,874	$86.32	$74.72	15%
1997	$473.45	$424.79	$3,968,704,661	$88.58	$79.47	16%
1998	$498.10	$446.91	$4,040,247,225	$90.64	$81.33	15%
1999	$514.84	$463.47	$4,197,087,981	$94.77	$85.31	16%

Considering Charitable Choice

Eileen W. Lindner, Editor

The primary legislative basis for federal assistance to the poor was appreciably amended with the passage of the Personal Responsibility and Work Opportunity Act of 1996. Within this new and complex law section 104 established what has become known as the "Charitable Choice" provision. At its heart this provision requires states to permit faith-based organizations (FBOs) to be eligible, along with other nonprofit organizations, to provide contracted social services. Further, the section forbids states from requiring a faith-based organization to "alter its form of internal governance or remove religious arts, icons, scripture or other symbols" as a condition for serving as a contracted provider of social services.

The *Yearbook of American & Canadian Churches* annually seeks to identify trends and developments observable within the American religious landscape. From its inception Charitable Choice has demonstrated an unusual potential to affect such trends and developments. The brief treatment of Charitable Choice which follows is intended to suggest some of the issues at stake and highlight ways in which research has begun to inform the myriad discussions that will be occasioned by the decision of FBOs to choose Charitable Choice. To that end it considers three factors relating to the Charitable Choice provision: the political climate that nurtured the development of the provision; the experiences of FBOs under the provision; and the initial research undertaken to analyze aspects of the consequences of the provision. This modest contribution to the national debate owes much to the labor of a number of investigators who have pioneered in exploring the after effects of this welfare reform provision. It is hoped it will serve to quicken and deepen interest—particularly among church agencies—in assessing the consequences, intended and otherwise, of choosing Charitable Choice.

A Peculiar Lineage

The political will to formulate and enact the Charitable Choice provision of the welfare reform law came from a somewhat unexpected quarter. As University of Arizona sociologist Mark Chaves has noted: "The Charitable Choice section of the Welfare Reform Legislation was sponsored by Senator John Ashcroft, Republican of Missouri, and initiatives inspired by this legislation have been actively promoted by prominent conservative organizations such as the Christian Coalition and The Family Research Council" (1999b; p. 843). Chaves and others have suggested that this support was motivated, at least in part, by a desire to see broader church involvement in meeting the needs of the poor as well as by an interest in "redirecting public resources to religious organizations" (1999b; p. 837).

Such potential motivating factors must be located historically in the context of discussions of welfare reform during the Newt Gingrich years in Congress. This period was marked by a concern for a private-public partnership with a resultant decrease in the overall size of governmental structures. The enduring legacy of the George H. W. Bush Administration, with its emphasis on the "Points of Light" and its unbridled enthusiasm for voluntary service, contributed more than a little to the move toward Charitable Choice. In 1996 the divisive mood in the nation made a rightward movement by the Clinton Administration a political necessity for passage of welfare reform legislation. The President was thoroughly criticized by liberal organizations over the bill as a whole, with many condemning it as punitive toward the poor. FBOs that are generally considered liberal criticized the Charitable Choice provision of the bill in particular. Mainline churches and allied religious liberty groups sounded a shrill warning concerning the possibility of Charitable Choice's corrosive impact upon the wall of church-state separation.

More than one observer has since remarked on the ironic nature of the sponsorship of and the opposition to the Charitable Choice provision. The very subset of American Christians whose life experience and theology have predisposed them to be wary of entanglement with government urged the provision's passage. Those mainline churches that have until recently enjoyed religious cultural hegemony were most persistent in their cautions concerning the dangers of public monies being expended through private sectarian channels. Thus it was, with this confusing political and ecclesial lineage, that the Charitable Choice provision became law.

Choosing Charitable Choice

The origins of the Charitable Choice provision might well have led one to predict that religious conservatives would enthusiastically give leadership to congregational participation in local social service provisions while liberal-leaning congregations demurred. However, such a prediction would be contradicted by a review of actual developments over the first four years of the provision's tenure. Moreover, it is now evident that other factors beyond church-state theory and liberal vs. conservative social thought are determinative. While to date no nationwide study has thoroughly investigated the demographic profile of all participating congregations much less examined the correlation of belief and practice, some compelling early work has been done.

Mark Chaves (1999a) concluded that larger congregations, especially those that are predominantly African American, "are most likely to seek public monies." This finding has been corroborated by the work of Arthur E. Farnsley (1999), updated through The Polis Center of Indianapolis. At least two other studies confirm and extend the findings that although many congregations provide some form of social service ministry only a small percentage do so in a manner and degree sufficient to obtain public monies and conform to the requirements pertaining thereto. Susan Grettenberger (1997), a Michigan State University investigator, studied 400 United

Methodist Churches and found the type and extent of social services provided to be limited in scope and directed particularly to specific populations. The work of Robert Wuthnow (1988), who examined linkages between church and faith-based nonprofits, found that congregations' capacities to provide social services were enhanced or even made possible only through their association with nonprofit agencies. Such agencies possess the requisite financial and administrative capability congregations often lack.

Amy L. Sherman offered an overview of the early years of implementing Charitable Choice in July 2000 (2000a). Her conclusion that opponents' worst fears about Charitable Choice have not been realized might well have been accompanied by the assertion that neither have its proponents' greatest hopes been fulfilled. The law's provisions contain potentially confusing directives concerning FBOs that only more time and greater experiential learning are likely to correct. Many observers believe that even with such evolving clarity a host of church-state implications will ultimately require attention.

Refinancing Mission

The early research that has been published gives ample evidence of the importance of careful analysis of the consequences of the Charitable Choice law. Through this provision and its aftermath local congregations—FBOs, in social science parlance—have been "discovered" by governmental agencies, philanthropic foundations and researchers alike. It is not certain that they will ever be the same again.

The investigations of Ram Cnaan and his colleagues at the University of Pennsylvania contribute much to the discussions at this point. In a superb summary of extant research Cnaan et al. (1999) present many of the implications from this major shift in governmental approach to religious based organizations. In particular Cnaan points out the lack of knowledge regarding FBOs on the part of the social work profession and calls for a new engagement across the professional disciplines of social work, clergy, researchers and governmental agencies. In a study of nearly 900 congregations in Philadelphia, Cnaan (2000a) found only 7 percent of clergy were familiar with the Charitable Choice provisions although nearly two thirds thought their congregations would be willing to apply for such funds. Mark Chaves (1999b) found three quarters of clergy unfamiliar with the Charitable Choice provisions in the law; however, only about 36 percent of his respondents expressed a willingness on the part of their congregations to apply to use such governmental funds. The disparity in the findings of Chaves and Cnaan may be attributable to several factors, especially methods of sampling, geographical spread, and difference in timeframe.

More significant than research methodology is the focus of the studies, namely, the willingness and capacity of local congregations to respond to social needs. Although most churches take pride in their commitment to serve the indigent at their doorstep they lack the capacity for sustained work with larger numbers of persons on an indeterminate basis. The present research points up the need for government planners to take cognizance of these congregational realities when projecting the ultimate ability of FBOs to provide services. In 1998, the scope of Charitable Choice was extended to include community services block grants and a broad range of governmental programs, with further expansion projected. Governmental expectations may well outstrip FBOs willingness and capacity for such service.

A number of conferences called either by governmental or religious organizations have sought to sharpen the national debate concerning Charitable Choice. At New York's Riverside Church conference HUD Secretary Andrew Cuomo enthusiastically announced the increase in HUD assistance administered by FBOs to $1 billion in 2001. At the same conference the Reverend Calvin O. Butts, Pastor of New York's Abyssinian Baptist Church, noted the difficult balancing act churches face when they try to carry out community ministries within the bounds of governmental programs. Given Abyssinian's extensive involvement in such ministries, Reverend Butts' cautions should be heeded by both FBOs and governmental agencies.

Putting Faith in Faith Based Organizations

The changes wrought by the Charitable Choice provision are apt to have long-term consequences for governmental agencies, FBOs, and the poor themselves for some time to come. Careful longitudinal research should be initiated to gauge the consequences that may result from this public-private partnership. In addition, research should be designed and implemented to shed light on the extent of changes in church-state relationships that may occur.

The *Yearbook of American & Canadian Churches* believes the national debate concerning Charitable Choice will best be served by sound research. Among other elements that warrant study are the following:

- A further examination and measurement of the willingness and capacity of local FBOs to provide services, including identification of FBOs by socio-economic status, geographical distribution, and faith tradition.
- Study of FBOs that begin and later cease to provide contracted services.
- Financial analysis of FBOs providing services (pre/post).
- Longitudinal comparative studies of clients served at/by FBOs and those receiving services in traditional settings.
- Pre/post Charitable Choice studies of outcomes of FBO sponsored programs that are not eligible for funding. Do such programs increase, decrease, or remain constant?
- Close identification and examination of church state relationships and case law arising thereunto.

Such research and the studies presently underway will contribute much to our national debate in seeking to provide the most effective services. It will also inform churches and other FBOs as they consider Charitable Choice within the larger context of religious faithfulness.

Bibliography

American Jewish Congress 2000. "AJ Congress and Texas Civil Rights Project Challenge Texas 'Charitable Choice' Program, 'Permeated' with Christianity, Violating Separation of Church and State." Press release, New York, July 24, 2000.

Ammerman, Nancy. *Congregation and Community.* New Brunswick, NJ: Rutgers University Press, 1997.

Chaves, Mark. "Congregations' Social Service Activities." *Charting Civil Society.* Washington, DC: The Urban Institute, 1999a.

————. "Religious congregations and welfare reform: Who will take advantage of charitable choice?" *American Sociological Review,* 64:836-846, 1999b.

Cnaan, Ram A. *Keeping Faith in the City: Survey Results on 887 Congregations.* Philadelphia: University of Pennsylvania, Center for Research on Religion and Urban Civil Society, 2000a.

————. "Keeping Faith in the City II: How 887 Philadelphia Congregations Serve Their Needy Neighbors Including the Children and Families of Prisoners." *Draft CRRUCS Report 2000-3.* Philadelphia: University of Pennsylvania, Center for Research on Religion and Urban Civil Society, 2000b.

Cnaan, Ram A., with Rodney Rodgers, Harold Dean Trulear, and Gaynor Yancey. "Managing local religious congregations in America: Contextual necessities and leadership challenge." Paper presented at the fourth International Research Symposium on Public Management–IRSPM 2000: Panel on Organization and Management of Voluntary, Nonprofit Organizations and NGO's, Rotterdam, Holland, April 10-11, 2000c.

Cnaan, Ram A., with R. J. Wineburg, and S. C. Boddie, *The newer deal: Social work and religion in partnership.* New York: Columbia University Press, 1999.

Etindi, D. "Charitable choice and its implications for faith-based organizations." *The Welfare Reformer,* 1 (1):6-11, 1999.

Farnsley, Arthur E. II. "Research Note: Grant Applications from Faith-Based Organizations." Indianapolis: The Polis Center, Indiana University Purdue University Indianapolis, 1999.

Grettenberger, S., and P. Hovmand. "The role of churches in human services: United Methodist churches in Michigan." Paper presented at the 26th annual meeting of the Association for research on Nonprofit Organizations and Voluntary Action, Indianapolis, IN, 1997.

A Guide to Charitable Choice: The Rules of Section 104 of the 1996 Federal Welfare Law Governing State Cooperation with Faith-based Social-Service Providers. Washington, DC: The Center for Public Justice; and Annandale, Virginia: The Christian Legal Society's Center for Law and Religious Freedom, 1997.

Hill, R. B. *Report on study of church-based human services.* Baltimore: Associated Black Charities, 1998.

Hodgkinson, Virginia A., and Murray S. Weitzman. *From Belief to Commitment: The Community Service Activities and Finances of Religious Congregations in the United States, 1993 Edition.* Washington, DC: Independent Sector, 1993.

Kuzma, A. L. "Faith-based providers partnering with government: Opportunity and temptation." *Journal of Church and State,* 4:1-37, 2000.

Marcum, John P. "Social Justice and Social Welfare: Report for the August 1997 Presbyterian Panel." Louisville, Kentucky: Research Services, Presbyterian Church (U.S.A.), 1997.

Matsui, Elena, and Joseph Chuman, "The Case Against Charitable Choice." *Voice of Reason: The Newsletter of Americans for Religious Liberty,* 2 (71):2, 6, 2000.

Monsma, Stephen. *When Sacred and Secular Mix: Religious Nonprofit Organizations and Public Money.* Lanham, MD: Rowman & Littlefield, 1996.

Nathan, R. P., and T. Gais, *Implementing the personal responsibility act of 1996: A first look.* Albany, NY: Rockefeller Institute Press, 1999.

Printz, Tobi Jennifer. "Faith-based Service Providers in the Nation's Capital: Can They Do More?" No. 2 in *Charting Civil Society,* a series by the Center on Nonprofits and Philanthropy. Washington, DC: The Urban Institute, 1998.

Sherman, Amy L. "Churches as government partners: Navigating 'Charitable Choice.'" *The Christian Century,* 117 (20):716-721, 2000a.

―――. *The Growing Impact of Charitable Choice.* Washington, DC: Center for Public Justice, 2000b.

Wuthnow, Robert. *The Restructuring of American Religion: Society and Faith Since World War II.* Princeton: Princeton University Press, 1988.

II

DIRECTORIES

1. United States Cooperative Organizations, National

The organizations listed in this section are cooperative religious organizations that are national in scope. Regional cooperative organizations in the United States are listed in Directory 7, "United States Regional and Local Ecumenical Bodies."

The Alban Institute, Inc.

Founded in 1974, the Alban Institute, Inc. is a non-profit, non-denominational membership organization. Its mission is to work to encourage local congregations to be vigorous and faithful so that they may equip the people of God to minister within their faith communities and in the world. Through its book and periodical publishing, education programs, consulting and training services and research, the Alban Institute provides resources and services to congregations and judicatories of all denominations and their lay and ordained leaders.

The Institute has long been a pioneer in identifying, researching and publishing information about key issues in the religious world such as conflict management, clergy transition, and involuntary termination of clergy and lay leadership. The Institute's resources include over 100 book titles, over 40 courses offered nationally each year, and a staff of senior and regional consultants located across the country ready to assist local congregations. Individuals, congregations, and institutions support Alban's work and maintain their cutting-edge skills for ministry through membership in the Institute or as constituents and consumers of Alban's products and services.

Headquarters
7315 Wisconsin Ave., Ste. 1250 W., Bethesda, MD 20814-3211 Tel. (800)486-1318
Email: pwalker@alban.org
Website: www.alban.org
Media Contact, Marketing and Communications Director, Holly Hemphill

Officers
Pres., The Rev. James P. Wind, Ph.D.

American Bible Society

In 1816, pastors and laymen representing a variety of Christian denominations gathered in New York City to establish an organization "to disseminate the Gospel of Christ throughout the habitable world." Since that time the American Bible Society (ABS) has continued to provide God's Word, without doctrinal note or comment, wherever it is needed and in the language and format the reader can most easily use and understand. The ABS is the servant of the denominations and local churches. It provides Scriptures at exceptionally low costs in various attractive formats for their use in outreach ministries here in the United States and all across the world.

Today the ABS serves more than 100 denominations and agencies, and its board of trustees is composed of distinguished laity and clergy drawn from these Christian groups.

Fifty years ago the American Bible Society played a leading role in the founding of the United Bible Societies, a federation of 138 national Bible Societies around the world that enables global cooperation in Scripture translation, publication and distribution in more than 200 countries and territories. The ABS contributes approximately 45 percent of the support provided by the UBS to those national Bible Societies which request support to meet the total Scripture needs of people in their countries.

The work of the ABS is supported through gifts from individuals, local churches, denominations and cooperating agencies. Their generosity helped make the distribution of 287.2 million copies of the Scriptures during 1994, out of a total of 608 million copies of the Scriptures distributed by all member societies of the UBS.

Headquarters
National Service Center, 1865 Broadway, New York, NY 10023 Tel. (212)408-1200
Media Contact, Dir. Communications, Mike Maus, Tel. (212)408-1419 Fax (212)408-1456
Email: mmaus@americanbible.org
Website: www.americanbible.org

Officers
Chpsn., Sally Shoemaker Robinson
Vice-Chpsn., Harold Bennett
Pres., Dr. Eugene B. Habecker
Exec. Vice-Pres., Peter Bradley
Vice-Pres. for Scripture Publications, Maria I. Martinez

Vice-Pres. for Development and Communications, Arthur Caccese

Vice-Pres. for Finance and Administration, Patrick English

Acting Vice-Pres. for Marketing, John Cruz

Department Heads: Church Relations, Rev. Fred A. Allen; Scripture Publications, Assoc. Vice-Pres., Rev. Dr. David G. Burke; Volunteer Activities & Field Services, Dir., Frank Gomez; Catholic Ministries, Dir., Jeanette Russo; Human Resources, Dir., Steven King; Communications, Dir., Mike Maus; Scripture Production Services, Dir., Alain Sasson; Publications, Dir., David Singer; Development and Communications, Assoc. Vice-Pres., Jeffrey Towers; Finance and Administration, Assoc. Vice-Pres. and Controller, Donald Cavanaugh

American Council of Christian Churches

The American Council of Christian Churches is a Fundamentalist multidenominational organization whose purposes are to provide information, encouragement, and assistance to Bible-believing churches, fellowships, and individuals; to preserve our Christian heritage through exposure of, opposition to, and separation from doctrinal impurity and compromise in current religious trends and movements; to protect churches from religious and political restrictions, subtle or obvious, that would hinder their ministries for Christ; and to promote obedience to the inerrant Word of God.

Founded in 1941, The American Council of Christian Churches (ACCC) is a multi-denominational agency for fellowship and cooperation among Bible-believing churches in various denominations/fellowships: Bible Presbyterian Church, Evangelical Methodist Church, Fellowship of Fundamental Bible Churches (formerly Bible Protestant), Free Presbyterian Church of North America, Fundamental Methodist Church, General Association of Regular Baptist Churches, Independent Baptist Fellowship of North America, Independent Churches Affiliated, along with hundreds of independent churches. The total membership nears 2 million. Each denomination retains its identity and full autonomy, but cannot be associated with the World Council of Churches, National Council of Churches or National Association of Evangelicals.

Headquarters
P.O. Box 5455, Bethlehem, PA 18015 Tel. (610)865-3009 Fax (610)865-3033
Email: accc@juno.com
Website: www.amcouncilc.org
Media Contact, Exec. Dir., Dr. Ralph Colas

Officers
Pres., Dr. Richard A. Harris
Vice-Pres., Dr. John McKnight
Exec. Sec., Dr. Ralph Colas

Sec., Rev. Craig Griffith
Treas., William H. Worrilow, Jr.
Commissions: Chaplaincy; Education; Laymen; Literature; Missions; Radio & Audio Visual; Relief; Youth

American Friends Service Committee

Founded: 1917, Regional Groups: 9. Founded by and related to the Religious Society of Friends (Quakers) but supported and staffed by individuals sharing basic values regardless of religious affiliation. Attempts to relieve human suffering and find new approaches to world peace and social justice through nonviolence. Work in 22 countries includes development and refugee relief, peace education, and community organizing. Sponsors off-the-record seminars around the world to build better international understanding. Conducts programs with U.S. communities on the problems of minority groups such as housing, employment, and denial of legal rights. Maintains Washington, D.C., office to present AFSC experience and perspectives to policy-makers. Seeks to build informed public resistance to militarism and the military-industrial complex. A co-recipient of the Noble Peace Prize. Programs are multiracial, nondenominational, and international.

Divisions: Community Relations Unit, International Programs, Peacebuilding Unit

Headquarters
1501 Cherry St., Philadelphia, PA 19102 Tel. (215)241-7000 Fax (215)864-0104
Email: afscinfo@afsc.org
Website: www.afsc.org
Dir. of Media Relations

Officers
Presiding Clerk., Donald Gann
Treas., Kate Nicklin
Interim General Secretary, Don Reeves

The American Theological Library Association, Inc.

The American Theological Library Association, Inc. (ATLA) is a library association that works to improve theological and religious libraries and librarianship by providing continuing education, developing standards, promoting research and experimental projects, encouraging cooperative programs and publishing and disseminating research tools and aids. Founded in 1946, ATLA currently has a membership of over 245 institutions and 550 individuals.

Headquarters
820 Church St., Ste. 400, Evanston, IL 60201 Tel. (847)869-7788 Fax (847)869-8513
Email: Alta@alta.com
Website: www.atla.com
Media Contact, Dir. of Member Services

Pres., Milton J. (Joe) Coalter, Louisville Presbyterian Theological Seminary, 1646 Cowling Ave., Louisville, KY 40205-1370

Vice-Pres., William Hook, Vanderbilt Divinity School, 419 21st Avene S., Nashville, TN 37240-0007

Sec., Eileen Saner, Associated Mennonite Biblical Seminary, 3003 Benham Ave., Elkhart, IN 46517-1999

Exec. Dir. & CEO, Dennis A. Norlin, 820 Church St., Ste. 400, Evanston, IL 60201

American Tract Society

The American Tract Society is a nonprofit, interdenominational organization, instituted in 1825 through the merger of most of the then-existing tract societies. As one of the earliest religious publishing bodies in the United States, ATS has pioneered in the publishing of Christian books, booklets and leaflets. The volume of distribution has risen to 25-30 million pieces of literature annually. For free samples or a free catalog contact 1-800-54-TRACT.

Headquarters

P.O. Box 462008, Garland, TX 75046 Tel. (972)276-9408 Fax (972)272-9642

Media Contact, Vice-Pres. Marketing, Tom Friday

Officers

Chpsn., John A. Mawhinney

The American Waldensian Society

The American Waldensian Society (AWS) promotes ministry linkages, broadly ecumenical, between U.S. churches and Waldensian (Reformed)-Methodist constituencies in Italy and Waldensian constituencies in Argentina-Uruguay. Founded in 1906, AWS aims to enlarge mission discovery and partnership among overseas Waldensian-Methodist forces and denominational forces in the U.S.

AWS is governed by a national ecumenical board, although it consults and collaborates closely with the three overseas Waldensian-Methodist boards.

The Waldensian experience is the earliest continuing Protestant experience

Headquarters

475 Riverside Dr., Rm. 1850, New York, NY 10115 Tel. (212)870-2671 Fax (212)870-2499

Media Contact, Exec. Dir., Rev. Frank G. Gibson, Jr.

Officers

Pres., Rev. Laura R. Jervis

Vice-Pres., Rev. James O'Dell

Sec., Rev. Kent Jackson

Treas., Lon Haines

Exec. Dir., Rev. Frank G. Gibson, Jr.

Appalachian Ministries Educational Resource Center (AMERC)

The mission of AMERC is to promote contextual, cross-cultural education for theological students, faculties, and other Christian leaders. Working primarily through an ecumenical consortium of theological schools, AMERC supports experiential learning about the theological, spiritual, social, economic and environmental aspects of Appalachian culture, especially for rural and small town settings for ministry.

Since 1985 AMERC, a consortium of nearly 40 seminaries has provided quality educational programs and learning experiences for seminaries and other religious leaders interested in ministry in Appalachia and other rural areas. The centerpiece of these programs has been in-depth, contextually based dialogue with local people engaged in creative ministries, exploring with them social, economic, political, ecological, cultural, and religious issues. Intense theological reflection is used to understand these issues through the eyes of faith, equipping students and other leaders for ministry in the Appalachian context.

In the new millennium AMERC's form of ministry is changing. AMERC is now supporting its consortium of members by providing program grants, technical and library support, and leadership consultation. The consortium seminaries and other groups, in turn, design and offer an even wider variety of pilot programs in rural and small town ministry in the context of Appalachia. AMERC has launched into the first Grants Program for members of the consortium and hopes to fund 7 to 10 seminaries with up to $10,000 grants within the next year.

Headquarters

300 Harrison Rd., Berea, KY 40403 Tel. (859) 986-8789 Fax (859)986-2576

Media Contact: Rev. Dr. Bennett D. Page, Executive Director

Email: bpage@amerc.org

Website: www.amerc.org

Media Contact, Devel. Coord., Kathy Williams

Officers

Chair, Rev. Dr. Douglass Lewis, Wesley Theological Seminary

Vice Chair, Rev. Dr. Leon Carroll, Columbia Theological Seminary

Secretary, Ms. Tena Willemsma, Commission on Religion in Appalachia

Treasurer, Mr. Jim Strand, Berea College

The Associated Church Press

The Associated Church Press was organized in 1916. Its member publications include major Protestant, Catholic, and Orthodox groups in the U.S. and Canada. Some major ecumenical journals are also members. It is a professional

Christian journalistic association seeking to promote excellence among editors and writers, recognize achievements, and represent the interests of the religious press. It sponsors seminars, conventions, awards programs, and workshops for editors, staff people, and business managers. It is active in postal rates and regulations on behalf of the religious press.

Headquarters
Media Contact, Exec. Dir., Dr. John Stapert, P.O. Box 30215, Phoenix, AZ 85046-0215 Tel. (602)569-6371 Fax (602)569-6180
Email: john_stapert@ecunet.org

Officers
Pres., Roger Kahle, 8765 West Higgins Rd., Chicago , Il. 60631
Exec. Dir., Dr. John Stapert, P.O. Box 30215, Phoenix, AZ 85046-0215 Tel. (602)569-6371
Treas., Nena Asquith, P.O. Box 1245, Bethlehem, PA 18016-1245

The Associated Gospel Churches

Organized in 1939, The Associated Gospel Churches (AGC) endorses chaplains primarily for Fundamental Independent Baptist and Bible Churches to the U.S. Armed Forces. The AGC has been recognized by the U.S. Department of Defense for 61 years as an Endorsing Agency, and it supports a strong national defense. The AGC also endorses VA chaplains, police, correctional system and civil air patrol chaplains.

The AGC provides support for its associated constituent churches (Fundamental Independent Churches), seminaries, Bible colleges and missionaries.

The AGC believes in the sovereignty of the local church, the historic doctrines of the Christian faith and the infallibility of the Bible.

The AGC is a member of the National Conference on Ministry to the Armed Forces (NCMAF) and the Endorsers Conference for Veterans Affairs Chaplaincy (ECVAC).

Headquarters
Media Contact, Pres., George W. Baugham, D.D., National Hdqt., P.O. Box 733, Taylors, SC 29687 Tel. (864)268-9617 Fax (864)268-0166

Officers
Commission on Chaplains, Pres. and Chmn., Billy Baugham, D.D.
Vice-Pres., Rev. Chuck Flesher
Sec.-Treas., Eva Baugham
Executive Committee, Chaplain (Captain) James Poe, USN Member

ADRIS/Association for the Development of Religious Information Services

The Association for the Development of Religious Information Services was established in 1971 to facilitate coordination and cooperation among information services that pertain to religion. Its goal is a worldwide network that is interdisciplinary, inter-faith and interdenominational to serve both administrative and research applications. ADRIS publishes a newsletter and provides Internet consulting services toward these goals.

Headquarters
ADRIS Newsletter Office, P.O. Box 210735, Nashville, TN 37221-0735 Tel. (615)429-8744 Fax (508)632-0370
Email: editor@adris.org
Website: www.adris.org
Media Contact, Newsletter Ed., Edward W. Dodds, P.O. Box 210735, Nashville, TN 37221-0735 Tel. (615)429-8744 Fax (508) 632-0370

Association of Catholic Diocesan Archivists

The Association of Catholic Diocesan Archivists, which began in 1979, has been committed to the active promotion of professionalism in the management of diocesan archives. The Association meets annually: in the even years it has its own summer conference, in the odd years it meets in conjunction with the Society of American Archivists. Publications include Standards for Diocesan Archives, Access Policy for Diocesan Archives and the quarterly Bulletin.

Headquarters
Archives & Records Center, 711 West Monroe, Chicago, IL 60661 Tel. (312)831-0711 Fax (312)736-0488
Media Contact, Ms. Nancy Sandlebac

Officers
Episcopal Mod., ———
Pres., Msgr. Francis J. Weber, 15151 San Fernando Mission Blvd., Mission Hills, CA 91345 Tel. (818)365-1501
Vice-Pres., Dr. Charles Nolan, 1100 Chartres St., New Orleans, LA 70116 Tel. (504)529-2651 Fax (504)529-2001
Sec.-Treas., Sr. Catherine Louise LaCoste, C.S.J., 10291/2 Hayes Ave., San Diego, CA 92103 Tel. (619)298-6608
Bd. Members: Kinga Perzynska, P.O. Box 13124, Capital Station, Austin, TX 78711 Tel. (512)476-6296 Fax (512)476-3715; Timothy Cary, P.O. Box 07912, Milwaukee, WI 19807 Tel. (414)769-3407 Fax (414)769-3408; Lisa May, P.O. Box 907, 1700 San Jacinto, Houston, TX 77001 Tel. (713)659-5461 Fax (713)759-9151; John J. Treanor, 711 W. Monroe, Chicago, IL 60661 Tel. (312)736-5150 Fax (312)736-0488; Bernice Mooney, 27 C St., Salt Lake City, UT 84103-2397 Tel. (801)328-8641 Fax (801)328-9680
Newsletter Editor, Nancy Sandleback

Association of Gospel Rescue Missions

The Association of Gospel Rescue Missions (AGRM), formerly the International Union of Gospel Missions, is an association of 290 rescue missions and other ministries that serve more than 7 million homeless and needy people in the inner cities of the U.S., Canada and overseas each year. Since 1913, AGRM member ministries have offered emergency food and shelter, evangelical outreach, Christian counsel, youth and family services, prison and jail outreach, and rehabilitation and specialized programs for the mentally ill, the elderly, the urban poor and street youth. The AGRM operates RESCUE College, an Internet-based distance education program to prepare and train rescue mission workers. The AGRM sponsors Alcoholics Victorious, a network of Christian support groups.

Headquarters

1045 Swift, N. Kansas City, MO 64116-4127 Tel. (816)471-8020 Fax (816)471-3718
Email: agrm@agrm.org
Website: www.agrm.org
Media Contact, Exec. Dir., Rev. Stephen E. Burger or Phil Rydman

Officers

Exec. Dir., Rev. Stephen E. Burger
Pres., Dr. Malcolm C. Lee, P.O. Box 1112, Richmond, CA 94802 Tel. (510)215-4888 Fax (510)215-0178
Vice-Pres., Mr. Rick Alvis, Box 817, Indianapolis, IN 46206 Tel. (317)635-3575 Fax (317)687-3629
Sec.-Treas., Lorraine Minor, 1301 Wabash, Kansas City, MO 64127 Tel. (816)474-9380 Fax (816)231-7597

NATIONAL PROGRAM UNITS AND STAFF
Education, Rev. Michael Liimatta
Membership Services, Tammy Sharp
Newsletter and Magazine: Stephen E. Burger; Philip Rydman
Convention, Stephen E. Burger
Business Admn., Len Conner
Historian, Delores Burger
Exec. Sec., Madeleine Wooley
Communications & Development, Phillip Rydman
Expansion, Gary Meek
Educational Associate, Dru Gray

Association of Statisticians of American Religious Bodies

This Association was organized in 1934 and grew out of personal consultations held by representatives from The Yearbook of American Churches, The National (now Official) Catholic Directory, the Jewish Statistical Bureau, The Methodist (now The United Methodist), the Lutheran and the Presbyterian churches.

ASARB has a variety of purposes: to bring together those officially and professionally responsible for gathering, compiling, and publishing denominational statistics; to provide a forum for the exchange of ideas and sharing of problems in statistical methods and procedure; and to seek such standardization as may be possible in religious statistical data.

Headquarters

c/o John P. Marcum, Presbyterian Church (U.S.A.), 100 Witherspoon St., Rm. 2623, Louisville, KY 40202-1396 Tel. (502)569-5161 Fax (502)569-5501
Email: jackm@ctr.pcusa.org
Media Contact, Sec./Treas., John P. Marcum

Officers

Pres., Richard H. Taylor, United Church of Christ, 300 Weybosset Street, Providence, RI 02903 Tel. (401) 331-9844 Fax (401) 331-0023
1st Vice-Pres., Cliff Tharp, Southern Baptist Convention, 127 Ninth Ave. N., Nashville, TN 37220 Tel. (615)251-2517 Fax (615)251-5636
2nd Vice-Pres., Rich Houseal, Church of the Nazarene, 6401 The Paseo, Kansas City, MO 64131 Tel. (816)333-7000 Fax (816)361-5202
Sec./Treas., John P. Marcum, Presbyterian Church (U.S.A.), 100 Witherspoon St., Rm. 2623, Louisville, KY 40202-1396 Tel. (502)569-5161 Fax (502)569-5501
MEMBERS-AT-LARGE
Clifford Grammich, 3166 South Bentley Ave., Los Angeles, CA 90034-3008 Tel. (310) 444-1826
James Schwartz, UJA Federations of N.A., 111 Eighth Ave., Suite 11E, New York, NY 10011-5201 Tel. (212)284-6729 Fax (212)284-6805

The Association of Theological Schools in the United States and Canada

The Association of Theological Schools is the accrediting and program agency for graduate theological education in North America. Its member schools offer graduate professional and academic degrees for church-related professions.

Headquarters

10 Summit Park Drive, Pittsburgh, PA 15275-1103 Tel. (412)788-6505 Fax (412)788-6510
Email: ats@ats.edu
Website: www.ats.edu
Media Contact, Dir. Of Comm., Nancy Merrill, Tel. (412)788-6505

Officers

Pres., Martha J. Horne, Protestant Episcopal Theological Seminary in Virginia, Alexandria, VA
Vice-Pres., David L. Tiede, Luther Seminary, St. Paul, MN
Secretary, Clarence G. Newsome, Howard University School of Divinity, Washington, DC

23

Treasurer, Thomas E. Fahey, Ernst & Young, New York, NY

Staff
Executive Director, Daniel O. Aleshire

Blanton-Peale Institute

Blanton-Peale Institute is dedicated to helping people overcome emotional obstacles by joining mental health expertise with religious faith and values. The Blanton-Peale Graduate Institute provides advanced training in marriage and family therapy, psychotherapy and pastoral care for ministers, rabbis, sisters, priests and other counselors. The Blanton-Peale Counseling Centers provide counseling for individuals, couples, families and groups. Blanton-Peale also offers a nationwide telephone support service for clergy, social service agencies, and other employers and promotes interdisciplinary communication among theology, medicine and the behavioral sciences. Blanton-Peale was founded in 1937 by Dr. Norman Vincent Peale and psychiatrist Smiley Blanton, M.D.

Headquarters
3 W. 29th St., New York, NY 10001 Tel. (212) 725-7850 Fax (212)689-3212
Media Contact, ———

Officers
Chpsn., John Allen
Vice-Chpsn., Arthur Caliandro
Sec., Janet E. Hunt
Treas., Mary McNamara
Pres. & CEO, Dr. Holly Johnson

Bread For The World

Bread for the World is a nonprofit, nondenominational Christian citizen's movement of 45,000 members that advocates specific hunger policy changes and seeks justice for hungry people at home and abroad. Founded in 1974, Bread for the World is supported by more than 45 Protestant, Catholic and Evangelical denominations and church agencies. Rooted in the gospel of God's love in Jesus Christ, its 45,000 members write, call and visit their members of Congress to win specific legislative changes that help hungry people, and place the issue of hunger on the nation's policy agenda.

Bread for the World works closely with Bread for the World Institute. The Institute seeks to inform, educate, nurture and motivate concerned citizens for action on policies that affect hungry people.

Headquarters
50 F St., NW, Ste. 500, Washington, DC 20001 Tel. (202)639-9400 Fax (202)639-9401
Email: bread@bread.org
Website: www.bread.org
Media Contact, Aimee Moiso

Officers
Pres., Rev. David Beckmann
Bd. Chpsn., Chrisine Vladimiroff
Bd. Vice-Chpsn., Pablo Sanchez

Campus Crusade for Christ International

Campus Crusade for Christ International is an interdenominational, evangelistic and discipleship ministry dedicated to helping fulfill the Great Commission through the multiplication strategy of "win-build-send." Formed in 1951 on the campus of UCLA, the organization now includes 68 plus separate ministries and special projects reaching out to almost every segment of society. There are more than 20,500 staff members and 663,000 trained volunteers in 181 countries. The NewLife 2000 strategy helps to give every person on earth an opportunity to say "yes" to Jesus Christ by the end of the year 2000.

Headquarters
100 Lake Hart Dr., Orlando, FL 32832 Tel. (407) 826-2000 Fax (407)826-2120
Email: ofcom@ccci.org
Website: www.ccci.org
Media Contact, Sid Wright

Officers
Pres., William R. Bright
Exec. Vice-Pres., Stephen B. Douglass
Vice-Pres. of Admn. & Chief Fin. Officer, Kenneth P. Heckman
Vice-Pres. of Intl. Ministries, Bailey E. Marks

CARA-Center for Applied Research in the Apostolate

CARA-the Center for Applied Research in the Apostolate is a not-for-profit research organization of the Roman Catholic Church. It operates on the premise that not only theological principles but also findings of the social sciences must be the basis for pastoral care.

CARA's mission since its founding in 1964 has been "To discover, promote, and apply modern techniques and scientific informational resources for practical use in a coordinated and effective approach to the Church's social and religious mission in the modern world, at home and overseas."

CARA performs a wide range of research studies and consulting services. Since its roots are Roman Catholic, many of its studies are done for dioceses, religious orders, parishes, and the National Conference of Catholic Bishops. Interdenominational studies are also performed. Publishes The CARA Report, a research newsletter on Catholic Church related topics, four times a year and The Catholic Ministry Formation Directory, a guide and statistical compilation of enrollments for Catholic seminaries, diaconate formation programs, and lay ministry formation programs.

Georgetown University, Washington, DC 20057-1203 Tel. (202)687-8080 Fax (202)687-8083
Email: cara@gunet.georgetown.edu
Website: www.georgetown.edu/research/cara/index. html
Media Contact, Executive Director, Dr. Bryan Froehle

Officers
Bishop William B. Friend, Chair, CARA Board of Directors

Periodical
The CARA Report

Center for Parish Development

The Center for Parish Development is an ecumenical, nonprofit research and development agency whose mission is to help church bodies learn to become faithful expressions of God's mission in today's post-modern, post-Christendom world. Founded in 1968, the Center brings to its client-partners a strong theological orientation, a missional ecclesial paradigm with a focus on faithful Christian communities as the locus of mission, research-based theory and practice of major change, a systems approach, and years of experience working with national, regional, and local church bodies.

The Center staff provides research, consulting and training support for church organizations engaging in major change. The Center is governed by a 12-member Board of Directors.

Headquarters
5407 S. University Ave., Chicago, IL 60615 Tel. (773)752-1596
Email: cpd@missionalchurch.org
Website: www.missionalchurch.org
Media Contact, Administrative Coord., Marilyn R. Olson

Officers
Chpsn., Eugene L. Delves, 9142 S. Winchester Ave., Chicago, IL 60620
Vice-Chpsn., Pastor Gordon Nusz, First United Methodist Church, 777 West Eight Mile Road, Northville, MI 48167
Sec., Delton Krueger, 10616 Penn Ave. South, Bloomington, MN 55431
Exec. Dir., Paul M. Dietterich

Chaplaincy of Full Gospel Churches

The Chaplaincy of Full Gospel Churches (CFGC) is a unique coalition of 138 nondenominational churches and networks of churches united for the purpose of being represented in military and civilian chaplaincies. Since its inception in 1984, CFGC has grown rapidly, recently representing over 7.5 million American Christians.

Churches, fellowships and networks of churches which affirm the CFGC statement of faith that "Jesus is Savior, Lord and Baptizer in the Holy Spirit today, with signs, wonders and gifts following" may join the endorsing agency. CFGC represents its 138 member-networks of churches (consisting of over 60,000 churches nationwide) before the Pentagon's Armed Forces Chaplains Board, the National Conference of Ministry to the Armed Forces, Endorsers Conference for Veterans Affairs Chaplaincy, Federal Bureau of Prisons, Association of Professional Chaplains, and other groups requiring professional chaplaincy endorsement. The organization also ecclesiastically credentials professional counselors.

Headquarters
2715 Whitewood Dr., Dallas, TX 75233 Tel. (214)331-4373 Fax (214)333-4401
Email: cfgc@fastlane.net
Website: www.chaplaincyfullgospel.org
Media Contact, Rev. Dr. E. H. Jim Ammerman

Officers
Pres. & Dir., Rev. Dr. E. H. Jim Ammerman
Deputy Dir., Rev. Dr. Charlene Ammerman
Vice-Pres., Ed Leach

Christian Endeavor International

Christian Endeavor International is a Christ-centered, youth-oriented ministry which assists local churches in reaching young people with the gospel of Jesus Christ, discipling them in the Christian faith, and equipping them for Christian ministry and service in their local church, community and world. It trains youth leaders for effective ministry and provides opportunities for Christian inspiration, spiritual growth, fellowship, and service. Christian Endeavor International reaches across denominational, cultural, racial and geographical boundaries.

Headquarters
1221 East Broad St., P.O. Box 2106, Columbus, OH 43216-2106 Tel. (614)258-3947 Fax (614) 258-4950
Media Contact, Exec. Dir., Rev. David G. Jackson

Officers
Pres., Dr. Kent D. Maxwell
Exec. Dir., Rev. David G. Jackson

Christian Management Association

Christian Management Association provides management training and leadership resources for Christian organizations and larger churches. Its membership represents CEOs/executive directors, pastors, church administrators, finance officers and other managers from more than 1,600 organizations in the United States. CMA publishes a bi-monthly magazine, Christian Management Report, a monthly newsletter, an annual Who's Who in Christian Management Membership directory, and other resources. CMA also provides comprehensive training and strategic networking opportunities through CMA's annual leadership and management conference for Christian organizations, CEO Dialogues one-day roundtables, the all new School of Management (multiple sites), local chapter meetings, management books and audiotapes. Annual membership is open to Christian Organizations and individuals. Companies that provide products or services to Christian organizations and churches may apply for Business Membership. Contact CMA for a free membership information packet and sample publications.

Headquarters
P.O. Box 4638, Diamond Bar, CA 91765 Tel. (909)861-8861 Fax (909)860-8247
John Pearson, CEO
Media Contact, Director of Membership Development, Jackie Tsujimoto
Email: CMA@CMAonline.org
Website: www. CMAonline.org

Officers
Chairman, Mark G. Holbrook, President/CEO, Evangelical Christian Credit Union
Vice-Chairman, Frank Sommerville, Attorney, Weycer, Kaplan, Pulaski & Zuber, P.C.
Secretary, Robert Peterson, Retired Chief Financial Officer, Evangelical Free Church of America
Treas., James A. Canning, Vice-President Finance & Administration, World Vision International
CEO, John Pearson

A Christian Ministry in the National Parks
This ministry is recognized by over 40 Christian denominations and extends the ministry of Christ to the millions of people who live, work and vacation in our National Parks. Ministry Staff Members conduct services of worship in the parks on Sundays. The staff is employed by park concessionaires and have a full-time job in which their actions, attitudes, and commitment to Christ serve as witness. Room and board are provided at a minimal cost; minimum commitment of 90 days needed.

Headquarters
45 School Street, Boston, MA 02108 Tel. (617)720-5655 Fax (617)720-7899
Email: acmnp@juno.com
Website: www.coolworks.com/acmnp/
Media Contact, The Rev. Richard P. Camp, Jr.

Officers
Dir., The Rev. Richard P. Camp, Jr.

Church Growth Center: Home of the Church Doctor Ministries
The Church Growth Center is an interfaith, nonprofit, professional organization which exists to bring transformational change of the Christian church toward the effective implementation of the Lord's Great Commission, to make disciples of all people. This effort is done through consultations, resources, and educational events.

Founded in 1978 by Kent R. Hunter, president and chairman of the board, the Church Growth Center offers several services including church consultations by experienced consultants under the Creative Consultation Services arm, cutting edge resources through our bookstore, The Church Doctor"! Resource Center, and by providing educational events at churches and organizations in the way of providing speakers and resources at seminars, workshops, and conferences.

Other ministries under the arm of the Church Growth Center include Mission Teams International (taking teams overseas to train pastors to be more effective in their churches), The Church Doctor"! daily radio program (which is practical direction and helps for the lay person in the church), Nehemiah Guest Missionary House (where short-term missionaries may stay while learning church growth and working at the Center), and Strategies for Today's Leader (a quarterly magazine with timely thematic issues geared for pastors and leaders). The quarterly newsletter is the Church Doctor Report

Headquarters
1230 U. S. Highway Six, P.O. Box 145, Corunna, IN 46730 Tel. (219)281-2452 Fax (219)281-2167
Email: churchgrowth@juno.com
Website: www.churchdoctor.org
Media Contact, Assistant to Pres., Michelle Jones

Officers
Pres., Dr. Kent R. Hunter, D.min, Ph.D.
Vice-Pres., Rev. Paul Griebel, 312 S. Oak St., Kendallville, IN 46755
Sec.-Treas., Roger Miller, 1060 Park Dr., Turkey Lake, LaGrange, IN 46761

Church Women United in the U.S.A.
Church Women United in the U.S.A. is a grassroots ecumenical movement of one-half million Protestant, Orthodox, Roman Catholic and other Christian women, organized into more than 1,300 local and state units throughout the United States and Puerto Rico. Founded in 1941, CWU works in coalition with religious and secular groups on issues of peace and justice. A major program emphasis in the 1996 - 2000 Quadrenium is "Making the World Safer for Women and Children."

Headquarters
NATIONAL OFFICE
475 Riverside Dr., Ste. 500, New York, NY 10115 Tel. (800) CWU-5551 OR (212)870-2347 Fax (212)870-2338
Email: cwu@churchwomen.org
Website: www.churchwomen.org

Media Contact, Mary Stamp, Tel. (212) 870-2344, Email: mstamp@churchwomen.org

LEGISLATIVE OFFICE

CWU Washington Ofc., 110 Maryland Ave. NE, Rm. 108, Washington, DC 20002 Tel. (202) 544-8747, Fax (202)544-9133

Legislative Asst., Wash. Ofc., Tiffany L. Heath, Email: tlheath@churchwomen.org

UNITED NATIONS OFFICE

475 Riverside Dr., Ste. 500, New York, NY 10115 Tel. (212)661-3856

UN Ofc., Staff Liaison, Jeannie H. Lee, Email: jhlee@churchwomen.org

ADMINISTRATION

General Director, Dr. Kathleen S. Hurty, Email: khurty@churchwomen.org

Controller, Roberto Vazquez, rvazquez@churchwomen.org

Officers

Pres., Jerrye Champion, Scottsdale, AZ

Vice-Pres., Jane Erdahl, New York, NY

Sec.-Treas., Joan Regal, Maplewood, MN

PROGRAM MANAGERS

Ecumenical Celebrations, Jeanette Zaragoza De Leon

Ecumenical Development, Dir., Jeannie H. Lee

Leadership Development, Ascension Day

Regional Coordinators: Central, Helen Traudt, Lincoln, NE; East Central, Gladys Kapenga, Wyoming, MI; Mid-Atlantic, Judith Hill, Harrisburg, PA; Northeast, Marilyn Lariviere, Hyannis, MA; Northwest, Edna Best, Billings, MT; South Central, Mickey Simpson, Tulsa, OK; Southeast, Morene Williams, Athens, GA; Southwest, Winifred Hardy, Bailey, CO

Managing Editor, Elisabeth Young

Consultation on Church Union

Officially constituted in 1962, the Consultation on Church Union is a venture in reconciliation of nine American communions. It has been authorized to explore the formation of a uniting church, truly catholic, truly evangelical and truly reformed. In 1992 the participating bodies were African Methodist Episcopal Church, African Methodist Episcopal Zion Church, Christian Church (Disciples of Christ), Christian Methodist Episcopal Church, The Episcopal Church, International Council of Community Churches, Presbyterian Church (U.S.A.), United Church of Christ and The United Methodist Church. These churches are at present deciding whether to enter a relationship of covenanted communion, to be called "Churches Uniting in Christ" and is scheduled for inauguration in January 2002. At the January, 1999 Plenary, at St. Louis, Missouri, the Assembly affirmed the Visible Marks of Churches Uniting in Christ and the marks of the fuller unity sought by "entering into a new level of visible commitment" by openly inviting participating churches to enter into this new relationship in 2002 or "to be part-

ners in continuing relationship to realize fully that unity for which Christ prayed." This 18th Plenary dared to hope that other American Christian bodies may enter this dialogue, commending "to the churches the actions recommended in 'A call to Christian Commitment and Action to Combat Racism' approved by the 18th Plenary."

The Plenary Assembly is composed of 10 delegates and 10 associate delegates from each of the participating churches. Included also are observer-consultants from more than 20 other churches, other union negotiations and conciliar bodies. The Executive Committee is composed of the president, two representatives from each of the particiiating communions and the secretariat. The secretariat consists of the executive staff of the Consultation. In the fall of 1999, the National Office was moved from Princeton, New Jersey to Lowell, Massachusetts.

In addition to publishing documents commissioned by the Consultation, a Newsletter is distributed periodically to keep its constituency abreast of current ecumenical concerns facing the Consultation and to share examples of local initiatives in ecclesial cooperation. An Editorial Board prepares an annual Lenten Booklet of devotional meditations entitled: Liberation and Unity.

Headquarters

260 Gorham Street, Lowell, MA 01851

Mailing Address: Highland Station, P.O. Box 2143, Lowell, MA 01851

Tel (978)453-2842 Fax (978)441-0692

Media Contact, Associate General Secretary, The Rev. K. Gordon White

Officers

General Sec., The Rev. Dr. Michael Kinnamon

Associate General Sec., The Rev., K. Gordon White

Pres., The Rev. Dr. Jeffrey R. Newhall, 25 Francis St., P.O. Box 60074, Worcester, MA 01606-0074

Vice Pres., Bishop McKinley Young, 700 Martin Luther King Jr., Dr., SW, ITC P.O. Box 456, Atlanta, GA 30314-4143

Vice Pres., The Rev. Diane Kessler, Massachusetts Council of Churches, 14 Beacon St., Room 416, Boston, MA 02108

Sec., The Rev. Kathy Bannister, 204 W. First St., P.O. Box 327, Bison, KS 67502

REP. FROM PARTICIPATING CHURCHES

African Methodist Episcopal Church: Bishop Vinton R. Anderson, 4144 Lindell Blvd., Ste. 222, St. Louis, MO 63108; Bishop McKinley Young, 700 Martin Luther King Jr., Dr., SW, ITC P.O. Box 456, Atlanta, GA 30314-4143

African Methodist Episcopal Zion Church: Bishop Marshall H. Strickland, 2000 Cedar Circle Dr., Baltimore, MD 21228; Bishop Cecil Bishop, 2663 Oakmeade Dr., Charlotte, NC 28270

Christian Church (Disciples of Christ): Rev. Dr.

Robert K. Welsh., P.O. Box 1986, Indianapolis, IN 46206; Rev. Dr. Suzanne Webb, 7018 Putney Road, Arcadia, MI 49613-9600

Christian Methodist Episcopal Church: Bishop Charles Helton, 6524 16th St, NW, Washington, DC 20012; Dr. Vivian U. Robinson, 8th Episcopal Dist. Hdqt., 1256 Hernlen St., Augusta, GA 30901

The Episcopal Church: Rev. Lucinda Laird, St. Matthew's Episcopal Church, 330 N. Hubbards Lane, Louisville, KY 40207; Rt. Rev. Edwin F. Gulick, Jr., 425 S. Second Street, Louisville, KY 40202

Intl. Council of Community Churches: Mr. Abraham Wright, 1912-3 Rosemary Hills Drive, Silver Springs, MD 20910; The Rev. Dr. Jeffrey R. Newhall, 25 Francis St., P.O. Box 60074, Worcester, MA 01606-0074

Presbyterian Church (U.S.A.): Ms. Georgette Huie, McCormick Seminary, Presbyterian Church (USA) 5555 Woodlawn Ave., Chicago, IL 60737

United Church of Christ: Rev. Dr. Thomas E. Dipko, 319 Parkway Dr., Berea, OH 44017; Rev. Diane C. Kessler, Mass. Council of Churches, 14 Beacon St., Boston, MA 02108

The United Methodist Church: Bishop William B. Grove, 109 McDavid Lane, Charleston, W. Virginia 25311; Rev. Kathy Bannister, 204 W. First Street, P.O. Box 327, Bison, Kansas 67520

Evangelical Council for Financial Accountability

Founded in 1979, the Evangelical Council for Financial Accountability has the purpose of helping Christ-centered, evangelical, nonprofit organizations earn the public's trust through their ethical practices and financial accountability. ECFA assists its over 940 member organizations in making appropriate public disclosure of their financial practices and accomplishments, thus materially enhancing their credibility and support potential among present and prospective donors.

Headquarters

P.O. Box 17456, Washington, DC 20041-7456 Tel. (540)535-0103 Fax (540)535-0533
Email: info@ecfa.org
Website: www.ecfa.org
Media Contact, Pres., Paul D. Nelson

Officers

Pres., Paul D. Nelson
Vice-Pres., Donor & Member Services, Daniel D. Busby
Dir. of Member Review & Compliance, Lucinda Repass
V.P. Member Review & Compliance, Bill Altman

Evangelical Press Association

The Evangelical Press Association is an organization of editors and publishers of Christian periodicals which seeks to promote the cause of Evangelical Christianity and enhance the influence of Christian journalism.

Headquarters

314 Dover Rd., Charlottesville, VA 22901 Tel. (804)973-5941 Fax (804)973-2710
Email: 74463,272@compuserve.com
Website: www. epassoc.org
Media Contact, Exec. Dir., Ronald Wilson

Officers

Pres., David Neff, Christianity Today, 465 Gundersen Dr., Carol Stream, IL, 60188
Pres-Elect, Terry White, Inside Journal, PO Box 17429, Washington, DC 20041-0429
Treas., Lamar Keener, Christian Times, PO Box 2606, El Cajon, CA 92021
Sec., Jeanette Thomason, Aspire, 107 Kenner Ave., Nashville, TN 37205
Advisor, Dean Ridings, Christian Camp & Conference Journal, PO Box 62189, Colorado Springs, CO 80962-2189
Advisor, Brian Peterson, New Man, 600 Rinehart Rd., Lake Mary, FL 32746
Exec. Dir., Ronald Wilson

Friends World Committee for Consultation (Section of the Americas)

The Friends World Committee for Consultation (FWCC) was formed in 1937. There has been an American Section as well as a European Section from the early days and an African Section was organized in 1971. In 1974 the name, Section of the Americas, was adopted by that part of the FWCC with constituency in North, Central, and South America and in the Caribbean area. In 1985 the Asia-West Pacific Section was organized. The purposes of FWCC are summarized as follows: To facilitate loving understanding of diversities among Friends while discovering together, with God's help, a common spiritual ground; and to facilitate full expression of Friends' testimonies in the world.

Headquarters

Section of the Americas Headquarters
1506 Race St., Philadelphia, PA 19102 Tel. (215)241-7250 Fax (215)241-7285
Email: Americas@FWCC.Quaker.org
Media Contact, Exec. Sec., Cilde Grover
Latin American Office, Guerrero 223 Pte., Zona Centro, Cd. Mante, TAM 89800 Mexico

Glenmary Research Center

The Research Center is a department of the Glenmary Home Missioners, a Catholic society of priests and brothers. The Center was established in 1966 to serve the rural research needs of the Catholic Church in the United States. Its research has led it to serve ecumenically a wide variety of church bodies. Local case studies as well as quantitative research is done to understand better the diversity of contexts in the rural sections of the country. The Center's statistical profiles of the nation's counties cover both urban and rural counties.

Headquarters

1312 Fifth Ave. North, Nashville, TN 37208 Tel. (615)256-1905 Fax (615)251-1472
Email: GRC@Glenmary.org
Website: www.glenmary.org
Media Contact, ———

Officers

Pres., Rev. Gerald Dorn, P.O. Box 465618, Cincinnati, OH 45246-5618
1st Vice-Pres., Rev. Daniel Dorsey, P.O. Box 465618, Cincinnati, OH 45246-5618
2nd Vice-Pres., Bro. Jack Henn, P.O. Box 465618, Cincinnati, OH 45246-5618
Treas., Robert Knueven, P.O. Box 465618, Cincinnati, OH 45246-5618
Dir., Kenneth M. Sanchagrin, Ph.D.
Email: ksanchagrin@glenmary.org

Graymoor Ecumenical & Interreligious Institute (GEII)

Graymoor Ecumenical & Interreligious Institute has its roots in the Graymoor Ecumenical Institute, which was founded in 1967 by the Franciscan Friars of the Atonement, to respond to the Friars' historical concern for Christian Unity in light of the theological and ecumenical developments arising from the Second Vatican Council.

In 1991, in response to developments in both the Institute and the wider ecumenical scene, the Graymoor Ecumenical Institute was expanded into an information and service organization with a mission of Christian Unity and interreligious dialogue. Today, the Graymoor Ecumenical & Interreligious Institute employs several means to acomplish this goal. Among these are specialization desks for African-American Churches; Evangelical and Free Churches; Lutheran, Anglican, and Roman Catholic Affairs; Interreligious Dialogue; and Social Ecumenism. Another is the annual Week of Prayer of Christian Unity—a world-wide observance initiated in 1908 by the Rev. Paul Wattson, co-founder of the Society of the Atonement—the theme and text of which are now chosen and prepared by the Pontifical Council for Promoting Christian Unity and representatives of the World Council of Churches. The Institute publishes the monthly journal Ecumenical Trends—to keep clergy and laity abrest of developments in the ecumenical and interreligious movements; provides membership in, and collaboration with, national and local ecumenical and interreligious organizations and agencies; and cooperates with individuals engaged in ecumenical and interreligious work.

Over the years, the Graymoor Ecumenical & Interreligious Institute has sponsored and co-sponsored meetings, colloquia, and workshops in areas of ecumenical and interreligious dialogue. These have been as diverse as colloquia between African-American and Hispanic Pentecostal scholars; Christians, Muslims, and Jews; state Councils of Churches; and interfaith training workshops for Christian leaders.

Headquarters

475 Riverside Dr., Rm. 1960, New York, NY 10115-1999 Tel. (212)870-2330 Fax (212)870-2001
Email: lmnygeii@aol.com
Media Contact: Walter Gagne, SA, Graymoor, Route 9, PO Box 300, Garrison, NY 10524-0300 Tel. (845)424-3671 x. 3421 Fax (845)424-2160

Staff

Interreligious Affairs Desk, Dir., Elias D. Mallon, SA, Ph.D.
Lutheran, Anglican, Roman Catholic Affairs Research Desk, Assoc. Dir., Lorelei F. Fuchs, SA, MA, STL, Email: 100772,372@compuserv.com
African American Churches, Assoc. Dir., Paul Teresa Hennessee, SA, MA, Email: PTHennesse@aol.com
Evangelical & Free Churches, Assoc. Dir., Elizabeth H. Mallon, M.Div., Email: Edemallon@aol.com
Ecumenical Trends, Editor, Assoc. Dir., Keven McMorrow, SA, STD, Graymoor, Route 9, PO Box 300, Garrison, NY 10524-0300 Tel. (845)424-3671 ext. 3120, Email: Kmcmorrow@atonementfriars.org
Social Ecumenism/National Public Policy Ministries, Paul Ojibway, SA, MA, GEII/Washington Office: 516 G Street NE-B, Washington, DC 20002 Tel. (202)543-2800 Fax (202)547-8107
Email: briefing@voicesforjustice.org
Website: www.voicesforjustice.org
Graymoor, Route 9, PO Box 300, Garrison, NY 10524-0300 Tel. (845)424-2109 Fax (845)424-2163

Inter-Varsity Christian Fellowship of the U.S.A.

Inter-Varsity Christian Fellowship is a non-profit, interdenominational student movement that ministers to college and university students and faculty in the United States. Inter-Varsity began in the United States when students at the University of Michigan invited C. Stacey Woods, then General Secretary of the Canadian movement, to help establish an Inter-Varsity chapter on their campus. Inter-Varsity Christian Fellowship-USA was incorporated two years later, in 1941.

Inter-Varsity's uniqueness as a campus ministry lies in the fact that it is student-initiated and student-led. Inter-Varsity strives to build collegiate fellowships that engage their campus with the gospel of Jesus Christ and develop disciples

29

who live out biblical values. Inter-Varsity students and faculty are encouraged in evangelism, spiritual discipleship, serving the church, human relationships, righteousness, vocational stewardship and world evangelization. A triennial missions conference held in Urbana, Illinois, jointly sponsored with Inter-Varsity-Canada, has long been a launching point for missionary service.

Headquarters

6400 Schroeder Rd., P.O. Box 7895, Madison, WI 53707 Tel. (608)274-9001 Fax (608)274-7882

Media Contact, Dir. of Development Services, Carole Sharkey, P.O. Box 7895, Madison, WI 53707 Tel. (608)274-9001 Fax (608)274-7882

Officers

Pres. & CEO, Stephen A. Hayner

Vice-Pres., C. Barney Ford; Robert A. Fryling; Samuel Barkat; Ralph Thomas; Jim Malliet

Bd. Chpsn., Virginia Viola

Bd. Vice-Chpsn., E. Kenneth Nielson

Interfaith Impact for Justice and Peace

Interfaith Impact for Justice and Peace is the religious community's united voice in Washington. It helps Protestant, Jewish, Muslim and Catholic national organizations have clout on Capitol Hill and brings grassroots groups and individual and congregational members to Washington and shows them how to turn their values into votes for justice and peace.

Interfaith Impact for Justice and Peace has established the following Advocacy Networks to advance the cause of justice and peace: Justice for Women; Health Care; Hunger and Poverty; International Justice and Peace; Civil and Human Rights. The Interfaith Impact Foundation provides an annual Legislative Briefing for their members.

Members receive the periodic Action alerts on initiatives, voting records, etc., and a free subscription to the Advocacy Networks of their choice.

Headquarters

100 Maryland Ave. N.E., Ste. 200, Washington, DC 20002 Tel. (202)543-2800 Fax (202)547-8107

Media Contact, Jane Hull Harvey

Officers

Chpsn. of Bd., Jane Hull Harvey, The United Methodist Church

MEMBERS

African Methodist Episcopal Church
African Methodist Episcopal Zion Church
Alliance of Baptists
American Baptist Churches, USA: Washington Office; World Relief Office
American Ethical Union
American Muslim Council
Center of Concern

Christian Methodist Episcopal (CME) Church
Christian Church (Disciples of Christ)
Church of the Brethren
Church Women United
Commission on Religion in Appalachia
Episcopal Church
Episcopal Urban Caucus
Evangelical Lutheran Church in America
Federation of Southern Cooperatives/LAF
Federation for Rural Empowerment
Graymoor Ecumenical and Interreligious Institute
Jesuit Social Ministries
Maryknoll Fathers and Brothers
Moravian Church in America
National Council of Churches of Christ: Church World Service; Washington Office
National Council of Jewish Women

NETWORK

Peoria Citizens Committee
Presbyterian Church (U.S.A.)
Progressive National Baptist Convention
Presbyterian Hunger Fund
Reformed Church in America
Rural Advancement Fund
Society of African Missions
Southwest Organizing Project
Southwest Voter Registration/Education Project
Toledo Metropolitan Ministries
Union of American Hebrew Congregations
Unitarian Universalist Association
Unitarian Universalist Service Committee
United Church of Christ: Bd. for Homeland Ministries; Bd. for World Ministries; Hunger Action Ofc.; Ofc. of Church in Society
The United Methodist Church: Gen. Bd. of Church & Society; Gen. Bd. of Global Ministries Natl. Div.; Gen. Bd. of Global Ministries Women's Div.; Gen. Bd. of Global Ministries World Div.
Virginia Council of Churches
Western Organization of Resource Councils

Interreligious Foundation for Community Organization (IFCO)

IFCO is a national ecumenical agency created in 1966 by several Protestant, Roman Catholic and Jewish organizations, to be an interreligious, interracial agency for support of community organization and education in pursuit of social justice. Through IFCO, national and regional religious bodies collaborate in development of social justice strategies and provide financial support and technical assistance to local, national and international social-justice projects.

IFCO serves as a bridge between the churches and communities and acts as a resource for ministers and congregations wishing to better understand and do more to advance the struggles of the poor and oppressed. IFCO conducts workshops for community organizers and uses its national and international network of organizers, clergy and other professionals to act in the interest of justice.

Churches, foundations and individual donors

use IFCO services as a fiscal agent to make donations to community organizing projects.

IFCO's global outreach includes humanitarian aid shipments through its Pastors for Peace program to Cuba, Haiti, Nicaragua, Honduras, and Chiapas, Mexico.

Headquarters
402 W. 145th St., New York, NY 10031 Tel. (212)926-5757 Fax (212)926-5842
Email: IFCO@igc.org
Website: www. IFCOnews.org
Media Contact, Dir. of Communications, Gail Walker

Officers
Pres., Rev. Schuyler Rhodes
Vice President & Treasurer, Marilyn Clement

The Liturgical Conference

Founded in 1940 by a group of Benedictines, the Liturgical Conference is an independent, ecumenical, international association of persons concerned about liturgical renewal and meaningful worship. The Liturgical Conference is known chiefly for its periodicals, books, materials and sponsorship of regional and local workshops on worship-related concerns in cooperation with various church groups.

Headquarters
8750 Georgia Ave., Ste. 123, Silver Spring, MD 20910-3621 Tel. (301)495-0885
Email: litconf@aol.com
Media Contact, Exec. Dir., Robert Brancatelli

Officers
Pres., Eleanor Bernstein
Vice-Pres., Samuel Torvend
Sec., Robert Rimbo
Treas., Victor Cinson

The Lord's Day Alliance of the United States

The Lord's Day Alliance of the United States, founded in 1888 in Washington, D.C., is the only national organization whose sole purpose is the preservation and cultivation of Sunday, the Lord's Day, as a day of rest and worship. The Alliance also seeks to safeguard a Day of Common Rest for all people regardless of their faith. Its Board of Managers is composed of representatives from 25 denominations. It serves as an information bureau, publishes a magazine, Sunday, and furnishes speakers and a variety of materials such as pamphlets, a book, The Lord's Day, videos, posters, radio spot announcements, decals, cassettes, news releases, articles for magazines and television programs.

Headquarters
2930 Flowers Rd. S., Atlanta, GA 30341 Tel. (770)936-5376 Fax (770)936-5385
Media Contact, Exec. Dir. & Ed., Rev. Timothy A. Norton

Email: tnorton@ldausa.org
Website: www.ldausa.org

Officers
Exec. Dir. & Ed., Rev. Timothy A. Norton
Pres., Dr. Paul Craven, Jr.
Vice-Pres.: Charles Holland; Roger A. Kvam; Timothy E. Bird; John H. Schaal; William B. Shea; W. David Sapp
Sec., Rev. Donald Pepper
Treas., E. Larry Eidson

Lutheran World Relief

Lutheran World Relief (LWR) is an overseas development and relief agency based in New York City which responds quickly to natural and man-made disasters and supports more than 160 long-range development projects in countries throughout Africa, Asia, the Middle East and Latin America.

Founded in 1945 to act on behalf of Lutherans in the United States, LWR has as its mission "to support the poor and oppressed overseas in their efforts to meet basic human needs and participate with dignity and equity in the life of their communities; and to alleviate human suffering resulting from natural disaster, war, social conflict or poverty."

Headquarters
700 Light Street, Baltimore, MD 21230-3850, Tel. 410-230-2700
Email: lwr@lwr.org
Website: www.lwr.org/
Media Contact, Jonathan C. Frerichs

Officers
Pres., Kathryn F. Wolford

The Mennonite Central Committee

The Mennonite Central Committee is the relief and service agency of North American Mennonite and Brethren in Christ Churches. Representatives from Mennonite and Brethren in Christ groups make up the MCC, which meets annually in June to review its program and to approve policies and budget. Founded in 1920, MCC administers and participates in programs of agricultural and economic development, education, health, self-help, relief, peace and disaster service. MCC has about 900 workers serving in 50 countries in Africa, Asia, Europe, Middle East and South, Central and North America.

MCC has service programs in North America that focus both on urban and rural poverty areas. There are also North American programs focusing on such diverse matters as community conciliation, employment creation and criminal justice issues. These programs are administered by two national bodies-MCC U.S. and MCC Canada.

Contributions from North American Mennonite and Brethren in Christ churches provide the largest part of MCC's support. Other sources of financial support include the contributed earnings of volunteers, grants from private and government agencies and contributions from Mennonite churches abroad. The total income in 1999, including material aid contributions, amounted to $69.4 million.

MCC tries to strengthen local communities by working in cooperation with local churches or other community groups. Many personnel are placed with other agencies, including missions. Programs are planned with sensitivity to locally felt needs.

Headquarters

21 S. 12th St., P.O. Box 500, Akron, PA 17501-0500 Tel. (717)859-1151 Fax (717)859-2171
Canadian Office, 134 Plaza Dr., Winnipeg, MB R3T 5K9 Tel. (204)261-6381 Fax (204)269-9875
Email: mailbox@mcc.org
Website: www. mennonitecc.ca/mcc/
Media Contact, Exec. Dir., Ronald J.R. Mathies, P.O. Box 500, Akron, PA 17501 Tel. (717)859-1151 Fax (717)859-2171

Officers

Exec. Directors: Intl., Ronald J.R. Mathies; Canada, David Dyck; U.S.A., Jose Ortiz

National Association of Ecumenical and Interreligious Staff

NAEIS is an association of professional staff in ecumenical and interreligious work. Founded as the Association of Council Secretaries in 1940, the Association was widened to include program staff in 1971, and renamed the National Association of Ecumenical Staff. It has included staff of any faith engaged in interreligious work since 1994. NAEIS provides means for personal and professional growth, and for mutual support, through national and regional conferences, a newsletter and exchange among its membership.

NAEIS was established to provide creative relationships among them and to encourage mutual support and personal and professional growth. This is accomplished through training programs, through exchange and discussion of common concerns at conferences, and through the publication of the Corletter, in collaboration with NCCC Ecumenical Networks.

Headquarters

Currently best reached through Janet E. Leng, Membership Officer, P.O. Box 7093, Tacoma, WA 98406-0093. Tel. (253)759-0141
Email: Maeisjan@aol.com
Media contact: Dr. Jay T. Rock, Interfaith Relations Commission, NCCC USA, 475 Riverside Dr., Rm. 870, New York, NY 10115 Tel (212)870-2560 Fax (212)870-2158

Officers

Pres., Dr. Jay T. Rock, Interfaith Relations Commission, NCCC USA, 475 Riverside Dr., Rm. 870, New York, NY 10115 Tel (212)870-2560 Fax (212)870-2158
Vice-Pres., Julia Sibley Juras, South Carolina

Christian Action Council, P.O. Box 3248, Columbia, SC 29230-3248 Tel. (803)786-7115 Fax (803)786-7116
Imm. Past-Pres., Arthur Lee, Emergency Feeding Program, Church Council of Greater Seattle, PO Box 18145, Seattle, WA 98118-0145 Tel (206)723-0647
Sec., Dr. Paul Teresa Hennessee, Graymoor Ecumenical and Interreligious Institute, 475 Riverside Dr., New York, NY 10115, Tel (212) 870-2968 Fax (212) 870-2001
Tres., James W. Robinson, Tulsa Metropolitan Ministry, 221 South Nogales Ave., Tulsa, OK 74127-8721 Tel. (918)582-3147 Fax (918) 582-3159

The National Association of Evangelicals

The National Association of Evangelicals (NAE) is a voluntary fellowship of evangelical denominations, churches, organizations and individuals demonstrating unity in the body of Christ by standing for biblical truth, speaking with a representative voice, and serving the evangelical community through united action, cooperative ministry and strategic planning.

The association is comprised of approximately 43,000 congregations nationwide from 50 member denominations and fellowships, as well as several hundred independent churches. The membership of the association includes over 250 parachurch ministries and educational institutions. Through the cooperative ministry of these members, NAE directly and indirectly benefits over 27 million people. These ministries represent a broad range of theological traditions, but all subscribe to the distinctly evangelical NAE Statement of Faith. The association is a nationally recognized entity by the public sector with a reputation for integrity and effective service.

The cooperative ministries of the National Association of Evangelicals demonstrate the association's intentional desire to promote cooperation without compromise.

Headquarters

P.O. Box 1325, Azusa, CA 91702 Tel. (626)963-5966
NAE-Washington, 1001 Connecticut Ave., Suite 522, Washington, DC 20036 Tel. (202)789-1011 Fax (202)842-0392
Email: NAE@nae.net
Website: www.nae.net
Media Contact, Rev. John Mendez, (626)963-5966

Staff

President, Dr. Kevin Mannoia
Counsel, Forest Montgomery

MEMBER DENOMINATIONS

Advent Christian General Conference
Assemblies of God
Association of Vineyard Churches
Baptist General Conference

Brethren Church, The (Ashland, Ohio)
Brethren in Christ Church
Christian & Missionary Alliance
Christian Catholic Church (Evan. Protestant)
Christian Church of North America
Christian Reformed Church in North America
Christian Union
Church of God, Cleveland, TN
Church of God, Mountain Assembly
Church of the Nazarene
Church of the United Brethren in Christ
Churches of Christ in Christian Union
Congregational Holiness Church
Conservative Baptist Assoc. of America
Conservative Congregational Christian Conf.
Conservative Lutheran Association
Elim Fellowship
Evangelical Church of North America
Evangelical Congregational Church
Evangelical Free Church of America
Evangelical Friends Intl./North America
Evangelical Mennonite Church
Evangelical Methodist Church
Evangelical Presbyterian Church
Evangelistic Missionary Fellowship
Fellowship of Evangelical Bible Churches
Fire-Baptized Holiness Church of God of the
    Americas
Free Methodist Church of North America
General Association of General Baptists
Intl. Church of the Foursquare Gospel
Intl. Pentecostal Church of Christ
Intl. Pentecostal Holiness Church
Mennonite Brethren Churches, USA
Midwest Congregational Christian Fellowship
Missionary Church
Open Bible Standard Churches
Pentecostal Church of God
Pentecostal Free Will Baptist Church
Presbyterian Church in America
Primitive Methodist Church, USA
Reformed Episcopal Church
Reformed Presbyterian Church of N.A.
Salvation Army
Synod of Evangelical Fellowship Chapels of the
    Fellowship Deaconry, Inc.
Synod of Mid-America (Reformed Church in
    America)
Wesleyan Church
Worldwide Church of God

National Bible Association

The National Bible Association is an autonomous, interfaith organization of lay people that advocates regular Bible reading and sponsors National Bible Week (Thanksgiving week) each November. Program activities include public service advertising, distribution of nonsectarian literature and thousands of local Bible Week observances by secular and religious organizations. The Association also urges constitutionally acceptable use of the Bible in public school classrooms, i.e., the study of the Bible in literature. All support comes from individuals, corporations and foundations.

Founded in 1940 by a group of business and professional people, the Association offers daily Bible readings in several English and Spanish translations on its website and has the IRS nonprofit status of a 501(c)(3) educational association.

Headquarters
1865 Broadway, New York, NY 10023 Tel.
    (212)408-1390 Fax (212)408-1448
Email: info@nationalbible.org
Website: www.nationalbible.org
Media Contact, Pres., Thomas R. May

Officers
Cpsn., Stewart S. Furlong
Vice-Cpsn., Robert Cavalero
Pres., Thomas R. May
Treas., Paul Werner
Sec., J. Marshall Gage

The National Conference for Community and Justice

The National Conference for Community and Justice, founded in 1927 as the National Conference of Christians and Jews, is a human relations organization dedicated to fighting bias, bigotry and racism in America. The NCCJ promotes understanding and respect among all races, religions and cultures through advocacy, conflict resolution and education.

Programmatic strategies include interfaith and interracial dialogue, youth leadership workshops, workplace training, human relations research, and the building of community coalitions. NCCJ has 65 regional offices staffed by approximately 350 people. Nearly 200 members comprise the National Board of Advisors and members from that group form the 27-member National Board of Directors. Each regional office has its own Regional Board of Directors with a total of about 2,800. The National Board of Advisors meets once annually, the National Board of Directors at least three times annually.

Headquarters
475 Park Ave. South, New York, NY 10016 Tel.
    (212)545-1300 Fax (212)545-8053
Media Contact, Dir. of Communications, Joyce
    Dubensky

Officers
Pres. & CEO, Sanford Cloud, Jr.

National Conference on Ministry to the Armed Forces

The Conference is an incorporated civilian agency. Representation in the Conference with all privileges of the same is open to all endorsing or certifying agencies or groups authorized to provide chaplains for any branch of the Armed Forces.

The purpose of this organization is to provide

a means of dialogue to discuss concerns and objectives and, when agreed upon, to take action with the appropriate authority to support the spiritual ministry to and the moral welfare of Armed Forces personnel.

Headquarters
4141 N. Henderson Rd., Ste. 13, Arlington, VA 22203 Tel. (703)276-7905 Fax (703)276-7906 Email: jackw@erols.com & maureen.francis@tcs. wap.org
Media Contact, Jack Williamson

Staff
Coord., Jack Williamson
Admn. Asst., Maureen Francis

Officers
Chpsn., Rodger Venzke
Chpsn.-elect, Robert Vickers
Sec., J. Paul Jenson
Treas., Jacob Heerema
Committee Members: Catholic Rep., John J. Glynn; Protestant Rep., Jeannette Flynn; Jewish Rep., David Lapp; Orthodox Rep., Ted Boback; Member-at-Large, McKinley Young; Past Chair, Richard O. Stenbakken

National Council of the Churches of Christ in the U.S.A.
The National Council of the Churches of Christ in the U.S.A. is the preeminent expression in the United States of the movement toward Christian unity. The NCC's 36 member communions, including Protestant, Orthodox and Anglican church bodies, work together on a wide range of activities that further Christian unity, that witness to the faith, that promote peace and justice and that serve people throughout the world. Approximately 50 million U.S. Christians belong to churches that hold Council membership. The Council was formed in 1950 in Cleveland, Ohio, by the action of representatives of the member churches and by the merger of 12 previously existing ecumenical agencies, each of which had a different program focus. The roots of some of these agencies go back to the 19th century.

Headquarters
475 Riverside Dr., New York, NY 10115. Tel. (212)870-2141
Media Contact, Dir. of News Services, Ms. Carol J. Fouke, 475 Riverside Dr., Rm. 850, New York, NY 10115, Tel. (212)870-2252, Fax (212)870-2030
Website: www.ncccusa.org

Officers
GENERAL OFFICERS
Pres., The Honorable Andrew J. Young
Gen. Sec., Rev. Dr. Robert W. Edgar
Pres.-Elect, Ms. Elenie K. Huszagh, Esq.
Immediate Past Pres., Rt. Rev. Craig B. Anderson
Sec., Rev. Roberto Delgado

Treas., Mr. Philip Young
Vice-Pres., Church World Service and Witness: Rev. Patrick Mauney
Vice-Pres., National Ministries, Dr. Audrey Miller
Vice Pres. at Large: Bishop Jon S. Enslin, Rev. Dr. Bertrice Wood, Ms. Barbara Ricks Thompson
THE GENERAL SECRETARIAT
Tel. (212)870-2141 Fax (212)870-2817
Gen. Sec., Rev. Robert W. Edgar
Interim Dir. of Development, Mr. John A. Briscoe
Special Assistant to the Gen. Sec., Ms. Karen M. Hessel, Tel. (212)870-2421
YEARBOOK OF AMERICAN AND CANADIAN CHURCHES
Editor, Rev. Dr. Eileen W. Lindner, Deputy General Secretary for Research and Development Tel. (212)870-2333
Redevelopment and Technical Dir., Rev. Marcel A. Welty Tel. (212)870-2379
Assistant Editor, Mr. Nathan Hanson, Tel. (212) 870-2031 Fax (212)870-2817
WASHINGTON OFFICE
110 Maryland Ave. NE Washington, D.C. 20002. Tel. (202)544-2350. Fax (202)543-1297.
Dir., Ms. Brenda Girton-Mitchell, Esq.
COMMUNICATIONS COMMISSION
Tel. (212)870-2574 Fax (212)870-2030
Dir., News Services, Ms. Carol J. Fouke
Dir., Electronic Media, Rev. David W. Pomeroy
Communications Coordinator, Ms. Sarah Vilankulu
Design and Print Services, Manager, Mr. Sean Grandits
UNITY, EDUCATION, AND JUSTICE PROGRAM MINISTRIES
Faith and Order, Rev. Dr. William G. Rusch Tel. (212)870-2569
Interfaith Relations, Dr. Jay T. Rock, Tel. (212)870-2560
Orthodox Liaison, Mr. Gabriel Habib Tel. (202)-544-2350
Dir., Ministries in Christian Education, Rev. Patrice Rosner Tel. (212)870-2738
Ministries in Christian Education, Dr. Joe Leonard Tel. (212)870-2673
Environmental Justice, Rev. Richard Killmer Tel. (212)870-2385
Economic Justice, Rev. Richard Killmer
Racial Justice, Dir., Ms. Sammy Toineeta Tel., (212)870-2387
Justice for Women, Prog. Cood., Ms. Karen M. Hessel, Tel. (212)870-2421
Interfaith Center for Corporate Responsibility, Interim Dir., Tel. (212)870-2293
Natl. Farm Worker Ministry, Executive Director, Mary Dutcher Tel. (314)726-6470
ADMINISTRATION AND FINANCE
Tel. (212)870-2088 Fax (212)870-3112
Chief Financial Officer and Interim General Manager, Dr. Barbara Ellen Black

Financial Services
Controller, Mr. Chuck Chamberlayne, Tel. (212)870-2084
Dept. of Business Services, Tel. (212)870-2181
Dir., Ms. Melrose B. Corley Tel. (212)870-2267
Office of Human Resources, Tel. (212)870-2088
Coord., Human Resources, Ms. Judy Williams, Tel., (212)870-2089
Manager, Recruitment, Ms. Laura Williams, Tel. (212)870-2097
CHURCH WORLD SERVICE AND WITNESS
Tel. (212)870-2061 Fax (212)870-3523
Exec. Dir., Rev. John L. McCullough, Tel. (212)870-2175
Deputy Dir., Operations, Ms. Joanne Rendall, Tel. (219)264-3102 x. 332
Dir., Resource Development Department, Mr. Rhonnie Hemphill, Tel. (219)264-3102 x. 454
Interim Dir., Mission Relations & Witness Program, Mr. David Weaver, Tel. (212)870-2818
Dir., Education & Advocacy for International Justice & Human Rights, -vacant-
Interim Dir., Social Economic Development, Mr. Rick Santos, Tel. (212)870-2008
Dir., Emergency Response, Mr. Rick Augsburger, Tel. (212)870-3154
Dir., Immigration & Refugee Program, Rev. Wendy Pomeroy, Tel. (212)870-2167
CONSTITUENT BODIES OF THE NATIONAL COUNCIL (with membership dates)
African Methodist Episcopal Church (1950)
African Methodist Episcopal Zion Church (1950)
The Alliance of Baptists in the U.S.A. (2000)
American Baptist Churches in the U.S.A. (1950)
The Antiochian Orthodox Christian Archdiocese of North America (1966)
Armenian Apostolic Church of America, Diocese of the (1957)
Christian Church (Disciples of Christ) (1950)
Christian Methodist Episcopal Church (1950)
Church of the Brethren (1950)
Coptic Orthodox Church (1978)
The Episcopal Church (1950)
Evangelical Lutheran Church in America (1950)
Friends United Meeting (1950)
Greek Orthodox Archdiocese of America (1952)
Hungarian Reformed Church in America (1957)
Intl. Council of Community Churches (1977)
Korean Presbyterian Church in America, Gen. Assembly of the (1986)
Malankara Orthodox Syrian Church, Diocese of America (1998)
Mar Thoma Church (1997)
Moravian Church in America, Northern Province, Southern Province (1950)
National Baptist Convention of America, Inc. (1950)
National Baptist Convention, U.S.A., Inc. (1950)
National Missionary Baptist Convention of America (1995)
Orthodox Church in America (1950)

Philadelphia Yearly Meeting of the Religious Society of Friends (1950)
Polish Natl. Catholic Church of America (1957)
Presbyterian Church (U.S.A.) (1950)
Progressive Natl. Baptist Convention, Inc. (1966)
Reformed Church in America (1950)
Russian Orthodox Church in the U.S.A., Patriarchal Parishes of the (1966)
Serbian Orthodox Church in the U.S.A. & Canada (1957)
The Swedenborgian Church (1966)
Syrian Orthodox Church of Antioch(Archdiocese of the U.S. and Canada) (1960)
Ukrainian Orthodox Church of the U.S.A.(1950)
United Church of Christ (1950)
The United Methodist Church (1950)

National Institute of Business and Industrial Chaplains

NIBIC is the professional organization for workplace chaplains that includes members from a wide variety of denominations and work settings, including corporations, manufacturing plants, air and sea ports, labor unions and pastoral counseling centers. NIBIC has six membership categories, including Clinical, Professional, Affiliates and Organizational.

NIBIC works to establish professional standards for education and practice; promotes and conducts training programs; provides mentoring, networking and chaplaincy information; encourages research and public information dissemination; communicates with business leaders and conducts professional meetings. NIBIC publishes a quarterly newsletter and co-sponsors The Journal of Pastoral Care. A public membership meeting and training conference is held annually.

Headquarters

7100 Regency Square Blvd., Ste. 210, Houston, TX 77036-3202 Tel. (713)266-2456 Fax (713)266-0845
Email: info@nibic.com
Website: www. nibic.com
Media Contact, Rev. Diana C. Dale, 7100 Regency Square Blvd., Ste. 210, Houston, TX 77036-3202 Tel. (713)266-2456 Fax (713) 266-0845

Officers

Executive Dir., Rev. Diana C. Dale, D.Min.
Vice-Pres., Rev. Stephen Holden
President, Rev. Timothy Bancroft, D.Min.
Treas., Rev. Gregory Edwards

National Interfaith Cable Coalition, Inc.

The National Interfaith Cable Coalition, Inc. (NICC) was formed as a not-for-profit 501(c)3 corporation, in December, 1987, and is currently comprised of nearly 70 associated faith groups from the Jewish and Christian traditions.

35

In September 1988, NICC launched a religious cable network called VISN (Vision Interfaith Satellite Network), now known as Odyssey Network. Today, Odyssey is owned and operated by Crown Media Holdings, Inc., in which NICC is a strategic investor. Odyssey provides a mix of high-quality family entertainment and faith-based programming. NICC provides 30 hours a week of programming on the network.

In 2000, NICC adopted Faith & Values Media as its service mark and expanded its mission to include a significant Web presence (FaithAnd ValuesMedia.org) and plans for a full-time digital channel.

Headquarters

74 Trinity Place, Ste. 1550, New York, NY 10006 Tel. (212)406-4121 Fax (212)406-4105
Media Contact, Beverly Judge
Email: bjudge@mail.nicc-usa.org

Officers

Chair, Dr. Daniel Paul Matthews
Vice Chair, Ralph Hardy Jr., Esq.
Secretary, Rabbi Paul J. Menitoff
Treasurer, Betty Elam

Staff

President and CEO, Edward J. Murray
Vice President, Beverly Judge

National Interfaith Coalition on Aging

The National Interfaith Coalition on Aging (NICA), a constituent unit of the National Council on Aging, is composed of Protestant, Roman Catholic, Jewish and Orthodox national and regional organizations and individuals concerned about the needs of older people and the religious community's response to problems facing the aging population in the United States. NICA was organized in 1972 to address spiritual concerns of older adults through religious sector action.

Mission Statement: The National Interfaith Coalition on Aging (NICA), affiliated with the National Council on the Aging (NCOA) is a diverse network of religious and other related organizations and individual members which promotes the spiritual well being of older adults and the preparation of persons of all ages for the spiritual tasks of aging. NICA serves as a catalyst for new and effective research, networking opportunities, resource development, service provision, and dissemination of information.

Headquarters

c/o NCOA, 409 Third St., SW, 2nd Floor, Washington, DC 20024 Tel. (202)479-6655 Fax (202)479-0735
Media Contact, NCOA Dir. of Communications, Michael Reinemer

Officers

Chpsn., Rev. Dr. Richard H. Gentzler, Jr.

Chpsn.-Elect, Rev. Dr. Robert W. Carlson
Past Chpsn., Josselyn Bennett
Sec., Rev. Dr. James W. Ellor
Vol. Dir., Dr. Rita K. Chow

National Interfaith Committee for Worker Justice

The National Interfaith Committee for Worker Justice (NICWJ) is a network of fifty-six interfaith groups and people of faith who educate and mobilize the U.S. religious community on issues and campaigns to improve wages, benefits and working conditions for workers, especially low-wage workers. The organization rebuilds relationships between the religious community and organized labor.

The organization supports and organizes local interfaith worker justice groups around the country, publishes Faith Works six times a year providing congregations resources and updates on religion-labor work, coordinates the Poultry Justice project to improve conditions for poultry workers, and promotes healthy dialogue between management and unions in religious owned or sponsored health care facilities.

Headquarters

1020 West Bryn Mawr, 4th floor, Chicago, IL 60660-4627. Tel. (773)728-8400 Fax (773) 728-8409
Email: info@nicwj.org
Website: www.nationalinterfaith.org
Media Contact: Mr. Toure Muhammed

Officers

President, Bishop Jesse DeWitt (retired United Methodist Bishop)
Vice President, Bishop Howard Hubbard (Bishop of the Catholic Diocese of Albany)
Secretary-Treasurer, Rev. Jim Sessions (Union Community Fund)
Chair of Action & Issues Committee, Rev. Michael Rouse (Pastor, St. Catherine African Methodist Episcopal Zion Church)
Chair of Education Committee, Rabbi Robert Marx (Congregation Hakafa)
Chair of Board Development Committee, Ms. Evely Laser Shlensky (Committee on Social Action of Reform Judaism)

Staff

Executive Director, Ms. Kim Bobo
Education & Outreach Coordinator, Ms. Regina Botterill
Poultry Justice Coordinator, Ms. Miltoria Bey
North Carolina Poultry Justice Coordinator, Ms. Deborah Young
Religious Employers Project Coordinator, Sr. Barbara Pfarr, SSND and Sr. Denise Starkey, OP
Communications Coordinator, Mr. Toure Muhammed
Office Manager, Ms. Bridget Harris
Designer & Webmaster, Ms. Jana Winch

NETWORK AFFILIATES

ARIZONA
Phoenix Interfaith Committee for Worker Justice, 4302 N. 87th Pl., Scottsdale, AZ 85251; Tel. (602)946-5843; Contact: Mrs. Margaret Grannis

ARKANSAS
Western Arkansas Labor Coalition, P.O. Box 1122, Alma, AK 7921; Tel. (501)783-1149; Contact: Matt Joyce

Little Rock Religion and Labor Committee of Jobs with Justice, PO Box 477, Hampton, AK 71744; Tel. (840)783-1149; Fax (840)783-0512; Contact: Rev. Steve Copley

CALIFORNIA
Los Angeles Clergy and Laity United for Economic Justice, 548 S. Spring St., Suite 630, Los Angeles, CA 90013-2313; Tel. (213) 486-9880 x103; Fax (213)486-9886; Contact: Ms. Linda Lotz

San Jose Interfaith Council on Race, Religion, Economic & Social Justice, 2102 Almaden Rd., #107, Santa Clara, CA 95125; Tel. (408) 269-7872; Email: tic@atwork.org Coordinator: Poncho Guevara

DELAWARE
Delmarva Poultry Justice Alliance, c/o La Esperanza, 319 Race St., Georgetown, DE 19947; Tel. (302)854-9264; Fax (302)854-9277; Contact: Ms. Andrea Lukowsky

FLORIDA
Immokalee—Religious Leaders Concerned, 3619 Woodlake Drive, Bonita Springs, FL 34134; Tel. (941)495-1679; Fax (941)495-6595; Contact: Rhea Gray

South Florida Interfaith Committee for Worker Justice, 6801 NW 15th Ave., Miami, FL 33147; Tel. (305)835-9808; Fax (305)835-7227; Contact: Rev. Richard Bennett

ILLINOIS
Chicago Interfaith Committee on Worker Issues, 1020 West Bryn Mawr, Chicago, IL 60660-4627; Tel. (773)728-8400; Fax (773)728-8409; Contact: Rev. Richard Bundy or Ms. Kristi Sanford

INDIANA
Northwest Indiana—Calumet Project, 7128 Arizona Ave., Hammond, IN 46323-2223; Tel. (219)845-5008; Fax (219)845-5032; Contact: Mr. Steven Ashby

Central Indiana—St. Joseph Valley Project, 2015 W. Western, #209, South Bend, IN 46629; Tel. (219)287-3834; Fax (219)233-5543; Coordinator: Mr. Dan Lane

Indianapolis—Interfaith Committee for Worker Justice, c/o East Tenth United Methodist Church, 2327 East 10th St., Indianapolis, IN 46220-0530; Tel. (317)636-9017; Fax (317) 633-8368; Contact: Rev. Darren Cushman-Wood

KENTUCKY
Worker Rights Outreach & Kentucky Jobs with Justice, 1815 Fernwood Avenue, Louisville, KY 40205; Tel. (502)568-5600; Fax (502) 581-1437; Contact: Mr. Chris Sanders

MASSACHUSETTS
Massachusetts Interfaith Committee for Worker Justice, 33 Harrison Ave., 4th floor, Boston, MA 02111; Tel. (617)574-9296; Fax (617) 426-7684; Email: inalliance@aol.com; Contact: Dr. Jonathan Fine

Religion & Labor Committee, c/o Labor Guild of Boston, 883 Hancock St., Quincy, MA 02170; Tel. (617)786-1822; Fax (617)472-2486; Contact: Father Edward Boyle

Holy Cross Student Labor Action Committee, PO Box 840, College of the Holy Cross, Worcester, MA 01610; Email: mldorosa@holycross.edu

MICHIGAN
Detroit Interfaith Committee on Worker Issues, 1641 Webb, Detroit, MI 48206; Tel. (313) 869-1632; Fax (313)869-8266; Contact: Ms. Barbara Hunt

MISSOURI
Kansas City Religion and Labor Coalition, PO Box 240595, Kansas City, MO 64124; Tel. (816)861-0073; Fax (816)861-0071; Contact: Mr. Jerry Meszaros

Labor & Religion Committee of the Human Rights Commission, 3519 N. 14th St., St. Louis, MO 63107; Tel. (314)241-9165; Fax (314)436-9291; Contact Rev. Rich Creason

NEVADA
Las Vegas Interfaith Council for Worker Justice, 1630 S. Commerce St., Las Vegas, NV 89102; Tel. (702)386-5258; Fax (702)384-0845; Contact: Ms. Paula Tusiani

NEW HAMPSHIRE
Interfaith Committee for Worker Justice, PO Box 292, Goffstown, NH 03045; Tel. (603)497-5167; Contact: Fred Robinson

NEW YORK
Albany Capitol District Labor Religion Coalition, 159 Wolf Road, Albany, NY 12205; Tel. (518)459-5400; Fax (518)454-6411; Contact: Ms. Margaret Shirk

Buffalo Coalition for Economic Justice, 2123 Bailey Ave., Buffalo, NY 14211; Tel. (716) 894-2013; Contact: Ms. Joan Malone

New York City Labor-Religion Coalition, 40 Fulton St., 22nd Floor, New York, NY 10038; Tel. (212)406-2156, ext. 237; Fax (212)406-2296; Contact: Rabbi Michael Feinberg

New York City Staten Island Religion Labor Coalition, 32D Franklin Lane, Staten Island, NY 10306; Tel. (212)406-2156; Fax (212) 406-2296; Contact: Ms. Lilly Gioia

New York State Labor-Religion Coalition, 159 Wolf Road, Albany, NY 12205; Tel. (518)459-5400; Contact: Mr. Brian O'Shaughnessy

Syracuse Central New York Labor Religion Coalition, 614 James St., Syracuse, NY 13201; Tel. (315)445-1690; Fax (315)445-1690; Contact: Ms. Mary Hannick

NORTH CAROLINA

North Carolina Poultry Justice Alliance, 417 Arlington St., Greensboro, NC 27406; Tel. (336)271-4070; Email: jtaylor54@juno.com; Contact: Dr. Jerry Taylor

Pulpit Forum, 1310 MLK Dr., Greensboro, NC 27406; Tel. (336)272-8441; Fax (336)378-1165; Contact: Rev. W.F. Wright

OHIO

Central Ohio Religion-Labor Network, Office of Social Action, Diocese of Columbus, Columbus, OH 42315; Tel. (614)241-2541; Contact: Mr. Mark Huddy

Cincinnati Interfaith Committee on Worker Justice, c/o Social Action Office, 100 E. 8th St., Cincinnati, OH 45212; Tel. (513)421-3131; Fax (513)421-1582; Contact: Mr. Thomas Choquette

Cleveland Jobs with Justice, 20525 Center Ridge Rd., Rocky River, OH 44116; Tel. (440)333-6363; Fax (440)333-1491; Contact: Mr. Steve Cagan

OKLAHOMA

Labor-Religion Council of Oklahoma, PO Box 2009, Tulsa, OK 74101-2009; Tel. (918)587-3115; Fax (918)587-6692; Contact: Rev. Donald Brooks

OREGON

Eugene-Springfield Solidarity Network, 4355 Pinecrest Dr., Eugene, OR 97405; Tel. (541)345-3253; Fax (541)346-2790; Contact: Mr. Charles Spencer

PENNSYVANIA

Area Religious Task Force on the Economy, 5125 Tenn. Ave., Pittsburgh, PA 15224; Tel. (412)361-3022; Contact: Rev. Ted Erickson

TENNESSEE

Nashville Middle Tennessee Jobs with Justice, 516 Riverwood Circle, Nashville, TN 37216; Tel. (615)226-9420; Fax (615)227-3185; Contact: Ms. Laurie Bullock

Knoxville Religious Outreach Committee, Jobs with Justice, 1959 Highlander Way, New Market, TN 37820; Tel. (423)933-3443; Fax (423)933-3424; Contact: Rev. Jim Sessions

TEXAS

Brazos Valley Interfaith Alliance for Worker Justice, St. Mary's Catholic Church, 603 Church St., College Station, TX 77840; Tel. (409) 846-5717; Contact: Ms. Maureen Murray

Dallas Jobs with Justice, c/o Camp Wisdom UMC, 1300 W. Camp Wisdom Rd., Dallas, TX 75232; Tel. (972)224-4556; Fax (972)228-9434; Contact: Rev Charles Stovall

Houston Interfaith Committee for Worker Justice, c/o Worklife Ministries, 7100 Regency Sq., Suite 210, Houston, TX 77036; Tel. (713)266-2456; Fax (713)266-0845; Contact: Rev. Diana Dale

WASHINGTON

Washington Religious Labor Partnership, c/o Wash. Association of Churches, 419 Occidental Ave., South, #201, Seattle, WA 98104; Tel. (206)625-9790; Fax (206)625-9791; Contact: Rev. John Boonstra

WISCONSIN

Faith Community for Worker Justice, 2128 N. 73rd St., Wauwatosa, WI 53213; Tel. (414) 771-7250; Fax (414)771-0509; Contact: Mr. Bill Lange

Center on Conscience and War / NISBCO

CCW/NISBCO, formed in 1940, is a nonprofit service organization supported by individual contributions and related to more than thirty religious organizations. Its purpose is to defend and extend the rights of conscientious objectors to war and organized violence. NISBCO provides information on how to register for the draft and to document one's convictions and qualify as a conscientious objector, how to cope with penalties if one does not cooperate, and how to qualify as a conscientious objector while in the Armed Forces. It also provides more general information for counselors and the public about conscientious objection, military service and the operation of the draft. It provides information to and support of conscientious objectors in other countries.

As a national resource center it assists research in its area of interest including the peace witness of religious bodies. Its staff provides referral to local counselors and attorneys and professional support for them. Through publications and speaking, CCW/NISBCO encourages people to decide for themselves what they believe about participation in war and to act on the basis of the dictates of their own informed consciences. ·

Headquarters

1830 Connecticut Ave. NW, Washington, DC 20009-5732 Tel. (202)483-2220 Fax (202) 483-1246

Email: nisbco@nisbco.org
Website:www.nisbco.org
Media Contact, Exec. Dir., J.E. McNeil

Officers

Exec. Dir., J.E. McNeil
Chpsn., Jonathan Ogle
Sec., John Michael Sophos
Treas., Frank Massey

National Religious Broadcasters

National Religious Broadcasters is an association of 1,300 organizations which produce religious programs for radio and television and other forms of electronic mass media or operate stations carrying predominately religious programs. NRB member organizations are responsible for more than 75 percent of all religious radio and television in the United States, reaching an average weekly audience of millions by radio, television, and other broadcast media.

Dedicated to the communication of the Gospel, NRB was founded in 1944 to safeguard free and complete access to the broadcast media. By encouraging the development of Christian programs and stations, NRB helps make it possible for millions to hear the good news of Jesus Christ through the electronic media.

Headquarters

7839 Ashton Ave., Manassas, VA 20109 Tel. (703)330-7000 Fax (703)330-7100
Email: info@nrb.org
Website: www.nrb.org
Media Contact, Pres., Brandt Gustavson; Vice-Pres., Michael Glenn

Officers

Chmn., Wayne A. Pederson, Northwestern College Radio, St. Paul, MN
1st Vice Chmn., Glenn R. Plummer, Christian Television Network, Detroit, MI
2nd Vice Chmn., Michael D. Little, Christian Broadcasting Network, Virginia Beach, VA
Sec., William Skelton, Love Worth Finding Ministries, Memphis, TN
Treas., James A. Gwinn, CRISTA Ministries, Seattle, WA

National Woman's Christian Temperance Union

The National WCTU is a not-for-profit, non-partisan, interdenominational organization dedicated to the education of our nation's citizens, especially children and teens, on the harmful effects of alcoholic beverages, other drugs and tobacco on the human body and the society in which we live. The WCTU believes in a strong family unit and, through legislation, education and prayer, works to strengthen the home and family.

WCTU, which began in 1874 with the motto, "For God and Home and Every Land," is organized in 58 countries.

Headquarters

1730 Chicago Ave., Evanston, IL 60201 Tel. (708)864-1396
Website: www.wctu.org
Media Contact, Sarah F. Ward, Tel. 765-345-7600

Officers

Pres., Sarah F. Ward, 33 N. Franklin, Knightstown, IN 46148
Email: sarah@wctu.org
Vice-Pres., Rita Wert, 2250 Creek Hill Rd., Lancaster, PA 17601
Promotion Dir., Nancy Zabel, 1730 Chicago Ave., Evanston, IL 60201-4585
Treas., Faye Pohl, P.O. Box 739, Meade, KS 67864
Rec. Sec., Dorothy Russell, 18900 Nestueca Dr., Cloverdale, OR 97112

MEMBER ORGANIZATIONS

Loyal Temperance Legion (LTL), for boys and girls ages 6-12
Youth Temperance Council (YTC), for teens through college age

North American Baptist Fellowship

Organized in 1964, the North American Baptist Fellowship is a voluntary organization of Baptist Conventions in Canada and the United States, functioning as a regional body within the Baptist World Alliance. Its objectives are: (a) to promote fellowship and cooperation among Baptists in North America and (b) to further the aims and objectives of the Baptist World Alliance so far as these affect the life of the Baptist churches in North America. Its membership, however, is not identical with the North American membership of the Baptist World Alliance.

Church membership of the Fellowship bodies is more than 28 million.

The NABF assembles representatives of the member bodies once a year for exchange of information and views in such fields as evangelism and education, missions, stewardship promotion, lay activities and theological education. It conducts occasional consultations for denominational leaders on such subjects as church extension. It encourages cooperation at the city and county level where churches of more than one member group are located.

Headquarters

Baptist World Alliance Bldg., 6733 Curran St., McLean, VA 22101
Email: nabf@bwanet.org
Website: www. bwanet.org
Media Contact, Dr. Denton Lotz

Officers

Pres., Dr. Robert Ricker, 2002 S. Arlington Heights Rd., Arlington Heights, IL 60005
Vice-Pres., Dr. David Emmanuel Goatley, 300 I St., NE, Suite 104, Washington, DC 20002
Vice-Pres., Dr. Phillip Wise, 300 West Main St., Box 2025, Dothan, AL 36301
Vice-Pres., Dr. Robert Wilkins, 7185 Millcreek Dr. Mississauga, ON l5N 5R4, Canada

MEMBER BODIES

American Baptist Churches in the USA
Baptist General Conference
Canadian Baptist Federation
General Association of General Baptists
National Baptist Convention of America
National Baptist Convention, USA, Inc.
Progressive National Baptist Convention, Inc.
Seventh Day Baptist General Conference
North American Baptist Conference
Southern Baptist Convention

Oikocredit: Ecumenical Development Cooperative Society

Based in the Netherlands, EDCS is often called "the churches' bank for the poor." EDCS borrows funds from churches, religious communities and concerned individuals and re-lends the funds to enterprises operated by low-income communities. Launched in 1975 through an initiative of the World Council of Churches, EDCS is organized as a cooperative of religious institutions and is governed by annual membership meetings and an elected board of religious leaders and development and financial professionals.

An international network of 15 EDCS Regional Managers is responsible for lending funds to cooperative enterprises and microcredit institutions. At the present time over $50 million is at work in coffee shops, fishing enterprises, handicraft production, truck farming, and many other commercial ventures owned and operated by poor people.

EDCS is represented in the United States by the Ecumenical Development Corporation-USA (EDC-USA), a 501(c)3 non-profit corporation. American individuals and congregations can invest in EDCS by purchasing one, three, and five year notes paying 0-2% interest that are issued by EDC-USA.

U.S. Headquarters
475 Riverside Dr., 16th Floor, New York, NY 10115 Tel. (212)870-2725 Fax (212)870-2722 Email: edcusa@erols.com
Media Contact, Regional Manager for North America, The Rev. Louis L. Knowles

Officers, EDC-USA
Chpsn., The Rev. Dr. DarEll Weist
Vice-Chpsn., Thomas Dowdell
Treas., Bruce Foresman
Sec., Suzanne Sattler, IHM

Parish Resource Center, Inc.
Parish Resource Center, Inc. promotes, establishes, nurtures and accredits local Affiliate Parish Resource Centers. Affiliate centers educate, equip and strengthen subscribing congregations of all faiths by providing professional consultants, resource materials and workshops. The Parish Resource Center was founded in 1976. In 2000, there were six free-standing affiliates located in Lancaster, PA; Long Island, NY; South Bend, IN; Denver, CO; Dayton, OH and New York City. These centers serve congregations from 49 faith traditions.

Headquarters
633 Community Way, Lancaster, PA 17603 Tel. (717)299-2223 Fax (717)299-7229
Email: prcinc@redrose.net
Media Contact, Pres., Dr. D. Douglas Whiting

Officers
Chair, Richard J. Ashby, Jr.
Vice-Chair, Margaret M. Obrecht
Sec., Dr. Robert Webber
Treas., Stephen C. Eyre
Pres., Dr. D. Douglas Whiting

Pentecostal/Charismatic Churches of North America
The Pentecostal/Charismatic Churches of North America (PCCNA) was organized October 19, 1994, in Memphis, TN. This organizational meeting came the day after the Pentecostal Fellowship of North America (PFNA) voted itself out of existence in order to make way for the new fellowship.

The PFNA had been formed in October 1948 in Des Moines, IA. It was composed of white-led Pentecostal denominations. The move to develop a multiracial fellowship began when the PFNA Board of Administration initiated a series of discussions with African-American Pentecostal leaders. The first meeting was held July 10-11, 1992, in Dallas, TX. A second meeting convened in Phoenix, AZ, January 4-5, 1993. On January 10-11, 1994, 20 representatives from each of the two groups met in Memphis to make final plans for a Dialogue which was held in Memphis, October 1994.

This racial reconciliation meeting has been called "The Memphis Miracle." During this meeting the PFNA was disbanded, and the PCCNA was organized. The new organization quickly adopted the "Racial Reconciliation Manifesto." Subsequent meetings were held in Memphis, TN (1996), Washington, D.C. (1997), Tulsa, OK (1998), and Hampton, VA (1999).

Forty thousand copies of the PCCNA-sponsored magazine's inaugural issue of Reconciliation were published in June, 1998 and distributed to pastors in PCCNA-member churches. Dr. Harold D. Hunter and Dr. Cecil M. Robeck, Jr., are co-editors of this publication.

Headquarters
1910 W. Sunset Blvd. Ste. 200, Los Angeles, CA 90026-0176 Tel. (213)484-2400, ext. 309 Fax (213)413-3824
Email: comm@foursquare.org
Website: www. iphc.org/pccna/index.html
Media Contact, Dr. Ronald Williams

Executive Committee
Co-Chpsn., Bishop Gilbert E. Patterson, 240 E. Raines Rd., Memphis, TN 38109
Co-Chpsn., Rev. Thomas Trask, 1445 Boonville Ave., Springfield, MO 65802
1st. Vice-Chpsn., Bishop Barbara Amos, 1010 East 26th St., Norfolk, VA 23504
2nd Vice-Chpsn., Rev. Rev. Billy Joe Daugherty, 7700 S. Lewis, Tulsa, OK 74136-6600
Sec., Rev. Oswill Williams, 3720 N Keith Street, Cleveland, TN 37320
Treas., Dr. Ronald Williams, P.O. Box 26902, Los Angeles, CA 90026
Co-Editors of Reconciliation: Dr. Harold D. Hunter, PO Box 12609, Oklahoma City, OK 73157; Dr. Cecil M. Robeck, Jr., 135 North Oakland Ave., Pasadena, CA 91182
Members: Bishop Ithiel Clemmons, 221 Kingston Ave., Brooklyn, NY 11213; Rev. Bishop Rodderick Ceasar, 110-25 Buy Brewer Blvd., Jamaica Queens, NY 11433; Bishop George D. McKinney, 5825 Imperial Ave., San Diego, CA 92114; Bishop James Leggett, P.O. Box 12609, Oklahoma City, OK 73157; Dr.

Paul Walker, 2055 Mount Paran Rd., NW, Atlanta, GA 30327; Rev. Ann Gimenez, 640 Kempsville Rd., Virginia Beach, VA 23464
Advisors: Bishop B.E. Underwood, 172 Tanglewood South, Royston, GA 30662; Rev. Perry Gillum, 3720 N. Keith St., Cleveland, TN 37320; Dr. Vinson Synan, Regent University, P.O.Box 1056, Chesapeake, VA 23327; Dr. Ray Hughes, P.O.Box 2430, Cleveland, TN 37320

Project Equality, Inc.

Project Equality is a nonprofit national interfaith program for affirmative action and equal employment opportunity.

Project Equality serves as a central agency to receive and validate the equal employment commitment of suppliers of goods and services to sponsoring organizations and participating institutions, congregations and individuals. Employers filing an accepted Annual Participation Report are included in the Project Equality "Buyer's Guide."

Workshops, training events and consultant services in affirmative action, diversity, and equal employment practices in recruitment, selection, placement, transfer, promotion, discipline and discharge are also available to sponsors and participants.

Headquarters

Pres., 7132 Main St., Kansas City, MO 64114-1406 Tel. (816)361-9222 or toll free 1877-PE-IS-EEO Fax (816)361-8997
Email: KirkP@projectequality.org
Website: www.projectequality.org
Media Contact, Pres., Rev. Kirk P. Perucca

Officers

Chpsn., Donald Hayashi
Vice-Chpsn., Cheryl Hammond-Hopewell
Sec., Barbara George
Treas., Joan Green
Pres., Rev. Kirk P. Perucca

SPONSORS/ENDORSING ORGANIZATIONS

American Baptist Churches in the U.S.A.
American Friends Service Committee
American Jewish Committee
Assoc. Of Junior Leagues, Intl.
Central Conference of American Rabbis
Church of the Brethren
The Episcopal Church
Evangelical Lutheran Church in America
National Council of Churches of Christ in the U.S.A.
National Education Association
Presbyterian Church (U.S.A.)
Reorganized Church of Jesus Christ of Latter-Day Saints
The United Methodist Church
Unitarian Universalist Association
United Church of Christ

United Methodist Assoc. of Health & Welfare Ministries
YWCA of the USA

Protestant Radio and Television Center, Inc.

The Protestant Radio and Television Center, Inc. (PRTVC) is an interdenominational organization dedicated to the purpose of creating, producing, marketing and distributing audio-visual products for the nonprofit sector. Its primary constituency is religious, educational and service-oriented groups. The "Flagship" production is the weekly radio show "The Protestant Hour."

Chartered in 1949, PRTVC provides a state-of-the-art studio facility, professional staff and a talent pool for radio, TV, cassettes and other forms of media production.

Affiliate members include the Episcopal Radio & TV Foundation, Evangelical Lutheran Church in America, Presbyterian Church (U.S.A.), United Methodist Communications, Agnes Scott College, Candler School of Theology, Emory University and Columbia Theological Seminary.

Headquarters

1727 Clifton Rd., NE, Atlanta, GA 30329 Tel. (404)634-3324 Fax (404)634-3326
Media Contact, Sandra Rogers

Officers

Bd. Chpsn., Dr. Gerald Troutman
Vice-Chpsn., Dale VanCantfort
Pres., J. Paul Howard
Treas., William W. Horlock
Sec., Betty Chilton

The Religion Communicators Council, Inc.

RCC is an international, interfaith, interdisciplinary association of professional communicators who work for religious groups and causes. It was founded in 1929 and is the oldest non-profit professional public relations organization in the world. RCC's more than 600 members include those who work in communications and related fields for church-related institutions, denominational agencies, non- and inter-denominational organizations and communications firms who primarily serve religious organizations.

Members represent a wide range of faiths, including Presbyterian, Baptist, Methodist, Lutheran, Episcopalian, Mennonite, Roman Catholic, Seventh-day Adventist, Jewish, Salvation Army, Brethren, Bahá'í, Disciples, Latter-Day Saints and others.

On the national level, RCC sponsors an annual three-day convention, and has published six editions of a Religious Public Relations Handbook for churches and church organizations, and a videostrip, The Church at Jackrabbit Junction. Members receive a quarterly newsletter (Counselor). There are 11 regional chapters.

41

RCC administers the annual Wilbur Awards competition to recognize high quality coverage of religious values and issues in the public media. Wilbur winners include producers, reporters, editors and broadcasters nationwide. To recognize communications excellence within church communities, RCC also sponsors the annual DeRose-Hinkhouse Awards for its own members.

In 1970, 1980, 1990, and 2000 RCC initiated a global Religious Communications Congress bringing together thousands of persons from western, eastern and third-world nations who are involved in communicating religious faith.

Headquarters
475 Riverside Dr., Rm. 1948A, New York, NY 10115-1948 Tel. (212)870-2985 Fax (212) 870-3578
Email: rccrprc@interport.net
Website: www.rprc.org

Officers
Pres., Jeanean D. Merkel, Nat'l Leadership Conferences of Religious Orders, 808 Cameron Street, Silver Spring, MD 20910 Tel. (301) 588-4955
Vice-Pres., Rev. Eric Shafer, Evangelical Lutheran Church in America, 8765 West Higgins Road, Chicago, IL 60631 (773)380-2960

Religion In American Life, Inc.
Religion In American Life (RIAL) is a unique cooperative program of some 50 major national religious groups (Catholic, Eastern Orthodox, Jewish, Protestant, Muslim, etc.). It provides services for denominationally-supported, congregation-based outreach and growth projects such as the current Invite a Friend program. These projects are promoted through national advertising campaigns reaching the American public by the use of all media. The ad campaigns are produced by a volunteer agency with production/distribution and administration costs funded by denominations and business groups, as well as by individuals.

Since 1949, RIAL ad campaign projects have been among the much coveted major campaigns of The Advertising Council. This results in as much as $30 million worth of time and space in a single year, contributed by media as a public service. Through RIAL, religious groups demonstrate respect for other traditions and the value of religious freedom. The RIAL program also includes seminars and symposia, research and leadership awards.

Headquarters
36 MacArthur Dr., Old Greenwich, CT 06870 Tel. (203)637-1757 Fax (203)637-5706
Email: rabbirob94@aol.com
Website: www.rial.com
Media Contact, Exec. Admin., Randy M. Bucknoff Tel (203)637-1757

Executive Committee
Natl. Chpsn., Thomas S. Johnson, Chairman & CEO, Greenpoint Bank, NY
Chpsn. of Bd., Robert A. Wilson
Vice-Chpsns.: Bishop Khajag Barsamian, Primate (Armenian Church of America); The Rev. Dr. M. William Howard, (President, New York Theological Seminary); Most Rev. William Cardinal Keeler, (Archbishop of Baltimore); Rabbi Ronald B. Sobel, (Cong. Emanu-El of the City of N.Y.)
Sec., Sonia Francis, (The Episcopal Church)
Treas., Robertson H. Bennett

Staff
Pres. & CEO, Robert B. Lennick, Rabbi
Exec. Admin., Randy M. Bucknoff

Religion News Service
Religion News Service (RNS) has provided news and information to the media for almost 70 years. Owned by the Newhouse News Service, it is staffed by veteran jounalists who cover stories on all of the world religions as well as trends in ethics, morality and spirituality.

RNS provides a daily news service, a weekly news report, and photo and graphic services. The daily service is available via the AP Data Features wire, fax, Ecunet, or email. The weekly report is available by wire or email. Photos and graphics are supplied online.

Headquarters
1101 Connecticut Ave. NW, Ste. 350, Washington, DC 20036 Tel. (202)463-8777 Fax (202) 463-0033
Email: info@religionnews.com
Website: www. religionnews.com
Media Contact, David Anderson

Officers
Editor, David Anderson

Religion Newswriters Association
Founded in 1949, the RNA is a professional association of religion news editors and reporters on secular daily and weekly newspapers, news services, news magazines, radio and television stations. It sponsors five annual contests for excellence in religion news coverage in the secular press. Annual meetings are held anytime from late spring to early fall..

Headquarters
P.O. Box 2037, Westerville, OH 43086 Tel. (614)891-9001 Fax (614) 891-9774
Email: rnastuff@aol.com
Website: www.rna.org
Media Contact, Exec. Dir., Debra Mason

Officers
Pres., Gayle White, Journal Constitution, Atlanta, GA
1st Vice-Pres., David Briggs, Cleveland Plain Dealer

2nd Vice-Pres., Sandy Dolbee, San Diego Union Tribune, San Diego, CA
Treas., Jeff Sheler, U.S. News and World Report
Sec., ———

Religious Conference Management Association, Inc.

The Religious Conference Management Association, Inc. (RCMA) is an interfaith, non-profit, professional organization of men and women who have responsibility for planning and/or managing meetings, seminars, conferences, conventions, assemblies or other gatherings for religious organizations.

Founded in 1972, RCMA is dedicated to promoting the highest professional performance by its members and associate members through the mutual exchange of ideas, techniques and methods.

Today RCMA has more than 3,000 members and associate members.

The association conducts an annual conference and exposition which provides a forum for its membership to gain increased knowledge in the arts and sciences of religious meeting planning and management.

Headquarters
One RCA Dome, Ste. 120, Indianapolis, IN 46225 Tel. (317)632-1888 Fax (317)632-7909
Website: www.rcmaweb.org
Media Contact, Exec. Dir., Dr. DeWayne S. Woodring

Officers
Pres., Dr. Jack Stone, Church of the Nazarene, 6401 The Paswo, Kansas City, MO 64131-1213
Vice-Pres., Ms. Linda M. de Leon, General Conference Seventh-Day Adventist Church, 12501 Old Columbia Pike, Silver Spring, MD 20904
Sec.-Treas., Dr. Melvin Worthington, Natl. Assoc. of Free Will Baptists, P.O. Box 5002, Antioch, TN 37011-5002
Exec. Dir., Dr. DeWayne S. Woodring

United Ministries in Higher Education

United Ministries in Higher Education is a cooperative effort to provide religious programs and services to those engaged in higher education ministries.

Headquarters
7407 Steele Creek Rd., Charlotte, NC 28217 Tel. (704)588-2182 Fax (704)588-3652
Media Contact, Res. Sec., Linda Danby Freeman
Email: linda_freeman@ecunet.org

Officers
Treas., Linda Danby Freeman
Personnel Service, Kathy Carson, 11720 Borman Dr., Ste. 240, St. Louis, MO 63146 Tel. (314)991-3000 Fax (314)991-2957
Resource Center, Linda Danby Freeman

PARTICIPATING DENOMINATIONS
Christian Church (Disciples of Christ)
Presbyterian Church (U.S.A.)
United Church of Christ

United Religions Initiative

The purpose of the United Religions Initiative is to create the United Religions—a permanent public forum where people of many faiths gather in mutual respect to pursue justice, healing and peace, with reverence for all life. The United Religions will have global visibility and stature, and will be a vital presence in local communities all over the world. The goal of the United Religions Initiative was to give birth to the United Religions in June 2000.

In 1993, the Rt. Rev. William Swing, Bishop of the Episcopal Diocese of California, was asked by the United Nations to host an interfaith service to commemorate 50 years of political leaders working together daily for peace. As he thought of religion's role in armed conflicts all over the world, he wondered why there was no permanent forum where the world's religions leaders worked together daily for peace. If a United Nations, why not a United Religions?

During the next three years, Bishop Swing and a small interfaith group consulted with many leaders in interfaith dialogue and hosted an international youth conference. In 1996, Bishop Swing undertook a three-month pilgrimage around the world. The vision of a United Religions became part of a worldwide conversation rooted in over 100 years of international interfaith work.

Launched at its first global summit in San Francisco in June 1996, the United Religions Initiative has rapidly become one of the most ambitious and hopeful interreligious initiatives in the world. In the past two years, over 1,000 participants at six regional conferences on four continents, and three global summits have developed the vision of a United Religions. These grass-roots and global leaders from over 40 spiritual traditions have begun many pilot projects' models of a United Religions in action. In two years, world of the United Religions Initiative has reached more than a million people throughout the world. The United Religions Initiative has an active presence on every continent. Its global headquarters and interfaith Board of Directors are in San Francisco.

Headquarters
P.O. Box 29242, San Francisco, CA 94129-0242 Tel. (415)561-2300 Fax (415)562-2313
Email: office@united-religions.org
Website: www.united-religions.org
Media Contact: Barbara H. Hartford, Operations Manager

Staff
Exec Dir., The Rev. Cn. Charles Gibbs
Vice-Pres., The Rev. William Rankin

43

Operations Mgr., Ms. Barbara Hartford
Project Mgr., Ms. Sally Mahe Ackerly
Project Mgr., Mr. Paul Andrews
Latin American Coord., Fr. Luis Dolan
European Coord., Mr. Josef Boehle
SIGMA/African Coord., Mr. Godwin Hlatshwayo
SIGMA, Mr. David Cooperrider
SIGMA, Mr. Gurudev Khalsa
The Chaordic Alliance, Mr. Dee Hock
D.B. Robbins Consulting, Ms. Diane Robbins
Corporation for Positive Change, Ms. Diana Whitney
Youth Projects, Ms. Jennifer Peace

Board Members

Pres., Bishop William Swing
Chair, Ms. Rita Semel
Vice-Chair, Rev. Dr. Jack Lundin
Treas., Mr. Rick Murray
Sec., Rev. Paul Chaffee

Vellore Christian Medical College Board (USA), Inc.

The Vellore Christian Medical College Board (USA) has been linked since 1900 to the vision of a young American medical doctor, Dr. Ida S. Scudder, who founded Christian Medical College and Hospital in Vellore, India. Dr. Ida's vision was to train women in all the healing arts so that they could treat women and their families. Today after 100 years of teaching and service the College and Hospital is directed by an Indian woman, Dr. Joyce Ponnaiya. The Vellore Christian Medical College Board (USA) supports the work of Christian Medical College and Hospital in Vellore through exchange personnel programs including volunteers to Vellore and senior CMC staff receiving fellowships to study and work in the United States over 3 month periods. The Vellore Board also assists CMC&H with Capital Campaigns and high tech medical equipment.

Headquarters

475 Riverside Dr., Rm. 243, New York, NY 10115 Tel. (212)870-2640 Fax (212)870-2173
Email: usaboard@vellorecmc.org
Website: www.vellorecmc.org
Media Contact, President, Rev. William Salmond
Email: wsalmond@vellorecmc.org

Officers

Chair., Dr. Mani M. Mani, 5137 West 60th Terrace, Mission, KS 66205
Vice-Chair., Miriam Ballert, 7104 Olde Oak Ct., Prospect, KY 40059
Sec., Mrs. Edwina Youth, 211 Blue Ridge Dr., Levittown, PA 19057
Treas., Michael Holt, 352 Pines Lake Dr. East, Wayne, NJ 07470

The World Conference on Religion and Peace (WCRP/USA)

The World Conference on Religion and Peace in the United States (WCRP/USA) provides a forum for the nation's religious bodies based upon respect for religious differences. In today's world cooperation among religions offers an important opportunity to mobilize and coordinate the great moral and sociological capacities for constructive action inherent in religious communities.

WCRP/USA provides American religious bodies with opportunities for the following: to identify shared commitments to constructive social development, justice, and peace; to coordinate their efforts with other religious groups on behalf of widely-shared concerns; to design, undertake and evaluate joint action projects; and to communicate and collaborate with similar national religious forums organized by WCRP, and with other organizations as well, around the world.

Headquarters

WCRP/USA, 777 United Nations Plaza, New York, NY 10017 Tel. (212)338-9140 Fax (212) 983-0566
Email: wcrp_usa@wcrp.org
Website: www.wcrp.org

Officers

Sec. Gen., Mr. Antonios Kireopoulos
Moderator, V. Rev. Leonid Kishkovsky

World Council of Churches, United States Office

The United States Conference of the World Council of Churches was formed in 1938 when the WCC itself was still in the "Process of Formation." Henry Smith Leiper, an American with many national and international connections, was given the title of "Associate General Secretary" of the WCC and asked to carry out WCC work in the U.S. After the World Council of Churches was officially born in 1948 in Amsterdam, Netherlands, Leiper raised millions of dollars for WCC programs.

Today the U.S. Conference of the WCC is composed of representatives of U.S. member churches of the worldwide body. The U.S. Office of the WCC works to develop relationships among the churches, advance the work of WCC and interpret the council in the United States.

Headquarters

475 Riverside Dr., Rm. 915, New York, NY 10115 Tel. (212)870-2533 Fax (212)870-2528
Email: usa@wcc-coe.org
Website: www.wcc-coe.org/wcc/usoffice
Media Contact, Philip E. Jenks

Officers

WCC President from North America and Moderator, Rev. Kathryn Bannister, The United Methodist Church
Vice-Moderator, Bishop McKinley Young, African Methodist Episcopal Church
Vice-Moderator and Treasurer, The Rev. Leonid Kishkovsky, Orthodox Church in America

Exec. Dir., Jean S. Stromberg, Tel. (212)870-2522
Comm. & Publ. Officer, Philip E. Jenks, Tel. (212)870-3193
Office Admn., Sonia P. Omulepu, (212)870-2470

World Day of Prayer

World Day of Prayer is an ecumenical movement initiated and carried out by Christian women in 170 countries who conduct a common day of prayer on the first Friday of March to which all people are welcome. There is an annual theme for the worship service that has been prepared by women in a different country each year. For 2001 the women of Samoa have prepared a worship service on the theme, Informed Prayer, Prayerful Action" which is also the WDP motto. The offering at this service is gathered by each WDP National/Regional Committee and given to help people who are in need.

Headquarters

World Day of Prayer International Comm., 475 Riverside Dr., Rm. 560, New York, NY 10115 Tel. (212)870-3049 Fax (212)864-8648
Email: WDPIC@worlddayofprayer.net
Website:www.worlddayofprayer.net
Media Contact, Exec. Dir., Eileen King

Officers

Chairperson, Yvonne Harrison
Treasurer, Karen Prudente
North America, Susan Shank Mix (USA); Sylvia Lisk Vanhaverbeke (Canada)
Africa, Sarie Jansen; Karen Ngigi
Asia, Shunila Ruth; Jong Ok Lee
Caribbean, Waveney Benjamin; Neva Edwards
Europe, Inge Lise Lollike; Alena Naimanova
Latin America, Renee Carter; Inez Proverbs
Middle East, Aida Haddad; Nadia Menes
Pacific, Margaret Kenna; Gwen Tulo
Member at Large, Maria Gabriela Trimbitas

World Methodist Council-North American Section

The World Methodist Council, one of the 30 or so "Christian World Communions," shares a general tradition which is common to all Christians. The world organization of Methodists and related United Churches is comprised of 74 churches with roots in the Methodist tradition. These churches found in 130 countries have a membership of more than 34 million.

The Council's North American Section, comprised of ten Methodist and United Church denominations, provides a regional focus for the Council in Canada, the United States and Mexico. The North American Section meets at the time of the quinquennial World Conference and Council, and separately as Section between world meetings. The Section met in Rio de Janeiro, Brazil in August 1996 during the 17th World Methodist Conference to elect its officers for the 1997-2001 quinquennium. 2001-2006 officers will be elected in Brighton, England, July 2001.

North American Churches related to the World Methodist Council have a membership of approximately 16 million and a church community of more than 30 million.

Headquarters

P.O. Box 518, Lake Junaluska, NC 28745 Tel. (828)456-9432 Fax (828)456-9433
Email: wmc6@juno.com
Website: worldmethodistcouncil.org
Media Contact, Gen. Sec., Joe Hale

Officers

Section Pres., Bishop Neil L. Irons, 900 S. Arlington Ave., Rm. 214, Harrisburg, PA 17109-5097 Tel. (717)652-6705 Fax (717)652-5109
First Vice-Pres., Bishop Thomas L. Hoyt, CME Church
Vice-Pres.: Bishop John R. Bryant, AME Church; Bishop Cecil Bishop, AMEZ Church; Bishop Richard D. Snyder, Free Methodist Church; Bishop Gracela Alverez, Methodist Church in Mexico; Bishop Keith Elford, Free Methodist Church of Canada; Rev. Carol Hancock, United Church of Canada; Dr. Jack Stone, Church of the Nazarene; Dr. Earle L. Wilson, The Wesleyan Church; Chairman, Finance Committee, Dr. Donald V. Fites
Treas., Dr. James W. Holsinger, Jr.
Asst. Treas., Edna Alsdurf
General Sec., Dr. Joe Hale
World Officers from North America: Dr. Frances M. Alguire; Dr. Maxie D. Dunnam; Bishop Donald Ming

YMCA of the USA

The YMCA is one of the largest private voluntary organizations in the world, serving about 30 million people in more than 100 countries. In the United States, more than 2,000 local branches, units, camps and centers annually serve more than 14 million people of all ages, races and abilities. About half of those served are female. No one is turned away because of an inability to pay.

The Y teaches youngsters to swim, organizes youth basketball games and offers adult aerobics. But the Y represents more than fitness—it works to strengthen families and help people develop values and behavior that are consistent with Christian principles.

The Y offers hundreds of programs including day camp for children, child care, exercise for people with disabilities, teen clubs, environmental programs, substance abuse prevention, family nights, job training and many more programs from infant mortality prevention to overnight camping for seniors.

The kind of programs offered at a YMCA will vary; each is controlled by volunteer board

US COOPERATIVE ORGANIZATIONS

members who make their own program, policy, and financial decisions based on the special needs of their community. In its own way, every Y works to build strong kids, strong families, and strong communities.

The YMCA was founded in London, England, in 1844 by George Williams and friends who lived and worked together as clerks. Their goal was to save other live-in clerks from the wicked life of the London streets. The first members were evangelical Protestants who prayed and studied the Bible as an alternative to vice. The Y has always been nonsectarian and today accepts those of all faiths at all levels of the organization.

Headquarters
101 N. Wacker Dr., Chicago, IL 60606 Tel. (312) 977-0031 Fax (312)977-9063
Website: www.ymca.net
Media Contact, Media Relations Manager, Arnie Collins

Officers
Board Chpsn., Daniel E. Emerson
Exec. Dir., David R. Mercer
(Int.) Public Relations Assoc., Mary Pyke Gover

Young Women's Christian Association of the United States

The YWCA of the U.S.A. is comprised of 364 affiliates in communities and on college campuses across the United States. It serves one million members and program participants. It seeks to empower women and girls to enable them, coming together across lines of age, race, religious belief, economic and occupational status to make a significant contribution to the elimination of racism and the achievement of peace, justice, freedom and dignity for all people. Its leadership is vested in a National Board, whose functions are to unite into an effective continuing organization the autonomous member Associations for furthering the purposes of the National Association and to participate in the work of the World YWCA.

Headquarters
Empire State Building, 350 Fifth Ave., Ste. 301 New York, NY 10118 Tel. (212)273-7800 Fax (212)465-2281
Email: HN2062@handsnet.org
Website: www.ywca.org
Media Contact, Chief of Staff, Cynthia Sutliff

Officers
National Pres., Alexine Clement Jackson
Sec., Tina Maree Herrera
Chief Exec. Officer, Prema Mathai-Davis

Youth for Christ/USA

Founded in 1944, as part of the body of Christ, our vision is to see every young person in every people group in every nation have the opportunity to make an informed decision to be a follower of Jesus Christ and become a part of a local church.

There are 237 locally controlled YFC programs serving in cities and metropolitan areas of the United States.

YFC's Campus Life Club program involves teens who attend approximately 1,557 high schools in the United States. YFC's staff now numbers approximately 1,000. In addition, nearly 21,000 part-time and volunteer staff supplement the full-time staff. Youth Guidance, a ministry for nonschool-oriented youth includes group homes, court referrals, institutional services and neighborhood ministries. The year-round conference and camping program involves approximately 200,000 young people each year. Other ministries include DC Ministries, World Outreach, Project Serve, and Teen Moms. Independent, indigenous YFC organizations also work in 127 countries overseas.

Headquarters
U.S. Headquarters, P.O. Box 228822, Denver, CO 80222 Tel. (303)843-9000 Fax (303)843-9002
Canadian Organization, 1212-31 Avenue NE, #540, Calgary, AB T2E 7S8
Website: www.yfc.org
Media Contact, Pres., Roger Cross

Officers
United States, president, Roger Cross
Canada, Pres., -vacant-
Intl. Organization: Acting Pres., Jean-Jacques Weiler

2. Canadian Cooperative Organizations, National

In most cases the organizations listed here work on a national level and cooperate across denominational lines. Regional cooperative organizations in Canada are listed in Directory 8, "Canadian Regional and Local Ecumenical Bodies."

Aboriginal Rights Coalition (ARE)

ARC works towards the transformation of the relationship between Canadian society and Aboriginal peoples. Through education, research, advocacy and action, this coalition of national churches, faith bodies, and regional groups works in solidarity with Aboriginal peoples. ARC seeks to embody true partnership by building authentic alliances in the global struggle for Aboriginal justice.

Headquarters

153 Laurier Ave. East, 2nd Floor, Ottawa, ON K1N 6N8 Tel. (613)235-9956 Fax (613)235-1302
Email: arc@istar.ca
Media Contact, Natl. Coord., Ed Bianchi

Officers

Co-Chairs.: Richard Renshaw, Mildred Poplar
Natl. Coord., Ed Bianchi

MEMBER ORGANIZATIONS

Anglican Church of Canada
Canadian Conference of Catholic Bishops
Canadian Religious Conference
Council of Christian Reformed Churches in Canada
Evangelical Lutheran Church in Canada
Mennonite Central Committee
Oblate Conference in Canada
Presbyterian Church of Canada
Religious Society of Friends (Quakers)
Society of Jesus (Jesuits)
Canadian Unitarian Council
United Church of Canada

Alcohol and Drug Concerns Inc.

Alcohol and Drug Concerns is a registered, nonprofit, charitable organization that has a long association with the Christian Church. The organization's mission is to empower youth to make positive lifestyle choices relating to alcohol, tobacco, and other drugs.

The organization was granted a national charter in 1987, moving from an Ontario charter dating back to 1934. Among its services are: Choices F.I.T. (Fostering Independent Thinking) —a substance abuse prevention resource for grade 4 to 8 teachers; an Institute on Addiction Studies; Making the Leap—a substance abuse prevention resource for grade 7 to 8 teachers created by high school students; Drug and Alcohol Game Show for grades 6 to 9—a classroom activity; education and awareness courses for clients of the Ontario Ministry of Corrections.

Headquarters

4500 Sheppard Ave. E, Ste. 112, Toronto, ON M1S 3R6 Tel. (416)293-3400 Fax (416)293-1142
Email: info@concerns.ca
Website: www.concerns.ca
Media Contact, Robert Walsh, CEO

Officers

Pres., Jean Desgagne, Toronto
Treas., Peter Varley, Toronto
Vice-Pres., Nanci Harris, Toronto
Vice-Pres., Valerie Petroff, Oak Ridges
Vice-Pres., Heidi Stanley, Orillia
Past Pres., Larry Gillians, Napanee
CEO, Robert Walsh

Association of Canadian Bible Colleges

The Association brings into cooperative association Bible colleges in Canada that are evangelical in doctrine and whose objectives are similar. Services are provided to improve the quality of Bible college education in Canada and to further the interests of the Association by means of conferences, seminars, cooperative undertakings, information services, research, publications and other projects.

Headquarters

Box 4000, Three Hills, AB T0M 2N0 Tel. (403) 443-3051 Fax (403)443-5540
Media Contact, Sec./Treas., Peter Doell, Email: peter.doell@pbi.ab.ca

Officers

Pres., Larry J. McKinney, Tel. (204)433-7488 Fax (204)433-7158
Vice-Pres., Dr. Arthur Maxwell, Tel. (506)432-4400 Fax (506)432-4425
Sec./Treas., Peter Doell, Tel. (403)443-3051 Fax (403)443-5540
Members-at-Large: Nil Lavallee Tel. (705)748-9111 Fax (705)748-3931; Wendy Thomas Tel. (306) 545-1515 Fax (306)545-0201; Earl Marshall Tel. (519)651-2869; Fax (519)651-2820

Canadian Bible Society

As early as 1804, the British and Foreign Bible Society was at work in Canada. The oldest Bible Society branch is at Truro, Nova Scotia, and has been functioning continually since 1810. In 1904, the various auxiliaries of the British and Foreign Bible Society joined to form the Canadian Bible Society.

The Canadian Bible Society has 16 district offices across Canada, each managed by a District Secretary. The Society holds an annual meeting consisting of one representative from each district, plus an Executive Committee whose members are appointed by the General Board.

Each year contributions, bequests and annuity income of $11 million come from Canadian supporters. Through the Canadian Bible Society's membership in the United Bible Societies' fellowship, over 74 million Bibles, Testaments and Portions were distributed globally in 1994. At least one book of the Bible is now available in over 2090 languages.

The Canadian Bible Society is nondenominational. Its mandate is to translate, publish, distribute and encourage the use of the Scriptures, without doctrinal note or comment, in languages that can be easily read and understood.

Headquarters
10 Carnforth Rd., Toronto, ON M4A 2S4 Tel. (416)757-4171 Fax (416)757-3376
Media Contact, Communications Officer, Bruce Allen

Officers
National Director, The Rev. Fr. Greg Bailey

Canadian Centre for Ecumenism

The Centre has facilitated understanding and cooperation among believers of various Christian traditions and world religions since 1963. An active interdenominational Board of Directors meets annually.
Outreach:

ECUMENISM, a quarterly publication, develops central themes such as Rites of Passage, Sacred Space, Interfaith Marriages, Care of the Earth, etc. through contributions from writers of various churches and religions in addition to its regular ecumenical news summaries, book reviews and resources.

A specialized library is open to the public for consultation in the areas of religion, dialogue, evangelism, ethics, spirituality, etc.

Conferences and sessions are offered on themes such as Ecumenism and Pastoral Work, Pluralism, World Religions, Prayer and Unity.

Headquarters
2065 Sherbrooke St. W. Montreal, QC H3H 1G6 Tel. (514)937-9176 Fax (514)937-4986
Email: ccocce@total.net
Website: www.total.net/~ccocce

Officers
Media Contact, Bernice Baranowski
Associate Directors: Emmanuel Lapierre, O.P.; Diane Willey, N.D.S.
Director: Gilles Bourdeau, O.F.M.

Canadian Evangelical Theological Association

In May 1990, about 60 scholars, pastors and other interested persons met together in Toronto to form a new theological society. Arising out of the Canadian chapter of the Evangelical Theological Society, the new association established itself as a distinctly Canadian group with a new name. It sponsored its first conference as CETA in Kingston, Ontario, in May 1991.

CETA provides a forum for scholarly contributions to the renewal of theology and church in Canada. CETA seeks to promote theological work which is loyal to Christ and his Gospel, faithful to the primacy and authority of Scripture and responsive to the guiding force of the historic creeds and Protestant confessions of the Christian Church. In its newsletters and conferences, CETA seeks presentations that will speak to a general theologically-educated audience, rather than to specialists.

CETA has special interest in evangelical points of view upon and contributions to the wider conversations regarding religious studies and church life. Members therefore include pastors, students and other interested persons as well as professional academicians. CETA currently includes about 100 members, many of whom attend its annual conference in the early summer. It publishes the Canadian Evangelical Review and supports an active internet discussion group, which may be accessed through ceta-l@egroups.com.

Headquarters
Dr. Douglas Harink, The King's University College, 9125-50 Street, Edmonton, AB T6B 2H3
Media Contact, Dr. Douglas Harink

Officers
Pres., Dr. Douglas Harink
Sec./Treas., Dr. Tony Cummins
Editor, Canadian Evangelical Review, Dr. Archie Pell
Executive Member, Mr. John Franklin

Canadian Tract Society

The Canadian Tract Society was organized in 1970 as an independent distributor of Gospel leaflets to provide Canadian churches and individual Christians with quality materials proclaiming the Gospel through the printed page. It is affiliated with the American Tract Society, which encouraged its formation and assisted in its founding, and for whom it serves as an exclusive Canadian distributor. The CTS is a nonprofit international service ministry.

Headquarters
26 Hale Rd., P.O. Box 2156, Brampton, ON L6T 3S4 Tel. (905)457-4559 Fax (905)457-0529
Media Contact, Mgr., Donna Croft

Officers
Director/Sec., Robert J. Burns
Director, John Neufeld
Director, Patricia Burns

The Canadian Council of Churches

The Canadian Council of Churches was organized in 1944. Its basic purpose is to provide the churches with an agency for conference and consultation and for such common planning and common action as they desire to undertake. It encourages ecumenical understanding and action throughout Canada through local councils of churches. It also relates to the World Council of Churches and other agencies serving the worldwide ecumenical movement.

The Council has a Governing Board which meets semiannually and an Executive Committee. Program is administered through two commissions—Faith and Witness, Justice and Peace.

Headquarters

3250 Bloor St. West, 2nd Floor, Toronto, ON M8X 2Y4 Tel. (416)232-6070 Fax (416)236-4532

Media Contact, General Secretary

Email: ccchurch@web.net

Website: www.web.net/~ccchurch

Officers

Pres., Bishop Andre Vallee

Vice-Presidents: Rev. Michael Winnowski, Fr. Shenork Sovin, Ms. Karen MacKay Llewellyn

Treas., Nancy Bell

Treas. Emeritus, Mr. Jack Hart

Gen. Secretary., Ms. Janet Somerville

MEMBER CHURCHES:

The Anglican Church of Canada

The Armenian Orthodox Church-Diocese of Canada

Baptist Convention of Ontario and Quebec

British Methodist Episcopal Church*

Canadian Conference of Catholic Bishops

Christian Church (Disciples of Christ)

Coptic Orthodox Church of Canada

Christian Reformed Church in North America—Canadian Ministries

Ethiopian Orthodox Church in Canada

Evangelical Lutheran Church in Canada

Greek Orthodox Metropolis of Toronto, Canada

Orthodox Church in America, Diocese of Canada

Polish National Catholic Church

Presbyterian Church in Canada

Reformed Church in Canada

Religious Society of Friends-Canada Yearly Meeting

Salvation Army-Canada and Bermuda

The Ukrainian Orthodox Church

The United Church of Canada

*Associate Member

Canadian Society of Biblical Studies/Société Canadienne des Études Bibliques

The object of the Society shall be to stimulate the critical investigation of the classical biblical literatures, together with other related literature, by the exchange of scholarly research both in published form and in public forum.

Headquarters

Dept. of Religion and Culture, Wilfrid Laurier University, Waterloo, ON N2L 3C5 Tel. (519)884-0710, ext.3323 Fax (519)884-9387

Email: mdesjard@wlu.ca

Media Contact, Exec. Sec., Dr. Michel Desjardins

Officers

President (2000-01), John S. Kloppenborg Verbin, Faculty of Theology, St. Michael's College, 81 St. Mary Street, Toronto, ON M5S 1J4 Tel. (416)926-7267 Fax (416)926-7294, Email: kloppen@chass.utoronto.ca

Vice-Pres. (2000-01), Ehud Ben Zvi, Department of Comparative Literature, Religion and Film/Media Studies, University of Alberta, 347 Old Arts Building, Edmonton, AB T6G 2E6, Tel. (780)492-7183 Fax (780)492-2715, Email: ehud.ben.zvi@ualberta.ca

Exec. Secretary. (1997-02), Dr. Michel Desjardins, Dept. of Religion and Culture, Wilfrid Laurier University, Waterloo, ON N2L 3C5 Tel. (519)884-0710, ext.3323, Email: mdesjard@mach1.wlu.ca

Treas. (2000-03), Dietmar Neufeld, Department of Classical, Near Eastern and Religious Studies, University of British Columbia, Vancouver, BC V6T 1Z1, Tel. (604)822-4065 Fax (604)8229431, Email: dneufeld@interchange.ubc.ca

Programme Coord. (1998-01), Edith Humphrey, 42 Belmont, Aylmer, QC J9H 2M7 Tel. (819) 682-9257, Email: ehumphre@ccs.carleton.ca

Communications Officer (1999-02), John McLaughlin, Department of Theology and Religious Studies, Wheeling Jesuit University, Wheeling, WV 26003, Tel. (304)243-2310 Fax (304)243-2243, Email: mclaugh@wju.edu

Student Member-at-Large (1999-01), David A. Bergen, 7101 Huntercrest Rd., N.W., Calgary, AB T2K 4J9, Tel. (403)275-5369, Email: bergend@cadvision.com

The Church Army in Canada

The Church Army in Canada has been involved in evangelism and Christian social service since 1929.

Headquarters

397 Brunswick Ave., Toronto, ON M5R 2Z2 Tel. (416)924-9279 Fax (416)924-2931

Media Contact, National Dir., Capt. Walter W. Marshall

Officers

National Dir., Capt. R. Bruce Smith

Dir. of Training, Capt. Roy E. Dickson

Field Sec., Capt. Reed S. Fleming

Bd. Chmn., Ivor S. Joshua, C.A.

The Churches' Council on Theological Education in Canada: An Ecumenical Foundation

The Churches' Council (CCTE:EF) maintains an overview of theological education in Canada on behalf of its constituent churches and functions as a bridge between the schools of theology and the churches which they serve.

Founded in 1970 with a national and ecumenical mandate, the CCTE:EF provides resources for research into matters pertaining to theological education, opportunities for consultation and cooperation and a limited amount of funding in the form of grants for the furtherance of ecumenical theological education.

Headquarters

60 St. Clair Avenue E, Ste. 302, Toronto, ON M4T 1N5 Tel. (416)928-3223 Fax (416)928-3563

Media Contact, Exec. Dir., Dr. Stewart Gillan

Email: ccte@web.ca

Website: www.web.net/~ccte

Officers

Bd. of Dir., Chpsn., Dr. Richard C. Crossman, Waterloo Lutheran Seminary, 75 University Ave. W., Waterloo, ON N2L 3C5

Bd. of Dir., Vice-Chpsn., Sr. Ellen Leonard, CSJ, Univ. of St. Michaels's College, 81 St. Mary St., Toronto, ON M5S 1J4

Interim Treas., -vacant-

Exec. Dir., Dr. Stewart Gillan

MEMBER ORGANIZATIONS

The General Synod of the Anglican Church of Canada

Canadian Baptist Ministries

The Evangelical Lutheran Church in Canada

The Presbyterian Church in Canada

The Canadian Conference of Catholic Bishops

The United Church of Canada

Ecumenical Coalition for Economic Justice (ECEJ)

The Ecumenical Coalition for Economic Justice (ECEJ) enables member churches to have a more effective public voice in advocating for a just, moral and sustainable economy. ECEJ undertakes research, education and advocacy to promote economic policy alternatives that are grounded in a Christian perspective. Sponsoring denominations include: the Anglican Church of Canada, the Canadian Catholic Bishops Conference, the Evangelical Lutheran Church in Canada, the Presbyterian Church in Canada and the United Church of Canada. ECEJ also acts as a link to social movements and coalitions to bring a collective church presence to them and to inform our own analysis.

The program focus of the next three years will be to advance alternative economic policies which support our vision of an "economy of hope". This includes proposing different ways to assess economic prosperity, challenging the growth model, envisioning a new model for social programs in global economy, and presenting alternative fiscal and monetary policies.

ECEJ publishes a quarterly briefing paper on current issues, the Economic Justice Report, as well as education and action resources.

An Administrative Committee oversees ECEJ and is made up of representatives from the sponsoring denominations as well as participating members which currently include: the School Sisters of Notre Dame, the Scarboro Foreign Mission, and the Religious Society of Friends (Quaker).

Headquarters

77 Charles St. W, Ste. 402, Toronto, ON M5S 1K5 Tel. (416)921-4615 Fax (416)922-1419

Media Contact, Educ. & Communications, Jennifer Henry

Email:gattfly@web.net

Officers

Co-Chpsn., Doryne Kirby

Co-Chpsn., Jim Marshall

Staff

Research, John Dillon

Women & Economic Justice Programme, Kathryn Robertson

Education/Communication, Jennifer Henry

Administration/Finance, Diana Gibbs

Evangelical Fellowship of Canada

The Fellowship was formed in 1964. There are 31 denominations, 124 organizations, 1,200 local churches and 11,000 individual members.

Its purposes are: "Fellowship in the gospel" (Phil. 1:5), "the defence and confirmation of the gospel" (Phil. 1:7) and "the furtherance of the gospel" (Phil. 1:12). The Fellowship believes the Holy Scriptures, as originally given, are infallible and that salvation through the Lord Jesus Christ is by faith apart from works.

In national and regional conventions the Fellowship urges Christians to live exemplary lives and to openly challenge the evils and injustices of society. It encourages cooperation with various agencies in Canada and overseas that are sensitive to social and spiritual needs.

Headquarters

Office: 600 Alden Rd. Ste. 300, Markham, ON L3R 0E7 Tel. (905)479-5885 Fax (905)479-4742

Mailing Address: M.I.P. Box 3745, Markham, ON L3R 0Y4

Media Contact, Pres., Dr. Gary Walsh, 600 Alden Rd., Ste. 300, Markham, ON L3R 0E7 Tel. (905)479-5885 Fax (905)479-4742

Email: efc@efc-canada.com

Officers

Pres., Dr. Gary Walsh

Chair, Dr. Paul Magnus

Vice-Chair, Dr. Rick Penner
Treas., Lt. Col. David Luginbuhl
Past Pres., Dr. Brian Stiller

EXECUTIVE COMMITTEE

Rev. Scott Campbell; Rev. Carson Pue; Ms. Ruth
Andrews; Rev. Stewart Hunter; Ms.
Jacqueline Dugas; Dr. Rick Penner; Lt. Col.
David Luginbuhl; Dr. Ralph Richardson; Rev.
Abe Funk; Rev. Gillis Killam; Dr. Paul
Magnus; Rev. Winston Thurton

Task Force on Evangelism-(Vision Canada),
Interim Chair, Gary Walsh

Social Action Commission, Chpsn., Dr. James
Read

Education Commission, Chpsn., Dr. Glenn Smith

Women in Ministry Task Force, Chpsn., Rev.
Eileen Stewart-Rhude

Aboriginal Task Force, Co-Chairs, Ray Aldred;
Wendy Peterson

Religious Liberties Commission, Chpsn., Dr.
Paul Marshall

Task Force on Global Mission, Chpsn., Dr. Geoff
Tunnicliffe

Inter-Varsity Christian Fellowship of Canada

Inter-Varsity Christian Fellowship is a nonprofit, interdenominational student movement
centering on the witness to Jesus Christ in campus communities, universities, colleges and high
schools and through a Canada-wide Pioneer
Camping program. It also ministers to professionals and teachers through Nurses and Teacher
Christian Fellowship.

IVCF was officially formed in 1928-29 by the
late Dr. Howard Guinness, whose arrival from
Britain challenged students to follow the example of the British Inter-Varsity Fellowship by
organizing themselves into prayer and Bible
study fellowship groups. Inter-Varsity has
always been a student-initiated movement
emphasizing and developing leadership in the
campus to call Christians to outreach, challenging other students to a personal faith in Jesus
Christ and studying the Bible as God's revealed
truth within a fellowship of believers. A strong
stress has been placed on missionary activity,
and the triennial conference held at Urbana, IL
(jointly sponsored by U.S. and Canadian IVCF)
has been a means of challenging many young
people to service in Christian vocations. Inter-
Varsity works closely with and is a strong
believer in the work of local and national
churches.

Headquarters

Unit 17, 40 Vogell Rd., Richmond Hill, ON L4B
3N6 Tel. (905)884-6880 Fax (905)884-6550

Media Contact, Gen. Dir., Rob Regier

Officers

Gen. Dir., Rob Regier

Interchurch Communications

Interchurch Communications is made up of
the communication units of the Anglican Church
of Canada, the Evangelical Lutheran Church in
Canada, the Presbyterian Church in Canada, the
Canadian Conference of Catholic Bishops
(English Sector), and the United Church of
Canada. ICC members collaborate on occasional
video or print coproductions and on addressing
public policy issues affecting religious communications.

Headquarters

3250 Bloor St. W., Etobicoke, ON M8X 2Y4

Media Contact, Chpsn., Douglas Tindal,
Anglican Church of Canada, 600 Jarvis St.,
Toronto, ON M4Y 2J6 Tel. (416)924-9199 x.
286 Fax (416)968-7983

Email: doug.tindal@national.anglican.ca

MEMBERS

Mr. Douglas Tindal, Anglican Church of Canada,
600 Jarvis St., Toronto, ON M4Y 2J6 Tel.
(416)924-9199 ext.286 Fax (416)968-7983,
Email: dtindal@national.anglican.ca

Mr. William Kokesch, Canadian Conference of
Catholic Bishops, 90 Parent Ave., Ottawa, ON
K1N 7B1 Tel. (613)241-9461 Fax (613)241-
8117, Email: kokesch@cccb.ca

Mr. Merv Campone, Evangelical Lutheran
Church in Canada, 305-896 Cambie St.,
Vancouver, BC V6B 2P6 Tel. (604)888-4562
Fax (604)687-6593
Email: mcampone@spiritscall.com

Rev. Keith Knight, Presbyterian Church in
Canada, 50 Wynford Dr., Don Mills, ON M3C
1J7 Tel. (416)441-1111 Fax (416)441-2825,
Email: kknight@presbyterian.ca

Mr. Gordon How, United Church of Canada,
3250 Bloor St. W., Etobicoke, ON M8X 2Y4
Tel. (416)231-7680 Fax (416)231-3103,
Email: ghow@uccan.org

Religious Television Associates, 3250 Bloor St.
W., Etobicoke, ON M8X 2Y4 Tel. (416)231-
7680 Fax (416)232-6004

John Howard Society of Ontario

The John Howard Society of Ontario is a registered nonprofit charitable organization providing services to individuals, families and groups at
all stages in the youth and criminal justice system. The Society also provides community education on critical issues in the justice system and
advocacy for reform of the justice system. The
mandate of the Society is the prevention of crime
through service, community education, advocacy
and reform.

Founded in 1929, the Society has grown from
a one-office service in Toronto to 17 local
branches providing direct services in the major
cities of Ontario and a provincial office providing justice policy analysis, advocacy for reform
and support to branches.

51

6 Jackson Pl., Toronto, ON M6P 1T6 Tel. (416) 604-8412 Fax (416)604-8948
Media Contact, Exec. Dir., William Sparks

Officers
Pres., Susan Reid-MacNevin, Dept. of Sociology, Univ. Of Guelph, Guelph, ON N1G 2W1
Vice-Pres., Richard Beaupe, 4165 Fernand St., Hamner, ON B3A 1X4
Treas., Jack Battler, Waterloo, ON
Sec., Peter Angeline, OISE, 252 Bloor St. W., Toronto, ON
Exec. Dir., William Sparks

LOCAL SOCIETIES
Collins Bay; Hamilton; Kingston; Lindsay; London; Niagara; Oshawa; Ottawa; Peel; Peterborough; Sarnia; Sault Ste. Marie; Sudbury; Thunder Bay; Toronto; Waterloo; Windsor

John Milton Society for the Blind in Canada

The John Milton Society for the Blind in Canada is an interdenominational Christian charity whose mandate is producing Christian publications for Canadian adults or young people who are blind, deafblind or visually impaired. As such, it produces Insight, a large-print magazine, Insound, a cassette magazine and In Touch, a braille magazine. The John Milton Society also features an audio cassette library called the Library in Sound, which contains Christian music, sermons, seasonal materials and workshops.

Founded in 1970, the Society is committed to seeing that visually-impaired people receive accessible Christian materials by mail.

Headquarters
40 St. Clair Ave. E., Ste. 202, Toronto, ON M4T 1M9 Tel. (416)960-3953
Media Contact, Ex. Dir., The Rev. Barry R. Brown

Officers
Exec. Dir., The Rev. Barry R. Brown
Pres., The Rev. Ian Nichols

Lutheran Council in Canada

The Lutheran Council in Canada was organized in 1967 and is a cooperative agency of the Evangelical Lutheran Church in Canada and Lutheran Church-Canada.

The Council's activities include communications, coordinative service and national liaison in social ministry, chaplaincy and scout activity.

Headquarters
302-393 Portage Ave., Winnipeg, MB R3B 3H6 Tel. (204)984-9150 Fax (204)984-9185
Media Contact, Pres., Rev. Ralph Mayan, 3074 Portage Ave., Winnipeg, MB R3K 0Y2 Tel. (204)895-3433 Fax (204)897-4319
Email: lcc@mts.net

Officers
Pres.,Rev. Ralph Mayan
Treas., -vacant-
Sec., Rev. Leon C. Gilbertson
Vice Pres., Bishop Telmore Sartison

Mennonite Central Committee Canada (MCCC)

Mennonite Central Committee Canada was organized in 1964 to continue the work which several regional Canadian inter-Mennonite agencies had been doing in relief, service, immigration and peace. All but a few of the smaller Mennonite groups in Canada belong to MCC Canada.

MCCC is part of the Mennonite Central Committee (MCC) International which has its headquarters in Akron, Pa. from where most of the overseas development and relief projects are administered. In 1998-99 MCCC's income was $34 million, about 34 percent of the total MCC income. There were 383 Canadians out of a total of 893 MCC workers serving in North America and abroad during the same time period.

The MCC office in Winnipeg administers projects located in Canada. Domestic programs of Voluntary Service, Native Concerns, Peace and Social Concerns, Food Program, Employment Concerns, Ottawa Office, Victim/Offender Ministries, Mental Health and Immigration are all part of MCC's Canadian ministry. Whenever it undertakes a project, MCCC attempts to relate to the church or churches in the area.

Headquarters
134 Plaza Dr., Winnipeg, MB R3T 5K9 Tel. (204)261-6381 Fax (204)269-9875
Communications, Rick Fast, 134 Plaza Dr., Winnipeg, MT R3T 5K9 Tel. (204)261-6381 Fax (204)269-9875

Officers
Exec. Dir., Dave Dyck

Project Ploughshares

The founding of Project Ploughshares in 1976 was premised on the biblical vision of transforming the material and human wealth consumed by military preparations into resources for human development. An internationally recognized Canadian peace and justice organization, the Project undertakes research, education, and advocacy programs on common security, demilitarization, security alternatives, arms transfer controls, demobilization and peace building. Project Ploughshares is a project of the Canadian Council of Churches and is supported by national churches, civic agencies, affiliated community groups and more than 10,000 individuals.

Publications: the Ploughshares Monitor (quarterly), the Armed Conflicts Report (annual), Briefings and Working Papers (occasional).

Headquarters
Institute of Peace and Conflict Studies, Conrad

Grebel College, Waterloo, ON N2L 3G6 Tel. (519)888-6541 Fax (519)885-0806
Media Contact, Director, Ernie Regehr
Email:plough@ploughshares.ca
Website: www.ploughshares.ca

Officers
Chair, Walter Pitman
Treasurer, Philip Creighton

SPONSORING ORGANIZATIONS
Anglican Church of Canada
Canadian Catholic Organization for Development & Peace
Canadian Friends Service Committee
Canadian Voice of Women for Peace
Conrad Grebel College
Evangelical Lutheran Church in Canada
Mennonite Central Committee Canada
Presbyterian Church in Canada
United Church of Canada

Religious Television Associates

Religious Television Associates was formed in the early 1960s for the production units of the Anglican, Baptist, Presbyterian, Roman Catholic Churches and the United Church of Canada. In the intervening years, the Baptists have withdrawn and the Lutherans have come in. RTA provides an ecumenical umbrella for joint productions in broadcasting and development education. The directors are the heads of the Communications Departments participating in Interchurch Communications.

Headquarters
3250 Bloor St. W., Etobicoke, ON M8X 2Y4 Tel. (416)231-7680 ext. 4051 Fax (416)232-6004
Media Contact, Exec. Dir., Rod Booth
Email:rbooth@uccan.org

Officers
The Anglican Church of Canada
Canadian Conference of Catholic Bishops
The Canadian Council of Churches
The Evangelical Lutheran Church in Canada
The Presbyterian Church in Canada
The United Church of Canada

Scripture Union

Scripture Union is an international interdenominational missionary movement working in 130 countries.

Scripture Union aims to work with the churches to make God's Good News known to children, young people and families and to encourage people of all ages to meet God daily through the Bible and prayer.

In Canada, a range of daily Bible guides are offered to individuals, churches, and bookstores from age four through adult. Sunday School curriculum and various evangelism and discipling materials are also offered for sale.

A program of youth and family evangelism, including beach missions and community-based evangelistic holiday clubs, is also undertaken.

Headquarters
1885 Clements Rd., Unit 226, Pickering, ON L1W 3V4 Tel. (905)427-4947 Fax (905)427-0334
Email: sucan@istar.ca
Website: http://home.istar.ca/~sucan
Media Contact, Gen. Dir., John Irwin, Email: john_w_irwin@compuserve.com

DIRECTORS
Harold Murray, 216 McKinnon Pl. NE, Calgary, AB T2E 7B9

Student Christian Movement of Canada

The Student Christian Movement of Canada was formed in 1921 from the student arm of the YMCA. It has its roots in the Social Gospel movements of the late 19th and early 20th centuries. Throughout its intellectual history, the SCM in Canada has sought to relate the Christian faith to the living realities of the social and political context of each student generation.

The present priorities are built around the need to form more and stronger critical Christian communities on Canadian campuses within which individuals may develop their social and political analyses, experience spiritual growth and fellowship and bring Christian ecumenical witness to the university.

The Student Christian Movement of Canada is affiliated with the World Student Christian Federation.

Headquarters
310 Danforth Ave., Toronto, ON M4K 1N6 Tel. (416)463-4312 Fax (416)466-6854
Email: scmcan@web.net
Website: www.web.net/~scmcan/
Media Contact, Natl. Coord., Susannah Schmidt

Officers
Natl. Coord., Susannah Schmidt

Taskforce on the Churches and Corporate Responsibility

The Taskforce on the Churches and Corporate Responsibility is a national ecumenical coalition of the major churches in Canada. Official representatives from the General Synod of the Anglican Church of Canada, the Canadian Conference of Catholic Bishops, the Evangelical Lutheran Church in Canada, the Presbyterian Church in Canada, the Religious Society of Friends (Quakers), the United Church of Canada, CUSO, the YWCA, and a number of religious orders of women and men, serve as links between the Taskforce and the decision-making structures of the members. The Taskforce assists the members in implementing policies adopted by the churches in the areas of corporate responsibility. Among the policies and issues placed on the agenda of the Taskforce by the participating churches are: principles for global corporate responsibility and bench marks for measuring

53

business performance; corporate operating practices and codes of operation conduct; environmental reporting; human rights and Aboriginal land rights in relation to corporate conduct; social and environmental issues relative to corporate global citizenship; corporate governance issues; responsible investing issues.

Headquarters
129 St. Clair Ave., W., Toronto, ON M4V 1N5
   Tel. (416)923-1758 Fax (416)927-7554
Email: tccr@web.net
Website: web.net/~tccr
Media Contact, Coord., Daniel Gennarelli, Tel. (416)923-1758 Fax (416)927-7554

Officers
Coord., Daniel Gennarelli
Bd. Co-Chpsns.: Tim Ryan; David Hallman
Treas., Doug Peter
Chpsn., Corp. Governance Comm., Richard Soo
Co-Chpsns. Inter-Church Comm. on Ecology, Joy Kennedy, Jim Profit

MEMBERS
Anglican Church of Canada
Basilian Fathers
Baptist Convention Ontario/Quebec
Canadian Conference of Catholic Bishops
Canadian Religious Conference
Christian Reformed Church in Canada
Conference religieuse canadiene- Quebec
Congregation of Notre Dame
Evangelical Lutheran Church in Canada
Grey Sisters of the Immaculate Conception
Jesuit Fathers of Upper Canada
Les Soeurs de Sainte-Anne
Oblate Conference of Canada
Presbyterian Church in Canada
Redemptorist Fathers
Religious Hospitallers of St. Joseph
Religious Society of Friends (Quakers)
School Sisters of Notre Dame
Scarboro Foreign Mission Society
Sisterhood of St. John the Divine
Sisters of Charity-Mount St. Vincent
Sisters of Charity of the Immaculate Conception
Sisters of Mercy Generalate
Sisters of St. Ann, Victoria
Sisters of St. Joseph of Hamilton
Sisters of St. Joseph-Diocese of London
Sisters of Service of Canada
Sisters of St. Joseph-Sault Ste. Marie
Sisters of St. Joseph-Toronto
Sisters of the Holy Names of Jesus & Mary Windsor, ON
Sisters of Holy Names of Jesus and Mary, Longueil, P.Q.
Sisters of Providence of St. Vincent dePaul
Sisters of St. Martha
Toronto United Church Council
United Church of Canada
Ursulines of Chatham Union
Young Women's Christian Association

Ten Days for Global Justice
Supported by five of Canada's major Christian denominations. Ten Days is dedicated to helping people discover, examine and reflect on the ways global and domestic structures and policies promote and perpetuate poverty and injustice for the majority of the world's people. Ten Days is an education and action program that attempts to influence the policies and practice of Canadian churches, government, business, labour, education and the media.

Headquarters
77 Charles St. W. Ste. 401, Toronto, ON M5S
   1K5 Tel. (416)922-0591 Fax (416)922-1419
Email: tendays@web.net
Website: www.web.net/~tendays
Media Contact, Natl. Coord., Dennis Howlett

Staff
Natl. Coord., Dennis Howlett
Coord. for Leadership Dev. & Regional Communication, David Reid
Resource Coord., Julie Graham
Admn. Asst., Ramya Hemachandra

MEMBER ORGANIZATIONS
Anglican Church of Canada
Canadian Cath. Orgn. for Dev. & Peace
Evangelical Lutheran Church in Canada
Presbyterian Church in Canada
United Church of Canada

Women's InterChurch Council of Canada
Women's Inter-Church Council of Canada is a national Christian women's council that encourages women to grow in ecumenism, to strengthen ecumenical community, to share their spirituality and prayer, to engage in dialogue about women's concerns and to stand in solidarity with one another. The Council calls women to respond to national and international issues affecting women and to take action together for justice. WICC sponsors the World Day of Prayer and Fellowship of the Least Coin in Canada. Human rights projects for women are supported and a quarterly magazine "Making Waves" distributed.

Headquarters
Suite 201, 394 Bloor St. W, Toronto, ON M5S
   1X4 Tel. (416)929-5184 Fax (416)929-4064
Website: www.wicc.org
Media Contact, Communications Coordinator, Gillian Barfoot

Officers
Pres., Joyce Christie
Exec. Dir., Rev. Karen Hincke

CHURCH MEMBER BODIES
African Methodist Episcopal, Anglican Church of Canada, Baptist Convention of Ontario & Quebec, Christian Church (Disciples of Christ), Evangelical Lutheran Church in

Canada, Mennonite Central Committee, Presbyterian Church in Canada, Religious Society of Friends, Roman Catholic Church, Salvation Army in Canada, United Church of Canada

World Vision Canada

World Vision Canada is a Christian humanitarian relief and development organization. Although its main international commitment is to translate child sponsorship into holistic, sustainable community development, World Vision also allocates resources to help Canada's poor and complement the mission of the church.

World Vision's Reception Centre assists government-sponsored refugees entering Canada. The NeighbourLink program mobilizes church volunteers to respond locally to people's needs. A quarterly publication, Context, provides data on the Canadian family to help churches effectively reach their communities. The development education program provides resources on development issues. During the annual 30-Hour Famine, people fast for 30 hours while discussing poverty and raising funds to support aid programs.

Headquarters
6630 Turner Valley Rd., Mississauga, ON L5N 2S4 Tel. (905)821-3030 Fax (905)821-1356
Email:philip_maher@worldvision.ca
Website: www.worldvision.ca
Media Contact, Philip Maher, Tel. (905)567-2726

Officers
Pres., Dave Toycen
Vice-Pres.: Intl. & Govt. Relations, Linda Tripp; Natl. Programs, Don Posterski; Fin. & Admin., Charlie Fluit; Donor Development Group, Brian Tizzard

Young Men's Christian Association in Canada

The YMCA began as a Christian association to help young men find healthy recreation and meditation, as well as opportunities for education, in the industrial slums of 19th century England. It came to Canada in 1851 with the same mission in mind for young men working in camps and on the railways.

Today, the YMCA maintains its original mission, helping individuals to grow and develop in spirit, mind and body, but attends to those needs for men and women of all ages and religious beliefs. The YMCA registers 1.5 million participants in 250 communities that are served by 64 autonomous associations across Canada.

The program of each association differs according to the needs of the community, but most offer one or more programs in each of the following categories: health and fitness, child care, employment counselling and training,

recreation, camping, community support and outreach, international development and short-term accommodation.

The YMCA encourages people of all ages, races, abilities, income and beliefs to come together in an environment which promotes balance in life, breaking down barriers and helping to create healthier communities.

Headquarters
42 Charles St. E., 6th Floor., Toronto, ON M4Y 1T4 Tel. (416)967-9622 Fax (416)967-9618
Media Contact, Sol Kasimer

Officers
Chpsn., Ray Mantha
CEO, Sol Kasimer

Young Women's Christian Association of/du Canada

The YWCA of/du Canada is a national voluntary organization serving 44 YWCAs and YM-YWCAs across Canada. Dedicated to the development and improved status of women and their families, the YWCA is committed to service delivery and to being a source of public education on women's issues and an advocate of social change. Services provided by YWCAs and YM-YWCAs include adult education programs, residences and shelters, child care, fitness activities, wellness programs and international development education. As a member of the World YWCA, the YWCA of/du Canada is part of the largest women's organization in the world.

Headquarters
80 Gerrard St. E., Toronto, ON M5B 1G6 Tel. (416)593-9886 Fax (416)971-8084
Media Contact, Int. CEO, Margaret MacKenzie

Officers
Pres., Ann Mowatt

Youth for Christ/Canada

Youth For Christ is an interdenominational organization founded in 1944 by Torrey Johnson. Under the leadership of YFC's 11 national board of directors, Youth For Christ/Canada cooperates with churches and serves as a mission agency reaching out to young people and their families through a variety of ministries.

YFC seeks to have maximum influence in a world of youth through high-interest activities and personal involvement. Individual attention is given to each teenager through small group involvement and counselling. These activities and relationships become vehicles for communicating the message of the Gospel.

Headquarters
822-167 Lombard Ave., Winnipeg, MB R3B 0V3 Tel. (204)989-0056 Fax (204)989-0067

Officers
Natl. Dir., Randy L. Steinwand

3. Religious Bodies in the United States

The United States, with its staunch constitutional stance on religious freedom and successive waves of immigrants over the last three centuries, has proved to be a fertile soil for the development of varied Christian traditions. In the directory which follows, some 217 distinct church traditions are represented. Many of these groups represent the processes of dividing and reuniting that are a hallmark of the American religious contexts. Many churches listed here represent those with a long tradition in Europe, Africa, or Asia predating their American tenure. Others are American-born churches. The researcher may be helped by consulting the churches grouped by tradition at the end of this directory in the section entitled, "Religious Bodies in the United States Arranged by Families." In this section, all the Baptists bodies are listed together, all the Lutheran bodies, Methodists, etc.

The following directory information is supplied by the national headquarters of each church. Each listing contains a brief description of the church, followed by the national headquarters contact information, which includes a mailing address, telephone and fax numbers, email and website addresses (when available), and the name of the media contact. After the headquarters, there are data regarding the church officers or leaders, including names, titles, and contact information (when contact information differs from the headquarters). There is a staggering array of churches, each with its own form of organization; not all of them refer to their leaders as "officers." In some places, the reader will find the term "Bishops," "Board Members," or "Executives" in place of "Officers." Finally, when applicable, each entry contains a list of the names of church publications.

The churches are printed in alphabetical order by the official name of the organization. There are a few instances in which certain churches are more commonly known by another name. In such cases, the reader is referred incidentally within the text to the appropriate official name. Churches that are member communions of the National Council of Churches of Christ in the U.S.A. are marked with an asterisk (*).

Other useful information about the churches listed here can be found in other chapters or directories within the book. Statistical information for these churches can be found in the tables toward the end of this book in Chapter III. Further, more extensive information about the publications listed in this directory can be found in Directory 11, "Religious Periodicals in the United States." For a list of church websites, see Directory 5, "The Emerging Electronic Church."

The organizations listed here represent the denominations to which the vast majority of church members in the United States belong. It does not include all religious bodies functioning in the United States. *The Encyclopedia of American Religions* (Gale Research Inc., P.O. Box 33477, Detroit MI 48232-5477) contains names and addresses of additional religious bodies

Advent Christian Church

The Advent Christian Church is a conservative, evangelical denomination which grew out of the Millerite movement of the 1830s and 1840s. The members stress the authority of Scripture, justification by faith in Jesus Christ alone, the importance of evangelism and world missions and the soon visible return of Jesus Christ.

Organized in 1860, the Advent Christian Church maintains headquarters in Charlotte, N.C., with regional offices in Rochester, N. H., Princeton, N.C., Ellisville, MO., Lewiston, Idaho, and Lenoir, N.C. Missions are maintained in India, Nigeria, Ghana, Japan, Liberia, Croatia, New Zealand, Malaysia, the Philippines, Mexico, South Africa, Namibia, Honduras and Memphis, Tenn.

The Advent Christian Church maintains doctrinal distinctives in three areas: conditional immortality, the sleep of the dead until the return of Christ and belief that the kingdom of God will be established on earth made new by Jesus Christ.

Headquarters
P.O. Box 23152, Charlotte, NC 28227 Tel. (704) 545-6161 Fax (704)573-0712

Media Contact, Exec. Director, David E. Ross
Email: acpub@adventchristian.org

Officers
Pres., Rev. James Crouse, 326 9th St., Baraboo, WI 53913
Exec. Dir., David E. Ross
Sec., Rev. Thomas S. Warren II, 8912 Snow Hill Ln., Jacksonville, FL 32221
Appalachian Vice-Pres., Rev. James Lee, 1338 Delwood Dr. SW, Lenoir, NC 28645
Central Vice-Pres., Rev. Glenn Fell, 1525 Plainfield Rd., LaGrange, IL 60525
Eastern Vice-Pres., Rev. Glenn Rice, 130 Leighton St., Bangor, ME 04401
Southern Vice-Pres., Rev. Brent Ross, 3635 Andrea Lee Ct., Snellville, GA 30278-4941
Western Vice-Pres., Brad Neil, 4035 S. 275th Pl., Auburn, WA 98001
The Woman's Home & Foreign Mission Soc., Pres., Hazel Blackstone, 2141 Broadway, Bangor, ME 04901

Periodicals
Advent Christian News; The Advent Christian Witness; Insight; Maranatha; Henceforth...; Coast to Coast on Campus; Leadership Letter; Prayer and Praise

African Methodist Episcopal Church*

This church began in 1787 in Philadelphia when persons in St. George's Methodist Episcopal Church withdrew as a protest against color segregation. In 1816 the denomination was started, led by Rev. Richard Allen who had been ordained deacon by Bishop Francis Asbury and was subsequently ordained elder and elected and consecrated bishop.

Headquarters

1134 11th St., NW, Washington, DC 20001 Tel. (202)371-8700

Officers

Senior Bishop, Bishop John Hurst Adams, Presiding Bishop, Seventh Episcopal District, African Methodist Episcopal Church, 110 Pisgah Church Rd., Columbia, SC 29203 Tel. (803)935-0500, Fax (803)935-0830

Chief Ecumenical & Urban Affairs Officer, Bishop McKinley Young, AME, 700 Martin Luther King, Jr. Dr., SW, Atlanta, GA 30314-4143 Tel. 404-522-0800 Fax

President, General Board, Bishop Donald George K. Ming, Sixth Episcopal District, African Methodist Episcopal Church, 208 Auburn Ave., NW, Atlanta, GA 30303, Tel. 404-524-8279 Fax 404-524-0778

President, Council of Bishops 1999-2000, Bishop C. Garnett Henning, Sr. Nineteenth Episcopal District, African Methodist Episcopal Church, 9301 S. 11th Ave., Inglewood, CA 90305, 310-677-4779

President, Council of Bishops 2000-2001, Bishop William P. DeVeaux, Eighteenth Episcopal District, African Methodist Episcopal Church, 88660 Woodland Dr., Silver Springs, MD 20910 Tel. 301-585-8288 Fax 301-585-3192

General Secretary, Dr. Cecil W. Howard, 4144 Lindell Blvd., Suite 122, St. Louis, MO 63108, Tel. 314-534-5118, Fax 314-534-7419

Treasurer, Mr. Richard A. Lewis, 1134 11th St., NW, Washington, DC 20001, Tel. 202-371-8700, Fax 202-371-8735

President, Lay Organization, Mr. J. L. Williams, 1840 Francis St., Jacksonville, FL 32209, Tel. 904-765-9150, Fax 904-765-9156

Publisher, Dr. A. Lee Henderson, 500 8th Avenue, S., Suite 200, Nashville, TN 37203, Tel. 615-256-5882, Fax 613-244-7604

President, Women's Missionary Society, Dr. Dorothy Adams Peck, 1134 11th St., NW, Washington, DC 20001, Tel. 202-371-8886, Fax 202-371-8820

Director, Young People's Division, Ms. Adrienne A. Morris, Women's Missionary Society, 327 Washington Av., Wyoming, OH 45115, Tel. 513-821-1481 Fax 513-821-3073

Periodicals

The Christian Recorder; A.M.E. Church Review; Journal of Christian Education; Secret Chamber; Women's Missionary Magazine; Voice of Mission; YPD Newsletter

African Methodist Episcopal Zion Church*

The A.M.E. Zion Church is an independent body, having withdrawn from the John Street Methodist Church of New York City in 1796. The first bishop was James Varick.

Headquarters

Dept. of Records & Research, P.O. Box 32843, Charlotte, NC 28232 Tel. (704)332-3851 Fax (704)333-1769

Media Contact, Gen. Sec.-Aud., Dr. W. Robert Johnson, III

BOARD OF BISHOPS
OFFICERS

*President, Samuel Chuka Ekemam, Sr., Okigwe Rd., P.O. Box 1149, Owerri, Nigeria, West Africa; (011)234-83-232271

*NOTE: Presidency rotates every six months according to seniority.

Secretary., Bishop Marshall H. Strickland I, 2000 Cedar Circle Dr., Baltimore, MD 21215 Tel. (410)744-7330 Fax (410)788-5510

Asst. Sec., Bishop Clarence Carr, 2600 Normandy Dr., Greendale, MO 63121, Tel. (314)727-2931 Fax (314)727-0663

Treas., Bishop George Washington Carver Walker, Sr., 137 Talcott Notch Rd., Farmington, CT 06032 Tel.(860)676-8414 Fax (860)676-8424

MEMBERS

ACTIVE

Battle, Jr. George Edward, 8403 Dembridge Ln., Davidson, NC 28036 Tel. (704)895-2236 Office Tel. (704)332-7600 Fax (704)343-3745

Bishop, Cecil, 2663 Oakmeade Dr., Charlotte, NC 28270 Tel. (704)846-9370 Fax (704)846-9371

Brown, Warren Matthew, 22 Crowley Dr., Randolph, MA 02368 Tel. (781)961-2434 Fax (781)961-2939

Carr, Clarence, 2600 Normandy Dr., Greendale, MO 63121, Tel. (314)727-2931 Fax (314)727-0663

Ekeman, Sr., Samuel Chuka, 98 Okigwe Rd., PO Box 1149, Owerri, Nigeria West Africa Tel. (011)234-83-232271

Jarrett, Jr., Nathaniel, 7322 South Clyde Ave., Chicago, IL 60649 Tel. (773)684-8098 Fax (773)684-0810

Johnson, Joseph, 320 Walnut Point Dr., PO Box 608 Matthews, NC 28106 Tel. (704)849-0521 Fax (704)849-0571

Rochester, Enoch Benjamin, Office: Hwy. 130 South, Suite 2A, Cinnaminson, NJ 08077 Tel. (609)786-2555 Fax (609) 786-8568; Home: 129 Sagebush Dr., Belleville, IL 62221 Tel. (618)257-8481

Strickland I, Marshall Hayward, 2000 Cedar

Circle Dr., Baltimore, MD 21215 Tel. (410)744-7330 Fax (410)788-5510

Thompson, Richard Keith, 1420 Missouri Ave., N.W., Washington, DC 20011, Mailing Address: PO Box 55458, Washington, DC, 20040 Tel. (202)723-8993 Fax (202)722-1840

Walker, Sr., George Washington Carver, 137 Talcott Notch Rd., Farmington, CT 06032 Tel.(860)676-8414 Fax (860)676-8424

Williams, Milton Alexander, 12904 Canoe Court, Fort Washington, MD 20744 Tel. (301)292-0002 Fax (301)292-6655; Office: 2001 Ninth St., N.W., Suite 306, Box 322, Washington, DC 20001 Tel. (202)265-9590 Fax (202)265-9593

RETIRED

Foggie, Charles H., 1200 Windermere Dr., Pittsburgh, PA 15218 Tel. (412)242-5842

Hilliard , William Alexander, 690 Chicago Blvd., Detroit, MI 48202

Hoggard, James Clinton, 4515 Willard Ave., Apt, 2203, South Chevy Chase, MD 20815 Tel. (301)652-9010; Office: Howard University School of Divinity, 1400 Shepherd St., N.E., Suite 189/191, Washington, DC 20017 Tel. (202)635-6201

Miller, Sr., John Henry, Springdale Estates, 8605 Caswell Ct., Raleigh, NC 27612 Tel. (919)848-6915

Speaks, Ruben Lee, P.O. Box 986, Salisbury, NC 28145 Tel. (704)637-6018 Fax (704) 639-0059

EPISCOPAL ASSIGNMENTS

Piedmont Episcopal District: Blue Ridge, West Central North Carolina, Western North Carolina, and Jamaica Conferences: Bishop Cecil Bishop

North Eastern Episcopal District: New England, New York, Western New York, and Bahamas Islands Conferences: Bishop George W. Walker, Sr.

Mid-Atlantic II Episcopal District: East Tennessee-Virginia, India, London-Birmingham, Manchester-Midland, Philadelphia-Baltimore, and Virginia Conferences: Bishop Milton A. Williams

Eastern West Africa Episcopal District: Central Nigeria, Lagos-West Nigeria, Nigeria, Northern Nigeria, and Rivers Conferences: Bishop S. Chuka Ekemam, Sr.

Eastern North Carolina Episcopal District: Albemarle, Cape Fear, Central North Carolina, North Carolina, and Virgin Islands Conferences: Bishop George E. Battle, Jr.

South Atlantic Episcopal District: Georgia, Palmetto, Pee Dee, South Carolina, and South Georgia Conferences: Bishop Joseph Johnson

Alabama-Florida Episcopal District: Alabama, Cahaba, Central Alabama, North Alabama, South Alabama, West Alabama, Florida, and South Florida Conferences: Bishop Richard K. Thompson

Mid-West Episcopal District: Indiana, Kentucky, Michigan, Missouri, Tennessee, and South

Africa Conferences: Bishop Enoch B. Rochester

Mid-Atlantic I Episcopal District: Allegheny, New Jersey, Ohio, Guyana, Trinidad-Tobago, and Barbados Conferences: Bishop Marshall Haywood Strickland I

Western Episcopal District: Alaska, Arizona, California, Oregon-Washington, Southwest Rocky Mountain, and Colorado Conferences: Bishop Clarence Carr

Southwestern Delta: Arkansas, Louisiana, Oklahoma, South Mississippi, West Tennessee-Mississippi, and Texas Conferences: Bishop Nathaniel Jarrett

Western West Africa: Cote D'Ivore, East Ghana, Liberia, Mid-Ghana, and West Ghana Conferences: Bishop Warren Matthew Brown

General Officers and Departments

Dept. of Records & Research, Gen. Sec.-Aud., Dr. W. Robert Johnson, III, 401 E. Second St., Ste. 108, Charlotte, NC 28202 Tel. (704)332-3851 Fax (704)333-1769; Mailing Address: P.O. Box 32843, Charlotte, NC 28232; Email: j1gsa@aol.com

Dept. of Finance, CFO, Shirley Welch, 401 E. Second St., Ste. 101, Charlotte, NC 28202 Tel. (704)333-4847 Fax (704)333-6517; Mailing Address: P.O. Box 31005, Charlotte, NC 28231

Star of Zion, Michael Libsy, Editor, 401 E. Second St., Suite 106, Charlotte, NC 28202 Tel. (704)377-4329 Fax (704)377-4329 Fax (704)377-2809; E-mail: starozion@juno.com Mailing Address: PO Box 31005, Charlotte, NC 28231

A.M.E. Zion Quarterly Review and Historical Society: James D. Armstong, Sec.-Ed., 401 E. Second St., Suite 103, Charlotte, NC 28202 Tel. (704)334-0728 Fax (704)333-1769 Mailing Address: PO Box 33247, Charlotte, NC 28231

Dept. of Overseas Missions and Missionary Seer: Sec.-Ed., Dr. Kermit J. DeGraffenreidt, 475 Riverside Dr., Rm. 1935, New York, NY 10115 Tel. (212)870-2952 Fax (212)870-2808

Dept. Brotherhood Pensions & Min. Relief: Sec.-Treas., Dr. David Miller, 401 E. Second St., Suite 209, Charlotte, NC 28202 Tel. (704)333-3779 or 1-800-762-5106 Fax (704)333-3867P.O. Box 34454, Charlotte, NC 28234-4454

Christian Education Dept.: Gen. Sec., Rev. Raymon Hunt, 401 E. Second St., Suite 207, Charlotte, NC 28202 Tel. (704)332-9323 Fax (704)332-9332 E-mail: ced1amez@juno.com Mailing Address: P.O. Box 32305, Charlotte, NC 28232-2305

Dept. of Church School Literature: Ed., Dr. Mary A. Love, 401 E. Second St., Suite 208, Charlotte, NC 28202 Tel. (704)332-1034 Fax (704)333-1769 Mailing Address: P.O. Box 31005, Charlotte, NC 28231

Dept. of Church Extension & Home Mission: Sec-Treas., Dr. Lem Long, Jr., 401 E. Second St., Suite 104, Charlotte, NC 28202 Tel. (704)334-2519 Fax (704)334-3806 Mailing Address: P.O. Box 31005, Charlotte, NC 28231

Bureau of Evangelism: Dir., Rev. Darryl B. Starnes, Sr., 401 E. Second St., Suite 111, Charlotte, NC 28202 Tel. (704)342-3070 Fax (704)342-2389 Mailing Address: P.O. Box 33623, Charlotte, NC 28233-3623

Public Affairs and Convention Manager: Dir., Rev. George E. McKain, II, 943 West 1st North St., Summerville, SC 29483 Tel. (803) 873-2475

Dept. of Health & Social Concerns: Dir., Dr. Bernard H. Sullivan, P.O. Box 972, Gastonia, NC 28053 Tel. (704)866-0325 or (704)864-1791 Fax (704)864-7641

A.M.E. Zion Publishing House: Interim Gen. Mgr., Dr. David Miller, 401 E. Second St., Suite 106, Charlotte, NC 28202 Tel. (704)334-9596 Fax (704)334-9592; 1-800-343-9835 Mailing Address: PO Box 30714, Charlotte, NC 28230

Periodicals

Star of Zion; Quarterly Review; Church School Herald; Missionary Seer; Vision Focus

Albanian Orthodox Archdiocese in America

The Albanian Orthodox Church in America traces its origins to the groups of Albanian immigrants which first arrived in the United States in 1886, seeking religious, cultural and economic freedoms denied them in the homeland.

In 1908 in Boston, the Rev. Fan Stylian Noli (later Archbishop) served the first liturgy in the Albanian language in 500 years, to which Orthodox Albanians rallied, forming their own diocese in 1919. Parishes began to spring up throughout New England and the Mid-Atlantic and Great Lakes states. In 1922, clergy from the United States traveled to Albania to proclaim the self-governance of the Orthodox Church in the homeland at the Congress of Berat.

In 1971 the Albanian Archdiocese sought and gained union with the Orthodox Church in America, expressing the desire to expand the Orthodox witness to America at large, giving it an indigenous character. The Albanian Archdiocese remains vigilant for its brothers and sisters in the homeland and serves as an important resource for human rights issues and Albanian affairs, in addition to its programs for youth, theological education, vocational interest programs and retreats for young adults and women.

Headquarters

523 E. Broadway, S. Boston, MA 02127
Media Contact, Sec., Dorothy Adams, Tel. (617) 268-1275 Fax (617)268-3184

Officers

Metropolitan Theodosius, Tel. (617)268-1275
Chancellor, V. Rev. Arthur E. Liolin, 60 Antwerp St., East Milton, MA 02186 Tel. (617)698-3366
Lay Chpsn., William Poist, 40 Forge Village Rd., Westford, MA 01885 Tel. (978)392-0759
Treas., Cynthia Vasil Brown, 471 Capt. Eames Circle, Ashland, MA 01721 (508)881-0072

Albanian Orthodox Diocese of America

This Diocese was organized in 1950 as a canonical body administering to the Albanian faithful. It is under the ecclesiastical jurisdiction of the Ecumenical Patriarchate of Constantinople (Istanbul).

Headquarters

6455 Silver Dawn Lane, Las Vegas, NV 89118 Tel. (702)221-8245 Fax (702)221-9167
Media Contact, Rev. Ik. Ilia Katre

Officers

Vicar General, Rev. Ik. Ilia Katre

Allegheny Wesleyan Methodist Connection (Original Allegheny Conference)

This body was formed in 1968 by members of the Allegheny Conference (located in eastern Ohio and western Pennsylvania) of the Wesleyan Methodist Church, which merged in 1966 with the Pilgrim Holiness Church to form The Wesleyan Church.

The Allegheny Wesleyan Methodist Connection is composed of persons "having the form and seeking the power of godliness, united in order to pray together, to receive the word of exhortation, and to watch over one another in love, that they may help each other to work out their salvation." There is a strong commitment to congregational government and to holiness of heart and life. There is a strong thrust in church extension within the United States and in missions worldwide.

Headquarters

P.O. Box 357, Salem, OH 44460 Tel. (330)337-9376
Media Contact, Pres., Rev. Michael Marshall
Email: awmc@juno.com

Officers

Pres., Rev. Michael Marshall, P.O. Box 357, Salem, OH 44460
Vice-Pres., Rev. William Cope, 1827 Allen Drive, Salem, OH 44460
Sec., Rev. Ray Satterfield, Rt. 4, Box 300, Salem, WV 26426
Treas., James Kunselman, 2161 Woodsdale Rd., Salem, OH 44460

Periodicals

The Allegheny Wesleyan Methodist

The Alliance of Baptists in the U.S.A.*

The Alliance of Baptists is an alliance of individuals and churches dedicated to the preservation of historic Baptist principles, freedoms, and traditions, and to the expression of our ministry and mission through cooperative relationships with other Baptist bodies and the larger Christian community.

From its inception in early 1987, the Alliance has stood for those values that have distinguished the Baptist movement from its beginnings nearly four centuries ago—the freedom and accountability of every individual in matters of faith; the freedom of each congregation under the authority of Jesus Christ to determine its own ministry and mission; and religious freedom for all in relationship to the state.

Headquarters

1328 16th St. N.W., Washington, DC 20036 Tel. (202)745-7609 Fax (202)745-0023

Media Contact, Exec. Dir., Rev. Dr. Stan Hastey

Officers

Exec. Dir., Rev. Dr. Stan Hastey
Assoc. Dir., Jeanette Holt
Pres., The Rev. Paula Clayton Dempsey, Mars Hill, NC, (828)689-1128
Vice-Pres., Craig Henry, Monroe, LA (318)388-4400
Sec., David Gooch, Nashville, TN (615)321-0222

Publications

"connections"

The American Association of Lutheran Churches

This church body was constituted on November 7, 1987. The AALC was formed by laity and pastors of the former American Lutheran Church in America who held to a high view of Scripture (inerrancy and infallibility). This church body also emphasizes the primacy of evangelism and world missions and the authority and autonomy of the local congregation.

Congregations of the AALC are distributed throughout the continental United States from Long Island, N.Y., to Los Angeles. The primary decision-making body is the General Convention, to which each congregation has proportionate representation.

Headquarters

The AALC National Office, 10800 Lyndale Ave. S., Ste. 210, Minneapolis, MN 55420-5614 Tel. (612)884-7784 Fax (612)884-7894,

The AALC Regional Office, 2211 Maynard St., Waterloo, IA 50701 Tel. (319)232-3971 Fax (319)232-1523

Media Contact, Admn. Coord., Rev. Charles D. Eidum, 10800 Lyndale Ave. So., # 210 Minneapolis, MN 55420-5614, Tel. (612) 884-7784 FAX (612) 884-7894

Email: chuckAALC@aol.com
Website: www.taalc.org

Officers

Presiding Pastor, Rev. Thomas V. Addland, 10800 Lyndale Ave., So., #210, Minneapolis, MN 55420-5614, Tel. (612)884-7784 Fax (612)884-7894, Email: aadland@aol.com
Asst. Presiding Pastor, Rev. John A. Anderson, 310 Seventh St., Ames, IA 50010 Tel. (515) 232-3815
Sec., Rev. Dick Hueter, N9945 Highway 180, Wausaukee, WI 54177 Tel. (715)732-0327
Treas., Rev. Dale Zastrow, 700 Second Ave. NE, Minot, ND 58703 Tel. (701)839-7474

Periodicals

The Evangel

The American Baptist Association

The American Baptist Association (ABA) is an international fellowship of independent Baptist churches voluntarily cooperating in missionary, evangelistic, benevolent and Christian education activities throughout the world. Its beginnings can be traced to the landmark movement of the 1850s. Led by James R. Graves and J.M. Pendleton, a significant number of Baptist churches in the South, claiming a New Testament heritage, rejected as extrascriptural the policies of the newly formed Southern Baptist Convention (SBC). Because they strongly advocated church equality, many of these churches continued doing mission and benevolent work apart from the SBC, electing to work through local associations. Meeting in Texarkana, TX, in 1924, messengers from the various churches effectively merged two of these major associations, the Baptist Missionary Association of Texas and the General Association, forming the American Baptist Association.

Since 1924, mission efforts have been supported in Australia, Africa, Asia, Canada, Central America, Europe, India, Israel, Japan, Korea, Mexico, New Zealand, South America and the South Pacific. An even more successful domestic mission effort has changed the ABA from a predominantly rural southern organization to one with churches in 48 states.

Through its publishing arm in Texarkana, the ABA publishes literature and books numbering into the thousands. Major seminaries include the Missionary Baptist Seminary, founded by Dr. Ben M. Bogard in Little Rock, AR; Texas Baptist Seminary, Henderson, TX; Oxford Baptist Institute, Oxford, MS; and Florida Baptist Schools in Lakeland, FL.

While no person may speak for the churches of the ABA, all accept the Bible as the inerrant Word of God. They believe Christ was the virgin-born Son of God, that God is a triune God, that the only church is the local congregation of scripturally baptized believers and that the work of the church is to spread the gospel.

Headquarters

4605 N State Line Ave. Texarkana, TX 75503
Tel. (903) 792-2783

Media Contact: Jim Jones, Public Relations
Director

Email: bssc@abaptist.org

Officers

President: George Raley, 9890 Hwy 15, Rison,
AR 71665

Vice Presidents: Neal Clark, Rt. 1, Box 48A,
Daingerfield, TX 75638; John Owen, P.O. Box
142, Bryant, AR 72089; David Butimore Sr.,
1602 Winters Rd., Brementon, WA 98311

Recording Clerks: Larry Clements, 270 Tracy
Dr., Monticello, AR 71655; Lonnie Wiggins,
1114 Occidental St., Redlands, CA 92374

Publications: Editor in Chief, Bill Johnson; Bus.
Mgr., Wayne Sewell, 4605 N. State Line Ave.,
Texarkana, TX 75503

Meeting Arrangements Director: Edgar N.
Sutton, P.O. Box 240, Alexander, AR 72002

Sec.-Treas. of Missions: Randy Cloud, P.O. Box
1050 Texarkana, TX 75504

American Baptist Churches in the U.S.A.*

Originally known as the Northern Baptist
Convention, this body of Baptist churches
changed the name to American Baptist
Convention in 1950 with a commitment to "hold
the name in trust for all Christians of like faith
and mind who desire to bear witness to the historical Baptist convictions in a framework of
cooperative Protestantism."

In 1972 American Baptist Churches in the
U.S.A. was adopted as the new name. Although
national missionary organizational developments
began in 1814 with the establishment of the
American Baptist Foreign Mission Society and
continued with the organization of the American
Baptist Publication Society in 1824 and the
American Baptist Home Mission Society in
1832, the general denominational body was not
formed until 1907. American Baptist work at the
local level dates back to the organization by
Roger Williams of the First Baptist Church in
Providence, R. I. in 1638.

Headquarters

American Baptist Churches Mission Center
P.O. Box 851, Valley Forge, PA 19482-0851 Tel.
(610)768-2000 Fax (610)768-2320

Media Contact, Dir., Office of Comm., Richard
W. Schramm, Tel. (610)768-2077 Fax (610)
768-2320

Email: richard.schramm@abc-usa.org
Website: www.abc-usa.org

Officers

Pres., Trinette V. McCray
Vice-Pres., David Hunt
Budget Review Officer, Kenneth Hines
Interim Gen. Sec., Robert H. Roberts
Assoc. Gen. Sec.-Treas., Cheryl H. Wade

REGIONAL ORGANIZATIONS

Central Region, ABC of, Fred A. Ansell, 5833
SW 29th St., Topeka, KS 66614-2499

Chicago, ABC of Metro, William R. Nelson
(Interim), 28 E. Jackson Blvd., Ste. 210,
Chicago, IL 60604-2207

Cleveland Baptist Assoc., Dennis E. Norris, 1836
Euclid Ave., Ste. 603, Cleveland, OH 44115-
2234

Connecticut, ABC of, Lowell H. Fewster, 100
Bloomfield Ave., Hartford, CT 06105-1097

Dakotas, ABC of, Truman G. Sproles (Interim),
1524 S. Summit Ave., Sioux Falls, SD 57105-
1697

District of Columbia Bapt. Conv., W. Jere Allen,
1628 16th St., NW, Washington, DC 20009-
3099

Great Rivers Region, ABC of the, J. Dwight
Stinnett, P.O. Box 3786, Springfield, IL
62708-3786

Indiana, ABC of, Larry D. Mason, 1350 N.
Delaware St., Indianapolis, IN 46202-2493

Indianapolis, ABC of Greater, Larry D. Sayre,
1350 N. Delaware St., Indianapolis, IN 46202-
2493

Los Angeles, ABC of, Samuel S. Chetti, 605 W.
Olympic Blvd., Ste. 700, Los Angeles, CA
90015-1426

Maine, ABC of, Foster Williams (Interim), 107
Winthrop St., P.O. Box 617, Augusta, ME
04332-0617

Massachusetts, ABC of, Alfred J. Fletcher, 20
Milton St., Dedham, MA 02026-2967

Metropolitan New York, ABC of, James O.
Stallings, 475 Riverside Dr., Rm. 432, New
York, NY 10115-0432

Michigan, ABC of, Michael A. Williams, 4578 S.
Hagadorn Rd., East Lansing, MI 48823-5396

Mid-American Baptist Churches, Gary L.
Grogan, Ste. 15, 2400 86th St., Des Moines,
IA 50322-4380

Nebraska, ABC of, J. David Mallgren, 6404
Maple St., Omaha, NE 68104-4079

New Jersey, ABC of, Susan Gillies, 3752
Nottingham Way, Ste. 101, Trenton, NJ
08690-3802

New York State, ABC of, William A. Carlsen,
5842 Heritage Landing Dr., East Syracuse,
NY 13057-9359

Northwest, ABC of, 409 Third Ave. South, Suite
A, Kent, WA 98032-5843

Ohio, ABC of, C. Jeff Woods, 136 N. Galway
Dr., P.O. Box 376, Granville, OH 43023-0376

Oregon, ABC of, W. Wayne Brown, 0245 SW
Bancroft St., Ste. G, Portland, OR 97201-4270

Pacific Southwest, ABC of the, Dale V. Salico,
970 Village Oaks Dr., Ste. 101, Covina, CA
91724-3679

Pennsylvania & Delaware, ABC of, Clayton R.
Woodbury, 106 Revere Lane, Coatesville, PA
19320

Philadelphia Baptist Assoc., Larry K. Waltz, 100
N. 17th St., Philadelphia, PA 19103-2736

61

Pittsburgh Baptist Assoc., Lawrence O. Swain, 429 Forbes Ave., #1620, Pittsburgh, PA 15219-1604

Puerto Rico, Baptist Churches of, Miladys Oliveras (Interim) #21, San Juan, PR 00917

Rhode Island, ABC of, Donald R. Rasmussen, P.O. Box 330, Exeter, RI 02822

Rochester-Genesee Region, ABC of, W. Kenneth Williams, 151 Brooks Ave., Rochester, NY 14619-2454

Rocky Mountains, ABC of, Louise B. Barger, 3900 Wadsworth Blvd. Suite 365, Lakewood, CO 80235-2220

South, ABC of the, Walter L. Parrish, II, 5124 Greenwich Ave., Baltimore, MD 21229-2393

Vermont/New Hampshire, ABC of, Louis A. George, Wheeler Professional Park, One Oak Ridge Rd., Bldg. 3, Suite 4A, West Lebanon, NH 03784-3121

West, ABC of the, Paul D. Borden (Acting), 2420 Camino Ramon, Ste. 140, San Ramon, CA 94583-4207

West Virginia Baptist Convention, Lloyd D. Hamblin, Jr., P.O. Box 1019, Parkersburg, WV 26102-1019

Wisconsin, ABC of, Richard O. Goins (Interim) 15330 W. Watertown Plank Rd., Elm Grove, WI 53122-2391

BOARDS

Bd. of Educational Ministries: Exec. Dir., Jean B. Kim; Pres., Kevin Rose

American Baptist Assembly: Green Lake, WI 54941; Pres., Kenneth P. Giacoletto; Chpsn., Hector Gonzalez

American Baptist Historical Society: 1106 S. Goodman St., Rochester, NY 14620; or P.O. Box 851, Valley Forge, PA 19482-0851; Admn./ Archivist, Deborah B. VanBroekhoven; Pres., Beverly Davison

American Baptist Men: Dir., Z. Allen Abbott, Jr.; Pres., Larru Callahan

American Baptist Women's Ministries: Exec. Dir., Carol Franklin Sutton; Pres., Karen Selig

Ministerial Leadership Commission: Exec. Dir., Ivan George

Bd. of Intl. Ministries: Exec. Dir., John A. Sundquist; Pres., Stephen Hasper

Bd. of Natl. Ministries: Exec. Dir., Aidsand F. Wright-Riggins; Pres., Thomas Litwiler

Ministers & Missionaries Benefit Bd.: Exec. Dir., Sumner M. Grant; Pres., Mary H. Purcell, 475 Riverside Dr., New York, NY 10115

Minister Council: Dir., Carole (Kate) H. Harvey; Pres., G. Daniel Jones

Periodicals

Tomorrow Magazine; Baptist Leader; The Secret Place; American Baptist Quarterly; American Baptists In Mission

The American Carpatho-Russian Orthodox Greek Catholic Church*

The American Carpatho-Russian Orthodox Greek Catholic Church is a self-governing dio-cese that is in communion with the Ecumenical Patriarchate of Constantinople. The late Patriarch Benjamin I, in an official Patriarchal Document dated Sept. 19, 1938, canonized the Diocese in the name of the Orthodox Church of Christ.

Headquarters

312 Garfield St., Johnstown, PA 15906 Tel. (814)539-4207

Media Contact, Chancellor, V. Rev. Protopresbyter Frank P. Miloro, Tel. (814)539-8086 Fax (814)536-4699

Officers

Bishop, Metropolitan Nicholas Smisko

Chancellor, V. Rev. Protopresbyter Frank P. Miloro, 127 Chandler Ave., Johnstown, PA 15906

Treas., V. Rev. Protopresbyter Ronald A. Hazuda, 115 East Ave., Erie, PA 16503

Periodicals

The Church Messenger

American Catholic Church

The American Catholic Church was founded in 1988, and incorporated in 1989, as an alternative to the structures and strictures of the Roman Catholic Church, yet without denying basic catholic beliefs of faith and love, spirituality and community, prayer and sacramentality. The American Catholic Church is a federation of inde-pendent churches offering a progressive alterna-tive in the Catholic tradition. It is a newly formed rite, as in the tradition of the Orthodox churches of the Catholic tradition and the Old Catholic Church of Utrecht. It remains a Catholic Church, and its priests are considered Catholic priests.

Headquarters

Good Shepherd Rectory, P.O. Box 725, Hampton Bays, NY 11946 Tel. (516)723-201 Fax (516)723-0348

Media Contact, Archbishop, Most Rev. Robert J. Allmen, D.D.

Officers

Archbishop, Most Rev. Robert J. Allmen, D.D.

American Evangelical Christian Churches

Founded in 1944, the AECC is composed of individual ministers and churches who are united in accepting "Seven Articles of Faith." These seven articles are: the Bible as the written word of God; the Virgin birth; the deity of Jesus Christ; Salvation through the atonement; guidance of our life through prayer; the return of the Saviour; the establishment of the Millennial Kingdom.

The American Evangelical Christian Churches offers the following credentials: Certified Christian Worker, Commission to Preach, Licensed Minister and Ordained Minister to those who accept the Seven Articles of Faith, who put unity in Christ first and are approved by AECC.

A.E.C.C. seeks to promote the gospel through

its ministers, churches and missionary activities. Churches operate independently with all decisions concerning local government left to the individual churches.

The organization also has ministers in Canada, England, Bolivia, Philippines, Thailand, Brazil and South America.

Headquarters
P.O. Box 47312, Indianapolis, IN 46227 Tel. (863) 314-9370 Fax (863)314-9570
Media Contact, International Mod., Dr. Otis O. Osborne, 1421 Roseland Ave., Sebring, FL 33870 Tel. (863)314-9370
Email: alpha@strato.net
Website: www.aeccministries.com

Officers
INTERNATIONAL OFFICERS
Mod., Dr. Otis O. Osborne, 1421 Roseland Ave., Sebring, FL 33870 Tel. (863)314-9370
Sec., Dr. Charles Wasielewski, Box 51, Barton, NY 13734 Tel. (607)565-4074
Treas., Dr. S. Omar Overly, 2481 Red Rock Blvd., Grove City, OH 43123-1154 Tel. (614) 871-0710

REGIONAL MODERATORS
Northwest Region: Rev. Alvin House, PO Box 393, Darby MT 59829 Tel.(406)821-3141
Central-West Region: Rev. Charles Clark, Box 314, Rockport, IL 62370 Tel.(217)437-2507
Central Region: Dr. S. Omar Overly, 2481 Red Rock Blvd., Grove City, OH 43123-1154 Tel.(614)871-0710
Northeast Region: Rev. John Merrill, PO Box 183, East Smithfield, PA 18817 Tel.(717)596-4598
East Region: Rev. Larry Walker, PO Box 1165, Lillington, NC 27546 Tel.(919)893-9529
Southeast Region: Rev. James Fullwood, 207 5th Avenue, N.E., Lutz, FL 33549

STATE MODERATORS
Rev. James Brown: Maryland
Rev. John W. Coats: Delaware
Rev. Linda Felice: New York
Dr. Berton G. Heleine: Illinois
Rev. R. Eugene Hill: New Jersey
Rev. Kenneth Pope: Washington
Rev. Art Mirek: Michigan
Rev. Charles Jennings: Pennsylvania
Rev. Jerry Myers: Indiana

FOREIGN OUTREACH MINISTRIES
American Evangelical Christian Churches-Canada
Regional Moderator, Dr. Stephen K. Massey, 730 Ontario Street, Suite 709, Toronto, Ontario M4X 1N3, Canada (416) 323-9076
Philippine Evangelical Christian Churches
Director, Rev. Alan A. Olubalang, PO Box 540, Cotabato City, Philippines 9600
American Evangelical Christian Churches-Philippines

Regional Moderator, Rev. Oseas Andres, PO Box 2695, Central Post Office, 1166 Q.C. Metro Manila, Philippines 430-6549

Periodicals
The American Evangelical Christian Churches Newsletter- Monthly

American Rescue Workers
Major Thomas E. Moore was National Commander of Booth's Salvation Army when a dispute flared between Booth and Moore. Moore resigned from Booth's Army and due to the fact that Booth's Army was not incorporated at the time, Moore was able to incorporate under said name. The name was changed in 1890 to American Salvation Army. In 1913 the current name American Rescue Workers was adopted.

It is a national religious social service agency which operates on a quasimilitary basis. Membership includes officers (clergy), soldiers/adherents (laity), members of various activity groups and volunteers who serve as advisors, associates and committed participants in ARW service functions.

The motivation of the organization is the love of God. Its message is based on the Bible. This is expressed by its spiritual Ministry, the purposes of which are to preach the gospel of Jesus Christ and to meet human needs in his name without discrimination. It is a branch of the Christian Church . . . A Church with a Mission.

Headquarters
Operational Headquarters: 25 Ross Street, Williamsport, PA 17701 Tel. (570)323-8693 Fax (570)323-8694
National Field Office, 1209 Hamilton Blvd., Hagerstown, MD 21742 Tel. (301)797-0061
Media Contact, Natl. Communication Sec., Col. Robert N. Coles, Rev., Natl. Field Ofc., Fax (301) 797-1480

Officers
Commander-In-Chief & Pres. Of Corp., General Claude S. Astin, Jr. Rev
Chief of Staff, Col. Larry D. Martin
Natl. Bd. Pres., Col. George B. Gossett, Rev.
Ordination Committee, Chpsn., Gen. Paul E. Martin, (Emeritus) Rev.
Natl. Chief Sec., Major Dawn R. Astin, NQ-643 Elmira St., Williamsport, PA 17701

Periodicals
The Rescue Herald
Editor in Chief- Col. Robert N. Cole, Rev.

Amish—please see Old Order Amish Church

The Antiochian Orthodox Christian Archdiocese of North America*
The spiritual needs of Antiochian faithful in North America were first served through the

Syro-Arabian Mission of the Russian Orthodox Church in 1895. In 1895, the Syrian Orthodox Benevolent Society was organized by Antiochian immigrants in New York City. Raphael Hawaweeny, a young Damascene clergyman serving as professor of Arabic language at the Orthodox theological academy in Kazan, Russia, came to New York to organize the first Arabic-language parish in North America in 1895, after being canonically received under the omophorion of the head of the Russian Church in North America. Saint Nicholas Cathedral, now located at 355 State St. in Brooklyn, is considered the "mother parish" of the Archdiocese.

On March 12, 1904, Hawaweeny became the first Orthodox bishop to be consecrated in North America. He traveled throughout the continent and established new parishes. The unity of Orthodoxy in the New World, including the Syrian Greek Orthodox community, was ruptured after the death of Bishop Raphael in 1915 and by the Bolshevik revolution in Russia and the First World War. Unity returned in 1975 when Metropolitan Philip Saliba, of the Antiochian Archdiocese of New York, and Metropolitan Michael Shaheen of the Antiochian Archdiocese of Toledo, Ohio, signed the Articles of Reunification, ratified by the Holy Synod of the Patriarchate. Saliba was recognized as the Metropolitan Primate and Shaheen as Auxiliary Archbishop. A second auxiliary to the Metropolitan, Bishop Antoun Khouri, was consecrated at Brooklyn's Saint Nicholas Cathedral, in 1983. A third auxiliary, Bishop Basil Essey was consecrated at Wichita's St. George Cathedral in 1992. Two additional bishops were added in 1994: Bishop Joseph Zehlaoui and Bishop Demetri Khoury.

The Archdiocesan Board of Trustees (consisting of 60 elected and appointed clergy and lay members) and the Metropolitan's Advisory Council (consisting of clergy and lay representatives from each parish and mission) meet regularly to assist the Primate in the administration of the Archdiocese. Currently, there are 227 parishes and missions in the Archdiocese.

Headquarters

358 Mountain Rd., Englewood, NJ 07631 Tel. (201)871-1355 Fax (201)871-7954

Media Contact, Father Thomas Zain, 52 78th St., Brooklyn, NY 11209 Tel. (718)748-7940 Fax (718)855-3608

Officers

Primate, Metropolitan Philip Saliba
Auxiliary, Bishop Antoun Khouri
Auxiliary, Bishop Joseph Zehlaoui
Auxiliary, Bishop Basil Essey
Auxiliary, Bishop Demetri Khoury

Periodicals

The Word; Credo; Again Magazine

Apostolic Catholic Assyrian Church of the East, North American Dioceses

The Holy Apostolic Catholic Assyrian Church of the East is the ancient Christian church that developed within the Persian Empire from the day of Pentecost. The Apostolic traditions testify that the Church of the East was established by Sts. Peter, Thomas, Thaddaeus and Bartholomew from among the Twelve and by the labors of Mar Mari and Aggai of the Seventy. The Church grew and developed carrying the Christian gospel into the whole of Asia and islands of the Pacific. Prior to the Great Persecution at the hands of Tamer'leng the Mongol, it is said to have been the largest Christian church in the world.

The doctrinal identity of the church is that of the Apostles. The church stresses two natures and two Qnume in the One person, Perfect God-Perfect man. The church gives witness to the original Nicene Creed, the Ecumenical Councils of Nicea and Constantinople and the church fathers of that era. Since God is revealed as Trinity, the appellation "Mother of God" is rejected for the "Ever Virgin Blessed Mary Mother of Christ," we declare that she is Mother of Emmanuel, God with us!

The church has maintained a line of Catholicos Patriarchs from the time of the Holy Apostles until this present time. Today the present occupant of the Apostolic Throne is His Holiness Mar Dinkha IV, 120th successor to the See of Selucia Ctestiphon.

Headquarters

Catholicos Patriarch, His Holiness Mar Dinkha, IV, Metropolitanate Residence, The Assyrian Church of the East, Baghdad, Iraq

Media Contact, Rev. Chancellor C. H. Klutz, 7201 N. Ashland, Chicago, IL 60626 Tel. (773)465-4777 Fax (773)465-0776

Officers
BISHOPS- NORTH AMERICA

Diocese Eastern USA: His Grace Bishop Mar Aprim Khamis, 8908 Birch Ave., Morton Grove, IL 60053 Tel. (847)966-0617 Fax (847) 966-0012; Chancellor to the Bishop, Rev. Chancellor C. H. Klutz, 7201 N. Ashland, Chicago, IL 60626 Tel. (773)465-4777 Fax (773)465-0776

Diocese Western USA: ———, St. Joseph Cathedral, 680 Minnesota Ave., San Jose, CA 95125 Tel. (408)286-7377 Fax (408)286-1236

Diocese of Canada: His Grace Bishop Mar Emmanuel Joseph, St. Mary Cathedral, 57 Apted Ave., Weston, ON M9L 2P2 Tel. (416) 744-9311

Comm. on Inter-Church & Religious Ed.: His Grace Bishop Mar Bawai, Diocese of Seattle in WA, 165 NW 65th, Seattle, WA 98117 Tel. (206)789-1843

Periodicals

Qala min M'Dinkha (Voice from the East)

Apostolic Christian Church (Nazarene)

This body was formed in America by an immigration from various European nations, from a movement begun by Rev. S. H. Froehlich, a Swiss pastor, whose followers are still found in Switzerland and Central Europe.

Headquarters

Apostolic Christian Church Foundation, 1135 Sholey Rd., Richmond, VA 23231 Tel. (804) 222-1943 Fax (804)236-0642
Media Contact, Exec. Dir., James Hodges

Officers

Exec. Dir., James Hodges

Apostolic Christian Churches of America

The Apostolic Christian Church of America was founded in the early 1830s in Switzerland by Samuel Froehlich, a young divinity student who had experienced a religious conversion based on the pattern found in the New Testament. The church, known then as Evangelical Baptist, spread to surrounding countries. A Froehlich associate, Elder Benedict Weyeneth, established the church's first American congregation in 1847 in upstate New York. In America, where the highest concentration today is in the Midwest farm belt, the church became known as Apostolic Christian.

Church doctrine is based on a literal interpretation of the Bible, the infallible Word of God. The church believes that a true faith in Christ's redemptive work at Calvary is manifested by a sincere repentance and conversion. Members strive for sanctification and separation from worldliness as a consequence of salvation, not as a means to obtain it. Security in Christ is believed to be conditional based on faithfulness. Uniform observance of scriptural standards of holiness are stressed. Holy Communion is confined to members of the church. Male members are willing to serve in the military, but do not bear arms. The holy kiss is practiced and women wear head coverings during prayer and worship.

Doctrinal authority rests with a council of elders, each of whom serves as a local elder (bishop). Both elders and ministers are chosen from local congregations, do not attend seminary and serve without compensation. Sermons are delivered extemporaneously as led by the Holy Spirit, using the Bible as a text.

Headquarters

3420 N. Sheridan Rd., Peoria, IL 61604
Media Contact, secretary., William R. Schlatter, 14834 Campbell Rd., Defiance, OH 43512 Tel. (419) 393-2621

Officers

Sec., Elder (Bishop) William R. Schlatter, 14834 Campbell Rd., Defiance, OH 43512 Tel. (419) 393-2621

Periodicals

The Silver Lining

Apostolic Episcopal Church

Apostolic Episcopal Church was founded in 1925 by a former priest of the Episcopal Church in USA, Rev. Arthur W. Brooks. The orientation of the new church was definitely New Age and New Thought with an emphasis on healing and charismatic teachings. When Bishop Brooks passed to his eternal reward, his successor as Bishop of the Province of the East was Dr. Harold Jarvis, Mar Haroldus, who established the visiting Church Missions. The purpose of the visiting Church Missions was to visit daily in homes, hospitals, prisons, and places of business: the sick, shut-ins, discouraged, imprisoned and those in need of pastoral counseling. Free of charge each person received prayer, healing or consolation and literature as required. This is still the Church's main goal and work, along with its sacramental ministry.

In 1978 upon the retirement of Dr. Jarvis, the Rev. Francis C. Spataro, Founder & President of the Vilatte Guild, became both Priest-in-Charge and Administrator of the Province of the East. Fr. Francis had been ordained priest on December 26, 1976 by Archbishop Uladyslau at the American College & Seminary. After 14 years as Administrator, Fr. Francis was elected & consecrated the Bishop on October 31, 1992 in London at Christ the King Cathedral by Archbishop Bertil Persson assisted by Bishops George Boyer and Eric Eades. On Setember 13, 1995, Bishop Spataro also succeeded the deceased Dr. Paul Schultz as Rector Pro Provincial of the U.S. Council of the Order of Corporate Reunion.

The Order of Corporate Re-union, founded in 1874, is dedicated to the restoration of unity in the Holy Catholic Church, Eastern & Western. In the U.S.A. it publishes the Tover of St. Cassian and hosts ecumenical gatherings in various churches; it works closely with the Temple of Understanding, a global interfaith forum as well as with the World Peace Prayer Society. On June 12, 1994, it donated a Peace Pole to the Church of St. Joseph of Arimathea, Preston Hollow, N.Y. Present for the dedication ceremony in front of the Church were: Archbishop Bertil Persson, Mother Lucia L. Grosch, Bishop Francis C. Spataro and all the parishioners.

On August 21, 1993, Bishop Spataro assisted His Eminence Macario Ga, Obispo Maximo of the Iglesia Filipina Independiente to consecrate the new presiding archbishop of the continuing Anglican Church in the USA, M. Rev. H. Edwin Caudill in New York City at Holy Cross PNC Church in the East Village. Present were the heads of several independent Catholic & Orthodox Churches in New York City.

Headquarters

The Order of Corporate Reunion, 80-46 234

Street, Queens, NY 11427-2116 Tel. (718)740-4134; Holy Cross House 286 Union Ave., Brooklyn, NY 11211 (718) 387-2024

Media contact, Rt. Rev. Francis Spataro, Box 192B-1, Preston Hollow, NY 12469) Tel. (518) 239-5940 or Holy Cross House (above).

Office of The Tover of St. Cassian, 80-46 234 St., Queens, NY 11427-2116 Tel. (718)740-4131

Officers

Rt. Rev. Francis C. Spataro, President; Rt. Rev. Paget Mack, Coadjutor; Rt. Rev. Bertil Persson, Emeritus; Rt. Rev. Walter Walgraeve, E.U. Representative

Periodicals

The Tover of St. Cassian

Apostolic Faith Mission Church of God

The Apostolic Faith Mission Church of God was founded and organized July 10, 1906, by Bishop F. W. Williams in Mobile, Alabama.

Bishop Williams was saved and filled with the Holy Ghost at a revival in Los Angeles under Elder W. J. Seymour of The Divine Apostolic Faith Movement. After being called into the ministry, Bishop Williams went out to preach the gospel in Mississippi, then moved on to Mobile. On Oct. 9, 1915, the Apostolic Faith Mission Church of God was incorporated in Mobile under Bishop Williams, who was also the general overseer of this church.

Headquarters

Ward's Temple, 806 Muscogee Rd., Cantonment, FL 32533

Media Contact, Natl. Sunday School Supt., Elder Thomas Brooks, 3298 Toney Dr., Decatur, GA 30032 Tel. (404)284-7596

Officers

BOARD OF BISHOPS

Presiding Bishop, Donice Brown, 2265 Welcome Cir., Cantonement, FL 32535 Tel. (904)968-5225

Bishop T.C. Tolbert Sr., 226 Elston Ave., Anniston, AL, 36201; Bishop John Crum, 4236 Jackson St., Birmingham, AL, 35217; Bishop Samuel Darden, 25 Taunton Ave., Hyde Park, MA 02136; Bishop James Truss, P.O. Box 495, Lincoln, AL, 35096; Bishop T.C. Tolbert, Jr., 768 Grayton Rd., Ohatchee, AL 36271; Bishop T. L. Frye, 223 Carver, Atmore, AL 36502

NATIONAL DEPARTMENTS

Missionary Dept., Pres., Sarah Ward, Cantonment, FL

Youth Dept., Pres., Johnny Kennedy, Birmingham, AL

Sunday School Dept., Supt., Thomas Brooks, Decatur, GA

Mother Dept., Pres., Mother Bessie Davis, 1003 Northeast St., Pensacola, FL 32501

INTERNATIONAL DEPARTMENTS

Morobia, Liberia, Bishop Beter T. Nelson, Box 3646, Bush Rhode Islane, Morobia, Liberia

Apostolic Faith Mission of Portland, Oregon

The Apostolic Faith Mission of Portland, Oregon, was founded in 1907. It had its beginning in the Latter Rain outpouring on Azusa Street in Los Angeles in 1906.

Some of the main doctrines are justification by faith which is a spiritual new birth, as Jesus told Nicodemus and as Martin Luther proclaimed in the Great Reformation; sanctification, a second definite work of grace; the Wesleyan teaching of holiness; the baptism of the Holy Ghost as experienced on the Day of Pentecost and again poured out at the beginning of the Latter Rain revival in Los Angeles.

Mrs. Florence L. Crawford, who had received the baptism of the Holy Ghost in Los Angeles, brought this Latter Rain message to Portland on Christmas Day 1906. It has spread to the world by means of literature which is still published and mailed everywhere without a subscription price. Collections are never taken in the meetings and the public is not asked for money.

Camp meetings have been held annually in Portland, Oregon since 1907, with delegations coming from around the world.

Missionaries from the Portland headquarters have established churches in Korea, Japan, the Philippines and many countries in Africa.

Headquarters

6615 SE 52nd Ave., Portland, OR 97206 Tel. (503)777-1741 Fax (503)777-1743

Media Contact, Superintendent General, Dwight L. Baltzell

Website: www.apostolicfaith.org

Officers

President, Rev. Dwight L. Baltzell

Periodicals

Higher Way

Apostolic Lutheran Church of America

Organized in 1872 as the Solomon Korteniemi Lutheran Society, this Finnish body was incorporated in 1929 as the Finnish Apostolic Lutheran Church in America and changed its name to Apostolic Lutheran Church of America in 1962. This body stresses preaching the Word of God. There is an absence of liturgy and formalism in worship. A seminary education is not required of pastors. Being called by God to preach the Word is the chief requirement for clergy and laity. The church stresses personal absolution and forgiveness of sins, as practiced by Martin Luther, and the importance of bringing converts into God's kingdom.

OFFICE OF THE SECRETARY
332 Mt. Washington Way, Clayton, CA 94517-1546 Tel. (925)672-3320 Fax (925)673-0965
Media Contact, Secretary, Ivan M. Seppala

Officers
Chairman, Richard C. Juuti, RRI, Bentley, AB T0C 0J0, Canada
Treas., Ben Johnson, 98920 Keller Rd., Astoria, OR 97103

Periodicals
Christian Monthly

Apostolic Orthodox Catholic Church

The Christian Church was established by the Lord Jesus Christ and His Holy Apostles in Jerusalem in 29 A.D. From Jerusalem, the Church spread to other centers of the known world, including Constantinople, founded in 37 A.D. by St. Andrew the First-Called Holy Apostle. In 864, the Church of Constantinople introduced the Orthodox Christian Faith to present-day Russia. In 988, Rus' Prince Vladimir converted and declared Orthodoxy the State religion, while hundreds of thousands were baptized at Kiev. The resulting Russian Orthodox Church became the greatest safe-guard and body of Orthodox Christians in the world.

The history of American Orthodox Catholic Christianity began in 1794 when Russian Orthodox Church missionaries established the first Orthodox mission on North American soil at present-day Alaska. Their missionary efforts continued down the Pacific coast in 1824, then across the whole continent. Being the canonical founder of Orthodox Christianity in North America, the Russian Orthodox Church maintained and presided over all Orthodox missions, churches, and Christians throughout North America without question or challenge for over 100 years. However, the 1917 Bolshevik Revolution which resulted in severe persecution and imprisonment of the Russian Orthodox Mother Church also resulted in the unrestrained rise of old-country nationalism and great ethnic turbulence between Orthodox Catholic Christians and their churches in North America. They seperated and divided, often violently, along ethnic and nationalist lines with each creating their own old-world ethnic administrations. The once long-held unity and single Orthodox Church canonical administration in North America was destroyed.

The Apostolic Orthodox Catholic Church (AOCC) is canonically indigenous to North America and comprised of bishops, clergy and faithful possessing unbroken Apostolic Succession since the time of Jesus Christ's appointment of His Twelve Holy Apostles to the present day through American Orthodoxy's Luminary and Defender, Russian Orthodox Prelate-Archbishop Aftimios Ofiesh of Blessed Memory.

The AOCC has unquestionable Apostolic Succession passed on to its bishops through the Russian Orthodox Church by Archbishop Aftimios Ofiesh, his succeeding Bishops Sophronios Beshara and Christopher Contogeorge, and through consecrating support of such memorable Orthodox leaders as Albanian Orthodox Church Metropolitan Theophan Noli. The Apostolic Succession and Canonicity of these bishops and their successors was declared valid, authentic and independent by the Orthodox Church Ecumenical Patriarchate of Constantinople in 1945, and re-affirmed in 1951. English-speaking and non-ethnic restrictive, the AOCC's further validity is evidenced by its life, mind, discourse and teaching all being governed and directed in accordance with the Sacred Canons of the Most Ancient Holy Orthodox Catholic Church. The AOCC embraces the ideals and theology of Orthodoxy and freedom which Archbishop Aftimios Ofiesh stood for, taught and passed on by selfless devotion and love for Christ and His Church, and by his personal example.

Headquarters
AOCC Chancery, P.O. Box 1834, Glendora, CA 91740-1834 Tel. (626)335-7369
Media Contact, Rt. Rev. Fr. Bartimaeus, Archpriest, Ecumenical Relations Officer, 2324 9th Street, South, Great Falls, MT 59405 Tel/Fax (406)563-5426 AOCC

Officers
Presiding Bishop, Most Rev. Gorazd
Second-Presiding Bishop, Most Rev. Aftimios II
Bishop Secretary, Most Rev. Angelo
Archbishop, The Most Rev. Richard
Synod of Bishops & Dioceses:
Most Rev. Gorazd, Bishop of the Diocese of Los Angeles & Greater Pacific, P.O. Box 1834, Glendora, CA 91740-1834 Tel. (626)335-7369
Most Rev. Aftimios II, Bishop of the Diocese of the Rocky Mountains & Midwest, 4696 SE Horseshoe Ct., Salem, OR 97301 Tel. (503)375-6175, Email: BaftimII@aol.com,
Most Rev. Richard, Bishop of the Diocese of Indiana, 3615 Arizona Street # C, Lake Station, IN 46405
Most Rev. John, Bishop of the Diocese of New York, 4-20 Green Way Ave., Manorville, NY 11949 Tel. (516)878-4172
Most Rev. Angelo, Bishop of the Diocese of the Eastern States, 37 Shippee School House Rd., Foster, RI 02825 Tel. (401)647-2867
Most Rev. Alexei, Bishop of Monte Cristo Skete, P.O. Box 16591, Colorado Springs, CO 80935-6591

SEMINARY
Holy Trinity Apostolic Orthodox Catholic Seminary, PO Box 1834, Glendora, CA 91740-1834

Periodicals
Carpenter's Workshop

Apostolic Overcoming Holy Church of God, Inc.

The Right Reverend William Thomas Phillips (1893-1973) was thoroughly convinced in 1912 that Holiness was a system through which God wanted him to serve. In 1916 he was led to Mobile, Alabama, where he organized the Ethiopian Overcoming Holy Church of God. In April 1941 the church was incorporated in Alabama under its present title.

Each congregation manages its own affairs, united under districts governed by overseers and diocesan bishops and assisted by an executive board comprised of bishops, ministers, laymen and the National Secretary. The General Assembly convenes annually.

The church's chief objective is to enlighten people of God's holy Word and to be a blessing to every nation. The main purpose of this church is to ordain elders, appoint pastors and send out divinely called missionaries and teachers. This church enforces all ordinances enacted by Jesus Christ. The church believes in water baptism (Acts 2:38, 8:12, and 10:47), administers the Lord's Supper, observes the washing of feet (John 13:4-7), believes that Jesus Christ shed his blood to sanctify the people and cleanse them from all sin and believes in the resurrection of the dead and the second coming of Christ.

Headquarters

1120 N. 24th St., Birmingham, AL 35234

Media Contact, Dr. Juanita R. Arrington, Business Manager, A.O.H. Church of God Public Relations Department

Officers

Presiding Senior Bishop & Exec. Head, Rt. Rev. Jasper Roby

Assistant Presider for the Year 2000-2001, Bishop Joe Bennett

Periodicals

The People's Mouthpiece

Armenian Apostolic Church of America

Widespread movement of the Armenian people over the centuries caused the development of two seats of religious jurisdiction of the Armenian Apostolic Church in the World: the See of Etchmiadzin, in Armenia, and the See of Cilicia, in Lebanon.

In America, the Armenian Church functioned under the jurisdiction of the Etchmiadzin See from 1887 to 1933, when a division occurred within the American diocese over the condition of the church in Soviet Armenia. One group chose to remain independent until 1957, when the Holy See of Cilicia agreed to accept them under its jurisdiction.

Despite the existence of two dioceses in North America, the Armenian Church has always functioned as one church in dogma and liturgy.

Headquarters

Eastern Prelacy, 138 E. 39th St., New York, NY 10016 Tel. (212)689-7810 Fax (212)689-7168

Western Prelacy, 4401 Russel Ave., Los Angeles, CA 90027 Tel. (323)663-8273 Fax (323)663-0438

Media Contact, Vasken Ghougassian

Officers

Eastern Prelacy, Prelate, Archbishop Oshagan Choloyan

Eastern Prelacy, Chpsn., Jack Mardoian, Esq.

Western Prelacy, Prelate, Bishop Moushegh Mardirossian

Western Prelacy, Chpsn., Aesen Danielian, Esq.

DEPARTMENTS

Eastern Prelacy Offices, Executive Director, Vasken Ghougasian

AREC, Armenian Religious Educ. Council, Exec. Coord., Deacon Shant Kazanjian

ANEC, Armenian Natl. Educ. Council, Exec. Coord., Gilda Kupelian

Periodicals

Outreach

Armenian Apostolic Church, Diocese of America*

The Armenian Apostolic Church was founded at the foot of the biblical mountain of Ararat in the ancient land of Armenia, where two of Christ's Holy Apostles, Saints Thaddeus and Bartholomew, preached Christianity. In A.D. 303 the historic Mother Church of Etchmiadzin was founded by Saint Gregory the Illuminator, the first Catholicos of All Armenians. This cathedral still stands and serves as the center of the Armenian Church. A branch of this Church was established in North America in 1889. The first church building was consecrated in 1891 in Worcester, MA. The first Armenian Diocese was set up in 1898 by the then-Catholicos of All Armenians, Mgrditch Khrimian (Hairig). Armenian immigrants built the first Armenian church in the new world in Worcester, MA, under the jurisdiction of Holy Etchmiadzin.

In 1927, the churches and the parishes in California were formed into a Western Diocese and the parishes in Canada formed their own diocese in 1984. Other centers of major significance of the Armenian Apostolic Church are the Catholicate of Cilicia, now located in Lebanon, the Armenian Patriarchate of Jerusalem and the Armenian Patriarchate of Constantinople.

Headquarters

Eastern Diocese: 630 Second Ave., New York, NY 10016-4885 Tel. (212)686-0710 Fax (212) 779-3558

Western Diocese: 3325 North Glenoaks Blvd., Burbank, CA 91504 Tel. (818) 558-7474 FAX (818) 558-6333

Canadian Diocese: 615 Stuart Ave., Outremont, QC H2V 3H2 Tel. (514)276-9479 Fax (514)276-9960

Media Contact, Dir., Zohrab Information Ctr., V. Rev. Fr. Krikor Maksoudian, Eastern Diocese

Officers

Eastern Diocese
Primate, Archbishop Khajag Barsamian, Eastern Diocese Ofc.
Chancellor, Rev. Fr. Garabed Kochakian
Diocesan Council, Chpsn., Haig Dadourian, 415 Madison Ave., 7th Fl., New York, NY 10017
Western Diocese
Primate, His Em. Archbishop Vatche Hovsepian, Western Diocese Ofc.
Diocesan Council, Chpsn., Dn. Dr. Varouj Altebarmakian, 7290 North San Pedro, Fresno, CA 93011
Diocesan Council, Sec., Mr. John Yaldezian, 23221 Aetna St., Woodland Hills, CA 91367 Tel. (B) (818) 346-6163
Canadian Diocese
Primate, His Em. Archbishop Hovnan Derderian
Diocesan Council Chpsn, Mr. Takvor Hopyan, 20 Pineway,Blvd., Willowdale, ON M2H 1A1, Canada Tel. (B) (416) 222-2639
Diocesan Council secretary., Mr. Vahe Ketli, 750 Montpellier, # 909, St. Laurens, QC H4L 5A7, Canada Tel. (R) (514) 747-1347

Periodicals

The Armenian Church; The Mother Church

Assemblies of God

From a few hundred delegates at its founding convention in 1914 at Hot Springs, Ark., the Assemblies of God has become one of the largest church groups in the modern Pentecostal movement worldwide. Throughout its existence it has emphasized the power of the Holy Spirit to change lives and the participation of all members in the work of the church.

The revival that led to the formation of the Assemblies of God and numerous other church groups early in the 20th century began during times of intense prayer and Bible study. Believers in the United States and around the world received spiritual experiences like those described in the Book of Acts. Accompanied by baptism in the Holy Spirit and its initial physical evidence of "speaking in tongues," or a language unknown to the person, their experiences were associated with the coming of the Holy Spirit at Pentecost (Acts 2), so participants were called Pentecostals.

The church also believes that the Bible is God's infallible Word to man, that salvation is available only through Jesus Christ, that divine healing is made possible through Christ's suffering and that Christ will return again for those who love him. In recent years, this Pentecostal revival has spilled over into almost every denomination in a new wave of revival sometimes called the charismatic renewal.

Assemblies of God leaders credit their church's rapid and continuing growth to its acceptance of the New Testament as a model for the present-day church. Aggressive evangelism and missionary zeal at home and abroad characterize the denomination.

Assemblies of God believers observe two ordinances-water baptism by immersion and the Lord's Supper, or Holy Communion. The church is trinitarian, holding that God exists in three persons: Father, Son and Holy Spirit.

Headquarters

1445 Boonville Ave., Springfield, MO 65802 Tel. (417)862-2781 Fax (417)862-8558
Media Contact, Dir. of Public Relations, Juleen Turnage, Fax (417)862-5554

EXECUTIVE PRESBYTERY

Gen. Supt., Thomas E. Trask
Asst. Supt., Charles T. Crabtree
Gen. Sec., George O. Wood
Gen. Treas., James E. Bridges
Foreign Missions, Exec. Dir., John Bueno
Home Missions, Exec. Dir., Charles Hackett
Great Lakes, M. Wayne Benson, 250 Sorrento Dr., S.E., Byron Center, MI 49315
Gulf, Gene Jackson, PO Box 358, Madison, TN 37116
North Central, David Argue, 1111 Old Cheney Rd., Lincoln, NE 68512
Northeast, Almon Bartholomew, 13 Cedarwood Dr., Queensbury, NY 12804
Northwest, R. L. Brandt, 1601 Judd Circle, Billings, MT 59102
South Central, Armon Newburn, P.O. Box 13179, Oklahoma City, OK 73113
Southeast, Dan Betzer, 4701 Summerlin Rd., Ft. Myers, FL 33919
Southwest, Richard Dresselhaus, 8404 Phyllis Pl., San Diego, CA 92123
Language Area Spanish, Jesse Miranda, 3257 Thaxton, Hacienda Heights, CA 91745
Language Area Other, Nam Soo Kim, 130-30 31st Ave., 4th Fl, Flushing, NY 11354
Ethnic Fellowship, Spencer Jones, 7724 S. Racine Ave., Chicago, IL 60620

INTERNATIONAL HEADQUARTERS

Division of the Treasury, Gen. Treas., James E. Bridges
Division of Christian Education, Natl. Dir., LeRoy Bartel
Division of Church Ministries, Executive Liaison, Charles Crabtree
Division of Foreign Missions, Exec Dir., John Bueno
Division of Home Missions, Exec. Dir., Charles Hackett
Div. of Publication, Gospel Publishing House, Natl. Dir., Arlyn Pember

Periodicals

Enrichment: A Journal for Pentecostal Ministry; At Ease; Caring; High Adventure; Club Connection; Pentecostal Evangel; Christian Education Counselor; Woman's Touch; Heritage; On Course

Assemblies of God International Fellowship (Independent/Not Affiliated)

April 9, 1906 is the date commonly accepted by Pentecostals as the 20th-century outpouring of God's spirit in America, which began in a humble gospel mission at 312 Azusa Street in Los Angeles. This spirit movement spread across the United States and gave birth to the Independent Assemblies of God (Scandinavian). Early pioneers instrumental in guiding and shaping the fellowship of ministers and churches into a nucleus of independent churches included Pastor B. M. Johnson, founder of Lakeview Gospel Church in 1911; Rev. A. A. Holmgren, a Baptist minister who received his baptism of the Holy Spirit in the early Chicago outpourings, was publisher of Sanningens Vittne, a voice of the Scandinavian Independent Assemblies of God and also served as secretary of the fellowship for many years; Gunnar Wingren, missionary pioneer in Brazil; and Arthur F. Johnson, who served for many years as chairman of the Scandinavian Assemblies.

In 1935, the Scandinavian group dissolved its incorporation and united with the Independent Assemblies of God of the U.S. and Canada which by majority vote of members formed a new corporation in 1986, Assemblies of God International Fellowship (Independent/Not Affiliated).

Headquarters

6325 Marindustry Dr. , San Diego, CA 92121 Tel. (858)677-9701 Fax (858)677-0038

Media Contact, Exec. Dir. & Ed., Rev. T. A. Lanes

Email: agifellowship.org

Officers

Exec. Dir., Rev. T. A. Lanes

Sec., Rev. George E. Ekeroth

Treas., M. J. Ekeroth

Canada, Sec., Harry Nunn, Sr., 15 White Crest Ct., St. Catherines, ON 62N 6Y1

Periodicals

The Fellowship Magazine

Associate Reformed Presbyterian Church (General Synod)

The Associate Reformed Presbyterian Church (General Synod) stems from the 1782 merger of Associate Presbyterians and Reformed Presbyterians. In 1822, the Synod of the Carolinas broke with the Associate Reformed Church (which eventually became part of the United Presbyterian Church of North America).

The story of the Synod of the Carolinas began with the Seceder Church, formed in Scotland in 1733 and representing a break from the established Church of Scotland. Seceders, in America called Associate Presbyterians, settled in South Carolina following the Revolutionary War. They were joined by a few Covenanter congregations which, along with the Seceders, had protested Scotland's established church. The Covenanters took their name from the Solemn League and Covenant of 1643, the guiding document of Scotch Presbyterians. In 1790, some Seceders and Covenanters formed the Presbytery of the Carolinas and Georgia at Long Cane, S.C. Thomas Clark and John Boyse led in the formation of this presbytery, a unit within the Associate Reformed Presbyterian Church. The presbytery represented the southern segment of that church.

In 1822 the southern church became independent of the northern Associate Reformed Presbyterian Church and formed the Associate Reformed Presbyterian Church of the South. "Of the South" was dropped in 1858 when the northern group joined the United Presbyterian Church and "General Synod" was added in 1935. The General Synod is the denominations highest court; it is composed of all the teaching elders and at least one ruling elder from each congregation.

Doctrinally, the church holds to the Westminster Confession of Faith. Liturgically, the synod has been distinguished by its exclusive use of psalmody; in 1946 this practice became optional.

Headquarters

Associate Reformed Presbyterian Center, One Cleveland St., Greenville, SC 29601-3696 Tel. (864)232-8297 Fax (864)271-3729

Media Contact, Principal Clk., Rev. C. Ronald Beard, D.D., 3132 Grace Hill Rd., Columbia, SC 29204 Tel. (803)787-6370.

The Rev. H. Neely Gaston, 741 Cleveland St. Greenville, SC 29601

Moderator: Rev. Dwight L. Pearson, D.D., PO Box 174, Chester, SC 29706-0174 Tel.(864)385-2228

Email: dragondraw@aol.com

AGENCIES AND INSTITUTIONS (In the A.R. Presbyterian Center in Greenville)

Admn. Ser. Dir., Ed Hogan

Christian Education, Dir., Dr. David Vickery

Church Extension, Dir., Rev. James T. Corbitt, D.D.

Publications, Editor, E. Benton Johnston

Treasurer, Guy H. Smith, III

World Witness, Bd. of Foreign Missions, Exec. Sec., John E. Mariner

OTHER INSTITUTIONS

Bonclarken Assembly, Dir., James T. Brice, 500 Pine St., Flat Rock, NC 28731 Tel. (704)692-2223

Erskine College, Pres., Rev. John L. Carson, Ph.D., Due West, SC 29639 Tel. (864)379-8759

Erskine Theological Seminary, Dean, Ralph J. Gore, Jr., Ph.D., Due West, SC 26939 Tel. (864) 379-8885

Periodicals
The Associate Reformed Presbyterian; The Adult Quarterly

The Association of Free Lutheran Congregations

The Association of Free Lutheran Congregations, rooted in the Scandinavian revival movements, was organized in 1962 by a Lutheran Free Church remnant which rejected merger with The American Lutheran Church. The original 42 congregations were joined by other like-minded conservative Lutherans, and there has been almost a sixfold increase in the number of congregations. Members subscribe to the Apostles', Nicene and Athanasian creeds; Luther's Small Catechism; and the Unaltered Augsburg Confession. The Fundamental Principles and Rules for Work (1897) declare that the local congregation is the right form of the kingdom of God on earth, subject to no authority but the Word and the Spirit of God.

Distinctive emphases are: (1) the infallibility and inerrancy of Holy Scriptures as the Word of God; (2) congregational polity; (3) the spiritual unity of all believers, resulting in fellowship and cooperation transcending denominational lines; (4) evangelical outreach, calling all to enter a personal relationship with Jesus Christ; (5) a wholesome Lutheran pietism that proclaims the Lordship of Jesus Christ in all areas of life and results in believers becoming the salt and light in their communities; (6) a conservative stance on current social issues.

A two-year Bible school and a theological seminary are in suburban Minneapolis. Mission support is channeled to churches in Brazil, Mexico, Canada, India, and Portugal.

Headquarters

3110 E. Medicine Lake Blvd., Minneapolis, MN 55441 Tel. (763)545-5631 Fax (763)545-0079
Media Contact, Pres., Rev. Robert L. Lee
Email: www.aflc.org

Officers

Pres., Rev. Robert L. Lee
Vice-Pres., Rev. Elden K. Nelson, 1633 Co. Rd. 8 SE, Kandiyohi, MN 56251
Sec., Rev. Brian Davidson, 3110 E. Medicine Lake Blvd., Minneapolis, MN 55441

Periodicals

The Lutheran Ambassador

Baptist Bible Fellowship International

Organized on May 24, 1950 in Fort Worth, Tex., the Baptist Bible Fellowship was founded by about 100 pastors and lay people who had grown disenchanted with the policies and leadership of the World Fundamental Baptist Missionary Fellowship, an outgrowth of the Baptist Bible Union formed in Kansas City in 1923 by fundamentalist leaders from the Southern Baptist, Northern Baptist and Canadian Baptist Conventions. The BBF elected W. E. Dowell as its first president and established offices and a three-year (now four-year with a graduate school) Baptist Bible College.

The BBF statement of faith was essentially that of the Baptist Bible Union, adopted in 1923, a variation of the New Hampshire Confession of Faith. It presents an infallible Bible, belief in the substitutionary death of Christ, his physical resurrection and his premillennial return to earth. It advocates local church autonomy and strong pastoral leadership and maintains that the fundamental basis of fellowship is a missionary outreach. The BBF vigorously stresses evangelism and the international missions office reports 901 adult missionaries working on 110 fields throughout the world.

There are BBF-related churches in every state of the United States, with special strength in the upper South, the Great Lakes region, southern states west of the Mississippi, Kansas and California. There are seven related colleges and one graduate school or seminary.

A Committee of Forty-Five, elected by pastors and churches within the states, sits as a representative body, meeting in three subcommittees, each chaired by one of the principal officers: an administration committee chaired by the president, a missions committee chaired by a vice-president and an education committee chaired by a vice-president.

Headquarters

World Mission Service Center
Baptist Bible Fellowship Missions Bldg., 720 E. Kearney St., Springfield, MO 65803 Tel. (417) 862-5001 Fax (417)865-0794
Mailing Address, P.O. Box 191, Springfield, MO 65801
Media Contact, Mission Dir., Dr. Bob Baird, P.O. Box 191, Springfield, MO 65801

Officers

Pres., Ken Gillming Sr., Cherry Street Baptist Church, 1201 S. Oak Grove Ave., Springfield, MO 65804
First Vice-Pres., Rev. Bill Monroe, Florence Baptist Temple, 2308 S. Irby Street, Florence, SC 29505-0809
Second Vice-Pres., Bill Dougherty, First Coast Baptist Church, 7587 Blanding Blvd., Jacksonville, FL 32244-5155
Sec., K. B. Murray, Millington Street Baptist Church, 1304 Millington St., Winfield, KS 67156
Treas., Wayne Guinn, Bethany Baptist Church, 1100 Dorchester Ave., Melborne, FL
Mission Dir., Dr. Bob Baird, P.O. Box 191, Springfield, MO 65801

Periodicals

The Baptist Bible Tribune; The Preacher; Global Partners

Baptist General Conference

The Baptist General Conference, rooted in the pietistic movement of Sweden during the 19th century, traces its history to Aug. 13, 1852. On that day a small group of believers at Rock Island, Illinois, under the leadership of Gustaf Palmquist, organized the first Swedish Baptist Church in America. Swedish Baptist churches flourished in the upper Midwest and Northeast, and by 1879, when the first annual meeting was held in Village Creek, Iowa, 65 churches had been organized, stretching from Maine to the Dakotas and south to Kansas and Missouri.

By 1871, John Alexis Edgren, an immigrant sea captain and pastor in Chicago, had begun the first publication and a theological seminary. The Conference grew to 324 churches and nearly 26,000 members by 1902. There were 40,000 members in 1945 and 135,000 in 1993.

Many churches began as Sunday schools. The seminary evolved into Bethel, a four-year liberal arts college with 1,800 students, and theological seminaries in Arden Hills, Minnesota. and San Diego, California. Missions and the planting of churches have been main objectives both in America and overseas. Today churches have been established in the United States, Canada and Mexico, as well as twenty countries overseas. In 1985 the churches of Canada founded an autonomous denomination, The Baptist General Conference of Canada.

The Baptist General Conference is a member of the Baptist World Alliance, the Baptist Joint Committee on Public Affairs and the National Association of Evangelicals. It is characterized by the balancing of a conservative doctrine with an irenic and cooperative spirit. Its basic objective is to seek the fulfillment of the Great Commission and the Great Commandment.

Headquarters

2002 S. Arlington Heights Rd., Arlington Heights, IL 60005 Tel. (847)228-0200 Fax (847)228-5376

Media Contact, Pres., Dr. Robert S. Ricker

Email: gmarsh@baptist

Website: www.bgc.bethel.edu

Officers

Pres. & Chief Exec. Officer, Dr. Robert Ricker

Exec, Vice-Pres., Ray Swatkowski

Vice-Pres. Of Ministry Partner Services, Dr. Lou Petrie

Vice-Pres. of Finance, Stephen R. Schultz

Vice Pres. of Church Enrichment, Dr. Jerry Sheveland

Vice-Pres. of Church Planting, Dr. Ronald Larson

OTHER ORGANIZATIONS

Bd. of Trustees: Bethel College & Seminary, Pres., Dr. George K. Brushaber, 3900 Bethel Dr., St. Paul, MN 55112

Periodicals

The Standard

Baptist Missionary Association of America

A group of regular Baptist churches organized in associational capacity in May, 1950, in Little Rock, Ark., as the North American Baptist Association. The name changed in 1969 to Baptist Missionary Association of America. There are several state and numerous local associations of cooperating churches. In theology, these churches are evangelical, missionary, fundamental and for the most part premillennial.

Headquarters

9219 Sibly Hole Rd., Little Rock, AR Tel. (501) 455-4977 Fax (501)455-3636

Mailing Address, P.O. Box 193920, Little Rock, AR 72219-3920

Media Contact, Dir. of Baptist News Service, Kenneth W. Vanderslice, P.O. Box 97, Jacksonville, TX 75766 Tel. (903)586-2501 Fax (903)586-0378

Officers

Pres., Ronald Morgan, 208 N. Arkansas St., Springhill, LA 71075-2704

Vice-Pres.: Leon J. Carmical, 85 Midway Church Rd., Sumrall, MS 39428; David T. Watkins, 1 Pineridge St., Magnolia, AR 71753

Rec. Sec.: Rev. Ralph Cottrell, P.O. Box 1203, Van, TX 75790; Don J. Brown, P.O. Box 8181, Laruel, MS 39441; James Ray Raines, 5609 N. Locust, N. Little Rock, AR 72116

DEPARTMENTS

Missions: Gen. Sec., Rev. F. Donald Collins, P.O. Box 193920, Little Rock, AR 72219-3920

Publications: Ed.-in-Chief, Rev. James L. Silvey, 311 Main St., P.O. Box 7270, Texarkana, TX 75505

Christian Education: Bapt. Missionary Assoc. Theological Sem., Pres., Dr. Charley Holmes, Seminary Heights, 1530 E. Pine St., Jacksonville, TX 75766

Baptist News Service: Dir., Rev. Kenneth W. Vanderslice, P.O. Box 97, Jacksonville, TX 75766

Life Word Broadcast Ministries: Dir., Rev. George Reddin, P.O. Box 6, Conway, AR 72032

Armed Forces Chaplaincy: Exec. Dir., Bobby C. Thornton, P.O. Box 240, Flint, TX 75762

BMAA Dept. of Church Ministries: Donny Parish, P.O. Box 10356, Conway, AR 72033

Daniel Springs Encampment: James Speer, P.O. Box 310, Gary, TX 75643

Ministers Resource Services: Craig Branham, 4001 Jefferson St., Texarkana, TX 75501

OTHER ORGANIZATIONS

Baptist Missionary Assoc. Brotherhood: Pres., Bill Looney, 107 Bearskin Dr., Sherwood, AR 72120

National Women's Missionary Auxiliary: Pres., Mrs. Bill Skinner, RR1 Box 213 B, Mineola, TX 75773-9742 Tel. 903-365-2465

Periodicals

The Gleaner

Beachy Amish Mennonite Churches

The Beachy Amish Mennonite Church was established in 1927 in Somerset County, Pa. following a division in the Amish Mennonite Church in that area. As congregations in other locations joined the movement, they were identified by the same name. There are currently 97 churches in the United States, 9 in Canada and 34 in other countries. Membership in the United States is 7,059, according to the 1996 Mennonite Yearbook.

Beachy Churches believe in one God eternally existent in three persons (Father, Son and Holy Spirit); that Jesus Christ is the one and only way to salvation; that the Bible is God's infallible Word to us, by which all will be judged; that heaven is the eternal abode of the redeemed in Christ; and that the wicked and unbelieving will endure hell eternally.

Evangelical mission boards sponsor missions in Central and South America, Belgium, Ireland, and in Kenya, Africa.

The Mission Interests Committee, founded in 1953 for evangelism and other Christian services, sponsors homes for handicapped youth and elderly people, mission outreaches among the North American Indians in Canada and a mission outreach in Europe.

Headquarters

Media Contact, David L. Miller, P.O. Box 73, Partridge, KS 67566 Tel. (316)567-2376

Officers

Amish Mennonite Aid: Sec.-Treas., Vernon Miller, 2675 U.S. 42 NE, London, OH 43140 Tel. (614)879-8616

Mission Interests Committee: Sec.-Treas., Melvin Gingerich, 42555 900W, Topeka, IN 46571 Tel. (219)593-9090

Choice Books of Northern Virginia: Supervisor, Simon Schrock, 4614 Holly Ave., Fairfax, VA 22030 Tel. (703)830-2800

Calvary Bible School: HC 61, Box 202, Calico Rock, AR 72519 Tel. (501)297-8658; Sec.-Treas., Elmer Gingerich, HC 74, Box 282, Mountain View, AR 72560 Tel. (501)296-8764

Penn Valley Christian Retreat, Bd. Chmn., Wayne Schrock, RR 2, Box 165, McVeytown, PA 17015 Tel. (717)529-2935

Periodicals

The Calvary Messenger

Berean Fundamental Church

Founded 1932 in North Platte, Nebraska, this body emphasizes conservative Protestant doctrines.

Headquarters

Box 6103, Lincoln, NE 68506 Tel. (402)489-8056 Fax (402)489-8056

Media Contact, Pres., Pastor Doug Shada

Officers

Pres., Doug Shada

Vice-Pres., Richard Crocker, 419 Lafayette Blvd., Cheyenne, WY 82009 Tel. (307)635-5914

Sec., Roger Daum, 1510 O Street, Cozad, NE 69130 Tel. (308)784-3675

Treas., Virgil Wiebe, P.O. Box 6103, Lincoln, NE 68506

Exec. Advisor, Curt Lehman, Tel. (402)483-4840

Exec. Advisor, Carl M. Goltz, P.O. Box 397, North Platte, NE 69103 Tel. (308)532-6723

The Bible Church of Christ, Inc.

The Bible Church of Christ was founded on March 1, 1961 by Bishop Roy Bryant, Sr. Since that time, the Church has grown to include congregations in the United States, Africa and India. The church is trinitarian and accepts the Bible as the divinely inspired Word of God. Its doctrine includes miracles of healing, deliverance and the baptism of the Holy Ghost.

Headquarters

1358 Morris Ave., Bronx, NY 10456 Tel. (718) 588-2284 Fax (718) 992-5597

Media Contact, Pres., Bishop Roy Bryant, Sr

Website: www.thebiblechurchofchrist.org

Officers

Pres., Bishop Roy Bryant, Sr.

V. Pres., Asst. Bishop Derek G. Owens

Sec., Sissieretta Bryant, Treas., Elder Artie Burney

EXECUTIVE TRUSTEE BOARD

Chpsns.: Elder Alberto L. Hope, 1358 Morris Ave., Bronx, NY 10456, Tel. (718)588-2284; Bishop Derek G. Owens, 100 W. 2nd St., Mount Vernon, NY 10550 Tel. (914)664-4602

Exec. Admn., Sr. Hermenia Benjamin,

Deacon Tommy Robinson, Presiding Elders: Delaware, Elder Edward Cannon, R R Box 70-B5, Diamond Acre, Dagsboro, DE 19939 Tel. (302)732-3351; Virginia, Elder Jesse Alston, 221 Keith Rd., Newport News, VA 23606 Tel. (804)930-2445; Monticello, 104 Waverly Ave., Monticello, NY 12701; Mount Vernon, Elder Artie Burney

OTHER ORGANIZATIONS

Bookstore: Mgr., Evangelist Beryl C. Foster, Tel. (718)293-1928

Evangelism: Intl. Pres., Evangelist Gloria Gray

Foreign Missions: Pres., Sr. Autholene Smith

Food Pantry: Dir., Evangelist Susie Jones

Home Missions: Pres., Evangelist Mary Jackson

Minister of Music: Ray Brown

Prison Ministry Team: Pres., Evangelist Marvin Lowe

Public Relations: Deacon Abraham Jones

Publications: Dir., Deaconess Betty Hamilton

Sunday Schools: Gen. Supt., Elder A. M. Jones

Theological Institute: Pres., Dr. Roy Bryant, Sr.; Dean, Elder A. M. Jones

Vessels Unto Honor Deliverance Ministries: Pres., Evangelist Antoinette Cannaday

Women's Committee: Natl. Chpsn., Sissieretta Bryant

Youth: 100 W. 2nd St., Mount Vernon, NY 10550; Bronx, Elder Anita Robinson, 1358 Morris Ave., Bronx, NY 10456, Tel. (718)588-2284; Annex, Elder Reginald Gullette, 1069 Morris Ave., Bronx, NY 10456 Tel. (718)992-4653; Bishop Derek Owens, Pastor, Minister Monica Hope, Assistant, 1140 Congress St., Schenetady, NY 12303; India, Dr. B. Veeraswamy, 46-7-34, Danavaya Peta, Rajahmunry, India, 533103; Haiti, Antoine Polycarpe, P.O. Box 197, Port-au-Prince, Haiti; St. Croix, Elder Floyd Thomas, 1-J Diamond Ruby, P.O. Box 5183, Sunny Isles, Christiansted, St. Croix Tel. (809)778-1002

Periodicals

The Voice; The Gospel Light; The Challenge

Bible Fellowship Church

The Bible Fellowship Church grew out of divisions in the Mennonite community in Pennsylvania in the 1850s. Traditional church leadership resisted the freedom of expression and prayer meetings initiated by several preachers and church leaders. These evangelical Mennonites formed the Evangelical Mennonite Society. Over the next two decades various like minded groups in Canada, Ohio and Pennsylvania joined the Society.

In 1959 the Conference became the Bible Fellowship Church and new articles of faith were ratified. They now hold a unique combination of Reformed doctrines with insistence on "Believer Baptism" and Premillennialism.

Headquarters

Bible Fellowship Church, 3000 Fellowship Dr., Whitehall, PA 18052

Media Contact, David J. Watkins, Greater Bible Fellowship Church, 693 Church Rd., Graterford, PA 19426 Tel. (610)489-9389

Officers

Chmn., Randall A. Grossman

Vice-Chmn., William G. Schlonecker

Sec., David A. Thomann

Asst. Sec., Robert W. Smock

BOARDS AND COMMITTEES

Bd. of Dir., Bible Fellowship Church

Bd. of Christian Education

Board of Extension

Bible Fellowship Church Homes, Inc.

Board of Pensions

Board of Pinebrook Bible Conference

Board of Missions

Board of Publication and Printing

Bd. of Victory Valley Camp

Board of Higher Education

Periodicals

Fellowship News

Bible Holiness Church

This church came into being about 1890 as the result of definite preaching on the doctrine of holiness in some Methodist churches in southeastern Kansas. It became known as The Southeast Kansas Fire Baptized Holiness Association. The name was changed in 1945 to The Fire Baptized Holiness Church and in 1995 to Bible Holiness Church. It is entirely Wesleyan in doctrine, episcopal in church organization and intensive in evangelistic zeal.

Headquarters

600 College Ave., Independence, KS 67301 Tel. (316)331-3049

Media Contact, Gen. Supt., Leroy Newport

Officers

Gen. Supt., Leroy Newport

Gen. Sec., Wayne Knipmeyer, Box 457, South Pekin, IL 61564

Gen. Treas., Robert Davolt, 1323 Laura, Wichita, KS 67211

Periodicals

The Flaming Sword; John Three Sixteen

Bible Way Church of Our Lord Jesus Christ World Wide, Inc.

This body was organized in 1957 in the Pentecostal tradition for the purpose of accelerating evangelistic and foreign missionary commitment and to effect a greater degree of collective leadership than leaders found in the body in which they had previously participated.

The doctrine is the same as that of the Church of Our Lord Jesus Christ of the Apostolic Faith, Inc., of which some of the churches and clergy were formerly members.

This organization has churches and missions in Africa, England, Guyana, Trinidad and Jamaica, and churches in 25 states in America. The Bible Way Church is involved in humanitarian as well as evangelical outreach with concerns for urban housing, education and economic development.

Headquarters

4949 Two-Notch Rd., Columbia, SC 29204 Tel. (800)432-5612 Fax (803)691-0583

Media Contact, Chief Apostle, Presiding Bishop Huie Rogers

Officers

Presiding Bishop, Bishop Huie Rogers, 4949 Two Notch Rd., Columbia, SC 29204 Tel. (800)432-5612 Fax (803)691-0583

Gen. Sec., Bishop Edward Williams, 5118 Clarendon Rd., Brooklyn, NY 11226 Tel. (718)451-1238

Brethren in Christ Church

The Brethren in Christ Church was founded in Lancaster County, Pa. in about the year 1778 and was an outgrowth of the religious awakening which occurred in that area during the latter part of the 18th century. This group became known as "River Brethren" because of their original location near the Susquehanna River. The name "Brethren in Christ" was officially adopted in 1863. In theology they have accents of the Pietist, Anabaptist, Wesleyan and Evangelical movements.

Headquarters
General Church Office, P.O. Box A, Grantham, PA 17027 Tel. (717)697-2634 Fax (717) 697-7714
Media Contact, Mod., Dr. Warren L. Hoffman, Tel. (717)697-2634 Fax (717)697-7714

Officers
Mod., Dr. Warren L. Hoffman, P.O. Box A, Grantham, PA 17027 Tel. (717)697-2634 Fax (717)697-7714
Gen. Sec., Rev. Kenneth O. Hoke
Tresurer, Allen Carr

OTHER ORGANIZATIONS
General Conference Board: Chpsn., Mark Garis, 504 Swartley Rd., Hatfield, PA 19440
Bd. for Media Ministries: Chpsn., Harold Chubb, P.O. Box 189, Nappanee, IN 46550
Bd. for World Missions: Chpsn., David Hall, 996 East Hight St., Elizabethtown, PA 17022 Fax 1; Exec. Dir., Rev. John Brubaker, P.O. Box 390, Grantham, PA 17027-0390
Jacob Engle Foundation Bd. of Dir.: CEO, Julie Stout, CPA
Pension Fund Trustees: Chpsn., Donald R. Zook
Bd. for Stewardship Services: Chpsn., Donald J. Winters, 2404 Willow Glen Dr., Lancaster, PA 17602; Exec. Dir., Rev. Phil Keefer, Box A, Grantham, PA 17027
Publishing House: Exec. Dir., Roger Williams, Evangel Press, P.O. Box 189, Nappanee, IN 46550

Periodicals
Evangelical Visitor; Yes!

Brethren Church (Ashland, Ohio)
The Brethren Church (Ashland, Ohio) was organized by progressive-minded German Baptist Brethren in 1883. They reaffirmed the teaching of the original founder of the Brethren movement, Alexander Mack, and returned to congregational government.

Headquarters
524 College Ave., Ashland, OH 44805 Tel. (419) 289-1708 Fax (419)281-0450
Media Contact, Editor of Publications, Richard C. Winfield
Email: brethren@brethrenchurch.org
Website: www.brethrenchurch.org

Officers
Executive Dir., Dr. Emanuel W. Sandberg
Dir. of Missionary Ministries, Rev. Reilly Smith
Dir. of Congregational Ministries, Dr. Dan Lawson
Dir. of Pastoral Ministries, Rev. David Cooksey
Dir. of Administrative Services, Mr. Stanley Gentle

Director of Publications, Rev. Richard C. Winfield

Periodicals
The Brethren Evangelist

The Catholic Church
The largest single body of Christians in the United States, The Catholic Church is under the spiritual leadership of His Holiness the Pope. Its establishment in America dates back to the priests who accompanied Columbus on his second voyage to the New World. A settlement, later discontinued, was made in 1565 at St. Augustine, Florida. The continuous history of this Church in the Colonies began at St. Mary's in Maryland, in 1634.

Headquarters

INTERNATIONAL ORGANIZATION
His Holiness the Pope, Bishop of Rome, Vicar of Jesus Christ, Supreme Pontiff of the Catholic Church.
Pope John Paul II, Karol Wojtyla (born May 18, 1920; installed Oct. 22, 1978)

APOSTOLIC NUNCIO TO THE UNITED STATES
Archbishop Gabriel Montalvo, 3339 Massachusetts Ave., N.W., Washington, DC 20008 Tel. (202)333-7121 Fax (202)337-4036

U.S. ORGANIZATION
National Conference of Catholic Bishops, 3211 Fourth St., Washington, DC 20017-1194 (202)541-3000
The National Conference of Catholic Bishops (NCCB) is a canonical entity operating in accordance with the Vatican II Decree, Christus Dominus. Its purpose is to foster the Church's mission to mankind by providing the Bishops of this country with an opportunity to exchange views and insights of prudence and experience and to exercise in a joint manner their pastoral office.

Officers

NATIONAL CONFERENCE OF CATHOLIC BISHOPS (NCCB)

GENERAL SECRETARIAT
General Sec., Msgr. Dennis M. Schnurr
General Sec. Elect, Msgr. Willaim P. Fay
Assoc. Gen. Sec., Sr. Sharon A. Euart, RSM; Mr. Bruce E. Egnew

Officers
Pres., Bishop Joseph A. Fiorenza
Vice-Pres., Bishop Wilton D. Gregory
Treas., Bishop Henry J. Mansell
Sec., Archbishop Harry J. Flynn

NCCB STANDING COMMITTEES
Administrative Committee: Chmn., Bishop Joseph A. Fiorenza
Executive Committee: Chmn., Bishop Joseph A. Fiorenza

75

Committee on Budget and Finance: Chmn., Bishop Henry J. Mansell

Committee on Personnel: Bishop Wilton D. Gregory

Committee on Priorities and Plans: Chmn., Bishop Joseph A. Fiorenza

Subcommittee on the Third Millennium: Chmn., Bishop Wilton D. Gregory

African American Catholics: Chmn., Bishop J. Terry Steib, SVD

American Bishops' Overseas Appeal: Chmn., Bishop Joseph A. Fiorenza

American College Louvain: Chmn., Bishop Edward K. Braxton

Boundaries of Dioceses and Provinces: Chmn., Bishop Joseph A. Fiorenza

Canonical Affairs: Chmn., Bishop A. James Quinn

Church in Latin America: Interim Chmn., Bishop Raymundo J. Pena

Consecrated Life: Chmn., Bishop Joseph J. Gerry, OSB

Diaconate: Chmn., Bishop Gerald F. Kicanas

Doctrine: Chmn., Archbishop Daniel E. Pilarczyk

Ecumenical and Interreligious Affairs: Chmn., Bishop Tod D. Brown

Evangelization: Chmn., Bishop Michael W. Warfel

Hispanic Affairs: Chmn., Bishop Arthur N. Tafoya

Home Missions: Chmn., Bishop Edward J. Slattery

Laity: Chmn., Bishop John J. McRaith

Subcommittee on Lay Ministry: Chmn., Bishop Joseph P. Delaney

Subcommittee on Youth and Young Adults: Chmn., Bishop Kevin M. Britt

Liturgy: Chmn., Archbishop Oscar H. Lipscomb

Marriage and Family Life: Chmn., Bishop Anthony J. O'Connell

Migration: Chmn., Bishop Nicholas A. DiMarzio

North American College Rome: Chmn., Archbishop Daniel A. Cronin

Pastoral Practices: Chmn., Bishop Stephen E. Blaire

Priestly Formation: Chmn., Bishop George H. Niederauer

Priestly Life and Ministry: Chmn., Bishop Richard C. Hanifen

Pro-Life Activities: Chmn., William Cardinal Keeler

Relationship Between Eastern and Latin Catholic Churches: Chmn., Bishop Basil H. Losten

Science and Human Values: Chmn., Bishop John S. Cummins

Selection of Bishops: Chmn., Bishop Joseph A. Fiorenza

Vocations: Chmn., Archbishop Roger L. Schwietz, OMI

Woman in Society and in the Church: Chmn., Archbishop John G. Vlazny

World Mission: Chmn., Bishop Curtis J. Guillory, SVD

NCCB AD HOC COMMITTEES

Agricultural Issues: Chmn., Bishop William S. Skylstad

Aid to the Church in Central and Eastern Europe: Chmn., Adam Cardinal Maida

Bishops' Life and Ministry: Chmn., Bishop William S. Skylstad

Catholic Charismatic Renewal: Chmn., Bishop Sap G. Jacobs

Diocesan Audits: Chmn., Bishop Joseph P. Delaney

Economic Concerns of the Holy See: Chmn., Archbishop James P. Keleher

Forum on the Principles of Translation: Chmn., Archbishop Jerome G. Hanus, OSB

Health Care Issues and the Church: Chmn., Bishop Joseph L. Charron, CPPS

Implementation of Ex Corde Ecclesiae: Chmn., Bishop John J. Leibrecht

Subcommittee on Implementation of Ex Corde Ecclesiae: Chmn., Anthony Cardinal Bevilacqua

Native American Catholics: Chmn., Bishop Donald E. Pelotte, SSS

Nomination of Conference Officers: Chmn., Bishop George H. Niederauer

Oversee the Use of the Catechism: Chmn., Archbishop Daniel M. Buechlein, OSB

Publishing and Promotion Services: Chmn., Bishop James A. Griffin

Review of Scripture Translations: Chmn., Bishop Richard J. Sklba

Revision of Statutes and Bylaws: Chmn., Archbishop Daniel E. Pilarczyk

Sexual Abuse: Chmn., Bishop John F. Kinney

Shrines: Chmn., Archbishop James P. Keleher

Stewardship: Chmn., Bishop Sylvester D. Ryan

UNITED STATES CATHOLIC CONFERENCE (USCC), 3211 Fourth St., Washington, DC 20017, Tel. (202)541-3000

The United States Catholic Conference is a civil entity of the U.S. Catholic Bishops assisting them in their service to the Church in the United States by uniting the people of God where voluntary, collective action on a broad diocesan level is needed. The USCC provides an organizational structure and the resources needed to insure coordination, cooperation and assistance in the public, educational and social concerns of the church at the national, regional, state and, as appropriate, diocesan levels.

GENERAL SECRETARIAT

General Sec., Msgr. William P. Fay

General Sec. Elect, Msgr. William P. Fay

Assoc. Gen. Sec., Sr. Sharon A. Euart, RSM, Mr. Bruce Egnew

Officers

Pres., Bishop Joseph A. Fiorenza

Vice-Pres., Bishop Wilton D. Gregory

Treas., Bishop Henry J. Mansell

Sec., Archbishop Harry J. Flynn

USCC EXECUTIVE COMMITTEES

Administrative Board: Chmn., Bishop Joseph A. Fiorenza

Executive Committee: Chmn., Bishop Joseph A. Fiorenza

Committee on Budget and Finance: Chmn. Bishop Henry J. Mansell

Committee on Personnel: Chmn., Bishop Wilton D. Gregory

Committee on Priorities and Plans: Chmn., Bishop Joseph A. Fiorenza

USCC DEPARTMENTAL COMMITTEES

Catholic Campaign for Human Development: Chmn., Bishop John J. Leibrecht

Communications: Chmn., Bishop Robert N. Lynch

Domestic Policy: Chmn., Roger Cardinal Mahony

International Policy: Chmn., Bernard Cardinal Law

Education: Chmn., Bishop Donald W. Wuerl

Advisory Committee on Public Policy and Catholic Schools: Chmn., Bishop Donald W. Wuerl

Bishops and Catholic College and University Presidents: Chmn., Bishop Donald W. Wuerl

Catechesis: Chmn., Bishop Donald W. Wuerl

Sapientia Christiana: Chmn., Bishop John P. Boles

For information on related organizations and individual dioceses, consult the Official Catholic Directory (published annually by P.J. Kenedy and Sons) and the NCCB/USCC website (www.nccbuscc.org).

Periodicals

Newspapers: *National Catholic Register; National Catholic Reporter; Our Sunday Visitor; The Wanderer*

Magazines: *America; Catholic Digest; The Catholic Worker; Church; Columbia; Commonweal; Crisis; The Living Light; New Oxford Review; Origins; The Pope Speaks; St. Anthony Messenger; Theology Digest; U.S. Catholic; La Voz Catolica; Worship*

Christ Catholic Church

The church is a catholic communion established in 1968 to minister to the growing number of people who seek an experiential relationship with God and who desire to make a total commitment of their lives to God. The church is catholic in faith and tradition. Participating cathedrals, churches and missions are located in several states.

Headquarters

405 Kentling Rd., Highlandville, MO 65669 Tel. (417)443-3951

Media Contact, Archbishop, Most Rev. Karl Pruter

Officers

Archbishop, Most Rev. Karl Pruter, P.O. Box 98, Highlandville, MO 65669 Tel. (417)443-3951

Periodicals

St. Willibrord Journal

Christ Community Church (Evangelical-Protestant)

This church was founded by the Rev. John Alexander Dowie on Feb. 22, 1896 at Chicago, Ill. In 1901 the church founded the city of Zion, IL, and moved their headquarters there. Theologically, the church is rooted in evangelical orthodoxy. The Scriptures are accepted as the rule of faith and practice. Other doctrines call for belief in the necessity of repentance for sin and personal trust in Christ for salvation.

The Christ Community Church is a denominational member of The National Association of Evangelicals. It has work in six other nations in addition to the United States. Branch ministries are found in Tonalea, Arizona and Lindenhurst, Illinois.

Headquarters

2500 Dowie Memorial Dr., Zion, IL 60099 Tel. (847)746-1411 Fax (847)746-1452

Officers

Senior Pastor, Ken Langley

Christadelphians

The Christadelphians are a body of people who believe the Bible to be the divinely inspired word of God, written by "Holy men who spoke as they were moved by the Holy Spirit" (2 Peter 1:21). They believe that the Old Testament presents God's plan to establish His Kingdom on earth in accord with the promises He made to Abraham and David; and that the New Testament declares how that plan works out in Jesus Christ, who died a sacrificial death to redeem sinners. They believe in the personal return of Jesus Christ as King, to establish "all that God spoke by the mouth of his holy prophets from of old" (Acts 3:21). They believe that at Christ's return many of the dead will be raised by the power of God to be judged. Those whom God deems worthy will be welcomed into eternal life in the Kingdom on earth. Christadelphians believe in the mortality of man; in spiritual rebirth requiring belief and immersion in the name of Jesus; and in a godly walk in this life. They have no ordained clergy, and are organized in a loose confederation of autonomous congregations (ecclesias) in approximately 100 countries. They are conscientiously apposed to participation in war. They endeavor to be enthusiastic in work, loyal in marriage, generous in giving, dedicated in preaching, and cheerful in living.

The denomination was organized in 1844 by a medical doctor, John Thomas, who came to the United States from England in 132, having survived a near shipwreck in a violent storm. This experience affected him profoundly, and he vowed to devote his life to a search for the truth of God and a future hope from the Bible.

Headquarters
Media Contact, Trustee, Norman D. Zilmer, Christadelphian Action Society, 1000 Mohawk Dr., Elgin, IL 60120-3148 Tel. (847)741-5253 Fax (847)888-3334
Email: Nzilmer@aol.com
Website: www.christadelphia.org

Leaders
(Co-Ministers) Norman Fadelle, 815 Chippewa Dr., Elgin, IL 60120; Norman D. Zilmer, 1000 Mohawk Dr., Elgin, IL 60120

Periodicals
Christadelphian Tidings; Christadelphian Advocate

Christian Brethren (also known as Plymouth Brethren)
The Christian Brethren began in the 1820s as an orthodox and evangelical movement in the British Isles and is now worldwide. The name Plymouth Brethren was given by others because the group in Plymouth, England, was a large and influential congregation. In recent years the term Christian Brethren has replaced Plymouth Brethren for the "open" branch of the movement in Canada and British Commonwealth countries and to some extent in the United States.

The unwillingness to establish a denominational structure makes the autonomy of local congregations an important feature of the movement. Other features are weekly observance of the Lord's Supper and adherence to the doctrinal position of conservative, evangelical Christianity.

In the 1840s the movement divided. The "exclusive" branch, led by John Nelson Darby, stressed the interdependency of congregations. Since disciplinary decisions were held to be binding on all assemblies, exclusives had subdivided into seven or eight main groups by the end of the century. Since 1925 a trend toward reunification has reduced that number to three or four. The "open" branch of the movement was led by George Müller of orphanage fame. It stressed evangelism and foreign missions. Now the larger of the two branches, it has never experienced world-wide division.

CORRESPONDENT
James A. Stahr, 327 W. Prairie Ave., Wheaton, Il 60187-3408 Tel. (630)665-3757

RELATED ORGANIZATIONS
Interest Ministries, P.O. Box 940, Prospect Heights, IL 60070
Christian Missions in Many Lands, Box 13, Spring Lake, NJ 07762
Stewards Foundation, 14275 Midway Rd., Ste. 285, Addison, TX 75001
International Teams, 411 W. River Rd., Elgin, IL 60123
Emmaus Bible College, 2570 Asbury Rd., Dubuque, IA 52001
Stewards Ministries, 18-3 E. Dundee Rd., Ste. 100, Barrington, IL 60010

Christian Church (Disciples of Christ) in the United States and Canada*
Born on the American frontier in the early 1800s as a movement to unify Christians, this body drew its major inspiration from Thomas and Alexander Campbell in western Pennsylvania and Barton W. Stone in Kentucky. Developing separately, the "Disciples, under Alexander Campbell, and the "Christians," led by Stone, united in 1832 in Lexington, Ky.

The Christian Church (Disciples of Christ) is marked by informality, openness, individualism and diversity. The Disciples claim no official doctrine or dogma. Membership is granted after a simple statement of belief in Jesus Christ and baptism by immersion—although most congregations accept transfers baptized by other forms in other denominations. The Lord's Supper—generally called Communion—is open to Christians of all persuasions. The practice is weekly Communion, although no church law insists upon it.

Thoroughly ecumenical, the Disciples helped organize the National and World Councils of Churches. The church is a member of the Consultation on Church Union. The Disciples and the United Church of Christ have declared themselves to be in "full communion" through the General Assembly and General Synod of the two churches. Official theological conversations have been going on since 1967 directly with the Roman Catholic Church, and since 1987 with the Russian Orthodox Church.

Disciples have vigorously supported world and national programs of education, agricultural assistance, urban reconciliation, care of persons with retardation, family planning and aid to victims of war and calamity. Operating ecumenically, Disciples' personnel or funds work in more than 100 countries outside North America.

Three manifestations or expressions of the church (general, regional and congregational) operate as equals, with strong but voluntary covenantal ties to one another. Entities in each manifestation manage their own finances, own their own property, and conduct their own programs. A General Assembly meets every two years and has voting representation from each congregation.

Headquarters
Disciples Center, 130 E. Washington St., P.O. Box 1986, Indianapolis, IN 46206-1986 Tel. (317)635-3100 Fax (317)635-3700
Media Contact, Dir. of News & Information, Cliff Willis
Email: cmiller@oc.disciples.org
Website: www.disciples.org

Officers
Gen. Minister & Pres., Richard L. Hamm
Mod., Paul D. Rivers, 850 Oxford Ct., Valley Stream, NY 11580

1st Vice-Mod., Lanny C. Lawler, First Christian Church, 650 McCallie Ave., Chattanooga, TN 37403

2nd Vice-Mod., Minnie L. Smith, P.O. Box 1148, Hannibal, MO 63401

General Officers

Gen. Minister & Pres., Richard L. Hamm

Assoc. Gen. Minister & Vice Pres., William H. Edwards

Assoc. Gen. Min. for Admn., Donald B. Manworren

Assoc. Gen Min. & Admin. Sec. Of the National Convention, John R. Foulkes, Sr.

ADMINISTRATIVE UNITS

Bd. of Church Extension: Pres., James L. Powell, 130 E. Washington St., P.O. Box 7030, Indianapolis, IN 46207-7030 Tel. (317)635-6500 Fax (317)635-6534

Christian Bd. of Publ. (Chalice Press): Pres., Cyrus N. White, 1316 Convention Plaza Dr., P.O. Box 179, St. Louis, MO 63166-0179 Tel. (314)231-8500 or (800)668-8016 Fax (314) 231-8524

Christian Church Foundation, Inc.: Pres., James P. Johnson, Fax (317)635-1991

Church Finance Council, Inc.: Pres., Lois Artis Murray

Council on Christian Unity, Inc.: Pres., Robert K. Welsh, Tel. (317)713-2586 Fax (317)713-2588

Disciples of Christ Historical Society: Pres., Peter M. Morgan, 1101 19th Ave. S., Nashville, TN 37212-2196 Tel. (615)327-1444 Fax (615)327-1445

Division of Higher Education: Pres., Dennis L. Landon, 11720 Borman Dr., Ste. 240, St. Louis, MO 63146-4191 Tel. (314)991-3000 Fax (314)991-2957

Division of Homeland Ministries: Pres., Ann Updegraff Spleth, Fax (317)635-4426

Division of Overseas Ministries: Pres., Patricia Tucker Spier, Fax (317)635-4323

National Benevolent Association: Pres., Cindy Dougherty, 11780 Borman Dr., St. Louis, MO 63146-4157 Tel. (314)993-9000 Fax (314)993-9018

Pension Fund: Pres., Arthur A. Hanna, 130 E. Washington St., Indianapolis, IN 46204-3645 Tel. (317)634-4504 Fax (317)634-4071

REGIONAL UNITS OF THE CHURCH

Alabama-Northwest Florida: Regional Minister, John P. Mobley, 1336 Montgomery Hwy. S., Birmingham, AL 35216-2799 Tel. (205)823-5647 Fax (205)823-5673

Arizona: Regional Minister, Dennis L. Williams, 4423 N. 24th St., Ste 700, Phoenix, AZ 85016-5544 Tel. (602)468-3815 Fax (602)468-3816

Arkansas: Regional Min./Pres., Barbara E. Jones, 9302 Geyer Springs Rd., P.O. Box 191057, Little Rock, AR 72219-1057 Tel. (501)562-6053 Fax (501)562-7089

California North-Nevada: Int. Regional Min./Pres., Charles R. Blaisdell, 9260 Alcosta Blvd., C-18, San Ramon, CA 94583-4143 Tel. (510)556-9900 Fax (510)556-9904

Canada: Exec. Director, Stan Litke, 40 Midlake Blvd., SE, Box 48068, Calgary, AB T2X 3C9 Tel. (403)254-8413 Fax (403)254-6178

Capital Area: Regional Minister, Wm. Chris Hobgood, 11501 Georgia Ave., Ste. 400, Wheaton, MD 20902 Tel. (301)942-8266 Fax (301)942-8366

Central Rocky Mountain Region: Int. Exec. Regional Minister, John D. Wolfersberger, 2950 Tennyson #300, P.O. Box 12186, Denver, CO 80212 Tel. (303)561-1790 Fax (303)561-1795

Florida: Regional Minister, William C. Morrison, 924 N. Magnolia Ave., Ste. 200, Orlando, FL 32803 Tel. (407)843-4652 Fax (407)843-0272

Georgia: Regional Minister, Tom W. Neal, 2370 Vineville Ave., Macon, GA 31204-3163 Tel. (912)743-8649 or (800)755-0485Fax (912) 741-1508

Idaho-South: Regional Minister, Larry Crist, 6465 Sunrise Ave., Nampa, ID 83686 Tel. (208)468-8976 Fax (208)468-8973

Illinois and Wisconsin: Regional Minister/Pres., Herbert L. Knudsen, 1011 N. Main St., Bloomington, IL 61701-1753 Tel. (309)828-6293 Fax (309)829-4612

Indiana: Regional Minister, C. Edward Weisheimer, 1100 W. 42nd St., Indianapolis, IN 46208-3375 Tel. (317)926-6051 Fax (317) 931-2034

Kansas: Regional Minister/Pres., Patsie Sweeden, 2914 S.W. MacVicar Ave., Topeka, KS 66611-1787 Tel. (785)266-2914 Fax (785) 266-0174

Kansas City, Greater: Regional Min./Pres., Paul J. Diehl, Jr., 5700 Broadmoor, Ste. 205, Mission, KS 66202-2405 Tel. (913)432-1414 Fax (913)432-3598

Kentucky: Gen. Minister, A. Guy Waldrop, 1125 Red Mile Rd., Lexington, KY 40504-2660 Tel. (859)233-1391 Fax (395)233-2079

Louisiana: Transitional Regional Minister, Zena S. McAdams, 3524 Holloway Prairie Rd., Pineville, LA 71360-5816 Tel. (318)443-0304 Fax (318)449-1367

Michigan: Regional Minister, Morris Finch, Jr., 2820 Covington Ct., Lansing, MI 48912-4830 Tel. (517)372-3220 Fax (517)372-2705

Mid-America Region: Int. Regional Minister, David L. Webb, Hwy. 54 W., P. O. Box 104298, Jefferson City, MO 65110-4298 Tel. (573)636-8149 Fax (573)636-2889

Mississippi: Regional Minister, William E. McKnight, 1619 N. West St., P.O. Box 4832, Jackson, MS 39296-4832 Tel. (601)352-6774 Fax (601)355-1221

Montana: Regional Minister, Karen Frank-Plumlee, 1019 Central Ave., Great Falls, MT 59401-3784 Tel. (406)452-7404

Nebraska: Regional Ministers, Kenneth W. Moore, 1268 S. 20th St., Lincoln, NE 68502-1699 Tel. (402)476-0359 or (800)580-8851 Fax (402)476-0350

North Carolina: Regional Minister, Rexford L. Horne, 509 N.E. Lee St., P.O. Box 1568, Wilson, NC 27894 Tel. (252)291-4047 Fax (252)291-3338

Northeastern Region: Co-Assoc. Regional Ministers, Sharon T. Hart, Lonnie F. Oates, & Ariel Rodriguez, 475 Riverside Dr., Rm. 1950, New York, NY 10115 Tel. (212)870-2734 Fax (870)2735

Northwest Region: Regional Minister/Pres., Jack Sullivan, Jr., 6558-35th Ave. SW, Seattle, WA 98126-2899 Tel. (206)938-1008 Fax (206) 933-1163

Ohio: Regional Pastor/Pres., Howard M. Ratcliff, 38007 Butternut Ridge Rd., P.O. Box 299, Elyria, OH 44036-0299 Tel. (440)458-5112 Fax (440)458-5114

Oklahoma: Regional Pastor, Thomas R. Jewell, 301 N.W. 36th St., Oklahoma City, OK 73118-8661 Tel. (405)528-3577 Fax (405)528-3584

Oregon: Regional Minister, Mark K. Reid, 0245 S.W. Bancroft St., Ste. F, Portland, OR 97201-4267 Tel. (503)226-7648 Fax (503)228-6983

Pacific Southwest Region: Regional Minister/Pres., Don W. Shelton, 2401 N. Lake Ave., Altadena, CA 91001-2418 Tel. (818)296-0385 Fax (818)296-1280

Pennsylvania: Regional Minister, W. Darwin Collins, 670 Rodi Rd., Pittsburgh, PA 15235-4524 Tel. (412)731-7000 Fax (412)731-4515

South Carolina: Interim Regional Minister, Carl R. Flock, 1098 E. Montague Ave., North Charleston, SC 29405-4837 Tel. (803)554-6886 Fax (803)554-6886

Southwest Region: Regional Minister, Ralph Glenn, 3209 S. University Dr., Fort Worth, TX 76109-2239 Tel. (817)926-4687 Fax (817) 926-5121

Tennessee: Regional Minister/Pres., Glen J. Stewart, 3700 Richland Ave., Nashville, TN 37205-2499 Tel. (615)269-3409 Fax (615)269-3400

Upper Midwest Region: Regional Minister/Pres., Richard L. Guentert, 3300 University Ave., P.O. Box 1024, Des Moines, IA 50311-1024 Tel. (515)255-3168 Fax (515)255-2625

Virginia: Regional Minister, Lee Parker, 518 Brevard St., Lynchburg, VA 24501 Tel. (804) 846-3400 Fax (804)528-4919

West Virginia: Regional Minister, William B. Allen, P.O. Box 264, Parkersburg, WV 26102-0264 Tel. (304)428-1681 Fax (304)428-1684

Periodicals

The Disciple; Vanguard; Mid-Stream: An Ecumenical Journal

Christian Church of North America, General Council

Originally known as the Italian Christian Church, its first General Council was held in 1927 at Niagara Falls, N.Y. This body was incorporated in 1948 at Pittsburgh, Pa., and is described as Pentecostal but does not engage in the "the excesses tolerated or practiced among some churches using the same name."

The movement recognizes two ordinances-baptism and the Lord's Supper. Its moral code is conservative and its teaching is orthodox. Members are exhorted to pursue a life of personal holiness, setting an example to others. A conservative position is held in regard to marriage and divorce. The governmental form is, by and large, congregational. District and National officiaries, however, are referred to as Presbyteries led by Overseers.

The group functions in cooperative fellowship with the Italian Pentecostal Church of Canada and the Evangelical Christian Churches-Assemblies of God in Italy. It is an affiliate member of the Pentecostal Fellowship of North America and of the National Association of Evangelicals.

Headquarters

1294 Rutledge Rd., Transfer, PA 16154-2299 Tel. (724)962-3501 Fax (724)962-1766

Exec. Sec., Terri Metcalfe; Admin. Asst., Chris Marini

Officers

Executive Bd., Gen. Overseer, Rev. John DelTurco, P.O. Box 1198, Hermitage, PA 16148

Exec. Vice-Pres., Rev. Charles Gay, 26 Delafield Dr., Albany, NY 12205

Asst. Gen. Overseers: Rev. Joseph Shipley 44-19 Francis Lewis Blvd., Bayside, NY 11361; Rev. Vincent Prestigiacomo, 21 Tyler Hill Rd., Jaffrey, NH 03452; Rev. Charles Gay, 26 Delafield Dr., Albany, NY 12205; Rev. Michael Trotta, 224 W. Winter Ave., New Castle, PA 16101; Rev. Douglas Bedgood, Sr., 442 Trinidad Ln., Teadkwood Village, Largo, FL 33770

DEPARTMENTS

Benevolence, Rev. John Del Turco, P.O. Box 1198, Hermitage, PA 16148

Home Missions, Rev. John Ferguson

Faith, Order & Credentials, Rev. Rev. Charles Gay, 26 Delafield Dr., Albany, NY 12205

Missions, Rev. David Verzilli, 4875 Shadow Oak, Youngstown, OH 44515

Publications Relations, Rev. John Tedesco, 1188 Heron Rd., Cherry Hill, NJ 08003

Lay Ministries: Rev. Eugene De Marco, 155 Scott St., New Brighton, PA 15066

Education: Rev. Lucian Gandolfo, 1030 Fairfield Circle, Clarks Summit, PA 18411

Periodicals

Vista

Christian Churches and Churches of Christ

The fellowship, whose churches were always strictly congregational in polity, has its origin in the American movement to "restore the New

Testament church in doctrine, ordinances and life" initiated by Thomas and Alexander Campbell, Walter Scott and Barton W. Stone in the early 19th century.

Headquarters
Media Contact, No. American Christian Convention Dir., Rod Huron, 4210 Bridgetown Rd., Box 11326, Cincinnati, OH 45211 Tel. (513) 598-6222 Fax (513)598-6471

CONVENTIONS
North American Christian Convention: Dir., Rod Huron, 4210 Bridgetown Rd., Box 11326, Cincinnati, OH 45211 Tel. (513)598-6222; NACC Mailing Address, Box 39456, Cincinnati, OH 45239

National Missionary Convention, Coord., Walter Birney, Box 11, Copeland, KS 67837 Tel. (316)668-5250

Eastern Christian Convention, Kenneth Meade, 5300 Norbeck Rd., Rockville, MD 20853 Tel. (301)460-3550

Periodicals
Christian Standard; Restoration Herald; Horizons; The Lookout

The Christian Congregation, Inc.

The Christian Congregation is a denominational evangelistic association that originated in 1787 and was active on the frontier in areas adjacent to the Ohio River. The church was an unincorporated organization until 1887. At that time a group of ministers who desired closer cooperation formally constituted the church. The charter was revised in 1898 and again in 1970.

Governmental polity basically is congregational. Local units are semi-autonomous. Doctrinal positions, strongly biblical, are essentially universalist in the sense that ethical principles, which motivate us to creative activism, transcend national boundaries and racial barriers. A central tenet, John 13:34-35, translates to such respect for sanctity of life that abortions on demand, capital punishment and all warfare are vigorously opposed. All wars are considered unjust and obsolete as a means of resolving disputes.

Early leaders were John Chapman, John L. Puckett and Isaac V. Smith. Bishop O. J. Read was chief administrative and ecclesiastic officer for 40 years until 1961. Rev. Dr. Ora Wilbert Eads has been general Superintendent since 1961. Ministerial affiliation for independent clergymen is provided.

Headquarters
812 W. Hemlock St., LaFollette, TN 37766
Media Contact, Gen. Supt., Rev. Ora W. Eads, D.D., Tel. (423)562-6330

Officers
Gen. Supt., Rev. Ora W. Eads, D.D.

Christian Methodist Episcopal Church*

On December 16, 1870 the General Conference of the Methodist Church South approved the request of its colored membership for the formation of their conferences into a separate ecclesiastical body, which became the Colored Methodist Episcopal Church in America. In 1954, at its General Conference in Memphis, Tennessee it was overwhelmingly voted to change the term "Colored" to "Christian". On January 3, 1956 the official name became the Christian Methodist Episcopal Church.

Headquarters
First Memphis Plaza, 4466 Elvis Presley Blvd., Memphis, TN 38116
Media Contact, Exec. Sec., Attorney Juanita Bryant, 3675 Runnymede Blvd., Cleveland Hts., OH 44121, Tel. (216)382-3559 Fax (216) 382-3516, Email: juanbr4law@aol.com

Officers
Exec. Sec., Attorney Juanita Bryant, 3675 Runnymede Blvd., Cleveland Hts., OH 44121, Tel. (216)382-3559 Fax (216)382-3516, Email: juanbr4law@aol.com
Sec. Gen. Conf., Rev. John Gilmore, Mt. Olive CME Church, 538 Linden Ave., Memphis, TN 38126

OTHER ORGANIZATIONS
Christian Education: Gen. Sec., Dr. Ronald M. Cunningham, 4466 Elvis Presley Blvd., Ste. 214, Box 193, Memphis, TN 38116-7100 Tel. (901)345-0580 Fax (901)345-4118
Lay Ministry: Gen. Sec., Dr. Victor Taylor, 9560 Drake Ave., Evenston, IL 60203, Tel. 800-782-4335 x. 6029, Fax (312)345-6056, email: victav@idt.net
Evangelism & Missions: Gen. Sec., Dr. Willie C. Champion, 102 Pearly Top Dr., Glen Heights, TX 75154 Tel. (214)372-9505
Finance: Sec., Joseph C. Neal, Jr., P.O. Box 75085, Los Angeles, CA 90075 Tel. (323)233-5050
Editor, The Christian Index: Dr. Kenneth E. Jones, P.O. Box 431, Fairfield, AL 35064, Tel. (205)929-1640 Fax (205)791-1910, Email: Goodoc@aol.com
Publication Services: Gen. Sec., Rev. William George, 4466 Elvis Presley Blvd., Memphis, TN 38116 Tel. (901)345-0580 Fax (901)767-8514
Personnel Services: Gen. Sec., Dr. N. Charles Thomas, P.O. Box 9, Memphis, TN 38101-0074 Tel. (901)345-4120
Women's Missionary Council: Pres., Judith E. Grant, 723 E. Upsal St., Philadelphia, PA 19119 Tel. (215)843-7742

BISHOPS
First District: Bishop William H. Graves, Sr., 4466 Elvis Presley Blvd., Ste. 222, Memphis, TN 38116 Tel. (901)345-0580

Second District: Bishop Nathaniel L. Linsey, 5115 Rollman Estate Dr., Cincinnati, OH 45236 Tel. (513)772-8622

Third District: Bishop Dotcy I. Isom, Jr., 5925 W. Florissant Ave., St. Louis, MO 63136 Tel. (314)381-3111

Fourth District: Bishop Thomas L. Hoyt, Jr., 109 Holcomb Dr., Shreveport, LA 71103 Tel. (318) 222-6284

Fifth District: Bishop Paul A.G. Stewart, Sr., 310 18th St., N, Ste. 400D, Birmingham, AL 35203 Tel. (205)655-0346

Sixth District: Bishop Othal H. Lakey, 2001 M.L. King, Jr. Dr. SW, Ste. 423, Atlanta, GA 30310 Tel. (404)752-7800

Seventh District: Bishop Charles L. Helton 6524 16th St., NW, Washington, DC 20012 and 5337 Ruth Dr., Charlotte, NC 28215 Tel. (704)536-8067

Eighth District: Bishop Marshall Gilmore, Sr., 1616 E. Illinois, Dallas, TX 75216 Tel. (214) 372-9073

Ninth District: Bishop E. Lynn Brown, 3844 W. Slauson Ave., Ste. 1, Los Angeles, CA 90043 Tel. (213)294-3830

Tenth District: Bishop Lawrence L. Reddick III, PO Box 27147, Memphis, TN 38167, Tel. (901)274-1070

Retired: Bishop Caesar D. Coleman, 1000 Longmeadow Ln., DeSoto, TX 75115, Bishop Richard O. Bass, Sr., 1556 Delton Pl., Midfield, AL 35228; Bishop Oree Broomfield, Sr., 3505 Springrun Dr., Decatur, GA 30032

Periodicals

The Christian Index; The Missionary Messenger

The Christian and Missionary Alliance

The Christian and Missionary Alliance was formed in 1897 by the merger of two organizations begun in 1887 by Dr. Albert B. Simpson, The Christian Alliance and the Evangelical Missionary Alliance. The Christian and Missionary Alliance is an evangelical church which stresses the sufficiency of Jesus as Savior, Sanctifier, Healer, and Coming King and has earned a worldwide reputation for its missionary accomplishments. The Canadian districts became autonomous in 1981 and formed The Christian and Missionary Alliance in Canada.

NATIONAL OFFICE

P.O. Box 35000, Colorado Springs, CO 80935-3500 Tel. (719)599-5999 Fax (719)593-8692
Media Contact, Rev. Robert L. Niklaus

Officers

Pres., Rev. Peter N. Nanfelt, D.D.
Corp. Vice Pres., Rev. Abraham H. Poon, D. Min
Corp. Sec., Rev. David L. Goodin
Vice Pres. for Administration, Rev. Randall B. Corbin, D. Min.
Vice Pres., for Advancement, Rev. John P. Stumbo

Vice Pres. for International Ministries, Rev. Robert L. Fetherlin, D. Min.
Vice Pres. For National Church Ministries, Rev. Donald A. Wiggins, D. Min.
Vice Pres. For Operations/Finance, Mr. Duane A. Wheeland, CPA

Board of Managers

Chpsn., to be elected August 2000
Vice-Chpsn., Rev. Rockwell L. Dillaman

DISTRICTS

Cambodian: Rev. Nareth May, 1616 S. Palmetto Ave., Ontario, CA 91762, Tel. 909-988-9434

Central: Dr. Gordon F. Meier, 1218 High St., Wadsworth, OH 44281, Tel. 303-336-2911

Central Pacific: Rev. Edward (Ted) A. Cline, 715 Lincoln Ave., Woodland, CA 95695 Tel. 530-662-2500

E. Pennsylvania: Rev. Francis L. Leonard, 1200 Spring Garden Dr., Middletown, PA 17057, Tel. 717-985-9240

Great Lakes: Dr. Donald A Wiggins, 2250 Huron Parkway, Ann Arbor, MI 48104 Tel. 734-677-8555

Haitian North: Rev. Sainvilus Point Du Jour, P.O. Box 791, Nyack, NY 10960, Tel. 914-578-1804

Haitian South: Rev. Brave L. Laverdure, 2922 Oak Vista Way SW, Lawrenceville, GA 30044, Tel. 770-931-0456

Hmong: Rev. Chong-Neng Thao, 12287 Pennsylvania St., Thornton, CO 80241, Tel. 303-252-1793

Korean: Rev. P. Gil Kim, 713 W. Commonwealth Ave., Ste. C, Fullerton, CA 92832, Tel. 714-879-5201

Laotian: Rev. Bouathong Vangsoulatda, 715 Lincoln Ave., Woodland, CA 95695, Tel. 530-406-1189

Metropolitan: Rev. John F. Soper, 349 Watchung Ave., North Plainfield, NJ 07060, Tel. 908-668-8421

MidAmerica: Rev. Douglas L. Grogan, 1301 S. 119th St., Omaha, NE 68144, Tel. 402-330-1888

Mid-Atlantic: Rev. John E. Zuch, Jr., P.O. Box 1217, Frederick, MD 21702, Tel. 301-620-9934

Midwest: Dr. M. Fred Polding, 260 Glen Ellyn Road, Bloomingdale, IL 60108, Tel. 630-893-1355

Native American: Rev. Craig S. Smith, 19019 N. 74th Dr., Glendale, AZ 85308, Tel. 623-561-8134

New England: Dr. Richard E. Bush, P.O. Box 288, South Easton, MA 02375 Tel. 508-238-3820

Northeastern: Rev. David J. Phillips, 6275 Pillmore Dr., Rome, NY 13440 Tel. 315-336-4720

Northwestern: Rev. Craig L. Strawser, 1813 Lexington Ave., N., Roseville, MN 55113 Tel. 651-489-1391

Ohio Valley, Dr. David F. Presher, 4050

Executive Park Dr., #402, Cincinnati, OH 45241, Tel. 513-733-4833

Pacific NW, Rev. Kelvin J. Gardiner, P.O. Box 1030, Canby, OR 97013 Tel. 503-266-2238

Puerto Rico: Rev. Luis Felipa, P.O. Box 191794, San Juan, PR 00919-1794, Tel. 787-281-0101

Rocky Mountain: Rev. Delbert McKenzie, 2545 St. Johns Ave., Billings, MT 59102 Tel. 406-656-4233

South Atlantic: Rev. L. Ferrell Towns, 10801 Johnston Rd., Ste. 125, Charlotte, NC 28226, Tel. 704-543-0470

South Pacific: Rev. Bill J. Vaughn, 4130 Adams St., Ste. A, Riverside, CA 92504 Tel. 909-351-0111

Southeastern: Dr. Mark T. O' Farrell, P.O. Box 720430, Orlando, FL 32872-0430 Tel. 407-823-9662

Southern: Rev. A. Eugene Hall, 5998 Deerfoot Parkway, Trussville, AL 35173 Tel. 205-661-9585

Southwestern: Rev. Daniel R. Wetzel, 5600 E. Loop 820 South Ste. 100, Fort Worth, TX 76119 Tel. 817-561-0879

Spanish Central: Rev. Jose Bruno, 260 Glen Ellyn Rd., Bloomingdale, IL 60108 Tel. 630-924-7171

Spanish Eastern: Rev. Marcelo Realpe, 3133 Central Ave. Suite 202, Union City, NJ 07087, Tel. 201-866-6676

Spanish Western: Rev. Douglas M. Domier, P.O. Box 3805, Dana Point, CA 92629 Tel. 949-489-3816

Vietnamese: Rev. Quang B. Nguyen, 2275 W. Lincoln Ave., Anaheim, CA 92801 Tel. 714-491-8007

W. Great Lakes: Rev. Gary E. Russell, W6107 Aerotech Dr., Appleton, WI 54914, Tel. 920-734-1123

W. Pennsylvania, Rev. Palmer L. Zerbe, 600 Chestnut & Sutton Streets, Punxsutawney, PA 15767, Tel. 814-938-6920

NATIONAL ETHNIC ASSOCIATIONS

African-American: Exec. Sec., Rev. Gus H. Brown, 688 Diagonal Rd., Akron, OH 44320 Tel. 330-376-4654

Chinese: Exec. Sec., Rev. Peter Chu, 14209 Secluded Ln., N. Potomac, MD 20878 Tel. 301-294-8067

Filipino: Exec. Sec., Rev. Abednego Ferrer, 166 W. Harder Rd., Hayward, CA 94544 Tel. 510-887-6261

ETHNIC/CULTURAL MINISTRIES

Arab & South Asian: Rev. Joseph S. Kong, P.O. Box 35000, Colorado Springs, CO 80935 Tel. 719-599-5999 x. 2052

Dega: Mr. Glik Rahlan, 713 Highgate Pl., Raleigh, NC 27610 Tel. 919-821-2351

Alliance Jewish Ministries Association: Rev. Abraham Sandler, 9820 Woodfern Rd., Philadelphia, PA 19115 Tel. 215-676-5122

Periodicals

Alliance Life

Christian Reformed Church in North America

The Christian Reformed Church represents the historic faith of Protestantism. Founded in the United States in 1857 and active in Canada since 1908, it asserts its belief in the Bible as the inspired Word of God, and is creedally united in the Belgic Confession (1561), the Heidelberg Catechism (1563), and the Canons of Dort (1618-19).

Headquarters

2850 Kalamazoo Ave., SE, Grand Rapids, MI 49560 Tel. (616)224-0744 Fax (616)224-5895

Media Contact, Gen. Sec., Dr. David H. Engelhard

Website: www.crcna.org

Officers

Gen. Sec., Dr. David H. Engelhard

Exec. Dir. of Ministries, Dr. Peter Borgdorff

Canadian Ministries Director, -vacant-, 3475 Mainway, PO Box 5070 STN LCR 1, Burlington, ON L7R 3Y8

Director of Finance and Administration, Kenneth Horjus

OTHER ORGANIZATIONS

The Back to God Hour: Dir. of Ministries, Dr. Calvin L. Bremer, International Headquarters, 6555 W. College Dr., Palos Heights, IL 60463

Christian Reformed Home Missions: Dir., Rev. John A. Rozeboom

Christian Reformed World Missions, US: Dir., Rev. Merle Den Bleyker

Christian Ref. World Missions, Canada: Dir., Albert Karsten, 3475 Mainway, P.O. Box 5070 STN LCR 1, Burlington, ON L7R 3Y8

Christian Reformed World Relief, US: Dir., Andrew Ryskamp

Christian Reformed World Relief, Canada: Dir., H. Wayne deJong, 3475 Mainway, P.O. Box 5070 STN LCR 1, Burlington, ON L7R 3Y8

CRC Publications: Dir., Gary Mulder

Ministers' Pension Fund: Admn., Kenneth Horjus

Periodicals

The Banner

Christian Union

Organized in 1864 in Columbus, Ohio, the Christian Union stresses the oneness of the Church with Christ as its only head. The Bible is the only rule of faith and practice and good fruits the only condition of fellowship. Each local church governs itself.

Headquarters

c/o Christian Union Bible College, P.O. Box 27, Greenfield, OH 45123 Tel. (513)981-2897

Media Contact, Pres., Dr. Joseph Harr, 3025 Converse-Roselm Rd., Grover Hill, OH 45849 Tel. (419)587-3226

Officers

Pres., Dr. Joseph Harr

83

Vice-Pres., Rev. Harold McElwee, P.O. Box 132, Milo, IA 50166 Tel. (419)822-4261

Sec., Rev. Joseph Cunningham, 1005 N. 5th St., Greenfield, OH 45123 Tel. (513)981-3476

Asst. Sec., Rev. Earl Mitchell, 17500 Hidden Valley Rd., Independence, MO 64057 Tel. (816)373-3416

Treas., Rev. Lawrence Rhoads, 902 N.E. Main St., West Union, OH 45693 Tel. (513)544-2950

Church of the Brethren*

German pietists-anabaptists founded the Church of the Brethren in 1708 under Alexander Mack in Schwarzenau, Germany. They entered the colonies in 1719 and settled at Germantown, Pa. They have no other creed than the New Testament, hold to principles of nonviolence, temperance and volunteerism and emphasize religion in daily life.

Headquarters

Church of the Brethren General Offices, 1451 Dundee Ave., Elgin, IL 60120 Tel. (847)742-5100 Fax (847)742-6103

New Windsor Service Center, 500 Main Street, P.O. Box 188, New Windsor, MD 21776-0188 Tel. (410)635-6464 Fax (410)635-8789

Washington Office, 337 N. Carolina Ave. SE, Washington, DC 20003 Tel. (202)546-3202 Fax (202)544-5852

Media Contact, Staff for Interpretation, Howard Royer, Elgin Ofc.

Officers

Mod., Phill Carlos Archbold

Mod.-Elect, Paul Grout

Sec., Cathy Huffman

GENERAL BOARD STAFF

Ofc. of Ex. Dir.: Ex. Dir., Judy Mills Reimer; Manager of Office Operations, Jon Kobel; Coordinator of Human Resources, Elsie Holderread

LEADERSHIP TEAM

Exec. Director, Judy Mills Reimer

Treas. & Director of Centralized Resources, Judy E. Keyser

Director & Publisher of Brethren Press, Wendy McFadden

Director of Congregational Life Ministries, Glenn F. Timmons

Director of Global Mission Partnerships, Mervin Keeney

Director of Brethren Service Center, Stanley J. Noffsinger

Periodicals

Messenger

Church of Christ

Joseph Smith and five others organized the Church of Christ on April 6, 1830 at Fayette, New York. In 1864 this body was directed by revelation through Granville Hedrick to return in 1867 to Independence, Missouri to the "consecrated land" dedicated by Joseph Smith. They did so and purchased the temple lot dedicated in 1831.

Headquarters

Temple Lot, 200 S. River St., P.O. Box 472, Independence, MO 64051 Tel. (816)833-3995

Media Contact, Gen. Church Rep., William A. Sheldon, P.O. Box 472, Independence, MO 64051 Tel. (816)833-3995

Officers

Council of Apostles, Secy., Apostle Smith N. Brickhouse, P.O. Box 472, Independence, MO 64051

Gen. Bus. Mgr., Bishop Alvin Harris, P.O. Box 472, Independence, MO 64051

Periodicals

Zion's Advocate

The Church of Christ (Holiness) U.S.A.

The Church of Christ (Holiness) U.S.A. has a Divine commission to propagate the gospel throughout the world, to seek the conversion of sinners, to reclaim backsliders, to encourage the sanctification of believers, to support divine healing, and to advance the truth for the return of our Lord and Savior Jesus Christ. This must be done through proper organization.

The fundamental principles of Christ's Church have remained the same. The laws founded upon these principles are to remain unchanged. The Church of Christ (Holiness) U.S.A. is representative in form of government; therefore, the final authority in defining the organizational responsibilities rests with the national convention. The bishops of the church are delegated special powers to act in behalf of or speak for the church. The pastors are ordained ministers, who under the call of God and His people, have divine oversight of local churches. However, the representative form of government gives ministry and laity equal authority in all deliberate bodies. With the leadership of the Holy Spirit, Respect, Loyalty and Love will greatly increase.

Headquarters

329 East Monument Street, P.O. Box 3622, Jackson, MS 39207 Tel. (601)353-0222 Fax (601)353-4002

Media Contact, Maurice D. Bingham, Ed. D., Senior Bishop

BOARD OF BISHOPS

Senior Bishop, Maurice D. Bingham, Ed. D.

Eastern Diocese, Bishop Lindsay E. Jones

North Central Diocese, Elder Bennett Wolfe

Northern Diocese, Bishop Emery Lindsay

Pacific Northwest Diocese, Bishop Robert Winn

South Central Diocese, Bishop Joseph Campbell

Southeastern Diocese, Bishop Victor P. Smith

Southwestern Diocese, Bishop Vernon Kennebrew
Western Diocese, Bishop Robert Winn
Board Member, Bishop James K. Mitchell

Church of Christ, Scientist

The Church of Christ, Scientist, was founded in 1879 by Mary Baker Eddy "to commemorate the word and works of our Master [Christ Jesus], which should reinstate primitive Christianity and its lost element of healing" (Church Manual, p. 17). Central to the Church's mission is making available worldwide Mrs. Eddy's definitive work on health and Bible-based Christian healing, Science and Health with key to the scriptures, as well as its publications, Internet sites, and broadcast programs, all of which respond to humanity's search for spiritual answers to today's pressing needs.

The Church also maintains an international speakers' bureau to introduce the public to Christian Science and Mrs. Eddy. Christian Science practitioners, living in hundreds of communities worldwide, are available full-time, to pray with anyone seeking comfort and healing. And Christian Science teachers hold yearly classes for those interested in a more specific understanding of how to practice the Christian Science system of healing.

The worldwide activities and business of the Church are transacted by a five-member Board of Directors in Boston. About 2000 congregations, each democratically organized and governed, are located in approximately 75 countries. The church has no clergy. Worship services are conducted by lay persons elected to serve as Readers. Each church maintains a Reading Room—a bookstore open to the community for spiritual inquiry and research; and a Sunday School where young people discuss the contemporary relevance of ideas from the Bible and Science and Health.

Headquarters

The First Church of Christ, Scientist, 175 Huntington Ave., Boston, MA 02115
Media Contact, Mgr., Comm. on Publication, Gary A. Jones, Tel. (617)450-3301 Fax (617)450-3325
Website: www.tfccs.com

Officers

Bd. of Directors: Virginia S. Harris; Walter D. Jones; Olga M. Chaffee, John Lewis Selover; Paul D. Grimes
President, Jean Stark Hebenstreit
Treas., Walter D. Jones
Clk., Olga M. Chaffee
First Reader, J. Thomas Black
Second Reader, Patricia Tupper Hyatt

Periodicals

The Christian Science Monitor (website: www. csmonitor.com); The Christian Science Journal; Christian Science Sentinel; The

Herald of Christian Science (13 languages); Christian Science Quarterly Bible Lessons in 16 languages and English Braille

Church of God (Anderson, Indiana)

The Church of God (Anderson, Indiana) began in 1881 when Daniel S. Warner and several associates felt constrained to forsake all denominational hierarchies and formal creeds, trusting solely in the Holy Spirit as their overseer and the Bible as their statement of belief. These people saw themselves at the forefront of a movement to restore unity and holiness to the church, not to establish another denomination, but to promote primary allegiance to Jesus Christ so as to transcend denominational loyalties.

Deeply influenced by Wesleyan theology and Pietism, the Church of God has emphasized conversion, holiness and attention to the Bible. Worship services tend to be informal, accentuating expository preaching and robust singing.

There is no formal membership. Persons are assumed to be members on the basis of witness to a conversion experience and evidence that supports such witness. The absence of formal membership is also consistent with the church's understanding of how Christian unity is to be achieved—that is, by preferring the label Christian before all others.

The Church of God is congregational in its government. Each local congregation is autonomous and may call any recognized Church of God minister to be its pastor and may retain him or her as long as is mutually pleasing. Ministers are ordained and disciplined by state or provincial assemblies made up predominantly of ministers. National program boards serve the church through coordinated ministries and resource materials.

There are Church of God congregations in 89 foreign countries, most of which are resourced by one or more missionaries. There are slightly more Church of God adherents overseas than in North America. The heaviest concentration is in the nation of Kenya.

General Offices

Box 2420, Anderson, IN 46018-2420 Tel. (765)642-0256 Fax (765)642-5652
Media Contact, Communications Coordinator, Church of God Ministries, Don Taylor

CHURCH OF MINISTRIES

Includes Congregational Ministries, Resource & Linking Ministries and Outreach Ministries
Email: dtaylor@chog.org
Website: www.chog.org

OTHER ORGANIZATIONS

Bd. of Church Extension, Pres., J. Perry Grubbs, Box 2069, Anderson, IN 46018
Women of the Church of God, Natl. Coord., Linda J. Mason, Box 2328, Anderson, IN 46018
Bd. of Pensions, Exec. Sec.-Treas., Jeffrey A. Jenness, Box 2299, Anderson, IN 46018

Periodicals
Inform; Church of God Missions; The Shining Light; Metro Voice

The Church Of God In Christ

The Church of God in Christ was founded in 1907 in Memphis, Tennessee, and was organized by Bishop Charles Harrison Mason, a former Baptist minister who pioneered the embryonic stages of the Holiness movement beginning in 1895 in Mississippi.

Its founder organized four major departments between 1910-1916: the Women's Department, the Sunday School, Young Peoples Willing Workers and Home and Foreign Mission.

The Church is trinitarian and teaches the infallibility of scripture, the need for regeneration and subsequent baptism of the Holy Ghost. It emphasizes holiness as God's standard for Christian conduct. It recognizes as ordinances Holy Communion, Water Baptism and Feet Washing. Its governmental structure is basically episcopal with the General Assembly being the Legislative body.

Headquarters

Mason Temple, 938 Mason St., Memphis, TN 38126 Tel. (901)947-9300

Mailing Address, P.O. Box 320, Memphis, TN 38101

Temple Church Of God In Christ, 672 S. Lauderdale St., Memphis, TN 38126 Tel. (901)527-9202

GENERAL OFFICES

Office of the Presiding Bishop: Presiding Bishop, Bishop Chandler D. Owens, Tel. (901)947-9338

Office of the General Secretary: Gen. Sec., Bishop W. W. Hamilton, (901)947-9358

Office of the Financial Secretary: Sec., Bishop Frank O. White, Tel. (901)947-9310

Office of the Treasurer: Treasurer, Bishop Samuel L. Lowe, Tel. (901)947-9381

Office of the Board of Trustees: Chmn., Elder Dwight Green, Tel. (901)947-9326

Office of the Chief Operating Officer at World Headquarters: Elder A.Z. Hall, Jr., 930 Mason Street, Memphis, TN Tel. (901)947-9358

Office of the Clergy Bureau: Dir., Bishop W. W. Hamilton, Tel. (901)974-9358

Office of Supt. of National Properties: Supt., Elder Marles Flowers, Tel. (901)947-9330

Office of Accounting: Chief Financial Officer, Ms. Sylvia H. Law, Tel. (901)947-9361

Department of Evangelism: Pres., Elder Richard White, Atlanta, GA, Tel. (404)361-7020

Department of Missions: Pres. Bishop Carlis L. Moody, Tel. (901)947-9316; Vice Pres., Elder Jesse W. Denny

Dept. of Music: Pres., Ms. LuVoinia Whittley, 20205 Augusta Dr., Olympia Fields, IL 60461 Tel. (312)626-1970

Dept. of Sunday Schools: Gen. Supt., Bishop Jerry Macklin, 1027 W. Tennyson Rd., Hayward, CA 94544 (510)783-9377

Dept. of Women: Pres.-Gen. Supervisor, Mother Willie Mae Rivers, P.O. Box 1052, Memphis, TN 38101, Tel. (901)775-0600

Dept. of Youth (Youth Congress): Pres., Elder J. Drew Sheard, 7045 Curtis Dr., Detroit, MI 48235, Tel. (313)864-7170

Church of God in Christ Book Store: Mgr., Geraldine Miller, 285 S. Main St., Memphis, TN 38103 Tel. (901)947-9304

Church of God in Christ Publishing House: CEO, Dr. David A. Hall, Sr., Tel. (901)947-9342

Board of Publications: Chmn., Bishop R.L.H. Winbush, Tel. (901)947-9342

Periodicals
The Whole Truth; The Voice of Missions

Church of God in Christ, International

The Church of God in Christ, International was organized in 1969 in Kansas City, Mo., by 14 bishops of the Church of God in Christ of Memphis, Tenn. The doctrine is the same, but the separation came because of disagreement over polity and governmental authority. The Church is Wesleyan in theology (two works of grace) but stresses the experience of full baptism of the Holy Ghost with the initial evidence of speaking with other tongues as the Spirit gives utterance.

Headquarters

170 Adelphi St., Brooklyn, NY 11205 Tel. (718) 625-9175

Media Contact, Natl. Sec., Rev. Sis. Sharon R. Dunn

Officers

Presiding Bishop, Most Rev. Carl E. Williams, Sr.

Vice-Presiding Bishop, Rt. Rev. J. P. Lucas, 90 Holland St., Newark, NJ 07103

Sec.-Gen., Deacon Dennis Duke, 360 Colorado Ave., Bridgeport, CT 06605

Exec. Admn., Horace K. Williams, Word of God Center, Newark, NJ

Women's Dept., Natl. Supervisor, Evangelist Elvonia Williams

Youth Dept., Pres., Dr. Joyce Taylor, 137-17 135th Ave., S., Ozone Park, NY 11420

Music Dept., Pres., Isaiah Heyward

Bd. of Bishops, Chpsn., Bishop J. C. White, 360 Colorado Ave., Bridgeport, CT 06605

Church of God in Christ, Mennonite

The Church of God in Christ, Mennonite was organized in Ohio in 1859 by the evangelist-reformer John Holdeman. The church unites with the faith of the Waldenses, Anabaptists and other such groups. Emphasis is placed on obedience to the teachings of the Bible, including the doctrine of the new birth and spiritual life, noninvolvement in government or the military, head-coverings for the women, beards for the men and separation from the world shown by simplicity in clothing, homes, possessions and life-style. The church has a worldwide membership of about 18,300, most of them in the United States and Canada.

Headquarters
P.O. Box 313, 420 N. Wedel Ave., Moundridge, KS 67107 Tel. (316)345-2532 Fax (316)345-2582

Media Contact, Dale Koehn, P.O. Box 230, Moundridge, KS 67107 Tel. (316)345-2532 Fax (316)345-2582

Periodicals
Messenger of Truth

Church of God (Cleveland, Tennessee)

It is one of America's oldest Pentecostal churches founded in 1886 as an outgrowth of the holiness revival under the name Christian Union. In 1907 the church adopted the organizational name Church of God. It has its foundation upon the principles of Christ as revealed in the Bible. The Church of God is Christian, Protestant, foundational in its doctrine, evangelical in practice and distinctively Pentecostal. It maintains a centralized form of government and a commitment to world evangelization.

Headquarters
P.O. Box 2430, Cleveland, TN 37320 Tel. (423) 472-3361 Fax (423)478-7066

Media Contact, Dir. of Communications, Michael L. Baker, Tel. (423)478-7112 Fax (423)478-7066

EXECUTIVES
Gen. Overseer, R. Lamar Vest
Asst. Gen. Overseers, G. Dennis McGuire; T. L. Lowery; Bill F. Sheeks
Secretary General, Gene D. Rice

DEPARTMENTS
Benefits Board, CEO, Arthur Rhodes
Business & Records, Dir., Julian B. Robinson
Care and Affirmation, Dir., John D. Nichols
Chaplains Commission, Dir., Robert D. Crick
Communications/Media Ministries: Director, Michael L. Baker
Education—European Bible Seminary, Dir., John Sims
Education—Hispanic Institute of Ministry, Dir., Jose D. Montanez
Education—International Bible College, Pres., Cheryl Busse
Education—Lee University, Pres., C. Paul Conn
Education—Patten College, Chancellor, Bebe Patten
Education—Puerto Rico Bible School, Pres., Ildefonso Caraballo
Education—School of Ministry, Chancellor, Paul L. Walker

Education—Theological Seminary, President, Donald M. Walker
Evangelism & Home Missions, Dir., Orville Hagan
Evangelism—Black Ministries, Dir., Asbury R. Sellers
Evangelism—Cross-Cultural Min., Dir., Wallace J. Sibley
Evangelism—Hispanic Ministry, Dir., Esdras Betancourt
Evangelism—Native American Ministries, Dir., Douglas M. Cline
Lay Ministries, Dir., Leonard Albert
Legal Services, Dir., Dennis W. Watkins
Men/Women of Action, Dir., Hugh Carver
Ministerial Development, Dir., Larry G. Hess
Ministry to Israel, Dir., J. Michael Utterback
Ministry to the Military, Dir.,Robert A. Moore
Music Ministries, Dir., Delton Alford
Pentecostal Resource Center, Director, Frances Arrington
Publications, Dir., Daniel F. Boling
Stewardship, Dir., Al Taylor
Women's Ministries, Director, Rebecca J. Jenkins
World Missions, Dir., Lovell R. Cary
Youth & Christian Education, Dir., John D. Childers

Periodicals
Church of God Evangel; Church of God Evangelica; Save Our World; Ministry Now Profiles

Church of God by Faith, Inc.

Founded 1914, in Jacksonville Heights, Florida., by Elder John Bright, this church believes the word of God as interpreted by Jesus Christ to be the only hope of salvation and Jesus Christ the only mediator for people.

Headquarters
3220 Haines St., P.O. Box 3746, Jacksonville, FL 32206 Tel. (904)353-5111 Fax (904)355-8582
Media Contact, Ofc. Mgr., Sarah E. Lundy

Officers
Presiding Bishop, James E. McKnight, P.O. Box 121, Gainesville, FL 32601
Treas., Elder Theodore Brown, 93 Girard Pl., Newark, NJ 07108
Ruling Elders: Elder John Robinson, 300 Essex Dr., Ft. Pierce, FL 33450; Elder D. C. Rourk, 207 Chestnut Hill Dr., Rochester, NY 14617
Exec. Sec., Elder George Matthews, 8834 Camphor Dr., Jacksonville, FL 32208

Church of God General Conference (Oregon, IL and Morrow, GA)

This church is the outgrowth of several independent local groups of similar faith. Some were in existence as early as 1800, and others date their beginnings to the arrival of British immigrants around 1847. Many local churches carried the name Church of God of the Abrahamic Faith. State and district conferences of these groups were formed as an expression of mutual cooperation. A national organization was instituted at Philadelphia in 1888. Because of strong convictions on the questions of congregational rights and authority, however, it ceased to function until 1921, when the present General Conference was formed at Waterloo, Iowa.

The Bible is accepted as the supreme standard of faith. Adventist in viewpoint, the second (premillenial) coming of Christ is strongly emphasized. The church teaches that the kingdom of God will be literal, beginning in Jerusalem at the time of the return of Christ and extending to all nations. Emphasis is placed on the oneness of God and the Sonship of Christ, that Jesus did not pre-exist prior to his birth in Bethlehem and that the Holy Spirit is the power and influence of God. Membership is dependent on faith, repentance and baptism by immersion.

The work of the General Conference is carried on under the direction of the board of directors. With a congregational church government, the General Conference exists primarily as a means of mutual cooperation and for the development of yearly projects and enterprises.

The headquarters and Bible College were moved to Morrow, Ga. in 1991.

Headquarters

P.O. Box 100,000, Morrow, GA 30260 Tel. (404)362-0052 Fax (404)362-9307
Media Contact, Pres., David Krogh
Email: info@abc-coggc.org
Website: www.abc-coggc.org

Officers

Chpsn., Joe E. James, 100 Buck Dr., Piedmont, SC 29673
Vice-Chpsn., Charles Bottolfs, 43137 Happywoods Rd., Hammond, LA 70403
Pres., David Krogh, Georgia Ofc.
Sec., Pastor Greg Demmitt, 825 E. Drake Dr., Tempe, AZ 85283
Treas., Robert Huddlestun, 16440 Fairfield Ln., Granger, IN 46530

OTHER ORGANIZATIONS

Bus. Admn., Controller, Gary Burnham, Georgia Ofc.
Atlanta Bible College, Pres., David Krogh, Georgia Ofc.

Periodicals

The Restitution Herald; A Journal From the Radical Reformation; Church of God Progress Journal

Church of God, Mountain Assembly, Inc.

The church was formed in 1895 and organized in 1906 by J. H. Parks, S. N. Bryant, Tom Moses and William Douglas.

Headquarters

164 N. Florence Ave., P.O. Box 157, Jellico, TN 37762 Tel. (423)784-8260 Fax (423)784-3258
Media Contact, Gen. Sec.-Treas., Rev. Alfred Newton, Jr.
Email: cgmahdq@jellico.com
Website: www.cgmahdq.org

Officers

Gen. Overseer, Rev. Cecil Johnson
Asst. Gen. Overseer/World Missions Dir., Rev. Lonnie Lyke
Gen. Sec.-Treas., Rev. Alfred Newton, Jr.
Youth Ministries & Camp Dir., Rev. Ken Ellis

Periodicals

The Gospel Herald

Church of God of Prophecy

The Church of God of Prophecy is one of the churches that grew out of the work of A. J. Tomlinson in the first half of the twentieth century. Historically it shares a common heritage with the Church of God (Cleveland, Tennessee) and is in the mainstream of the classical Pentecostal-holiness tradition.

At the death of A. J. Tomlinson in 1943, M. A. Tomlinson was named General Overseer and served until retirement in 1990. He emphasized unity and fellowship unlimited by racial, social or political differences. The present general overseer, Billy D. Murray, Sr., is committed to promoting Christian unity world evangelization.

At the death of A.J. Tomlinson in 1943, M.A. Tomlinson was named General Overseer and served until his retirement in 1990. He emphasized unity and fellowship unlimited by racial, social, or political differences. The next General Overseer, Billy D. Murray, Sr., who served from 1990 until his retirement in 2000, emphasized a commitment to the promotion of Christian unity and world evangelization. In July 2000, Fred S. Fisher, Sr. was duly selected to serve as the fourth General Overseer of the Church of God of Prophecy.

From its beginnings, the Church has based its beliefs on "the whole Bible, rightly divided," and has accepted the Bible as God's Holy Word, inspired, inerrant and infallible. The church is firm in its commitment to orthodox Christian belief. The Church affirms that there is one God, eternally existing in three persons: Father, Son and Holy Spirit. It believes in the deity of Christ, His virgin birth, His sinless life, the physical miracles He performed, His atoning death on the cross, His bodily resurrection, His ascension to the right hand of the Father and his Second coming. The church professes that salvation results from grace alone through faith in Christ, that regeneration by the Holy Spirit is essential for the salvation of sinful men, and that sanctification by the blood of Christ makes possible personal holiness. It affirms the present ministry of the Holy Spirit by Whose indwelling believers are able to live godly lives and have power for service. The church believes in, and promotes, the ultimate unity of believers as prayed for by Christ in John 17. The church stresses the sanctity of human life and is committed to the sanctity of the marriage bond and the importance of strong, loving Christian families. Other official teachings include Holy Spirit baptism with tongues as initial evidence; manifestation of the spiritual gifts; divine healing; premillenial second-coming of Christ; total abstinence from the use of tobacco, alcohol and narcotics; water baptism by immersion; the Lord's supper and washing of the saints' feet; and a concern for moderation and holiness in all dimensions of lifestyle.

The Church is racially integrated on all levels, including top leadership. Women play a prominent role in church affairs, serving in pastoral roles and other leadership positions. The church presbytery has recently adopted plurality of leadership in the selection of a General Oversight Group. This group consists of eight bishops located around the world who, along with the General Overseer, are responsible for inspirational leadership and vision casting for the church body.

The Church has local congregations in all 50 states and more than 100 nations worldwide. Organizationally there is a strong emphasis on international missions, evangelism, youth and children's ministries, women's and men's ministries, stewardship, communications, publishing, leadership development and discipleship.

CHURCH OF GOD OF PROPHECY INTERNATIONAL OFFICES

P.O. Box 2910, Cleveland, TN 37320-2910
Media Contact, Betty J. Fisher, Tel. (423)559-5100 Fax (423)559-5108
Email: betty@cogop.org
Website: www.cogop.org

Officers

General Oversight Group: Gen. Overseer, Bishop Fred S. Fisher, Sr.; General Presbyters: Sherman Allen, Sam Clements, Daniel Corbett, Clayton Endecott, Miguel Mojica, José Reyes, Sr., Felix Santiago, Brice Thompson
International Offices Ministries Dirs.: Finance, Communications, and Publishing, Oswill Williams; Global Outreach and Administrative Asst. to the General Presbyters, Randy Howard; Leadership Development and Discipleship Ministries, Larry Duncan.

Periodicals

White Wing Messenger; Victory (Youth Magazine/ Sunday School Curriculum); The Happy Harvester

The Church of God (Seventh Day), Denver, Colorado

The Church of God (Seventh Day) began in southwestern Michigan in 1858, when a group of Sabbath-keepers led by Gilbert Cranmer refused to give endorsement to the visions and writings of Ellen G. White, a principal in the formation of the Seventh-Day Adventist Church. Another branch of Sabbath-keepers, which developed near Cedar Rapids, Iowa, in 1860, joined the Michigan church in 1863 to publish a paper called The Hope of Israel, the predecessor to the Bible Advocate, the church's present publication. As membership grew and spread into Missouri and Nebraska, it organized the General Conference of the Church of God in 1884. The words "Seventh Day" were added to its name in 1923. The headquarters of the church was in Stanberry, Missouri, from 1888 until 1950, when it moved to Denver.

The Church teaches salvation is a gift of God's grace, and is available solely by faith in Jesus Christ, the Savior; that saving faith is more than mental assent, it involves active trust and repentance from sin. Out of gratitude, Christians will give evidence of saving faith by a lifestyle that conforms to God's commandments, including the seventh-day Sabbath, which members observe as a tangible expression of their faith and rest in God as their Creator and Redeemer. The church believes in the imminent, personal, and visible return of Christ; that the dead are in an unconscious state awaiting to be resurrected, the wicked to be destroyed, and the righteous to be rewarded to eternal life in the presence of God on a restored earth. The church observes two ordinances: baptism by immersion and an annual Communion service accompanied by foot washing.

Headquarters

330 W. 152nd Ave., P.O. Box 33677, Denver, CO 80233 Tel. (303)452-7973 Fax (303)452-0657
Media Contact, Pres., Whaid Rose
Email: offices@cog7.org
Website: www.cog7.org

MINISTRIES

Missions Ministries, Dr., William Hicks: Church Planting Dir., Mike Vlad; Home Missions Dir., Ralph Diaz; Missions Abroad, Dir., Victor Burford
Publications/Bible of Advocate Press, Dir., John Crisp
Summit School of Theology, Dir., Jerry Griffin
Young Adult Ministry, Dir., Becky Riggs
Youth Ministry, Dirs., Kurt & Kristi Lang
Women's Ministry, Dir., Mary Ling
Spring Vale Academy (Para Church Ministry) Dir., John Tivald

Periodicals

The Bible Advocate

The Church of Illumination

The Church of Illumination was organized in 1908 for the express purpose of establishing congregations at large, offering a spiritual, esoteric, philosophic interpretation of the vital biblical teachings, thereby satisfying the inner spiritual needs of those seeking spiritual truth, yet permitting them to remain in, or return to, their former church membership.

Headquarters
Beverly Hall, 5966 Clymer Rd., Quakertown, PA 18951 Tel. (800)779-3796
Media Contact, Dir. General, Gerald E. Poesnecker, P.O. Box 220, Quakertown, PA 18951 Tel. (215)536-7048 Fax (215) 536-7058
Email: bevhall@comcat.com
Website: www.soul.org

Officers
Dir.-General, Gerald E. Poesnecker, P.O. Box 220, Quakertown, PA 18951

The Church of Jesus Christ (Bickertonites)
This church was organized in 1862 at Green Oak, Pa., by William Bickerton, who obeyed the Restored Gospel under Sidney Rigdon's following in 1845.

Headquarters
Sixth & Lincoln Sts., Monongahela, PA 15063 Tel. (412)258-3066
Media Contact, Exec. Sec., John Manes, 2007 Cutter Dr., McKees Rocks, PA 15136 Tel. (412)771-4513

Officers
Pres., Dominic Thomas, 6010 Barrie, Dearborn, MI 48126
First Counselor, Paul Palmieri, 319 Pine Dr., Aliquippa, PA 15001 Tel. (412)378-4264
Second Counselor, Robert Watson, Star Rt. 5, Box 36, Gallup, NM 87301
Exec. Sec., John Manes, 2007 Cutter Dr., McKees Rocks, PA 15136 Tel. (412)771-4513

Periodicals
The Gospel News

The Church of Jesus Christ of Latter-day Saints
This church was organized April 6, 1830, at Fayette, N.Y., by Joseph Smith. Members believe Joseph Smith was divinely directed to restore the gospel to the earth, and that through him the keys to the Aaronic and Melchizedek priesthoods and temple work also were restored. Members believe that both the Bible and the Book of Mormon (a record of the Lord's dealings with His people on the American continent 600 B.C. - 421 A.D.) are scripture. Membership is over eleven million.

In addition to the First Presidency, the governing bodies of the church include the Quorum of the Twelve Apostles, the Presidency of the Seventy, the Quorums of the Seventy and the Presiding Bishopric.

Headquarters
47 East South Temple St., Salt Lake City, UT 84150 Tel. (801)240-1000 Fax (801)240-1167
Media Contact, Dir., Media Relations, Michael Otterson, Tel. (801)240-4378 Fax (801)240-1167
Website: www.lds.org

Officers
Pres., Gordon B. Hinckley
1st Counselor, Thomas S. Monson
2nd Counselor, James E. Faust
Council of the Twelve Apostles: Pres., Boyd K. Packer; L. Tom Perry; David B. Haight; Neal A. Maxwell; Russell M. Nelson; Dallin H. Oaks; M. Russell Ballard; Joseph B. Wirthlin; Richard G. Scott; Robert D. Hales; Jeffrey R. Holland; Henry B. Eyring

AUXILIARY ORGANIZATIONS
Sunday Schools, Gen. Pres., Harold G. Hillam
Relief Society, Gen. Pres., Mary Ellen Smoot
Young Women, Gen. Pres., Margaret Nadauld
Young Men, Gen. Pres., Jack H. Goaslind
Primary, Gen. Pres., Patricia P. Pinegar

Periodicals
The Ensign; Liahona; The New Era; Friend Magazine

Church of the Living God (Motto: Christian Workers for Fellowship)
The Church of the Living God was founded by William Christian in April 1889 at Caine Creek, Ark. It was the first Black church in America without Anglo-Saxon roots and not begun by white missionaries.

Christian was born a slave in Mississippi on Nov. 10, 1856 and grew up uneducated. In 1875 he united with the Missionary Baptist Church and began to preach. In 1888 he left the Baptist Church and began what was known as Christian Friendship Work. Believing himself to have been inspired by the Spirit of God through divine revelation and close study of the Scriptures, he was led to the truth that the Bible refers to the church as The Church of the Living God (I Tim. 3:15).

The church believes in the infallibility of the Scriptures, is Trinitarian and believes there are three sacraments ordained by Christ: baptism (by immersion), the Lord's Supper (unleavened bread and water) and foot washing.

The Church of the Living God, C.W.F.F., believes in holiness as a gift of God subsequent to the New Birth and manifested only by a changed life acceptable to the Lord.

Headquarters
430 Forest Ave., Cincinnati, OH 45229 Tel. (513)569-5660
Media Contact, Chief Bishop, W. E. Crumes

EXECUTIVE BOARD
Chief Bishop, W. E. Crumes
Vice-Chief Bishop, Robert D. Tyler, 3802 Bedford, Omaha, NE 68110

Exec. Sec., Bishop C. A. Lewis, 1360 N. Boston, Tulsa, OK 73111

Gen. Sec., Gwendolyn Robinson, 8611 S. University, Chicago, IL 60619

Gen. Treas., Elder Harry Hendricks, 11935 Cimarron Ave., Hawthorne, CA 90250

Bishop E. L. Bowie, 2037 N.E. 18th St., Oklahoma City, OK 73111

Chaplain, Bishop E. A. Morgan, 735 S. Oakland Dr., Decatur, IL 65525;

Bishop Luke C. Nichols, Louisville, KY

Bishop Jeff Ruffin, Phoenix, AZ

Bishop R. S. Morgan, 12100 Greystone Terr., Oklahoma City, OK 73120

Bishop S. E. Shannon, 1034 S. King Hwy., St. Louis, MO 63110

Bishop J. C. Hawkins, 3804 N. Temple, Indianapolis, IN 46205

Overseer, Elbert Jones, 4522 Melwood, Memphis, TN 38109

NATIONAL DEPARTMENTS
Convention Planning Committee
Young People's Progressive Union
Christian Education Dept.
Sunday School Dept.
Natl. Evangelist Bd.
Natl. Nurses Guild
Natl. Women's Work Dept.
Natl. Music Dept.
Gen. Sec. Ofc.

Periodicals
The Gospel Truth

Church of the Lutheran Brethren of America

The Church of the Lutheran Brethren of America was organized in December 1900. Five independent Lutheran congregations met together in Milwaukee, Wisconsin, and adopted a constitution patterned very closely on that of the Lutheran Free Church of Norway.

The spiritual awakening in the Midwest during the 1890s crystallized into convictions that led to the formation of a new church body. Chief among the concerns were church membership practices, observance of Holy Communion, confirmation practices and local church government.

The Church of the Lutheran Brethren practices a simple order of worship with the sermon as the primary part of the worship service. It believes that personal profession of faith is the primary criterion for membership in the congregation. The Communion service is reserved for those who profess faith in Christ as savior. Each congregation is autonomous and the synod serves the congregations in advisory and cooperative capacities.

The synod supports a world mission program in Cameroon, Chad, Japan and Taiwan. Approximately 40 percent of the synodical budget is earmarked for world missions. A growing home mission ministry is planting new congregations in the United States and Canada. Affiliate organizations operate several retirement/nursing homes, conference and retreat centers.

Headquarters
1020 Alcott Ave., W., Box 655, Fergus Falls, MN 56538 Tel. (218)739-3336 Fax (218)739-5514
Media Contact, Pres., Rev. Robert M. Overgaard

Officers
Pres., Rev. Robert M. Overgaard, Sr.
Vice-Pres., Rev. David Rinden
Sec., Rev. Richard Vettrus, 707 Crestview Dr., West Union, IA 52175
Exec. Dir. of Finance, Bradley Martinson
Lutheran Brethren Schools, Pres., Rev. Joel Egge, Lutheran Brethren Schools, Box 317, Fergus Falls, MN 56538
World Missions, Exec. Dir., Rev. Matthew Rogness
Home Missions, Exec. Dir., Rev. Armin Jahr
Church Services, Exec. Dir., Rev. Brent Juliot
Youth Ministries, Exec. Dir., Nathan Lee

Periodicals
Faith & Fellowship

Church of the Lutheran Confession

The Church of the Lutheran Confession held its constituting convention in Watertown, S.D., in August of 1960. The Church of the Lutheran Confession was begun by people and congregations who withdrew from church bodies that made up what was then known as the Synodical Conference over the issue of unionism. Following such passages as I Corinthians 1:10 and Romans 16:17-18, the Church of the Lutheran Confession holds the conviction that mutual agreement with the doctrines of Scripture is essential and necessary before exercise of church fellowship is appropriate.

Members of the Church of the Lutheran Confession uncompromisingly believe the Holy Scriptures to be divinely inspired and therefore inerrant. They subscribe to the historic Lutheran Confessions as found in the Book of Concord of 1580 because they are a correct exposition of Scripture.

The Church of the Lutheran Confession exists to proclaim, preserve and spread the saving truth of the gospel of Jesus Christ, so that the redeemed of God may learn to know Jesus Christ as their Lord and Savior and follow him through this life to the life to come.

Headquarters
501 Grover Rd., Eau Claire, WI 54701 Tel. (715)836-6622
Media Contact, Pres., Daniel Fleischer Tel.(361)241-5147
Email: JohnHLau@juno.com
Website: www.clclutheran.org

Officers
Pres., Rev. Daniel Fleischer, 201 Princess Dr., Corpus Christi, TX 78410-1615

Vice-Pres., Rev. John Schierenbeck, 3015 Ave. K NW, Winter Haven, FL 33881

Mod., Prof. Ronald Roehl, 515 Ingram Dr. W., Eau Claire, WI 54701

Sec., Rev. James Albrecht, 102 Market St., P.O. Box 98 Okebena, MN 55432-2408

Treas., Lowell Moen, 3455 Jill Ave., Eau Claire, WI 54701

Archivist, Prof. David Lau, 507 Ingram Dr., Eau Claire, WI 54701

Statistician, Dr. James Sydow, 7863 Alden Way, Fridley, MN 55432-2408

Periodicals
The Lutheran Spokesman; Journal of Theology

Church of the Nazarene

The Church of the Nazarene resulted from the merger of three independent holiness groups. The Association of Pentecostal Churches in America, located principally in New York and New England, joined at Chicago in 1907 with a largely West Coast body called the Church of the Nazarene and formed the Pentecostal Church of the Nazarene. A southern group, the Holiness Church of Christ, united with the Pentecostal Church of the Nazarene at Pilot Point, Texas, in 1908. In 1919 the word "Pentecostal" was dropped from the name. Principal leaders in the organization were Phineas Bresee, William Howard Hoople, H. F. Reynolds and C. B. Jernigan. The first congregation in Canada was organized in November 1902 by Dr. H. F. Reynolds in Oxford, Nova Scotia.

The Church of the Nazarene emphasizes the doctrine of entire sanctification or Christian Holiness. It stresses the importance of a devout and holy life and a positive witness before the world by the power of the Holy Spirit. Nazarenes express their faith through evangelism, compassionate ministries, and education.

Nazarene government is representative, a studied compromise between episcopacy and congregationalism. Quadrennially, the various districts elect delegates to a general assembly at which six general superintendents are elected.

The international denomination has 9 liberal arts colleges, two graduate seminaries, 43 Bible colleges, two schools of nursing, and a junior college. The church maintains over 600 missionaries in 119 world areas. World services include medical, educational and religious ministries. Books, periodicals and other Christian literature are published at the Nazarene Publishing House. The church is a member of the Christian Holiness Partnership and the National Association of Evangelicals.

Headquarters
6401 The Paseo, Kansas City, MO 64131 Tel. (816)333-7000 Fax (816)822-9071

Media Contact, Gen. Sec./Headquarters Operations Officer (HOO), Dr. Jack Stone, Tel. (816)333-7000, Ext. 2517

Officers
Gen. Supts.: John A. Knight; William J. Prince; James H. Diehl; Paul G. Cunningham; Jerry D. Porter; Jim L. Bond

Gen. Sec. (HOO), Jack Stone

Gen. Treas. (HFO), Robert Foster

OTHER ORGANIZATIONS

General Bd.: Sec., Jack Stone; Treas., Robert Foster

Evangelism & Church Growth Div., Dir., Bill Sullivan

Chaplaincy Min., Dir., Curt Bowers

Pastoral Min., Dir., Wilbur Brannon

Communications Div., Dir., Michael Estep

NCN Productions, Dir., David Anderson

World Literature Ministries, Dir., Ray Hendrix

Int. Bd. of Educ., Ed. Commissioner, Jerry Lambert

Pensions & Benefits Services USA & Intl., Don Walter

Stewardship Development, Dir., Steve Weber

Sunday School Min. Div., Dir., Talmadge Johnson

Adult Min., Dir., David Felter

Children's Min., Dir., Lynda Boardman

Cirriculum Dir., Randy Cloud

NYI Min., Dir., Fred Fullerton

World Mission Div., Dir., Louie Bustle

Nazarene World Mission Soc., Dir., Nina Gunter

Mission Strategy, Dir., Tom Nees

Periodicals
Holiness Today; Preacher's Magazine; Cross Walk; Grow Magazine

Church of Our Lord Jesus Christ of the Apostolic Faith, Inc.

This church body was founded by Bishop R.C. Lawson in Columbus, Ohio, and moved to New York City in 1919. It is founded upon the teachings of the apostles and prophets, Jesus Christ being its chief cornerstone.

Headquarters
2081 Adam Clayton Powell Jr. Blvd., New York, NY 10027 Tel. (212)866-1700

Media Contact, Exec. Sec., Bishop T. E. Woolfolk, P.O. Box 119, Oxford, NC 27565 Tel. (919)693-9449 Fax (919)693-6115

Officers
Board of Apostles: Chief Apostle, Bishop William L. Bonner;

Presiding Apostle, Bishop Gentle L. Groover; Bishop Frank S. Solomon;

Vice-Presider, Bishop Matthew A. Norwood; Bishop James I. Clark, Jr.; Bishop Wilbur L. Jones; Bishop J. P. Steadman

Bd. of Bishops, Chmn., Bishop Henry A. Moultrie II

Bd. of Presbyters, Pres., Elder Michael A. Dixon

Exec. Sec., Bishop T. E. Woolfolk

Natl. Rec. Sec., Bishop Fred Rubin, Sr.

Natl. Fin. Sec., Bishop Clarence Groover

Natl. Corr. Sec., Bishop Raymond J. Keith, Jr.
Natl Treas., Elder Richard D. Williams

Periodicals
Contender for the Faith; Minute Book

Church of the United Brethren in Christ

The Church of the United Brethren in Christ had its beginning with Philip William Otterbein and Martin Boehm, who were leaders in the revival movement in Pennsylvania and Maryland from the late 1760s into the early 1800s.

On Sept. 25, 1800, they and others associated with them formed a society under the name of United Brethren in Christ. Subsequent conferences adopted a Confession of Faith in 1815 and a constitution in 1841. The Church of the United Brethren in Christ adheres to the original constitution as amended in 1957, 1961 and 1977.

Headquarters
302 Lake St., Huntington, IN 46750 Tel. (219) 356-2312 Fax (219)356-4730
Media Contact, Communications Dir., Steve Dennie
Email: sdennie@ub.org
Website: www.ub.org

Officers
Bishop, Dr. Ray A. Seilhamer
Gen. Treas./Office Mgr., Marda J. Hoffman
Dept. of Education, Dir., Dr. G. Blair Dowden
Dept. of Church Services, Dir., Rev. Paul Hirschy
Dept. of Missions, Dir., Rev. Kyle McQuillen

Churches of Christ

Churches of Christ are autonomous congregations whose members appeal to the Bible alone to determine matters of faith and practice. There are no central offices or officers. Publications and institutions related to the churches are either under local congregational control or independent of any one congregation.

Churches of Christ shared a common fellowship in the 19th century with the Christian Churches/Churches of Christ and the Christian Church (Disciples of Christ). Fellowship was gradually estranged following the Civil War due to theistic evolution, higher critical theories, centralization of church-wide activities through a missionary society and addition of musical instruments.

Members of Churches of Christ believe in one God, one Lord and Savior, Jesus Christ, one Holy Spirit, one body or church of God, one baptism by immersion into Christ, one faith revealed in the Holy, inspired, inerrant scriptures and one hope of eternal life based on the grace of God in Christ and a response by each individual of faith and obedience to God's gracious instructions in scripture. The New Testament pattern is followed for salvation and church membership, church organization and standards of Christian living.

Headquarters
Media Contact, Ed., Gospel Advocate, Dr. F. Furman Kearley, 1404 Mockingbird Ln., Corsicana, TX 75110

Periodicals
Action; Christian Woman; Christian Bible Teacher; The Christian Chronicle; Firm Foundation; Gospel Advocate; Guardian of Truth; Restoration Quarterly; 21st Century Christian; Upreach; Rocky Mountain Christian; The Spiritual Sword; Word and Work

Churches of Christ in Christian Union

Organized in 1909 at Washington Court House, Ohio, as the Churches of Christ in Christian Union, this body believes in the new birth and the baptism of the Holy Spirit for believers. It is Wesleyan, with an evangelistic and missionary emphasis.

The Reformed Methodist Church merged with the Churches of Christ in Christian Union in 1952.

Headquarters
1426 Lancaster Pike, Box 30, Circleville, OH 43113 Tel. (614)474-8856 Fax (614)477-7766
Media Contact, Dir. of Comm., Rev. Ralph Hux

Officers
Gen. Supt., Dr. Daniel Tipton
Asst. Gen. Supt., Rev. Ron Reese
Gen. Treas.,
Gen. Bd. of Trustees: Chpsn., Dr. Daniel Tipton; Vice-Chpsn., Rev. Ron Reese
District Superintendents: West Central District, Rev. Ron Reese; South Central District, Rev. Don Spurgeon; Northeast District, Rev. Don Seymour; West Indies District, Rev. Stafford Prosper

Periodicals
The Evangelical Advocate

Churches of God, General Conference

The Churches of God, General Conference (CGGC) had its beginnings in Harrisburg, Pa., in 1825.

John Winebrenner, recognized founder of the Church of God movement, was an ordained minister of the German Reformed Church. His experience-centered form of Christianity, particularly the "new measures" he used to promote it, his close connection with the local Methodists, his "experience and conference meetings" in the church and his 'social prayer meetings" in parishioners' homes resulted in differences of opinion and the establishment of new congregations. Extensive revivals, camp meetings and mission endeavors led to the organization of additional congregations across central Pennsylvania and westward through Ohio, Indiana, Illinois and Iowa.

In 1830 the first system of cooperation between local churches was initiated as an "eldership" in eastern Pennsylvania. The organization of other elderships followed. General Eldership was organized in 1845, and in 1974 the official name of the denomination was changed from General Eldership of the Churches of God in North America to its present name.

The Churches of God, General Conference, is composed of 16 conferences in the United States and 1 conference in Haiti. The polity of the church is presbyterial in form. The church has mission ministries in the southwest among native Americans and is extensively involved in church planting and whole life ministries in Bangladesh, Brazil, Haiti and India.

The General Conference convenes in business session triennially. An Administrative Council composed of 16 regional representatives is responsible for the administration and ministries of the church between sessions of the General Conference.

Headquarters

Legal Headquarters, United Church Center, Rm. 213, 900 S. Arlington Ave., Harrisburg, PA 17109 Tel. (717)652-0255

Administrative Offices, General Conf. Dir., Pastor Wayne W. Boyer, 700 E. Melrose Ave., P.O. Box 926, Findlay, OH 45839 Tel. (419)424-1961 Fax (419)424-3343

Media Contact, Editor, Martin A. Cordell, P.O. Box 926, Findlay, OH 45839 Tel. (419) 424-1961 Fax (419)424-3343

Email: director@cggc.org

Website: www.cggc.org

Officers

Pres., Glenn E. Beatty, 1114 Circle Dr., Latrobe, PA 15650 Tel. (412)539-9400

Journalizing Sec., Dr. C. Darrell Prichard, 2412 Sweetwater Dr., Findlay, OH 45840 Tel. (419)424-9777

Treas., Robert E. Stephenson, 700 E. Melrose Ave., P.O. Box 926, Findlay, OH 45839 Tel. (419)424-1961

DEPARTMENTS

Cross-Cultural Ministries, Pastor Don Dennison
Pensions, Mr. James P. Thomas
Denominational Communications, Martin A. Cordell
Church Renewal, Pastor Keith L. Raderstorf
Church Planting, Pastor Charles A. Hirschy
Youth & Family Life Ministries, Susan L. Callaway

Periodicals

The Church Advocate; The Gem; The Missionary Signal

Congregational Holiness Church

This body was organized in 1921 and embraces the doctrine of Holiness and Pentecost. It carries on mission work in Mexico, Honduras, Costa Rica, Cuba, Brazil, Guatemala, India, Nicaragua, El Salvador, Venezula, Panama, and Chile.

Headquarters

3888 Fayetteville Hwy., Griffin, GA 30223 Tel. (404)228-4833 Fax (404)228-1177

Media Contact, Gen. Supt., Bishop Chet Smith

Website: www.ch.church.com

EXECUTIVE BOARD

Gen. Supt., Bishop Chet Smith
1st Asst. Gen. Supt., Rev. William L. Lewis
2nd Asst. Gen. Supt., Rev. Wayne Hicks
Gen. Sec., Rev. Leslee Bailey
Gen. Treas., Rev. Ronald Wilson

Periodicals

The Gospel Messenger

Conservative Baptist Association of America (CBAmerica)

The Conservative Baptist Association of America (now known as CBAmerica) was organized May 17, 1947 at Atlantic City, N.J. The Old and New Testaments are regarded as the divinely inspired Word of God and are therefore infallible and of supreme authority. Each local church is independent, autonomous and free from ecclesiastical or political authority.

CBAmerica provides wide-ranging support to its affiliate churches and individuals through nine regional associations. CBA offers personnel to assist churches in areas such as growth and health conflict resolution and financial analysis. The association supports its clergy with retirement planning, referrals for new places of ministry and spiritual counseling. The Conservative Baptist Women's Ministries assists women in the church to be effective in their personal growth and leadership.

Each June or July there is a National Conference giving members an opportunity for fellowship, inspiration and motivation.

Headquarters

1501 W. Mineral Ave., Suite B, Littleton, CO 80120-5612, Tel. (888)627-1995 or (720)283-3030 Fax (720)283-3333

Media Contact, Executive Administrator, Rev. Ed Mitchell

Email: cba@cbamerica.org

Website: www.cbamerica.org

OTHER ORGANIZATIONS

CBInternational, Exec. Dir., Dr. Hans Finzel, 1501 W. Mineral Ave., Littleton, CO 80120-5612

Mission to the Americas, Exec. Dir., Rev. Rick Miller, Box 828, Wheaton, IL 60189

Conservative Baptist Higher Ed. Council, Dr. Brent Garrison, Southwestern College, 2625 E. Cactus Rd., Phoenix, AZ 85032

Periodicals

Spectrum; Front Line

Conservative Congregational Christian Conference

In the 1930s, evangelicals within the Congregational Christian Churches felt a definite need for fellowship and service. By 1945, this loose association crystallized into the Conservative Congregational Christian Fellowship, committed to maintaining a faithful, biblical witness.

In 1948 in Chicago, the Conservative Congregational Christian Conference was established to provide a continuing fellowship for evangelical churches and ministers on the national level. In recent years, many churches have joined the Conference from backgrounds other than Congregational. These churches include Community or Bible Churches and churches from the Evangelical and Reformed background that are truly congregational in polity and thoroughly evangelical in conviction. The CCCC welcomes all evangelical churches that are, in fact, congregational. The CCCC believes in the necessity of a regenerate membership, the authority of the Holy Scriptures, the Lordship of Jesus Christ, the autonomy of the local church and the universal fellowship of all Christians.

The Conservative Congregational Christian Conference is a member of the World Evangelical Congregational Fellowship (formed in 1986 in London, England) and the National Association of Evangelicals.

Headquarters
7582 Currell Blvd., Ste. #108, St. Paul, MN 55125 Tel. (651)739-1474 Fax (651)739-0750
Media Contact, Conf. Min., Rev. Clifford R. Christensen

Officers
Pres., Rev. Edward Whitman, 59 Province Rd., Barrington, NH 03825
Vice-Pres., Rev. Larry Scovil, 317 W. 40th Street, Scottsbluff, NE 69361
Conf. Min., Rev. Clifford R. Christensen, 457 S. Mary St., Maplewood, MN 55119
Controller, Mr. Orrin Bailey, 4260 East Lake Rd., Muskegon, MI 49444
Treas., Rev. Tay Kersey, 8450 Eastwood Rd., Moundsview, MN 55112
Sec., Rev. Peter Murdy, 4 Plympton St., Middleboro, MA 02346
Editor, Mr. Bill Nygren, P.O. Box 423, La Pointe, WI 54850
Historian, Rev. Milton Reimer, 507 Central Ave., New Rockford, ND 58356

Periodicals
Foresee

Conservative Lutheran Association

The Conservative Lutheran Association (CLA) was originally named Lutheran's Alert National (LAN) when it was founded in 1965 by 10 conservative Lutheran pastors and laymen

meeting in Cedar Rapids, Iowa. Its purpose was to help preserve from erosion the basic doctrines of Christian theology, including the inerrancy of Holy Scripture. The group grew to a worldwide constituency, similarly concerned with maintaining the doctrinal integrity of the Bible and the Lutheran Confessions.

Headquarters
Trinity Lutheran Church, 4101 E. Nohl Ranch Rd., Anaheim, CA 92807 Tel. (714)637-8370
Media Contact, Pres., Rev. P. J. Moore
Email: PastorPJ@ix.netcom.com

Officers
Pres., Rev. P. J. Moore, 4101 E. Nohl Ranch Rd., Anaheim, CA 92807 Tel. (714)637-8370
Vice-Pres., Rev. Dr. R. H. Redal, 409 Tacoma Ave. N., Tacoma, WA 98403 Tel. (206)383-5528
Faith Seminary, Dean, Rev. Dr. Michael J. Adams, 3504 N. Pearl St., P.O. Box 7186, Tacoma, WA 98407 Tel. (888)777-7675 Fax (206)759-1790

Coptic Orthodox Church*

This body is part of the ancient Coptic Orthodox Church of Egypt which is currently headed by His Holiness Pope Shenouda III, 116th Successor to St. Mark the Apostle. Egyptian immigrants have organized many parishes in the United States. Copts exist outside Egypt in Ethiopia, Europe, Asia, Australia, Canada and the United States. The total world Coptic community is estimated at 27 million. The church is in full communion with the other members of The Oriental Orthodox Church Family, The Syrian Orthodox Church, Armenian Orthodox Church, Ethiopian Orthodox Church, the Syrian Orthodox Church in India and the Eritrean Orthodox Church.

Headquarters
427 West Side Ave., Jersey City, NJ 07304 Tel. (201)333-0004 Fax (201)333-0502
Media Contact, Fr. Abraam D. Sleman

CORRESPONDENT
Fr. Abraam D. Sleman

Cumberland Presbyterian Church

The Cumberland Presbyterian Church was organized in Dickson County, Tennessee, on Feb. 4, 1810. It was an outgrowth of the Great Revival of 1800 on the Kentucky and Tennessee frontier. The founders were Finis Ewing, Samuel King and Samuel McAdow, ministers in the Presbyterian Church who rejected the doctrine of election and reprobation as taught in the Westminster Confession of Faith.

By 1813, the Cumberland Presbytery had grown to encompass three presbyteries, which constituted a synod. This synod met at the Beech Church in Sumner County, Tenn., and formulated a "Brief Statement" which set forth the points

95

in which Cumberland Presbyterians dissented from the Westminster Confession. These points are:

1. That there are no eternal reprobates;
2. That Christ died not for some, but for all people;
3. That all those dying in infancy are saved through Christ and the sanctification of the Spirit;
4. That the Spirit of God operates on the world, or as coextensively as Christ has made atonement, in such a manner as to leave everyone inexcusable.

From its birth in 1810, the Cumberland Presbyterian Church grew to a membership of 200,000 at the turn of the century. In 1906 the church voted to merge with the then-Presbyterian Church. Those who dissented from the merger became the nucleus of the continuing Cumberland Presbyterian Church.

Headquarters

1978 Union Ave., Memphis, TN 38104 Tel. (901)276-4572 Fax (901)272-3913

Media Contact, Stated Clk., Rev. Robert D. Rush, Fax (901)276-4578

Email: assembly@cumberland.org

Website: www.cumberland.org

Officers

Mod., Bob G. Roberts, 7309 Ledoux, Fort Worth, TX 76134 Tel. (817)293-2691

Stated Clk., Rev. Robert D. Rush, Tel.(901)276-4572 Fax (901) 276-4578

General Assembly Council, Exec. Dir., Davis Gray, Tel.(901)276-4572 x. 3316 Fax (901) 272-3913

INSTITUTIONS

Cumberland Presbyterian Children's Home, Exec. Dir., Rev. Dr. Judy Keith, Drawer G, Denton, TX 76202 Tel. (940)382-5112 Fax (940)387-0821; E-mail: cpch@gte.net

Cumberland Presbyterian Center, Tel.(901)276-4572 Fax (901)272-3913

Memphis Theological Seminary, Pres., Dr. Larry Blakeburn, 168 E. Parkway S., Memphis, TN 38104 Tel. (901)458-8232 Fax (901)452-4051; E-mail: wa4mff@aol.com

Bethel College, Pres., Dr. Robert Prosser, 325 Cherry St., McKenzie, TN 38201 Tel. (901)352-4004 Fax (901)352-4069; E-mail: rprosser@bethel-college.edu

Historical Foundation, Archivist, Susan K. Gore, 1978 Union Avenue, Memphis, TN 38104, Tel. 901-276-8602 Fax 901-272-3913

BOARDS

Bd. of Christian Education, Exec. Dir., Claudette Pickle

Bd. of Missions, Exec. Dir., Rev. Michael Sharpe

Bd. of Stewardship, Exec. Sec., Rev. Richard Magrill

Bd. Of the Cumberland Presbyterian, Editor, Mrs. Pat Pottorrff Richards

Periodicals

The Cumberland Presbyterian; The Missionary Messenger

Cumberland Presbyterian Church in America

This church, originally known as the Colored Cumberland Presbyterian Church, was formed in May 1874. In May 1869, at the General Assembly meeting in Murfreesboro, Tennessee, Moses Weir of the Black delegation sucessfully appealed for help in organizing a separate African church so that: Blacks could learn self-reliance and independence; they could have more financial assistance; they could minister more effectively among Blacks; and they could worship close to the altar, not in the balconies. He requested that the Cumberland Presbyterian Church organize Blacks into presbyteries and synods, develop schools to train black clergy, grant loans to assist Blacks to secure hymnbooks, Bibles and church buildings and establish a separate General Assembly.

In 1874 the first General Assembly of the Colored Cumberland Presbyterian Church met in Nashville. The moderator was Rev. P. Price and the stated clerk was Elder John Humphrey.

The denomination's General Assembly, the national governing body, is organized around its three program boards and agencies: Finance, Publication and Christian Education, and Missions and Evangelism. Other agencies of the General Assembly are under these three program boards.

The church has four synods (Alabama, Kentucky, Tennessee and Texas), 15 presbyteries and 153 congregations. The CPC extends as far north as Cleveland, Ohio, and Chicago, as far west as Marshalltown, Iowa, and Dallas, Tex., and as far south as Selma, Ala.

Headquarters

Media Contact, Stated Clk., Rev. Dr. Robert Stanley Wood, 226 Church St., Huntsville, AL 35801 Tel. (205)536-7481 Fax (205)536-7482

Officers

Mod., Rev. Endia Scruggs, 1627 Carroll Rd., Harvest, AL 35749

Stated Clk., Rev. Dr. Robert Stanley Wood, 226 Church St., Huntsville, AL 35801 Tel. (205) 536-7481

SYNODS

Alabama, Stated Clk., Arthur Hinton, 511 10th Ave. N.W., Aliceville, AL 35442

Kentucky, Stated Clk., Mary Martha Daniels, 8548 Rhodes Ave., Chicago, IL 60619

Tennessee, Stated Clk., Elder Clarence Norman, 145 Jones St., Huntington, TN 38334

Texas, Stated Clk., Arthur King, 2435 Kristen, Dallas, TX 75216

Periodicals

The Cumberland Flag

Elim Fellowship

The Elim Fellowship, a Pentecostal Body established in 1947, is an outgrowth of the Elim Missionary Assemblies formed in 1933.

It is an association of churches, ministers and missionaries seeking to serve the whole Body of Christ. It is of Pentecostal conviction and charismatic orientation, providing ministerial credentials and counsel and encouraging fellowship among local churches. Elim Fellowship sponsors leadership seminars at home and abroad and serves as a transdenominational agency sending long-term, short-term and tent-making missionaries to work with national movements.

Headquarters

1703 Dalton Rd., Lima, NY 14485 Tel. (716)582-2790 Fax (716)624-1229
Media Contact, Gen. Sec., Paul Anderson
Email: 75551.743@compuserve.com
Website: www.ElimFellowship.org

Officers

Gen. Chairman, Bernard J. Evans
Asst. Gen. Chairman, George Veach
Gen. Treas., Michael McDonald

Periodicals

Elim Herald

Episcopal Church*

The Episcopal Church entered the colonies with the earliest settlers at Jamestown, Va., in 1607 as the Church of England. After the American Revolution, it became autonomous in 1789 as The Protestant Episcopal Church in the United States of America. (The Episcopal Church became the official alternate name in 1967.) Samuel Seabury of Connecticut was elected the first bishop and consecrated in Aberdeen by bishops of the Scottish Episcopal Church in 1784.

In organizing as an independent body, the Episcopal Church created a bicameral legislature, the General Convention, modeled after the new U.S. Congress. It comprises a House of Bishops and a House of Deputies and meets every three years. A 38-member Executive Council, which meets three times a year, is the interim governing body. An elected presiding bishop serves as Primate and Chief Pastor.

After severe setbacks in the years immediately following the Revolution because of its association with the British Crown and the fact that a number of its clergy and members were Loyalists, the church soon established its own identity and sense of mission. It sent missionaries into the newly settled territories of the United States, establishing dioceses from coast to coast, and also undertook substantial missionary work in Africa, Latin America and the Far East. Today, the overseas dioceses are developing into independent provinces of the Anglican Communion, the worldwide fellowship of 36 churches in communion with the Church of England and the Archbishop of Canterbury.

The beliefs and practices of The Episcopal Church, like those of other Anglican churches, are both Catholic and Reformed, with bishops in the apostolic succession and the historic creeds of Christendom regarded as essential elements of faith and order, along with the primary authority of Holy Scripture and the two chief sacraments of Baptism and Eucharist.

EPISCOPAL CHURCH CENTER

815 Second Ave., New York, NY 10017 Tel. (212)716-6240 or (800)334-7626 Fax (212)867-0395 or (212)490-3298
Media Contact, Dir. of News & Info., James Solheim, (212)922-5385
Website: www.ecusa.anglican.org

Officers

Presiding Bishop & Primate, Most Rev. Frank Tracy Griswold III
Vice Pres & Assist. to the Presiding Bishop for Administration, Patricia C. Mordecai
Assistant to the Presiding Bishop for Communication, Barbara L. Braver
Assistant to the Presiding Bishop for Program, Ms. Sonia Francis
Treas., Stephen C. Duggan
Canon to the Primate and Presiding Bishop, The Rev. Canon Carlson Gerdau
House of Deputies: Pres., Pamela P. Chinnis
Exec. Officer of the General Convention, Sec. Of the House of Deputies, Sec. Of the Domestic and Foreign Missionary Society, and Sec. Of the Executive Council, The Rev. Rosemari Sullivan

OFFICE OF THE PRESIDING BISHOP

Presiding Bishop, Most Rev. Frank Tracy Griswold III, 212-922-5322
Vice Pres. Assistant to the Presiding Bishop for Administration, Patricia Mordecai, 212-922-5313
Canon to the Presiding Bishop, Rev. Canon Carl Gerdau, 212-922-5282
Exec. Dir., Church Deployment Office, The Rev. James G. Wilson, 212-922-5251
Coordinator for Ministry Development, The Rev. Dr. Melford E. Holland, Jr., 212-922-5246
Exec. Dir., Office of Pastoral Dev., Rt. Rev. F. Clayton Mathews, 212-716-6163
Exec. Sec., General Board of Examining Chaplains, The Rev. Locke E. Bowman Jr., 919-489-1422
Suffragan Bishop for the Armed Forces, Rt. Rev. Charles L. Keyser, 212-922-5240
Suffragan Bishop for American Churches in Europe, Rt. Rev. Jeffery Rowthorn, 011-33-1-472-01792
Dir., Ecumenical and Interfaith Relations, The Rev. Canon David W. Perry, 212-716-6220

ADMINISTRATION AND FINANCE

Treasurer of the Domestic and Foreign Missionary Society and of the General Convention, Stephen C. Duggan, 212-922-5296

Controller, Thomas Hershkowitz, 212-922-5366

Archivist, Mark Duffy, 800-525-9329

Human Resources, John Colon, 212-922-5158

SERVICE, EDUCATION AND WITNESS

Asst. to the Presiding Bishop for Program, Sonia Francis, 212-922-5198

Dir., Anglican and Global Relations, The Rev. Canon Patrick Mauney, 212-716-6223

Dir., Congregational Ministries, Rev. Winston Ching, 212-922-5344

Editor, Episcopal Life, Jerry Hames, 212-716-6009

Interim Dir., Media Services, The Rev. Clement Lee, 212-922-5386

Dir., News & Information, James Solheim, 212-922-5385

Dir., Migration Ministries, Richard Parkins, 212-716-6252

Dir., Peace & Justice Ministries, The Rev. Brian Grieves, 212-922-5207

Dir., Ministries to the Young & Young Adult Ministries Staff Officer, Thomas Chu, 212-922-5267

Exec Dir., Presiding Bishop's Fund for World Relief, Sandra Swan, 212-716-6020

BISHOPS IN THE U.S.A.

(C)= Coadjutor; (S)= Suffragan; (A)= Assistant

Address: Right Reverend

Presiding Bishop & Primate, Most Rev. Frank Tracy Griswold III; Pastoral Dev., Rt. Rev. Harold Hopkins; S. Bishop for Chaplaincies to Military\Prisons\Hosp., Rt. Rev. Charles L. Keyser 212-922-5240

Alabama: Henry N. Parsley, Jr., 521 N. 20th St., Birmingham, AL 35203, 205-715-2066

Alaska: Mark MacDonald, David Elsensohn, 1205 Denali Way, Fairbanks, AK 99701-4137, 907-452-3040

Albany: Daniel W. Herzog, 68 S. Swan St., Albany, NY 12210-2301, 518-465-4737

Arizona: Robert Shahan, 114 W. Roosevelt, Phoenix, AZ 85003-1406, 602-254-0976

Arkansas: Larry E. Maze, P.O. Box 162668, Little Rock, AR 72216-4668, 501-372-2168

Atlanta: Frank Kellog Allan, 2744 Peachtree Rd. N.W., Atlanta, GA 30363, 404-365-1010

Bethlehem: Paul Marshall, 333 Wyandotte St., Bethlehem, PA 18015, 610-691-5655

California: William E. Swing, 1055 Taylor St., San Francisco, CA 94115, 415-288-9712

Central Florida: John H. Howe, 1017 E. Robinson St., Orlando, FL 32801, 407-423-3567

Central Gulf Coast: Charles F. Duvall, P.O. Box 13330, Pensacola, FL 32591-3330, 904-434-7337

Central New York: David B. Joslin, 310 Montgomery St., Ste. 200, Syracuse, NY 13202, 315-474-6596

Central Pennsylvania: Michael Creighton, P.O. Box 11937, Harrisburg, PA 17108, 717-236-5959

Chicago: William D. Persell, 65 E. Huron St., Chicago, IL 60611, 312-751-4200

Colorado: William J. Winterrowd, 1300 Washington St., Denver, CO 80203, 303-837-1173

Connecticut: Clarence N. Coleridge, 1335 Asylum Ave., Hartford, CT 06105, 203-233-4481

Dallas: James M. Stanton, 1630 Garrett St., Dallas, TX 75206, 214-826-8310

Delaware: Wayne P. Wright, 2020 Tatnall St., Wilmington, DE 19802, 302-656-5441

East Carolina: Clifton Daniel III, P.O. Box 1336, Kinston, NC 28501, 919-522-0885

East Tennessee: Charles Von Rosenberg, 401 Cumberland Ave., Knoxville, TN 37902-2302, 615-521-2900

Eastern Michigan: Edward Leidel, 4611 Swede Ave., Midland, MI 48642, 517-752-6020

Eastern Oregon: Rustin R. Kimsey, P.O. Box 620, The Dalles, OR 97058, 541-298-4477

Easton: Martin G. Townsend, P.O. Box 1027, Easton, MD 21601, 410-822-1919

Eau Claire: Keith B. Whitmore, 510 S. Farwell St., Eau Claire, WI 54701, 715-835-3331

El Camino Real: Richard Shimpfky, P.O. Box 1903, Monterey, CA 93940, 408-394-4465

Florida: Stephen H. Jecko, 325 Market St., Jacksonville, FL 32202, 904-356-1328

Fond du Lac: Russell E. Jacobus, P.O. Box 149, Fond du Lac, WI 54936, 414-921-8866

Fort Worth: Jack Iker, 6300 Ridgelea Pl., Ste. 1100, Fort Worth, TX 76116, 817-738-9952

Georgia: Henry Louttit, Jr., 611 East Bay St., Savannah, GA 31401, 912-236-4279

Hawaii: Richard Chang, 229 Queen Emma Square, Honolulu, HI 96813, 808-536-7776

Idaho: Harry B. Bainbridge, P.O. Box 936, Boise, ID 83701, 208-345-4440

Indianapolis: Catherine M. Waynick, 1100 W. 42nd St., Indianapolis, IN 46208, 317-926-5454

Iowa: C. Christopher Epting, 225 37th St., Des Moines, IA 50312, 515-277-6165

Kansas: William E. Smalley, 833-35 Polk St., Topeka, KS 66612, 913-235-9255

Kentucky: Edwin F. Gulick, 600 E. Maine, Louisville, KY 40202, 502-584-7148

Lexington: Don A. Wimberly, P.O. Box 610, Lexington, KY 40586, 606-252-6527

Long Island: Orris G. Walker, 36 Cathedral Ave., Garden City, NY 11530, 516-248-4800

Los Angeles: Frederick H. Borsch; Chester Talton, (S), P.O. Box 2164, Los Angeles, CA 90051, 213-482-2040

Louisiana: Charles E. Jenkins, 1623 7th St., New Orleans, LA 70115-4411, 504-895-6634

Maine: Chilton Knudsen, 143 State St., Portland, ME 04101, 207-772-1953

Maryland: Bob Ihloff, 4 East University Pkwy., Baltimore, MD 21218-2437, 410-467-1399

Massachusetts: M. Thomas Shaw, SSJE; Barbara Harris, (S), 138 Tremont St., Boston, MA 02111, 617-482-5800

98

Michigan: R. Stewart Wood, Jr., 4800 Woodward Ave., Detroit, MI 48201, 313-832-4400

Milwaukee: Roger J. White, 804 E. Juneau Ave., Milwaukee, WI 53202, 414-272-3028

Minnesota: James L. Jelinek; 430 Oak Grove St., #306, Minneapolis, MN 55403, 612-871-5311

Mississippi: Alfred C. Marble, P.O. Box 23107, Jackson, MS 39225-3107, 601-948-5954

Missouri: Hays Rockwell, 1210 Locust St., St. Louis, MO 63103, 314-231-1220

Montana: Charles I. Jones, 515 North Park Ave., Helena, MT 59601, 406-442-2230

Nebraska: James E. Krotz, 200 N. 62nd St., Omaha, NE 68132, 402-341-5373

Nevada: Stewart C. Zabriskie, P.O. Box 6357, Reno, NV 89513, 702-737-9190

New Hampshire: Douglas E. Theuner, 63 Green St., Concord, NH 03301, 603-224-1914

New Jersey: Joe M. Doss, 808 W. State St., Trenton, NJ 08618

New York: Richard F. Grein, 1047 Amsterdam Ave., New York, NY 10025, 212-316-7413

Newark: John Shelby Spong; Jack McKelvey, (S), 24 Rector St., Newark, NJ 07102, 201-622-4306

North Carolina: Robert C. Johnson, Jr., 201 St. Albans Dr., Raleigh, NC 27619, 919-787-6313

North Dakota: Andrew H. Fairfield, P.O. Box 10337, Fargo, ND 58106-0337, 701-235-6688

Northern California: Jerry A. Lamb, P.O. Box 161268, Sacramento, CA 95816, 916-442-6918

Northern Indiana: Michael P. Basden, 117 N. Lafayette Blvd., South Bend, IN 46601, 219-233-6489

Northern Michigan: James Kelsey, 131 E. Ridge St., Marquette, MI 49855, 906-228-7160

Northwest Texas: C. Wallis Ohl, Jr., P.O. Box 1067, Lubbock, TX 79408, 806-763-1370

Northwestern Pennsylvania: Robert D. Rowley, 145 W. 6th St., Erie, PA 16501, 814-456-4203

Ohio: J. Clark Grew; Arthur B. Williams, (S), 2230 Euclid Ave., Cleveland, OH 44115, 216-771-4815

Oklahoma: Robert M. Moody; William J. Cox, (A), 924 N. Robinson, Oklahoma City, OK 73102, 405-232-4820

Olympia: Vincent W. Warner, P.O. Box 12126, Seattle, WA 98102, 206-325-4200

Oregon: Robert Louis Ladehoff, P.O. Box 467, Portland, OR 97034, 503-636-5613

Pennsylvania: Charles Bennison (Coady), 240 S. 4th St., Philadelphia, PA 19106, 215-627-6434

Pittsburgh: Robert W. Duncan, Jr., 325 Oliver Ave., Pittsburgh, PA 15222, 412-281-6131

Quincy: Keith L. Ackerman, 3601 N. North St., Peoria, IL 61604, 309-688-8221

Rhode Island: Geralyn Wolf, 275 N. Main St., Providence, RI 02903, 401-274-4500

Rio Grande: Terence Kelshaw, 4304 Carlisle St. NE, Albuquerque, NM 87107, 505-881-0636

Rochester: William G. Burrill, 935 East Ave., Rochester, NY 14607, 716-473-2977

San Diego: Gethin B. Hughes, St. Paul's Church, 2728 6th Ave., San Diego, CA 92103, 619-291-5947

San Joaquin: John-David Schofield, 4159 East Dakota Ave., Fresno, CA 93726, 209-244-4828

South Carolina: Edward L. Salmon, P.O. Box 20127, Charleston, SC 29413-0127, 843-722-4075

South Dakota: Creighton Robertson, 500 S. Main St., Sioux Falls, SD 57102-0914, 605-338-9751

Southeast Florida: Calvin O. Schofield, Jr., 525 NE 15th St., Miami, FL 33132, 305-373-0881

Southern Ohio: Herbert Thompson, Jr.; Kenneth Price, (S), 412 Sycamore St., Cincinnati, OH 45202, 513-421-0311

Southern Virginia: David C. Bane, Jr., 600 Talbot Hall Rd., Norfolk, VA 23505, 804-423-8287

Southwest Florida: Rogers S. Harris, P.O. Box 491, St. Petersburg, FL 33731, 941-776-1018

Southwestern Virginia: John B. Lipscomb, P.O. Box 2279, Roanoke, VA 24009, 703-342-6797

Spokane: Frank J. Terry, 245 E. 13th Ave., Spokane, WA 99202, 509-624-3191

Springfield: Peter H. Beckwith, 821 S. 2nd St., Springfield, IL 62704, 217-525-1876

Tennessee: Bertram M. Herlong, One LaFleur Bldg., Ste. 100, 50 Vantage Way, Nashville, TN 37228, 615-251-3322

Texas: Claude E. Payne, 3203 W. Alabama St., Houston, TX 77098, 713-520-6444

Upper South Carolina: Dorsey F. Henderson, Jr., P.O. Box 1789, Columbia, SC 29202, 803-771-7800

Utah: Carolyn Irish, 231 E. First St. S., Salt Lake City, UT 84111, 801-322-4131

Vermont: Mary Adelia McLeod, Rock Point, Burlington, VT 05401, 802-863-3431

Virginia: Peter J. Lee; Clayton Matthews, (S), 110 W. Franklin St., Richmond, VA 23220, 804-643-8451

Washington: Ronald Haines; Jane H. Dixon, (S), Episc. Church House, Mt. St. Alban, Washington, DC 20016, 202-537-6555

West Missouri: John Buchanan, P.O. Box 413216, Kansas City, MO 64141, 816-471-6161

West Tennessee: James M. Coleman, 692 Poplar Ave., Memphis, TN 38105, 901-526-0023

West Texas: James E. Folts; Earl N. MacArthur, (S), P.O. Box 6885, San Antonio, TX 78209, 210-824-5387

West Virginia: John H. Smith, P.O. Box 5400, Charleston, WV 25361-0400, 304-344-3597

Western Kansas: Vernon Strickland, P.O. Box 2507, Salina, KS 67402, 913-825-1626

Western Louisiana: Robert J. Hargrove, Jr., P.O. Box 2031, Alexandria, LA 71309-2031, 318-442-1304

Western Massachusetts: Gordon P. Scruton, 37 Chestnut St., Springfield, MA 01103, 413-737-4786

99

Western Michigan: Edward L. Lee, 2600 Vincent Ave., Kalamazoo, MI 49008, 616-381-2710

Western New York: J. Michael Garrison, 1114 Delaware Ave., Buffalo, NY 14209, 716-881-0660

Western North Carolina: Robert H. Johnson, P.O. Box 369, Black Mountain, NC 28711, 704-669-2921

Wyoming: Bruce H. Johnson, 104 S. 4th St., Laramie, WY 82070, 307-742-6606

Am. Churches in Europe-Jurisdiction: Jeffery Rowthorn, The American Cathedral, 23 Avenue Georges V, 75008, Paris, France

Navajoland Area Mission: Steven Plummer, P.O. Box 40, Bluff, UT 84512, 505-327-7549

Periodicals

Episcopal Life

The Episcopal Orthodox Church

This Church was established in 1963 as a self-governing Anglican Body, known then as the Anglican Orthodox Church. It has been described as the "much more conservative cousin" of the Episcopal Church USA in NBC News anchor, Tom Brokaw's best seller, The Greatest Generation. The Church upholds orthodox theology and traditional liturgical practice, using the 1928 Book of Common Prayer and the Authorized Version of the Bible for public worship. The Church holds to the Thirty-Nine Artlicles of Religion and confesses the fundamental doctrines of the historic Christian Faith: the Virgin Birth, the Atonement, the Resurrection, the Trinity, and salvation by faith in Christ alone. In 1967, the Church authorized the creation of the worldwide Orthodox Anglican Communion, a global fellowship of traditionalist Anglican Bishops and clergy, with ministries in Europe, Africa, Asia, and South America. In 1975 the Church established Cranmer Seminary to train Godly men for Holy Orders. The seminary became the first of its kind to offer distance-delivered and internet-based learning opportunities for students around the world. In 1999 the name of the Church was changed to the Episcopal Orthodox Christian Archdiocese of America (The Episcopal Orthodox Church), to reflect the strong growth experienced by this body in the 1990's. On April 30, 2000, the Most Reverend Dr. Scott E. McLaughlin became the fourth Presiding Bishop of the Church and Metropolitan of the Orthodox Anglican Communion.

Headquarters

The Chancery of the Archdiocese

2558 Hickory Tree Road, Winston-Salem, NC 27127-9145 Tel. (336)775-9866 Fax (336)775-9867

Media Contact, The Most Rev. Dr. Scott McLaughlin

Email: episcopalorthodox1@msn.com

Website: www.Episcopalorthodox.org

Officers

Presiding Bishop, The Most Rev. Dr. Scott E. McLaughlin, The Chancery of the Archdiocese, 2558 Hickory Tree Road, Winston-Salem, NC 27127-9145 Tel. (336)775-9866 Fax (336)775-9867

Periodicals

The Episcopal Orthodox Encounter; The Cranmer Theological Review

The Estonian Evangelical Lutheran Church

For information on the Estonian Evangelical Lutheran Church (EELC), please see the listing in Chapter 4, "Religious Bodies in Canada."

Headquarters

383 Jarvis St., Toronto, ON M5B 2C7

The Evangelical Church

The Evangelical Church was born June 4, 1968 in Portland, Oregon, when 46 congregations and about 80 ministers, under the leadership of V. A. Ballantyne and George Millen, met in an organizing session. Within two weeks a group of about 20 churches and 30 ministers from the Evangelical United Brethren and Methodist churches in Montana and North Dakota became a part of the new church. Richard Kienitz and Robert Strutz were the superintendents.

Under the leadership of Superintendent Robert Trosen, the former Holiness Methodist Church became a part of the Evangelical Church in 1969, bringing its membership and a flourishing mission field in Bolivia. The Wesleyan Covenant Church joined in 1977, with its missionary work in Mexico, in Brownsville, Texas and among the Navajos in New Mexico.

The Evangelical Church in Canada, where T. J. Jesske was superintendent, became an autonomous organization on June 5, 1970. In 1982, after years of discussions with the Evangelical Church of North America, a founding General Convention was held at Billings, Montana, where the two churches united. In 1993 the Canadian conference merged with the Canadian portion of the Missionary Church to form the Evangelical Missionary Church. The new group maintains close ties with their American counterparts. Currently there are nearly 150 U.S. congregations of the Evangelical Church. The headquarters is located in Minneapolis, Minnesota.

The following guide the life, program and devotion of this church: faithful, biblical and sensible preaching and teaching of those truths proclaimed by scholars of the Wesleyan-Arminian viewpoint; an itinerant system which reckons with the rights of individuals and the desires of the congregation; local ownership of all church properties and assets.

The church is officially affiliated with the Christian Holiness Partnership, the National

Association of Evangelicals, Wycliffe Bible Translators, World Gospel Mission and OMS International. The denomination has nearly 150 missionaries.

Headquarters
7733 West River Rd., Minneapolis, MN 55444
Tel. (612)561-0886 Fax (612)561-0774
Media Contact, Gen. Supt., John F. Sills

Officers
Gen. Supt., Dr. John F. Sills
Dir. of Missions, Rev. Duane Erickson

Periodicals
HeatBeat; The Evangelical Challenge

The Evangelical Church Alliance

What is known today as the Evangelical Church Alliance began in 1887 under the name "World's Faith Missionary Association." Years later, on March 28, 1928, a nonprofit organization was incorporated in the state of Missouri under the same name. In October, 1931, the name "Fundamental Ministerial Association" was chosen to reflect the organization's basis of unity.

On July 21, 1958, during the annual convention at Trinity Seminary and Bible College in Chicago, Illinois, a more comprehensive constitution was created and the name was changed to "The Evangelical Church Alliance."

The ECA licenses and ordains ministers who are qualified providing them with credentials from a recognized ecclesiastical body; provides training courses through the Bible Extension Institute for those who have not had the opportunity to attend Seminary or Bible School; provides Associate Membership for churches and Christian organizations giving opportunity for fellowship and networking with other evangelical ministers and organizations who share the same goals and mission, while remaining autonomous; provides Regional Conventions and an Annual International Convention where members can find fellowship, encouragement and training; cooperates with churches in finding new pastors when they have openings.

ECA is an international, nonsectarian, Evangelical organization.

Headquarters
205 W. Broadway St., P.O. Box 9, Bradley, IL 60915 Tel. (815)937-0720 Fax (815)937-0001
Media Contact, Pres./CEO, Dr. George L. Miller

Officers
Pres./CEO, Dr. George L. Miller

Periodicals
The Evangel

The Evangelical Congregational Church

This denomination had its beginning in the movement known as the Evangelical Association,

organized by Jacob Albright in 1800. A division which occurred in 1891 in the Evangelical Association resulted in the organization of the United Evangelical Church in 1894. An attempt to heal this division was made in 1922, but a portion of the United Evangelical Church was not satisfied with the plan of merger and remained apart, taking the above name in 1928. This denomination is Wesleyan-Arminian in doctrine, evangelistic in spirit and Methodist in church government, with congregational ownership of local church property.

Congregations are located from New Jersey to Illinois. A denominational center, a retirement village and a seminary are located in Myerstown, Pennsylvania. Three summer youth camps and four camp meetings continue evangelistic outreach. A worldwide missions movement includes conferences in North East India, Liberia, Mexico, Costa Rica, and Japan. The denomination is a member of National Association of Evangelicals.

Headquarters
Evangelical Congregational Church Center, 100 W. Park Ave., Myerstown, PA 17067 Tel. (800)866-7581 Fax (717)866-7383
Media Contact, Bishop, Rev. Michael W. Sigman, Tel. (717)866-7581
Email: eccenter@eccenter.com
Website: www.eccenter.com/church/

Officers
Presiding Bishop, Rev. Michael W. Sigman
1st Vice-Chpsn., Rev. Gary Brown
Sec., Rev. Robert J. Stahl
Asst. Sec.: Rev. Gregory Dimick, Hatfield, PA; Rev. Bruce Ray, Chicago, IL
Treas., Norma Minnich, Reedsville, PA
E.C.C. Retirement Village, Supt., Rev. Bruce Hill, Fax (717)866-6448
Evangelical School of Theology, Pres., Dr. Kirby N. Keller, Fax (717)866-4667

OTHER ORGANIZATIONS
Administrative Council: Chpsn., Bishop Michael W. Sigman; Vice-Chpsn., Rev. Keith R. Miller; Treas., Norma Minnich
Div. of Evangelism & Spiritual Care, Chpsn., Bishop Michael W. Sigman
Div. of Church Ministries & Services, Chpsn., Rev. Keith R. Miller
Div. of Missions, Chpsn., Rev. John Ragsdale
Bd. of Pensions: Pres., William Kautz, New Cumberland, PA; Business Mgr., Rev. Keith R. Miller, Myerstown, PA 17067

Periodicals
Doors and Windows; Window on the World (EC Missions)

The Evangelical Covenant Church

The Evangelical Covenant Church has its roots in historic Christianity as it emerged during the Protestant Reformation, in the biblical instruction of the Lutheran State Church of Sweden and in the great spiritual awakenings of the 19th century.

The Covenant Church adheres to the affirmations of the Protestant Reformation regarding the Holy Scriptures, believing that the Old and the New Testament are the Word of God and the only perfect rule for faith, doctrine and conduct. It has traditionally valued the historic confessions of the Christian church, particularly the Apostles' Creed, while at the same time emphasizing the sovereignty of the Word over all creedal interpretations. It has especially cherished the pietistic restatement of the doctrine of justification by faith as basic to its dual task of evangelism and Christian nurture. It recognizes the New Testament emphasis upon personal faith in Jesus Christ as Savior and Lord, the reality of a fellowship of believers which acknowledges but transcends theological differences, and the belief in baptism and the Lord's Supper as divinely ordained sacraments of the church.

While the denomination has traditionally practiced the baptism of infants, in conformity with its principle of freedom it has also recognized the practice of believer baptism. The principle of personal freedom, so highly esteemed by the Covenant, is to be distinguished from the individualism that disregards the centrality of the Word of God and the mutual responsibilities and disciplines of the spiritual community.

Headquarters

5101 N. Francisco Ave., Chicago, IL 60625 Tel. (773)784-3000 Fax (773)784-4366
Media Contact, Pres., Dr. Glenn R. Palmberg

Officers

Pres., Dr. Glenn R. Palmberg
Vice-Pres., Rev. Stanley R. Henderson
Sec., Rev. Mary C. Miller
Treas., Dean A. Lundgren

ADMINISTRATIVE BOARDS

Bd. of Christian Educ. & Discipleship: Exec. Dir., Rev. Doreen L. Olson
Bd. of Church Growth & Evangelism: Exec. Dir., Rev. Gary B. Walter
Bd. of Covenant Women Ministries: Exec. Dir., Rev. Ruth Y. Hill
Bd. of Human Resources: Advisory Member, Rev. Mary C. Miller
Bd. of the Ministry: Exec. Dir., Rev. Donn N. Engebretson
Bd. of Pensions: Dir. of Pensions, Rev. Mary C. Miller
Bd. of Communication: Exec. Dir., Donald L. Meyer
Bd. of World Mission: Exec. Dir., Rev. James W. Gustafson
Bd. of Benevolence: Pres. of Covenant Ministries of Benevolence, Paul V. Peterson, 5145 N. California Ave., Chicago, IL 60625
North Park University: Pres., Dr. David G. Horner, 3225 W. Foster Ave., Chicago, IL 60625; North Park Theological Seminary: Pres. and Dean, Dr. John E. Phelan Jr.

SERVICE ORGANIZATIONS

National Covenant Properties: Pres., David W. Johnson, 5101 N. Francisco, Chicago, IL 60625 Tel. (773)784-3000
Covenant Trust Company: Pres., Gilman G. Robinson, 5101 N. Francisco, Chicago, IL 60625 Tel. (773)784-9911

REGIONAL CONFERENCES OF THE E.C.C.

Central Conference: Supt., Rev. Herbert M. Freedholm, 3319 W. Foster Ave., Chicago, IL 60625 Tel. (773)267-3060
East Coast Conference: Supt., Rev. Robert C. Dvorak, 52 Missionary Rd., Cromwell, CT 06416 Tel. (860)635-2691
Great Lakes Conference: Supt., Rev. David S. Dahlberg, 70 W. Streetsboro St., P.O. Box 728, Hudson, OH 44236 Tel. (330)655-9345
Midwest Conference: Supt., Rev. Kenneth P. Carlson, 13304 W. Center Rd. #229, Omaha, NE 68144 Tel. (402)334-3060
North Pacific Conference: Supt., Rev. Mark A. Novak, 9311 SE 36th St., Ste 120, Mercer Island, WA 98040 Tel. (206)275-3903
Northwest Conference: Supt., Rev. Paul Erickson, 4721 E. 31st St., Minneapolis, MN 55406 Tel. (612)721-4893
Pacific Southwest Conference: Supt., Rev. Evelyn M. R. Johnson, 1333 Willow Pass Rd., Ste 212, Concord, CA 94502 Tel. (925)677-2140
Southeast Conference: Supt., Rev. Kurt A. Miericke, 1759 W. Broadway St., #7, Oviedo, FL 32765 Tel. (407)977-8009
E.C.C. of Canada: Supt., Rev. Jeffrey Anderson, 2791 Pembina Hwy, Winnipeg, MN R3T 2H5 Tel. (204) 269-3437
Midsouth Region: Conference Developer, Rev. Garth T Bolinder, 8411 Greenwood Circle, Lenexa, KS 66215 Tel. (785)888-1825
E.C.C. of Alaska: Field Dir., Rev. Paul W. Wilson, P.O. Box 770749, Eagle River, AK 99577 Tel. (907)694-6348

Periodicals

Covenant Companion; Covenant Quarterly; Covenant Home Altar

The Evangelical Free Church of America

In October 1884, 27 representatives from Swedish churches met in Boone, Iowa, to establish the Swedish Evangelical Free Church. In the fall of that same year, two Norwegian-Danish groups began worship and fellowship (in Boston and in Tacoma) and by 1912 had established the Norwegian-Danish Evangelical Free Church Association. These two denominations, representing 275 congregations, came together at a merger conference in 1950.

The Evangelical Free Church of America is an

association of local, autonomous churches across the United States and Canada, blended together by common principles, policies and practices. A 12-point statement addresses the major doctrines but also provides for differences of understanding on minor issues of faith and practice.

Overseas outreach includes 500 missionaries serving in 31 countries.

Headquarters
901 East 78th St., Minneapolis, MN 55420-1300 Tel. (612)854-1300 Fax (612)853-8488
Media Contact, Exec. Dir. of Ministry Advancement, Timothy Addington

Officers
Acting Pres./Exec. Vice-Pres., Rev. William Hamel
Moderator, Ronald Aucutt, 3417 Silver Maple Pl., Falls Church, VA 22042
Vice-Moderator, Rev. Mark J. Wold, 41827 Higgins Way, Fremont, CA 94539
Sec., Dr. Roland Peterson, 235 Craigbrook Way, NE, Fridley, MN 55432
Vice-Sec., Rev. William S. Wick, 92 South Main, Northfield, VT 05663
Chief Fin. Ofc., Robert Peterson
Exec. Dir., Evangelical Free Church Mission, Dr. Ben Swatsky
Assoc. Dir. of Mission USA, Rev. Steve Hudson

Periodicals
Evangelical Beacon; Pursuit

Evangelical Friends International —North American Region
The organization restructured from Evangelical Friends Alliance in 1990 to become internationalized for the benefit of its world-wide contacts. The North America Region continues to function within the United States as EFA formerly did. The organization represents one corporate step of denominational unity, brought about as a result of several movements of spiritual renewal within the Society of Friends. These movements are: (1) the general evangelical renewal within Christianity, (2) the new scholarly recognition of the evangelical nature of 17th-century Quakerism, and (3) EFA, which was formed in 1965.

The EFA is conservative in theology and makes use of local pastors. Sunday morning worship includes singing, Scripture reading, a period of open worship and a sermon by the pastor.

Headquarters
5350 Broadmoor Cir. NW, Canton, OH 44709 Tel. (330)493-1660 Fax (330)493-0852
Media Contact, Gen. Supt., Dr. John P. Williams, Jr.

YEARLY MEETINGS
Evangelical Friends Church, Eastern Region, Wayne Ickes, 5350 Broadmoor Cir., N.W., Canton, OH 44709 Tel. (330)493-1660 Fax (330)493-0852

Rocky Mountain YM, John Brawner, 3350 Reed St., Wheat Ridge, CO 80033 Tel. (303)238-5200 Fax (303)238-5200
Mid-America YM, Duane Hansen, 2018 Maple, Wichita, KS 67213 Tel. (316)267-0391 Fax (316)267-0681
Northwest YM, Mark Ankeny, 200 N. Meridian St., Newberg, OR 97132 Tel. (503)538-9419 Fax (503)538-9410
Alaska YM, Sam Williams, P.O. Box 687, Kotzebue, AK 99752 Tel. (907)442-3906
Friends Church Southwest, YM, Linda Coop, P.O. Box 1607, Whittier, CA 90609-1607 Tel. (562)947-2883 Fax (562)947-9385

Periodicals
The Friends Voice

Evangelical Lutheran Church in America*
The Evangelical Lutheran Church in America (ELCA) was organized April 30-May 3, 1987, in Columbus, Ohio, bringing together the 2.25 million-member American Lutheran Church, the 2.85 million-member Lutheran Church in America, and the 100,000-member Association of Evangelical Lutheran Churches.

The ELCA is, through its predecessors, the oldest of the major U.S. Lutheran churches. In the mid-17th century, a Dutch Lutheran congregation was formed in New Amsterdam (now New York). Other early congregations were begun by German and Scandinavian immigrants to Delaware, Pennsylvania, New York and the Carolinas.

The first Lutheran association of congregations, the Pennsylvania Ministerium, was organized in 1748 under Henry Melchior Muhlenberg. Numerous Lutheran organizations were formed as immigration continued and the United States grew.

In 1960, the American Lutheran Church (ALC) was created through a merger of an earlier American Lutheran Church, formed in 1930, the Evangelical Lutheran Church, begun in 1917, and the United Evangelical Lutheran Church in America started in 1896. In 1963 the Lutheran Free Church, formed in 1897, merged with the ALC.

In 1962, the Lutheran Church in America (LCA) was formed by a merger of the United Lutheran Church, formed in 1918, with the Augustana Lutheran Church, begun in 1860, the American Evangelical Lutheran Church, founded in 1872, and the Finnish Lutheran Church or Suomi Synod, founded in 1891.

The Association of Evangelical Lutheran Churches arose in 1976 from a doctrinal split with the Lutheran Church-Missouri Synod.

The ELCA, through its predecessor church bodies, was a founding member of the Lutheran World Federation, the World Council of Churches, and the National Council of the Churches of Christ in the USA.

103

The church is divided into 65 geographical areas or synods. These 65 synods are grouped into nine regions for mission, joint programs and service.

Headquarters

8765 W. Higgins Rd., Chicago, IL 60631 Tel. (773)380-2700 Fax (773)380-1465
Media Contact, Dir. for News, John Brooks, Tel. (773)380-2958 Fax (773)380-2406
Email: info@elca.org
Website: www.elca.org

Officers

Presiding Bishop, Rev. Dr. H. George Anderson
Sec., Rev. Dr. Lowell G. Almen
Treas., Richard L. McAuliffe
Vice-Pres., Dr. Addie J. Butler
Exec. for Admn., Rev. Dr. Robert N. Bacher
Office of the Bishop: Exec. Assts. for Federal Chaplaincies, Rev. Lloyd W. Lyngdal; Exec. Asst., Ms. Myrna J. Sheie

DIVISIONS

Div. for Congregational Min.: Co-Exec. Dir., Rev. Mark R. Moller-Gunderson; Co-Exec. Dir., Rev. M. Wyvetta Bullock; Bd. Chpsn., Mr. Ronald C. Bruggeman; Lutheran Youth Organization, Pres., Leota Thomas-Breitfeld
Div. for Higher Educ. & Schools: Exec. Dir., Rev. Dr. Leonard G. Schultze; Bd. Chpsn., Rev. John G. Andreasen
Div. for Global Mission: Exec. Dir., Rev. Bonnie L. Jensen; Bd. Chpsn., Ms. Shai Celeste
Div. for Ministry: Exec. Dir., Rev. Dr. Joseph M. Wagner; Bd. Chpsn., Mr. Kevin J. Boatright
Div. for Outreach: Exec. Dir., Rev. Dr. Richard A. Magnus, Jr.; Bd. Chpsn., Ms. Dorothy Baumgartner
Div. for Church in Society: Exec. Dir., Rev. Charles S. Miller, Jr.; Chpsn., Rev. Dr. James M. Childs, Jr.

COMMISSIONS

Comm. for Multicultural Ministries: Exec. Dir., Rev. Frederick E.N. Rajan; Chpsn., Rev. W. Arthur Lewis
Comm. for Women: Exec. Dir., Joanne Chadwick; Chpsn., Rev. Janet M. Corpus

CHURCHWIDE UNITS

Conference of Bishops: Asst. to the Bishop, Rev. Kathie Bender Schwich; Chpsn., Rev. Donald J. McCoid
ELCA Foundation: Exec. Dir., The Rev. Donald M. Hallberg, Chpsn., Mr. David D. Swartling
ELCA Publishing House: Exec. Dir., Rev. Marvin L. Roloff; Bd. Chpsn., Mr. Richard E. Lodmill
ELCA Bd. of Pensions: Exec. Dir., John G. Kapanke; Bd. Chpsn, Mr. Earl L. Mummert
Women of the ELCA: Exec. Dir., Catherine I. H. Braasch; Bd. Chpsn., Ms. Linda Chinnia

DEPARTMENTS

Dept. for Communication, Dir., Rev. Eric C. Shafer

Dept. for Ecumenical Affairs, Dir., Rev. Daniel F. Martensen; Committee Chpsn., Ms. Kristen E. Kvam
Dept. for Human Resources, Dir., Ms. Else Thompson
Dept. for Research & Evaluation, Dir., Dr. Kenneth W. Inskeep
Dept. for Synodical Relations, Dir., Rev. Kathie Bender Schwich

SYNODICAL BISHOPS

Region 1

Alaska, Rev. Ronald D. Martinson, 1847 W. Northern Lights Blvd., #2, Anchorage, AK 99517-3343 Tel. (907)272-8899 Fax (907) 274-3141
Northwest Washington, Rev. Donald H. Maier, 5519 Pinney Ave. N, Seattle, WA 98103-5899 Tel. (206)783-9292 Fax(206)783-9833
Southwestern Washington, Rev. David C. Wold, 420 121st St., S., Tacoma, WA 98444-5218 Tel. (253)535-8300 Fax (253)535-8315
Eastern Washington-Idaho, Rev. Martin D. Wells, 314 South Spruce St., Ste. A, Spokane, WA 99204-1098 Tel. (509)838-9871 Fax (509) 838-0941
Oregon, Rev. Paul R. Swanson, 2800 N. Vancouver Ave., Ste. 101, Portland, OR 97227-1643 Tel. (503) 413-4191 Fax (503)413-2407
Montana, Rev. Dr. Mark R. Ramseth, 2415 13th Ave. S., Great Falls, MT 59405-5199 Tel. (406)453-1461 Fax (406)761-4632
Int. Regional Coord., Mr. Steven H. Lansing, Region 1, 766-B John St., Seattle, WA 98109-5186 Tel. (206)624-0093 Fax (206)626-0987

Region 2

Sierra Pacific, Rev. Robert W. Mattheis, 401 Roland Way, #215, Oakland, CA 94621-2011 Tel. (510)430-0500 Fax (510)430-8730
Southern California (West), Bishop, Rev. Paul W. Egertson, 1300 E. Colorado St., Glendale, CA 91205-1498 Tel. (818)507-9591 Fax (818) 507-9627
Pacifica, Rev. Murray D. Finck, 23655 Via Del Rio, Ste. B, Yorba Linda, CA 92887-2738 Tel. (714)692-2791 Fax (714)692-9317
Grand Canyon, Rev. Dr. Howard E. Wennes, INTERCHURCH CENTER 4423 N. 24th St., Ste. 400, Phoenix, AZ 85016-5544 Tel. (602)957-3223 Fax (602)956-8104
Rocky Mountain, Rev. Allan C. Bjornberg, 455 Sherman St., Ste. 160, Denver, CO 80203 Tel. (303)777-6700 Fax (303)733-0750
Region 2, Ms. Margaret Schmitt Ajer, Region 2, 3755 Avocado Blvd., Suite 411, La Mesa, CA 91941 Tel. (619)460-9312 Fax (619) 360-9314

Region 3

Western North Dakota, Rev. Duane C. Danielson, 1614 Capitol Way, P.O. Box 370, Bismarck, ND 58502-0370 Tel. (701)223-5312 Fax(701)223-1435
Eastern North Dakota, Rev. Richard J. Foss,

104

1703 32nd Ave., S., Fargo, ND 58103-5936 Tel. (701)232-3381 Fax (701)232-3180

South Dakota, Rev. Andrea F. DeGroot-Nesdahl, Augustana College, 29th & S. Summit, Sioux Falls, SD 57197-0001 Tel. (605)336-4011 Fax (605)336-4028

Northwestern Minnesota, Rev. Arlen D. Hermodson, Concordia College, 901 8th St. S., Moorhead, MN 56562-0001 Tel. (218)299-3019 Fax (218)299-3363

Northeastern Minnesota, Rev. E. Peter Strommen, 1025 London Rd., Ste. B, Duluth, MN 55802 Tel. (218)724-4424 Fax (218)724-4393

Southwestern Minnesota, Rev. Stanley N. Olson, 175 E. Bridge St., P.O. Box 499, Redwood Falls, MN 56283-0499 Tel. (507)637-3904 Fax (507)637-2809

Minneapolis Area, Rev. David W. Olson, 122 W. Franklin Ave., Ste. 600, Minneapolis, MN 55404-2474 Tel. (612)870-3610 Fax (612)870-0170

Saint Paul Area, Rev. Mark S. Hanson, 105 W. University Ave., St. Paul, MN 55103-2094 Tel. (651)224-4313 Fax (651)224-5646

Southeastern Minnesota, Rev. Glenn W. Nycklemoe, Assisi Heights, 1001 14th St. NW, Ste. 300, Rochester, MN 55901-2511 Tel. (507)280-9457 Fax (507)280-8824

Regional Coord., Rev. Craig A. Boehlke, Region 3, Luther Seminary, 2481 Como Ave., St. Paul, MN 55108-1445 Tel. (651)649-0454 Fax (651)641-3425

Region 4

Nebraska, Rev. David L. DeFreese, 4980 S. 118th St., Ste. D, Omaha, NE 68137-2220 Tel. (402)896-5311 Fax (402)896-5354

Central States, Rev. Dr. Charles H. Maahs, 6400 Glenwood St., Ste. 210, Shawnee Mission, KS 66202-4021 Tel. (913)362-0733 Fax (913)362-0317 (M-F)

Arkansas-Oklahoma, Rev. Floyd M. Schoenhals, 6911 S. 66th E. Ave., Ste. 200, Tulsa, OK 74133-1748 Tel. (918)492-4288 Fax (918)491-6275

Northern Texas-Northern Louisiana, Rev. Dr. Kevin S. Kanouse, 1230 Riverbend Dr., Ste. 105, P.O. Box 560587, Dallas, TX 75356-0587 Tel. (214)637-6865 Fax (214)637-4805

Southwestern Texas, Rev. Ray Tiemann, 8919 Tesoro Dr., Ste. 109, P.O. Box 171270, San Antonio, TX 78217-8270 Tel. (210)824-0068 Fax (210)824-7009

Texas-Louisiana Gulf Coast, Rev. Paul J. Blom, 12707 N. Freeway, #580, Houston, TX 77060-1239 Tel. (281)873-5665 Fax (281)875-4716

Regional Coord., Rev. Ann E. Helmke, Region 4, 415 Oakleaf, San Antonio, TX, 78209, Tel. (210)244-8034 Fax (210)828-5881

Region 5

Metropolitan Chicago, Rev. Kenneth R. Olsen, 1420 West Dickens Ave., Chicago, IL 60614-3004 Tel. (773)248-0021 Fax (773)248-8455

Northern Illinois, Rev. Gary M. Wollersheim, 103 W. State St., Rockford, IL 61101-1105 Tel. (815) 964-9934 Fax (815)964-2295

Central/Southern Illinois, Rev. Warren A. Freiheit, 524 S. Fifth St., Springfield, IL 62701-1822 Tel. (217)753-7915 Fax (217) 753-7976

Southeastern Iowa, Rev. Philip L. Hougen, 2635 Northgate Dr., P.O. Box 3167, Iowa City, IA 52244-3167 Tel. (319)338-1273 Fax (319) 351-8677

Western Iowa, Rev. Curtis H. Miller, 318 E. Fifth St., P.O. Box 577, Storm Lake, IA 50588-0577 Tel. (712)732-4968 Fax (712)732-6540

Northeastern Iowa, Rev. Steven L. Ullestad, 201-20th St. SW, P.O. Box 804, Waverly, IA 50677-0804 Tel. (319)352-1414 Fax (319) 352-1416

Northern Great Lakes, Rev. Thomas A. Shrenes, 1029 N. Third St., Marquette, MI 49855-3588 Tel. (906)228-2300 Fax (906)228-2527

Northwest Synod of Wisconsin, Rev. Robert D. Berg, 12 W. Marshall St., P.O. Box 730, Rice Lake, WI 54868-0730 Tel. (715)234-3373 Fax (715)234-4183

East-Central Synod of Wisconsin, Rev. James A. Justman, 16 Tri-Park Way, Appleton, WI 54914-1658 Tel. (920)734-5381 Fax (920) 734-5074

Greater Milwaukee, Rev. Peter Rogness, 1212 S. Layton Blvd., Milwaukee, WI 53215-1653 Tel. (414)671-1212 Fax (414)671-1756

South-Central Synod of Wisconsin, Rev. Dr. Jon S. Enslin, 2909 Landmark Pl., Ste. 202, Madison, WI 53713-4237 Tel. (608)270-0201 Fax (608)270-0202

La Crosse Area, Rev. April Ulring Larson, 3462 Losey Blvd. S., La Crosse, WI 54601-7217 Tel. (608)788-5000 Fax (608)788-4916

Regional Coord., Rev. Carl R. Evenson, Region 5, 675 Deerwood Dr., Ste. 4., Neenah, WI 54956-1629 Tel. (920)720-9880 Fax (920) 720-9881

Region 6

Southeast Michigan, Rev. Robert A. Rimbo, 218 Fisher Bldg., 3011 W. Grand Ave., Detroit, MI 48202-3011 Tel. (313)875-1881 Fax (313) 875-1889

North/West Lower Michigan, Rev. Gary L. Hansen, 801 S. Waverly Rd., Ste. 201, Lansing, MI 48917-4254 Tel. (517)321-5066 Fax (517)321-2612

Indiana-Kentucky, Rev. James R. Stuck, 911 E. 86th St., Ste. 200, Indianapolis, IN 46240-1840 Tel. (317)253-3522 Fax (317)254-5666

Northwestern Ohio, Rev. Marcus C. Lohrmann, 621 Bright Rd., Findlay, OH 45840-6987 Tel. (419) 423-3664 Fax (419)423-8801

Northeastern Ohio, Rev. Marcus J. Miller, 282 W. Bowery St., 3rd Fl., Akron, OH 44307-2504 Tel. (330)253-1500 Fax (330)253-2199

Southern Ohio, Rev. Dr. Callon W. Holloway, Jr.,

300 S. 2nd St., Columbus, OH 43215-5001 Tel. (614)464-3532 Fax (614)464-3422

Regional Coord., Marilyn McCann Smith, Region 6, PO Box 91, 119 1/2 N. Main St. Bluffton, OH 45817 Tel. (419)369-4006 Fax (419)369-4007

Region 7

New Jersey, Rev. E. Roy Riley, Jr., 1930 State Hwy. 33, Hamilton Square, Trenton, NJ 08690-1799 Tel. (609) 586-6800 Fax (609) 586-1597

New England, Rev. Margaret G. Payne, 20 Upland St., Worcester, MA 01607-1624 Tel. (508)791-1530 Fax (508)797-9295

Metropolitan New York, Rev. Stephen P. Bouman, 475 Riverside Dr., New York, NY 10115 Tel. (212)870-3313 Fax (212)870-3376

Upstate New York, Rev. Dr. Lee M. Miller, 3049 E. Genesee St., Syracuse, NY 13224-1699 Tel. (315)446-2502 Fax (315)446-4642

Northeastern Pennsylvania, Rev. Dr. David R. Strobel, 4865 Hamilton Blvd., Wescosville, PA 18106-9705 Tel. (610)395-6891 Fax (610) 398-7083

Southeastern Pennsylvania, Rev. Roy G. Almquist, 506 Haws Ave., Norristown, PA 19401-4543 Tel. (610)278-7342 Fax (610) 696-2782

Slovak Zion, Rev. Juan Cobrda, 8340 N. Oleander Ave., Niles, IL 60714 Tel. (847)965-2475 Fax (847)583-8015

Regional Coord., Rev. Caleb D. Harms, Lutheran Theol. Seminary at Philadelphia, Hagan Hall, 7301 Germantown Ave., Philadelphia, PA 19119-6319 Tel. (215)248-4616 Fax (215) 248-7377

Region 8

Northwestern Pennsylvania, Rev. Paull E. Spring, Rte. 257, Salina Rd., P.O. Box 338, Seneca, PA 16346-0338 Tel. (814)677-5706 Fax (814)676-8591

Southwestern Pennsylvania, Rev. Donald J. McCoid, 9625 Perry Hwy., Pittsburgh, PA 15237-5590 Tel. (412)367-8222 Fax (412) 369-8840

Allegheny, Rev. Gregory R. Pile, 701 Quail Ave., Altoona, PA 16602-3010 Tel. (814)942-1042 Fax (814)941-9259

Lower Susquehanna, Rev. Dr. Guy S. Edmiston, Jr., 900 S. Arlington Ave., Ste. 208, Harrisburg, PA 17109-5031 Tel. (717)652-1852 Fax (717)652-2504

Upper Susquehanna, Rev. Dr. A. Donald Main, Rt. 192 & Reitz Blvd., P.O. Box 36, Lewisburg, PA 17837-0036 Tel. (570)524-9778 Fax (570)524-9757

Delaware-Maryland, Rev. Dr. H. Gerard Knoche, 700 Light St., Baltimore, MD 21230-3850 Tel. (410)230-2860 Fax (410)230-2871

Metropolitan Washington, D.C., Rev. Theodore F. Schneider, 1030-15th St., NW, Ste 1010, Washington, DC 20005-1503 Tel. (202)408-8110 Fax (202)408-8114

West Virginia-Western Maryland, Rev. Ralph W. Dunkin, The Atrium, 503 Morgantown Avenue, Ste. 100, Fairmont, WV 26554-4374 Tel. (304)363-4030 Fax (304)366-9846

Regional Coord., Rev. James E. Miley, Lutheran Theological Sem. at Gettysburg, 61 Seminary Ridge, Gettysburg, PA 17325-1795 Tel. (717)334-3033 Fax (717)334-0323

Region 9

Virginia, Rev. James F. Mauney, Roanoke College, Bittle Hall, P.O. Drawer 70, Salem, VA 24153-0070 Tel. (540)389-1000 Fax (540) 389-5962

North Carolina, Rev. Leonard H. Bolick, 1988 Lutheran Synod Dr., Salisbury, NC 28144-4480 Tel. (704)633-4861 Fax (704)638-0508

South Carolina, Rev. David A. Donges, 1003 Richland St., P.O. Box 43, Columbia, SC 29202-0043 Tel. (803)765-0590 Fax (803) 252-5558

Southeastern, Rev. Ronald B. Warren, 100 Edgewood Ave., NE, Ste. 1600, Atlanta, GA 30303 Tel. (404)589-1977 Fax (404)521-1980

Florida-Bahamas, Rev. William B. Trexler, 3838 W. Cypress St., Tampa, FL 33607-4897 Tel. (813)876-7660 Fax (813)870-0826

Caribbean, Rev. Francisco L. Sosa, PMB Num 359, 425 Carr 693, Ste. 1, Dorado, PR 00646-4802 Tel. (787) 273-8300 Fax (787)796-3365

Regional Coord., Dr. Dorothy L. Jeffcoat, Region 9, Lutheran Theological Southern Seminary, 4201 N. Main St., Columbia, SC 29203 Tel. (803)754-2879 Fax (803)786-6499

Periodicals

The Lutheran; Lutheran Partners; Lutheran Woman Today; Seeds for the Parish

Evangelical Lutheran Synod

The Evangelical Lutheran Synod had its beginning among the Norwegian settlers who brought with them their Lutheran heritage. The Synod was organized in 1853. It was reorganized in 1918 by those who desired to adhere to the synod's principles not only in word but also in deed.

The Synod owns and operates Bethany Lutheran College and Bethany Lutheran Theological Seminary. It has congregations in 20 states and maintains foreign missions in Peru, Chile, the Czech Republic and Ukraine. It operates a seminary in Lima, Peru and in Ternopil, Ukraine.

Headquarters

6 Browns Court, Mankato, MN 56001 Tel. (507) 344-7356 Fax (507)344-7426

Media Contact, Pres., Rev. George Orvick

Email: gorvick@blc.edu

Website: www.EvLuthSyn.org

Officers

Pres., Rev. George Orvick, 6 Browns Ct., Mankato, MN 56082

Sec., Rev. Craig Ferkenstad, Rt. 3, Box 40, St. Peter, MN 56082

Treas., LeRoy W. Meyer, 1038 S. Lewis Ave., Lombard, IL 60148

OTHER ORGANIZATIONS

Lutheran Synod Book Co., Bethany Lutheran College, 700 Luther Dr., Mankato, MN 56001

Bethany Lutheran Theological Seminary, 6 Browns Court, Mankato, MN 56001

Periodicals

Lutheran Sentinel; Lutheran Synod Quarterly; Young Branches; ELS Educator; Oak Leaves; Mission News

Evangelical Mennonite Church

The Evangelical Mennonite Church is an American denomination in the European free church tradition, tracing its heritage to the Reformation period of the 16th century. The Swiss Brethren of that time believed that salvation could come only by repentance for sins and faith in Jesus Christ; that baptism was only for believers; and that the church should be separate from controls of the state. Their enemies called them Anabaptists, since they insisted on rebaptizing believers who had been baptized as infants. As the Anabaptist movement spread to other countries, Menno Simons became its principal leader. In time his followers were called Mennonites.

In 1693 a Mennonite minister, Jacob Amman, insisted that the church should adopt a more conservative position on dress and style of living and should more rigidly enforce the "ban" - the church's method of disciplining disobedient members. Amman's insistence finally resulted in a division within the South German Mennonite groups; his followers became known as the Amish.

Migrations to America, involving both Mennonites and Amish, took place in the 1700s and 1800s, for both religious and economic reasons.

The Evangelical Mennonite Church was formed in 1866 out of a spiritual awakening among the Amish in Indiana. It was first known as the Egly Amish, after its founder Bishop Henry Egly. Bishop Egly emphasized regeneration, separation and nonconformity to the world. His willingness to rebaptize anyone who had been baptized without repentance created a split in his church, prompting him to gather a new congregation in 1866. The conference, which has met annually since 1895, united a number of other congregations of like mind. This group became The Defenseless Mennonite Church in 1898 and has been known as the Evangelical Mennonite Church since 1948.

Headquarters

1420 Kerrway Ct., Fort Wayne, IN 46805 Tel. (219)423-3649 Fax (219)420-1905

Media Contact, Admn. Asst., Lynette Augsburger

Officers

Pres., Rev. Donald W. Roth

Chpsn.., Rev. Doug Habegger, 1050 S. Fourth St., Morton, IL 61550

Vice-Chpsn., Rev. Bryce Winteregg, 11331 Coldwater Rd., Ft. Wayne, IN 46845

Sec., Gene Rupp, c/o Taylor University, 236 W. Reade Ave., Upland, IN 46989

Treas., Elmer Lengacher, 11507 Bull Rapids Rd., Harlan, IN 46743

Periodicals

EMC Today

Evangelical Methodist Church

The Evangelical Methodist Church was organized in 1946 at Memphis, Tenn., largely as a movement of people who opposed modern liberalism and wished for a return to the historic Wesleyan position. In 1960, it merged with the Evangel Church (formerly Evangelistic Tabernacles) and with the People's Methodist Church in 1962.

Headquarters

P.O. Box 17070, Indianapolis, IN 46217 Tel. (317)780-8017 Fax (317)780-8078

Media Contact, Gen. Conf. Sec.-Treas., Rev. James A. Coulston

Officers

Gen. Supt., Dr. Edward W. Williamson

Gen. Conf. Sec.-Treas., Rev. James A. Coulston

Evangelical Presbyterian Church

The Evangelical Presbyterian Church (EPC), established in March 1981, is a conservative denomination of 9 geographic presbyteries - 8 in the United States and one in Argentina. From its inception with 12 churches, the EPC has grown to 197 churches with a membership of over 63,000.

Planted firmly within the historic Reformed tradition, evangelical in spirit, the EPC places high priority on church planting and development along with world missions. Sixty-one missionaries serve the church's mission.

Based on the truth of Scripture and adhering to the Westminster Confession of Faith plus its Book of Order, the denomination is committed to the "essentials of the faith." The historic motto "In essentials, unity; in nonessentials, liberty; in all things charity" catches the irenic spirit of the EPC, along with the Ephesians theme, "truth in love."

The Evangelical Presbyterian Church is a member of the World Alliance of Reformed Churches, National Association of Evangelicals, World Evangelical Fellowship and the Evangelical Council for Financial Accountability.

Headquarters

Office of the General Assembly, 29140 Buckingham Ave., Ste. 5, Livonia, MI 48154 Tel. (734)261-2001 Fax (734)261-3282

107

Media Contact, Stated Clk., Rev. Michael Glodo, 29140 Buckingham Ave., Ste. 5, Livonia, MI 48154 Tel. (734)261-2001 Fax (734)261-3282 Email: EPCHURCH@epc.org
Website: www.epc.org

Officers

Mod., Mr. John Graham, III, 11 Huntington Rd., SW, Rome, GA 30165
Administration Committee, Chmn., Dr. James McGuire, Ward Presbyterian Church, 40000 Six Mile Rd., Northville, MI 48167
Stated Clk., Rev. Michael Glodo

PERMANENT COMMITTEES

Board of Pension & Benefits, Chmn., Dr. Orin Littlejohn, 100 Azelea Way, Marshall, TX 75672
Committee on Admn., Chmn., Dr. James McGuire, Ward Presbyterian Church, 40000 Six Mile Rd., Northville, MI 48167
Committee on Fraternal Relations, Chmn.,
Committee on National Outreach, Chmn., Rev. Rodger Woodworth, New Hope EPC, 2710 Shadeland Ave., Pittsburgh, PA 15212
Committee on Presbytery Review, Chmn., Rev. George Woodcock, 27665 Yvette, Warren, MI 48167
Committee on World Outreach, Chmn., Dr. James McGuire, Ward Presbyterian Church, 40000 Six Mile Rd., Northville, MI 48167
Committee on Ministerial Vocation, Chmn.,
Comm. on Christian Educ. & Publ., Chmn., Rev. David Ruff, Forest Hill EPC, 7224 Park Rd., Charlotte, NC 28210
Committee on Women's Ministries, Chmn., Mrs. Vicki Oliver 18414 Glastonbury Dr., Livonia, MI 48152
Committee on Theology, Chmn., Mr. Charles Haden, 10709 Old Coach Rd., Houston, TX 77024
Committee on Student and Young Adult Ministries, Chmn., Rev. James Byrne, Fourth Presbyterian Church, 5500 River Rd., Bethesda, MD 20816

PRESBYTERIES

Central South, Stated Clk., Rev. Dennis Flach, New Covenant Evangelical Presbyterian Church, P.O. Box 842, Natchez, MS 39121
East, Stated Clk., Dr. Frank Johnson, 136 Chaucer Pl., Cherry Hills, NJ 08003
Florida, Stated Clk., Rev. Robert Garment, Trinity EPC, 5150 Oleander, Ft. Pierce, FL 34982
Mid-America, Stated Clk., Mr. Dexter Kuhlman, 1926 Prospector Ridge, Ballwin, MO 63011
Mid-Atlantic, Stated Clk., Dr. Howard Shockley, 58 Bear Trail, Fairview, NC 28730
Midwest, Stated Clk., Mr. Alton Bennett, 33604 Grand River, Farmington, MI 48335
Southeast, Stated Clk., Rev. Russ Ragon, Lookout Valley Pres. Church, 435 Patten Chapel Rd., Chattanooga, TN 37419

West, Stated Clk., Mr. Cecil Mathews, 6137 E. Hinsdale Ct., Englewwod, CO 80111
St. Andrews, Stated Clk., Rev. Juan Jose Mejias, San Antonio de Padua Mission Church, Godoy Cruz 99, 1718 San Antonio de Padua, Pica, Buenos Aires, Argentina

Periodicals

Reflections Magazine (3/year)

Fellowship of Evangelical Bible Churches

Formerly known as Evangelical Mennonite Brethren, this body emanates from the Russian immigration of Mennonites into the United States, 1873-74. Established with the emphasis on true repentance, conversion and a committed life to Jesus as Savior and Lord, the conference was founded in 1889 under the leadership of Isaac Peters and Aaron Wall. The founding churches were located in Mountain Lake, Minnesota, and in Henderson and Janzen, Nebraska. The conference has since grown to a fellowship of 44 churches with approximately 4,500 members in Argentina, Canada, Paraguay and the United States.

Foreign missions have been a vital ingredient of the total ministry. Today missions constitute about 35 percent of the total annual budget, with one missionary for every 30 members in the home churches. The conference does not develop and administer foreign mission fields of its own, but actively participates with existing evangelical "faith" mission societies. The conference has representation on several mission boards and has missionaries serving under approximately 40 different agencies around the world.

The church is holding fast to the inerrancy of Scripture, the deity of Christ and the need for spiritual regeneration of man from his sinful natural state by faith in the death, burial and resurrection of Jesus Christ as payment for sin. Members look forward to the imminent return of Jesus Christ and retain a sense of urgency to share the gospel with those who have never heard of God's redeeming love.

Headquarters

5800 S. 14th St., Omaha, NE 68107 Tel. (402) 731-4780 Fax (402)731-1173
Admn., Robert L. Frey, 5800 S. 14th St., Omaha, NE 68107 Tel. (402)731-4780 Fax (402)731-1173
Email: febcoma@aol.com

Officers

Pres., Rev. Gerald Epp, P.O. Box 86, Waldheim, SK S0K 4R0 Tel. (306)945-2023 Email: ggepp@sk.sympatico.ca
Vice-President, Rev. Frank Wiens, P.O. Box 50773, Billings, MT 59105-0773 Tel. (406) 254-6961, Email: fcwen@aol.com
Rec. Sec., Stan Seifert, 35351 Munroe Ave., Abbotsford, BC V3G 1L4 Tel. (604)852-3253 Fax (604)852-7887

Admn., Robert L. Frey, 5800 South 14th St., Omaha, NE 68107-3584 Tel. (402)731-4780 Fax (402)731-1173 Email: febcoma@aol.com

Ministries Coordinator, Harvey Schultz, 3011 3rd Ave. East, P.O. Box 8, Waldheim, SK S0K 4R0, Tel. (306)945-2220 Fax (306)945-2088, Email: hesals@aol.com

Commission on Churches, Chpsn., Rev. Bob Vogt, 495 Evergreen Ave., Box 21861, Steinbach, MB R5G 1B5, Tel. [O](204)326-3561, [H](204)346-2642 Fax (204)326-5420, Email: sbachemb@mts.net

Commission on Education, Chpsn., Rev. Harvey Gilbert, 5112 N. 86th St., Omaha, NE 68134-2814, Tel. (402)571-3541 Email: hgilbert@radiks.net

Commission on Missions, Chpsn., Martin Fast, SR 266, Box 9, Frazer, MT 59225 Tel. (406)392-5722, Email: mkfast@juno.com

Commission of Trustees, Chpsn., William Janzen, 6212 Country Club Rd., Omaha, NE 68152-2057 Tel. [O] (402)397-7812, [H] (402)571-2352 Fax (204)397-2113

Commission on Church Planting, Chpsn., Rev. Randy Smart, Box 111, Stuartburn, MB R0A 2B0 Tel. [O](204)425-3383 [H](204)425-3990 Email: smartr@mb.sympatico.ca

Comm. on Women's Ministries, Chpsn., Ruth Epp, Box 86, Waldheim, SK S0K 4R0 Tel. (306)945-2023, E-mail: ggepp@sk.sympatico.ca

Periodicals

Gospel Tidings

Fellowship of Fundamental Bible Churches

The churches in this body represent the 1939 separation from the Methodist Protestant Church, when some 50 delegates and pastors (approximately one-third of the Eastern Conference) withdrew to protest the union of the Methodist Protestant Church with the Methodist Episcopal Church and the Methodist Episcopal Church South, and what they considered the liberal tendencies of those churches. These churches subsequently changed their name to the Bible Protestant Church. In 1985, this group again changed its name to the Fellowship of Fundamental Bible Churches to more accurately define their position.

As fundamentalists, this group strongly adheres to the historic fundamentals of the faith, including the doctrine of separation. This group accepts a literal view of the Bible and, consequently, accepts premillennial theology and a pre-tribulational rapture.

The churches are currently located in New Jersey, New York, Pennsylvania, Virginia, Michigan, and California. It is a fellowship of independent Bible and Baptist churches. Baptism, by immersion, and the Lord's Supper, as a memorial, are recognized as ordinances.

There are currently 21 churches representing 1500 members. This constituent body is a member of the American Council of Christian Churches.

The Fellowship of Fundamental Bible Churches owns and operates Tri-State Bible Camp and Conference Center in Montague, New Jersey, oversees a mission board called Fundamental Bible Missions, and conducts a Bible Institute called Fundamental Bible Institute.

Headquarters

P.O. Box 206, Penns Grove, NJ 08069

Media Contact, Sec., Rev. Edmund G. Cotton, 80 Hudson St., Port Jervis, NY 12771 Tel. (914)856-7695

Email: edgc@pikeonline.net

Officers

Pres., Rev. Mark Franklin, 284 Whig Lane, Monroeville, NJ 08343 Tel. (609)881-0057

Vice-Pres., Rev. Gary Myers, P.O. Box 191, Meshoppen, PA 18630 Tel. (717)833-4898

Sec., Rev. Edmund G. Cotton, 80 Hudson St., Port Jervis, NY 12771 Tel. (914)856-7695

Treas., Ken Thompson, 501 N. Main Street, Elmer, NJ 08318 (865)358-0515

Fellowship of Grace Brethren Churches

A division occurred in the Church of the Brethren in 1882 on the question of the legislative authority of the annual meeting. It resulted in the establishment of the Brethren Church under a legal charter requiring congregational government. This body divided in 1939 with the Grace Brethren establishing headquarters at Winona Lake, Ind., and the Brethren Church at Ashland, Ohio.

Headquarters

Media Contact, Fellowship Coord., Rev. Thomas Avey, P.O. Box 386, Winona Lake, IN 46590 Tel. (219)269-1269 Fax (219)269-4066

Email: fgbc@fgbc.org

Website: www.fgbc.org

Officers

Mod., Dr. Galen Wiley, 22713 Ellsworth Ave., Minerva, OH 44657

1st Mod.-Elect, Dr. James Custer, 2515 Carriage Rd., Powell, OH 43065

2nd Mod.-Elect, Dr. Ron Manahan, 2316 E. Kemo Ave., Warsaw, IN 46580

Fellowship Coord., Rev. Thomas Avey, P.O. Box 386, Winona Lake, IN 46590 Tel. (219)269-1269 Fax (219)269-4066

Sec., Fellowship Coord., Rev. Thomas Avey, P.O. Box 386, Winona Lake, IN 46590

Treas., Thomas Staller, 2311 S. Cost-a-Plenty Drive, Warsaw, IN 46580

OTHER BOARDS

Grace Brethren International Missions, Exec. Dir., Rev. Tom Julien, P.O. Box 588, Winona Lake, IN 46590

Grace Brethren Home Missions, Exec. Dir., Larry Chamberlain, P.O. Box 587, Winona Lake, IN 46590

Grace College & Seminary, Pres., Ronald E. Manahan, 200 Seminary Dr., Winona Lake, IN 46590 Tel. (210)372-5100

Brethren Missionary Herald Co., Pub. & Gen. Mgr., James Bustram, P.O. Box 544, Winona Lake, IN 46590

CE National, Exec. Dir., Rev. Ed Lewis, P.O. Box 365, Winona Lake, IN 46590

Grace Brethren Navajo Ministries, Dir., Steve Galegor, Counselor, NM 87018

Grace Village Retirement Community, Admn., Jeff Carroll, P.O. Box 337, Winona Lake, IN 46590

Natl. Fellowship of Grace Brethren Ministries, Pres., Dr. Steve Taylor, 132 Summerall Ct., Aiken, SC 29801 Women's Missionary Council, Pres., Janet Minnix, 3314 Kenwick Tr., S.W., Roanoke, VA, 24015

Grace Brethren Men International, Pres., Morgan Burgess, 163 N. Franklin St., Delaware, OH 43015

Free Christian Zion Church of Christ

This church was organized in 1905 at Redemption, Ark., by a company of African-American ministers associated with various denominations. Its polity is in general accord with that of Methodist bodies.

Headquarters

1315 S. Hutchinson St., Nashville, AR 71852 Tel. (501)845-4933

Media Contact, Gen. Sec., Shirlie Cheatham

Officers

Chief Pastor, Willie Benson, Jr.

Free Methodist Church of North America

The Free Methodist Church was organized in 1860 in Western New York by ministers and laymen who had called the Methodist Episcopal Church to return to what they considered the original doctrines and lifestyle of Methodism. The issues included human freedom (anti-slavery), freedom and simplicity in worship, free seats so that the poor would not be discriminated against and freedom from secret oaths (societies) so the truth might be spoken freely at all times. The founders emphasized the teaching of the entire sanctification of life by means of grace through faith.

The denomination continues to be true to its founding principles. It communicates the gospel and its power to all people without discrimination through strong missionary, evangelistic and educational programs. Six colleges, a Bible college and numerous overseas schools train the youth of the church to serve in lay and ministerial roles.

Its members covenant to maintain simplicity in life, worship, daily devotion to Christ, responsible stewardship of time, talent and finance.

Headquarters

World Ministries Center: 770 N. High School Rd., Indianapolis, IN 46214 Tel. (317)244-3660 Fax (317)244-1247

Mailing Address, P.O. Box 535002, Indianapolis, IN 46253 Tel. (800)342-5531

Media Contact, Yearbook Ed., P.O. Box 535002, Indianapolis, IN 46253

Officers

Bishops: Robert Nxumalo; Noah Nzeyimana; Richard D. Snyder; Luis Uanela Nhaphale; Jim Tuan; Teodoro Reynoso; Joseph F. James; Roger W. Haskins; Leslie Krober

Gen. Conf. Sec., Melvin J. Spencer

Admn. & Finance, Gen. Dir., Gary M. Kilgore

Growth Ministries, Gen. Dir., David Harvey

Light & Life Communications, Publisher, John E. Van Valin

Light & Life Magazine, Ed., Doug Newton

Higher Education, Gen. Sec., Timothy M. Beuthin

Men's Ministries, Exec. Dir., Lucien E. Behar

Free Methodist Foundation, Stanley B. Thompson

Women's Ministries Intl., Pres., Beth Webb

World Missions, Gen. Dir., Larry Houck

Periodicals

Light and Life Magazine; Free Methodist World Mission People

Friends General Conference

Friends General Conference (FGC) is an association of fourteen yearly meetings open to all Friends meetings which wish to be actively associated with FGC's programs and services. Friends General Conference includes Baltimore, Canadian, Illinois, Lake Erie, New England, New York, Northern, Ohio Valley, Philadelphia, South Central and Southeastern Yearly Meetings; Alaska Friends Conference, Southern Appalachian Yearly Meeting and Association, and Piedmont Friends Fellowship; plus seven independently affiliated monthly meetings. Friends General Conference is primarily a service organization with the stated purpose of nurturing the spiritual life within its constituency of predominantly unprogrammed Friends. FGC offers services to all Friends, but has no authority over constituent meetings. A Central Committee, to which constituent Yearly Meetings name appointees (in proportion to membership), and its Executive Committee, are responsible for the direction of FGC's programs and services which include a bookstore, conferences, and traveling ministires program. The 1995 Central Committee approved the following Minute of Purpose:

Friends General Conference is a Quaker organization in the unprogrammed tradition of the Religious Society of Friends which primarily serves affiliated yearly and monthly meetings. It is our experience that:

**Faith is based on direct experience of God.

**Our lives witness this experience individually and corporately.

**By answering that of God in everyone, we build and sustain inclusive community.

Friends General Conference provides resources and opportunities that educate and invite members and attenders to experience, individually and corporately, God's living presence, and to discern and follow God's leadings. Friends General Conference reaches out to seekers and to other religious bodies inside and outside the Religious Society of Friends.

Headquarters
1216 Arch St., 2B, Philadelphia, PA 19107 Tel. (215)561-1700 Fax (215)561-0759
Media Contact, Gen. Sec., Bruce Birchard
Email: friends@fgcquaker.org
Website: www.fgcquaker.org

Officers
Gen. Sec., Bruce Birchard
Presiding Clerk, Janice Domanik
Treas., Mike Hubbart

YEARLY MEETINGS
Alaska Friends Conference, Clerk, Charlotte Basham, P.O. Box 25078, Ester, AK 99725 Tel. (907)479-2006; Email: ffcsb@aurora.alaska.edu
*Baltimore, Clerk, Lamar Matthew, 17100 Quaker Ln., Sandy Spring, MD 20860 Tel. (301)774-7663; Email: dianajbym@igc.org
*Canadian: Clerk, Gordan McClure, 91A Fourth Ave., Ottawa, ON K1S 2L1 Tel. (613)235-8553; Email: cym@web.net Website: www.web.net/~cym
Illinois, Clerk, Elizabeth Mertic, 21898 Brentwood Lane, Lake Villa, IL 60046, Email: jnurenberg@xcel.com
Lake Erie, Clerk, Janet Smith, 121 Cherry St., Perrysburg, OH 43551 Tel. (419) 874-6738, Email: jesmith@glasscity.net
*New England, Clerk, Anne Kriebel, 901 Pleasant St., Worcester, MA 01602-1908 Tel. (508) 754-6760, Email: neym@ultranet.com
*New York, Clerk, Victoria B. Cooley, 15 Rutherford Pl., New York, NY 10003 Tel. (212)673-5750, Email: nyym@compuserve.com
Northern: Co-Clerks, Lorene Ludy and Jean Eden, 510 S. Dickinson, Madison, WI 53703, Tel. (608) 251-3375, Email: ludyeden@danenet.wicip.org
Ohio Valley, Clerk, Christine Snyder, 7897 Rain Tree Rd., Centerville, OH 45459 Tel. (937)433-6204, Email: snydervc@aol.com
Philadelphia, Clerk, Arlene Kelly, 1515 Cherry St., Philadelphia, PA 19102 Tel. (215)241-7210, Email: joanb@pym.org
Piedmont Friends Fellowship, Clerk, David Bailey, 1712 Lakemont Dr., Greensboro, NC

27410 Tel. (336)854-1225, Email: DLLOYD-BAI@aol.com
South Central, Clerk, Jan Michael, 1422 S. Western Stillwater, OK 74074-6832 Tel. (405)624-0778
*Southeastern, Clerk, Stephen Angell, Annie McPherson, Staff, 4002 NW 16th Pl., Gainsville, FL 32605 Tel. (352)336-7689; Email: SEYM@juno.com
Southern Appalachian, Clerk, Penelope Wright, P.O. Box 1164, Bristol, TN 37621-1164 Tel. (540)628-5852; Email: pennywright@earthlink.net
*also affiliated with Friends United Meeting

Periodicals
Friends Journal

Friends United Meeting*
Friends United Meeting was organized in 1902 (the name was changed in 1963 from the Five Years Meeting of Friends) as a loose confederation of North American yearly meetings to facilitate a united Quaker witness in missions, peace work and Christian education.

Today Friends United Meeting is comprised of 27 member yearly meetings representing about half the Friends in the world. FUM's current work includes programs of mission and service and congregational renewal. FUM publishes Christian education curriculum, books of Quaker history and religious thought and a magazine, Quaker Life.

Headquarters
101 Quaker Hill Dr., Richmond, IN 47374-1980 Tel. (765)962-7573 Fax (765)966-1293
Media Contact, Interim General Secretary, Wayne Carter
Email: info@fum.org
Website: www.fum.org

Officers
Presiding Clk., Stan Bauer
Treas., John Bell
Interim Gen. Sec., Wayne Carter

DEPARTMENTS
World Missions, Assoc. Sec., Retha McCutchen
North American Ministries, Interim Assoc. Sec., Barbara Mays
Quaker Hill Bookstore, Mgr., Tonya Abrams
Friends United Press, Ed., Barbara Mays

YEARLY MEETINGS
Baltimore Yearly Meeting, 17100 Quaker Ln., Sandy Spring, MD 20860 Tel. (301)774-7663 (800)962-4766 Fax (301)774-7084 Lamar Matthew, clerk; Frank Massey, Gen. Sec.
Bware Yearly Meeting, P.O. Box 179, Suna, Kenya; Epainitus Adego, Gen Supt.
Canadian Yearly Meeting: 91-A Fourth Ave., Ottawa ON K1S 2L1, Canada; Tel. and Fax (613)235-8553; Gordon McClure, clerk
Central Yearly Meeting, P.O. Box 1510,

Kakamega, Kenya, East Africa, Joseph Andugu, Gen. Sec.

Cuba Yearly Meeting, Ave. Libertad #110, Puerto Padre, Las Tunas, Cuba; Maria Renya Yi, President

East Africa Yearly Meeting of Friends, P.O. Box 35, Tiriki, Kenya, East Africa; Matthew Tsimbaji, Clerk, Thomas Ilote, Gen. Sec., Erastus Kesohole, Gen Supt.

East Africa Yearly Meeting of Friends (North), P.O. Box 544, Kitale, Kenya, East Africa; Henry Mayabe, Gen. Sec., Titus Adira, Gen. Supt.

East Africa Yearly Meeting of Friends (South), P.O. Box 160, Vihiga, Kenya, East Africa; Joseph Kisia, Clerk; Lam Kisanya Osodo, Gen. Sec., Gilbert Akenga Oyando, Gen. Supt.

Elgon East Yearly Meeting, P.O. Box 2322, Kitale, Kenya, East Africa; Maurice Simiyu, Gen. Sec.

Elgon Religious Soociety of Friends, P.O. Box 4, Wibuye, Kenya, East Africa, Tom Isiye, General Sec., John Ngoya, Gen. Supt., Charles Mbachi, Presiding Clerk

Indiana Yearly Meeting, 4715 N. Wheeling Ave., Muncie, IN 47304-1222; Tel. (765)284-6900 Fax (765)284-8925; Susan Kirkpatrick, Clerk; Alan Weinacht, Gen. Supt.

Iowa Yearly Meeting, Box 657, Oskaloosa, IA 52577; Tel. (515)673-9717 Fax (515)673-9718; Margaret Stoltzfus, Clerk, Kevin Mortimer, Gen. Superintendent

Jamaica Yearly Meeting, 4 Worthington Ave., Kingston 5, Jamaica WI; Tel. (809)926-7371

Kakamega Yearly Meeting, P.O. Box 465, Kakamega, Kenya, East Africa; Jonathan Shisanya, Gen. Sec.

Lugari Yearly Meeting, Lugari Farmers Training Centre, P.O. Box 438, Turbo, Kenya, East Africa; Samson Atsya, Gen. Sec.

Malava Yearly Meeting, P.O. Box 26, Malava, Kenya, East Africa; Enoch Shinachi, Gen. Sec.

Nairobi Yearly Meeting, P.O. Box 8321, Nairobi, Kenya, East Africa; Stanley Ndezwa, Clerk, Aggrey Mukilima, Gen. Supt.

Nandi Yearly Meeting, P.O. Box 102, Kapsabet, Kenya, East Africa; Fredrick Inyangu, Presiding clk.

Nebraska Yearly Meeting, 423 S. Tinker St., Hominy, OK 74035; Tel. (918)885-2714; David Nagle, Clerk

New England Yearly Meeting, 901 Pleasant St., Worcester, MA 01602 Tel. (508)754-6760; Elizabeth Muench, Clerk; Jonathan Vogel-Borne, Field Secretary

New York Yearly Meeting, 15 Rutherford Pl., New York, NY 10003 Tel. (212)673-5750; Victoria B. Cooley, Clerk; Helen Garay Toppins, Admin. Sec.

North Carolina Yearly Meeting, 5506 W. Friendly Ave., Greensboro, NC 27410; Tel. (336)292-6957; Brent McKinney, Clerk; John Porter, Gen. Superintendent

Southeastern Yearly Meeting, 4002 NW 16th Pl., Gainsville, FL 32605; Tel. (352)336-7689; Cecilia Yocum, Clerk, Annie McPhearson, Sec.

Tanzania Yearly Meeting, P.O. Box 151, Mugumu, Serengeti, Tanzania; Joshua Lavuna Oguma, Gen. Sec.

Uganda Yearly Meeting, P.O. Box 605, Kampala, Uganda, East Africa; Samuel Wefwafwa, Gen. Sec.

Vokoli Yearly Meetings, P.O. Box 266, Wodanga, Vokoli, Kenya, 0331 45033; Javan Mirembe, Gen. Sec., Hannington Mbaco, Presiding Clerk, Timonakita, Gen Supt.

Western Yearly Meeting, P.O. Box 70, Plainfield, IN 46168; Tel. (317)839-2789 and 839-2849 Fax (317)839-2616; Charles Heavilin, Clerk; Curt Shaw, Gen. Superintendent

Wilmington Yearly Meeting, Pyle Center Box 1194, Wilmington, OH 45177; Tel. (937)382-2491 Fax (937)382-7077; Gary Farlow, Clerk; Rudy Haag, Ex. Sec.

Periodicals

Quaker Life

Evangelical Friends International—North American Region is listed under "E".

Philadelphia Yearly Meeting of the Religious Society of Friends is listed under "P".

Religious Society of Friends (Conservative) is listed under "R".

Religious Society of Friends (Unaffiliated Meetings) is listed under "R".

Full Gospel Assemblies International

The Full Gospel Assemblies International was founded in 1962 under the leadership of Dr. Charles Elwood Strauser. The roots of Full Gospel Assemblies may be traced to 1947 with the beginning of the Full Gospel Church of Coatesville, Pennsylvania. As an Assemblies of God Pentecostal church, the Full Gospel Church of Coatesville was active in evangelization and educational ministries to the community. In service to the ministers and students of the Full Gospel Church ministries, the Full Gospel Trinity Ministerial Fellowship was formed in 1962, later changing its name to Full Gospel Assemblies International.

Retaining its original doctrine and faith, Full Gospel Assemblies is Trinitarian and believes in the Bible as God's infallible Word to all people, in baptism in the Holy Spirit according to Acts 2, in divine healing made possible by the sufferings of our Lord Jesus Christ and in the imminent return of Christ for those who love him.

The body of Full Gospel Assemblies is an evangelical missionary fellowship sponsoring ministry at home and abroad, composed of self governing ministries and churches. Congregations, affiliate ministries and clerical bodies are located throughout the United States and over 30 countries of the world.

Headquarters
3170 Lincoln Hwy, Parkesburg, PA
Mailing Address, P.O. Box 1230, Coatesville, PA 19320 Tel. (610)857-2357
Media Contact, Simeon Strauser

Officers
Gen. Supt., Dr. AnnaMae Strauser
Exec. Dir of Admn., Simeon Strauser
Exec. Dir. of Ministry, J. Victor Fisk
Exec. Sec., Betty Stewart
National Ministers Council & Trustees: Chpsn., Simeon Strauser, Sadsburyville, PA; Donald Campbell, Mt. Morris, PA; David Treat, Cape Coral, FL; Carol Strauser, Parkesburg, PA; Edward Popovich, Burgetstown, PA; Archie Neale, Pittsburgh, PA; J. Victor Fisk, Appolo, PA

Periodicals
Full Gospel Ministries Outreach Report

Full Gospel Fellowship of Churches and Ministers International
In the early 1960s a conviction grew in the hearts of many ministers that there should be closer fellowship between the people of God who believed in the apostolic ministry. At the same time, many independent churches were experiencing serious difficulties in receiving authority from the IRS to give governmentally accepted tax-exempt receipts for donations.

In September 1962 a group of ministers met in Dallas, Texas, to form a Fellowship to give expression to the essential unity of the Body of Christ under the leadership of the Holy Spirit—a unity that goes beyond individuals, churches or organizations. This was not a movement to build another denomination, but rather an effort to join ministers, churches and ministry organizations of like mind across denominational lines.

To provide opportunities for fellowship and to support the objectives and goals of local and national ministries, regional conventions and an annual international convention are held.

Headquarters
100 N. Belt Line Rd., Irving, TX 75061 Tel. (214)492-1254
Media Contact, Exec. Sec., Dr. Chester P. Jenkins

Officers
Pres., Dr. Don Arnold, P.O. Box 324, Gadsden, AL 35901
1st Vice-Pres., Dr. Ray Chamberlain
Exec. Sec., Dr. Chester P. Jenkins
Treas., Rev. Gene Evans P.O. Box 813, Douglasville, GA 30133
CFO, Dr. S.K. Biffle, 4325 W. Ledbetter Dr.

Ofc. Sec., Ms. Lanita Isbell & Nita Biffle
Vice-Pres. at Large: Rev. Maurice Hart, P.O. Box 4316, Omaha, NE 68104; Rev. Don Westbrook, 3518 Rose of Sharon Rd., Durham, NC 27705
Chmn. of Evangelism, David Ellis
Past Pres., Dr. James Helton

REGIONAL VICE-PRESIDENTS
Southeast, Rev. Gene Evans, P.O. Box 813, Douglasville, GA 30133
South Central, Rev. Robert J. Miller, P.O. Box 10621, Killeen, TX 76547
Southwest, Rev. Don Shepherd, 631 Southgate Rd., Sacramento, CA 95815
Northeast, Rev. David Ellis, 3636 Winchester Rd., Allertown, PA 18104
North Central, Rev. Raymond Rothwell, P.O. Box 367, Eaton, OH 45320
Northwest, Rev. Ralph Trask, 3212 Hyacinth NE, Salem, OR 97303

Periodicals
Fellowship Tidings

Fundamental Methodist Church, Inc.
This group traces its origin through the Methodist Protestant Church. It withdrew from The Methodist Church and organized on August 27, 1942.

Headquarters
1034 N. Broadway, Springfield, MO 65802
Media Contact, Dist. Supt., Rev. Ronnie Howerton, 1952 Highway H, Monett, MO 65708 Tel. (417)235-3849

Officers
Treas., Wayne Blades, Rt. 1, Crane, MO 65633 Tel. (417)723-8123
Sec., Betty Nicholson, Rt. 2, Box 397, Ash Grove, MO 65604 Tel. (417)672-2268
Dist. Supt., Rev. Ronnie Howerton, 1952 Highway H, Monett, MO 65708 Tel. (417)235-3849

General Assembly of the Korean Presbyterian Church in America*
This body came into official existence in the United States in 1976 and is currently an ethnic church, using the Korean and English language.

Headquarters
General Assembly of the Korean Presbyterian Church in America
17200 Clark Ave., Bellflower, CA 90706
Tel. (714)816-1100 Fax (714)816-1120

Officers
Moderator, Rev. In Hwa Sohn, 6021 Franconia Rd., Alexandria, VA 22310 Tel. (703)922-6064
General Secretary, Rev. Seung Koo Choi, 3146 W. Ball Rd., #31, Anaheim, CA 92804 Tel. (714)816-1100

General Association of General Baptists

Similar in doctrine to those General Baptists organized in England in the 17th century, the first General Baptist churches were organized on the Midwest frontier following the Second Great Awakening. The first church was established by the Rev. Benoni Stinson, in 1823 at Evansville, Ind.

Stinson's major theological emphasis was general atonement - "Christ tasted death for every man." The group also allows for the possibility of apostasy. It practices open communion and believer's baptism by immersion.

Called "liberal" Baptists because of their emphasis on the freedom of man, General Baptists organized a General Association in 1870 and invited other "liberal" Baptists (e.g., "Free Will" and Separate Baptists) to participate.

The policy-setting body is composed of delegates from local General Baptist churches and associations. Each local church is autonomous but belongs to an association. The group currently consists of more than 60 associations in 16 states, as well as several associations in the Philippines, Guam, Saipan, Jamaica and India. Ministers and deacons are ordained by a presbytery.

A number of boards continue a variety of missions, schools and other support ministries. General Baptists belong to the Baptist World Alliance, the North American Baptist Fellowship and the National Association of Evangelicals.

Headquarters

100 Stinson Dr., Poplar Bluff, MO 63901 Tel. (573)785-7746 Fax (573)785-0564
Media Contact, Exec. Dir., Dr. Ron Black

Officers

Mod., Rev. Phil Warren
Clk., Rev. Tommy Roberts
Exec. Dir., Dr. Ron Black

OTHER ORGANIZATIONS

International Missions, Dir., Rev. Jack Eberhardt
National Missions, Dir., Rev. Ron Byrd
Women's Ministries, Dir., Sandra Trivitt
Nursing Home Admn., Wanda Britt, Rt. #2, Box 230, Campbell, MO 63933
University Bd., Pres., Dr. James Murray, Oakland City University, 143 N. Lucretia, Oakland City, IN 47660
Congregational Ministries, Dir., Rev. Mike Warren, 100 Stinson Dr., Poplar Bluff, MO 63901
Pastoral Ministries, Dir., Rev. Fred Brittain, 100 Stinson Dr., Poplar Bluff, MO 63901
Admin./Financial Services, Financial Officer, Linda McDonough, 100 Stinson Dr., Poplar Bluff, MO 63901
Stinson Press, Inc., Pres., Rev. Dale Bates, 400 Stinson Dr., Poplar Bluff, MO 63901
Oakview Heights Continuing Care, Administrator, Rev. Jack Cole, 1320 West 9th St., Mt. Carmel, IL 62863

Compassionate Care Adoption Agency, Dir., Dr. John Clanton, Rt. 3, Box 12B, Oakland City, IN 47660

Periodicals

General Baptist Messenger; Capsule; Voice; Church Talk; Pastor Talk; The Servant

General Association of Regular Baptist Churches

This association was founded in May, 1932, in Chicago by a group of churches which had withdrawn from the Northern Baptist Convention (now the American Baptist Churches in the U.S.A.) because of doctrinal differences. Its Confession of Faith, which it requires all churches to subscribe to, is essentially the old, historic New Hampshire Confession of Faith with a premillennial ending applied to the last article.

The churches of the General Association of Regular Baptist Churches voluntarily join together to accomplish four goals. (1) Champion Biblical truth—committed to communication with the whole counsel of God in its timeless relevance. (2) Impact the world for Christ—obeying the Lord's Great Commission to take the life-changing gospel to the entire world. (3) Perpetuate its Baptist heritage—faithfully promoting its Scriptural legacy and identity. (4) Advancing GARBC churches—strengthening existing churches and planting new churches for the purposes of evangelism and edification.

Headquarters

1300 N. Meacham Rd., Schaumburg, IL 60173 Tel. (847)843-1600 Fax (847)843-3757
Media Contact, Natl. Rep., Dr. John Greening
Email: garbc@garbc.org
Website: www.garbc.org

Officers

Chpsn., Rev. Bryce Augsburger
Vice-Chpsn., Rev. W. David Warren
Treas., Dr. David Gower
Sec., Rev. David Strope
Natl. Rep., Dr. John Greening

Periodicals

Baptist Bulletin

General Church of the New Jerusalem

The General Church of the New Jerusalem, also called the New Church, was founded in 1897. It is based on the teachings of the 18th Century scientist Emanuel Swedenborg, and stresses the oneness of God, who is the Lord Jesus Christ, and a life of faith and love in service to others, in true married love, and in life after death.

Headquarters

P.O. Box 711, Bryn Athyn, PA 19009 Tel. (215) 938-2620
Media Contact, Ed., Church Journal, Donald L.

Rose, Box 277, Bryn Athyn, PA 19009 Tel. (215)947-6225 Fax (215)947-3078
Email: svsimpso@newchurch.edu
Website: www.newchurch.org

Officers

Presiding Bishop, Rt. Rev. P. M. Buss
Sec., Susan V. Simpson
Treas., Daniel T. Allen

Periodicals

New Church Life

General Conference of Mennonite Brethren Churches

A small group, requesting that closer attention be given to prayer, Bible study and a consistent lifestyle, withdrew from the larger Mennonite Church in the Ukraine in 1860. Anabaptist in origin, the group was influenced by Lutheran pietists and Baptist teachings and adopted a quasi-congregational form of church government. In 1874 and years following, small groups of these German-speaking Mennonites left Russia, settled in Kansas and then spread to the Midwest west of the Mississippi and into Canada. Some years later the movement spread to California and the West Coast. In 1960, the Krimmer Mennonite Bretheren Conference merged with this body.

Today the General Conference of Mennonite Brethren Churches conducts services in many European languages as well as in Vietnamese, Mandarin and Hindi. It works with other denominations in missionary and development projects in 25 countries outside North America.

Headquarters

4812 E. Butler Ave., Fresno, CA 93727 Tel. (209)452-1713 Fax (209)452-1752
Media Contact, Exec. Sec., Marvin Hein

Officers

Mod., Ed Boschman, 12630 N. 103rd Ave., Suite 215, Sun City, AZ 85351
Asst. Mod., Herb Kopp, 200 McIvor Ave., Winnipeg, NB R20 028
Sec., Valerie Rempel
Exec. Sec., Marvin Hein

Periodicals

Christian Leader; Mennonite Bretheren Herald

Grace Gospel Fellowship

The Grace Gospel Fellowship was organized in 1944 by a group of pastors who held to a dispensational interpretation of Scripture. Most had ministries in the Midwest. Two prominent leaders were J. C. O'Hair of Chicago and Charles Baker of Milwaukee. Subsequent to 1945, a Bible Institute was founded (now Grace Bible College of Grand Rapids, Mich.), and a previously organized foreign mission (now Grace Ministries International of Grand Rapids) was affiliated with the group. Churches have now been established in most sections of the country. The body has remained a fellowship, each church being autonomous in polity. All support for its college, mission and headquarters is on a contributory basis.

The binding force of the Fellowship has been the members' doctrinal position. They believe in the Deity and Saviorship of Jesus Christ and subscribe to the inerrant authority of Scripture. Their method of biblical interpretation is dispensational, with emphasis on the distinctive revelation to and the ministry of the apostle Paul.

Headquarters

Media Contact, Pres., Roger G. Anderson, 2125 Martindale SW, P.O. Box 9432, Grand Rapids, MI 49509 Tel. (616)245-0100 Fax (616)241-2542
Email: ggfinc@aol.com

Officers

Pres., Roger G. Anderson

OTHER ORGANIZATIONS

Grace Bible College, Pres., Rev. Bruce Kemper, 1011 Aldon St. SW, Grand Rapids, MI 49509
Grace Ministries Intl., Exec. Dir., Dr. Samuel Vinton, 2125 Martindale Ave. SW, Grand Rapids, MI 49509
Prison Mission Association, Gen. Dir., Nathan Whitham, P.O. Box 1587, Port Orchard, WA 98366-0140
Grace Publications Inc., Exec. Dir., Roger G. Anderson, 2125 Martindale Ave. SW, Grand Rapids, MI 49509
Bible Doctrines to Live By, Exec. Dir., Lee Homoki, P.O. Box 2351, Grand Rapids, MI 49501

Periodicals

Truth

Greek Orthodox Archdiocese of America*

The Greek Orthodox Archdiocese of America is under the jurisdiction of the Ecumenical Patriarchate of Constantinople in Istanbul. It was chartered in 1922 by the State of New York and has 523 parishes in the United States. The first Greek Orthodox Church was founded in New Orleans in 1864.

Headquarters

8-10 E. 79th St., New York, NY 10021 Tel. (212) 570-3500 Fax (212)570-3569
Media Contact: Fr. Mark Arey, Executive Director, Dept. of Communications, Tel. (212)570-3571 Fax (212)570-3598

ARCHDIOCESAN COUNCIL

Primate of the Greek Orthodox Archdiocese of America and Exarch of the Atlantic and Pacific Oceans, His Eminence Archbishop Dimitrios

SYNOD OF BISHOPS

Most Rev. Metropolitan Iakovos of Krinis, Diocese of Chicago, 40 E. Burton Place, Chicago, IL 60610

Most Rev. Metropolitan Anthony of Dardanelles, Diocese of San Francisco, 372 Santa Clara Avenue, San Francisco, CA 94127

Most Rev. Metropolitan Maximos of Aenos, Diocese of Pittsburgh, 5201 Ellsworth Avenue, Pittsburgh, PA 15232

Most Rev. Metropolitan Methodios of Aneon, Diocese of Boston, 162 Goddard Avenue, Brookline, MA 02146

Most Reverend Metropolitan Isaiah of Proikonisou, Diocese of Denver, 4310 E. Alameda Avenue, Denver, CO 80222

AUXILIARY BISHOPS

His Grace Bishop Alexios of Troas, Archdiocesan Vicar, Diocese of Atlanta; His Grace Bishop Dimitrios of Xanthos, Archdiocese, New York, NY; His Grace Bishop of George of Komanon, Bethesda, MD

EXECUTIVE COMMITTEE

John A. Catsimatidis, Vice Chairman, New York, NY; Peter J. Pappas, Sec., Syosset, NJ; Andrew A. Athens, Chicago, IL; George Behrakis, Tewksbury, MA; Michael G. Cantonis, Tarpon Springs, FL; Harry J. Pappas, Visalia, CA; James J. Paulos, Dallas, TX; George E. Safiol, Weston, MA

ARCHDIOCESE OF NEW YORK; Office of the Archbishop; Office of the Chief Secretariat; Office of the Chancellor: Chancellor, V. Rev. Protopresbyter George G. Passias

ARCHDIOCESAN DEPARTMENTS

Archives; Archdiocese Benefits Committee; Archons, Order of St. Andrew; Dept. of Communications: GOTelecom, Internet Ministries, News & Information, Office of Publications, ORTHODOX OBSERVER (bi-monthly publication); Education & Culture; Finance; Inter-Orthodox & Ecumenical Affairs; Internet Ministries; Ionian Village; Leadership 100 Endowment Fund; Management Information Systems; Registry; Religious Education/DOXA; Stewardship Ministries/LOGOS; Youth & Young Adult Ministries

ORGANIZATIONS/ INSTITUTIONS

All Saints Center; Archdiocesan Presbyters Council; Diocesan and Parish Summer Camps; Greek Orthodox Young Adult League (GOYAL); Hellenic Cultural Center; Hellenic College/Holy Cross Greek Orthodox School of Theology; Holy Cross Bookstore; Inter-Church/Inter-Faith Marriage Committee; National Ladies Philoptochos Society; National Sisterhood of Presbyters; National Forum of Greek Orthodox Church Musicians; Orthodox Christian Mission Center; Patriarch Athenagoras National Institute; Patriarch Athenagoras Orthodox Institute at the Graduate Theological Union; Standing Conference of Canonical Orthodox Bishops in the Americas (SCOBA): Chairman, His Eminence Archbishop Spyridon; St. Basil Academy; St. Michael's Home- Quality Care for the Elderly; St. Nicholas Ranch and Retreat Center; St. Photios National Shrine

OTHER JURISDICTIONS OF THE ECUMENICAL PATRIARCHATE IN THE USA

Albanian Orthodox Diocese in America; Belarusian Council of Orthodox Churches in North America; American Carpatho-Russian Orthodox Greek Catholic Diocese of the USA; Ukrainian Orthodox Church of the USA

The Holy Eastern Orthodox Catholic and Apostolic Church in North America, Inc.

Called by many independents The 1927 Aftimios Church, this Church was canonically established Feburary 2, 1927 by the Russian Synod of Bishops in North America with approval of the Russian Patriarch. Archbishop Aftimios Ofiesh of the Syrian mission was appointed first Archbishop President of this Church by the Russian Synod. The Church was incorporated on Febuary 1, 1928 by Archbishop Aftimios and seven others in Boston and continues today. This Church was established to serve the English speaking Orthodox Community in the New World and to be the anchor of the orthodoxy in North America. The short name listed in our Constitution is the "American Orthodox Catholic Church" and the Synod approved the name "Orthodox Metropolitanate in North America" when the title of the Archbishop President was changed to Metropolitan. We are mainly a western rite Church today but some clergy still offer the Eastern Liturgy.

Headquarters

Presently a temporary see in Arkansas: All Saints Parish, P.O. Box 477, Mtn. View, AR 72560 Tel. (870) 269-2912

(Soon to acquire property in New Mexico for National Church Headquarters and shrine.)

Primate: Metropolitan Victor
Email: theocacna@webtv.net
Website: www.theocacna.org

NORTH AMERICAN HOLY SYNOD

Archbishop Victor
Mar Kepha
Archbishop Lawrence
Bishop Gerald

SYNOD ADVISORS

Archbishop Joseph
Archbishop James
Bishop Donald

Holy Ukrainian Autocephalic Orthodox Church in Exile

This church was organized in a parish in New York in 1951 by Ukrainian laymen and clergy who settled in the Western Hemisphere after World War II. In 1954 two bishops, immigrants from Europe, met with clergy and laymen and formally organized the religious body.

Headquarters
103 Evergreen St., W. Babylon, NY 11704

Officers
Admn., Rt. Rev. Serhij K. Pastukhiv, Tel. (516) 669-7402

House of God, Which is the Church of the Living God, the Pillar and Ground of the Truth, Inc.

This body, founded by Mary L. Tate in 1919, is episcopally organized.

Headquarters
1301 N. 58th St., Philadelphia, PA 19131
Media Contact, Sec., Rose Canon, 515 S. 57th St., Philadelphia, PA 19143 Tel. (215)474-8913

Officers
Bishop, Raymond W. White, 6107 Cobbs Creek Pkwy., Philadelphia, PA 19143 Tel. (215)748-6338

Hungarian Reformed Church in America*

A Hungarian Reformed Church was organized in New York in 1904 in connection with the Reformed Church of Hungary. In 1922, the Church in Hungary transferred most of its congregations in the United States to the Reformed Church in the U.S. Some, however, preferred to continue as an autonomous, self-supporting American denomination, and these formed the Free Magyar Reformed Church in America. This group changed its name in 1958 to Hungarian Reformed Church in America.

This church is a member of the World Alliance of Reformed Churches, Presbyterian and Congregational, the World Council of Churches and the National Council of Churches of Christ.

Headquarters
Bishop's Office, 13 Grove St., Poughkeepsie, NY 12601 Tel. (914)454-5735

Officers
Bishop, Rt. Rev. Alexander Forro
Chief Lay-Curator, Prof. Stephen Szabo, 464 Forest Ave., Paramus, NJ 07652
Gen. Sec. (Clergy), Rt. Rev. Stefan M. Torok, 331 Kirkland Pl., Perth Amboy, NJ 08861 Tel. (908)442-7799
Gen Sec. (Lay), Zoltan Ambrus, 3358 Maple Dr., Melvindale, MI 48122
Eastern Classes: Dean (Senior of the Deans,

Chair in Bishop's absence), Very Rev. Imre Bertalan, 10401 Grosvenor Pl., #1521, Rockville, MD 20852 Tel. (301)493-5036 Fax (301)571-5111; Lay-Curator, Balint Balogh, 519 N. Muhlenberg St., Allentown, PA 18104
New York Classes: Supervisor, Rt. Rev. Alexander Forro; Lay-Curator, Laszlo B. Vanyi, 229 E 82nd St., New York, NY 10028
Western Classes: Dean, V. Rev. Andor Demeter, 3921 W. Christy Dr., Phoenix, AZ 85029; Lay-Curator, Zolton Kun, 2604 Saybrook Dr., Pittsburgh, PA 15235

Periodicals
Magyar Egyhaz

Hutterian Brethren

Small groups of Hutterites derive their names from Jacob Hutter, a 16th-century Anabaptist who taught true discipleship after accepting Jesus as Saviour, advocated communal ownership of property and was burned as a heretic in Austria in 1536.

Many believers are of German descent and still use their native tongue at home and in church. Much of the denominational literature is produced in German and English. "Colonies" share property, practice non-resistance, dress plainly, do not participate in politics and operate their own schools. There are 428 colonies with 42,000 members in North America. Each congregation conducts its own youth work through Sunday school. Until age 15, children attend German and English school which is operated by each colony. All youth ages 15 to 20 attend Sunday school. They are baptized as adults upon confession of faith, around age 20.

Headquarters
Media Contact, Philip J. Gross, 3610 N. Wood Rd., Reardon, WA 99029 Tel. (509)299-5400 Fax (509)299-3099
Email: philsjg@juno.com

Officers
Smiedleut Chmn., No. 1, Jacob Waldner-Blumengard Colony, Box 13 Plum Coulee, MB R0G 1R0 Tel. (204)829-3527
Smiedleut Chmn., No. 2, Jacob Wipf, Spring Creek Colony, 36562 102 Street, Forbes, ND 58439 Tel. (701)358-8621
Dariusleut, Chmn., No. 1, Martin Walter, Springpoint Colony, Box 249, Pincher Creek, AB T0K 1W0 Phone (403)553-4368
Lehrerleut, Chmn., Rev. John Wipf, Rosetown Colony, Box 1509, Rosetown, SK S0L 2V0 Tel. (306)882-3344

IFCA International, Inc.

This group of churches was organized in 1930 at Cicero, Illinois, by representatives of the American Council of Undenominational Churches and representatives of various independent churches. The founding churches and members had separated themselves from various denominational affiliations.

The IFCA provides a way for independent churches and ministers to unite in close fellowship and cooperation, in defense of the fundamental teachings of Scripture and in the proclamation of the gospel of God's grace.

Headquarters

3520 Fairlanes, Grandville, MI 49418 Tel. (616) 531-1840 Fax (616)531-1814
Mailing Address, P.O. Box 810, Grandville, MI 49468-0810
Media Contact, Exec. Dir., Rev. Les C. Lofquist
Email: office@ifca.org
Website: www.ifca.org

Officers

Exec. Dir., Rev. Les C. Lofquist
Pres., Dr. Robert Graves, Santa Rosa, CA

Periodicals

The Voice

International Church of the Foursquare Gospel

Founded by Aimee Semple McPherson in 1927, the International Church of the Foursquare Gospel proclaims the message of Jesus Christ the Savior, Healer, Baptizer with the Holy Spirit and Soon-coming King. Headquartered in Los Angeles, this evangelistic missionary body of believers consists of nearly 1,907 churches in the United States and Canada.

The International Church of the Foursquare Gospel is incorporated in the state of California and governed by a Board of Directors who direct its corporate affairs. A Foursquare Cabinet, consisting of the Corporate Officers, Board of Directors and District Supervisors of the various districts of the Foursquare Church in the United States and other elected or appointed members, serves in an advisory capacity to the President and the Board of Directors.

Each local Foursquare Church is a subordinate unit of the International Church of the Foursquare Gospel. The pastor of the church is appointed by the Board of Directors and is responsible for the spiritual and physical welfare of the church. To assist and advise the pastor, a church council is elected by the local church members.

Foursquare Churches seek to build strong believers through Christian education, Christian day schools, youth camping and ministry, Foursquare Women International who support and encourage Foursquare missionaries abroad, radio and television ministries, the Foursquare World Advance Magazine and 276 Bible Colleges worldwide.

Worldwide ministries remains the focus of the Foursquare Gospel Church with 26,139 churches and meeting places, 37,919 national Foursquare pastors/leaders and 3,331,561 members and adherents in 107 countries around the globe. The Church is affiliated with the Pentecostal/Charismatic Churches of North America, National Association of Evangelicals and the World Pentecostal Fellowship.

Headquarters

1910 W. Sunset Blvd., Ste. 200, P.O. Box 26902, Los Angeles, CA 90026-0176 Tel. (213)989-4234 Fax (213)989-4590
Media Contact, Editor, Dr. Ron Williams
Website: www.foursquare.org

CORPORATE OFFICERS

Pres., Dr. Paul C. Risser
Vice-Pres., Dr. Clifford Hanes
Gen. Supvr., Rev. Jared Roth
Dir. of Missions Intl., Rev. Michael Larkin
Sec., Rev. Herbert Schneidau
Treas., Mr. Brent Morgan
Bd. of Directors: Dr. Paul C. Risser; Rev. Ralph Torres; Rev. Naomi Beard; Rev. Arthur Gray; Mark Simon; Rev. Alan Eastland; Rev. Lolita Frederick; Rev. Steve Overman; Rev. James Cecil; Rev. Ron Pinkston; Rev. Ivy Stanton
District Supervisors: Eastern, Dr. Dewey Morrow; Great Lakes, Dr. Fred Parker; Midwest, Rev. Larry Spousta; Northwest, Dr. Tom Ferguson; South Central, Rev. Dennis Easter; Southeast, Rev. Glenn Burris, Jr.; Southern California, Rev. James C. Scott, Jr.; Southwest, Rev. Don Long; Western, Rev. Robert Booth
Foursquare Cabinet: Composed of Corp. Officers; Board of Directors; District Supervisors, Cabinet: Thomas A. Baker, Cosette M. Conaway; James P. Freund; Mark T. Harris; Eric D. Hulet; Parnell M. Lovelace, Jr.; Mary L. Phillips; David W. Wing; Enrique Zone; Richard E. Scott; Jac W. Hayford; Ron D. Mehl; Jesus De Paz; Ted Roberts; Roger Al Whitlow; Rosa Wijesiriwardena

SUPPORT MINISTRIES

Natl. Dept. of Youth, Natl. Youth Minister, Rev. Jerry Dirmann
Natl. Dept. of Chr. Educ., Dir., Rev. Rick Wulfestieg

Periodicals

Foursquare World Advance

International Council of Community Churches*

This body is a fellowship of locally autonomous, ecumenically minded, congregationally governed, non-creedal Churches. The Council came into being in 1950 as the union of two former councils of community churches, one formed of black churches known as the Biennial Council of Community Churches in the United States and elsewhere and the other of white churches known as the National Council of Community Churches.

Headquarters

21116 Washington Pky., Frankfort, IL 60423-3112 Tel. (815)464-5690 Fax (815)464-5692

Media Contact, Exec. Dir., Rev. Michael E. Livingston

Officers

Pres., Rev. Judson Souers
Vice-Pres., Abraham Wright
Vice-Pres., Grace O'Neal
Sec., Rev. Herbert Freitag
Treas., Martha Nolan

OTHER ORGANIZATIONS

Commission on Laity and Church Relations, Dr. Michael Donahue

Commission on Ecumenical Relations, Rev. Herman Harmelink

Commission on Clergy Relations, Rev. David Matthews

Commission on Faith, Justice & Mission, Rev. Dr. Kate Epperly

Women's Christian Fellowship, Pres., Brenda Swanson

Samaritans (Men's Fellowship), Pres., Don Fair

Young Adult Fellowship, Pres., Corwin Mason

Youth Fellowship, Pres., Megan Depan

Periodicals

The Christian Community; The Inclusive Pulpit

The International Pentecostal Church of Christ

At a General Conference held at London, Ohio, Aug. 10, 1976, the International Pentecostal Assemblies and the Pentecostal Church of Christ consolidated into one body, taking the name International Pentecostal Church of Christ.

The International Pentecostal Assemblies was the successor of the Association of Pentecostal Assemblies and the International Pentecostal Missionary Union. The Pentecostal Church of Christ was founded by John Stroup of Flatwoods, Ketucky, on May 10, 1917 and was incorporated at Portsmouth, Ohio, in 1927. The International Pentecostal Church of Christ is an active member of the Pentecostal/Charismatic Churches of North America, as well as a member of the National Association of Evangelicals.

The priorities of the International Pentecostal Church of Christ are to be an agency of God for evangelizing the world, to be a corporate body in which people may worship God and to be a channel of God's purpose to build a body of saints being perfected in the image of His Son.

The Annual Conference is held each year during the first full week of August in London, Ohio.

Headquarters

2245 St. Rt. 42 SW, P.O. Box 439, London, OH 43140 Tel. (740)852-4722 Fax (740)852-0348

Media Contact, Gen. Overseer, Clyde M. Hughes

Email: hqipcc@aol.com

EXECUTIVE COMMITTEE

Gen. Overseer, Clyde M. Hughes, P.O. Box 439, London, OH 43140 Tel. (740)852-4722 Fax (740)852-0348

Asst. Gen. Overseer, B.G. Turner, RR5, Box 1286, Harpers Ferry, WV 25425 Tel. (304)535-221 Fax (304)535-1357

Gen. Sec., Asa Lowe, 513 Johnstown Rd., Chesapeake, VA 23322 Tel. (757)547-4329

Gen. Treas., Ervin Hargrave, P.O. Box 439, London, OH 43140 Tel. (740)852-4722 Fax (740)852-0348

Dir. of Global Missions, Dr. James B. Keiller, P.O. Box 18145, Atlanta, GA 30316 Tel. (404)627-2681 Fax (404)627-0702

DISTRICT OVERSEERS

Blue Ridge District, Clyde M. Hughes, P.O. Box 439, London, OH 43140 Tel. (740)852-4722 Fax (740)852-0348

Central District, Ervin Hargrave, P.O. Box 439, London, OH 43140 Tel. (740)852-4722 Fax (740)852-0348

Mid-Eastern District, H. Gene Boyce, 705 W. Grubb St., Hertford, NC 27944 Tel. (252)426-5403

Mountain District, Terry Lykins, P.O. Box 131, Staffordsville, KY 41256 Tel. (606)297-3282

New River District, Calvin Weikel, RR. 2, Box 300, Ronceverte, WV 24970 Tel. (304)647-4301

North Central District, Edgar Kent, P.O. Box 275, Hartford, MI 49057 Tel. (616)621-3326

North Eastern District, Wayne Taylor, 806 8th St., Shenandoah, VA 22849 Tel. (540) 652-8090

South Eastern District, Frank Angie, 2507 Old Peachtree Rd., Duluth, GA 30097 Tel. (770) 476-5196

Tri-State District, Cline McCallister, 5210 Wilson St., Portsmouth, OH 45662 Tel. and Fax (740)776-6357

OTHER ORGANIZATIONS

Beulah Heights Bible College, Pres., Samuel R. Chand, P.O. Box 18145, Atlanta, GA 30316 Tel. (404)627-2681 Fax (404)627-0702

Women's Ministries, Gen. Pres., Janice Boyce, 121 W. Hunters Tr., Elizabeth City, NC 27909 Tel. and Fax (252)338-3003

Pentecostal Ambassadors, Dustin Hughes, National Youth Dir., P.O Box 439, London, OH 43140 Tel. (740)852-0448 Fax (740)852-0348

National Christian Education Dept., Dir., Dustin Hughes, P.O. Box 439, London, OH 43140 Tel. (740)852-0448 Fax (740)852-0348

Periodicals

The Bridegroom's Messenger; The Pentecostal Leader

International Pentecostal Holiness Church

This body grew out of the National Holiness Association movement of the last century, with roots in Methodism. Beginning in the South and Midwest, the church represents the merger of the

Fire-Baptized Holiness Church founded by B. H. Irwin in Iowa in 1895; the Pentecostal Holiness Church founded by A. B. Crumpler in Goldsboro, North Carolina, in 1898; and the Tabernacle Pentecostal Church founded by N. J. Holmes in 1898.

All three bodies joined the ranks of the pentecostal movement as a result of the Azusa Street revival in Los Angeles in 1906 and a 1907 pentecostal revival in Dunn, N.C., conducted by G. B. Cashwell, who had visited Azusa Street. In 1911 the Fire-Baptized and Pentecostal Holiness bodies merged in Falcon, N.C., to form the present church; the Tabernacle Pentecostal Church was added in 1915 in Canon, Georgia.

The church stresses the new birth, the Wesleyan experience of sanctification, the pentecostal baptism in the Holy Spirit, evidenced by speaking in tongues, divine healing and the premillennial second coming of Christ.

Headquarters
P.O. Box 12609, Oklahoma City, OK 73157-2609 Tel. (405)787-7110 Fax (405)789-3957
Media Contact, Admn. Asst.

Officers
E-mail: jdl@iphc.org (for Bishop Leggett)
Website: www.iphc.org
Gen. Supt., Bishop James D. Leggett
Vice Chpsn./Asst. Gen. Supt., Rev. M. Donald Duncan
Asst. Gen. Supt., Dr. Ronald Carpenter
Asst. Gen. Supt., Rev. Paul Howell
Gen. Sec.-Treas., Rev. Jack Goodson

OTHER ORGANIZATIONS
The Publishing House (LifeSprings), Gen. Admn., Greg Hearn, Franklin Springs, GA 30639
Women's Ministries, Exec. Dir., Mary Belle Johnson
Men's Ministries, General. Dir., Col. Jack Kelley, P.O. Box 53307, Fayetteville, NC 28305-3307

Periodicals
IssacharFile; Helping Hand; Evangelism USA; Worldorama; CEM Connection

Jehovah's Witnesses
Modern-day Jehovah's Witnesses began in the early 1870s when Charles Taze Russell was the leader of a Bible study group in Allegheny City, Pennsylvania. In July 1879, the first issue of Zion's Watch Tower and Herald of Christ's Presence (now called The Watchtower) appeared. In 1884 Zion's Watch Tower Tract Society was incorporated, later changed to Watch Tower Bible and Tract Society. Congregations spread into other states and followers witnessed from house to house.

By 1913, printed sermons were in four languages in 3,000 newspapers in the United States, Canada and Europe. Hundreds of millions of books, booklets and tracts were distributed. Publication of the magazine now known as Awake! Began in 1919. Today, it is published in more than 80 languages and has a circulation of upwards of 19,000,000. In 1931 the name Jehovah's Witnesses, based on Isaiah 43:10-12, was adopted.

During the 1930s and 1940s Jehovah's Witnesses fought many court cases in the interest of preserving freedom of speech, press, assembly and worship. They have won a total of 43 cases before the United States Supreme Court. A missionary training school was established in 1943, and it has been a major factor in the international expansion of the Witnesss. There are now 5.6 million Witnesses in 232 lands (1997).

Jehovah's Witnesses believe in one almighty God, Jehovah, who is the Creator of all things.They believe in Jesus Christ as God's Son, the first of His creations. While Jesus is now an immortal spirit in heaven, ruling as King of God's Kingdom, he is still subject to his heavenly Father, Jehovah God. Christ's human life was sacrificed as a ransom to open up for obedient mankind the opportunity of eternal life. With Christ in heaven, 144,000 individuals chosen from among mankind will rule in righteousness over an unnumbered great crowd who will survive the destruction of wickedness and receive salvation into an earth cleansed of evil. (Rev. 7:9,10; 14:1-5). These, along with the resurrected dead, will transform the earth into a global earthly paradise and will have the prospect of living forever on it.

Headquarters
25 Columbia Heights, Brooklyn, NY 11201-2483 Tel. (718)560-5600
Media Contact, Public Affairs Office, James Pellechia

Officers
Pres. Watch Tower Bible and Tract Society of Pennsylvania, Milton G. Henschel

The Latvian Evangelical Lutheran Church in America
This body was organized into a denomination on Aug. 22, 1975 after having existed as the Federation of Latvian Evangelical Lutheran Churches in America since 1955. This church is a regional constituent part of the Lutheran Church of Latvia Abroad, a member of the Lutheran World Federation and the World Council of Churches.

The Latvian Evangelical Lutheran Church in America works to foster religious life, traditions and customs in its congregations in harmony with the Holy Scriptures, the Apostles', Nicean and Athanasian Creeds, the unaltered Augsburg Confession, Martin Luther's Small and Large Catechisms and other documents of the Book of Concord.

The LELCA is ordered by its Synod (General Assembly), executive board, auditing committee and district conferences.

Headquarters

2140 Orkla Dr., Golden Valley, MN 55427 Tel. (612)722-0174 Email: ucepure@aol.com
Media Contact, Juris Pulins, 9531 Knoll Top Rd., Union, IL 60180 Tel. (815)923-5919
Email: pulins@flash.net

Officers

Pres., Rev. Uldis Cepure, Tel. (612)546-3712
Vice-Pres., Rev. Anita Varsbergs, 9908 Shelburne Terr., 312, Gathersburg, MD 20878 Tel. (301) 251-4151
2nd Vice-Pres., Daira Cilnis, 19222 Beckford Pl., Northridge, CA 91324 Tel. (818)349-8023
Sec.,Girts Kugars, 5209 Douglas Ave., Kalamazoo, MI 49004 Tel. (616)381-3798
Treas., Vilmars Beinikis, 17 John Dr., Old Bethpage, NY 11804 Tel. (516)293-8432

Periodicals

Cela Biedrs; Lelba Zinas

The Liberal Catholic Church— Province of the United States of America

The Liberal Catholic Church was founded Feb. 13, 1916 as a reorganization of the Old Catholic Church in Great Britain with the Rt. Rev. James I. Wedgwood as the first Presiding Bishop. The first ordination of a priest in the United States was Fr. Charles Hampton, later a Bishop. The first Regionary Bishop for the American Province was the Rt. Rev. Irving S. Cooper (1919-1935).

Headquarters

Pres., The Rt. Rev. William S.H. Downey, 1206 Ayers Ave., Ojai, CA 93023 Tel. (805)646-2573 Fax (805)646-2575
Media Contact, Regionary Bishop, The Rt. Rev. William S.H. Downey
Email: bshp052497@aol.com
Website: www.thelcc.org

Officers

Pres. & Regionary Bishop, The Rt. Rev. William S.H. Downey
Vice-Pres., Rev. L. Marshall Heminway, P.O. Box 19957 Hampden Sta., Baltimore, MD 21211-0957
Sec. (Provincial), Rev. Lloyd Worley, 1232 24th Avenue Ct., Greeley, CO 80631 Tel. (303)356-3002
Provost, Rev. Lloyd Worley
Treas., Rev. Milton Shaw

BISHOPS

Regionary Bishop for the American Province, The Rt. Rev. William S.H. Downey
Aux. Bishops of the American Province: Rt. Rev. Dr. Robert S. McGinnis, Jr., 3612 N. Labarre Rd., Metaire, LA 70002; Rt. Rev. Joseph L. Tisch, P.O. Box 1117, Melbourne, FL 32901; Rt. Rev. Dr. Hein VanBeusekom, 12 Krotona Hill, Ojai, CA 93023; Rt. Rev. Ruben

Cabigting, P.O. Box 270, Wheaton, IL 60189; The Rt. Rev. Lawrence Smith 9740 S. Avers Ave., Evergreen Park, IL.

Periodicals

Ubique

The Lutheran Church-Missouri Synod (LCMS)

The Lutheran Church-Missouri Synod, which was founded in 1847, has more than 6,000 congregations in the United States and works in 64 other countries. It has 2.6 million members and is the second-largest Lutheran denomination in North America.

Christian education is offered for all ages. The North American congregations operate the largest elementary and secondary school systems of any Protestant denomination in the nation, and 14,961 students are enrolled in 12 LCMS institutions of higher learning.

Traditional beliefs concerning the authority and interpretation of Scripture are important. The synod is known for mass-media outreach through "The Lutheran Hour" on radio, "This Is The Life" dramas on television, and the products of Concordia Publishing House, the third-largest Protestant publisher, whose Arch Books children's series has sold more than 58 million copies.

An extensive network of more than 1,000 volunteers in 58 work centers produces Braille, large-type, and audiocassette materials for the blind and visually impaired. Fifty-nine of the Eighty-five deaf congregations affiliated with U.S. Lutheran denominations are LCMS; and many denominations use the Bible lessons prepared for developmentally disabled persons.

The involvement of women is high, although they do not occupy clergy positions. Serving as teachers, deaconesses and social workers, women comprise approximately 48 percent of total professional workers.

The members' responsibility for congregational leadership is a distinctive characteristic of the synod. Power is vested in voters' assemblies, generally comprised of adults of voting age. Synod decision making is given to the delegates at triennial national and district conventions, where the franchise is equally divided between lay and pastoral representatives.

Headquarters

The Lutheran Church-Missouri Synod, International Center, 1333 S. Kirkwood Rd., St. Louis, MO 63122-7295
Media Contact, Dir., News & Information, Rev. David Mahsman, Tel. (314)996-1227; Director, Public Relations, Mr. David Strand, (314)996-1229; Manager, News Bureau, Mr. Joe Isenhower, (314)996-1231, Fax (314) 996-1126
Email: infocenter@lcms.org
Website: www.lcms.org

Officers

Pres., Dr. A.L. Barry

121

1st Vice-Pres., Dr. Robert T. Kuhn
2nd Vice-Pres., Dr. Robert King
3rd Vice-Pres., Dr. William C. Weinrich
4th Vice-Pres., Dr. Roger D. Pittelko
5th Vice-Pres., Dr. Wallace Schulz
Sec., Dr. Raymond L. Hartwig
Treas., Mr. Paul Middeke
Admn. Officer of Bd. of Dir., Dr. Bradford L. Hewitt
Exec. Dir., Human Resources, Barb Ryan
Bd. of Directors: Dr. Karl L. Barth, Milwaukee, WI; Rev. Roosevelt Gray, Detroit, MI; Dr. Betty Duda, Oviedo, FL; Richard Peters, Amery, WI; Clifford A. Dietrich, Fort Wayne, IN; Ernest E. Garbe, Dieterich, IL; Dr. Jean Garton, Benton, AR; Oscar H. Hanson, Lafayette, CA; Ted Kober, Billings, MT; Dr. Donald K. Muchow, Austin, TX, Chairman; Rev. Ulmer Marshall, Jr., Mobile, AL; Christian Preus, Plymouth, MN; Dr. Edwin Trapp, Jr., Dallas, TX

BOARDS AND COMMISSIONS

Communication Services, Exec. Dir., -vacant-
Mission Services, Exec. Dir., Dr. Glenn O'Shoney
Higher Education Services, Exec. Dir., Dr. William F. Meyer
Human Care Ministries, Exec. Dir., -vacant-
Worker Benefit Plans, Exec. Dir., Dan A. Leeman
Lutheran Church-Missouri Synod Foundation, Pres., -vacant-
Lutheran Church Ext. Fund-Missouri Synod, Pres., Merle Freitag
Congregational Services, Exec. Dir., Dr. Le Roy Wilke
Black Ministries Services, Exec. Dir., Dr. Bryant Clancy

ORGANIZATIONS

Concordia Publishing House, Pres./CEO, Dr. Stephen Carter, 3558 S. Jefferson Ave., St. Louis, MO 63118-3968
Concordia Historical Institute, Dir., Rev. Daniel Preus, Concordia Seminary, 801 De Mun Ave., St. Louis, MO 63105
Intl. Lutheran Laymen's League, Exec. Dir., Rodger W. Hebermehl, 2185 Hampton Ave., St. Louis, MO 63139-2983
KFUO Radio, Exec. Dir., -vacant-
Intl. Lutheran Women's Missionary League, Pres., Virginia Von Seggern, 3558 S. Jefferson Ave., St. Louis, MO 63118-3910

Periodicals

The Lutheran Witness; Reporter

Malankara Orthodox Syrian Church, Diocese of America*

The American Diocese of the Malankara Orthodox Syrian Church is in full accord with the Mother Church- Malankara Orthodox Syrian Church, also known as the Indian Orthodox Church. The diocese is a national or missionary entity of the Indian Orthodox Church. The Malankara Orthodox Syrian Church established an American diocese in 1978 to serve her immigrant members in America. This diocese is a new phenomenon with great challenges and potentials, composed of immigrant Indian Orthodox members and their American born children. Now that some years have passed, the immigrant church is entering into an indigenous era with the second generation Indian Orthodox members. Currently there are 60 parishes, 68 clergy and about 12,000 members of this church in the United States. The diocese is still growing with immigrants and native-born members.

The Malankara Orthodox Syrian Church has claimed its roots in the Apostolic ministry of Apostle St. Thomas, who was martyred in India, since 52 AD. Although there is not much available about the early history of the Indian Church, it is known that later it was influenced by Roman Catholicism and then Protestant missionaries of the post Reformation period. During the sixteenth century, there arose an increased relationship with the Oriental churches with the arrival of Syrian Bishops. Although different segments of Christianity have been flourishing in India, the Church maintained a close faith in the Non-Chalcedonian councils.

The Malankara Orthodox Syrian Church got its name: "Malankara" from Maliankara, a near-by town of Dodungalloor where St. Thomas is believed to have arrived in 52 AD; "Orthodox" comes from the faith of the fathers- non Chalcedonian faith; "Syrian" comes from its connection with the Syrian Orthodox Church's traditions, practices, liturgy, language, and liturgical calendar.

Headquarters

80-34 Commonwealth Boulevard
Bellerose, NY 11426
Tel. (718) 470-9844
Fax (718) 470-9219
Media Contact, His Grace Mathews Mar Barnabas, Diocesan Metropolitan

Officers

Diocesan Metropolitan, His Grace Mathews Mar Barnabas

Mar Thoma Syrian Church of India*

According to tradition, the Mar Thoma Church was established as a result of the apostolic mission of St. Thomas the apostle in 52 AD. Church history attests to the continuity of the community of faithful, throughout the long centuries in India. The liturgy and faith practices of the Church were based on the relationship between the Church in Kerala, India, which St. Thomas founded, with the East-Syrian and Persian Churches. This started in the 3rd century and continued up to the 16th century. In the 17th century, the Malabar Church of St. Thomas (as the

122

Church in Kerala was known) renewed her relationship with the Orthodox Patriarchate of Antioch as part of the resistance to forced Latinization by the Portuguese. This process also led to the development of the Kerala Episcopacy, whereby the first Indian Bishop Mar Thoma I was consecrated in Kerala.

The Mar Thoma Church retains her Eastern Orthodoxy. She follows an Orthodox (true) worship form and liturgy, believes in the catholicity of grace, is missionary and evangelistic in approach. She derives Episcopal succession from the Syrian Orthodox Church of Antioch and follows Eastern Reformed Theology. She is independent, autonomous, and indigenous, constitutionally combining democratic values and Episcopal authority. She has been in full communion with the Anglican Church since 1954.

The Diocese of North America was organized in 1988 in order to serve the needs of the immigrant community. It has a membership of around five thousand families in sixty five parishes.

Headquarters

Sinai Mar Thoma Center, 2320 S. Merrick Avenue, Merrick, New York 11566 Tel. (516)377-3311 Fax (516)377-3322

Officers

Diocesan Bishop: The Rt. Rev. Dr. Zacharias Mar Theophilus Episcopa

Diocesan/Bishop's Sec.: The Rev. Oommen Philip

Diocesan Treasurer: Kuruvilla Cherian, CPA

Mennonite Church

The Mennonite Church is currently working with two other North American Mennonite denominations—the General Conference Mennonite Church and the Conference of Mennonites in Canada—to form the new, United Mennonite Church, organized as U.S. and Canadian bodies. The three have adopted the same vision statement and the Confession of Faith in a Mennonite Perspective. Some staff members are already jointly appointed. An Executive Board for Mennonite Church USA and a General Board for Mennonite Church Canada were elected in July 1999. Further decisions will be made in summer 2001.

The Mennonite Church in North America traces its beginnings to the Protestant Reformation. Conrad Grebel, Georg Blaurock and a small band of radical believers baptized one another in Zurich, Switzerland, on Jan. 21, 1525. First nicknamed Anabaptists (Rebaptizers) by their opponents, they preferred the term Brothers and Sisters in Christ. They later took their name from the Dutch priest Menno Simons, who joined the movement in 1536.

The Mennonites' refusal to conform to majesterial decrees, including bearing of arms and the swearing of oaths, attracted fierce animosity. Thousands were martyred for their beliefs in nearly a century of persecution. They moved to many places, including the United States and Canada, where some arrived as early as 1683.

North American Mennonites began their first home mission program in Chicago, Illinois in 1893 and their first overseas mission program in India in 1899. Since the 1920s the church has established extensive emergency relief and development services in conjunction with its mission program.

Mennonites hold that the Word of God is central and that new life in Christ is available to all who believe. Adult "Believers" baptism is practiced, symbolizing a conscious decision to follow Christ. Mennonites take seriously Christ's command to witness in word and deed. They stress that Christians need the support of a faith community for encouragement and growth. They view the teachings of Jesus as directly applicable to their lives. Mennonites generally refuse to serve in the military or to use violent resistance.

The largest body of Mennonites in North America, the Mennonite Church is a member of the Mennonite and Brethren in Christ World Conference, a worldwide fellowship, and the Mennonite Central Committee, an international relief and service agency. Individuals and program agencies participate in a variety of ecumenical activities at various levels of church life.

Headquarters

421 S. Second St., Ste. 600, Elkhart, IN 46516 Tel. (219)294-7131 Fax (219)293-3977, Email: mcgb@juno.com

Media Contact, J. Ron Byler, Associate Gen. Sec.

Email: rbyler@juno.com

Officers

Mod., Lee Snyder, 259 Brookwood Dr., Bluffton, OH 45817

Mod. Elect, Ervin Stutzman, 1200 Park Rd., Harrisonburg, VA 22802

Sec., Duane Oswald, 1111 E. Herndon Ave., Suite 308, Fresno, CA 93720-3100

Member at large, James M. Harder, P.O. Box 191, North Newton, KS 67117

Member at large, Roy Williams, 22642 Newfield Ct., Land O'Lakes, FL 34639

Exec. Bd., Gen. Sec., George B. Stoltzfus

Historical Cmte., Dir., John E. Sharp, 1700 S. Main, Goshen, IN 46526 Tel. (219)535-7477 Fax (219)535-7477, Email: johnes@hoshen.edu

Peace & Justice Committee, Susan Mark Landis, Minister of Peace and Justice, P.O.Box 173, Orville, OH 44667 Tel. (330) 683-6844 Fax (330) 683-6844, Email: mcpjc@ssnet.com

Bd. of Congregational Min., Pres., James H. Waltner, Box 1245, Elkhart, IN 46515 Tel. (219)294-7523 Fax (219)293-1892, Email: mbcma@juno.com

Bd. of Educ., Pres., Orville L. Yoder, Box 1142, Elkhart, IN 46515 Tel. (219)389-0018 Fax (219)293-7446, Email: sand.lb@juno.com

123

Bd. of Missions, Pres., Stanley W. Green, Box 370, Elkhart, IN 46515 Tel. (219)294-7523, Fax (219)294-8669, Email: barbara@mbm.org

Mutual Aid Bd., Pres., Howard L. Brenneman, 1110 North Main, P.O. Box 483, Goshen, IN 46526 Tel. (219)533-9511 Fax (219)533-5264, Email: mma@mma-online.org

Mennonite Publication Bd., Publisher, J. Robert Ramer, 616 Walnut Ave., Scottdale, PA 15683 Tel. (412)887-8500 Fax (412)887-3111, Email: info@mph.org

Periodicals

The Mennonite; Builder; Christian Living; Rejoice!; Mennonite Historical Bulletin; Mennonite Quarterly Review; On the Line; Purpose; Story Friends

Mennonite Church, The General Conference

The General Conference Mennonite Church is currently working with two other North American Mennonite denominations—the Mennonite Church and the Conference of Mennonites in Canada—to form the new, united Mennonite Church, organized as U.S. and Canadian bodies. The three have adopted the same vision statement and the Confession of Faith in a Mennonite Perspective. Some staff members are already jointly appointed. An Executive Board for Mennonite Church USA and a General Board for Mennonite Church Canada were elected in July 1999. Further decisions will be made in summer 2001.

The General Conference Mennonite Church was formed in 1860, uniting Mennonites throughout the United States who were interested in doing missionary work together. Today 65,500 Christians in 400 member congregations in Canada, the United States and three countries in South America try to follow the way of Jesus in their daily lives.

The conference consists of people of many ethnic backgrounds—including Swiss and German, Russian and Dutch, Native American, African American, Hispanic, Chinese, Vietnamese and Laotian.

The basic belief and practice of the conference come from the life and teachings of Jesus Christ, the early church of the New Testament and the Anabaptists of the 16th-century Reformation. Thus the conference seeks to be evangelical, guided by the Bible, led by the Holy Spirit and supported by a praying, discerning community of believers in congregations and fellowships. Peace, or shalom, is at the very heart of members, who seek to be peacemakers in everyday life.

The Mennonite vision statement reads, "God calls us to be followers of Jesus Christ and, by the power of the Holy Spirit, to grow as communities of grace, joy, and peace, so that God's healing and hope flow through us to the world."

Headquarters

722 Main, P.O. Box 347, Newton, KS 67114 Tel. (316)283-5100 Fax (316)283-0454

Media Contact, Dir. of Communications, David Linscheid; Email: gcmc@gcmc.org

Email: gcmc@gcmc.org

Website: www.southwind.net/~gcmc

OFFICERS & STAFF, MENNONITE CHURCH USA

Moderator, Lee Snyder, 259 Brookwood Drive, Bluffton, OH 45817

Moderator-elect, Ervin Stutzman, 374 Donegal Springs Rd., Mount Joy, PA 17552

Secretary, Duane Oswald, 1111 E. Herndon Ave., Suite 308, Fresno, CA 93720-3100

Member at Large, James M. Harder, P.O. Box 191, North Newton, KS 67117

Member at Large, Roy Williams, 22642 Newfield Ct., Land O'Lakes, FL 34639

General Secretary, George Stoltzfus, 421 S. 2nd Street, Suite 600, Elkhart, IN 46516

Gen. Sec., James Schrag, 722 Main St., Newton, KS 67114

Ministerial Leadership Committee, Dir. of Ministerial Leadership, Keith Harder, 722 Main St., Newton, KS 67114

OTHER ORGANIZATIONS RELATED TO GENERAL CONFERENCE MENNONITE CHURCH

Commission on Education, Exec. Sec., Dennis Good

Commission on Home Ministries, Exec., Sec. Lois Barrett

Commission on Overseas Mission, Exec. Sec., Ron Flaming

Division of General Services

Business Manager and Treas., Ted Stuckey; Communications Dir., Cynthia Snider

Faith and Life Press, Manager, Dennis Good

Mennonite Women, Exec. Coord., Lara Hall Blosser

Mennonite Men, Coord., Jim Gingerich

Periodicals

The Mennonite (published jointly with the Mennonite Church)

The United Methodist Church is listed under "U".

The Metropolitan Church Association, Inc.

Organized after a revival movement in Chicago in 1894 as the Metropolitan Holiness Church, this organization was chartered as the Metropolitan Church Association in 1899. It has Wesleyan theology.

Headquarters

323 Broad St., Lake Geneva, WI 53147 Tel. (414)248-6786

Media Contact, Pres., Rev. Warren W. Bitzer

Officers
Pres., Rev. Warren W. Bitzer
Vice-Pres. & Sec., Elbert L. Ison
Treas., Gertrude J. Puckhaber

Periodicals
The Burning Bush

The Missionary Church

The Missionary Church was formed in 1969 through a merger of the United Missionary Church (organized in 1883) and the Missionary Church Association (founded in 1898). It is evangelical and conservative with a strong emphasis on missionary work and church planting.

There are three levels of church government with local, district and general conferences. There are 11 church districts in the United States. The general conference meets every two years. The denomination operates one college in the United States.

Headquarters
3811 Vanguard Dr., P.O. Box 9127, Ft. Wayne, IN 46899-9127 Tel. (219)747-2027 Fax (219) 747-5331
Media Contact, Pres., Dr. John Moran
Email: mcdenomusa@aol.com
Website: www.mcusa.org

Officers
Pres., Dr. John Moran
Vice-Pres., Rev. William Hossler
Sec., Rev. Dave Engbrecht
Treas., Milt Gerber
Director of Church Planting, Rev. Robert Ransom
Director of World PartnersUSA: Rev. David Mann
Director of Discipling Ministries, Rev. Tom Swank
Dir. of Ad. Services, David Von Gunten
Director of Financial Services, Neil Rinehart
Youth Dir., Eric Liechty
Children's Dir., Mrs. Pam Merillat
Resource & Curriculum, Dr. Duane Beals
Family Life Dir., Christine Crocker
Marketing & Communication Dir.
Sunday School/Body Building Dir., Bob Keller
Senior Adult Ministry Dir., Dr. Charles Cureton
Missionary Men Liaison, Rev. Ron Phipps
Missionary Women Intl., Pres., Barbara Reffey
Missionary Church Investment Foundation, Mr. Eric Smith

Periodicals
Emphasis on Faith and Living; Priority

Moravian Church in America (Unitas Fratrum)*

In 1735 German Moravian missionaries of the pre-Reformation faith of Jan Hus came to Georgia, in 1740 to Pennsylvania, and in 1753 to North Carolina. They established the American Moravian Church, which is broadly evangelical, ecumenical, liturgical, "conferential" in form of government and has an episcopacy as a spiritual office. The Northern and Southern Provinces of the church operate on a semi-autonomous basis.

Headquarters
Denominational offices or headquarters are called the Provincial Elders' Conference.
See addresses for Northern and Southern Provinces:

NORTHERN PROVINCE

Headquarters
1021 Center St., P.O. Box 1245, Bethlehem, PA 18016-1245 Tel. (610)867-7566 Fax (610)866-9223
Media Contact, Rev. R. Burke Johnson

PROVINCIAL ELDERS' CONFERENCE
Pres., Rev. R. Burke Johnson
Vice-Pres./Sec. (Eastern Dist.), Rev. David L. Wickmann
Vice-Pres. (Western Dist.), Rev. Lawrence Christianson
Comptroller, Theresa E. Kunda, 1021 Center St., P.O. Box 1245, Bethlehem, PA 18016-1245
Eastern District Pres., Rev. David L. Wickmann, P.O. Box 1245, Bethlehem, PA 18016-1245
Western District Pres., Rev. Lawrence Christianson, P.O. Box 386, Sun Prairie, WI 53590
Pacific Southwest District Pres., Mr. Paul Detilla, 9600 Lemdran, Downey, CA 90240
Canadian District Pres., Mr. Graham Kerslake, 10910 Harvest Lake Way, NE, Calgary, AB T3K 4L1

SOUTHERN PROVINCE

Headquarters
459 S. Church St., Winston-Salem, NC 27101 or Mailing address: Drawer O, Winston-Salem, NC 27108 Tel. (336)725-5811 Fax (336)723-1029
Email: rsawyer@mcsp.org
Website: www.moravian.org (for Moravian Church, Northern and Southern Province)

PROVINCIAL ELDERS' CONFERENCE
Pres., Rev. Dr. Robert E. Sawyer
Vice President, Rev. Lane A. Sapp
Sec. Mr. George Johnson
Treas., Mr. Richard Cartner, Drawer M, Salem Station, Winston-Salem, NC 27108
Other Members: Mrs. Betsy R. Bombick, Rev. Tom Shelton
Asst. to Pres., Robert Hunter

ALASKA PROVINCE
P.O. Box 545, Bethel, AK 99559
Email: burke@mcnp.org
Website: www.moravian.org

Officers

Pres., Rev. Frank Chingliak
Vice-Pres., Rev. Peter Green
Sec., Sarah Owens
Treas., Juanita Asicksik
Dir. of Theological Education, Rev. Will Updegrove

Periodicals

The Moravian

Mormons-please see The Church of Jesus Christ of Latter-day Saints.

National Association of Congregational Christian Churches

This association was organized in 1955 in Detroit, Michigan, by delegates from Congregational Christian Churches committed to continuing the Congregational way of faith and order in church life. Participation by member churches is voluntary.

Headquarters

P.O. Box 1620, Oak Creek, WI 53154 Tel. (414)764-1620 Fax (414)764-0319
Media Contact, Assoc. Exec. Sec., Rev. Dr. Donald P. Olsen, 8473 So. Howell Ave., Oak Creek, WI 53154 Tel. (414)764-1620 Fax (414)764-0319
Email: naccc@naccc.org
Website: www.naccc.org/

Officers

Exec. Sec., Rev. Dr. Douglas L. Lobb, 8473 South Howell Ave., Oak Creek, WI 53154
Assoc. Exec. Secs., Rev. Phil Jackson and Rev. Dr. Donald P. Olsen

Periodicals

The Congregationalist

National Association of Free Will Baptists

This evangelical group of Arminian Baptists was organized by Paul Palmer in 1727 at Chowan, North Carolina. Another movement (teaching the same doctrines of free grace, free salvation and free will) was organized June 30, 1780, in New Durham, N.H., but there was no connection with the southern organization except for a fraternal relationship.

The northern line expanded more rapidly and extended into the West and Southwest. This body merged with the Northern Baptist Convention Oct. 5, 1911, but a remnant of churches reorganized into the Cooperative General Association of Free Will Baptists Dec. 28, 1916, at Pattonsburg, Mo.

Churches in the southern line were organized into various conferences from the beginning and finally united in one General Conference in 1921.

Representatives of the Cooperative General Association and the General Conference joined Nov. 5, 1935 to form the National Association of Free Will Baptists.

Headquarters

5233 Mt. View Rd., Antioch, TN 37013-2306 Tel. (615)731-6812 Fax (615)731-0771
Mailing Address, P.O. Box 5002, Antioch, TN 37011-5002
Media Contact, Exec. Sec., Melvin Worthington

Officers

Exec. Sec., Dr. Melvin Worthington
Mod., Rev. Carl Cheshier, PO Box 7208, Moore, OK 73153

DENOMINATIONAL AGENCIES

Free Will Baptist Foundation, Exec. Dir., William Evans
Free Will Baptist Bible College, Pres., Dr. Tom Malone
Foreign Missions Dept., Dir., Rev. James Forlines
Home Missions Dept., Dir., Trymon Messer
Bd. of Retirement, Dir., Rev. William Evans
Historical Commission, Chpsn., Dr. Thomas Marberry
Comm. for Theological Integrity, Chpsn., Rev. Leroy Forlines, P.O. Box 50117, Nashville, TN 37205
Music Commission, Chpsn., Rev. Randy Sawyer, 2316 Union Rd., Gastonia, NC 28054
Media Comm., Chpsn., Rev. Steve Faison, PO Box 295, Cedar Springs, GA 31732
Sunday School & Church Training Dept., Dir., Dr. Alton Loveless
Women Nationally Active for Christ, Exec. Sec., Majorie Workman
Master's Men Dept., Dir., Rev. Tom Dooley

Periodicals

Attack, A Magazine for Christian Men; Contact; Free Will Bible College Bulletin; Co-Laborer; Free Will Baptist Gem; Heartbeat; AIM

National Baptist Convention of America, Inc.*

The National Baptist Convention of America, Inc., was organized in 1880. Its mission is articulated through its history, constitution, articles of incorporation and by-laws. The Convention (corporate churches) has a mission statement with fourteen (14) objectives including: fostering unity throughout its membership and the world Christian community by proclaiming the gospel of Jesus Christ; validating and propagating the Baptist doctrine of faith and practice, and its distinctive principles throughout the world; and harnessing and encouraging the scholarly and Christian creative skills of its membership for Christian writing and publications.

Headquarters

Media Contact, Liaison Officer, Dr. Richard A.

Rollins, 777 S. R.L. Thornton Fwy., Ste. 205, Dallas, TX 75203 Tel. (214)946-8913 Fax (214)946-9619

Officers

Pres., Dr. E. Edward Jones, 1327 Pierre Ave., Shreveport, LA 71103 Tel. (318)221-3701 Fax (318)222-7512

Gen. Rec. Sec., Dr. Clarence C. Pennywell, 2016 Russell Rd., Shreveport, LA 71107

Corres. Sec., Rev. E. E. Stafford, 6614 South Western Ave., Los Angeles, CA 90047

Liaison Officer, Dr. Richard A. Rollins, 777 So. R.L. Thornton Frwy., Ste. 205, Dallas, TX 75203 Tel. (214)946-8913 Fax (214)946-9619

Pres. Aide, Rev. Dr. Joe R. Gant, 5823 Ledbetter St., Shreveport, LA 77108

Periodicals

The Lantern

National Baptist Convention, U.S.A., Inc.*

The older and parent convention of black Baptists, this body is to be distinguished from the National Baptist Convention of America.

Headquarters

1700 Baptist World Center Dr., Nashville, TN 37207 Tel. (615)228-6292 Fax (615)226-5935

Officers

Pres., Dr. William J. Shaw, 1700 Baptist World Center Dr., Nashville, TN 37207 Tel. (615)228-6292 Fax (615)226-5935

Gen. Sec., Dr. Roscoe Cooper, Jr., 300 Grace St., Richmond, VA 23220-4908 Tel. (804)643-0192

Periodicals

Mission Herald

National Missionary Baptist Convention of America*

The National Missionary Baptist Convention of America was organized in 1988 as a separate entity from the National Baptist Convention of America, Inc., after a dispute over control of the convention's publishing efforts. The new organization intended to remain committed to the National Baptist Sunday Church School and Baptist Training Union Congress and the National Baptist Publishing Board.

The purpose of the National Missionary Baptist Convention of America is to serve as an agency of Christian education, church extension and missionary efforts. It seeks to maintain and safeguard full religious liberty and engage in social and economic development.

Headquarters

1404 E. Firestone, Los Angeles, CA 90001 Tel. (213)582-0090

Media Contact, Dr. W. T. Snead, Sr.

Officers

Pres., Dr. W. T. Snead, Sr.

Vice-Pres., At-large, Dr. Harvey E. Leggett, 866 Monroe St., Ypsilanti, MI 48197

Vice-Pres., Ecumenical Affairs, Dr. F. Benjamin Davis, 1535 Dr. A.J. Brown Blvd. N., Indianapolis, IN 46202

Vice-Pres., Auxiliaries, T. J. Prince, 2219 Sea Island Dr., Dallas, TX 75232

Vice-Pres., Boards, Dr. O. E. Piper, 4220 W. 18th St., Chicago, IL 60623

Vice-Pres., Financial Affairs, J. A. Boles, 2001 South J St., Tacoma, WA 98405

Pres., National Baptist Publishing Bd., Dr. T. B. Boyd, III, 6717 Centennial Blvd., Nashville, TN 37209

Gen. Sec., Dr. Melvin V. Wade, 4269 S. Figueroa, Los Angeles, CA 90037

Corres. Sec., Dr. H. J. Johnson, 2429 South Blvd., Dallas, TX 75215

Treas., Dr. W. N. Daniel, 415 W. Englewood Ave., Chicago, IL 60612

Rec. Sec., Dr. Lonnie Franks, Crocker, TX

National Organization of the New Apostolic Church of North America

This body is a variant of the Catholic Apostolic Church which began in England in 1830. The New Apostolic Church distinguished itself from the parent body in 1863 by recognizing a succession of Apostles.

Headquarters

3753 N. Troy St., Chicago, IL 60618

Media Contact, Sec. & Treas., Ellen E. Eckhardt, Tel. (773)539-3652 Fax (773)478-6691

Website: www.nak.org

Officers

Pres., Rev. Erwin Wagner, 330 Arlene Pl., Waterloo, ON N2J 2G6

First Vice-Pres., Rev. Richard C. Freund, 1 Mikel Ln., Glen Head, NY 11545-1591

Second Vice-Pres., Rev. Leonard E Kolb, 4522 Wood St., Erie, PA 16509-1639

Treas. & Sec., Ellen E. Eckhardt, 6380 N. Indian Rd., Chicago, IL 60646

Asst. Sec., Rev. John E. Doderer, 3753 N. Troy St., Chicago, IL 60618

National Primitive Baptist Convention, Inc.

Throughout the years of slavery and the Civil War, the African American population of the South worshipped with the white population in their various churches. At the time of emancipation, their white brethren helped them establish their own churches, granting them letters of fellowship, ordaining their deacons and ministers and helping them in other ways.

The doctrine and polity of this body are quite similar to that of white Primitive Baptists, yet there are local associations and a national convention, organized in 1907.

Each church is independent and receives and

127

controls its own membership. This body was formerly known as Colored Primitive Baptists.

Headquarters
6433 Hidden Forest Dr., Charlotte, NC 28213 Tel. (704)596-1508
Media Contact, Elder T. W. Samuels

Officers
Natl. Convention, Pres., Elder T. W. Samuels, Tel. (704)596-3153
Natl. Convention, Vice-Pres., Elder Ernest Ferrell, Tallahassee, FL
Natl. Convention, Chmn. Bd. of Dirs., Elder Ernest Ferrell, Tallahassee, FL
Natl. Church School Training Union, Pres., Jonathan Yates, Mobile, AL
Natl. Ushers Congress, Pres., Bro. Carl Batts, 21213 Garden View Dr., Maple Heights, OH 44137
Publishing Bd., Chpsn., Elder E. W. Wallace, Creamridge, NJ
Women's Congress, Pres., Betty Brown, Cocoa Beach, FL
Natl. Laymen's Council, Pres., Densimore Robinson, Huntsville, AL
Natl. Youth Congress, Pres., Robert White, Trenton, NJ

National Spiritualist Association of Churches
This organization is made up of believers that Spiritualism is a science, philosophy and religion based upon the demonstrated facts of communication between this world and the next.

Headquarters
NSAC General Offices, Rev. Sharon L. Snowman, Secretary, P.O. Box 217, Lily Dale, NY 14752-0217
Media Contact, Mr. Robert Egby, 720 Almonesson, Westville, NJ 08093
Email: nsac@nsac.org
Website: www.nsac.org

Officers
Pres., Rev. Barbara Thurman, 200 Marina Vista Rd., Larkspur, CA 94939-2144
Vice-Pres., Rev. Pamla Ashlay, 11811 Watertown Plank Rd., Milwaukee, WI 53226
Sec., Rev. Sharon L. Snowman, P.O. Box 217, Lily Dale, NY 14752 Tel. (716)595-2000 Fax (716)595-2020
Treas., Rev. Lelia Cutler, 7310 Medfield St. #1, Norfolk, VA 23505

OTHER ORGANIZATIONS
Bureau of Educ., Supt., Rev. Catherine Snell, 17 Ann Court, Kings Park, NY 11754
Bureau of Public Relations, Mr. Robert Egby, 720 Almonesson, Westville, NJ 08093
The Stow Memorial Foundation, Sec., Rev. Sharon L. Snowman, P.O. Box 217, Lily Dale, NY 14752 Tel. (716)595-2000 Fax (716)595-2020

Spiritualist Benevolent Society, Inc., P.O. Box 217, Lily Dale, NY 14752

Periodicals
The National Spiritualist Summit; Spotlight

Netherlands Reformed Congregations
The Netherlands Reformed Congregations organized denominationally in 1907. In the Netherlands, the so-called Churches Under the Cross (established in 1839, after breaking away from the 1834 Secession congregations) and the so-called Ledeboerian churches (established in 1841 under the leadership of the Rev. Ledeboer, who seceded from the Reformed State Church), united in 1907 under the leadership of the then 25-year-old Rev. G. H. Kersten, to form the Netherlands Reformed Congregations. Many of the North American congregations left the Christian Reformed Church to join the Netherlands Reformed Congregations after the Kuyperian presupposed regeneration doctrine began making inroads.

All Netherlands Reformed Congregations, office-bearers and members subscribe to three Reformed Forms of Unity: The Belgic Confession of Faith (by DeBres), the Heidelberg Catechism (by Ursinus and Olevianus) and the Canons of Dort. Both the Belgic Confession and the Canons of Dort are read regularly at worship services, and the Heidelberg Catechism is preached weekly, except on church feast days.

Headquarters
Media Contact, Synodical Clk., Rev. C. Vogelaar, 2281 Mapleleaf Terrace, Grand Rapids, MI 49505 Tel. (616)742-5929 Fax (616)742-5930

OTHER ORGANIZATIONS
Netherlands Reformed Book and Publishing, 1233 Leffingwell NE, Grand Rapids, MI 49505

Periodicals
The Banner of Truth; Paul (mission magazine); *Insight Into* (for young people); *Learning and Living* (for school and home)

The New Church-please see General Church of the New Jerusalem.

North American Baptist Conference
The North American Baptist Conference was begun by immigrants from Germany. The first church was organized by the Rev. Konrad Fleischmann in Philadelphia in 1843. In 1865 delegates of the churches met in Wilmot, Ontario, and organized the North American Baptist Conference. Today only a few churches still use the German language, mostly in a bilingual setting.

The Conference meets in general session once every three years for fellowship, inspiration and to conduct the business of the Conference through elected delegates from the local churches. The General Council, composed of representatives of the various Associations and Conference organizations and departments, meets annually to determine the annual budget and programs for the Conference and its departments and agencies. The General Council also makes recommendations to the Triennial Conference on policies, long-range plans and election of certain personnel, boards and committees.

Approximately 65 missionaries serve in Brazil, Cameroon, Japan, Mexico, Nigeria, Philippines, and Russia.

Ten homes for the aged are affiliated with the Conference and 12 camps are operated on the association level.

Headquarters
1 S. 210 Summit Ave., Oakbrook Terrace, IL 60181 Tel. (630)495-2000 Fax (630)495-3301
Media Contact, Marilyn Schaer

Officers
Mod., Rev. Harvey Wilkie
Vice-Mod., Mr. Gordon Unger
Exec. Dir., Dr. Philip Yntema
Treas., Jackie Loewer

OTHER ORGANIZATIONS
Intl. Missions Dept., Dir., Ron Salzman
Home Missions Dept., Dir., Rev. Bob Walther
Church Extension Investors Fund, Dir., Les D. Collins

Periodicals
NABtoday

North American Old Roman Catholic Church (Archdiocese of New York)
This body is identical with the Roman Catholic Church in faith but differs from it in discipline and worship. The Mass is offered with the appropriate rite either in Latin or in the vernacular. All other sacraments are taken from the Roman Pontifical. This jurisdiction allows for married clergy.

PRIMATIAL HEADQUARTERS
Box 021647 GPO, Brooklyn, NY 11202-0036 Tel. (718)855-0600
Media Contact, Chancellor, Most Rev. Albert J. Berube

Officers
Primate, The Most Rev. Herve L. Quessy
Chancellor, Most Rev. Albert J. Berube
Diocese of New York: Ordinary, Most Rev. Albert J. Berube
Diocese of Montreal & French Canada: Ordinary, Most Rev. Herve L. Quessy

Old German Baptist Brethren
This group separated from the Church of the Brethren (formerly German Baptist Brethren) in 1881 in order to preserve and maintain historic Brethren Doctrine.

Headquarters
Vindicator Ofc. Ed., Steven L. Bayer, 6952 N. Montgomery County Line Rd., Englewood, OH 45322-9748 Tel. (937)884-7531

Periodicals
The Vindicator

Old Order Amish Church
The congregations of this Old Order Amish group have no annual conference. They worship in private homes. They adhere to the older forms of worship and attire. This body has bishops, ministers and deacons.

INFORMATION
Der Neue Amerikanische Calendar, c/o Raber's Book Store, 2467 C R 600, Baltic, OH 43804
Telephone Contact, LeRoy Beachy, Beachy Amish Mennonite Church, 4324 SR 39, Millersburg, OH 44654 Tel. (216)893-2883

Old Order (Wisler) Mennonite Church
This body arose from a separation of Mennonites dated 1872, under Jacob Wisler, in opposition to what were thought to be innovations.

The group is in the Eastern United States and Canada. Each state, or district, has its own organization and holds semi-annual conferences.

Headquarters
Media Contact, Amos B. Hoover, 376 N. Muddy Creek Rd., Denver, PA 17517 Tel. (717)484-4849 Fax (717)484-104

Open Bible Standard Churches
Open Bible Standard Churches originated from two revival movements: Bible Standard Conference, founded in Eugene, Oregon, under the leadership of Fred L. Hornshuh in 1919, and Open Bible Evangelistic Association, founded in Des Moines, Iowa, under the leadership of John R. Richey in 1932.

Similar in doctrine and government, the two groups amalgamated on July 26, 1935 as "Open Bible Standard Churches, Inc." with headquarters in Des Moines, Iowa.

The original group of 210 ministers has enlarged to incorporate over 2,479 ministers and 1,397 churches in 36 countries. The first missionary left for India in 1926. The church now ministers in Asia, Africa, South America, Europe, Canada, Mexico, Central America, and the Caribbean Islands.

Historical roots of the parent groups reach back to the outpouring of the Holy Spirit in 1906 at Azusa Street Mission in Los Angeles and to the full gospel movement in the Midwest. Both groups were organized under the impetus of pentecostal revival. Simple faith, freedom from fanaticism, emphasis on evangelism and missions and free fellowship with other groups were characteristics of the growing organizations.

The highest governing body of Open Bible Standard Churches meets biennially and is composed of all ministers and one voting delegate per 100 members from each church. A National Board of Directors, elected by the national and regional conferences, conducts the business of the organization. Official Bible College is Eugene Bible College in Oregon.

Open Bible Standard Churches is a charter member of the National Association of Evangelicals and of the Pentecostal/Charismatic Churches of North America. It is a member of the Pentecostal World Conference.

NATIONAL OFFICE
2020 Bell Ave., Des Moines, IA 50315 Tel. (515)288-6761 Fax (515)288-2510
Media Contact, Exec. Dir., Communications & Resources, Jeff Farmer, Tel. (515)288-6761 Fax (515)288-2510
Email: info@openbible.org
Website: www. openbible.org

Officers
Pres., Jeffrey E. Farmer
Sec.-Treas., Teresa A. Beyer
Dir. of Intl. Min., Paul V. Canfield

Periodicals
Message of the Open Bible

The (Original) Church of God, Inc.

This body was organized in 1886 as the first church in the United States to take the name "The Church of God." In 1917 a difference of opinion led this particular group to include the word (Original) in its name. It is a holiness body and believes in the whole Bible, rightly divided, using the New Testament as its rule and government.

Headquarters
P.O. Box 592, Wytheville, VA 24382
Media Contact, Gen. Overseer, Rev. William Dale, Tel. (800)827-9234

Officers
Gen. Overseer, Rev. William Dale
Asst. Gen. Overseer, Rev. Alton Evans

Periodicals
The Messenger

The Orthodox Church in America*

The Orthodox Church of America entered Alaska in 1794 before its purchase by the United States in 1867. Its canonical status of independence (autocephaly) was granted by its Mother Church, the Russian Orthodox Church, on April 10, 1970, and it is now known as The Orthodox Church in America.

Headquarters
P.O. Box 675, Syosset, NY 11791-0675 Tel. (516)922-0550 Fax (516)922-0954
Media Contact, Dir. of Communications, V. Rev. John Matusiak
Email: jjm@oca.org
Website: www.oca.org

Officers
Primate, Archbishop of Washington, Metropolitan of All America & Canada, Most Blessed Theodosius
Chancellor, V. Rev. Robert S. Kondratick, P.O. Box 675, Syosset, NY 11791 Tel. (516)922-0550 Fax (516)922-0954

SYNOD
Chpsn., His Beatitude Theodosius, P.O. Box 675, Syosset, NY 11791
Archbishop of New York, Most Rev. Peter, 33 Hewitt Ave., Bronxville, NY 10708
Archbishop of Pittsburgh & Western PA, Most Rev. Kyrill, P.O. Box R, Wexford, PA 15090
Archbishop of Dallas, Archbishop Dmitri, 4112 Throckmorton, Dallas, TX 75219
Archbishop of Philadelphia, Archbishop Herman, St. Tikhon's Monastery, South Canaan, PA 18459
Aux. Bishop of Anchorage, Rt. Rev. Innocent, P.O. Box 240805, Anchorage, AK 99524-0805
Archbishop of Detroit, Rt. Rev. Nathaniel, P.O. Box 309, Grass Lake, MI 49240-0309
Bishop of Midwest, Rt. Rev. Job, 605 Iowa St., Oak Park, IL 60302
Bishop of San Francisco, Rt. Rev. Tikhon, 649 North Robinson St., Los Angeles, CA 90026
Bishop of Ottawa and Canada, Rt. Rev. Seraphim, P.O. Box 179, Spencerville, ON K0E 1X0 Tel. (613)925-5226
Auxiliary Bishop, Titular Bishop of Bethesda, Rt. Rev. Mark, 9511 Sun Pointe Dr., Boynton Beach, FL 33437
Auxiliary Bishop for the Diocese of Alaska, Rt. Rev. Innocent, 513 E. 24th St., Ste. #3, Ancorage, AK 99503 Tel. (907) 279-0025

Periodicals
The Orthodox Church

The Orthodox Presbyterian Church

On June 11, 1936, certain ministers, elders and lay members of the Presbyterian Church in the U.S.A. withdrew from that body to form a new denomination. Under the leadership of the late Rev. J. Gresham Machen, noted conservative New Testament scholar, the new church determined to continue to uphold the Westminster Confession of Faith as traditionally understood by Presbyterians and to engage in proclamation of the gospel at home and abroad.

The church has grown modestly over the

years and suffered early defections, most notably one in 1937 that resulted in the formation of the Bible Presbyterian Church under the leadership of Dr. Carl McIntire. It now has congregations throughout the states of the continental United States.

The denomination is a member of the North American Presbyterian and Reformed Council and the International Council of Reformed Churches.

Headquarters
607 N. Easton Rd., Bldg. E, Box P, Willlow Grove, PA 19090-0920 Tel. (215)830-0900 Fax (215)830-0350
Media Contact, Stated Clerk, Rev. Donald J. Duff
E-mail: duff.1@opc.org
Website: www.opc.org

Officers
Moderator of General Assembly, The Rev. Larry G. Mininger, 818 East Harbour Ct., Ocoee, FL 34761-3116
Stated Clk., Rev. Donald J. Duff

Periodicals
New Horizons in the Orthodox Presbyterian Church

Patriarchal Parishes of the Russian Orthodox Church in the U.S.A.*
This group of parishes is under the direct jurisdiction of the Patriarch of Moscow and All Russia, His Holiness Aleksy II, in the person of a Vicar Bishop, His Grace Mercurius, Bishop of Zaraisk.

Headquarters
St. Nicholas Cathedral, 15 E. 97th St., New York, NY 10029 Tel. (212)831-6294 Fax (212)427-5003
Media Contact, Sec. to the Bishop, Boris Komaishko, Tel. (212)996-6638
Email: bmercurius@ruscon.com

Officers
Bishop Boris Komaishko

Pentecostal Assemblies of the World, Inc.
This organization is an interracial Pentecostal holiness of the Apostolic Faith, believing in repentance, baptism in Jesus's name and being filled with the Holy Ghost, with the evidence of speaking in tongues. It originated in the early part of the century in the Middle West and has spread throughout the country.

Headquarters
3939 Meadows Dr., Indianapolis, IN 46205 Tel. (317)547-9541
Media Contact, Admin., John E. Hampton, Fax (317)543-0512

Officers
Presiding Bishop, Norman L. Wagner

Asst. Presiding Bishop, James E. Tyson
Bishops: Arthus Brazier; George Brooks; Ramsey Butler; Morris Golder; Francis L. Smith, Francis L.; Brooker T. Jones; C. R. Lee; Robert McMurray; Philip L. Scott; William L. Smith; Samuel A. Layne; Freeman M. Thomas; James E. Tyson; Charles Davis; Willie Burrell; Harry Herman; Jeremiah Reed; Jeron Johnson; Clifton Jones; Robert Wauls; Ronald L. Young; Henry L. Johnson; Leodis Warren; Thomas J. Weeks; Eugene Redd; Thomas W. Weeks, Sr.; Willard Saunders; Davis L. Ellis; Earl Parchia; Vanuel C. Little; Norman Wagner; George Austin; Benjamin A. Pitt; Markose Thopil; John K. Cole; Peter Warkie; Norman Walters; Alphonso Scott; David Dawkins
Gen. Sec, Dr. Aletha Cushinberry
Assist. Gen Sec., Suffragan Bishop Noel Jones
Gen. Treas., Elder James Loving
Asst. Treas., Dist. Eld. Charles Ellis III

Periodicals
Christian Outlook

Pentecostal Church of God
Growing out of the pentecostal revival at the turn of the century, the Pentecostal Church of God was organized in Chicago on Dec. 30, 1919, as the Pentecostal Assemblies of the U.S.A. The name was changed to Pentecostal Church of God in 1922; in 1934 it was changed again to The Pentecostal Church of God of America, Inc.; and finally the name became the Pentecostal Church of God (Inc.) in 1979.

The International Headquarters was moved from Chicago, Illinois to Ottumwa, Iowa, in 1927, then to Kansas City, Missoui, in 1933 and finally to Joplin, Missouri, in 1951.

The denomination is evangelical and pentecostal in doctrine and practice. Active membership in the National Association of Evangelicals and the Pentecostal/Charismatic Churches North America is maintained.

The church is Trinitarian in doctrine and teaches the absolute inerrancy of the Scripture from Genesis to Revelation. Among its cardinal beliefs are the doctrines of salvation, which includes regeneration; divine healing, as provided for in the atonement; the baptism in the Holy Ghost, with the initial physical evidence of speaking in tongues; and the premillennial second coming of Christ.

Headquarters
4901 Pennsylvania, P.O. Box 850, Joplin, MO 64802 Tel. (417)624-7050 Fax (417)624-7102
Media Contact, Gen. Sec., Dr. Ronald R. Minor
Email: pcg@pcg.org

Officers
Gen. Supt., Dr. James D. Gee
Gen. Sec., Dr. Ronald R. Minor

OTHER GENERAL EXECUTIVES
Dir. of World Missions, Rev. John K. Norvell

131

Dir. of Indian Missions, Dr. C. Don Burke
Dir. of Youth Ministries, Rev. Reggie O. Powers
Dir. of Home Missions/Evangelism, Dr. H. O. (Pat) Wilson

ASSISTANT GENERAL SUPERINTENDENTS
Northwestern Division, Rev. Jamie J. Joiner
Southwestern Division, Rev. Lloyd L. Naten
North Central Division, Rev. Donald R. Dennis
South Central Division, Rev. E. L. Redding
Northeastern Division, Rev. Thomas E. Branham
Southeastern Division, Rev. C.W. Goforth

OTHER DEPARTMENTAL OFFICERS
Bus. Mgr., Rev. Alan Greagrey
Director of Women's Ministry, Diana L. Gee
Christian Educ., Dir., Mrs. Billie Palumbo

Periodicals
The Pentecostal Messenger; Spirit

Pentecostal Fire-Baptized Holiness Church
Organized in 1918, this group consolidated with the Pentecostal Free Will Baptists in 1919. It maintains rigid discipline over members.

Headquarters
P.O. Box 261, La Grange, GA 30241-0261 Tel. (706)884-7742
Media Contact, Gen. Mod., Wallace B. Pittman, Jr.

Officers
Gen. Treas., K. N. (Bill) Johnson, P.O. Box 1528, Laurinburg, NC 28352 Tel. (919)276-1295
Gen. Sec., W. H. Preskitt, Sr., Rt. 1, Box 169, Wetumpka, AL 36092 Tel. (205)567-6565
Gen. Mod., Wallace B. Pittman, Jr.
Gen. Supt. Mission Bd., Jerry Powell, Rt. 1, Box 384, Chadourn, NC 28431

Periodicals
Faith and Truth

The Pentecostal Free Will Baptist Church, Inc.
The Cape Fear Conference of Free Will Baptists, organized in 1855, merged in 1959 with The Wilmington Conference and The New River Conference of Free Will Baptists and was renamed the Pentecostal Free Will Baptist Church, Inc. The doctrines include regeneration, sanctification, the Pentecostal baptism of the Holy Ghost, the Second Coming of Christ and divine healing.

Headquarters
P.O. Box 1568, Dunn, NC 28335 Tel. (910)892-4161 Fax (910)892-6876
Media Contact, Gen. Supt., Preston Heath
Email: pheath@intrstar.net

Officers
Gen. Supt., Rev. Preston Heath

Asst. Gen. Supt., Rev. Reynolds Smith
Gen. Sec., Rev. Horace Johnson
Gen. Treas., Dr. W. L. Ellis
Christian Ed. Dir., Rev. Murray King
World Witness Dir., Rev. Dock Hobbs
Gen. Services Dir., Danny Blackman
Ministerial Council Dir., vacant
Ladies' Auxiliary Dir., Dollie Davis
Heritage Bible College, Pres., Dr. W. L. Ellis
Crusader Youth Camp, Dir., Rev. Murray King

OTHER ORGANIZATIONS
Heritage Bible College
Crusader Youth Camp
Blessings Bookstore, 1006 W. Cumberland St., Dunn, NC 28334 Tel. (910)892-2401
Cape Fear Christian Academy, Rt 1 Box 139, Erwin, NC 28339 Tel. (910)897-5423

Periodicals
The Messenger

Philadelphia Yearly Meeting of the Religious Society of Friends*
PYM traces its roots to the yearly meeting of 1681 in Burlington, New Jersey. For more than three centuries, PYM has served Monthly Meetings and Quarterly Meetings throughout eastern Pennsylvania, southern New Jersey, northern Maryland and Delaware. In general, the activities of PYM are organized under five Standing Committees: Standing Committee on Worship and Care; Standing Committee on Education; Standing Committee on Peace and Concerns; Standing Committee on Support and Outreach; Standing Committee on General Services.

Headquarters
Philadelphia Yearly Meeting, 1515 Cherry Street, Philadelphia, PA 19102-1479 Tel. (215)241-7000 Fax (215)567-2096
Website: www.pym.org

Officers
Gen. Sec., Thomas Jeavons
Clerk, Standing Committee on Worship and Care, D. Craig Trueblood, Email: worship@pym.org
Clerk, Standing Committee on Education, Rachel Bull (610)358-5926, Email: rabat-bull@aol.com or education@pym.org
Clerk, Standing Committee on Peace and Concerns, Elizabeth R. Marsh, Email: peace@pym.org
Clerk, Standing Committee on Support and Outreach, Sandra Gibbs Horne, Email: out-reach@pym.org
Clerk, Standing Committee on General Services, Sandra Moyer, Email: services@pym.org

Pillar of Fire
The Pillar of Fire was founded by Alma Bridwell White in Denver on Dec. 29, 1901 as the Pentecostal Union. In 1917, the name was

changed to Pillar of Fire. Alma White was born in Kentucky in 1862 and taught school in Montana where she met her husband, Kent White, a Methodist minister, who was a University student in Denver.

Because of Alma White's evangelistic endeavors, she was frowned upon by her superiors, which eventually necessitated her withdrawing from Methodist Church supervision. She was ordained as Bishop and her work spread to many states, to England, and since her death to Liberia, West Africa, Malawi, East Africa, Yugoslavia, Spain, India and the Philippines.

The Pillar of Fire organization has a college and two seminaries stressing Biblical studies. It operates eight separate schools for young people. The church continues to keep in mind the founder's goals and purposes.

Headquarters
P.O. Box 9159, Zarephath, NJ 08890 Tel. (908) 356-0102
Western Headquarters, 1302 Sherman St., Denver, CO 80203 Tel. (303)427-5462
Media Contact, 1st Vice Pres., Robert B. Dallenbach, 3455 W. 83 Ave., Westminster, CO 80030 Tel. (303)427-5462 Fax (303)429-0910

Officers
Pres. & Gen. Supt., Bishop Donald J. Wolfram
1st Vice-Pres. & Asst. Supt., Bishop Robert B. Dallenbach
2nd Vice-Pres./Sec.-Treas., Lois R. Stewart
Trustees: Kenneth Cope; Elsworth N. Bradford; S. Rea Crawford; Lois Stewart; Dr. Donald J. Wolfram; Robert B. Dallenbach; June Blue

Periodicals
The Pillar Monthly

Polish National Catholic Church of America*
After a number of attempts to resolve differences regarding the role of the laity in parish administration in the Roman Catholic Church in Scranton, Pennsylvania, this Church was organized in 1897. With the consecration to the episcopacy of the Most Rev. F. Hodur, this Church became a member of the Old Catholic Union of Utrecht in 1907.

Headquarters
Office of the Prime Bishop, 1004 Pittston Ave., Scranton, PA 18505 Tel. (570)346-9131
Media Contact, Prime Bishop, Most Rev. John F. Swantek, 1002 Pittston Ave., Scranton, PA 18505 Tel. (570)346-9131 Fax (570)346-2188

Officers
Prime Bishop, Most Rev. John F. Swantek, 115 Lake Scranton Rd., Scranton, PA 18505
Central Diocese: Bishop, Rt. Rev. Casimir Grotnik, 529 E. Locust St., Scranton, PA 18505
Eastern Diocese: Bishop, Rt. Rev. Thomas J. Gnat, 166 Pearl St., Manchester, NH 03104

Buffalo-Pittsburgh Diocese: Bishop, Rt. Rev. Thaddeus S. Peplowski, 5776 Broadway, Lancaster, NY 14086
Western Diocese: Rt. Rev. Robert M. Nemkovich, 920 N. Northwest Hwy., Park Ridge, IL 60068; Rt. Rev. Jan Dawidziok (Auxilliery Bp.) 1901 Wexford Ave., Parma, OH 44134
Canadian Diocese: Bishop, Sede Vacante, 186 Cowan Ave., Toronto, ON M6K 2N6
Ecumenical Officer, V. Rev. Marcell Pytlarz

Periodicals
God's Field; Polka

Presbyterian Church in America
The Presbyterian Church in America has a strong commitment to evangelism, to missionary work at home and abroad and to Christian education.

Organized in December 1973, this church was first known as the National Presbyterian Church but changed its name in 1974 to Presbyterian Church in America (PCA).

The PCA made a firm commitment on the doctrinal standards which had been significant in presbyterianism since 1645, namely the Westminster Confession of Faith and Catechisms. These doctrinal standards express the distinctives of the Calvinistic or Reformed tradition.

The PCA maintains the historic polity of Presbyterian governance, namely rule by presbyters (or elders) and the graded courts which are the session governing the local church. The presbytery is responsible for regional matters and the general assembly for national matters. The PCA has taken seriously the position of the parity of elders, making a distinction between the two classes of elders, teaching and ruling.

In 1982, the Reformed Presbyterian Church, Evangelical Synod (RPCES) joined the PCA. It brought with it a tradition that had antecedents in Colonial America. It also included Covenant College in Lookout Mountain, Georgia, and Covenant Theological Seminary in St. Louis, both of which are national denominational institutions of the PCA.

Headquarters
1852 Century Pl., Atlanta, GA 30345-4305 Tel. (404)320-3366 Fax (404)329-1275
Media Contact: Rev. J. Robert Fiol
Email: info@ac.pca-atl.org
Website: www.pcanet.org

Officers
Mod., Rev. Kennedy Smartt
Stated Clk., Dr. L. Roy Taylor, 1852 Century Pl., Ste. 190, Atlanta, GA 30345-4305 Tel. (404)320-3366

PERMANENT COMMITTEES
Admn., Dr. L. Roy Taylor, 1852 Century Pl., Ste. 190, Atlanta, GA 30345-4305 Tel. (404) 320-3366 Fax (404)329-1275

133

Christian Educ. & Publ., Dr. Charles Dunahoo, 1852 Century Pl., Ste. 190, Atlanta, GA 30345-4305 Tel. (404)320-3388

Mission to North America, Dr. Cortez Cooper, 1852 Century Pl., Ste. 205, Atlanta, GA 30345-4305 Tel. (404)320-3330

Mission to the World, Dr. Paul D. Kooistra, 1852 Century Pl., Ste. 201, Atlanta, GA 30345-4305 Tel. (404)320-3373

Presbyterian Church (U.S.A.)*

The Presbyterian Church (U.S.A.) was organized June 10, 1983, when the Presbyterian Church in the United States and the United Presbyterian Church in the United States of America united in Atlanta. The union healed a major division which began with the Civil War when Presbyterians in the South withdrew from the Presbyterian Church in the United States of America to form the Presbyterian Church in the Confederate States.

The United Presbyterian Church in the United States of America had been created by the 1958 union of the Presbyterian Church in the United States of America and the United Presbyterian Church of North America. Of those two uniting bodies, the Presbyterian Church in the U.S.A. dated from the first Presbytery organized in Philadelphia, about 1706. The United Presbyterian Church of North America was formed in 1858, when the Associate Reformed Presbyterian Church and the Associate Presbyterian Church united.

Strongly ecumenical in outlook, the Presbyterian Church (U.S.A.) is the result of at least 10 different denominational mergers over the last 250 years. A restructure, adopted by the General Assembly meeting in June 1993, has been implemented. The Presbyterian Church (U.S.A.) dedicated its new national offices in Louisville, Kentucky in 1988.

Headquarters

100 Witherspoon St., Louisville, KY 40202 Tel. (888)728-7228 Fax (502)569-5018

Media Contact, Assoc. Dir. for Communications, Gary W. Luhr, Tel. (502)569-5515 Fax (502) 569-8073

Email: presytel@pcusa.org

Website: www.pcusa.org

Officers

Mod., Syngman Rhee

Vice-Mod., Rebecca McElroy

Stated Clk., Clifton Kirkpatrick

Assoc. Stated Clks., Frederick Hueser, Jr., C. Fred Jenkins

THE OFFICE OF THE GENERAL ASSEMBLY

Tel. (888)728-7228 x. 5424 Fax (502)569-8005

Stated Clk., Clifton Kirkpatrick

Strategic Operations, Dir., Gradye Parsons

Middle Governing Body Relations, Coord., Gary Torrens

Dept. of the Stated Clerk, Dir., Loyda Aja

Dept. of Constitutional Services, Dir., C. Fred Jenkins

Ecumenical & Agency Relations, Dir., Robina Winbush

Dept. of Communication & Technology, Dir., Kerry Clements

Dept. of Hist., Philadelphia: 425 Lombard St., Philadelphia, PA 19147 Tel. (215)627-1852 Fax (215)627-0509; Dir., Frederick J. Heuser, Jr.; Deputy Dir., Margery Sly; Deputy Dir., Michelle Francis, PO Box 849, Montreat, NC 28757

GENERAL ASSEMBLY COUNCIL

Exec. Dir., John J. Detterick

Deputy Exec. Dir., Kathy Luekert

Worldwide Ministries Division, Dir., Marian McClure

Congregational Ministries Division, Dir., Donald G. Campbell

National Ministries Division, Dir., Curtis A. Kearns, Jr.

Mission Support Services Dir., Joey Bailey

BOARD OF PENSIONS

200 Market St., Philadelphia, PA 19103-3298, Tel. (800)773-7752 Fax (215)587-6215

Chpsn. of the Bd., Earldean V. S. Robbins

Pres., & CEO, Robert W. Maggs, Jr.

PRESBYTERIAN CHURCH (U.S.A.) FOUNDATION

200 E. Twelfth St., Jeffersonville, IN 47130 Tel. (812)288-8841 Fax (502)569-5980

Chpsn. of the Bd., James Henderson

Pres. & CEO, Robert E. Leech

PRESBYTERIAN CHURCH (U.S.A.) INVESTMENT & LOAN PROGRAM, INC.

Tel. (800)903-7457 Fax (502)569-8868

Chpsn. of the Board, Ben McAnally

Pres. & CEO, Kenneth G.Y. Grant

PRESBYTERIAN PUBLISHING CORPORATION

Chpsn. of the Bd., Robert Bohl

Pres. & CEO, Davis Perkins

SYNOD EXECUTIVES

Alaska-Northwest, Rev. Gary Skinner, 217 6th Ave. N., Seattle, WA 98109 Tel. (206)448-6403

Boriquen in Puerto Rico, Rev. Harry Fred Del Valle, Ave. Hostos Edificio 740, Cond. Medical Center Plaza, Ste. 216, Mayaguez, PR 00680 Tel. (787)832-8375

Covenant, Rev. Lowell Simms, 6172 Busch Blvd., Ste. 3000, Columbus, OH 43229-2564 Tel. (614)436-3310

Lakes & Prairies, Rev. Margaret J. Thomas, 8012 Cedar Ave. S., Bloomington, MN 55425-1210 Tel. (612)854-0144

Lincoln Trails, Rev. Verne E. Sindlinger, 1100 W. 42nd St., Indianapolis, IN 46208-3381 Tel. (317)923-3681

Living Waters, P. David Snellgrove, 318

Seaboard Ln, Ste. 205, Franklin, TN 37067, Tel. (615)261-4008

Mid-America, Rev. John L. Williams, 6400 Glenwood, Ste. 111, Overland Park, KS 66202-4072 Tel. (913)384-3020

Mid-Atlantic, Rev. William Stewart, Jr. Interim, P.O. Box 27026, Richmond, VA 23261-7026 Tel. (804) 342-0016

Northeast, Rev. Robert Howell White, Jr., 5811 Heritage Landing Dr., East Syracuse, NY 13057-9360 Tel. (315)446-5990

Pacific, Stephen Jenks, 8 Fourth St., Petaluma, CA 94952-3004 Tel. (707)765-1772

Rocky Mountains, Rev. Richard O. Wyatt, 3025 West 37th Ave., Ste.206, Denver, CO 80211-2799 Tel. (303)477-9070

South Atlantic, Floyd N. Rhodes, 118 E. Monroe St., Ste. 3, Jacksonville, FL 32202 Tel. (904)356-6070

Southern California & Hawaii, Rev. John N. Langfitt, 1501 Wilshire Blvd., Los Angeles, CA 90017-2293 Tel. (213)483-3840

Southwest, Jane DeVries, 4423 N. 24th St., Ste. 800, Phoenix, AZ 85016 Tel. (602)468-3800

The Sun, Rev. Judy R. Fletcher (Interim), 920 S. I 35 E, Denton, TX 76205-7898 Tel. (940)382-9656

The Trinity, Rev. Thomas M. Johnston, Jr., 3040 Market St., Camp Hill, PA 17011-4599 Tel. (717)737-0421

Periodicals

American Presbyterians: Journal of Presbyterian History; Presbyterian News Service "News Briefs"; Church & Society Magazine; Horizons; Monday Morning; Presbyterians Today; Interpretation; Presbyterian Outlook

Primitive Advent Christian Church

This body split from the Advent Christian Church. All its churches are in West Virginia. The Primitive Advent Christian Church believes that the Bible is the only rule of faith and practice and that Christian character is the only test of fellowship and communion. The church agrees with Christian fidelity and meekness; exercises mutual watch and care; counsels, admonishes, or reproves as duty may require and receives the same from each other as becomes the household of faith. Primitive Advent Christians do not believe in taking up arms.

The church believes that three ordinances are set forth by the Bible to be observed by the Christian church: (1) baptism by immersion; (2) the Lord's Supper, by partaking of unleavened bread and wine; (3) feet washing, to be observed by the saints' washing of one another's feet.

Headquarters

Media Contact, Sec.-Treas., Roger Wines, 1971 Grapevine Rd., Sissonville, WV 25320 Tel. (304)988-2668

Officers

Pres., Herbert Newhouse, 7632 Hughart Dr., Sissonville, WV 25320 Tel. (304)984-9277

Vice-Pres., Roger Hammons, 273 Frame Rd., Elkview, WV 25071 Tel. (304)965-6247

Sec. & Treas., Roger Wines, 1971 Grapevine Rd., Sissonville, WV 25320 Tel. (304)988-2668

Primitive Baptists

This large group of Baptists, located throughout the United States, opposes all centralization and modern missionary societies. They preach salvation by grace alone.

Headquarters

P.O. Box 38, Thornton, AR 71766 Tel. (501)352-3694

Media Contact, Elder W. Hartsel Cayce

Officers

Elder W. Hartsel Cayce

Elder Lasserre Bradley, Jr., Box 17037, Cincinnati, OH 45217 Tel. (513)821-7289

Elder S. T. Tolley, P.O. Box 68, Atwood, TN 38220 Tel. (901)662-7417

Periodicals

Baptist Witness; The Christian Baptist; The Primitive Baptist; For the Poor

Primitive Methodist Church in the U.S.A.

Hugh Bourne and William Clowes, local preachers in the Wesleyan Church in England, organized a daylong meeting at Mow Cop in Staffordshire on May 31, 1807, after Lorenzo Dow, an evangelist from America, told them of American camp meetings. Thousands attended and many were converted but the Methodist church, founded by the open-air preacher John Wesley, refused to accept the converts and reprimanded the preachers.

After waiting for two years for a favorable action by the Wesleyan Society, Bourne and Clowes established The Society of the Primitive Methodists. This was not a schism, Bourne said, for "we did not take one from them…it now appeared to be the will of God that we…should form classes and take upon us the care of churches in the fear of God." Primitive Methodist missionaries were sent to New York in 1829. An American conference was established in 1840.

Missionary efforts reach into Guatemala, Spain and other countries. The denomination joins in federation with the Evangelical Congregational Church, the United Brethren in Christ Church and the Southern Methodist Church and is a member of the National Association of Evangelicals.

The church believes the Bible is the only true rule of faith and practice, the inspired Word of God. It believes in one Triune God, the Deity of Jesus Christ, the Deity and personality of the Holy Spirit, the innocence of Adam and Eve, the

Fall of the human race, the necessity of repentance, justification by faith of all who believe, regeneration witnessed by the Holy Spirit, sanctification by the Holy Spirit, the second coming of the Lord Jesus Christ, the resurrection of the dead and conscious future existence of all people and future judgments with eternal rewards and punishments.

Headquarters
Media Contact, Pres., Rev. Wayne Yarnall, 1045 Laurel Run Rd., Wilkes-Barre, PA 18702 Tel. (570)472-3436 Fax (570)472-9283
Email: pmconf@juno.com

Officers
Pres., Rev. Wayne Yarnall, 1045 Laurel Run Rd., Wilkes-Barre, PA 18702 Tel. (570)472-3436 Fax (570)472-9283
Vice-Pres., Rev. Kerry R. Ritts, 723 Preston Ln., Hatboro, PA 19040
General. Secretary.: Rev. David Allen, Jr., 1199 Lawrence St., Lowell, MA 01852-5526 Tel. (978) 453-2052
Email: pahson@banet.net
Treas., Mr. Raymond C. Baldwin, 18409 Mill Run Ct., Leesburg, VA 20176-4583
Email: Rbaldwin32@aol.com

Progressive National Baptist Convention, Inc.*
This body held its organizational meeting in Cincinnati in November, 1961. Subsequent regional sessions were followed by the first annual session in Philadelphia in 1962.

Headquarters
601 50th Street, N.E., Washington, DC 20019 Tel. (202)396-0558 Fax (202)398-4998
Media Contact, Gen. Sec., Dr. Tyrone S. Pitts

Officers
Pres., Dr. Bennett W. Smith, Sr., St. John Baptist Church, 184 Goodell St., Buffalo, NY 14204
Gen. Sec., Dr. Tyrone S. Pitts

OTHER ORGANIZATIONS
Dept. of Christian Education, Exec. Dir., Dr. C. B. Lucas, Emmanuel Baptist Church, 3815 W. Broadway, Louisville, KY 40211
Women's Dept., Mildred Wormley, 218 Spring St., Trenton, NJ 08618
Home Mission Bd., Exec. Dir., Rev. Archie LeMone, Jr.
Congress of Christian Education, Pres., Rev. Harold S. Diggs, Mayfield Memorial Baptist Church, 700 Sugar Creek Rd. W., Charlotte, NC 28213
Baptist Global Mission Bureau, Dr. Ronald K. Hill, 161-163 60th St., Philadelphia, PA 19139
Nannie Helen Burroughs School, Tel. (202)398-5266

Periodicals
Baptist Progress

Protestant Reformed Churches in America
The Protestant Reformed Churches (PRC) have their roots in the sixteenth century Reformation of Martin Luther and John Calvin, as it developed in the Dutch Reformed churches. The denomination originated as a result of a controversy in the Christian Reformed Church in 1924 involving the adoption of the "Three Points of Common Grace." Three ministers in the Christian Reformed Church, the Reverends Herman Hoeksema, George Ophoff, and Henry Danhof, and their consistories (Eastern Avenue, Hope, and Kalamazoo, respectively) rejected the doctrine. Eventually these men were deposed, and their consistories were either deposed or set outside the Christian Reformed Church. The denomination was formed in 1926 with three congregations. Today the denomination is comprised of some twenty-seven churches (more than 6,000 members) in the USA and Canada.

The presbyterian form of church government as determined by the Church Order of Dordt is followed by the PRC. The doctrinal standards of the PRC are the Reformed confessions "the Heidelberg Catechism, Belgic Confession of Faith, and Canons of Dordrecht. The doctrine of the covenant is a cornerstone of their teaching. They maintain an unconditional, particular covenant of grace that God establishes with His elect.

Headquarters
16511 South Park Ave., South Holland, IL 60473 Tel. (708)333-1314
Media Contact, Stat. Clk., Don Doezema, 4949 Ivanrest Ave., Grandville, MI 49418 Tel. (616) 531-1490
Email: doezema@prca.org

Officers
Stat. Clk., Don Doezema

Periodicals
The Standard Bearer

Quakers-please see Friends.

Reformed Church in America*
The Reformed Church in America was established in 1628 by the earliest settlers of New York. It is the oldest Protestant denomination with a continuous ministry in North America. Until 1867 it was known as the Reformed Protestant Dutch Church.

The first ordained minister, Domine Jonas Michaelius, arrived in New Amsterdam from The Netherlands in 1628. Throughout the colonial period, the Reformed Church lived under the authority of the Classis of Amsterdam. Its churches were clustered in New York and New Jersey. Under the leadership of Rev. John Livingston, it became a denomination independent of the authority of the Classis of Amsterdam in 1776. Its geographical base was broadened in the 19th century by the immigration of Reformed Dutch and German settlers in the midwestern United States. The Reformed Church now spans the United States and Canada.

The Reformed Church in America accepts as its standards of faith the Heidelberg Catechism, Belgic Confession and Canons of Dort. It has a rich heritage of world mission activity. It claims to be loyal to reformed tradition which emphasizes obedience to God in all aspects of life.

Although the Reformed Church in America has worked in close cooperation with other churches, it has never entered into merger with any other denomination. It is a member of the World Alliance of Reformed Churches, the World Council of Churches and the National Council of the Churches of Christ in the United States of America. In 1998 it also entered into a relationship of full communion with the Evangelical Lutheran Church in America, Presbyterian Church (U.S.A.), and the United Church of Christ by way of the Formula of Agreement.

Headquarters

475 Riverside Dr., New York, NY 10115 Tel. (212)870-2841 Fax (212)870-2499

Media Contact, Dir., Communication and Production Services, Kim Nathan Baker, 4500 60th St. SE, Grand Rapids, MI 49512, Tel. (616)698-7071 Fax (616)698-6606

Email: kbaker@rca.org

Website: www.rca.org

OFFICERS AND STAFF OF GENERAL SYNOD

Pres., Carol Mutch, 475 Riverside Dr., 18th Floor, New York, NY 10115

General Synod Council: Mod., Greg Mast

Gen. Sec., Wesley Granberg- Michaelson, 475 Riverside Dr., 18th Floor, New York, NY 10115

Policy, Planning & Admn. Serv., Dir. & Assistant Sec., Kenneth R. Bradsell

Ministry & Personnel Services, Dir., Vernon Hoffs

Evangelism & Church Dev. Ser., Richard Welscott

Finance Services, Treas., Susan Converse

Congregational Ser., Dir., Jeffrey Japinga

Mission Services, Dir., Bruce Menning

African-American Council, Exec. Dir., Glen Missick

Council for Hispanic Ministries, Exec. Sec., Luis Perez

Native American Indian Ministries Council, -vacant-

Council for Pacific/Asian-American Min., Exec. Sec., Ella Campbell

OTHER ORGANIZATIONS

Bd. Of Benefits Services: Pres., to be elected 10/00; Sec., Wesley Granberg-Michaelson

RCA Foundation Dir., -vacant-

RCA Building and Extension Fund, Fund Executive, Paul Karssen

Reformed Church Women's Ministries, Exec. Dir., Arlene Waldorf

Periodicals

Perspectives; The Church Herald

Reformed Church in the United States

Lacking pastors, early German Reformed immigrants to the American colonies were led in worship by "readers." One reader, schoolmaster John Philip Boehm, organized the first congregations near Philadelphia in 1725. A Swiss pastor, Michael Schlatter, was sent by the Dutch Reformed Church in 1746. Strong ties with the Netherlands existed until the formation of the Synod of the German Reformed Church in 1793.

The Eureka Classis, organized in North and South Dakota in 1910 and strongly influenced by the writings of H. Kohlbruegge, P. Geyser and J. Stark, refused to become part of the 1934 merger of the Reformed Church with the Evangelical Synod of North America, holding that it sacrificed the Reformed heritage. (The merged Evangelical and Reformed Church became part of the United Church of Christ in 1957.) Under the leadership of pastors W. Grossmann and W. J. Krieger, the Eureka Classis in 1942 incorporated as the continuing Reformed Church in the United States.

The growing Eureka Classis dissolved in 1986 to form a Synod with four regional classes. An heir to the Reformation theology of Zwingli and Calvin, the Heidelberg Catechism, the Belgic Confession and the Canons of Dort are used as the confessional standards of the church. The Bible is strictly held to be the inerrant, infallible Word of God.

The RCUS supports Dordt College, Mid-America Reformed Seminary, New Geneva Theological Seminary, West Minster Theological Seminary in California, and Hope Haven. The RCUS is the official sponsor to the Reformed Confessing Church of Zaire.

Headquarters

Media Contact, Rev. Frank Walker Th.M., 5601 Spring Blossom St., Bakersfield, CA 93313-6041 Tel. (661)827-9885

Email: fhw@iname.com

Website: www.rcus.org

Officers

Pres., Rev. Vernon Pollema, 235 James Street, Shafter, CA 93263 Tel. (661)746-6907

Vice-Pres., Rev. Robert Grossmann, Th.M., 1905 200th St., Garner, IA 50438 Tel. (515)923-3060

Stated Clk., Rev. Frank Walker Th.M., 5601 Spring Blossom St., Bakersfield, CA 93313-6025 Tel. (661)827-9885

Treas., Clayton Greiman, 2115 Hwy. 69, Garner, IA 50438 Tel. (515)923-2950

Periodicals

Reformed Herald

Reformed Episcopal Church

The Reformed Episcopal Church was founded December 2, 1873 in New York City by Bishop George D. Cummins, an assistant bishop in the Protestant Episcopal Church from 1866 until 1873. Cummins and other evangelical Episcopalians viewed with alarm the influence of the Oxford Movement in the Protestant Episcopal Church, for the interest it stimulated in Roman Catholic ritual and doctrine and for intolerance it bred toward evangelical Protestant doctrine.

Throughout the late 1860s, evangelicals and ritualists clashed over ceremonies and vestments, exchanges of pulpits with clergy of other denominations, the meaning of critical passages in the Book of Common Prayer, interpretation of the sacraments and validity of the Apostolic Succession.

In October, 1873, other bishops publicly attacked Cummins in the church newspapers for participating in an ecumenical Communion service sponsored by the Evangelical Alliance. Cummins resigned and drafted a call to Episcopalians to organize a new Episcopal Church for the "purpose of restoring the old paths of their fathers." On Dec. 2, 1873, a Declaration of Principles was adopted and Dr. Charles E. Cheney was elected bishop to serve with Cummins. The Second General Council, meeting in May 1874 in New York City, approved a Constitution and Canons and a slightly amended version of the Book of Common Prayer. In 1875, the Third General Council adopted a set of Thirty-Five Articles.

Cummins died in 1876. The church had grown to nine jurisdictions in the United States and Canada at that time. The Reformed Episcopal Church is a member of the National Association of Evangelicals.

Headquarters

7372 Henry Ave., Philadelphia, PA 19128-1401 Tel. (215)483-1196 Fax (215)483-5235
Media Contact, Rt. Rev. Leonard Riches
Media Contact, Rt. Rev. Royal U. Grote, Jr., Church Growth Office, 211 Byrne Ave., Houston, TX 77009 Tel. (713)862-4929
Email: nicaea@aol.com
Website: www.geopages.com/capitolhill/1125/

Officers

Pres. & Presiding Bishop, Rt. Rev. Leonard W. Riches
Vice-Pres., Rt. Rev. Royal U. Grote, Jr.
Sec., Rev. Walter Banek
Treas., Rev. Jon W. Abboud

OTHER ORGANIZATIONS

Bd. of Foreign Missions: Pres., Dr. Barbara J. West, 316 Hunters Rd., Swedesboro, NJ 08085 Tel. (609) 467-1641
Bd. of Natl. Church Extension: Pres., Rt. Rev. Royal U. Grote, Jr., 211 Byrne Ave., Houston, TX 77009 Tel. (713)862-4929
Publication Society: Pres., Rt. Rev. Gregory K. Hotchkiss, 318 Main St., Somerville, NJ 08876 Tel. (908)725-2678 Fax (908)725-4641; Orders, Rev. Jonathan S. Riches, 7372 Henry Ave., Philadelphia, PA 19128 25-956-0655
The Reapers: Pres., Susan Higham, 472 Leedom St., Jenkintown, PA 19046
Committee on Women's Work: Pres., Joan Workowski, 1162 Beverly Rd., Rydal, PA 19046

BISHOPS

William H.S. Jerdan, Jr., 414 W. 2nd South St., Summerville, SC 29483
Sanco K. Rembert, P.O. Box 20068, Charleston, SC 29413
Franklin H. Sellers, Sr., 81 Buttercup Ct., Marco Island, FL 33937-3480
Leonard W. Riches, Sr., 85 Smithtown Rd., Pipersville, PA 18947 Tel. (215)483-1196 Fax (215)294-8009
Royal U. Grote, Jr., 211 Byrne Ave., Houston, TX 77009
James C. West, Sr., 408 Red Fox Run, Summerville, SC 29485
Robert H. Booth, 1611 Park Ave., #212, Quakertown, PA 18951
Gregory K. Hotchkiss, 318 E. Main St., Somerville, NJ 08876
George B. Fincke, 155 Woodstock Circle, Vacaville, CA 95687-3381
Daniel R. Morse, 11259 Wexford Dr., Eads, TN 38025
Michael Fedechko, Box 2532, New Liskeard, ON P0J 1P0
Charles W. Dorrington, 626 Blanshard St., Victoria, BC V8W 3G6
Ted Follows, 626 Blanshard St., Victoria, BC V8W 3G6
Daniel G. Cox, 9 Hilltop Pl., Baltimore, MD 21228
Ray R. Sutton, 3421 Madison Park Blvd., Shreveport, LA 71104

Periodicals

Reformed Episcopalians

Reformed Mennonite Church

This is a small group of believers in Pennsylvania, Ohio, Michigan, Illinois, and Ontario, Canada who believe in non-resistance of evil, and non-conformity to the world and who practice separation from unfaithful worship. They believe that Christian unity is the effect of brotherly love and are of one mind and spirit. Their church was established in 1812 by John Herr who agreed with the teachings of Menno Simon as well as those of Jesus Christ.

Headquarters

Lancaster County only, Reformed Mennonite Church, 602 Strasburg Pike, Lancaster, PA 17602

Media Contact, Bishop, Glenn M. Gross, Tel. (717)697-4623

Officers

Bishop Glenn M. Gross, 906 Grantham Rd., Mechanicsburg, PA 17055

Reformed Methodist Union Episcopal Church

The Reformed Methodist Union Episcopal church was formed after a group of ministers withdrew from the African Methodist Episcopal Church following a dispute over the election of ministerial delegates to the General Conference.

These ministers organized the Reformed Methodist Union church during a four-day meeting beginning on January 22, 1885 at Hills Chapel (now known as Mt. Hermon RMUE church), in Charleston, South Carolina. The Rev. William E. Johnson was elected president of the new church. Following the death of Rev. Johnson in 1896, it was decided that the church would conform to regular American Methodism (the Episcopacy). The first Bishop, Edward Russell Middleton, was elected, and "Episcopal" was added to the name of the church. Bishop Middleton was consecrated on Dec. 5, 1896, by Bishop P. F. Stephens of the Reformed Episcopal Church.

Headquarters

1136 Brody Ave., Charleston, SC 29407

Media Contact, Gen. Secretary, Brother Willie B. Oliver, P.O. Box 1995, Orangeburg, SC 29116 Tel. (803)536-3293

Officers

Bishop, Rt. Rev. Leroy Gethers, Tel. (803)766-3534

Asst. Bishop, Rt. Rev. Jerry M. DeVoe, Jr.

Gen. Sec., Brother Willie B. Oliver

Treas., Rev. Daniel Green

Sec. of Education, Rev. William Polite

Sec. of Books Concerns, Sister Ann Blanding

Sec. of Pension Fund, Rev. Joseph Powell

Sec. of Church Extension, Brother William Parker

Sec. of Sunday School Union, Sister Wine

Sec. of Mission, Rev. Warren Hatcher

Reformed Presbyterian Church of North America

Also known as the Church of the Covenanters, this church's origin dates back to the Reformation days of Scotland when the Covenanters signed their "Covenants" in resistance to the king and the Roman Church in the enforcement of state church practices. The Church in America has signed two "Covenants" in particular, those of 1871 and 1954.

Headquarters

Media Contact, Stated Clk., Louis D. Hutmire, 7408 Penn Ave., Pittsburgh, PA 15208 Tel. (412)731-1177 Fax (412)731-8861

Officers

Mod., Rev. William J. Edgar, 25 Lawrence Rd., Broomall, PA 19008 Tel. (610) 353-1371

Clk., J. Bruce Martin, 310 Main St., Ridgefield Park, NJ 07660 Tel. (201) 440-5993

Asst. Clk., Raymond E. Morton, 411 N. Vine St., Sparta, IL 62286 Tel. (618)443-3419

Stated Clk., Louis D. Hutmire, 7408 Penn Ave., Pittsburgh, PA 15208 Tel. (412)731-1177

Periodicals

The Covenanter Witness

Reformed Zion Union Apostolic Church

This group was organized in 1869 at Boydton, Va., by Elder James R. Howell of New York, a minister of the A.M.E. Zion Church, with doctrines of the Methodist Episcopal Church.

Headquarters

Rt. 1, Box 64D, Dundas, VA 23938 Tel. (804) 676-8509

Media Contact, Bishop G. W. Studivant

Officers

Exec. Brd., Chair, Rev. Hilman Wright, Tel. (804)447-3988

Sec., Joseph Russell, Tel. (804)634-4520

Religious Society of Friends (Conservative)

These Friends mark their present identity from separations occurring by regions at different times from 1845 to 1904. They hold to a minimum of organizational structure. Their meetings for worship, which are unprogrammed and based on silent, expectant waiting upon the Lord, demonstrate the belief that all individuals may commune directly with God and may share equally in vocal ministry.

They continue to stress the importance of the Living Christ and the experience of the Holy Spirit working with power in the lives of individuals who obey it.

YEARLY MEETINGS

North Carolina YM, Robert Gosner, P.O. Box 489, Woodland, NC 27897 Tel. (252)587-2571

Iowa YM: Deborah Frisch, Clerk, 916 41st Street, Des Moines, Iowa 50312-2612

Ohio YM, S. S. Smith, Clerk, 61830 Sandy Ridge Road, Barnesville, OH 43713

Religious Society of Friends (Unaffiliated Meetings)

Though all groups of Friends acknowledge the same historical roots, 19th-century divisions in theology and experience led to some of the current organizational groupings. Many newer yearly

139

meetings, often marked by spontaneity, variety and experimentation and hoping for renewed Quaker unity, have chosen not to identify with past divisions by affiliating in traditional ways with the larger organizations within the Society. Some of these unaffiliated groups have begun within the past 25 years.

YEARLY MEETINGS

Central Yearly Meeting (I), Supt., Jonathan Edwards, 5597 West County Rd., 700 N., Ridgeville, IN 47380

Intermountain Year'y Meeting(I), Clerk, Ted Church, 4 Arco, N.W., Albuquerque, NM 87120 Tel. (505)898-5305

North Pacific Yearly Meeting (I), Contact:, Helen Dart, 3311 NW Polk, Corvallis, OR 97330 Tel. (206)633-4860

Pacific Yearly Meeting (I), Clerk, Margaret Moss Man, 2151 Vine St., Berkeley, CA 94709

Periodicals

Friends Bulletin

Reorganized Church of Jesus Christ of Latter Day Saints

This church was founded April 6, 1830, by Joseph Smith, Jr., and reorganized under the leadership of the founder's son, Joseph Smith III, in 1860. The church, with headquarters in Independence, Missouri, is established in 36 countries in addition to the United States and Canada. A biennial world conference is held in Independence, Missouri. The current president is W. Grant McMurray. The church has a worldwide membership of approximately 245,000.

Headquarters

World Headquarters, P.O. Box 1059, Independence, MO 64051 Tel. (816)833-1000 Fax (816)521-3096

Media Contact, Publ. Rel. Commissioner, Susan Naylor

Officers

First Presidency: Pres., W. Grant McMurray; Counselor, Kenneth N. Robinson; Counselor, Peter A. Judd

Council of 12 Apostles, Pres., A. Alex Kahtava

Presiding Bishopric: Presiding Bishop, Larry R. Norris; Counselor, Orval G. Fisher; Counselor, Stephen M. Jones

Presiding Evangelist, Danny A. Belrose

World Church Sec., A. Bruce Lindgren

Public Relations, Susan Naylor

Periodicals

Saints Herald; Restoration Witness

The Roman Catholic Church-please see The Catholic Church.

Romanian Orthodox Church in America

The Romanian Orthodox Church in America is an autonomous Archdiocese chartered under the name of "Romanian Orthodox Archdiocese in America."

The diocese was founded in 1929 and approved by the Holy Synod of the Romanian Orthodox Church in Romania in 1934. The Holy Synod of the Romanian Orthodox Church of July 12, 1950, granted it ecclesiastical autonomy in America, continuing to hold only dogmatical and canonical ties with the Holy Synod and the Romanian Orthodox Patriarchate of Romania.

In 1951, approximately 40 parishes with their clergy from the United States and Canada separated from this church. In 1960, they joined the Russian Orthodox Greek Catholic Metropolia, now called the Orthodox Church in America, which reordained for these parishes a bishop with the title "Bishop of Detroit and Michigan."

The Holy Synod of the Romanian Orthodox Church, on June 11, 1973, elevated the Bishop of Romanian Orthodox Missionary Episcopate in America to the rank of Archbishop.

Headquarters

19959 Riopelle St., Detroit, MI 48203 Tel. (313) 893-8390

Media Contact, Archdiocesan Dean & Secretary, V. Rev. Fr. Nicholas Apostola, 44 Midland St., Worcester, MA 01602-4217 Tel. (508)799-0040 Fax (508)756-9866

Officers

Archbishop, His Eminence Victorin Ursache

Vicar, V. Rev. Archim. Dr. Vasile Vasilachi, 45-03 48th Ave., Woodside, Queens, NY 11377 Tel. (718)784-4453

Inter-Church Relations, Dir., Rev. Fr. Nicholas Apostola, 14 Hammond St., Worcester, MA 01610 Tel. (617)799-0040

Sec., V. Rev. Fr. Nicholas Apostola, 44 Midland St., Worcester, MA 01602 Tel. (508)756-9866 Fax (508)799-0040

Periodicals

Credinta-The Faith

The Romanian Orthodox Episcopate of America

This body of Eastern Orthodox Christians of Romanian descent was organized in 1929 as an autonomous Diocese under the jurisdiction of the Romanian Patriarchate. In 1951 it severed all relations with the Orthodox Church of Romania. Under the canonical jurisdiction of the autocephalous Orthodox Church in America since 1970, it enjoys full administrative autonomy and is headed by its own Bishop.

Headquarters

P.O. Box 309, Grass Lake, MI 49240-0309 Tel. (517) 522-4800 Fax (517)522-5907

Media Contact, Ed./Sec., Dept. of Publications, Rev. Deacon David Oancea, P.O. Box 185, Grass Lake, MI 49240-0185 Tel. (517)522-3656 Fax (517)522-5907

Email: roeasolia@aol.com
Website: www.roea.org

Officers

Ruling Bishop, His Eminence Archbishop Nathaniel Popp

Dean-Michigan, The V. Rev. Fr. Laurence Lazar, 18430 W 9 Mile Rd., Southfield, MI 48075-4032 Tel. (248)356-4144

Dean-Pacific Coast, The V. Rev. Fr. Constantin Alesce, P.O. Box 65853, Los Angeles, CA 90065-0853 Tel. (818)361-2750

Dean-Atlantic Seaboard, The V. Rev. Fr. Mircea Marinescu, 222 Park Ave., Quakertown, PA 18951-1634 Tel. (215)804-0645

Dean-Midwest, The V. Rev. Fr. Simion Pavel, 5825 N Mozart St., Chicago, IL 60659-3801 Tel. (773)878-0873

Dean-Ohio & Western Pennsylvania, The V. Rev. Fr. Panteleimon Stanciu, 1427 33rd St. NE, Canton, OH 44717-1547 Tel. (330)452-1940

Dean-South, The V. Rev. Fr. Dumitru Viorel Sasu, 6055 SW 19th St., Miramar, FL 33023-2906 Tel. (954)986-9866

OTHER ORGANIZATIONS

The American Romanian Orthodox Youth, Pres., Tom Rosco, 625 Centralia St., Dearborn Heights, MI 48127-3736

Assoc. of Romanian Orthodox Ladies' Aux., Pres., Mary Ellen Rosco, 625 Centralia St., Dearborn Hts., MI 48127-3736

Orthodox Brotherhood U.S.A., Pres., Eugenia Peru, 16732 Merriman Rd., Livonia, MI 48154-3162 Tel. (734)525-3558

Orthodox Brotherhood of Canada, Pres., Gloria Buchanan, 26 Mill Bay, Regina, SK S4N 1L6, Canada

Periodicals

Solia-The Herald; Calendarul Solia (annual); *Good News- Buna Vestire* (quarterly)

The Russian Orthodox Church Outside of Russia

This group was organized in 1920 to unite in one body of dioceses the missions and parishes of the Russian Orthodox Church outside of Russia. The governing body, set up in Constantinople, was sponsored by the Ecumenical Patriarchate. In November 1950, it came to the United States. The Russian Orthodox Church Outside of Russia emphasizes being true to the old traditions of the Russian Church. It is not in communion with the Moscow Patriarchate.

Headquarters

75 E. 93rd St., New York, NY 10128 Tel. (212)534-1601 Fax (212)426-1086

Media Contact, Dep. Sec., Bishop Gabriel

SYNOD OF BISHOPS

Pres., His Eminence Metropolitan Vitaly

Sec., Archbishop of Syracuse and Trinity, Laurus

Dep. Sec., Bishop of Manhattan, Gabriel, Tel. (212)722-6577

Periodicals

Living Orthodoxy; Orthodox Family; Orthodox Russia (Russian); Orthodox Voices; Pravoslavnaya Rus; Pravoslavnaya Zhisn; Orthodox America

The Salvation Army

The Salvation Army, founded in 1865 by William Booth (1829-1912) in London, England, and introduced into America in 1880, is an international religious and charitable movement organized and operated on a paramilitary pattern and is a branch of the Christian church. To carry out its purposes, The Salvation Army has established a widely diversified program of religious and social welfare services which are designed to meet the needs of children, youth and adults in all age groups.

Headquarters

615 Slaters Ln., Alexandria, VA 22313 Tel. (703)684-5500 Fax (703)684-5538

Media Contact, Community Relations & Devel., Lt. Colonel Tom Jones, Tel. (703)684-5521 Fax (703)684-5538

Officers

Natl. Commander, Commissioner John A. Busby

Natl. Chief Sec., Col. Tom Lewis

Natl. Community Relations, Dir., Lt. Colonel Tom Jones

TERRITORIAL ORGANIZATIONS

Central Territory: 10 W. Algonquin Rd., Des Plaines, IL 60016 Tel. (847)294-2000 Fax (847)294-2299; Territorial Commander, Commissioner Lawrence Moretz

Eastern Territory: 440 W. Nyack Rd., P.O. Box C-635, West Nyack, NY 10994 Tel. (914)620-7200 Fax (914)620-7766; Territorial Commander, Commissioner Joe Noland

Southern Territory: 1424 Northeast Expressway, Atlanta, GA 30329 Tel. (404)728-1300 Fax (404)728-1331; Territorial Commander, Commissioner Raymond A. Cooper

Western Territory: 180 E. Ocean Blvd., Long Beach, CA Tel. (562)436-7000 Fax (562)491-8792; Territorial Commander, Commissioner David Edwards

Periodicals

The War Cry

The Schwenkfelder Church

The Schwenkfelders are the spiritual descendants of the Silesian nobleman Caspar Schwenkfeld von Ossig (1489-1561), a scholar, reformer, preacher and prolific writer who endeavored to aid in the cause of the Protestant Reformation. A contemporary of Martin Luther, John Calvin, Ulrich Zwingli and Phillip Melanchthon, Schwenkfeld sought no following, formulated no creed and did not attempt to organize a church based on his beliefs. He labored for liberty of religious belief, for a fellowship of all believers and for one united Christian church.

141

He and his cobelievers supported a movement known as the Reformation by the Middle Way. Persecuted by state churches, ultimately 180 Schwenkfelders exiled from Silesia emigrated to Pennsylvania. They landed at Philadelphia Sept. 22, 1734. In 1782, the Society of Schwenkfelders, the forerunner of the present Schwenkfelder Church, was formed. The church was incorporated in 1909.

The General Conference of the Schwenkfelder Church is a voluntary association for the Schwenkfelder Churches at Palm, Worcester, Lansdale, Norristown and Philadelphia, Pennsylvania.

They practice adult baptism and dedication of children, and observe the Lord's Supper regularly with open Communion. In theology, they are Christo-centric; in polity, congregational; in missions, world-minded; in ecclesiastical organization, ecumenical.

The ministry is recruited from graduates of colleges, universities and accredited theological seminaries. The churches take leadership in ecumenical concerns through ministerial associations, community service and action groups, councils of Christian education and other agencies.

Headquarters
105 Seminary St., Pennsburg, PA 18073 Tel. (215)679-3103
Media Contact, Dennis Moyer

Officers
Mod., John Graham, Collegeville, PA 19426
Sec., Frances Witte, Central Schwenkfelder Church, Worcester, PA 19490
Treas., Syl Rittenhouse, 1614 Kriebel Rd., Lansdale, PA 19446

Periodicals
The Schwenkfeldian

Separate Baptists in Christ
The Separate Baptists in Christ are a group of Baptists found in Indiana, Ohio, Kentucky, Tennessee, Virginia, West Virginia, Florida and North Carolina dating back to an association formed in 1758 in North Carolina and Virginia.

Today this group consists of approximately 100 churches. They believe in the infallibility of the Bible, the divine ordinances of the Lord's Supper, feetwashing, baptism and that those who endureth to the end shall be saved.

The Separate Baptists are Arminian in doctrine, rejecting both the doctrines of predestination and eternal security of the believer.

At the 1991 General Association, an additional article of doctrine was adopted. "We believe that at Christ's return in the clouds of heaven all Christians will meet the Lord in the air, and time shall be no more," thus leaving no time for a literal one thousand year reign. Seven associations comprise the General Association of Separate Baptists.

Headquarters
Media Contact, Clk., Greg Erdman, 10102 N. Hickory Ln., Columbus, IN 47203 812-526-2540
Email: mail@separatebaptist.org
Website: www.separatebaptist.org

Officers
Mod., Rev. Jim Goff, 1020 Gagel Ave., Louisville, KY 40216
Asst. Mod., Rev. Jimmy Polston, 785 Kitchen Rd., Mooresville, IN 46158 Tel. (317)831-6745
Clk., Greg Erdman, 10102 N. Hickory Ln., Columbus, IN 47203 Tel. (812)526-2540
Asst. Clk., Rev. Mattew Cowan, 174 Oak Hill School Rd., Lot 30, Smiths Grove, KY 42171 Tel. (270)678-5599

Serbian Orthodox Church in the U.S.A. and Canada*
The Serbian Orthodox Church is an organic part of the Eastern Orthodox Church. As a local church it received its autocephaly from Constantinople in 1219 A.D.

In 1921, a Serbian Orthodox Diocese in the United States of America and Canada was organized. In 1963, it was reorganized into three dioceses, and in 1983 a fourth diocese was created for the Canadian part of the church. The Serbian Orthodox Church in the USA and Canada received its administrative autonomy in 1928. However, it remains canonically an integral part of the Serbian Orthodox Patriarchate with its see in Belgrade. The Serbian Orthodox Church is in absolute doctrinal unity with all other local Orthodox Churches.

Headquarters
St. Sava Monastery, P.O. Box 519, Libertyville, IL 60048 Tel. (847)367-0698

BISHOPS
Metropolitan of Midwestern America, Most Rev. Metropolitan Christopher
Bishop of Canada, Georgije, 5A Stockbridge Ave., Toronto, ON M8Z 4M6 Tel. (416)231-4009
Bishop of Eastern America, Rt. Rev. Bishop Mitrophan, P.O. Box 368, Sewickley, PA 15143 Tel. (412)741-5686
Diocese of Western America, Bishop Jovan, 2541 Crestline Terr., Alhambra, CA 91803 Tel. (818)264-6825

OTHER ORGANIZATIONS
Brotherhood of Serbian Orth. Clergy in U.S.A. & Canada, Pres., V. Rev. Nedeljko Lunich, Joliet, IL, Merrilville, IN
Federation of Circles of Serbian Sisters
Serbian Singing Federation

Periodicals
The Path of Orthodoxy

142

Seventh-day Adventist Church

The Seventh-day Adventist Church grew out of a worldwide religious revival in the mid-19th century. People of many religious persuasions believed Bible prophecies indicated that the second coming or advent of Christ was imminent.

When Christ did not come in the 1840s, a group of these disappointed Adventists in the United States continued their Bible studies and concluded they had misinterpreted prophetic events and that the second coming of Christ was still in the future. This same group of Adventists later accepted the teaching of the seventh-day Sabbath and became known as Seventh-day Adventists. The denomination organized formally in 1863.

The church was largely confined to North America until 1874, when its first missionary was sent to Europe. Today, over 46,000 congregations meet in 204 countries. Membership exceeds 10 million and increases between five and six percent each year.

In addition to a mission program, the church has the largest worldwide Protestant parochial school system with approximately 5,800 schools with more than 1,055,000 students on elementary through college and university levels.

The Adventist Development and Relief Agency (ADRA) helps victims of war and natural disasters, and many local congregations have community service facilities to help those in need close to home.

The church also has a worldwide publishing ministry with 56 printing facilities producing magazines and other publications in over 300 languages and dialects. In the United States and Canada, the church sponsors a variety of radio and television programs, including Christian Lifestyle Magazine, It Is Written, Breath of Life, Ayer, Hoy, y Mañana, Voice of Prophecy, and La Voz de la Esperanza.

The North American Division of Seventh-day Adventist includes 58 Conferences which are grouped together into 9 organized Union Conferences. The various Conferences work under the general direction of these Union Conferences.

Headquarters

12501 Old Columbia Pike, Silver Spring, MD 20904-6600 Tel. (301)680-6000

Media Contact, Dir., Archives & Statistics, Bert Haloviak

WORLD-WIDE OFFICERS

Pres., Jan Paulsen
Sec., Matthew A. Bediako
Treas., Robert L. Rawson

WORLD-WIDE DEPARTMENTS

Adventist Chaplaincy Ministries, Dir., Richard O. Stenbakken
Children's Ministries, Dir., Virginia L. Smith
Education, Dir., Humberto M. Rasi
Communication, Dir., Rajmund Dabrowski
Family Ministries, Dir., Ronald M. Flowers
Health and Temperance, Dir., Allan R. Handysides
Ministerial Assoc., Dir., James A. Cress
Public Affairs & Religious Liberty, Dir., John Graz
Publishing, Dir., Jose Luis Campos
Sabbath School & Personal Ministries, James W. Zackrison
Stewardship, Dir., Benjamin C. Maxson
Trust Services, Jeffrey K. Wilson
Women's Ministries, Ardis D. Stenbakken
Youth, Baraka G. Muganda

NORTH AMERICAN OFFICERS

Pres., Don C. Schneider
Vice-Pres.: Debra Brill; Clarence E. Hodges; Cyril Miller; Richard C. Osborn; Manuel Vasquez
Sec., Harold W. Baptiste
Assoc. Sec., Rosa T. Banks
Treas., Juan R. Prestol
Assoc. Treas.: Marshall Chase; Del L. Johnson; Kenneth W. Osborn

NORTH AMERICAN ORGANIZATIONS

Atlantic Union Conf.: P.O. Box 1189, South Lancaster, MA 01561-1189; Pres., Benjamin D. Schoun
Canada: Seventh-day Adventist Church in Canada (see Ch. 4)
Columbia Union Conf.: 5427 Twin Knolls Rd., Columbia, MD 21045; Pres., Harold L. Lee
Lake Union Conf.: P.O. Box C, Berrien Springs, MI 49103; Pres., Godon L. Retzer
Mid-America Union Conf.: P.O. Box 6128, Lincoln, NE 68506; Pres., Charles Sandefur
North Pacific Union Conf.: Pres., Jere D. Patzer, P.O. Box 16677, Portland, OR 97216;
Pacific Union Conf.: P.O. Box 5005, Westlake Village, CA 91359; Pres., Thomas J. Mostert, Jr
Southern Union Conf.: P.O. Box 849, Decatur, GA 30031; Pres., Malcolm D. Gordon
Southwestern Union Conf.: P.O. Box 4000, Burleson, TX 76097; Pres., Max A. Trevino

Periodicals

ADRA Works; Advent View; The Adventist Chaplain; Adventist Review; ASI Magazine; ASI Update; Audit Trails; AWR Transmissions; AWR Current; AWRecorder; AWResource; Children's Friend; Christian Record; Client Connection; College and University Dialogue; Collegiate Quarterly; Cornerstone Youth Resource Magazine; Cornerstone Connections; Elder's Digest; Encounter; For God and Country; Geoscience Reports; Guide; Insight; It is Written Channels; The Journal of Adventist Education; Kid's Ministry Ideas; Liberty; Lifeglow; Listen; Literature Evangelist; Message; Ministry; Mission—children, youth, adult; Origins; Our Little Friend; Primary

Treasure; Publishing Mirror; Sabbath School Teaching Aids; Sabbath School Program Helps; Sabbath School Leadership; Shabbat Shalom; Shepherdess International Journal; Signs of the Times; The Student; Telenotes; Vibrant Life; Voice of Prophecy News; The Window; Winner; Women of Spirit; Young and Alive; Youth Ministry ACCENT

Seventh Day Baptist General Conference, USA and Canada

Seventh Day Baptists emerged during the English Reformation, organizing their first churches in the mid-1600s. The first Seventh Day Baptists of record in America were Stephen and Ann Mumford, who emigrated from England in 1664. Beginning in 1665 several members of the First Baptist Church at Newport, R.I. began observing the seventh day Sabbath, or Saturday. In 1671, five members, together with the Mumfords, formed the first Seventh Day Baptist Church in America at Newport.

Beginning about 1700, other Seventh Day Baptist churches were established in New Jersey and Pennsylvania. From these three centers, the denomination grew and expanded westward. They founded the Seventh Day Baptist General Conference in 1802.

The organization of the denomination reflects an interest in home and foreign missions, publications and education. Women have been encouraged to participate. From the earliest years religious freedom has been championed for all and the separation of church and state, advocated.

Seventh Day Baptists are members of the Baptist World Alliance and Baptist Joint Committee. The Seventh Day Baptist World Federation has 17 member conferences on six continents.

Headquarters

Seventh Day Baptist Center, 3120 Kennedy Rd., P.O. Box 1678, Janesville, WI 53547-1678 Tel. (608)752-5055 Fax (608)752-7711
Media Contact, Ex. Sec., Calvin Babcock
Email: sdbgen@inwave.com
Website: www.seventhdaybaptist.org

OTHER ORGANIZATIONS

Seventh Day Baptist Missionary Society, Exec. Dir., Kirk Looper, 119 Main St., Westerly, RI 02891
Seventh Day Bapt. Bd. of Christian Ed., Exec. Dir., Dr. Ernest K. Bee, Jr., Box 115, Alfred Station, NY 14803
Women's Soc. of the Gen. Conference, Pres., Mrs. Ruth Probasco, 858 Barrett Run Rd., Bridgeton, NJ 08302
American Sabbath Tract & Comm. Council, Dir. of Communications, Rev. Kevin J. Butler, 3120 Kennedy Rd., P.O. Box 1678, Janesville, WI 53547
Seventh Day Baptist Historical Society, Historian, Don A. Sanford, 3120 Kennedy Rd., P.O. Box 1678, Janesville, WI 53547

Seventh Day Baptist Center on Ministry, Dir. of Pastoral Services, Rev. Rodney Henry, 3120 Kennedy Rd., P.O. Box 1678, Janesville, WI 53547

Periodicals

Sabbath Recorder

Southern Baptist Convention

The Southern Baptist Convention was organized on May 10, 1845, in Augusta, Georgia. Cooperating Baptist churches are located in all 50 states, the District of Columbia, Puerto Rico, American Samoa and the Virgin Islands. The members of the churches work together through 1,219 district associations and 41 state conventions and/or fellowships. The Southern Baptist Convention has an Executive Committee and 12 national agencies - four boards, six seminaries, one commission, and one auxiliary organization.

The purpose of the Southern Baptist Convention is "to provide a general organization for Baptists in the United States and its territories for the promotion of Christian missions at home and abroad and any other objects such as Christian education, benevolent enterprises, and social services which it may deem proper and advisable for the furtherance of the Kingdom of God". (Constitution, Article II)

The Convention exists in order to help the churches lead people to God through Jesus Christ.

From the beginning, there has been a mission desire to share the Gospel with the peoples of the world. The Cooperative Program is the basic channel of mission support. In addition, the Lottie Moon Christmas Offering for Foreign Missions and the Annie Armstrong Easter Offering for Home Missions support Southern Baptists' world mission programs.

In 1998, there were over 4,800 foreign missionaries serving in 154 foreign countries and over 5,000 home missionaries serving within the United States.

In 1987, the Southern Baptist Convention adopted themes and goals for the major denominational emphasis of Bold Mission Thrust for 1990-2000. Bold Mission Thrust is an effort to enable every person in the world to have opportunity to hear and to respond to the Gospel of Christ by the year 2000.

Headquarters

901 Commerce St., Nashville, TN 37203 Tel. (615)244-2355
Media Contact, Vice-Pres. for Convention Relations, A. William Merrell, Tel. (615)244-2355 Fax (615)782-8684
Email: bmerrell@sbc.net
Website: www.sbc.net

Officers

Pres., James Merritt
Recording Sec., John Yeats, P.O. Box 12130, Oklahoma City, OK 73112

Executive Committee: Pres., Morris H. Chapman; Vice-Pres., Business & Finance, Jack Wilkerson; Vice-Pres., Convention News, Will Hall; Vice-Pres., Convention Relations, A. William Merrell; Vice-Pres., Convention Policy, Augie Boto; Vice-Pres., Cooperative Program, David E. Hankins

GENERAL BOARDS AND COMMISSION

International Mission Board: Pres., Jerry A. Rankin, Box 6767, Richmond, VA 23230 Tel. (804)353-6655

North American Mission Board: Pres., Robert E. Reccord, 4200 No. Point Pkwy., Alpharetta, GA 30202 Tel. (770) 410-6519

Annuity Board: Pres., O. S. Hawkins, P.O. Box 2190, Dallas, TX 75221 Tel. (214)720-0511

LifeWay Christian Resources: Pres., James T. Draper, Jr. 127 Ninth Ave. N., Nashville, TN 37234 Tel. (615)251-2605

Ethics and Religious Liberty Commission: Pres., Richard D. Land, 901 Commerce St., Nashville, TN 37203 Tel. (615)244-2495

STATE CONVENTIONS

Alabama, Rick Lance, 2001 E. South Blvd., Montgomery, AL 36116 Tel. (334)288-2460

Alaska, Cloyd Sullins, 1750 O'Malley Rd., Anchorage, AK 99516 Tel. (907)344-9627

Arizona, Steve Bass, 3031 W. Northern Ave., Ste. 131, Phoenix, AZ 85052 Tel. (602)864-0337

Arkansas, Emil Turner, P.O. Box 552, Little Rock, AR 72203 Tel. (501)376-4791

California, Fermin A. Whittaker, 678 E. Shaw Ave., Fresno, CA 93710 Tel. (209)229-9533

Colorado, David T. Bunch, 7393 So. Alton Way, Englewood, CO 80112 Tel. (303)771-2480

District of Columbia, W. Jere Allen, 1628 16th St. NW, Washington, DC 20009 Tel. (202)265-1526

Florida, John Sullivan, 1230 Hendricks Ave., Jacksonville, FL 32207 Tel. (904)396-2351

Georgia, Dr. J. Robert White, 2930 Flowers Rd., S, Atlanta, GA 30341 Tel. (770)455-0404

Hawaii, O. W. Efurd, 2042 Vancouver Dr., Honolulu, HI 96822 Tel. (808)946-9581

Illinois, Bob Wiley, P.O. Box 19247, Springfield, IL 62794 Tel. (217)786-2600

Indiana, Charles W. Sullivan, P.O. Box 24189, Indianapolis, IN 46224 Tel. (317)241-9317

Iowa Southern Baptist Convention, O. Wyndell Jones, Suite #27, 2400 86th St., Des Moines, IA 50322 Tel. (515)278-4369

Kansas-Nebraska, R. Rex Lindsay, 5410 W. Seventh St., Topeka, KS 66606 Tel. (785)273-4880

Kentucky, Bill Mackey, P.O. Box 43433, Middletown, KY 40243 Tel. (502)245-4101

Louisiana, Dean Doster, P.O. Box 311, Alexandria, LA 71309 Tel. (318)448-3402

Maryland-Delaware, Charles R. Barnes, 10255 Old Columbia Rd., Columbia, MD 21046 Tel. (410)290-5290

Michigan, Michael Collins, 15635 W. 12 Mile Rd., Southfield, MI 48076 Tel. (248)557-4200

Minnesota-Wisconsin, William C. Tinsley, 519 16th St. SE, Rochester, MN 55904 Tel. (507)282-3636

Mississippi, James R. Futral, P.O. Box 530, Jackson, MS 39205 Tel. (601)968-3800

Missouri, James L. Hill, 400 E. High Street, Jefferson City, MO 65101 Tel. (573)635-7931

Nevada, David F. Meacham, 406 California Ave., Reno, NV 89509 Tel. (702)786-0406

New England, Kenneth R. Lyle, 5 Oak Ave., Northboro, MA 01532 Tel. (508)393-6013

New Mexico, Claude W. Cone, P.O. Box 485, Albuquerque, NM 87103 Tel. (505)924-2300

New York, J. B. Graham, 6538 Collamer Rd., East Syracuse, NY 13057 Tel. (315)433-1001

North Carolina, James H. Royston, 205 Convention Dr., Cary, NC 27511 Tel. (919)467-5100

Northwest, Jeff Iorg, 3200 NE 109th Ave., Vancouver, WA 98682 Tel. (360)882-2100 x. 121

Ohio, Exec. Dir., Jack P. Kwok, 1680 E. Broad St., Columbus, OH 43203 Tel. (614)258-8491

Oklahoma, Anthony L. Jordan, 3800 N. May Ave., Oklahoma City, OK 73112 Tel. (405) 942-3800

Pennsylvania-South Jersey, David C. Waltz, 4620 Fritchey St., Harrisburg, PA 17109 Tel. (717)652-5856

South Carolina, B. Carlisle Driggers, 190 Stoneridge Dr., Columbia, SC 29210 Tel. (803)765-0030

Tennessee, James M. Porch, P.O. Box 728, Brentwood, TN 37024 Tel. (615)371-2090

Texas, William M. Pinson, 333 N. Washington, Dallas, TX 75246 Tel. (214)828-5300

Southern Baptists of Texas, James W. Richards, P.O. Box 168585, Irving, TX 75106 Tel. (972)953-0878

Utah-Idaho, Jim Harding, P.O. Box 1347, Draper, UT 84020 Tel. (801)572-5350

Baptist General Association of Virginia, Reginald M. McDonough, P.O. Box 8568, Richmond, VA 23226 Tel. (804)672-2100

Southern Baptist Conservatives of Virginia, H. Doyle Chauncey, 4191 Innslake Dr., Ste 2U, Glen Allen, VA 23060 Tel. (804)270-1848

West Virginia, Jere L. Phillips, Number One Missions Way, Scott Depot, WV 25560 Tel. (304)757-0944

Wyoming, John W. Thomason, P.O. Box 4779, Casper, WY 82604 Tel. (307)472-4087

FELLOWSHIPS

Dakota Southern Baptist Fellowship, W.D. "Doc" Lindsey, Interim,, P.O. Box 7187, Bismarck, ND 58502 Tel. (701)255-3765

Montana Southern Baptist Fellowship, C. Clyde Billingsley, P.O. Box 99, Billings, MT 59103 Tel. (406)252-7537

Canadian Convention of Southern Baptists, Gerry Taillon, Postal Bag 300, Cochrane, Alberta T0L 0W0 Tel. (403)932-5688

145

Periodicals
The Commission; SBC Life; On Mission

Southern Methodist Church

Organized in 1939, this body is composed of congregations desirous of continuing in true Biblical Methodism and preserving the fundamental doctrines and beliefs of the Methodist Episcopal Church, South. These congregations declined to be a party to the merger of the Methodist Episcopal Church, The Methodist Episcopal Church, South and the Methodist Protestant Church into The Methodist Church.

Headquarters

P.O. Box 39, Orangeburg, SC 29116-0039 Tel. (803)536-1378 Fax (803)535-3881
Media Contact, Pres., Rev. Bedford F. Landers
Email: smchq@juno.com

Officers

Pres., Rev. Bedford F. Landers
Admn. Asst. to Pres., Philip A. Rorabaugh
Director of Foreign Missions, Rev. Franklin D. McLellan, P.O. Box 39, Orangeburg, SC 29116-0039
Southern Methodist College Pres., Rev. Daniel H. Shapley, PO Box 1027, Orangeburg, SC 29116-1027
The Eastern Conf., Vice-Pres., Rev. John T. Hucks, Jr., 221 Pinewood Dr., Rowesville, SC 29133
Alabama-Florida-Georgia Conf., Vice-Pres., Rev. Glenn A Blank, 2275 Scenic Highway, Apt. 109, Pensacola, FL 32502
Mid-South Conf., Vice-Pres., Rev. Dr. Ronald R. Carrier, 5030 Hillsboro Rd., Nashville, TN 37215
South-Western Conf., Vice-Pres., Rev. Ira Schilling, 106 Albert Dr., Haughton, LA 71037
Gen. Conf., Treas., Rev. Philip A. Rorabaugh, P.O. Drawer A, Orangeburg, SC 29116-0039

Periodicals

The Southern Methodist

Sovereign Grace Believers

The Sovereign Grace Believers are a contemporary movement which began its stirrings in the mid-1950s when some pastors in traditional Baptist churches returned to a Calvinist-theological perspective.

The first "Sovereign Grace" conference was held in Ashland, Kentucky, in 1954 and since then, conferences of this sort have been sponsored by various local churches on the West Coast, Southern and Northern states and Canada. This movement is a spontaneous phenomenon concerning reformation at the local church level. Consequently, there is no interest in establishing a Reformed Baptist "Convention" or "Denomination." Each local church is to administer the keys to the kingdom.

Most Sovereign Grace Believers formally or informally relate to the "First London" (1646), "Second London" (1689) or "Philadelphia" (1742) Confessions.

There is a wide variety of local church government in this movement. Many Calvinist Baptists have a plurality of elders in each assembly. Other Sovereign Grace Believers, however, prefer to function with one pastor and several deacons.

Membership procedures vary from church to church, but all require a credible profession of faith in Christ and proper baptism as a basis for membership.

Calvinistic Baptists financially support gospel efforts (missionaries, pastors of small churches at home and abroad, literature publication and distribution, radio programs, etc.) in various parts of the world.

Headquarters

Media Contact, Corres., Jon Zens, P.O. Box 548, St. Croix Falls, WI 54024 Tel. (651)465-6516 Fax (651)465-5101
Email: jon@searchingtogether.org
Website: www.searchingtogether.org

Periodicals

Searching Together

The Swedenborgian Church*

Founded in North America in 1792 as the Church of the New Jerusalem, the Swedenborgian Church was organized as a national body in 1817 and incorporated in Illinois in 1861. Its biblically-based theology is derived from the spiritual, or mystical, experiences and exhaustive biblical studies of the Swedish scientist and philosopher Emanuel Swedenborg (1688-1772).

The church centers its worship and teachings on the historical life and the risen and glorified present reality of the Lord Jesus Christ. It looks with an ecumenical vision toward the establishment of the kingdom of God in the form of a universal Church, active in the lives of all people of good will who desire and strive for freedom, peace and justice for all. It is a member of the NCCC and active in many local councils of churches.

With churches and groups throughout the United States and Canada, the denomination's central administrative offices and its seminary— Swedenborg School of Religion—are located in Newton, Massachusetts. Affiliated churches are found in Africa, Asia, Australia, Canada, Europe, the United Kingdom, Japan, South Korea and South America. Many philosophers and writers have acknowledged their appreciation of Swedenborg's teachings.

Headquarters

11 Highland Ave., Newtonville, MA 02460 Tel. (617)969-4240 Fax (617)964-3258

Media Contact, Central Ofc. Mgr., Martha Bauer
Email: manager@swedenborg.org
Website: www.swedenborg.org

Officers

Pres., Rev. Ronald P. Brugler, 489 Franklin St., N., Kitchener, ON, Canada N2A 1Z2

Vice-Pres., Christine Laitner, 10 Hanna Court, Midland, MI 48642

Rec. Sec., Gloria Toot, 10280 Gentlewind Dr., Montgomery, OH 45242

Treas., Lawrence Conant, 57 Grant St., W. Bridgewater, MA 02379

Ofc. Mgr., Martha Bauer

Periodicals

The Messenger; Our Daily Bread

Syrian (Syriac) Orthodox Church of Antioch*

The Syrian Orthodox Church of Antioch traces its origin to the Patriarchate established in Antioch by St. Peter the Apostle. It is under the supreme ecclesiastical jurisdiction of His Holiness the Syrian Orthodox Patriarch of Antioch and All the East, now residing in Damascus, Syria. The Syrian Orthodox Church—composed of several archdioceses, numerous parishes, schools and seminaries—professes the faith of the first three Ecumenical Councils of Nicaea, Constantinople and Ephesus, and numbers faithful in the Middle East, India, the Americas, Europe and Australia.

The first Syrian Orthodox faithful came to North America during the late 1800s, and by 1907 the first Syrian Orthodox priest was ordained to tend to the community's spiritual needs. In 1949, His Eminence Archbishop Mor Athanasius Y. Samuel came to America and was soon appointed Patriarchal Vicar. The Archdiocese was officially established in 1957. In 1995, the Archdiocese of North America was divided into three separate Patriarchal Vicariates (Eastern United States, Western United States and Canada), each under a hierarch of the Church. There are 19 official archdiocesan parishes and three mission congregations in the United States, located in California, District of Columbia, Florida, Illinois, Massachusetts, Michigan, New Jersey, New York, Oregon, Rhode Island and Texas. In Canada, there are five official parishes: three in the Province of Ontario and two in the Province of Quebec and a mission congregation in the Province of Alberta.

Headquarters

Archdiocese for the Eastern U.S., 260 Elm Avenue, Teaneck, NJ 07666 Tel. (201)801-0660 Fax (201)801-0603

Archdiocese of Los Angeles and Environs, 417 E. Fairmont Rd., Burbank, CA 91501 Tel. (818)845-5089 Fax (818)845-5436

Media Contact, Archdiocesan Gen. Sec., V. Rev. Chorepiscopus John Meno, 260 Elm Ave., Teaneck, NJ 07666 Tel. (201)907-0122 Fax (201)907-0551

Email: syrianoc@syrianorthodoxchurch.org
Website: www.syrianorthodoxchurch.org

Officers

Archdiocese for Eastern U.S.: Archbishop, Mor Cyril Aphrem Karim

Archdiocese of Los Angeles and Environs: Archbishop, Mor Clemis Eugene Kaplan

Triumph the Church and Kingdom of God in Christ Inc. (International)

This church was given through the wisdom and knowledge of God to the Late Apostle Elias Dempsey Smith on Oct. 20, 1897, in Issaquena County, Mississippi, while he was pastor of a Methodist church.

The Triumph Church, as this body is more commonly known, was founded in 1902. Its doors opened in 1904 and it was confirmed in Birmingham, Alabama, with 225 members in 1915. It was incorporated in Washington, D.C. in 1918 and currently operates in 31 states and overseas. The General Church is divided into 13 districts, including the Africa District.

Triumphant doctrine and philosophy are based on the principles of life, truth and knowledge; the understanding that God is in man and expressed through man; the belief in manifested wisdom and the hope for constant new revelations. Its concepts and methods of teaching the second coming of Christ are based on these and all other attributes of goodness.

Triumphians emphasize that God is the God of the living, not the God of the dead.

Headquarters

213 Farrington Ave. S.E., Atlanta, GA 30315

Media Contact, Bishop C. W. Drummond, 7114 Idlewild, Pittsburg, PA 15208 Tel. (412)731-2286

Officers

Chief Bishop, Bishop C. W. Drummond, 7114 Idlewild, Pittsburgh, PA 15208 Tel. (412)731-2286

Gen. Bd of Trustees, Chmn., Bishop Leon Simon, 1028 59th St., Oakland, CA 94608 Tel. (415)652-9576

Gen. Treas., Bishop Hosea Lewis, 1713 Needlewood Ln., Orlando, FL 32818 Tel. (407) 295-5488

Gen. Rec. Sec., Bishop Zephaniah Swindle, Box 1927, Shelbyville, TX 75973 Tel. (409)598-3082

True Orthodox Church of Greece (Synod of Metropolitan Cyprian), American Exarchate

The American Exarchate of the True (Old Calendar) Orthodox Church of Greece adheres to the tenets of the Eastern Orthodox Church, which considers itself the legitimate heir of the historical Apostolic Church.

When the Orthodox Church of Greece adopted

147

the New, or Gregorian, Calendar in 1924, many felt that this breach with tradition compromised the Church's festal calendar, based on the Old, or Julian, Calendar, and its unity with world Orthodoxy. In 1935, three State Church Bishops returned to the Old Calendar and established a Synod in Resistance, the True Orthodox Church of Greece. When the last of these Bishops died, the Russian Orthodox Church Abroad consecrated a new Hierarchy for the Greek Old Calendarists and, in 1969, declared them a Sister Church.

In the face of persecution by the State Church, some Old Calendarists denied the validity of the Mother Church of Greece and formed two synods, now under the direction of Archbishop Chrysostomos of Athens and Archbishop Andreas of Athens. A moderate faction under Metropolitan Cyprian of Oropos and Fili does not maintain communion with the Mother Church of Greece, but recognizes its validity and seeks a restoration of unity by a return to the Julian Calendar and traditional ecclesiastical polity by the State Church. About 1.5 million Orthodox Greeks belong to the Old Calendar Church.

The first Old Calendarist communities in the United States were formed in the 1930s. The Exarchate under Metropolitan Cyprian was established in 1986. Placing emphasis on clergy education, youth programs, and recognition of the Old Calendarist minority in American Orthodoxy, the Exarchate has encouraged the establishment of monastic communities and missions. Cordial contacts with the New Calendarist and other Orthodox communities are encouraged. A center for theological training and Patristic studies has been established at the Exarchate headquarters in Etna, California.

In July 1994, the True Orthodox Church of Greece (Synod of Metropolitan Cyprian), the True Orthodox Church of Romania, the True Orthodox Church of Bulgaria, and the Russian Orthodox Church Abroad entered into liturgical union, forming a coalition of traditionalist Orthodox bodies several million strong.

Headquarters

St. Gregory Palamas Monastery, P.O. Box 398, Etna, CA 96027-0398 Tel. (530)467-3228 Fax (530) 467-5828

Media Contact, Exarch in America, His Eminence, Archbishop Chrysostomos

Officers

Acting Synodal Exarch in America, His Grace Bishop Auxentios

Chancellor of the Exarchate, The Very Rev. Raphael Abraham, 3635 Cottage Grove Ave. S.E., Cedar Rapids, IA 52403-1612

Periodicals

Orthodox Tradition (quarterly theological journal)

Ukrainian Orthodox Church of the U.S.A.*

The Ukrainian Orthodox Church of the U.S.A. has its origin in the ancient lands of Rus-Ukraine (present day Ukraine). It was to the inhabitants of these lands that the Apostle Andrew first preached the Gospel. Christianization began early in the history of Rus-Ukraine by missionaries from the Orthodox Christian See of Constantinople. In 988 AD, the Saintly Prince Volodymyr, crowned a process of Christian Evangelization begun in the 4th century, by personally accepting Orthodox Christianity and inspiring his subjects to do the same. The baptism of Volodymyr, his household and the inhabitants of Kyiv, altered the face of Kyivan Rus-Ukraine and Slavic history for all time. Kyiv became the spiritual heart of Orthodox Christians in Rus-Ukraine. It was from this See that missionaries were sent into every corner of St. Volodymyr's realm. Through their efforts the Gospel was preached and new communities were established. The Mother Church of Kyiv and its See of Saint Sophia, modeled after Constantinople's See of the same name, gave birth to many Orthodox Christian centers and communities in the west, east and north of the Dnipro river, among them the Orthodox Christian See of Moscow, Russia (Rosia).

The Ukrainian Orthodox Church of U.S.A. ministers to the needs of the faithful whose ancestral roots are in Ukraine. The Church found haven in America in the early 1920's. Its first bishop, Metropolitan Ioan (John) Teodorovych, arrived from Ukraine in 1924 and shepherded the Church as Metropolitan until his death in 1971. His successor, Archbishop Mstyslav, arrived in the U.S.A. in 1950, and shepherded the Church as Metropolitan from 1971 until his death in 1993. It was Metropolitan Mstyslav who, as a consequence of Ukraine's independence, was named Patriarch of Kyiv and All Ukraine, in 1990. Previous to 1996 there were two Ukrainian Orthodox jurisdictions in the U.S.A. Formal unification of the Ukrainian Orthodox Church of the U.S.A., shepherded by His Beatitude Metropolitan Constantine, and the Ukrainian Orthodox Church of America, shepherded by His Grace Bishop Vsevolod, was concluded in November 1996.

Headquarters

P.O. Box 495, South Bound Brook, NJ 08880, Tel. (732)356-0090 Fax (732)356-5556

Media Contact: His Eminence Antony, Archbishop of New York, Consistory President

Email: uocofusa@aol.com

Website: www.uocofusa.org

Officers

Metropolitan, His Beatitude Constantine, 1803 Sidney Street, Pittsburgh, PA 15203

CENTRAL EPARCHY:

EPARCHIAL BISHOP: Metropolitan Constantine Eparchial Seat: St. Volodymyr Cathedral, Parma, Ohio. 5913 State Road, Parma, OH 44134 Tel: (216)885-1509 States embraced: Florida, Georgia, Ohio, Western Pennsylvania

EASTERN EPARCHY: Eparchial Bishop: Archbishop Antony. Eparchial Seat: St. Volodymyr Cathedral, New York, NY. 160 West 82nd St. New York, NY 10024 Tel: (212)873-8550 States embraced: Connecticut, Delaware, Massachusetts, Maryland, New Jersey, New York, Pennsylvania and Rhode Island

WESTERN EPARCHY: Eparchial Bishop: Archbishop Vsevolod Eparchial Seat: St. Volodymyr Cathedral, Chicago, Illinois. 2230-50 West Cortez St. Chicago, IL 60622 Tel: (312)278-2827 States embraced: Arizona, California, Colorado, Illinois, Indiana, Michigan, Minnesota, North Dakota, Nebraska, Oregon, Washington, Wisconsin, Ontario Province

COUNCIL OF THE METROPOLIA

Metropolitan Constantine - Chairman Achbishop AntonyAchbishop Vsevolod

METROPOLITAN COUNCIL MEMBERS

Archimandrite ANDRIJ - Vice-chairman

Protopresbyter William DIAKIW

Protopresbyter Frank ESTOCIN

Protopresbyter Nestor KOWAL

Protopresbyter Taras CHUBENKO

Protopriest John NAKONACHNY

Rev. Fr. Michael KOCHIS

Eng. Emil SKOCYPEC

Dr. Gayle WOLOSCHAK - Secretary

Dr. George KRYWOLAP- Secretary

Dr. Anatole LYSYJ

Ms. Olga LISKIWSKY-MORGAN

Dr. Paul MICEVYCH

LTC (Ret.) Stephen HALLICK-HOLUTIAK

Ms. Helen Greenleaf - UOL President

Mrs. Nadia MIRCHUK - United Sisterhood President

Eng. Michael Heretz - St. Andrew Society Pres.

CONSISTORY

Consistory President, His Eminence Antony, Archbishop of New York, P.O. Box 495, South Bound Brook, NJ 08880, Tel. (732)356-0090 Fax (732)356-5556, Email: uocofusa@aol.com

Vice Pres., V. Rev. Willam DIAKIW

Sec., V. Rev. Frank ESTOCIN

Treas., Mr. Emil SKOCYPEC

Member, V. Rev. John Nakonachny

Member, V. Rev. Myron Oryhon

Member, Dr. George Krywolap

Unitarian Universalist Association of Congregations

The Unitarian Universalist Association (UUA), created in 1961 through a merger of the Universalist Church of America with the American Unitarian Association, combines two liberal religious traditions. The religion traces its roots back to Europe where in 1569, the Transylvanian king, John Sigismund (1540-1571), issued an edict of religious freedom. The religious philosophy led to the organization of the Universalists in this country in 1793, and the Unitarians (organized here in 1825).

Founders of Universalism believed in universal salvation, while founders of Unitarianism believed in the unity of God (as opposed to the Trinity). Today, Unitarian Universalism is a liberal, creedless religion with Judeo-Christian roots. It draws also from Eastern, humanist, and other religious traditions, and encourages its members to seek religious truth out of their own reflection and experience. The denomination teaches tolerance and respect for other religious viewpoints, and affirms the worth and dignity of every person.

The Unitarian Universalist Association consists of over 1,055 congregations located principally in the United States and Canada, with over 217,000 members, and is served by more than 1,400 ministers. The Association is the fastest-growing liberal religion in North America, and this year completed its seventeenth consecutive year of growth. Each member congregation within the UUA is governed independently. The Association is made up of 22 Districts (served by a District Executive who is a member of the UUA staff) in North America, with each congregation having district affiliation. The Association is governed by an elected Board of Trustees, chaired by an elected Moderator. An elected President, three vice presidents, and directors of five departments form the Executive Staff which administers the daily activities of the Association.

The General Assembly, held each June in a different UUA District, serves as the Association's annual business meeting. The UUA includes Departments of Ministry; Religious Education; Congregational, District and Extension Services; Communications; Development; and Faith in Action. The World, published bi-monthly, is the denominational journal. Beacon Press, an internationally honored publishing house, is wholly owned by the Unitarian Universalist Association.

Headquarters

25 Beacon Street, Boston, MA 02108, Tel. (617) 742-2100, Fax (617) 367-323

Media Contact, John Hurley, Director of Information, Tel. (617)742-2100 x. 131

Email: jhurley@uua.org

Website: www.uua.org

Officers

President, The Rev. Dr. John A. Buehrens

Moderator, Denise T. Davidoff

Executive Vice President, Kathleen C. Montgomery

Periodicals
UU World; InterConnections

United Christian Church

The United Christian Church originated about 1864. There were some ministers and laymen in the United Brethren in Christ Church who disagreed with the position and practice of the church on infant baptism, voluntary bearing of arms and belonging to oath-bound secret combinations. This group developed into United Christian Church, organized at a conference held in Campbelltown, Pennsylvania, on May 9, 1877. The principal founders of the denomination were George Hoffman, John Stamn and Thomas Lesher. Before they were organized, they were called Hoffmanites.

The United Christian Church has district conferences, a yearly general conference, a general board of trustees, a mission board, a board of directors of the United Christian Church Home, a camp meeting board, a young people's board and local organized congregations.

It believes in the Holy Trinity and the inspired Holy Scriptures with the doctrines they teach. The church practices the ordinances of Baptism, Holy Communion and Foot Washing.

It welcomes all into its fold who are born again, believe in Jesus Christ as Savior and Lord and have received the Holy Spirit.

Headquarters

c/o John P. Ludwig, Jr., 523 W. Walnut St., Cleona, PA 17042 Tel. (717)273-9629
Media Contact, Presiding Elder, John P. Ludwig, Jr.

Officers

Presiding Elder, Elder John P. Ludwig, Jr.
Conf. Sec., Mr. Lee Wenger, 1625 Thompson Ave., Annville, PA 17003
Conf. Moderator, Elder Gerald Brinser, 2360 Horseshoe Pike, Annville, PA 17003

OTHER ORGANIZATIONS

Mission Board: Pres., Elder John P. Ludwig, Jr.; Sec., Elder David Heagy, 4129 Oak St., Lebanon, PA 17042; Treas., LeRoy Bomgardner, 1000 Bomgardner Lane, Annville, PA 17003

United Church of Christ*

The United Church of Christ was constituted on June 25, 1957 by representatives of the Congregational Christian Churches and of the Evangelical and Reformed Church, in Cleveland, Ohio.

The Preamble to the Constitution states: "The United Church of Christ acknowledges as its sole head, Jesus Christ...It acknowledges as kindred in Christ all who share in this confession. It looks to the Word of God in the Scriptures, and to the presence and power of the Holy Spirit...It claims...the faith of the historic Church expressed in the ancient creeds and reclaimed in the basic insights of the Protestant Reformers. It affirms the responsibility of the Church in each generation to make this faith its own in...worship, in honesty of thought and expression, and in purity of heart before God....it recognizes two sacraments: Baptism and the Lord's Supper."

The creation of the United Church of Christ brought together four unique traditions:

(1) Groundwork for the Congregational Way was laid by Calvinist Puritans and Separatists during the late 16th-early 17th centuries, then achieved prominence among English Protestants during the civil war of the 1640s. Opposition to state control prompted followers to emigrate to the United States, where they helped colonize New England in the 17th century. Congregationalists have been self-consciously a denomination from the mid-19th century.

(2) The Christian Churches, an 18th-century American restorationist movement emphasized Christ as the only head of the church, the New Testament as their only rule of faith, and "Christian" as their sole name. This loosely organized denomination found in the Congregational Churches a like disposition. In 1931, the two bodies formally united as the Congregational Christian Churches.

(3) The German Reformed Church comprised an irenic aspect of the Protestant Reformation, a second generation of Reformers drew on the insights of Zwingli, Luther and Calvin to formulate the Heidelberg Catechism of 1563. People of the German Reformed Church began immigrating to the New World early in the 18th century, the heaviest concentration in Pennsylvania. Formal organization of the American denomination was completed in 1793. The church spread across the country. In the Mercersburg Movement, a strong emphasis on evangelical catholicity and Christian unity was developed.

(4) In 19th-century Germany, Enlightenment criticism and Pietist inwardness decreased longstanding conflicts between religious groups. In Prussia, a royal proclamation merged Lutheran and Reformed people into one United Evangelical Church (1817). Members of this new church way migrated to America. The Evangelicals settled in large numbers in Missouri and Illinois, emphasizing pietistic devotion and unionism; in 1840 they formed the German Evangelical Church Society in the West. After union with other Evangelical church associations, in 1877 it took the name of the German Evangelical Synod of North America.

On June 25, 1934, this Synod and the Reformed Church in the U.S. (formerly the German Reformed Church) united to form the Evangelical and Reformed Church. They blended the Reformed tradition's passion for the unity of the church and the Evangelical tradition's commitment to the liberty of conscience inherent in the gospel.

Headquarters

700 Prospect Avenue, Cleveland, OH 44115 Tel. (216)736-2100 Fax (216)736-2103

Media Contact, Rev. Robert Chase, 700 Prospect Ave., Cleveland, OH 44115 Tel. (216)736-2173 Fax (216)736-2223

Email: langa @ucc.org

Website: www.ucc.org

Officers

Exec. Minister, Wider Church Ministries, Mr. Dale L. Bishop

Exec. Minister, Justice and Witness Ministries, Ms. Bernice Powell Jackson

Exec. Minister, Local Church Ministries, Rev. Jose A. Malayang

Chair, Executive Council, Mr. David D. Anderson

Vice Chair, Executive Council, Rev. Kekapa P. K. Lee

Mod., General Synod, Rev. Nancy S. Taylor

Asst. Mod., General Synod, Mr. Richard M. Harter

Asst. Mod., General Synod, Ms. Sammy Toineeta

ORGANIZATIONS

Office of General Ministries, National Office, 700 Prospect Avenue, Cleveland, Ohio 44115. Tel: 216-736-2100 Fax 216-736-2103: Associate General Minister, Ms. Edith A. Guffey; General Minister and President, Rev. John H. Thomas; Executive Associate to the Associate General Minister, Mr. Bill G. Hendricks; Executive Associate and Team Leader, Covenantal Relations Ministry, Rev. C. Nozomi Ikuta

Justice and Witness Ministries, National Offices (as above), Tel 216-736-3700 Fax 216-736-3703: Franklinton Center at Bricks, PO Box 220, Whitakers, NC Tel 252-437-1723 Fax 252-437-1278: Washington Office, 110 Maryland Avenue, NE, Washington, DC. Tel 202-543-1517 Fax 202-543-5994: Executive Minister, Ms. Bernice Powell Jackson; Executive Associate, Rev. F. Allison Phillips

Local Church Ministries, Tel 216-736-3800 Fax 216-736-3803. Executive Minister, Rev. Jose A. Malayang

Wider Church Ministries, National Offices (as above), Tel 216-736-3200 Fax 216-736-3203: 475 Riverside Drive, New York, NY 10115: Disciples of Christ Division of Overseas Ministries, PO Box 1986, Indianapolis, IN 46206. Tel 317-635-3100 Fax 317-635-4323: Executive Minister, Mr. Dale L. Bishop; Executive Associate to the Executive Minister, Rev. Joan Ishibashi

Pension Boards, Main Office, 475 Riverside Drive, New York, NY 10115. Tel 212-870-2777 Fax 212-870-2877; National Office, 700 Prospect Avenue, Cleveland, OH 44115. Tel 216-736-2271 Fax 216-736-2274: Executive Vice President, Mrs. Joan F. Brannick

United Church Foundation, Inc., 475 Riverside Drive, New York, NY 10115. Tel 212-870-2582 Fax 212-870-2366: Executive Vice President, Mr. Donald G. Hart

Council for American Indian Ministry, 471 3rd Street, Box 412, Excelsior, MN 55331. Tel 612-474-3532: Executive Director, Rev. Armin L. Schmidt

Council for Health and Human Services Ministries, National Office (as above). Tel 216-736-2250 Fax 216-736-2251: Executive Director, Rev. Bryan W. Sickbert

CONFERENCES

Western Region

California, Nevada, Northern, Rev. Mary Susan Gast, 9260 Alcosta Blvd., #C18, San Ramon, CA 94583-4143

California, Southern, Rev. Daniel F. Romero, 2401 N. Lake Ave., Altadena, CA 91001

Hawaii, Rev. David P. Hansen, 15 Craigside Pl., Honolulu, HI 96817

Montana-Northern Wyoming, Rev. John M. Schaeffer, 2016 Alderson Ave., Billings, MT 59102

Central Pacific, Rev. Hector Lopez, 0245 SW Bancroft St., Ste. E, Portland, OR 97201

Rocky Mountain, Rev. Lynne E. Simxcox Fitch, 7000 Broadway, Ste. 420, ABS Bldg., Denver, CO 80221

Southwest, Rev. Ann C. Rogers-Witte, 4423 N. 24th St., Ste. 600, Phoenix, AZ 85016

Washington-North Idaho, 720 14th Ave. E., Seattle, WA 98102; Rev. Randall Hyvonen, S. 412 Bernard St., Spokane, WA 99204

West Central Region

Iowa, Rev. Susan J. Ingham, 600 42nd St., Des Moines, IA 50312

Kansas-Oklahoma, Rev. John H. Krueger, 1248 Fabrique, Wichita, KS 67218

Minnesota, Rev. William Kaseman, 122 W. Franklin Ave., Rm. 323, Minneapolis, MN 55404

Missouri, Rev. A. Gayle Engel, 461 E. Lockwood Ave., St. Louis, MO 63119

Nebraska, Rev. George S. Worcester, 825 M St., Lincoln, NE 68508

North Dakota, Rev. Jack J. Seville, Jr., 227 W. Broadway, Bismarck, ND 58501

South Dakota, Rev. Gene E. Miller, 3500 S. Phillips Ave., #121, Sioux Falls, SD 57105-6864

Great Lakes Region

Illinois, Rev. Charlene Burch, 1840 Westchester Blvd., Westchester, IL 60154

Illinois South, Rev. Ronald L. Eslinger, Box 325, 1312 Broadway, Highland, IL 62249

Indiana-Kentucky, Rev. Stephen C. Gray, 1100 W. 42nd St., Indianapolis, IN 46208

Michigan, Rev. Kent J. Ulery, P.O. Box 1006, East Lansing, MI 48826

Ohio, Rev. Ralph C. Quellhorst, 6161 Busch Blvd., #95, Columbus, OH 43229

Wisconsin, Rev. Frederick R. Trost, 4459 Gray Rd., Box 495, De Forest, WI 53532-0495

151

Southern Region

Florida, Rev. M. Douglas Borko, 222 E. Welbourne Ave., Winter Park, FL 32789

South Central, Rev. Mark H. Miller, 6633 E. Hwy. 290, #200, Austin, TX 78723-1157

Southeast, Rev. Timothy C. Downs, 756 W. Peachtree St., NW, Atlanta, GA 30308

Southern, Rev. Herman Haller, 217 N. Main St., Box 658, Graham, NC 27253

Middle Atlantic Region

Central Atlantic, Rev. John R. Deckenback, 916 S. Rolling Rd., Baltimore, MD 21228

New York, Rev. C. Jack Richards, The Church Center, Rm. 202, 3049 E. Genesee St., Syracuse, NY 13224

Penn Central, Rev. Lyle J. Weible, The United Church Center, Rm. 126, 900 S. Arlington Ave., Harrisburg, PA 17109

Penn Northeast, Rev. Daniel A. Vander PLOEG, 431 Delaware Ave., P.O. Box 177, Palmerton, PA 18071

Penn Southeast, Rev. Franklin R. Mittman, Jr., 505 Second Ave., P.O. Box 400, Collegeville, PA 19426

Penn West, Rev. Kenneth G. Leishner, 320 South Maple Ave., Greensburg, PA 15601

Puerto Rico, Rev. Luis Rosario, Box 8609, Caguas, PR 00762

New England Region

Connecticut, Rev. Davida Foy Crabtree, 125 Sherman St., Hartford, CT 06105

Maine, Rev. Jean M. Alexander, Rev. David R. Gaewski, 68 Main St., P.O. Box 966, Yarmouth, ME 04096

Massachusetts, Rev. Erwin R. Bode, Jr., P.O. Box 2246, 1 Badger Rd., Framingham, MA 01701

New Hampshire: Rev. Carole C. Carlson; Rev. Benjamin C. L. Crosby; Rev. John W. Lynes, 314 S. Main, P.O. Box 465, Concord, NH 03302

Rhode Island, Rev. H. Dahler Hayes, 56 Walcott St., Pawtucket, RI 02860

Vermont, Rev. Arnold I. Thomas, 285 Maple St., Burlington, VT 05401

Nongeographic

Calvin Synod, Rev. Louis Medgyesi, 607 Plum St., Fairport Harbor, OH 44077

Periodicals

United Church News; Common Lot; Courage in the Struggle for Justice and Peace

United Holy Church of America, Inc.

The United Holy Church of America, Inc. is an outgrowth of the great revival that began with the outpouring of the Holy Ghost on the Day of Pentecost. The church is built upon the foundation of the Apostles and Prophets, Jesus Christ being the cornerstone.

During a revival of repentence, regeneration and holiness of heart and life that swept through the South and West, the United Holy Church was born. The founding fathers had no desire to establish a denomination but were pushed out of organized churches because of this experience of holiness and testimony of the Spirit-filled life.

On the first Sunday in May 1886, in Method, North Carolina, what is today known as the United Holy Church of America, Inc. was born. The church was incorporated on Sept. 25, 1918.

Baptism by immersion, the Lord's Supper and feet washing are observed. The premillennial teaching of the Second Coming of Christ, Divine healing, justification by faith, sanctification as a second work of grace and Spirit baptism are accepted.

Headquarters

5104 Dunstan Rd., Greensboro, NC 27405 Tel. (336)621-0669

Media Contact, Gen. Statistician, Ms. Jacquelyn B. McCain, 1210 N. Euclid Ave., Apt. A, St. Louis, MO 63113-2012, Tel. 314-367-8351 Fax 314-367-1835

Email: books@mohistory.org

GENERAL ADMINISTRATION

Gen. Pres., The Rt. Rev. Odell McCollum, 707 Woodmark Run, Gahanna, OH 43230, Tel. 614-475-4713, Rax 614-475-4713

Gen. Vice Pres., Bishop Elijah Williams, 901 Briarwood St., Reidsville, NC 27320 Tel. (919) 349-7275

Gen. 2nd Vice-Pres., The Rt. Rev. Kenneth O. Robinson, Sr., 33 Springbrook Road, Nanuet, NY 10954-4423, Tel. 914-425-8311, Fax 914-352-2686

Gen. Rec. Sec., Rev. Mrs. Elsie Harris, 2304 Eighth Street, Portsmouth, VA 23704, Tel 757-399-0926

Asst. Rec. Sec., Mrs. Cassandra Jones, 3869 JoAnn Drive, Cleveland, OH 44122, Tel. 216-921-0097

Gen. Fin. Sec., Vera Perkins-Hughes, P.O. Box 6194, Cleveland, OH Tel. (216) 851-7448

Asst. Fin. Sec., Bertha Williams, 4749 Shaw Dr., Wilmington, NC 28405 Tel. (919)395-4462

Gen. Corres. Sec., Ms. Gwendolyn Lane, 3069 Hudson Street, Columbus, OH 43219

Gen. Treas., Louis Bagley, 8779 Wales Dr., Cincinnati, OH 45249 Tel. (513)247-0588

GENERAL OFFICERS

Gen Pres. Missionary Dept., Rev. Ardelia M. Corbett, 519 Madera Dr., Youngstown, OH 44504 Tel. (216)744-3284

Gen. Evangelism & Extension Dept., Pres., Elder Clifford R. Pitts, 3563 North 14th St., Milwaukee, WI 53206, Tel. 414-244-1319

Gen. Bible Church School Dept., Superintendent, Robert L. Rollins, 1628 Avondale Ave., Toledo, OH 43607 Tel. (419)246-4046

Gen. Y.P.H.A., Pres., Elder James W. Brooks, Rt. 3 Box 105, Pittsboro, NC 27312 Tel. (919)542-5357

Gen. Ushers Department, Pres., Ms. Sherly M. Hughes, 1491 East 191st Street, #H-604, Euclid, OH 44117, Tel. 216-383-0038

Gen. Educ. Dept., Elder Roosevelt Alston, 168 Willow Creek Run, Henderson, NC 27636, Tel, 919-438-5854

Gen. Music Dept., Chair, Rosie Johnson, 2009 Forest Dale Dr., Silver Spring, MD 20932

Gen. Historian, Dr. Chester Gregory, Sr., 1302 Lincoln Woods Dr., Baltimore, MD 21228, Tel. 410-788-5144

Gen. Counsel, Mr. Joe L. Webster, Esquire, Attorney-At-Law, P.O. Box 2301, Chapel Hill, NC 27515-2301, Tel. 919-542-5150

UHCA Academy, Dir., Ms. Stephanie Davis, The United Holy Church of America, Inc., 5104 Dunstan Road, Greensboro, NC 27405, Tel. 336-621-0069

Gen. Statistician, Ms. Jacquelyn B. McCain, 1210 N. Euclid Ave., Apt. A, St. Louis, MO 63113-2012, Tel. 314-367-8351 Fax 314-367-1835

PRESIDENTS OF CONVOCATIONAL DISTRICTS

Barbados District; The Rt. Rev. Jestina Gentles, 5 West Ridge St., Britton's Hill, St. Michael, BH2 Barbados, West Indies, Tel. 246-427-7185

Bermuda Dist., The Rt. Rev. Calvin Armstrong, P.O. Box 234, Paget, Bermuda, Tel. 441-296-0828 or 441-292-8383

Central Western Dist., Bishop Bose Bradford, 6279 Natural Bridge, Pine Lawn, MO 63121 Tel. (314)355-1598

Ghana, West Africa Dist., The Rt. Rev. Robert Blount, 231 Arlington Av., Jersey City, NJ 07035, Tel. 201-433-5672

New England Dist., The Rt. Rev. Lowell Edney, 85 Woodhaven St., Mattapan, MA 02126, Tel. 617-296-5366

Northern Dist., The Rt. Rev. Kenneth O. Robinson, Sr., 33 Springbrook Rd., Nanuet, NY 10954, Tel. 914-425-8311

Northwestern Dist., The Rt. Rev. M. Daniel Borden, 8655 North Melody Lane, Macedonia, OH 44056, Tel. 330-468-0270

Pacific Coast Dist., The Rt. Rev. Irvin Evans, 235 Harvard Rd., Linden, NJ 07036, Tel. 908-925-6138

Southeastern Dist., The Rt. Rev. James C. Bellamy, 1825 Rockland Dr., SE, Atlanta, GA 30316, Tel. 404-241-1821

Southern Dist.- Goldsboro, The Rt. Rev. Ralph E. Love, Sr., 200 Barrington Rd., Greenville, NC 27834, Tel. 252-353-0495

Southern Dist.- Henderson, The Rt. Rev. Jesse Jones, 608 Cecil Street, Durham, NC 27707, Tel. 919-682-8249

St. Lucia Dist., The Rt. Rev. Carlisle Collymore, P.O. Box 51, Castries, St. Lucia, West Indies, Tel. 758-452-5835

Virginia Dist., The Rt. Rev. Albert Augson, 1406 Melton Ave., Richmond, VA 23223, Tel. 804-222-0463

West Virginia Dist., The Rt. Rev. Alvester McConnell, Route 3, Box 263, Bluefield, WV 24701, Tel. 304-248-8046

Western North Carolina Dist., The Rt. Rev. Elijah Williams, 901 Briarwood St., Reidsville, NC 27320-7020, Tel. 336-349-7275

Periodicals

The Holiness Union; The United Holy Church General Church Organ

United House of Prayer

The United House of Prayer was founded and organized as a hierarchical church in the 1920s by the late Bishop C. M. Grace, who had built the first House of Prayer in 1919 in West Wareham, MA, with his own hands. The purpose of the organization is to establish, maintain and perpetuate the doctrine of Christianity and the Apostolic Faith throughout the world among all people; to erect and maintain houses of prayer and worship where all people may gather for prayer and to worship the almighty God in spirit and in truth, irrespective of denomination or creed, and to maintain the Apostolic faith of the Lord and Savior, Jesus Christ.

Headquarters

1117 7th St. NW, Washington, DC 20001 Tel. (202)289-0238 Fax (202)289-8058

Media Contact, Apostle S. Green

Officers

CEO, Bishop S. C. Madison, 1665 N. Portal Dr. NW, Washington, DC 20012 Tel. (202)882-3956 Fax (202)829-4717

NATIONAL PROGRAM STAFF

The General Assembly, Presiding Officer, Bishop S. C. Madison, 1665 N. Portal Dr. NW, Washington, DC 20012 Tel. (202)882-3956 Fax (202)829-4717

General Council Ecclesiastical Court, Clerk, Apostle R. Price, 1665 N. Portal Dr. NW, Washington, DC 20012 Tel. (202)882-3956 Fax (202)829-4717

Annual Truth & Facts Publication, Exec. Editor, Bishop S. C. Madison, 1665 N. Portal Dr. NW, Washington, DC 20012 Tel. (202)882-3956 Fax (202)829-4717

Nationwide Building Program, General Builder, Bishop S. C. Madison, 1665 N. Portal Dr. NW, Washington, DC 20012 Tel. (202)882-3956 Fax (202)829-4717

Special Projects, Dir., Apostle S. Green

The United Methodist Church*

The United Methodist Church was formed April 23, 1968, in Dallas by the union of The Methodist Church and The Evangelical United Brethren Church. The two churches shared a common historical and spiritual heritage. The Methodist Church resulted in 1939 from the unification of three branches of Methodism - the Methodist Episcopal Church, the Methodist

153

Episcopal Church, South, and the Methodist Protestant Church.

The Methodist movement began in 18th-century England under the preaching of John Wesley, but the Christmas Conference of 1784 in Baltimore is regarded as the date on which the organized Methodist Church was founded as an ecclesiastical organization. It was there that Francis Asbury was elected the first bishop in this country.

The Evangelical United Brethren Church was formed in 1946 with the merger of the Evangelical Church and the Church of the United Brethren in Christ, both of which had their beginnings in Pennsylvania in the evangelistic movement of the 18th and early 19th centuries. Philip William Otterbein and Jacob Albright were early leaders of this movement among the German-speaking settlers of the Middle Colonies.

Headquarters

Information: InfoServ, United Methodist Information Service, Dir., Mary Lynn Holly, Tel. 1-800-251-8140

Media Contact, Dir., United Methodist News Service, Thomas S. McAnally,

Tel. (615)742-5470 Fax (615)742-5469

Email: infoserv@umcom.umc.org

Website: www.umc.org

Officers

Gen. Conference, Sec., Carolyn M. Marshall, 204 N. Newlin St., Veedersburg, IN 47987

Council of Bishops: Pres., Bishop William B. Oden, P.O. Box 600127, Dallas, TX 75360-0127 (3300 Mockingbird Ln, Ste 316, Dallas Tx 75205) Tel. (214)522-6741 Fax (214)528-4435 Email: bishop_dallas@mail.smu.edu, Sec., Bishop Sharon Zimmerman Rader, 750 Windsor St., Ste 303, Sun Prairie, WI 53590, Toll Free Tel. (800)240-7328 Tel. (608)837-8526 Fax (608)837-0281, Email: EpiscopalOffice @WisconsinUMC.org

BISHOPS AND CONFERENCE COUNCIL DIRECTORS

North Central Jurisdiction

Sec., Judith McCartney, 240 N. Sandusky St., Delaware, OH 43015 Tel. (614)363-0864

Dakotas: Bishop Michael J. Coyner, 815 25th St. S., Fargo, ND 58103-2303 Tel. (701)232-2241 Fax (701)232-2615; Richard W. Fisher, 1331 W. University Ave., P.O. Box 460, Mitchell, SD 57301-0460 Tel. (605)996-6552 Fax (605)996-1766

Detroit: Bishop Donald A. Ott, Tel. (248)559-7000 Fax (248)569-4830; Jeffery Regan, 21700 Northwestern Hwy., Ste. 1200, Southfield, MI 48075-4917 Tel. (248)559-7000 Fax (248)569-4830

East Ohio: Bishop Jonathan D. Keaton, Tel. (330)499-3972 Fax (330)499-3279; Judith A. Olin, 8800 Cleveland Ave. NW, P.O. Box 2800, North Canton, OH 44720 Tel. (330)499-3972 Fax (330)499-3279

Illinois Great Rivers: Bishop Sharon Brown Christopher, 400 Chatham Rd., Ste. 100, Springfield, IL 62704 Tel. (217)726-8071 Fax (217)726-8074; Rev. Raymond P. Owens, P.O. Box 515, Bloomington, IL 61702-0515 Tel. (309)828-5092 Fax (309)829-8369

Iowa: Bishop Charles W. Jordan, Tel. (515)283-1991 Fax (515)283-8672; Don Mendenhall, 500 E. Court Ave., Ste. C, Des Moines, IA 50309-2019 Tel. (515)283-1991 Fax (515)288-1906

Minnesota: Bishop John L. Hopkins, Tel. (612)870-4007 Fax (612)870-3587; James H. Perry, 122 W. Franklin Ave., #400, Minneapolis, MN 55404-2472 Tel. (612)870-0058 Fax (612)870-1260

North Indiana: Bishop Woodie W. White, 1100 W. 42nd St., Indianapolis, IN 46208 Tel. (317)924-1321 Fax (317)924-4859; Steven Burris, P.O. Box 869, Marion, IN 46952 Tel. (765)664-5138 Fax (765)664-2307

Northern Illinois: Bishop C. Joseph Sprague, 77 W. Washington St., Ste. 1820, Chicago, IL 60602 Tel. (312)346-9766 Fax (312)214-9031; Phillip Blackwell, 8765 W. Higgins Rd., Ste. 650, Chicago, IL 60631 Tel. (773)380-5060 Fax (773)380-5067

South Indiana: Bishop Woodie W. White, 1100 W. 42nd St., Indianapolis, IN 46208 Tel. (317)924-1321 Fax (317)924-4859; Susan W.N. Ruach, Box 5008, Bloomington, IN 47407-5008 Tel. (812)336-0186 Fax (812)336-0216

West Michigan: Bishop Donald A. Ott, 21700 Northwestern Hwy., Ste. 1200, Southfield, MI 48075-4917 Tel. (248)559-7000 Fax (810)569-4830; John R. Thompson, P.O. Box 6247, Grand Rapids, MI 49516-6247 Tel. (616)459-4503 Fax (616)459-0191

West Ohio: Bishop Judith Craig, Tel. (614)844-6200 Fax (614)781-2625; Stanley T. Ling, 32 Wesley Blvd., Worthington, OH 43085 Tel. (614)844-6200 Fax (614)781-2642

Wisconsin: Bishop Sharon Z. Rader, 750 Windsor St., Ste. 303, Sun Prairie, WI 53590 Tel. (608)837-8526 Fax (608)837-0281; Jane Follmer Zekoff, P.O. Box 620, Sun Prairie, WI 53590-0620 Tel. (608)837-7328 Fax (608)837-8547

Northeastern Jurisdiction

Baltimore-Washington: Bishop Felton Edwin May, 110 Maryland Ave., NE, Ste. 311, Washington, DC 20002 Tel. (202)546-3110 Fax (202)546-3186; Marcus Matthews, 9720 Patuxent Woods Dr., Ste. 100, Columbus, MD 21046 Tel. (410)309-3400 Fax (410)309-9430

Central Pennsylvania: Bishop Neil L. Irons, Tel. (717)652-6705 Fax (717)652-5109; G. Edwin Zeiders, 900 S. Arlington Ave., Harrisburg, PA 17109-5086 Tel. (717)652-0460 Fax (717)652-3499

Eastern Pennsylvania: Bishop Peter D. Weaver, Tel. (610)666-9090 Fax (610)666-9181;

Michelle Barlow, P.O. Box 820, Valley Forge, PA 19482-0820 Tel. (610)666-9090 Fax (610) 666-9093

New England: Bishop Susan W. Hassinger, PO Box 249, Lawrence, MA 01842-0449 Tel. (978)682-7555 Fax (978)682-9555; Lornagrace Stuart, PO Box 249, Lawrence, MA 01842-0449 Tel. (978)682-7555 Fax (978)682-9555

New York: Bishop Ernest S. Lyght, Tel. (914) 684-6922 Fax (914)997-1628; Clayton Miller, 252 Bryant Ave., White Plains, NY 10605 Tel. (914)997-1570 Fax (914)684-6874

North Central New York: Bishop Hae-Jong Kim, 1010 East Ave., Rochester, NY 14607 Tel. (716)271-3400 Fax (716)271-3404; c/o CCOM Director, P.O. Box 1515, Cicero, NY 13039 Tel. (315)699-8715 Fax (315)699-8774

Northern New Jersey: Bishop Alfred Johnson, 112 W. Delaware Ave., Pennington, NJ 08534 Tel. (609)737-3940 Fax (609)737-6962; Sherrie Dobbs, 22 Madison, Madison, NJ 07940 Tel. (201)377-3800 Fax (201)765-9868

Peninsula-Delaware: Bishop Peter D. Weaver, P.O. Box 820, Valley Forge, PA 19482-0820 Tel. (610)666-9090 Fax (610)666-9181; Jonathan Baker, 139 N. State St., Dover, DE 19901 Tel. (302)674-2626 Fax (302)674-1573

Southern New Jersey: Bishop Alfred Johnson, 112 W. Delaware Ave., Pennington, NJ 08534 Tel. (609)737-3940 Fax (609)737-6962; John A. Janka, 1995 E. Marlton Pike East, Cherry Hill, NJ 08003-1893 Tel. (609)424-1700 Fax (609)424-9282

Troy: Bishop Susan M. Morrison, 215 Lancaster St., Albany, NY 12210-1131 Tel. (518)426-0386 Fax (518)426-0347; Garry Campbell, P.O. Box 560, Saratoga Springs, NY 12866 Tel. (518)584-8214 Fax (518)584-8378

West Virginia: Bishop S. Clifton Ives, 900 Washington St., East, Charleston, WV 25301 Tel. (304)344-8330 Fax (304)344-8330; Randall Flanagan, P.O. Box 2313, Charleston, WV 25328 Tel. (304)344-8331 Fax (304)344-8338

Western New York: Bishop Hae-Jong Kim, 1010 East Ave., Rochester, NY 14607 Tel. (716)271-3400 Fax (716)271-3404; James M. Pollard, 8499 Main St., Buffalo, NY 14221 Tel. (716)633-8558 Fax (716)633-8581

Western Pennsylvania: Bishop George W. Bashore, Tel. (724)776-2300 Fax (724)776-1355; Larry Homitsky, PO Box 5002, Cranberry Township, PA 16066 Tel. (724)776-2300 Fax (724)776-1355

Wyoming: Bishop Susan M. Morrison, 215 Lancaster St., Albany, NY 12210-1131 Tel. (518) 426-0386 Fax (518)426-0347; Charles Johns, 1700 Monroe St., Endicott, NY 13761-0058 Tel. (607)757-0608 Fax (607)757-0752

South Central Jurisdiction

Exec. Sec.: Thalia Matherson, 5646 Milton St., #240, Dallas, TX 75206 Tel. (214)692-9081

Central Texas: Bishop Joe A. Wilson, Tel. (817) 877-5222 Fax (817)332-4609; Henry Radde, 464 Bailey, Ft. Worth, TX 76107-2153 Tel. (817)877-5222 Fax (817)338-4541

Kansas East: Bishop Albert F. Mutti, Tel. (913) 272-0587 Fax (913)272-9135; Dale L. Fooshee, P.O. Box 4187, Topeka, KS 66604-0187 Tel. (913)272-9111 Fax (913)272-9135

Kansas West: Bishop Albert F. Mutti, P.O. Box 4187, Topeka, KS 66604 Tel. (913)272-0587 Fax (913)272-9135; Barbara Sheldon, 9440 E. Boston, #150, Wichita, KS 67207-3600 Tel. (316)684-0266 Fax (316)684-0044

Little Rock: Bishop Janice K. Riggle Huie, 723 Center St., Little Rock, AR 72201-4399 Tel. (501)324-8019 Fax (501)324-8018; Lewis T. See, Jr., 715 Center St., Ste. 202, Little Rock, AR 72201 Tel. (501)324-8027 Fax (501)324-8018

Louisiana: Bishop Dan E. Solomon, Tel. (504) 346-1646 Fax (504)387-3662; Leslie Nichols Akin, 527 North Blvd., Baton Rouge, LA 70802-5720 Tel. (504)346-1646 Fax (504) 383-2652

Missouri East: Bishop Ann B. Sherer, PO Box 6039, Chesterfield, MO 63006 Tel. (314) 891-8001 Fax (314)891-8003; Elmer E. Revelle, 870 Woods Mill Rd., #400, Ballwin, MO 63011 Tel. (314)891-1207 Fax (314)891-1211

Missouri West: Bishop Ann B. Sherer, PO Box 6039, Chesterfield, MO 63006 Tel. (314)891-8001 Fax (314)891-8003; Keith T. Berry, 1512 Van Brunt Blvd., Kansas City, MO 64127 Tel. (816)241-7650 Fax (816)241-4086

Nebraska: Bishop Joel L. Martinez, Tel. (402) 466-4955 Fax (402)466-7931; Mel Luetchens, P.O. Box 4553, Lincoln, NE 68504 Tel. (402)464-5994 Fax (402)466-7931

New Mexico: Bishop Alfred L. Norris, Tel. (505)255-8786 Fax (505)255-8738; James E. Large, 7920 Mountain Rd. NE, Albuquerque, NM 87110-7805 Tel. (505)255-8786 Fax (505) 255-8738

North Arkansas: Bishop Janice K. Riggle Huie, 723 Center St., Little Rock, AR 72201-4399 Tel. (501)324-8019 Fax (501)324-8018; Lewis T. See, 715 Center St., Ste. 202, Little Rock, AR 72201 Tel. (501)324-8034 Fax (501) 324-8018

North Texas: Bishop William B. Oden, 3300 Mockingbird Ln., P.O. Box 600127, Dallas, TX 75360-0127 Tel. (214)522-6741 Fax (214) 528-4435; Mary Brooke Casad, P.O. Box 516069, Dallas, TX 75251-6069 Tel. (972)490-3438 Fax (972) 490-7216

Northwest Texas: Bishop Alfred L. Norris, 7920 Mountain Rd. NE, Albuquerque, NM 87110-7805 Tel. (505)255-8786 Fax (505)255-8738; Louise Schock, 1415 Ave. M, Lubbock, TX 79401-3939 Tel. (806)762-0201 Fax (806) 762-0205

Oklahoma: Bishop Bruce P. Blake, Tel. (405)525-2252 Fax (405)525-2216; David

155

Severe, 2420 N. Blackwelder, Oklahoma City, OK 73106-1499 Tel. (405)525-2252 Fax (405) 525-4164

Oklahoma Indian Missionary: Bishop Bruce P. Blake, 2420 N. Blackwelder Ave., Oklahoma City, OK 73106-1499 Tel. (405)525-2252 Fax (405)525-2216; David L. Severe, 2420 N. Blackwelder Ave., Oklahoma City, OK 73106-1499 Tel. (405)525-2252 Fax (405)525-2216

Rio Grande: Bishop Raymond H. Owen, P.O. Box 781688, San Antonio, TX 78278 Tel. (210)408-4500 Fax (210)408-4515; Francisco Estrada, P.O. Box 781974, San Antonio, TX 78278 Tel. (210)408-5313 Fax (210)408-4515

Southwest Texas: Bishop Raymond H. Owen, P.O. Box 781688, San Antonio, TX 78278 Tel. (210)408-4500 Fax (210)408-4501; Jerry Jay Smith, P.O. Box 78149, San Antonio, TX 78278 Tel. (210)408-4500 Fax (210)408-4501

Texas: Bishop J. Woodrow Hearn, Tel. (713)529-7736 Fax (713)521-3724; James Foster, 5215 Main St., Houston, TX 77002-9792 Tel. (713) 521-9383 Fax (713)521-3724

Southeastern Jurisdiction

Exec. Dir.: Gordon C. Goodgame, P.O. Box 67, Lake Junaluska, NC 28745 Tel. (704)452-2881

Alabama-West Florida: Bishop William W. Morris, 424 Interstate Park Dr., Montgomery, AL 36109 Tel. (334)277-1787 Fax (334)277-0109; James William Carpenter, P.O. Drawer 700, Andalusia, AL 36420-0700 Tel. (334)222-3127 Fax (334)222-0469

Florida: Bishop Cornelius L. Henderson, P.O. Box 1747, Lakeland, FL 33802-1747 Tel. (941) 688-4427 Fax (941)687-0568; James Jennings, P.O. Box 3767, Lakeland, FL 33802 Tel. (941) 688-5563 Fax (941)680-1912

Holston: Bishop Ray W. Chamberlain, Jr., P.O. Box 51787, Knoxville, TN 37950-1787 Tel. (423)525-1809 Fax (423)673-4474; Calvin W. Maas, P.O. Box 1178, Johnson City, TN 37605-1178 Tel. (423)928-2156 Fax (423)928-8807

Kentucky: Bishop Robert C. Morgan, 2000 Warrington Way, #280, Louisville, KY 40222 Tel. (502)425-4240 Fax (502)426-5181; Rhoda Peters, 2000 Warrington Way, #280, Louisville, KY 40222 Tel. (502)425-3884 Fax (502)426-5181

Memphis: Bishop Kenneth L. Carder, 520 Commerce St., Ste. 201, Nashville, TN 37203 Tel. (615)742-8834 Fax (615)742-3726; Benny Hopper, PO Box 1257, Jackson, TN 38302 Tel. (901)427-8589 Fax (901)423-2419

Mississippi: Bishop Marshall L. Meadows, Jr., P.O. Box 931, Jackson, MS 39205-0931 Tel. (601)948-4561 Fax (601)948-5981; c/o CCOM Dir., P.O. Box 1147, Jackson, MS 39215 Tel. (601) 354-0515 Fax (601)948-5982

North Alabama: Bishop Robert E. Fannin, Tel. (205)322-8665 Fax (205)322-8938; Michael Stewart, 898 Arkadelphia Rd., Birmingham, AL 35204 Tel. (205)226-7954 Fax (205)226-7975

North Carolina: Bishop Marion M. Edwards, P.O. Box 10955, Raleigh, NC 27605-0955 Tel. (919)832-9560 Fax (919)834-7989; Hope Morgan Ward, P.O. Box 10955, Raleigh, NC 27605-0955 Tel. (919)832-9560 Fax (919)834-7989

North Georgia: Bishop G. Lindsey Davis, Tel. (404)659-0002 Fax (404)577-0068; Douglas Brantley, 159 Ralph McGill Blvd. NE, Atlanta, GA 30308 Tel. (404)659-0002 Fax (404) 577-0131

Red Bird Missionary: Bishop Robert C. Morgan, 2000 Warrington Way, #280, Louisville, KY 40222 Tel. (502)425-4240 Fax (502)426-5181; Ruth Wiertzema, 6 Queendale Ctr., Beverly, KY 40913 Tel. (606)598-5915 Fax (606)598-6405

South Carolina: Bishop J. Lawrence McCleskey, Tel. (803)786-9486 Fax (803)754-9327; Charles L. Johnson, Sr., 4908 Colonial Dr., Columbia, SC 29203 Tel. (803)786-9486 Fax (803)691-0220

South Georgia: Bishop Richard C. Looney, P.O. Box 13616, Macon, GA 31208-3616 Tel. (912) 738-0048 Fax (912)738-9033; James T. Pennell, P.O. Box 20408, St. Simons Island, GA 31522-0008 Tel. (912)638-8626 Fax (912)638-5258

Tennessee: Bishop Kenneth L. Carder, 520 Commerce St., Ste. 201, Nashville, TN 37203 Tel. (615)742-8834 Fax (615)742-3726; Randall C. Ganues, P.O. Box 120607, Nashville, TN 37212 Tel. (615)329-1177 Fax (615)329-0884

Virginia: Bishop Joe E. Pennel, Jr., Tel. (804) 359-9451 Fax (804)358-7736; F. Douglas Dillard, P.O. 11367, Richmond, VA 23230-1367 Tel. (804)359-9451 Fax (804)359-5427

Western North Carolina: Bishop Charlene P. Kammerer, P.O. Box 18750, Charlotte, NC 28218 Tel. (704)535-2260 Fax (704)567-6117; Thomas R. Sigmon, P.O. Box 18005, Charlotte, NC 28218-0005 Tel. (704)535-2260 Fax (704) 567-6117

Western Jurisdiction

Alaska Missionary: Bishop Edward W. Paup, 1505 SW 18th Ave., Portland, OR 97201-2599 Tel. (503)226-1530 Fax (503)228-3189; Dale Kelley, 3402 Wesleyan Dr., Anchorage, AK 99508-4866 Tel. (907)333-5050 Fax (907) 333-2304

California-Nevada: Bishop Melvin G. Talbert, Tel. (916)374-1510 Fax (916)372-5544; James H. Corson, P.O. Box 980250, West Sacramento, CA 95798-0250 Tel. (916)374-1516 Fax (916)372-5544

California-Pacific: Bishop Roy I. Sano, Tel. (626)568-7300 Fax (626)796-7297; Marilynn Huntington, P.O. Box 6006, Pasadena, CA 91102 Tel. (626)568-7300 Fax (626)796-7297

Desert Southwest: Bishop William W. Dew, Jr.,

Tel. (602)266-6956 Fax (602)266-5343; Thomas G. Butcher, 1550 E. Meadowbrook Ave., Ste. 200, Phoenix, AZ 85014-4040 Tel. (602)266-6956 Fax (602)266-5343

Oregon-Idaho: Bishop Edward W. Paup, 1505 SW 18th Ave., Portland, OR 97201-2599 Tel. (503) 226-7931 Fax (503)228-3189; James Wenger-Monroe, 1505 SW 18th Ave., Portland, OR 97201-2599 Tel. (503) 226-7931 Fax (503)226-4158

Pacific Northwest: Bishop Elias G. Galvan, 2112 Third Ave. Ste. 301, Seattle, WA 98121-2333 Tel. (206)728-7674 Fax (206)728-8442; Daniel P. Smith, 2112 Third Ave., Ste. 300, Seattle, WA 98121-2333 Tel. (206)728-7462 Fax (206) 728-8442

Rocky Mountain: Bishop Mary Ann Swenson; Tel. (303)733-5035 Fax (303)733-5047; Gary M. Keene, 2200 S. University Blvd., Denver, CO 80210-4797 Tel. (303)733-3736 Fax (303)733-1730

Yellowstone: Bishop Mary Ann Swenson, 2200 S. University Blvd., Denver, CO 80210-4797 Tel. (303)733-5035 Fax (303)733-5047; Thomas Boller, P.O. Box 2540, Billings, MT 59103 Tel. (406)256-1385 Fax (406)256-4948

AGENCIES

Judicial Council: Pres., Tom Matheny; Sec., Sally Curtis AsKew, P.O. Box 58, Bogart, GA 30622 Tel. (770)725-1543 Fax (770)725-1685

Council on Finance & Administration: Pres., Bishop Richard C. Looney; Gen. Sec., Sandra Kelley Lackore, 1200 Davis St., Evanston, IL 60201-4193 Tel. (847)869-3345 Fax (847)869-6972

Council on Ministries: Pres., Bishop J. Woodrow Hearn; Gen. Sec., C. David Lundquist, 601 W. Riverview Ave., Dayton, OH 45406 Tel. (937) 227-9400 Fax (937)227-9407

Board of Church & Society: Pres., Bishop Charles W. Jordan; Gen. Sec., Thomas White Wolf Fassett, 100 Maryland Ave. NE, Washington, DC 20002 Tel. (202)488-5623 Fax (202)488-5619

Board of Discipleship: Pres., Bishop Mary Ann Swenson; Gen. Sec., Karen Greenwaldt, P.O. Box 840, Nashville, TN 37202 Tel. (615)340-7200 Fax (615)304-7006

Board of Global Ministries: Pres., Bishop Dan E. Solomon; Gen. Sec., Randolph Nugent, 475 Riverside Dr., New York, NY 10115 Tel. (212)870-3600 Fax (212)870-3748

Board of Higher Education & Ministry: Pres., Bishop William B. Oden; Gen. Sec., Roger Ireson, P.O. Box 871, Nashville, TN 37202 Tel. (615)340-7400 Fax (615)340-7048

Board of Pension & Health Benefits: Pres., Bishop Bruce P. Blake; Gen. Sec., Barbara Boigegrain, 1201 Davis St., Evanston, IL 60201 Tel. (847) 869-4550 Fax (847)475-5061

Board of Publications: Chpsn., W. Randolph Smith; United Methodist Publishing House,

Pres. & Publisher, Neil M. Alexander, P.O. Box 801, Nashville, TN 37202 Tel. (615)749-6000 Fax (615)749-6079

Commission on Archives & History: Pres., Bishop Emilio de Carvalho; Gen. Sec., Charles Yrigoyen, P.O. Box 127, Madison, NJ 07940 Tel. (973)408-3189 Fax (973)408-3909

Comm. Christian Unity/Interrel. Concerns: Pres., Bishop Roy I. Sano; Gen. Sec., Bruce Robbins, 475 Riverside Dr., Rm. 1300, New York, NY 10115 Tel. (212)749-3553 Fax (212)749-3556

Comm. on Communication/UM Communications: Pres., Bishop Sharon Z. Rader; Gen. Sec., Judith Weidman, 810 12th Ave. S., Nashville, TN 37203 Tel. (615)742-5400 Fax (615)742-5469

Commission on Religion & Race: Pres., Bishop S. Clifton Ives; Gen. Sec., Barbara R. Thompson, 100 Maryland Ave. NE, Washington, DC 20002 Tel. (202)547-2271 Fax (202)547-0358

Commission on the Status & Role of Women: Pres., Joyce Waldon Bright; Gen. Sec., Stephanie Anna Hixon; Cecelia M. Long, 1200 Davis St., Evanston, IL 60201 Tel. (847)869-7330 Fax (847)869-1466

Commission of United Methodist Men: Pres., Bishop Raymond H. Owen; Gen. Sec., Joseph L. Harris, PO Box 860, Nashville, TN 37202-0860 Tel. (615)340-7145 Fax (615)340-1770

Periodicals

Mature Years; El Intérprete; New World Outlook; Newscope; Interpreter; Methodist History; Christian Social Action; Pockets; Response; Social Questions Bulletin; United Methodist Reporter; United Methodist Review; Quarterly Review; Alive Now; Circuit Rider; El Aposento Alto; Weavings:A Journal of the Christian Spiritual Life; The Upper Room

United Pentecostal Church International

The United Pentecostal Church International came into being through the merger of two oneness Pentecostal organizations—the Pentecostal Church, Inc., and the Pentecostal Assemblies of Jesus Christ. The first of these was known as the Pentecostal Ministerial Alliance from its inception in 1925 until 1932. The second was formed in 1931 by a merger of the Apostolic Church of Jesus Christ with the Pentecostal Assemblies of the World.

The church contends that the Bible teaches that there is one God who manifested himself as the Father in creation, in the Son in redemption and as the Holy Spirit in regeneration; that Jesus is the name of this absolute deity and that water baptism should be administered in his name, not in the titles Father, Son and Holy Ghost (Acts 2:38, 8:16, and 19:6).

157

The Fundamental Doctrine of the United Pentecostal Church International, as stated in its Articles of Faith, is "the Bible standard of full salvation, which is repentance, baptism in water by immersion in the name of the Lord Jesus Christ for the remission of sins, and the baptism of the Holy Ghost with the initial sign of speaking with other tongues as the Spirit gives utterance."

Further doctrinal teachings concern a life of holiness and separation, the operation of the gifts of the Spirit within the church, the second coming of the Lord and the church's obligation to take the gospel to the whole world.

Headquarters

8855 Dunn Rd., Hazelwood, MO 63042 Tel. (314)837-7300 Fax (314)837-4503

Media Contact, Gen. Sec.-Treas., Rev. C. M. Becton

Officers

Gen. Supt., Rev. Nathaniel A. Urshan

Asst. Gen. Supts.: Rev. Kenneth Haney, 7149 E. 8 Mile Rd., Stockton, CA 95212; Jesse Williams, P.O. Box 64277, Fayetteville, NC 28306

Gen. Sec.-Treas., Rev. C. M. Becton

Dir. of Foreign Missions, Rev. Harry Scism

Gen. Dir. of Home Missions, Rev. Jack Cunningham

Editor-in-Chief, Rev. J. L. Hall

Gen. Sunday School Dir., Rev. E. J. McClintock

OTHER ORGANIZATIONS

Pentecostal Publishing House, Mgr., Rev. Marvin Curry

Youth Division (Pentecostal Conquerors), Pres., Brian Kinsey, Hazelwood, MO 63042

Ladies Auxiliary, Pres., Gwyn Oakes, P.O. Box 247, Bald Knob, AR 72010

Harvestime Radio Broadcast, Dir., Rev. J. Hugh Rose, 698 Kerr Ave., Cadiz, OH 43907

Stewardship Dept., Contact Church Division, Hazelwood, MO 63042

Education Division, Supt., Rev. Arless Glass, 4502 Aztec, Pasadena, TX 77504

Public Relations Division, Contact Church Division, Hazelwood, MO 63042

Historical Society & Archives

Periodicals

World Harvest Today; The North American Challenge; Homelife; Conqueror; Reflections; Forward

The United Pentecostal Churches of Christ

In a time when the Church of Jesus Christ is challenged to send the "Evening Light Message" to the uppermost part of the Earth, a group of men and women came together on May 29, 1992 at the Pentecostal Church of Christ in Cleveland, Ohio to form what is now called The United Pentecostal Churches of Christ.

Organized and established by Bishop Jesse Delano Ellis, II, the United Pentecostal Churches of Christ is about the business of preparing people to see the Lord of Glory. The traditional barriers of yesteryear must not keep saints or like faith apart ever again and this fellowship of Pentecostal, Apostolic Independent Churches have discovered the truth of Our Lord's Prayer in the seventeenth chapter of Saint John: "that they may all be One."

The United Pentecostal Churches of Christ is a fellowship of holiness assemblies which has membership in the universal Body of Christ. As such, we preserve the message of Christ's redeeming love through His atonement and declare holiness of life to be His requirement for all men who would enter into the Kingdom of God. We preach repentence from sin, baptism in the Name of Jesus Christ, a personal indwelling of the Holy Spirit, a daily walk with the Lord and life after death. Coupled with the cardinal truths of the Church are the age old customs of ceremony and celebration.

Headquarters

10515 Chester Ave., (at University Circle), Cleveland, OH 44106 Tel. (216)721-5935 Fax (216)721-6938

Contact Person, Asst. Gen. Sec., Rev. W. Michelle James Williams

REGIONAL OFFICE

493-5 Monroe St., Brooklyn, New York 11221 Tel. (718)574-4100 Fax (718)574-8504

Contact Person, Asst. Gen. Sec., Rev. Rodney McNeil Johnson

Officers

Presiding Bishop and Gen. Overseer, Bishop J. Delano Ellis, II, Cleveland, OH

Asst. Presiding Bishop, Bishop Carl Halloway Montgomery, II, Baltimore, MD

Secretary Gen., Bishop James R. Chambers, Brookyn, NY

Supervisor of Women's Department, Rev. Sabrina J. Ellis, Cleveland, OH

Pres. Of Pentecostal Youth Congress, Overseer Gregory Dillard, Chicago, IL

Periodicals

THE PENTECOSTAL FLAME

United Zion Church

A branch of the Brethren in Christ which settled in Lancaster County, Pennsylvania, the United Zion Church was organized under the leadership of Matthias Brinser in 1855.

Headquarters

United Zion Retirement Community, 722 Furnace Hills Pk., Lititz, PA 17543

Media Contact, Bishop, Carl Eberly, 270 Clay School Rd., Ephrata, PA 17522 Tel. (717)733-3932

Officers

Gen. Conf. Mod., Bishop Carl Eberly, 270 Clay

School Rd., Ephrata, PA 17522 Tel. (717)733-3932

Asst. Mod., Rev. John Leisey

Gen. Conf. Sec., Rev. Clyde Martin

Gen. Conf. Treas., Kenneth Kleinfelter, 919 Sycamore Lane, Lebanon, PA 17042

Periodicals
Zion's Herald

Unity of the Brethren

Czech and Moravian immigrants in Texas (beginning about 1855) established congregations which grew into an Evangelical Union in 1903, and with the accession of other Brethren in Texas, into the Evangelical Unity of the Czech-Moravian Brethren in North America. In 1959, it shortened the name to the original name used in 1457, the Unity of the Brethren (Unitas Fratrum, or Jednota Bratrska).

Headquarters
4009 Hunter Creek, College Station, TX 77845

Media Contact, Sec. of Exec. Committee, Ginger McKay, 148 N. Burnett, Baytown, TX 77520

Officers
Pres., Kent Laza, 4009 Hunter Creek, College Station, TX 77845

1st Vice Pres., Rev. Michael Groseclose, 902 Church St., Belleville, TX 77418 Tel. (512)365-6890

Sec. of Exec. Committee, Ginger McKay, 148 N. Burnett, Baytown, TX 77520

Fin. Sec., Rev. Joseph Polasek, 4241 Blue Heron, Bryan, TX 77807

Treas., Arranna Jakubik, P.O. Box 408, Snook, TX 77878

OTHER ORGANIZATIONS
Bd. of Christian Educ., Dr., Donald Ketcham, 900 N. Harrison, West, TX 76691

Brethren Youth Fellowship, Pres., Jamie Brooke Bryan, 1231 Four Corners, West, TX 76691

Friends of the Hus Encampment, Jim Baletka, 727 San Benito, College Station, TX 77845

Christian Sisters Union, Pres., Janet Pomykal, P.O. Box 560, Brenham, TX 77834

Sunday School Union, Pres., Dorothy Kocian, 107 S. Barbara Dr., Waco, TX 76705

Youth Director, Kimberly Stewart, 1500 Lawnmont Dr., Apt. 208, Round Rock, TX 78664

Periodicals
Brethren Journal, Editor, Rev.Milton Maly, 6703 FM 2502, Brenham, TX 77833; Bus Mngr., Jean Maly, 6703 FM 2502, Brenham, TX 77833

Universal Fellowship of Metropolitan Community Churches

The Universal Fellowship of Metropolitan Community Churches was founded Oct. 6, 1968 by the Rev. Troy D. Perry in Los Angeles, with a particular but not exclusive outreach to the gay community. Since that time, the Fellowship has grown to include congregations throughout the world.

The group is Trinitarian and accepts the Bible as the divinely inspired Word of God. The Fellowship has two sacraments, baptism and holy communion, as well as a number of traditionally recognized rites such as ordination.

This Fellowship acknowledges "the Holy Scriptures interpreted by the Holy Spirit in conscience and faith, as its guide in faith, discipline, and government." The government of this Fellowship is vested in its General Council (consisting of Elders and District Coordinators), clergy and church delegates, who exert the right of control in all of its affairs, subject to the provisions of its Articles of Incorporation and By-Laws.

Headquarters
8704 Santa Monica Blvd. 2nd Floor, West Hollywood, CA 90069-4548 Tel. (310)360-8640 x. 215 Fax (310)360-8680

Media Contact, Dir. of Communications, Maaza Mengiste

Email: communications@ufmcchq.com

Website: www.ufmcchq.com

Officers
Mod., Rev. Elder Troy D. Perry

Vice-Mod., Rev. Elder Nancy L. Wilson

Treas., Rev. Elder Donald Eastman

Clk., Rev. Elder Darlene Garner

Elder Clarke Friesen, P.O. Box 90685, Tucson, AZ 85752

Rev. Elder Nori Rost, 214 S. Prospect St., Colorado Springs, CO 80903

Rev. Elder Hong Kia Tan, 72 Fleet Rd., Hampstead, London, NW3 2QT England

Deputy Chief Executive Officer, Margaret Mahlman, 8704 Santa Monica Blvd., 2nd Floor, West Holywood, CA 90069-4548

Dir., Communications, Maaza Mengiste, 8704 Santa Monica Blvd., 2nd Floor, West Hollywood, CA 90069-4548

Chief Officer, Office of Ecumenical and Interreligious Concerns, Rev. Gwynne Guibord, 4311 Wilshire Blvd., Ste. 308, Los Angeles, CA 90010 Tel. (213)932-1516

OTHER COMMISSIONS & COMMITTEES
Min. of Global Outreach, Field Dir., Rev. Judy Dahl

Commission on the Laity, Chpsn., Mel Johnson

Clergy Credentials & Concerns, Admn., Rev. Justin Tanis

UFMCC AIDS Ministry: AIDS Liaison., Rev. Robert Griffin

Periodicals
Keeping in Touch; UFMCC E-Mail News Service (FREE)

Volunteers of America

Volunteers of America, founded in 1896 by Ballington and Maud Booth, provides spiritual and material aid for those in need in more than 300 communities across the United States. As one of the nation's largest and most diversified human-service organizations, Volunteers of America offers more than 400 programs for the elderly, families, youth, alcoholics, drug abusers, offenders and the disabled.

Headquarters
1660 Duke St., Alexandria, VA 22314-3324 Tel. (800)899-0089

Officers
Chpsn., Walt Patterson
Pres., Charles W. Gould

Periodicals
Spirit

The Wesleyan Church

The Wesleyan Church was formed on June 26, 1968, through the union of the Wesleyan Methodist Church of America (1843) and the Pilgrim Holiness Church (1897). The headquarters was established at Marion, Ind., and relocated to Indianapolis in 1987.

The Wesleyan movement centers around the beliefs, based on Scripture, that the atonement in Christ provides for the regeneration of sinners and the entire sanctification of believers. John Wesley led a revival of these beliefs in the 18th century.

When a group of New England Methodist ministers led by Orange Scott began to crusade for the abolition of slavery, the bishops and others sought to silence them. This led to a series of withdrawals from the Methodist Episcopal Church. In 1843, the Wesleyan Methodist Connection of America was organized and led by Scott, Jotham Horton, LaRoy Sunderland, Luther Lee and Lucius C. Matlack.

During the holiness revival in the last half of the 19th century, holiness replaced social reform as the major tenet of the Connection. In 1947 the name was changed from Connection to Church and a central supervisory authority was set up.

The Pilgrim Holiness Church was one of many independent holiness churches which came into existence as a result of the holiness revival. Led by Martin Wells Knapp and Seth C. Rees, the International Holiness Union and Prayer League was inaugurated in 1897 in Cincinnati. Its purpose was to promote worldwide holiness evangelism and the Union had a strong missionary emphasis from the beginning. It developed into a church by 1913.

The Wesleyan Church is now spread across most of the United States and Canada and 63 other countries. The Wesleyan World Fellowship was organized in 1972 to unite Wesleyan mission bodies developing into mature churches. The Wesleyan Church is a member of the Christian Holiness Partnership, the National Association of Evangelicals and the World Methodist Council.

Headquarters
P.O. Box 50434, Indianapolis, IN 46250 Tel. (317)570-5100
Media Contact, Gen. Sec., Dr. Ronald D. Kelly, Tel. (317)570-5154 Fax (317)570-5280
Email: gensecoff@aol.com
Website: www.wesleyan.org

Officers
Gen. Supts.: Dr. Earle L. Wilson; Dr. David W. Holdren; Dr. Thomas E. Armiger
Gen. Sec., Dr. Ronald D. Kelly
Gen. Treas., Donald M. Frase
Gen. Director of Communications, Dr. Norman G. Wilson
Gen. Publisher, Mr. Don Cady
Evangelism & Church Growth, Gen. Dir., Dr. B. Marlin Mull
World Missions, Gen. Dir., Dr. Donald L. Bray
Local Church Educ., Gen. Dir., Dr. Ray E. Barnwell, Sr.
Student Ministries, Gen. Dir., Rev. Ross DeMerchant
Education & the Ministry, Gen. Dir., Rev. Kerry D. Kind
Estate Planning, Gen. Dir., Rev. Howard B. Castle
Wesleyan Pension Fund, Gen. Dir., Mr. Bobby L. Temple
Wesleyan Investment Foundation, Gen. Dir., Dr. John A. Dunn

Periodicals
Wesleyan Woman; The Wesleyan Advocate; Wesleyan World

Wesleyan Holiness Association of Churches

This body was founded Aug. 4, 1959 near Muncie, Indiana by a group of ministers and laymen who were drawn together for the purpose of spreading and conserving sweet, radical, scriptural holiness. These men came from various church bodies. This group is Wesleyan in doctrine and standards.

Headquarters
1141 North US Hwy 27, Fountain City, IN 47341-9757 Tel. (765)584-3199
Media Contact, Gen. Sec.-Treas., Rev. Robert W. Wilson, RR3 Box 218, Selinsgrove, PA 17870

Officers
Gen. Supt., Rev. John Brewer
Asst. Gen. Supt., Rev. Jack W. Dulin, 3 Crescent Dr., Wabash, IN
Gen. Sec.-Treas., Rev. Robert W. Wilson, RR3 Box 218, Selinsgrove, PA 17870 Tel. (717)966-4147
Gen. Youth Pres., Rev. Nathan Shockley, 504 W. Tyrell St., St. Louis, MI 48880 Tel. (517)681-2591

Periodicals
Eleventh Hour Messenger

Wisconsin Evangelical Lutheran Synod

Organized in 1850 at Milwaukee, Wisconsin, by three pastors sent to America by a German mission society, the Wisconsin Evangelical Lutheran Synod still reflects its origins, although it now has congregations in 50 states and three Canadian provinces. It supports missions in 26 countries.

The Wisconsin Synod federated with the Michigan and Minnesota Synods in 1892 in order to more effectively carry on education and mission enterprises. A merger of these three Synods followed in 1917 to give the Wisconsin Evangelical Lutheran Synod its present form.

Although at its organization in 1850 WELS turned away from conservative Lutheran theology, today it is ranked as one of the most conservative Lutheran bodies in the United States. WELS confesses that the Bible is the verbally inspired, infallible Word of God and subscribes without reservation to the confessional writings of the Lutheran Church. Its interchurch relations are determined by a firm commitment to the principle that unity of doctrine and practice are the prerequisites of pulpit and altar fellowship and ecclesiastical cooperation. It does not hold membership in ecumenical organizations.

Headquarters

2929 N. Mayfair Rd., Milwaukee, WI 53222 Tel.
(414)256-3888 Fax (414)256-3899
Dir. of Communications, Rev. Gary Baumler
Email: webbin@sab.wels.net
Website: www.wels.net

Officers

Pres., Rev. Karl R. Gurgel
1st Vice-Pres., Rev. Richard E. Lauersdorf
2nd Vice-Pres., Rev. Jon Mahnke, 5828 Santa Teresa Blvd., San Jose CA 95123
Sec., Rev. Douglas L. Bode, 1005 E. Broadway, Prairie du Chien, WI 53821

OTHER ORGANIZATIONS

Executive Dir. Of Support Services, Mr. Douglas R. Wellumson
Bd. for Ministerial Education, Admn., Rev. Peter Kruschel
Bd. for Parish Services, Admn., Rev. Wayne Mueller
Bd. for Home Missions, Admn., Rev. Harold J. Hagedorn
Bd. for World Missions, Admn., Rev. Daniel Koelpin

Periodicals

Wisconsin Lutheran Quarterly; Forward in Christ; Lutheran Leader; The Lutheran Educator; Mission Connection

Religious Bodies in the United States Arranged by Families

The following list of religious bodies appearing in the Directory Section of the *Yearbook* shows the "families" or related clusters into which American religious bodies can be grouped. For example, there are many communions that can be grouped under the heading "Baptist" for historical and theological reasons. It should not be assumed, however, that all denominations under one family heading are necessarily consistent in belief or practice. The family clusters tend to represent historical factors more often than theological or practical ones. These family categories provide one of the major pitfalls when compiling church statistics because there is often a tendency to combine the statistics by "families" for analytical and comparative purposes. Such combined totals are deeply flawed, even though they are often used as variables for sociological analysis. The arrangement by families offered here is intended only as a general guide for conceptual organization when viewing the broad sweep of American religious culture.

Religious bodies that can not be categorized under family headings appear alphabetically and are not indented in the following list.

Adventist Bodies

Advent Christian Church
Church of God General Conference (Oregon, IL and Morrow, GA)
Primitive Advent Christian Church
Seventh-day Adventist Church

American Catholic Church
American Evangelical Christian Churches
American Rescue Workers

Anglican Bodies

The Anglican Orthodox Church
Episcopal Church
Reformed Episcopal Church

Apostolic Christian Church (Nazarene)
Apostolic Christian Churches of America
Apostolic Episcopal Church

Baptist Bodies

The Alliance of Baptists in the U.S.A.
The American Baptist Association
American Baptist Churches in the U.S.A.
Baptist Bible Fellowship International
Baptist General Conference
Baptist Missionary Association of America
Conservative Baptist Association of America
General Association of General Baptists
General Association of Regular Baptist Churches
National Association of Free Will Baptists
National Baptist Convention of America, Inc.
National Baptist Convention, U.S.A., Inc.
National Missionary Baptist Convention of America
National Primitive Baptist Convention, Inc.
North American Baptist Conference
Primitive Baptists
Progressive National Baptist Convention, Inc.
Separate Baptists in Christ
Seventh Day Baptist General Conference, USA and Canada

Southern Baptist Convention
Sovereign Grace Believers

Berean Fundamental Church

Brethren (German Baptists)

Brethren Church (Ashland, Ohio)
Church of the Brethren
Fellowship of Grace Brethren Churches
Old German Baptist Brethren

Brethren, River

Brethren in Christ Church
United Zion Church

The Catholic Church
Christ Community Church (Evangelical-Protestant)
Christadelphians
Christian Brethren (also known as Plymouth Brethren)
The Christian Congregation, Inc.
The Christian and Missionary Alliance
Christian Union
The Church of Christ (Holiness) U.S.A.
Church of Christ, Scientist
The Church of Illumination
Church of the Living God
Church of the Nazarene

Churches of Christ—Christian Churches

Christian Church (Disciples of Christ)
Christian Churches and Churches of Christ
Churches of Christ
Churches of Christ in Christian Union

Churches of God

Church of God (Anderson, Indiana)
The Church of God (Seventh Day), Denver, Colorado

Church of God by Faith, Inc.
Churches of God, General Conference

Churches of the New Jerusalem

General Church of the New Jerusalem
The Swedenborgian Church

**Conservative Congregational Christian
Conference**

Eastern Orthodox Churches

Albanian Orthodox Archdiocese in America
Albanian Orthodox Diocese of America
The American Carpatho-Russian Orthodox
Greek Catholic Church
The Antiochian Orthodox Christian
Archdiocese of North America
Apostolic Catholic Assyrian Church of the
East, North American Dioceses
Apostolic Orthodox Catholic Church
Greek Orthodox Archdiocese of America
The Holy Eastern Orthodox Catholic and
Apostolic Church in North America, Inc.
Holy Ukrainian Autocephalic Orthodox
Church in Exile
The Orthodox Church in America
Patriarchal Parishes of the Russian Orthodox
Church in the U.S.A.
The Romanian Orthodox Church in America
The Romanian Orthodox Episcopate of
America
The Russian Orthodox Church Outside of
Russia
Serbian Orthodox Church in the U.S.A. and
Canada
True Orthodox Church of Greece (Synod of
Metropolitan Cyprian), American
Exarchate
Ukrainian Orthodox Church of America
(Ecumenical Patriarchate)
Ukrainian Orthodox Church of the U.S.A.

The Evangelical Church Alliance
The Evangelical Church
The Evangelical Congregational Church
The Evangelical Covenant Church
The Evangelical Free Church of America
Fellowship of Fundamental Bible Churches
Free Christian Zion Church of Christ

Friends

Evangelical Friends International—North
American Region
Friends General Conference
Friends United Meeting
Philadelphia Yearly Meeting of the Religious
Society of Friends
Religious Society of Friends (Conservative)
Religious Society of Friends (Unaffiliated
Meetings)

Grace Gospel Fellowship
**House of God, Which is the Church of the
Living God, the Pillar and Ground of the
Truth, Inc.**
**Independent Fundamental Churches of
America/ IFCA International, Inc.**
**International Council of Community
Churches**
Jehovah's Witnesses

Latter Day Saints (Mormons)

Church of Christ
The Church of Jesus Christ of Latter-day
Saints
The Church of Jesus Christ (Bickertonites)
Reorganized Church of Jesus Christ of Latter
Day Saints

**The Liberal Catholic Church—Province of
the United States of America**

Lutheran Bodies

The American Association of Lutheran
Churches
Apostolic Lutheran Church of America
The Association of Free Lutheran
Congregations
Church of the Lutheran Brethren of America
Church of the Lutheran Confession
Conservative Lutheran Association
The Estonian Evangelical Lutheran Church
Evangelical Lutheran Church in America
Evangelical Lutheran Synod
The Latvian Evangelical Lutheran Church in
America
The Lutheran Church—Missouri Synod
Wisconsin Evangelical Lutheran Synod

Mennonite Bodies

Beachy Amish Mennonite Churches
Bible Fellowship Church
Church of God in Christ, Mennonite
Evangelical Mennonite Church
Fellowship of Evangelical Bible Churches
General Conference of Mennonite Brethren
Churches
Hutterian Brethren
Mennonite Church
Mennonite Church, The General Conference
Old Order (Wisler) Mennonite Church
Old Order Amish Church
Reformed Mennonite Church

Methodist Bodies

African Methodist Episcopal Church
African Methodist Episcopal Zion Church
Allegheny Wesleyan Methodist Connection
(Original Allegheny Conference)
Bible Holiness Church
Christian Methodist Episcopal Church
Evangelical Methodist Church

163

Free Methodist Church of North America
Fundamental Methodist Church, Inc.
Primitive Methodist Church in the U.S.A.
Reformed Methodist Union Episcopal Church
Reformed Zion Union Apostolic Church
Southern Methodist Church
The United Methodist Church
The Wesleyan Church

The Metropolitan Church Association, Inc.
The Missionary Church

Moravian Bodies

Moravian Church in America (Unitas Fratrum)
Unity of the Brethren

National Association of Congregational Christian Churches
National Organization of the New Apostolic Church of North America
National Spiritualist Association of Churches
North American Old Roman Catholic Church (Archdiocese of New York)

Old Catholic Churches

Christ Catholic Church

Oriental Orthodox Churches

Armenian Apostolic Church of America
Armenian Apostolic Church, Diocese of America
Coptic Orthodox Church
Syrian Orthodox Church of Antioch

Pentecostal Bodies

Apostolic Faith Mission of Portland, Oregon
Apostolic Faith Mission Church of God
Apostolic Overcoming Holy Church of God, Inc.
Assemblies of God
Assemblies of God International Fellowship (Independent/Not affiliated)
The Bible Church of Christ, Inc.
Bible Way Church of Our Lord Jesus Christ World Wide, Inc.
Christian Church of North America, General Council
Church of God of Prophecy
Church of God (Cleveland, Tennessee)
Church of God in Christ, International
The Church Of God In Christ
The (Original) Church of God, Inc.
Church of God, Mountain Assembly, Inc.
Church of Our Lord Jesus Christ of the Apostolic Faith, Inc.
Congregational Holiness Church
Elim Fellowship
Full Gospel Assemblies International
Full Gospel Fellowship of Churches and Ministers International

International Church of the Foursquare Gospel
The International Pentecostal Church of Christ
International Pentecostal Holiness Church
Open Bible Standard Churches
Pentecostal Assemblies of the World, Inc.
Pentecostal Church of God
Pentecostal Fire-Baptized Holiness Church
The Pentecostal Free Will Baptist Church, Inc.
Pillar of Fire
United Holy Church of America, Inc.
United Pentecostal Church International
The United Pentecostal Churches of Christ

Polish National Catholic Church of America

Presbyterian Bodies

Associate Reformed Presbyterian Church (General Synod)
Cumberland Presbyterian Church
Cumberland Presbyterian Church in America
Evangelical Presbyterian Church
General Assembly of the Korean Presbyterian Church in America
The Orthodox Presbyterian Church
Presbyterian Church (U.S.A.)
Presbyterian Church in America
Reformed Presbyterian Church of North America

Reformed Bodies

Christian Reformed Church in North America
Hungarian Reformed Church in America
Netherlands Reformed Congregations
Protestant Reformed Churches in America
Reformed Church in America
Reformed Church in the United States
United Church of Christ

The Salvation Army
The Schwenkfelder Church

Thomist Churches

Malankara Orthodox Syrian Church, Diocese of America
Mar Thoma Syrian Church of India

Triumph the Church and Kingdom of God in Christ Inc. (International)
Unitarian Universalist Association of Congregations

United Brethren Bodies

Church of the United Brethren in Christ
United Christian Church

United House of Prayer
Universal Fellowship of Metropolitan Community Churches
Volunteers of America
Wesleyan Holiness Association of Churches

4. Religious Bodies in Canada

A large number of Canadian religious bodies were organized by immigrants from Europe and elsewhere, and a smaller number sprang up originally on Canadian soil. In the case of Canada, moreover, many denominations that overlap the U.S.-Canada border have headquarters in the United States.

A final section in this directory lists churches according to denominational families. This can be a helpful tool in finding a particular church if you don't know the official name. Complete statistics for Canadian churches are found in the statistical section in Chapter 3: Table 1 contains membership figures, and Table 4 contains giving figures. Addresses for periodicals are found in the directory entitled, "Religious Periodicals in Canada."

Amish—please see Old Order Amish Church.

The Anglican Church of Canada

Anglicanism came to Canada with the early explorers such as Martin Frobisher and Henry Hudson. Continuous services began in Newfoundland about 1700 and in Nova Scotia in 1710. The first Bishop, Charles Inglis, was appointed to Nova Scotia in 1787. The numerical strength of Anglicanism was increased by the coming of American Loyalists and by massive immigration both after the Napoleonic wars and in the later 19th and early 20th centuries.

The Anglican Church of Canada has enjoyed self-government for over a century and is an autonomous member of the worldwide Anglican Communion. The General Synod, which normally meets triennially, consists of the Archbishops, Bishops and elected clerical and lay representatives of the 30 dioceses. Each of the Ecclesiastical Provinces—Canada, Ontario, Rupert's Land and British Columbia—is organized under a Metropolitan and has its own Provincial Synod and Executive Council. Each diocese has its own Diocesan Synod.

Headquarters

Church House, 600 Jarvis St., Toronto, ON M4Y 2J6 Tel. (416)924-9192 Fax (416)968-7983, Website: www.anglican.ca

Media Contact, Dir. of Information Resources, Douglas Tindal

General Email: info@national.anglican.ca

Email: dtindal@national.anglican.ca

GENERAL SYNOD OFFICERS

Primate of the Anglican Church of Canada, Most Rev. Michael G. Peers

Prolocutor, Rev. Rodney O. Andrews

Gen. Sec., Ven. James B. Boyles

Treas., Gen. Synod, Mr. James Cullen

DEPARTMENTS AND DIVISIONS

Faith, Worship & Ministry, Dir., Rev. Canon Alyson Barnett-Cowan

Financial Management and Dev., Dir., Mr. James Cullen

Inform. Resources Dir., Mr. Douglas Tindal

Partnerships, Dir., Dr. Eleanor Johnson

Pensions, Dir., Mrs. Jenny Mason

Primate's World Relief and Dev. Fund, Dir., Mr. Andrew Ignatieff

METROPOLITANS (ARCHBISHOPS)

Ecclesiastical Province of: Canada, The Most Rev. Arthur G. Peters, 5732 College St., Halifax, NS B3H 1X3; Rupert's Land, The Most Rev. Thomas O. Morgan, Box 1965, Saskatoon, SK S7K 3S5 Tel. (306)244-5651 Fax (306)933-4606, Email: diocese.stoon@sk.sympatico.ca; British Columbia, The Most Rev. David P. Crawley, 1876 Richter St., Kelowna, BC V1Y 2M9 Tel. (250)762-3306 Fax (250)762-4150; Ontario, -vacant-

DIOCESAN BISHOPS

Algoma: The Rt. Rev. Ronald Ferris, Box 1168, Sault Ste. Marie, ON P6A 5N7 Tel. (705)256-5061 Fax (705)946-1860, Email: dioceseofalgoma@on.aibn.com

Arctic: The Rt. Rev. Christopher Williams, 4910 51st St., Box 1454, Yellowknife, NT X1A 2P1 Tel. (867)873-5432 Fax (867)873-8478, Email: cwill@internorth.com

Athabasca: The Right Rev. John R. Clarke, Box 6868, Peace River, AB T8S 1S6 Tel. (780)624-2767 Fax (780)624-2365, Email: bpath@telusplanet.net

Brandon: The Rt. Rev. Malcolm A.W. Harding, Box 21009 WEPO, Brandon, MB R7B 3W8 Tel. (204)727-7550 Fax (204)727-4135, Email: bishopbdn@escape.ca

British Columbia: The Rt. Rev. Barry Jenks, 900 Vancouver St., Victoria, BC V8V 3V7 Tel. (250)386-7781 Fax (250)386-4013, Email: bishop@acts.bc.ca

Caledonia: The Rt. Rev. John E. Hannen, Box 278, Prince Rupert, BC V8J 3P6 Tel. (250)624-6013 Fax (250)624-4299, Email: bishopj@citytel.net

Calgary: Archbishop, The Rt. Rev. Barry C.B. Hollowell, #560, 1207 11th Ave., SW, Calgary, AB T3C 0M5, Tel. (403)243-3673 Fax (403) 243-2182, Diocesan Email: synod@calgary.anglican.ca

Cariboo: The Right Rev. James D. Cruickshank, 5-618 Tranquille Rd., Kamloops, BC V2B 3H6 Tel. (250)376-0112 Fax (250)376-1984, Email: cariboo@sageserve.com

Central Newfoundland: -vacant-, Email: bishop-central@nfld.net

Eastern Newfoundland and Labrador: The Rt. Rev. Donald F. Harvey, 19 King's Bridge Rd., St. John's, NF A1C 3K4 Tel. (709)576-6697 Fax (709)576-7122, Email: dharvey@anglicanenl.nf.net

Edmonton: The Rt. Rev. Victoria Matthews, 10033 - 84 Ave., Edmonton, AB T6E 2G6 Tel. (780)439-7344 Fax (780)439-6549, Email: synod@freenet.edmonton.ab.ca

Fredericton: The Rt. Rev. William J. Hockin, 115 Church St., Fredericton, NB E3B 4C8 Tel. (506)459-1801 Fax (506)459-8475, Email: bishfton@nbnet.nb.ca

Huron: -vacant-, One London Place, 903-255 Queens Ave., London, ON N6A 5R8 Tel. (519)434-6893 Fax (519)673-4151, Email: bishops@wwdc.com

Keewatin: The Rt. Rev. Gordon Beardy, 915 Ottawa St., Keewatin, ON P0X 1C0 Tel. (807)547-3353 Fax (807)547-3356 Email: keewatin@kenora.com

Kootenay: Archbishop, The Most Rev. David P. Crawley, 1876 Richter St., Kelowna, BC V1Y 2M9 Tel. (250)762-3306 Fax (250)762-4150, Email: diocese_of_kootenay@telus.net

Montreal: The Rt. Rev. Andrew S. Hutchison, 1444 Union Ave., Montreal, QC H3A 2B8 Tel. (514)843-6577 Fax (514)843-3221, Email: bishops.office@montreal.anglican.ca

Moosonee: The Rt. Rev. Caleb J. Lawrence, Box 841, Schumacher, ON P0N 1G0 Tel. (705)360-1129 Fax (705)360-1120, Email: lawrence@ntl.sympatico.ca

New Westminster: The Rt. Rev. Michael C. Ingham, 580-401 W. Georgia St., Vancouver, BC V6B 5A1 Tel. (604)684-6306 Fax (604)684-7017, Email: michael_ingham@ecunet.org

Niagara: The Rt. Rev. Ralph Spence, 252 James St. N., Hamilton, ON L8R 2L3 Tel. (905)527-1278 Fax (905)527-1281

Nova Scotia: The Most Rev. Arthur G. Peters, 5732 College St., Halifax, NS B3H 1X3 Tel. (902)420-0717 Fax (902)425-0717, Email: diocese@fox.nstn.ca

Ontario: The Rt. Rev. Peter Mason, 90 Johnson St., Kingston, ON K7L 1X7 Tel. (613)544-4774 Fax (613)547-3745, Email: pmason@ontario.anglican.ca

Ottawa: The Rt. Rev. Peter R. Coffin, 71 Bronson Ave., Ottawa, ON K1R 6G6 Tel. (613)232-7124 Fax (613)232-7088

Qu'Appelle: The Rt. Rev. Duncan D. Wallace, 1501 College Ave., Regina, SK S4P 1B8 Tel. (306)522-1608 Fax (306)352-6808, Email: quappelle@sk.sympatico.ca

Quebec: The Rt. Rev. Bruce Stavert, 31 rue des Jardins, Quebec, QC G1R 4L6 Tel. (418)692-3858 Fax (418)692-3876, Email: diocese_of_quebec@sympatico.ca

Rupert's Land: Rt. Rev. Donald D. Phillips, 935 Nesbitt Bay, Winnipeg, MB R3T 1W6 Tel. (204)453-6130 Fax (204)452-3915, Email: bishop@rupertsland.anglican.ca

Saskatchewan: The Rt. Rev. Anthony Burton, 1308 5th Ave. East, Prince Albert, SK S6V 2H7 Tel. (306)763-2455 Fax (306)764-5172, Email: burton@sk.sympatico.ca

Saskatoon: The Archbishop, Most Rev. Thomas O. Morgan, Box 1965, Saskatoon, SK S7K 3S5 Tel. (306)244-5651 Fax (306)933-4606, Email: diocese.stoon@sk.sympatico.ca

Toronto: The Rt. Rev. Terence E. Finlay, 135 Adelaide St. East, Toronto, ON M5C 1L8 Tel. (416)363-6021 Fax (416)363-3683, Email: tfinlay@toronto.anglican.ca

Western Newfoundland: The Rt. Rev. Leonard Whitten, 25 Main St., Corner Brook, NF A2H 1C2 Tel. (709)639-8712 Fax (709)639-1636, Email: dsown@nf.sympatico.ca

Yukon: The Rt. Rev. Terry Buckle, Box 4247, Whitehorse, YT Y1A 3T3 Tel. (867)667-7746 Fax (867)667-6125, Email: dioyuk@yukon.net

Periodicals
Anglican Journal (National Newspaper); Ministry Matters

The Antiochian Orthodox Christian Archdiocese of North America

The approximately 100,000 members of the Antiochian Orthodox community in Canada are under the jurisdiction of the Antiochian Orthodox Christian Archdiocese of North America with headquarters in Englewood, N.J. There are churches in Edmonton, Winnipeg, Halifax, London, Ottawa, Toronto, Windsor, Montreal, Saskatoon, Hamilton, Vancouver, Charlottetown, PEI.

Headquarters
Metropolitan Philip Saliba, 358 Mountain Rd., Englewood, NJ 07631 Tel. (201)871-1355 Fax (201)871-7954

Website: www.antiochian.com

Media Contact, Rev. Fr. Thomas Zain, 52 78th St., Brooklyn, NY 11209 Tel. (718)748-7940 Fax (718)855-3608

Periodicals
The Word; Again; Handmaiden

Apostolic Christian Church (Nazarene)

This church was formed in Canada as a result of immigration from various European countries. The body began as a movement originated by the Rev. S. H. Froehlich, a Swiss pastor, whose followers are still found in Switzerland and Central Europe.

Headquarters
Apostolic Christian Church Foundation, 1135 Sholey Rd., Richmond, VA 23231 Tel. (804)222-1943

Media Contact, James Hodges

The Apostolic Church in Canada

The Apostolic Church in Canada is affiliated with the worldwide organization of the Apostolic Church with headquarters in Great Britain. A product of the Welsh Revival (1904 to 1908), its Canadian beginnings originated in Nova Scotia in 1927. Today its main centers are in Nova Scotia, Ontario and Quebec. This church is evangelical, fundamental and Pentecostal, with special emphasis on the ministry gifts listed in Ephesians 4:11-12.

Headquarters
27 Castlefield Ave., Toronto, ON M4R 1G3
Media Contact, Pres., Rev. John Kristensen, 685 Park St. S., Peterborough, ON K9J 3S9 Tel. (705)742-1618
Website: www.apostolic.ca

Officers
Pres., Rev. John Kristensen, 685 Park St. S., Peterborough, ON K9J 3S9 Tel. (705)742-1618
Natl. Sec., Rev. J. Karl Thomas, 22 Malamute Cres., Scarborough, ON M1T 2C7 Tel. (416) 298-0977

Periodicals
Canadian News Up-Date; The News Magazine of the Apostolic Church in Canada

Apostolic Church of Pentecost of Canada Inc.

This body was founded in 1921 at Winnipeg, Manitoba, by Pastor Frank Small. Doctrines include belief in eternal salvation by the grace of God, baptism of the Holy Spirit with the evidence of speaking in tongues, water baptism by immersion in the name of the Lord Jesus Christ.

Headquarters
#119-2340 Pegasus Way NE, Calgary, AB T2E 8M5
E-mail: acop@acop.ca
Website: www.acop.ca
Media Contact, Admn., Rev. Wes Mills, Tel. (403)273-5777 Fax (403)273-8102

Officers
Mod., Rev. G. Killam
Admin., Rev. Wes Mills
Mission Director, Rev. Brian Cooper

Periodicals
Fellowship Focus; Harvest Time

Armenian Evangelical Church

Founded in 1960 by immigrant Armenian evangelical families from the Middle East, this body is conservative doctrinally, with an evangelical, biblical emphasis. The polity of churches within the group differ with congregationalism being dominant, but there are presbyterian Armenian Evangelical churches as well. Most of the local churches have joined main-line denominations. All of the remaining Armenian Evangelical (congregational or presbyterian) local churches in the United States and Canada have joined with the Armenian Evangelical Union of North America.

Headquarters
Armenian Evangelical Church of Toronto, 2851 John St., P.O. Box 42015, Markham, ON L3R 5R0 Tel. (905)305-8144
Media Contact, Chief Editor, Rev. Yessayi Sarmazian

A.E.U.N.A. Officers
Min. to the Union, Rev. Karl Avakian, 1789 E. Frederick Ave., Fresno, CA 93720
Mod., Rev. Bernard Geulsgeugian

Officers
Min., Rev. Yessayi Sarmazian

Periodicals
Armenian Evangelical Church

Armenian Holy Apostolic Church —Canadian Diocese

The Canadian branch of the ancient Church of Armenia founded in A.D. 301 by St. Gregory the Illuminator was established in Canada at St. Catharines, Ontario, in 1930. The diocesan organization is under the jurisdiction of the Holy See of Etchmiadzin, Armenia. The Diocese has churches in St. Catharines, Hamilton, Toronto, Ottawa, Vancouver, Mississauga, Montreal, Laval, Windsor, Halifax, Winnipeg, Edmonton and Calgary.

Headquarters
Diocesan Offices: Primate, Canadian Diocese, Archbishop Hovnan Derderian, 615 Stuart Ave., Outremont, QC H2V 3H2 Tel. (514)276-9479 Fax (514)276-9960, Email: adiocese@aol.com; Website: www.canarmdiocese.org
Media Contact, Exec. Dir., Arminé Keuchgerian; Silva Mangassarian, Secretary

Officers
Exec. Dir, Armine Keuchgerian
Sec., Silva Mangassarian
Webmaster, Garen Migirditzian

Associated Gospel Churches

The Associated Gospel Churches (AGC) traces its historical roots to the 1890s. To counteract the growth of liberal theology evident in many established denominations at this time, individuals and whole congregations seeking to uphold the final authority of the Scriptures in all matters of faith and conduct withdrew from those denominations and established churches with an evangelical ministry. These churches defended the belief that "all Scripture is given by inspiration of God" and also declared that the Holy Spirit gave the identical word of sacred writings of holy men of old, chosen by Him to be the channel of His revelation to man.

At first this growing group of independent churches was known as the Christian Workers' Churches of Canada, and by 1922 there was desire for forming an association for fellowship, counsel and cooperation. Several churches in southern Ontario banded together under the leadership of Dr. P. W. Philpott of Hamilton and Rev. H. E. Irwin, K. C. of Toronto.

When a new Dominion Charter was obtained on March 18, 1925, the name was changed to Associated Gospel Churches. Since that time the AGC has steadily grown, spreading across Canada by invitation to other independent churches of like faith and by actively beginning new churches.

Headquarters
3228 South Service Rd., Burlington, ON L7N 3H8 Tel. (905)634-8184 Fax (905)634-6283
E-mail: admin@agcofcanada.com
Website: www.agcofcanada.com
Media Contact, Rev. Tim Davis, c/o 3228 South Service Rd., Burlington, ON L7N 3H8 Tel. (905)634-8184 Fax (905)634-6283

Officers
Pres., Rev. A.F. (Bud) Penner, 3228 South Service Rd., Burlington, ON L7N 3H8 Tel. (905)634-8184 Fax (905)634-6283
Mod., Mrs. Debra Teakle, 2589 Noella Cres., Niagara Falls, ON L2J 3H7 Tel. (905)356-4767 Fax (same)
Sec.-Treas., Rev. Don Ralph, Box 3203, Stn. C, Hamilton, ON L8H 7K6 Tel. (905)549-4516

Association of Regular Baptist Churches (Canada)
The Association of Regular Baptist Churches was organized in 1957 by a group of churches for the purpose of mutual cooperation in missionary activities. The Association believes the Bible to be God's word, stands for historic Baptist principles, and opposes modern ecumenism.

Headquarters
130 Gerrard St. E., Toronto, ON M5A 3T4 Tel. (416)925-3261
Media Contact, Sec., Rev. W. P. Bauman, Tel. (416)925-3263 Fax (416)925-8305

Officers
Chmn., Rev. S. Kring, 67 Sovereen St., Delhi, ON N4B 1L7
Sec., Rev. W. P. Bauman

Baptist Convention of Ontario and Quebec
The Baptist Convention of Ontario and Quebec is a family of 386 churches in Ontario and Quebec, united for mutual support and encouragement and united in missions in Canada and the world.

The Convention was formally organized in 1888. It has two educational institutions—McMaster Divinty College founded in 1887, and the Baptist Leadership Education Centre at Whitby. The Convention works through the all-Canada missionary agency, Canadian Baptist Ministries. The churches also support the Sharing Way, its relief and development arm of Canadian Baptist Ministries.

Headquarters
195 The West Mall, Ste. 414, Etobicoke, ON M9C 5K1 Tel. (416)622-8600 Fax (416)622-2308
Media Contact, Exec. Min., Dr. Ken Bellous

Officers
Pres., Rev. Don Crisp
1st Vice-Pres., Rev. Ian Dixon
2nd Vice-Pres., Mrs. Brenda Mann
Treas./Bus. Admn., Nancy Bell
Exec. Min., Dr. Ken Bellous
Past Pres., Mr. Keith Hillyer

Periodicals
The Canadian Baptist

Baptist General Conference of Canada
The Baptist General Conference was founded in Canada by missionaries from the United States. Originally a Swedish body, BGC Canada now includes people of many nationalities and is conservative and evangelical in doctrine and practice.

Headquarters
4306-97 St. NW, Edmonton, AB T6E 5R9 Tel. (780)438-9127 Fax (780)435-2478
Media Contact, Exec. Dir., Rev. Abe Funk

Officers
Exec. Dir., Rev. Abe Funk, 4306-97 St. NW, Edmonton, AB T6E 5R9 Tel. (780)438-9127 Fax (780)435-2478
Exec. Dir., Gordon Sorensen, BGC Stewardship Foundation

DISTRICTS
Baptist Gen. Conf.- Central Canada: Exec. Min., Dr. Alf Bell, 19-130 Ulster St., Winnipeg, MB R3T 3A2 Tel. (204)261-9113 Fax (204)261-9176
Baptist General Conference in Alberta: Exec. Min., Dr. Cal Netterfield, 5011 122nd A St., Edmonton, AB T6H 3S8 Tel. (780)438-9126 Fax (780)438-5258
British Columbia Baptist Conference: Exec. Min., Rev. Walter W. Wieser, 7600 Glover Rd., Langley, BC V2Y 1Y1 Tel. (604)888-2246 Fax (604)888-0046
Baptist General Conf. in Saskatchewan: Exec. Min., Rev. Charles Lees

Baptist Union of Western Canada

Headquarters

302,902-11 Ave., SW, Calgary, AB T2R 0E7
Media Contact, Exec. Min., Dr. Gerald Fisher

Officers

Pres., Mr. Bill Mains, 4576 Rainer Crescent, Prince George, BC V2K 1X4
Exec. Minister, Dr. Gerald Fisher, 302, 902-11 Ave SW, Calgary, AB T2R 0E7
Alberta Area Minister, Rev. Ed Dyck, 302, 902-11 Ave SW, Calgary, AB T2R 0E7
BC Area Minister, Dr. Paul Pearce, 201, 20349-88th Ave., Langely, BC V1M 2K5
SK/MB Area Minister, Dr. Robert Krahn, 414 Cowley Place, Saskatoon, SK S7N 3X2
Carey Theological College, Principal, Dr. Brian Stelck, 5920 Iona Dr., Vancouver, BC V6T 1J6
Baptist Resources Centre, 302, 902-11 Ave SW, Calgary, AB T2R 0E7

The Bible Holiness Movement

The Bible Holiness Movement, organized in 1949 as an outgrowth of the city mission work of the late Pastor William James Elijah Wakefield, an early-day Salvation Army officer, has been headed since its inception by his son, Evangelist Wesley H. Wakefield, its bishop-general.

It derives its emphasis on the original Methodist faith of salvation and scriptural holiness from the late Bishop R. C. Horner. It adheres to the common evangelical faith in the Bible, the Deity and the atonement of Christ. It stresses a personal experience of salvation for the repentant sinner, of being wholly sanctified for the believer and of the fullness of the Holy Spirit for effective witness.

Membership involves a life of Christian love and evangelistic and social activism. Members are required to totally abstain from liquor and tobacco. They may not attend popular amusements or join secret societies. Divorce and remarriage are forbidden. Similar to Wesley's Methodism, members are, under some circumstances, allowed to retain membership in other evangelical church fellowships. Interchurch affiliations are maintained with a number of Wesleyan-Arminian Holiness denominations.

Year-round evangelistic outreach is maintained through open-air meetings, visitation, literature and other media. Noninstitutional welfare work, including addiction counseling, is conducted among minorities. There is direct overseas famine relief, civil rights action, environment protection and antinuclearism. The movement sponsors a permanent committee on religious freedom and an active promotion of Christian racial equality.

The movement has a world outreach with branches in the United States, India, Nigeria, Philippines, Ghana, Liberia, Cameroon, Kenya, Zambia, South Korea, Mulawi, and Tanzania. It also ministers to 89 countries in 42 languages through literature, radio and audiocassettes.

Headquarters

Box 223, Postal Stn. A, Vancouver, BC V6C 2M3 Tel. (250)492-3376
Media Contact, Bishop-General, Evangelist Wesley H. Wakefield, P.O. Box 223, Postal Station A, Vancouver, BC V6C 2M3 Tel. (250)492-3376

DIRECTORS

Bishop-General, Evangelist Wesley H. Wakefield, (Intl. Leader)
Evangelist M. J. Wakefield, Penticton, BC
Pastor Vincente & Mirasal Hernando, Phillipines
Pastor & Mrs. Daniel Stinnett, 1425 Mountain View W., Phoenix, AZ 85021
Evangelist I. S. Udoh, Abak, Akwalbom, Nigeria, West Africa
Pastor Richard & Laura Wesley, Protem, Monrovia, Liberia
Pastor Choe Chong Dee, Cha Pa Puk, S. Korea
Pastor S. A. Samuel, Andra, India
Pastors Heinz and Catherine Speitelsbach, Sardis, BC V2R 3W2
Pastor and Mrs. Daniel Vandee, Ghana, W. Africa

Periodicals

Hallelujah!

Brethren in Christ Church, Canadian Conference

The Brethren in Christ, formerly known as Tunkers in Canada, arose out of a religious awakening in Lancaster County, Pennsylvania late in the 18th century. Representatives of the new denomination reached Ontario in 1788 and established the church in the southern part of the present province. Presently the conference has congregations in Ontario, Alberta, Quebec and Saskatchewan. In theology they have accents of the Pietist, Anabaptist, Wesleyan and Evangelical movements.

Headquarters

Brethren in Christ Church, Gen. Ofc., P.O. Box A, Grantham, PA 17027-0901 Tel. (717)697-2634 Fax (717)697-7714
Canadian Headquarters, Bishop's Ofc., 2619 Niagara Pkwy., Ft. Erie, ON L2A 5M4 Tel. (905)871-9991
Media Contact, Mod., Dr. Warren L. Hoffman, Brethren in Christ Church Gen. Ofc.

Officers

Mod., Bishop Darrell S. Winger, 2619 Niagara Pkwy., Ft. Erie, ON L2A 5M4 Tel. (905)871-9991
Sec., Betty Albrecht, RR 2, Petersburg, ON N0B 2H0

Periodicals

Evangelical Visitor; "Yes", Shalom

British Methodist Episcopal Church of Canada

The British Methodist Episcopal Church was organized in 1856 in Chatham, Ontario and incorporated in 1913. It has congregations across the Province of Ontario.

Headquarters

430 Grey Street, London, ON N6B 1H3 Tel.

Media Contact, Gen. Sec., Rev. Jacqueline Collins, 47 Connolly St., Toronto, ON M6N 4Y5 Tel. (416)653-6339

Officers

Gen. Supt., Rt. Rev. Dr. Douglas Birse, R.R. #5, Thamesville, ON N0P 2K0, Tel. (519)692-3628

Asst. Gen. Supt., Maurice M. Hicks, 3 Boxdene Ave., Scarborough, ON M1V 3C9 Tel. (416)298-5715

Gen. Sec., Rev. Jacqueline Collins, 47 Connolly St., Toronto, ON M6N 4Y5 Tel. (416)653-6339

Gen. Treas., Ms. Hazel Small, 7 Wood Fernway, North York, ON M2J 4P6, Tel. (416)491-0313

Periodicals

B.M.E. Church Newsletter

Canadian and American Reformed Churches

The Canadian and American Reformed Churches accept the Bible as the infallible Word of God, as summarized in The Belgic Confession of Faith (1561), The Heidelberg Cathechism (1563) and The Canons of Dordt (1618-1619). The federation was founded in Canada in 1950 and in the United States in 1955.

Headquarters

Synod: 607 Dynes Rd., Burlington, ON L7N 2V4

Canadian Reformed Churches: Ebenezer Canadian Reformed Church, 607 Dynes Rd., Burlington, ON L7N 2V4

American Reformed Churches: American Reformed Church, 3167-68th St. S.E., Caledonia, MI 46316

Theological College, Dr. N. H. Gootjes, 110 W. 27th St., Hamilton, ON L9C 5A1 Tel. (905)575-3688 Fax (905)575-0799

Media Contact, Rev. G. Nederveen, 3089 Woodward Ave., Burlington, ON L7N 2M3 Tel. (905)681-7055 Fax (905)681-7055

Periodicals

Reformed Perspective: A Magazine for the Christian Family; In Holy Array; Evangel: The Good News of Jesus Christ; Clarion: The Canadian Reformed Magazine; Diakonia-A Magazine of Office-Bearers

Canadian Baptist Ministries

The Canadian Baptist Ministries has four federated member bodies: (1) Baptist Convention of Ontario and Quebec, (2) Baptist Union of Western Canada, (3) the United Baptist Convention of the Atlantic Provinces, (4) Union d'Églises Baptistes Françaises au Canada (French Baptist Union). Its main purpose is to act as a coordinating agency for the four groups for mission in all five continents.

Headquarters

7185 Millcreek Dr., Mississauga, ON L5N 5R4 Tel. (905)821-3533 Fax (905)826-3441

Website: www.cbmin.org

Media Contact, Communications, David Rogelstad

E-mail: daver@cbmin.org

Officers

Pres., Doug Coomas

Gen. Sec., Rev. Gart Nelson

E-mail: NelsonG@cbmin.org

Canadian Conference of Mennonite Brethren Churches

The conference was incorporated November 22, 1945.

Headquarters

3-169 Riverton Ave., Winnipeg, MB R2L 2E5 Tel. (204)669-6575 Fax (204)654-1865

Media Contact, Exec. Dir., Dave Wiebe

Officers

Mod., Jascha Boge, 261 Bonner Ave., Winnipeg, MB R2G 1B3 Tel. (204)663-1414

Asst. Mod., Ralph Gliege, Box 67, Hepburn, SK S0K 1Z0 Tel. (306)947-2030

Sec., Gerald Janzen, 32145 Austin Ave., Abbotsford, BC V2T 4P4

Periodicals

Mennonite Brethren Herald; Mennonitische Rundschau; IdeaBank; Le Lien; Expression; Chinese Herald

Canadian Convention of Southern Baptists

The Canadian Convention of Southern Baptists was formed at the Annual Meeting, May 7-9, 1985, in Kelowna, British Columbia. It was formerly known as the Canadian Baptist Conference, founded in Kamloops, British Columbia, in 1959 by pastors of existing churches.

Headquarters

Postal Box 300, Cochrane, AB T0L 0W0 Tel. (403)932-5688 Fax (403)932-4937

E-mail: office@ccsb.ca

Media Contact, Exec. Dir.-Treas., Rev. Gerald Taillon

Officers

Exec. Dir.-Treas., Gerald Taillon, 17 Riverview Close, Cochrane, AB T0L 0W4

Pres., Alan Braun, 334 Norton St., Penticton, BC V2A 4H7

170

The Baptist Horizon

Canadian District of the Moravian Church in America, Northern Province

The work in Canada is under the general oversight and rules of the Moravian Church, Northern Province, general offices for which are located in Bethlehem, Pennsylvania. For complete information, see "Religious Bodies in the United States" section of the *Yearbook*.

Headquarters

1021 Center St., P.O. Box 1245, Bethlehem, PA 18016-1245

Media Contact, Rev. R. Burke Johnson

Officers

Pres., Mr. Graham Kerslake, 10910 Harvest Lake Way NE, Calgary, AB T3K 4L1 Tel (403)508-7765 Fax (403)226-2467

Canadian Evangelical Christian Churches

The Canadian Evangelical Christian Churches is an international, full-gospel inter-denomination, which offers ministerial credentials to release men and women into the five-fold ministry to spread the Gospel, according to Ephesians 4:11,12. The congregations are associated through a common doctrine that is a combination of Calvinistic and Arminian beliefs. Each and every congregation is connected with CECC as congregational and ordination is supervised by the National Office.

Headquarters

General Superintendent, Rev. David P. Lavigne, 410-125 Lincoln Rd., Waterloo, ON N2J J2N, Tel. (519)725-5578 Fax (same)

Email: cecc@globalserve.net

Website: www.orc.ca~cecc

Officers

Gen. Supt., Rev. David P. Lavigne

Exec. Dir., Rev. Otto Ferber

Gen. Sec., Rev. Bill St. Pierre

Canadian Yearly Meeting of the Religious Society of Friends

Canadian Yearly Meeting of the Religious Society of Friends was founded in Canada as an offshoot of the Quaker movement in Great Britain and colonial America. Genesee Yearly Meeting, founded 1834, Canada Yearly Meeting (Orthodox), founded in 1867, and Canada Yearly Meeting, founded in 1881, united in 1955 to form the Canadian Yearly Meeting. Canadian Yearly Meeting is affiliated with Friends United Meeting and Friends General Conference. It is also a member of Friends World Committee for Consultation.

Headquarters

91A Fourth Ave., Ottawa, ON K1S 2L1 Tel. (613)235-8553 or (613)296-3222 Fax (613)235-1753

E-mail: cym@web.net

Website: www.web.net/-cym

Media Contact, Gen. Sec.-Treas.,—

Officers

Gen. Sec.-Treas.,—

Clerk: Gale Wills

Archivist, Jane Zavitz Bond

Archives, Arthur G. Dorland, Pickering College, 389 Bayview St., Newmarket, ON L3Y 4X2 Tel. (416)895-1700

Periodicals

The Canadian Friend; Quaker Concern

The Catholic Church in Canada

The largest single body of Christians in Canada, the Catholic Church is under the spiritual leadership of His Holiness the Pope. Catholicism in Canada dates back to 1534, when the first Mass was celebrated on the Gaspé Peninsula on July 7, by a priest accompanying Jacques Cartier. Catholicism had been implanted earlier by fishermen and sailors from Europe. Priests came to Acadia as early as 1604. Traces of a regular colony go back to 1608 when Champlain settled in Quebec City. The Recollets (1615), followed by the Jesuits (1625) and the Sulpicians (1657), began the missions among the native population. The first official Roman document relative to the Canadian missions dates from March 20, 1618. Bishop François de Montmorency-Laval, the first bishop, arrived in Quebec in 1659. The church developed in the East, but not until 1818 did systematic missionary work begin in western Canada.

In the latter 1700s, English-speaking Catholics, mainly from Ireland and Scotland, began to arrive in Canada's Atlantic provinces. After 1815 Irish Catholics settled in large numbers in what is now Ontario. The Irish potato famine of 1847 greatly increased that population in all parts of eastern Canada.

By the 1850s the Catholic Church in both English- and French-speaking Canada had begun to erect new dioceses and found many religious communities. These communities did educational, medical and charitable work among their own people as well as among Canada's native peoples. By the 1890s large numbers of non-English and non-French-speaking Catholics had settled in Canada, especially in the Western provinces. In the 20th century the pastoral horizons have continued to expand to meet the needs of what has now become a very multiracial church.

Headquarters

Media Contact, Dir. Communications Service, Rev. Mr. William Kokesch, Email: kokesch@ccb.ca

Dir. Service des Communications, Sylvain Salvas, Email: salvas@cccb.ca

Officers
General Secretariat of the Episcopacy
Secrétaire général (French Sector), Father Émilius Goulet
General Secretary (English Sector), Msgr. Peter Schonenbach
Assistant General Secretary (English Sector), Bede Martin Hubbard
Secrétaire général adjoint (French Sector), M. Gérald Baril

CANADIAN ORGANIZATION
Canadian Conference of Catholic Bishops/ Conférence des évêques catholiques du Canada, 90 Parent Ave., Ottawa, ON K1N 7B1 Tel. (613)241-9461 Fax (613)241-8117, Email: cecc@cccb.ca, Website: www.cccb.ca

EXECUTIVE COMMITTEE
National Level
Pres., His Eminence Jean-Claude Cardinal Turcotte (Montreal)
Vice-Pres., Most Rev. Gerald Wiesner, o.m.i. (Prince George)
Co-Treas.: Most Rev. Anthony F. Tonnos (Hamilton)

EPISCOPAL COMMISSIONS
National Level
Social Affairs, Mgr. Francois Thibodeau
Canon Law, Most Rev. Francis J. Spence
Relations with Assoc. of Priests, Religious, & Laity, Most Rev. Terrence Prendergast
Evangelization of Peoples, Mgr. André Gaumond
Ecumenism, Most Rev. Brendan O'Brien
Theology,——
Sector Level
Comm. sociales, Mgr. Robert Lebel
Social Comm., Most Rev. Fred Colli
Éducation chrétienne, Mgr. Paul Marchand
Christian Education, Most Rev. Anthony Tonnos
Liturgie, Mgr. Antoine Hacault
Liturgy, Most Rev. Marcel A.J. Gervais

OFFICES
Secteur français
Evangélisation des peuples, Dir., Mme. Adéle Bolduc
Office des communications sociales, Dir. général, M. Bertrand Ouellet
Office national de liturgie, coordonnateur, M. l'abbé Paul Boily, 3530, rue Adam, Montréal, QC H1W 1Y8 Tel. (514)522-4930 Fax (514)522-1557
Oecuménisme, Sr. Donna Geernaert
Services des communications, Dir., M. Sylvain Salvas
Service des Editions, Dir., Mme Johanne Gnassi
Théologie, Dir., P. Gilles Langevin
Tribunal d'appel du Canada, P. Pierre Allard, s.m.
Éducation chrétienne Dir., F. Jean-Claude Éthier

Affaires sociales, Dir., M. Joseph Gunn
English Sector
Natl. Liturgical Ofc., Dir., Sr. Donna Kelly, c.n.d.
Natl. Ofc. of Religious Educ., Dir., Bernadette Tourangeau
Evangelization of peoples, Dir., Ms. Adéle Bolduc
Ecumenism, Sr. Donna Geernaert
Theology Dir., P. Gilles Langevin, S.J.
Canadian Appeal Tribunal, P. Pierre Allard, s.m.
Communications Service, Dir., Rev. William Kokesch
Social Affairs, Dir., Joseph Gunn

REGIONAL EPISCOPAL ASSEMBLIES
Atlantic Episcopal Assembly: Pres., Mgr. André Richard; Vice-Pres., Most Rev. Raymond Lahey et Mgr. Francois Thibodeau; Sec.-Treas., Daniel Deveau, c.s.c., Tel. (506)758-2589 Fax (506)758-2580
Assemblée des évêques du Que: Prés., Mgr. Pierre Morissette; Vice-Pres., Mgr. Robert Ébacher; Sécretaire général, M. Guy St. Onge, prêtre; Secrétariat, 1225 Boulevard Saint Joseph est, Montréal, QC H2J 1L7 Tel. (514)274-4323 Fax (514)274-4383
Email: aeq@eveques.qc.ca
Ontario Conference of Catholic Bishops: Pres., Bishop Anthony Tonnos; Vice-Pres., Most Rev. Brendan O'Brien; Sec., Thomas J. Reilly; Secretariat, Ste. 800, 10 St. Mary St., Toronto, ON M4Y 1P9 Tel. (416)923-1423 Fax (416)923-1509
Email: occb@pathcom.com
Western Catholic Conference: Pres., Bishop Blaise Morand; Vice-Pres., Mgr. Raymond Roussin; Sec., Abbot Peter Novecosky, O.S.B., P.O. Box 10, Muenster, SK S0K 2Y0 Tel. (306)682-1788 Fax (306)682-1766

MILITARY ORDINARIATE
Ordinaire aux forces canadiennes: Mgr. Donald Thériault, National Defence Headquarters, Ottawa, ON K1A 0K2 Tel. (613)990- 7824 Fax (613)990-7824
Canadian Religious Conference: Sec. Gen., Sr. Hélène Robitaille, F.D.L.S., 219 Argyle St., Ottawa, ON K2P 2H4 Tel. (613)236-0824 Fax (613)236-0825
Email: crcn@web.net

Periodicals
Cahiers de Spiritualité Ignatienne; The Catholic Register; The Catholic Times (Montreal); Companion Magazine; Global Village Voice; Discover the Bible; L'Église Canadienne; The Monitor; National Bulletin on Liturgy; The New Freeman; Messenger (of the Sacred Heart); Foi et Culture (Bulletin natl. de liturgie) Liturgie; Prairie Messenger; Vie Liturgique; La Vie des Communautés religieuses; Relations; Présence; The Communicator; Scarboro Missions; Missions Today

Christ Catholic Church International

The Christ Catholic Church International, with Cathedral, churches, missions and oratories in Canada, the United States, Norway, Australia, Bosnia and Colombia South America, is an Orthodox-Catholic Communion tracing Apostolic Succession through the Old Catholic and Orthodox Catholic Churches.

The church ministers to a growing number of people seeking an experiential relationship with their Lord and Savior Jesus Christ in a Sacramental and Scripture based church. As one of the three founding members of FOCUS: Federation of Orthodox Catholic Churches United Sacramentally, CCCI is working to bring together Old and Orthodox Catholicism into one united church under the headship of Jesus Christ.

Headquarters

5165 Palmer Ave., P.O. Box 73, Niagara Falls, ON L2E 6S8 Tel. (905)354-2329 Fax (905)354-9934

E-mail: dwmullan@sympatico.ca

Website: www3.sympatico.ca/dwmullan

Media Contact, The Rt. Rev. John W. Brown, 1504-75 Queen St., Hamilton, ON L8R 3J3 Tel. (905)527-9089 Fax (905)354-9934

Officers

Presiding Bishop, The Most Rev. Donald Wm. Mullan, 6190 Barker St., Niagara Falls, ON L2E 1Y4

Archbishop, The Most Rev. Jose Ruben Garcia Matiz, Calle 52 Sur #24 A-35 - Bq. #1, Ap. 301, Santa Fe de Bogota, D.C., Colombia, South America

Episcopal Vicar, The Rt. Rev. John Wm. Brown, 1504-75 Queen St. N., Hamilton, ON L8R 3J3

Auxiliary Bishop, The Rt. Rev. Acie Angel, 1085 Wiethaupt Rd., Florissant, MO 63031

Auxiliary Bishop, The Rt. Rev. Curtis Bradley, 145 S. Garfield St., Denver, CO 80209

Auxiliary Bishop, The Rt. Rev. Gerard Laplante, 715 E. 51st Ave., Vancouver, BC V5X 1E2

Auxiliary Bishop, The Rt. Rev. Luis Fernando Hoyos Maldonado, A.A. 2437 Santa Fe de Bogota, D.C., Colombia, South America

Auxiliary Bishop, The Rt. Rev. L.M. McFerran, #206-6020 East Boulevard, Vancouver, BC C6M 3V5

Auxiliary Bishop, The Rt. Rev. Ronald K. Pace, 1411 Nursery Rd., Clearwater, FL 33756

Auxiliary Bishop, The Rt. Rev. Jose Moises Moncada Quevedo, A.A. 2437 Santa Fe de Bogota, D.C., Colombia, South America

Auxiliary Bishop, The Rt. Rev. Roger Robberstad, Pb 2624 St. Hanshaugen N-0131 Oslo, Norway

SEMINARY

St. Mary's Seminary: The Very Rev. Del Baier, 8287 Lamont, Niagara Falls, ON L2G 7L4 (offering on-site and correspondence programs)

The New Order of St. Francis: (Priests, Brothers and Sisters), Sec. General, Rev. Bro. Sean Ross, 5768 Summer St., Niagara Falls, ON L2G 1M2

Periodicals

St. Luke Magazine
The Franciscan

Christian Brethren (also known as Plymouth Brethren)

The Christian Brethren are a loose grouping of autonomous local churches, often called "assemblies." They are firmly committed to the inerrancy of Scripture and to evangelical doctrine of salvation by faith alone apart from works or sacrament. Characteristics and common elements are a weekly Breaking of Bread and freedom of ministry without a requirement of ordination. For their history, see "Religious Bodies in the United States" in the Directories section of this Yearbook.

CORRESPONDENT

James A Stahr, 327 W. Prairie Ave., Wheaton, IL 60187-3408 Tel. (630)665-3757

RELATED ORGANIZATIONS

Christian Brethren Church in the Province of Quebec, Exec. Sec., Marj Robbins, P.O. Box 1054, Sherbrooke, QC J1H 5L3 Tel. (819)820-1693 Fax (819)821-9287

MSC Canada, Administrator, William Yuille, 509-3950 14th Ave., Markham, ON L3R 0A9 Tel. (905)947-0468 Fax (905)947-0352

Vision Ministries Canada, Dir., Gord Martin, P.O. Box 28032, Waterloo, ON N2L 6J8 Tel. (519)725-1212 Fax (519)725-9421

Periodicals

News of Quebec

Christian Church (Disciples of Christ) in Canada

Disciples have been in Canada since 1810, and were organized nationally in 1922. This national church seeks to serve the Canadian context as part of the whole Christian Church (Disciples of Christ) in the United States and Canada.

Headquarters

128 Woolwich St., #202, P.O. Box 64, Guelph, ON N1H 6J6 Tel. (519)823-5190 Fax (519)823-5766

Media Contact, Exec. Min., Robert W. Steffer

Officers

Mod., Mervin Bailey, 1205 Jubilee Ave., Regina, SK S4S 3S7

Vice-Mod., John Dick, RR#4, Thamesdill, ON N0P 2K0

Exec. Min., Rev. Dr. Robert W. Steffer, P.O. Box 30013, 2 Quebec St., Guelph, ON N1H 8J5

Periodicals

Canadian Disciple

Christian and Missionary Alliance in Canada

A Canadian movement, dedicated to the teaching of Jesus Christ the Saviour, Sanctifier, Healer and Coming King, commenced in Toronto in 1887 under the leadership of the Rev. John Salmon. Two years later, the movement united with The Christian Alliance of New York, founded by Rev. A. B. Simpson, becoming the Dominion Auxiliary of the Christian Alliance, Toronto, under the presidency of the Hon. William H. Howland'. Its four founding branches were Toronto, Hamilton, Montreal, and Quebec. By Dec. 31, 1997, there were 386 churches across Canada, with 1211 official workers, including a worldwide missionary force of 240.

In 1980, the Christian and Missionary Alliance in Canada became autonomous. Its General Assembly is held every two years.

NATIONAL OFFICE

Box 7900 Stn. B, Willowdale, ON M2K 2R6 Tel. (905)771-6747 Fax (905) 771-9874
E-mail: nationaloffice@cmacan.org
Media Contact, Vice-Pres. General Services, Kenneth Paton

Officers

Pres., Dr. Arnold Cook, Box 7900, Postal Sta. B, Willowdale, ON M2K 2R6
Vice-Pres./Personnel & Missions, Rev. Wallace C.E. Albrecht
Vice-Pres./Fin., Paul D. Lorimer
Vice-Pres./Canadian Ministries, Rev. C. Stuart Lightbody
Vice-Pres./Gen. Services, Kenneth Paton

DISTRICT SUPERINTENDENTS

Canadian Pacific: Rev. Brian Thom
Western Canadian: Rev. Arnold Downey
Canadian Midwest: Rev. Bob Peters
Central Canadian: Rev. David Lewis
East Canadian District: Rev. Doug Wiebe
St. Lawrence: Rev. Yvan Fournier

Christian Reformed Church in North America

Canadian congregations of the Christian Reformed Church in North America have been formed since 1908. For detailed information about this denomination, please refer to the listing for the Christian Reformed Church in North America in Chapter 3, "Religious Bodies in the United States."

Headquarters

United States Office: 2850 Kalamazoo Ave., S.E., Grand Rapids, MI 49560 Tel. (616)224-0744 Fax (616)224-5895
Canadian Office: 3475 Mainway, P.O. Box 5070 STN LCR 1, Burlington, ON L7R 3Y8 Tel. (905)336-2920 Fax (905)336-8344
Website: www.crcna.org
Media Contact, Gen. Sec., Dr. David H.

Engelhard, U.S. Office; Director of Communication, Mr. Henry Hess, Canadian Office

Officers

Gen. Sec., Dr. David H. Engelhard, U.S. Office
Exec. Dir./Ministries, Dr. Peter Borgdorff, U.S.Office
Dir. of Fin.& Administration, Kenneth Horjus, U.S. Office

Periodicals

The Banner

Church of God (Anderson, Ind.)

This body is one of the largest of the groups which have taken the name "Church of God." Its headquarters are at Anderson, Indiana. It originated about 1880 and emphasizes Christian unity.

Headquarters

Western Canada Assembly, Chpsn., Hilda Nauenburg, 4717 56th St., Camrose, AB T4V 2C4 Tel. (780)672-0772 Fax (780)672-6888
Eastern Canada Assembly, Chpsn., Jim Wiebe, 38 James St., Dundas, ON L9H 2J6
E-mail: wcdncog@cable-lynx.net
Website: www.cable-lynx.net/~wcdncog
Media Contact for Western Canada, Church Service/Mission Coordinator, John D. Campbell, 4717 56th St., Camrose, AB T4V 2C4 Tel. (780)672-0772 Fax (780)672-6888

Periodicals

College News & Updates; The Gospel Contact; The Messenger

Church of God in Christ (Mennonite)

The Church of God in Christ, Mennonite was organized by the evangelist-reformer John Holdeman in Ohio. The church unites with the faith of the Waldenses, Anabaptists and other such groups throughout history. Emphasis is placed on obedience to the teachings of the Bible, including the doctrine of the new birth and spiritual life, noninvolvement in government or the military, a head-covering for women, beards for men and separation from the world shown by simplicity in clothing, homes, possessions and lifestyle. The church has a worldwide membership of about 18,300, largely concentrated in the United States and Canada.

Headquarters

P.O. Box 313, 420 N. Wedel Ave., Moundridge, KS 67107 Tel. (316)345-2532 Fax (316)345-2582
Media Contact, Dale Koehn, P.O.Box 230, Moundridge, KS 67107 Tel. (316)345-2532 Fax (316)345-2582

Periodicals

Messenger of Truth

174

Church of God (Cleveland, Tenn.)

It is one of America's oldest Pentecostal churches founded in 1886 as an outgrowth of the holiness revival under the name Christian Union. In 1907 the church adopted the organizational name Church of God. It has its foundation upon the principles of Christ as revealed in the Bible. The Church of God is Christian, Protestant, foundational in its doctrine, evangelical in practice and distinctively Pentecostal. It maintains a centralized form of government and a commitment to world evangelization.

The first church in Canada was extablished in 1919 in Scotland Farm, Manitoba. Paul H. Walker became the first overseer of Canada in 1931.

Headquarters

Intl. Offices: 2490 Keith St., NW, Cleveland, TN 37320 Tel. (423)472-3361 Fax (423)478-7066
Media Contact, Dir. of Communications, Michael L. Baker, P.O. Box 2430, Cleveland, TN 37320-2430 Tel. (423)478-7112 Fax (423)478-7066

EXECUTIVES

General Overseer: Paul L. Walker
Assistant General Overseers: R. Lamar Vest, G. Dennis McGuire, T.L. Lowery
General Secretary/Treasurer: Bill F. Sheeks
Canada-Eastern, Rev. Canute Blake, P.O. Box 2036, Brampton, ON L6T 3TO Tel. (905)793-2213 Fax (905)793-9173
Canada-Western, Rev. Raymond W. Wall, Box 54055, 2640 52 St. NE, Calgary, AB T1Y 6S6 Tel. (403)293-8817 Fax (403)293-8832
Canada-Quebec/Maritimes, Rev. Jacques Houle, 19 Orly, Granby, QC J2H 1Y4 Tel. (514)378-4442 Fax (514)378-8646

Periodicals

Church of God Evangel, Editorial Evangelica

The Church of God of Prophecy in Canada

In the late 19th century, people seeking God's eternal plan as they followed the Reformation spirit began to delve further for scriptural light concerning Christ and his church. A small group of people emerged which dedicated and covenanted themselves to God and one another to be the Church of God. On June 13, 1903, A.J. Tomlinson joined them during a period of intense prayer and Bible study. Under Tomlinson's dynamic leadership, the church enjoyed tremendous growth.

In 1923 two churches emerged. Those that opposed Tomlinson's leadership are known today in Canada as the New Testament Church of God. Tomlinson's followers are called the Church of God of Prophecy.

In Canada, the first Church of God of Prophecy congregation was organized in Swan River, Manitoba, in 1937. Churches are now established in British Columbia, Manitoba, Alberta, Saskatchewan, Ontario, Quebec and all 50 states.

The church accepts the whole Bible rightly divided, with the New Testament as the rule of faith and practice, government and discipline. The membership upholds the Bible as the inspired Word of God and believes that its truths are known by the illumination of the Holy Spirit. The Trinity is recognized as one supreme God in three persons—Father, Son and Holy Ghost. It is believed that Jesus Christ, the virgin-born Son of God, lived a sinless life, fulfilled his ministry on earth, was crucified, resurrected and later ascended to the right hand of God. Believers now await Christ's return to earth and the establishment of the millenial kingdom.

Headquarters

World Headquarters: Bible Place, P.O. Box 2910, Cleveland, TN 37320-2910
National Office: Bishop Adrian L. Varlack, P.O. Box 457, Brampton, ON L6V 2L4 Tel. (905)843-2379 Fax (905)843-3990
Media Contact, Bishop Mirriam Bailey, P.O. Box 457, Brampton, ON L6V 2L4 Tel. (905)843-2379 Fax (905)843-3990

Officers

Pres., Bishop Adrian L. Varlack
V. Pres & Sec., Aston R. Morrison
Asst. Sec. & Treas., Mirriam Bailey

Periodicals

Canada Update

The Church of Jesus Christ of Latter-day Saints in Canada

The Church has had a presence in Canada since the early 1830's. Joseph Smith and Brigham Young both came to Eastern Canada as missionaries. There are now 157,000 members in Canada in more than 400 congregations.

Leading the Church in Canada are the presidents of over 40 stakes (equivalent to a diocese). World headquarters is in Salt Lake City, UT (See U.S. Religious Bodies chapter of the Directories section of this *Yearbook*).

Headquarters

50 East North Temple St., Salt Lake City, UT 84150
Media Contact, Public Affairs Dir., Bruce Smith, 1185 Eglinton Ave., Box 116, North York, ON M3C 3C6 Tel. (416)424-2485 Fax (416)424-3326

Church of Jesus Christ of Latter-day Saints (Reorganized)—please see the Reorganized Church of Jesus Christ of Latter Day Saints.

Church of the Lutheran Brethren

The Church of the Lutheran Brethren of America was organized in December 1900. Five independent Lutheran congregations met together in Milwaukee, Wisconsin, and adopted a constitution patterned very closely to that of the Lutheran Free Church of Norway.

The spiritual awakening in the Midwest during the 1890s crystallized into convictions that led to the formation of a new church body. Chief among the concerns were church membership practices, observance of Holy Communion, confirmation practices and local church government.

The Church of the Lutheran Brethren practices a simple order of worship with the sermon as the primary part of the worship service. It believes that personal profession of faith is the primary criterion for membership in the congregation. The Communion service is reserved for those who profess faith in Christ as savior. Each congregation is autonomous and the synod serves the congregations in advisory and cooperative capacities.

The synod supports a world mission program in Cameroon, Chad, Japan and Taiwan. Approximately 40 percent of the synodical budget is earmarked for world missions. A growing home mission ministry is planting new congregations in the United States and Canada. Affiliate organizations operate several retirement/nursing homes, conference and retreat centers.

Headquarters

1020 Alcott Ave., W., P.O. Box 655, Fergus Falls, MN 56538 Tel. (218)739-3336 Fax (218)739-5514
E-mail: rmo@clba.org
Website: www.clba.org
Media Contact, Rev. Brent Juliot

Officers

Pres., Rev. Arthur Berge, 72 Midridge Close SE, Calgary, AB T2X 1G1
Vice-Pres., Rev. Luther Stenberg, PO Box 75, Hagen, SK S0J 1B0
Sec., Mr. Alvin Herman, 3105 Taylor Street E., Saskatoon, SK S7H 1H5
Treas., Edwin Rundbraaten, Box 739, Birch Hills, SK S0J 0G0
Youth Coord., Rev. Harold Rust, 2617 Preston Ave. S., Saskatoon, SK S7J 2G3

Periodicals

Faith and Fellowship

Church of the Nazarene in Canada

The first Church of the Nazarene in Canada was organized in November, 1902, by Dr. H. F. Reynolds. It was in Oxford, Nova Scotia. The Church of the Nazarene is Wesleyan Arminian in theology, representative in church government and warmly evangelistic.

Headquarters

20 Regan Rd., Unit 9, Brampton, ON L7A 1C3 Tel. (905)846-4220 Fax (905)846-1775
E-mail: nazarene@interlog.com
Website:http://web.1-888.com.nazarene/national/

Media Contact, Gen. Sec., Dr. Jack Stone, 6401 The Paseo, Kansas City, MO 64131 Tel. (816)333-7000 Fax (816)822-9071

Officers

Natl. Dir., Dr. William E. Stewart, 20 Regan Rd. Unit 9, Brampton, ON L7A 1C3 Tel. (905)846-4220 Fax (905)846-1775
Exec. Asst., John T. Martin, 20 Regan Rd. Unit 9, Brampton, ON L7A 1C3 Tel. (905)846-4220 Fax (905)846-1775
Chmn., Rev. Wesley G. Campbell, #205, 1255 56th St., Delta, BC V4L 2B9
Vice-Chmn., Rev. Ronald G. Fry, 1280 Finch Ave. W. Ste. 416, North York, ON M3J 3K6
Sec., Rev. Larry Dahl, 14320 94th St., Edmonton, AL T5E 3W2

Churches of Christ in Canada

Churches of Christ are autonomous congregations, whose members appeal to the Bible alone to determine matters of faith and practice. There are no central offices or officers. Publications and institutions related to the churches are either under local congregational control or independent of any one congregation.

Churches of Christ shared a common fellowship in the 19th century with the Christian Churches/Churches of Christ and the Christian Church (Disciples of Christ). Fellowship was broken after the introduction of instrumental music in worship and centralization of churchwide activities through a missionary society. Churches of Christ began in Canada soon after 1800, largely in the middle provinces. The few pioneer congregations were greatly strengthened in the mid-1800s, growing in size and number.

Members of Churches of Christ believe in the inspiration of the Scriptures, the divinity of Jesus Christ, and immersion into Christ for the remission of sins. The New Testament pattern is followed in worship and church organization.

Headquarters

Media Contact, Man. Ed., Gospel Herald, Eugene C. Perry, 4904 King St., Beansville, ON L0R 1B6 Tel. (416)563-7503 Fax (416)563-7503
E-mail: eperry9953@aol.com

Periodicals

Gospel Herald; Sister Triangle

Congregational Christian Churches in Canada

This body originated in the early 18th century when devout Christians within several denominations in the northern and eastern United States, dissatisfied with sectarian controversy, broke away from their own denominations and took the simple title "Christians." First organized in 1821 at Keswick, Ontario, the Congregational Christian Churches in Canada was incorporated on Dec. 4, 1989, as a national organization. In doctrine the body is evangelical, being governed by the Bible as the final authority in faith and practice. It believes that Christian character must be expressed in daily living; it aims at the unity of all true believers in Christ that others may believe in Him and be saved. In church polity, the body is democratic and autonomous. It is also a member of The World Evangelical Congregational Fellowship.

Headquarters
241 Dunsdon St. Ste. 405, Brantford, ON N3R 7C3 Tel. (519)751-0606 Fax (519)751-0852
Media Contact, Past Pres., Jim Potter, 8 Church St., Waldemar, ON L0N 1G0 Tel. (519)928-5561

Officers
Pres., Rev. Michael Shute
Exec. Dir., Rev. Bruce Robertson
Sec., Rev. Alan MacInnes

Periodicals
Spirit Catalyst Bi Monthly
Editor, Rev. Dr. Ross Bailey

The Coptic Orthodox Church in Canada

The Coptic Orthodox Church in North America was begun in Canada in 1964 and was registered in the province of Ontario in 1965. The Coptic Orthodox Church has spread rapidly since then. The total number of local churches in both Canada and the USA have reached seventy-four. Besides two dioceses were established a monastery with a bishop, monks and novices, as well as two theological seminaries.

The Coptic Orthodox Church is a hierarchical church and the administrative governing body of each local church is an elected Board of Deacons approved by the Bishop.

Headquarters
St. Mark's Coptic Orthodox Church, 41 Glendinning Ave., Scarborough, ON M1W 3E2 Tel. (416)494-4449 Fax (416)494-2631
Media Contact, Fr. Ammonius Guirguis, Tel. (416)494-4449 Fax (416)494-2631

Officers
Archpriest, Fr. Marcos A. Marcos
Officer, Fr. Ammonius Guirguis, 41 Glendinning Ave., Agincourt, ON M1W 3E2 Tel. (416)494-4449
Officer, Fr. Misael Ataalla

Disciples of Christ—please see Christian Church (Disciples of Christ) in Canada.

Doukhobars—please see Union of Spiritual Communities in Christ.

Elim Fellowship of Evangelical Churches and Ministers

The Elim Fellowship of Evangelical Churches and Ministers, a Pentecostal body, was established in 1984 as a sister organization of Elim Fellowship in the United States.

This is an association of churches, ministers and missionaries seeking to serve the whole body of Christ. It is Pentecostal and has a charismatic orientation.

Headquarters
379 Golf Road, RR#6, Brantford, ON N3T 5L8, Tel. (519)753-7266 Fax (519)753-5887
E-mail: elim@bfree.on.ca
Website: http://Bfree.ON.ca/comdir/churchs/elim
Ofc. Mgr., Larry Jones

Officers
Pres., Errol Alchin
Vice-Pres., John Woods, 3G Crestlea Cres. Nepean, ON N2G 4N1
Sec., Howard Ellis, 102 Ripley Cres., Kitchener, ON N2N 1V4
Treas., Aubrey Phillips, P.O. Box 208, Blairsville, GA 30512
President Emeritus, Carlton Spencer

COUNCIL OF ELDERS
Errol Alchin, Tel. (519)753-7266
Howard Ellis, Tel. (519)579-9844
Claude Favreau (819)477-7421
Aubrey Phillips, Tel. (706)745-2473
John Woods, Tel. (613)228-1796
Bernard Evans, Tel. (716)528-2790
Howard Ellis

The Estonian Evangelical Lutheran Church

The Estonian Evangelical Lutheran Church (EELC) was founded in 1917 in Estonia and reorganized in Sweden in 1944. The teachings of the EELC are based on the Old and New Testaments, explained through the Apostolic, Nicean and Athanasian confessions, the unaltered Confession of Augsburg and other teachings found in the Book of Concord.

Headquarters
383 Jarvis St., Toronto, ON M5B 2C7 Tel. (416)925-5465 Fax (416)925-5688
Media Contact, Archbishop, Rev. Udo Petersoo
Email: udo.petersoo@eelk.ee
Website: www.eelk.ee/~e.e.l.k./

Officers
Archbishop, The Rev. Udo Petersoo
Gen. Sec., Dean Edgar Heinsoo

Periodicals
Eesti Kirik

The Evangelical Covenant Church of Canada

A Canadian denomination organized in Canada at Winnipeg in 1904 which is affiliated with the Evangelical Covenant Church of America and with the International Federation of Free Evangelical Churches, which includes 31 federations in 26 countries.

This body believes in the one triune God as confessed in the Apostles' Creed, that salvation is received through faith in Christ as Saviour, that the Bible is the authoritative guide in all matters of faith and practice. Christian Baptism and the Lord's Supper are accepted as divinely ordained sacraments of the church. As descendants of the 19th century northern European pietistic awakening, the group believes in the need of a personal experience of commitment to Christ, the development of a virtuous life and the urgency of spreading the gospel to the "ends of the world."

Headquarters
2791 Pembina Highway, Winnipeg, MB R3T 2H5
Media Contact, Supt., Jeff Anderson

Officers
Supt., Rev. Jerome W. Johnson
Chpsn., Les Doell, RR 2, Wetaskiwin, AB T9A 1W9
Sec., Lori Koop, 6568 Claytonwood Pl., Surrey, BC V3S 7T5
Treas., Rod Johnson, Box 196, Norquay, SK S0A 2V0

Periodicals
The Covenant Messenger

Evangelical Free Church of Canada

The Evangelical Free Church of Canada traces its beginning back to 1917 when the church in Enchant, Alberta opened its doors. Today the denomination has nearly 144 churches from the West Coast to Quebec. Approximately 45 missionaries are sponsored by the EFCC in 10 countries. The Evangelical Free Church is the founding denomination of Trinity Western University in Langley, British Columbia. Church membership is 7,123, average attendance is 16,375.

Headquarters
Mailing Address, P.O. Box 850 LCD1, Langley, BC V3A 8S3 Tel. (604)888-8668 Fax (604)888-3108
Location, 7600 Glover Rd., Langley, BC
E-mail: efcc@twu.ca
Website: www.twu.ca/efcc/efcc.htm
Media Contact, Exec. Sec., Sharon Biro, P.O. Box 850 LCD1, Langley, BC V3A 8S3 Tel. (604)888-8668 Fax (604)888-3108

Officers
Pres., Dr. Richard J. Penner
Mod., William Dyck, Box 170, Fosston, SK, S0E 0V0

Periodicals
The Pulse

Evangelical Lutheran Church in Canada

The Evangelical Lutheran Church in Canada was organized in 1985 through a merger of The Evangelical Lutheran Church of Canada (ELCC) and the Lutheran Church in America-Canada Section.

The merger is a result of an invitation issued in 1972 by the ELCC to the Lutheran Church in America-Canada Section and the Lutheran Church-Canada. Three-way merger discussions took place until 1978 when it was decided that only a two-way merger was possible. The ELCC was the Canada District of the ALC until autonomy in 1967.

The Lutheran Church in Canada traces its history back more than 200 years. Congregations were organized by German Lutherans in Halifax and Lunenburg County in Nova Scotia in 1749. German Lutherans, including many United Empire Loyalists, also settled in large numbers along the St. Lawrence and in Upper Canada. In the late 19th century, immigrants arrived from Scandinavia, Germany and central European countries, many via the United States. The Lutheran synods in the United States have provided the pastoral support and help for the Canadian church.

Headquarters
302-393 Portage Avenue, Winnipeg, MB R3B 3H6 Tel. (204)984-9150 Fax (204)984-9185
Media Contact, Bishop, Rev. Telmor G. Sartison

Officers
Bishop, Rev. Telmor G. Sartison
Vice-Pres., Janet Morley
Sec., Mr. Robert H. Granke
Treas., Doreen Lecuyer

ASSISTANTS TO THE BISHOPS
Rev. Cynthia Halmarson
Rev. Richard Stetson

DIVISIONS AND OFFICES
Evangelical Lutheran Women, Pres., Lindy Wozniak
Exec. Dir., Ruth Vince

SYNODS
Alberta and the Territories: Bishop, Rev. Stephen P. Kristenson, 10014-81 Ave., Edmonton, AB T6E 1W8 Tel. (403)439-2636 Fax (403)433-6623
Eastern: Bishop, Rev. Michael J. Pryse, 50 Queen St. N., Kitchener, ON N2H 6P4 Tel. (519)743-1461 Fax (519)743-4291
British Columbia: Bishop, Rev. Raymond L. Schultz, 80-10th Ave., E., New Westminster, BC V3L 4R5 Tel. (604)524-1318 Fax (604)524-9255
Manitoba/Northwestern Ontario: Bishop, Rev. Richard M. Smith, 201-3657 Roblin Blvd., Winnipeg, MB R3G 0E2 Tel. (204)889-3760 Fax (204)869-0272
Saskatchewan: Bishop, Rev. Allan A. Grundahl, 601 Spadina Cres. E., Saskatoon, SK S7K 3G8 Tel. (306)244-2474 Fax (306)664-8677

Periodicals
Canada Lutheran; Esprit

178

The Evangelical Mennonite Conference

The Evangelical Mennonite Conference is a modern church of historic Christian convictions, tracing its indebtedness to the Radical Reformation, which, in turn, is rooted in the Protestant Reformation of the 16th century. The Centre of faith, and of Scripture, is found in Jesus Christ as Saviour and Lord.

The church's name was chosen in 1959. It's original name, Kleine Gemeinde, which means "small church", reflected its origins as a renewal movement among Mennonites in southern Russia. Klaas Reimer, a minister, was concerned about a decline of spiritual life and discipline in the church, and inappropriate involvement in the Napoleanic War. About 1812, Reimer and others began separate worship services, and two years later were organized as a small group.

Facing increasing government pressure, particularly about military service, the group migrated to North America in 1874 to 1875. Fifty families settled in Manitoba and 36 in Nebraska. Ties between the groups weakened and eventually the U.S. group gave up its KG identity. The KG survived several schisms and migrations, dating from its years in Russia through the 1940s.

As an evangelical church, The Evangelical Mennonite Conference holds that Scripture has final authority in faith and practice, a belief in Christ's finished work, and that assurance of salvation is possible. As Mennonite, the denomination has a commitment to discipleship, baptism upon confession of faith, community, social concern, non-violence and the Great Commission. As a conference, it seeks to encourage local churches, to work together on evangelism and matters of social concern, and relates increasingly well to other denominations.

In the year 2000 its membership surpassed 7,000, with many more people as treasured adherents and a wider circle of ministry influence. Membership is for people baptized on confession of faith (usually in adolescence or older). Children are considered safe in Christ until they reach an age where they are accountable for their own spiritual decision and opt out; they are considered part of the church, while full inclusion occurs upon personal choice.

The Conference has 53 churches from British Columbia to Ontario (33 in Manitoba) and roughly 135 mission workers in 25 countries. The cultural make-up of the Conference is increasingly diverse, though its Dutch-German background remains dominant nationally. Ten churches have pastors or leaders who are of non-Dutch-German background.

Some churches have a multiple leadership pattern (ministers and deacons can be selected from within the congregation); others have new patterns. Most churches support their leading minister full time. Its church governance moved from a bishop system to greater local congregational autonomy. It currently functions as a conference of churches with national boards, a conference council, and a moderator.

Women can serve on most national boards, as conference council delegates, as missionaries, and within a wide range of local church activities; while they can be selected locally, they cannot currently serve as nationally recognized or commissioned ministers.

It is a supporting member of Mennonite Central Committee and the Evangelical Fellowship of Canada. About 80 percent of its national budget goes toward mission work in Canada and other countries.

Headquarters

Box 1268, 440 Main St., Steinbach, MB R0A 2A0 Tel. (204)326-6401 Fax (204)326-1613
E-mail: emconf@mts.net
Media Contact, Conf. Pastor, John Koop

Officers

Acting Conf. Mod., Harvey Plett
General Sec., Len Barkman
Conference Pastor, David Thiessen
Bd. of Missions, Exec. Sec., Henry Klassen
Bd. of Missions, Foreign Sec., Lester Olfert
Bd. of Church Ministries, Exec. Sec./Editor, Terry M. Smith
Canadian Sec., Conf. Pastor, John Koop
Conference Youth Minister, Gerald Reimer

Periodicals

The Messenger

Evangelical Mennonite Mission Conference

This group was founded in 1936 as the Rudnerweider Mennonite Church in Southern Manitoba and organized as the Evangelical Mennonite Mission Conference in 1959. It was incorporated in 1962. The Annual Conference meeting is held in July.

Headquarters

Box 52059, Niakwa P.O., Winnipeg, MB R2M 5P9 Tel. (204)253-7929 Fax (204)256-7384
E-mail: emmc@mb.sympatico.ca
Media Contact, John Bergman, Box 206, Niverville, MB R0A 1E0 Tel. (204)388-4775
Fax (204)388-4775
E-mail: jbergman@mb.sympatico.ca

Officers

Mod., David Penner, 906-300 Sherk St., Leamington, ON N8H 4N7
Vice-Mod., Carl Zacharias, R.R. 1, Box 205, Winkler, MB R6W 4A1
Sec., Darrell Dyck, R.R. 1, Box 186, Winkler, MB R6W 4A1
Dir. of Conference Ministries, Jack Heppner
Dir. of Missions, Rev. Leonard Sawatzky
Business Admin., Henry Thiessen

179

OTHER ORGANIZATIONS

The Gospel Message: Box 1622, Saskatoon, SK S7K 3R8 Tel. (306)242-5001 Fax (306)242-6115; 210-401-33rd St. W., Saskatoon, SK S7L 0V5 Tel. (306)242-5001; Radio Pastor, Rev. Ed Martens

Periodicals

EMMC Recorder

The Evangelical Missionary Church of Canada

This denomination was formed in 1993 with the merger of The Evangelical Church of Canada and The Missionary Church of Canada. The Evangelical Missionary Church of Canada maintains fraternal relations with the worldwide body of the Missionary Church, Inc. and with the Evangelical Church of North America.The Evangelical Church of Canada was among those North American Evangelical United Brethern Conferences which did not join the EUB in merging with the Methodist Church in 1968. The Missionary Church of Canada is Anabaptist in heritage. Its practices and theology were shaped by the Holiness Revivals of the late 1800s. The Evangelical Missionary Church consists of 135 churches in two conferences in Canada.

Headquarters

4031 Brentwood Rd., NW, Calgary, AB T2L 1L1 Tel. (403)250-2759 Fax (403)291-4720

Media Contact, Exec. Dir., Missions and Administration, G. Keith Elliott

Email: evanmiss@emcc.ca

Officers

Pres., Rev. Mark Bolender, 1280 Ottawa St. S., Kitchener, ON N2E 1M1 Tel. (519)578-7275 Fax (519)578-7472

Canada East District, Dist. Supt., Rev. Phil Delsaut, 130 Fergus Ave., Kitchener, ON N2A 2H2 Tel. (519)894-9800

Canada West District, Dist. Supt., Rev. Walter Erion, 4031 Brentwood Rd., NW, Calgary, AB T2L 1L1 Tel. (403)250-2759 Fax (403)291-4720

The Fellowship of Evangelical Baptist Churches in Canada

This organization was founded in 1953 by the merging of the Union of Regular Baptist Churches of Ontario and Quebec with the Fellowship of Independent Baptist Churches of Canada.

Headquarters

679 Southgate Dr., Guelph, ON N1G 4S2 Tel. (519)821-4830 Fax (519)821-9829

Media Contact, Pres., Rev. Terry D. Cuthbert

E-Mail: president@fellowship.ca

Officers

Pres., Rev. Terry D. Cuthbert

Chmn., Rev. James A. Reese

Periodicals

B.C. Fellowship Baptist; The Evangelical Baptist; Intercom

Foursquare Gospel Church of Canada

The Western Canada District was formed in 1964 with the Rev. Roy Hicks as supervisor. Prior to 1964 it had been a part of the Northwest District of the International Church of the Foursquare Gospel with headquarters in Los Angeles, California.

A Provincial Society, the Church of the Foursquare Gospel of Western Canada, was formed in 1976; a Federal corporation, the Foursquare Gospel Church of Canada, was incorporated in 1981 and a national church formed. The provincial society was closed in 1994.

Headquarters

#100 8459 160th St., Surrey, BC V3S 3T9

E-mail: fgcc@canada.com

Media Contact, Pres. & Gen. Supervisor, Timothy J. Peterson, #100-8459 160th St., Surrey, BC V4N 1B4 Tel. (604)543-8414 Fax (604)543-8417

Officers

Pres. & Gen. Supervisor, Timothy J. Peterson

Periodicals

VIP Communique

Free Methodist Church in Canada

The Free Methodist Church was founded in New York in 1860 and expanded in 1880. It is Methodist in doctrine, evangelical in ministry and emphasizes the teaching of holiness of life through faith in Jesus Christ.

The Free Methodist Church in Canada was incorporated in 1927 after the establishment of a Canadian Executive Board. In 1959 the Holiness Movement Church merged with the Free Methodist Church. Full autonomy for the Canadian church was realized in 1990 with the formation of a Canadian General Conference. Mississauga, Ontario, continues to be the location of the Canadian Headquarters.

The Free Methodist Church ministers in 50 countries through its World Ministries Center in Indianapolis, Indiana.

Headquarters

4315 Village Centre Ct., Mississauga, ON L4Z 1S2 Tel. (905)848-2600 Fax (905)848-2603

E-mail: fmccan@inforamp.net

Website: www.fmc-canada.org

Media Contact, Mary-Elsie Fletcher

Officers

Bishop, Rev. Keith Elford

Dir. of Admn. Ser., Norman Bull

Dir. of Ministry Advancement, Rev. Mary-Elsie Fletcher

Supt., Personnel, Rev. Alan Retzman
Supt., Growth Ministries, Rev. Dr. Ron Bonar

Periodicals
The Free Methodist Herald

Free Will Baptists

As revival fires burned throughout New England in the mid- and late 1700s, Benjamin Randall proclaimed his doctrine of Free Will to large crowds of seekers. In due time, a number of Randall's converts moved to Nova Scotia. One such believer was Asa McGray, who was to become instrumental in the establishment of several Free Baptist churches. Local congregations were organized in New Brunswick. After several years of numerical and geographic gains, disagreements surfaced over the question of music, Sunday school, church offerings, salaried clergy and other issues. Adherents of the more progressive element decided to form their own fellowship. Led by George Orser, they became known as Free Christian Baptists.

The new group faithfully adhered to the truths and doctrines which embodied the theological basis of Free Will Baptists. Largely through Archibald Hatfield, contact was made with Free Will Baptists in the United States in the 1960s. The association was officially welcomed into the Free Will Baptist family in July 1981, by the National Association.

Headquarters
5233 Mt. View Rd., Antioch, TN 37013-2306 Tel. (615)731-6812 Fax (615)731-0771
Media Contact, Mod., Dwayne Broad, RR 3, Bath, NB E0J 1E0 Tel. (506)278-3771

Officers
Mod., Dwayne Broad
Promotional Officer, Dwayne Broad

General Church of the New Jerusalem

The Church of the New Jerusalem, also called The New Church, is a Christian Church founded on the Bible and the Writings of Emanuel Swedenborg (1688-1772). These Writings were first brought to Ontario in 1835 by Christian Enslin.

Headquarters
c/o Olivet Church, 279 Burnhamthorpe Rd., Etobicoke, ON M9B 1Z6 Tel. (416)239-3054 Fax (416)239-4935
E-mail: Mgladish@interlog.com
Website: www.newchurch.org
Media Contact, Exec. Vice-Pres., Rev. Michael D. Gladish

Officers
Pres., Rt. Rev. P. M. Buss, Bryn Athyn, PA 19009
Exec. Vice-Pres., Rev. Michael D. Gladish
Sec., Carolyn Bellinger, 110 Chapel Hill Dr., Kitchener, ON N2G 3W5

Treas., James Bellinger, 2 Shaver Court, Etobicoke, ON M9B 4P5

Periodicals
New Church Canadian

Greek Orthodox Metropolis of Toronto (Canada)

Greek Orthodox Christians in Canada are under the jurisdiction of the Ecumenical Patriarchate of Constantinople (Istanbul).

Headquarters
86 Overlea Blvd., Toronto, ON M4H 1C6 Tel. (416)429-5757 Fax (416)429-4588
E-mail: gocanada@total.net
Media Contact, Orthodox Way Committee

Officers
Metropolitan Archbishop of the Metropolis of Toronto (Canada), His Eminence Metropolitan Archbishop Sotirios

Periodicals
Orthodox Way

Independent Assemblies of God International (Canada)

This fellowship of churches has been operating in Canada for over 52 years. It is a branch of the Pentecostal Church in Sweden. Each church within the fellowship is completely independent.

Headquarters
1211 Lancaster St., London, ON N5V 2L4 Tel. (519)451-1751 Fax (519)453-3258
Media Contact, Gen. Sec., Rev. Harry Wuerch
E-mail: jwuerch@odyssey.on.ca

Officers
Gen. Sec., Rev. Harry Wuerch
Treas., Rev. David Ellyatt, 1795 Parkhurst Ave., London, ON N5V 2C4
E-mail: david.ellyatt@odyssey.on.ca

Periodicals
The Mantle

Independent Holiness Church

The former Holiness Movement of Canada merged with the Free Methodist Church in 1958. Some churches remained independent of this merger and they formed the Independent Holiness Church in 1960, in Kingston, Ontario. The doctrines are Methodist and Wesleyan. The General Conference is every three years, next meeting in 1998.

Headquarters
Rev. R. E. Votary, 1564 John Quinn Rd., R.R.1, Greely, ON K4P 1J9 Tel. (613)821-2237
Media Contact, Gen. Sec., Dwayne Reaney, 5025 River Rd. RR #1, Manotick, ON K4M 1B2 Tel. (613)692-3237

Officers
Gen. Supt., Rev. R. E. Votary, 1564 John Quinn Rd., Greeley, ON K4P 1J9

Gen. Sec., Dwayne Reaney
Additional Officers: E. Brown, 104-610 Pesehudoff Cresc., Saskatoon, SK S7N 4H5; D. Wallace, 1456 John Quinn Rd., R#1, Greely, ON K4P 1J9

Periodicals
Gospel Tidings

The Italian Pentecostal Church of Canada

This body had its beginnings in Hamilton, Ontario, in 1912 when a few people of an Italian Presbyterian Church banded themselves together for prayer and received a Pentecostal experience of the baptism in the Holy Spirit. Since 1912, there has been a close association with the teachings and practices of the Pentecostal Assemblies of Canada.

The work spread to Toronto, then to Montreal, where it also flourished. In 1959, the church was incorporated in the province of Quebec. The early leaders of this body were the Rev. Luigi Ippolito and the Rev. Ferdinand Zaffuto. The churches carry on their ministry in both the English and Italian languages.

Headquarters
6724 Fabre St., Montreal, QC H2G 2Z6 Tel. (514)593-1944 Fax (514)593-1835
Media Contact, Gen. Sec., Rev. John DellaForesta, 12216 Pierre Baillargeon, Montreal, QC H1E 6K1 Tel. (514)494-6969

Officers
Gen. Supt., Rev. Daniel Ippolito, 46 George Anderson Dr., Toronto, ON M6M 2Y8 Tel. (416)244-4005 Fax (416)244-0381
Gen. Sec., Rev. John DellaForesta, 12216 Pierre Baillargeon, Montreal, QC H1E 6K1 Tel. (514)494-6969
Gen. Treas., Rev. David Mortelliti, 6724 Fabre St., Montreal, QC H2G 2Z6 Tel. (514)593-1944 Fax (514)593-1835
Overseer, Rev. Mario Spiridigliozzi, 23 Wildwood Dr., Port Moody, BC V3H 4M4 Tel. (604)469-0788
Overseer, Rev. Tom Ciccarella, 1235 Minto Ave., LaSalle, ON N9J 3H0 Tel. (519)734-1340

Periodicals
Voce Evangelica/Evangel Voice

Jehovah's Witnesses

For details on Jehovah's Witnesses see "Religious Bodies in United States" in this edition of the *Yearbook*.

Headquarters
25 Columbia Heights, Brooklyn, NY 11201-2483 Tel. (718)560-5600 Fax (718)560-5619
Canadian Branch Office: Box 4100, Halton Hills, ON L7G 4Y4
Media Contact, Director, Public Affairs Office, James N. Pellechia

Media Contact, Public Affairs Office in Canada, Dennis Charland

Lutheran Church—Canada

Lutheran Church-Canada was established in 1959 at Edmonton, Alberta, as a federation of Canadian districts of the Lutheran Church - Missouri Synod; it was constituted in 1988 at Winnipeg, Manitoba, as an autonomous church.

The church confesses the Bible as both inspired and infallible, the only source and norm of doctrine and life and subscribes without reservation to the Lutheran Confessions as contained in the Book of Concord of 1580.

Headquarters
3074 Portage Ave., Winnipeg, MB R3K 0Y2 Tel. (204)895-3433 Fax (204)897-4319
Media Contact, Dir. of Comm., Ian Adnams

Officers
Pres., Rev. Ralph Mayan, 3074 Portage Ave., Winnipeg, MB R3K 0Y2
Vice-Pres., Rev. Dennis Putzman, 24 Valencia Dr., St. Catharines, ON L2T 3X8
2nd Vice-Pres., Rev. Daniel Rinderknecht, Box 1 Site 11 R.R. 4, Stony Plain, AB T7Z 1X4
3rd Vice-Pres., Rev. James Fritsche, 30 Dayton Dr., Winnipeg, MB R2J 3N1
Sec., Rev. William Ney, 4906 55th Ave., Stony Plain, AB T7Z 1B5
Treas., Allan Webster, C.A., 3074 Portage Ave., Winnipeg, MB R3K 0Y2

DISTRICT OFFICES
Alberta-British Columbia: Pres., Rev. D. Schiemann, 7100 Ada Blvd., Edmonton, AB T5B 4E4 Tel. (403)474-0063 Fax (403)477-9829
Central: Pres., Rev. T. Prachar, 1927 Grant Dr., Regina, SK S4S 4V6 Tel. (306)586-4434 Fax (306)586-0656
East: Pres., Rev. A. Maleske, 275 Lawrence Ave., Kitchener, ON N2M 1Y3 Tel. (519)578-6500 Fax (519)578-3369

Periodicals
The Canadian Lutheran

Mennonite Church Canada

Mennonite Church Canada began in 1902 as an organized fellowship of Mennonite immigrants from Russia clustered in southern Manitoba and around Rosthern, Saskatchewan. The first annual sessions were held in July, 1903. Its members hold to traditional Christian beliefs, believer's baptism and congregational polity. They emphasize practical Christianity: opposition to war, service to others and personal ethics. Further immigration from Russia in the 1920s and 1940s increased the group which is now located in all provinces from New Brunswick to British Columbia. In recent years a variety of other ethnic groups, including native Canadians, have joined the conference. This conference is affiliated with Mennonite Church USA whose offices are at Newton, Kansas.

Headquarters
600 Shaftesbury Blvd., Winnipeg, MB R3P 0M4 Tel. (204)888-6781 Fax (204)831-5675
Media Contact, Dan Dyck
Email: office@mennonitechurch.ca
Website: www.mennonitechurch.ca

Officers
Chpsn., Ron Sawatsky
Gen. Sec., Dan Nighswander

Periodicals
Canadian Mennonite

Mennonite Church (Canada)
This body has its origins in Europe in 1525 as an outgrowth of the Anabaptist movement. It was organized in North America in 1898. (See: Mennonite Church description in the section "Religious Bodies in the United States")

Headquarters
421 S. Second St., Ste. 600, Elkhart, IN 46516 Tel. (219)294-7131 Fax (219)293-3977
E-mail: mcgb@juno.com
Media Contact, J. Ron Byler, Associate General Secretary, Email: rbyler@juno.com

Periodicals
Canadian Mennonite (published jointly with Conference of Mennonites in Canada)

Moravian Church—please see Canadian District of the Moravian Church in America, Northern Province.

Mormans—please see the Church of Jesus Christ of Latter-Day Saints in Canada.

North American Baptist Conference
Churches belonging to this conference emanated from German Baptist immigrants of more than a century ago. Although scattered across Canada and the U.S., they are bound together by a common heritage, a strong spiritual unity, a Bible-centered faith and a deep interest in missions.

Note: The details of general organization, officers, and periodicals of this body will be found in the North American Baptist Conference directory in the "Religious Bodies in the United States" section of this *Yearbook*.

Headquarters
1 S. 210 Summit Ave., Oakbrook Terrace, IL 60181 Tel. (630)495-2000 Fax (630)495-3301
Media Contact, Marilyn Schaer

Officers
Exec. Dir., Dr. Philip Yntema

Periodicals
N.A.B. Today

The Old Catholic Church of Canada
The church was founded in 1948 in Hamilton, Ontario. The first bishop was the Rt. Rev. George Davis. The Old Catholic Church of Canada accepts all the doctrines of the Eastern Orthodox Churches and, therefore, not Papal Infallibility or the Immaculate Conception. The ritual is Western (Latin Rite) and is in the vernacular language. Celibacy is optional.

Headquarters
RR #1, Midland, ON L4R 4K3 Tel. (705)835-6940
Media Contact, Bishop, The Most Rev. David Thomson

Officers
Vicar General and Auxiliary Bishop, The Rt. Rev. A.C. Keating, PhD., 5066 Forest Grove Crest, Burlington, ON L7L GG6 Tel. (905)331-1113

Old Order Amish Church
This is the most conservative branch of the Mennonite Church and direct descendants of Swiss Brethren (Anabaptists) who emerged from the Reformation in Switzerland in 1525. The Amish, followers of Bishop Jacob Ammann, became a distinct group in 1693. They began migrating to North America about 1720; all of them still reside in the United States or Canada. They first migrated to Ontario in 1824 directly from Bavaria, Germany and also from Pennsylvania and Alsace-Lorraine. Since 1953 some Amish have migrated to Ontario from Ohio, Indiana and Iowa.

In 2000 there were 22 congregations in Ontario, each being autonomous. No membership figures are kept by this group, and there is no central headquarters. Each congregation is served by a bishop, two ministers and a deacon, all of whom are chosen from among the male members by lot for life.

CORRESPONDENT
Pathway Publishers, David Luthy, Rt. 4, Aylmer, ON N5H 2R3

Periodicals
Blackboard Bulletin; Herold der Wahreit; The Budget; The Diary; Die Botschaft; Family Life; Young Companion

Open Bible Faith Fellowship of Canada
This is an Evangelical, Full Gospel Fellowship of Churches and Ministries emphasizing evangelism, missions and the local church for success in the present harvest of souls. OBFF was chartered January 7, 1982.

Headquarters
Word of Life Church, P.O. Box 968, St. Catharines, ON L2R 6Z4 Tel. (905)646-0970
Media Contact, Exec. Dir., Randy Neilson

183

Officers

Pres., Peter Youngren
Exec. Dir., Randy Neilson
Sec., George Woodward
Treas., Ron Cosby

Orthodox Church in America (Canada Section)

The Archdiocese of Canada of the Orthodox Church in America was established in 1916. First organized by St. Tikhon, martyr Patriarch of Moscow, previously Archbishop of North America, it is part of the Russian Metropolia and its successor, the autocephalous Orthodox Church in America.

The Archdiocesan Council meets twice yearly, the General Assembly of the Archdiocese takes place every three years. The Archdiocese is also known as "Orthodox Church in Canada."

Headquarters

P.O. Box 179, Spencerville, ON K0E 1X0 Tel. (613)925-5226 (Office) (613)925-3004 (Home) Fax (613)925-1521
E-mail: zoe@recorder.ca

Officers

Bishop of Ottawa & Canada, The Rt. Rev. Seraphim Chancellor, V. Rev. Dennis Pinach, 17319
Treas., Nikita Lopoukhine, 55 Clarey Ave., Ottawa, ON K1S 2R6
Eastern Sec., Olga Jurgens, P.O. Box 179, Spencerville, ON K0E 1X0

ARCHDIOCESAN COUNCIL

Clergy Members: Rev. Lawrence Farley; V. Rev. Nicolas Boldireff; Rev. R.S. Kennaugh; Rev. Larry Reinheimer; V. Rev. John Tkachuk
Lay Members: Audrey Ewanchuk; Nicholas Ignatieff; David Grier; John Hadjinicolaou; Denis Lessard; Mother Sophia (Zion); David Rystephanuk
Ex Officio: Chancellor; Treas.; Eastern Sec.; Western Sec.

REPRESENTATIVES TO METROPOLITAN COUNCIL

V. Rev. John Tkachuk
Richard Schneider

Periodicals

Canadian Orthodox Messenger

Patriarchal Parishes of the Russian Orthodox Church in Canada

This is the diocese of Canada of the former Exarchate of North and South America of the Russian Orthodox Church. It was originally founded in 1897 by the Russian Orthodox Archdiocese in North America.

Headquarters

St. Barbara's Russian Orthodox Cathedral, 10105 96th St., Edmonton, AB T5H 2G3

Media Contact, Sec.-Treas., Victor Lopushinsky, #303 9566-101 Ave., Edmonton, AB T5H 0B4
Tel. (780)455-9071

Officers

Admn., Archbishop of Kashira, Most Rev. Mark, 10812-108 St., Edmonton, AB T5H 3A6 Tel. (780)420-9945

The Pentecostal Assemblies of Canada

This body is incorporated under the Dominion Charter of 1919 and is also recognized in the Province of Quebec as an ecclesiastical corporation. Its beginnings are to be found in the revivals at the turn of the century, and most of the first Canadian Pentecostal leaders came from a religious background rooted in the Holiness movements.

The original incorporation of 1919 was implemented among churches of eastern Canada only. In the same year, a conference was called in Moose Jaw, Saskatchewan, to which the late Rev. J. M. Welch, general superintendent of the then-organized Assemblies of God in the U.S., was invited. The churches of Manitoba and Saskatchewan were organized as the Western District Council of the Assemblies of God. They were joined later by Alberta and British Columbia. In 1921, a conference was held in Montreal, to which the general chairman of the Assemblies of God was invited. Eastern Canada also became a district of the Assemblies of God, joining Eastern and Western Canada as two districts in a single organizational union.

In 1920, at Kitchener, Ontario, eastern and western churches agreed to dissolve the Canadian District of the Assemblies of God and unite under the name The Pentecostal Assemblies of Canada.

Today the Pentecostal Assemblies of Canada operates throughout the nation and in about 30 countries around the world. Religious services are conducted in more than 25 different languages in the 1,100 local churches in Canada. Members and adherents number about 230,000. The number of local churches includes approximately 100 Native congregations.

Headquarters

6745 Century Ave., Mississauga, ON L5N 6P7 Tel. (905)542-7400 Fax (905)542-7313
Media Contact, Public Relations, Rev. W. A. Griffin
E-mail: wgriffin@paoc.org

Officers

Gen. Supt., Rev. William D. Morrow
Asst. Gen. Supt., Rev. E. Stewart Hunter
Gen. Sec.-Treas., Rev. David Ball

DISTRICT SUPERINTENDENTS

British Columbia: Rev. William R. Gibson, 5641 176 A St., Surrey, BC V3S 4G8 Tel. (604)576-9421 Fax (604)576-1499

Alberta: Rev. Lorne D. McAlister, 10585-111 St., #101, Edmonton, AB T5H 3E8 Tel. (403)426-0084 Fax (403)420-1318

Saskatchewan: Rev. Samuel O. Biro, 3488 Fairlight Dr., Saskatoon, SK S7M 3Z4 Tel. (306)652-6088 Fax (306)652-0199

Manitoba: Rev. Gordon V. Peters, 187 Henlow Bay, Winnipeg, MB R3Y 1G4 Tel. (204)488-6800 Fax (204)489-0499

Western Ontario: Rev. David Shepherd, 3214 S. Service Rd., Burlington, ON L7M 3J2 Tel. (905)637-5566 Fax (905)637-7558

Eastern Ontario and Quebec: Rev. Richard Hilsden, Box 13250, Kanata, ON K2K 1X4 Tel. (613)599-3422 Fax (613)599-7284

Maritime Provinces: Rev. David C. Slauenwhite, Box 1184, Truro, NS B2N 5H1 Tel. (902)895-4212 Fax (902)897-0705

BRANCH CONFERENCES

German Conference: Rev. Philip F. Kniesel, #310, 684 Belmont Ave., W, Kitchener, ON N2M 1N6

Slavic Conferences: Eastern District, Rev. A. Muravski, 44 Glenabbey Dr. Courtice, ON L1E 1B7; Western District, Rev. Michael Brandebura, 4108-134 Ave., Edmonton, AB T5A 3M2

Finnish Conference: Rev. E. Ahonen, 1920 Argyle Dr., Vancouver, BC V5P 2A8

Periodicals

Pentecostal Testimony; Resource: The National Leadership Magazine

The Pentecostal Assemblies of Newfoundland

This body began in 1911 and held its first meetings at Bethesda Mission at St. John's. It was incorporated in 1925 as The Bethesda Pentecostal Assemblies of Newfoundland and changed its name in 1930 to The Pentecostal Assemblies of Newfoundland.

Headquarters

57 Thorburn Rd., Box 8895, Stn. "A", St. John's, NF A1B 3T2 Tel. (709)753-6314 Fax (709)753-4945

Email: paon@paon.nf.ca

Media Contact, Gen. Supt., A. Earl Batstone, 57 Thorburn Rd., Box 8895, Stn. "A", St. John's, NF A1B 3T2

GENERAL EXECUTIVE OFFICERS

Gen. Supt. A. Earl Batstone, 57 Thorburn Rd., Box 8895, Stn. "A", St. John's, NF A1B 3T2

Gen. Sec.-Treas., Clarence Buckle, 57 Thorburn Rd., Box 8895, Stn. "A", St. John's, NF A1B 3T2

Ex. Dir. of Home Missions, Barry Q. Grimes, 57 Thorburn Rd., Box 8895, Stn. "A", St. John's, NF A1B 3T2

Ex. Dir. of Ch. Ministries, Robert H. Dewling, 57 Thorburn Rd., Box 8895, Stn. "A", St. John's, NF A1B 3T2

PROVINCIAL DIRECTORS

Sunday School Ministries, Alvin F. Peddle, Box 40, Baytona, NF A0G 2J0

Children's Ministries, Lorinda R. Moulton, Box 56, New Harbour, NF A0B 2P0

Women's Ministries, Nancy L. Hunter, 12 Harp Place, Paradise, NF A1L 1G9

Men's Ministries, Norman C. Joy, 2 Firgreen Ave., Mount Pearl, NF A1N 1T7

Youth Ministries, B. Dean Brenton, Box 21100, St. John's, NF A1B 3L5

Mature Adult Ministries, Clayton Rice, 29 Diana Rd., St. John's, NF A1B 1H7

Family Ministries, Eva M. Winsor, 26 Ireland Dr., Grand Falls-Windsor, NF A2A 2S6

AUXILIARY SERVICES

Chaplain for Institutions, Roy A. Burden, 293 Frecker Dr., St. John's, NF A1E 5T8

Pentecostal Senior Citizens Home Administrator, Beverley Bellefleur, Box 130, Clarke's Beach, NF A0A 1W0

Evergreen Manor, Summerford, NF A0G 4E0

Pastoral Enrichment Ministries, Gary D. & Eva M. Winsor, 26 Ireland Dr., Grand Falls-Windsor, NF A2A 2S6

Chaplain, Memorial University of Newfoundland, Gregory R. Dewling, Memorial University of Newfoundland, Box 102, St. John's, NF A1C 5S7

Emmanuel Convention Centre Administrator, Ronald M. Dicks, Box 1558, Lewisporte, NF A0G 3A0

World Missions Promotions, A. Scott Hunter, 12 Harp Place, Paradise, NF A1L 1G9

Managing Editor, Good Tidings, Burton K. Janes, 57 Thornburn Rd., Box 8895, Stn. "A", St. John's, NF A1B 3T2

Periodicals

Good Tidings

Plymouth Brethren—please see Christian Brethren.

Presbyterian Church in America (Canadian Section)

Canadian congregations of the Reformed Presbyterian Church, Evangelical Synod, became a part of the Presbyterian Church in America when the RPCES joined PCA in June 1982. Some of the churches were in predecessor bodies of the RPCES, which was the product of a 1965 merger of the Reformed Presbyterian Church in North America, General Synod and the Evangelical Presbyterian Church. Others came into existence later as a part of the home missions work of RPCES. Congregations are located in seven provinces, and the PCA is continuing church extension work in Canada. The denomination is committed to world evangelization and to a continuation of historic Presbyterianism. Its officers are required to subscribe to the Reformed faith as set forth in the Westminster Confession of Faith and Catechisms.

Headquarters

Media Contact, Correspondent, Doug Codling, Faith Reformed Presbyterian Church, 2581 E. 45th St., Vancouver, BC V5R 3B9 Tel. (604)438-8755

Periodicals

Equip for Ministry; Multiply; Network

Presbyterian Church in Canada

This is the nonconcurring portion of the Presbyterian Church in Canada that did not become a part of The United Church of Canada in 1925.

Headquarters

50 Wynford Dr., Toronto, ON M3C 1J7 Tel. (416)441-1111 Fax (416)441-2825
Website: www.presbycan.ca
Media Contact, Principal Clk., Rev. Stephen Kendall

Periodicals

Channels; The Presbyterian Message; Presbyterian Record; Glad Tidings; La Vie Chrétienne

Reformed Church in Canada

The Canadian branch of the Reformed Church in America consists of 41 churches organized under the Council of the Reformed Church in Canada and within the classis of Ontario (24 churches), British Columbia (10 churches), and Canadian Prairies (7 churches). The Reformed Church in America was established in 1628 by the earliest Dutch settlers in America as the Reformed Protestant Dutch Church. It is evangelical in theology and presbyterian in government.

Headquarters

Gen. Sec., Rev. Wesley Granberg- Michaelson, 475 Riverside Dr., Rm. 1812, New York, NY 10115 Tel. (212)870-2841 Fax (212)870-2499

Officers

Council of the Reformed Church in Canada, Exec. Sec., Rev. James Moerman, Reformed Church Center, RR #4, Cambridge, ON N1R 5S5 Tel. (519)622-1777
Media Contact, Dir., Communication and Production Services, Kim Nathan Baker, 4500 60th St., SE, Grand Rapids, MI 49512 Tel. (616)698-7071 Fax (616)698-6606

The Reformed Episcopal Church of Canada

The Reformed Episcopal Church is a separate entity. It was established in Canada by an act of incorporation given royal assent on June 2, 1886. It maintains the founding principles of episcopacy (in historic succession from the apostles), Anglican liturgy and Reformed doctrine and evangelical zeal. In practice it continues to recognize the validity of certain nonepiscopal orders

of evangelical ministry. The Church has reunited with the Reformed Episcopal Church and is now composed of two Dioceses in this body - the Diocese of Central and Eastern Canada and the Diocese of Western Canada and Alaska. The current Presiding Bishop is Bishop Leonard Riches in Philadelphia.

Headquarters

Box 2532, New Liskeard, ON P0J 1P0 Tel. (705)647-4565 Fax (705)647-4565
Email: fed@nt.net
Website: www.recus.org
Media Contact, Pres., Rt. Rev. Michael Fedechko, M.Div., D.D.

Officers

Pres., Rt. Rev. Michael Fedechko, 320 Armstrong St., New Liskeard, ON P0J 1P0
Sec., Janet Davidson, 224 Haliburton, New Liskeard, ON P0J 1P0

BISHOPS

Diocese of Central & Eastern Canada: Rt. Rev. Michael Fedechko, 320 Armstrong St., New Liskeard, ON P0J 1P0 Tel. (705)647-4565 Fax (705)647-4565
Diocese of Western Canada & Alaska: Rt. Rev. Charles W. Dorrington, 54 Blanchard St., Victoria, BC V8X 4R1 Tel. (604)744-5014 Fax (604)388-5891

Periodicals

The Messenger

Reinland Mennonite Church

This group was founded in 1958 when 10 ministers and approximately 600 members separated from the Sommerfelder Mennonite Church. In 1968, four ministers and about 200 members migrated to Bolivia. The church has work in five communities in Manitoba and one in Ontario

Headquarters

Bishop William H. Friesen, P.O. Box 96, Rosenfeld, MB R0G 1X0 Tel. (204)324-6339
Media Contact, Deacon, Henry Wiebe, Box 2587, Winkler, MB R6W 4C3 Tel. (204)325-8487

Reorganized Church of Jesus Christ of Latter Day Saints

Founded April 6, 1830, by Joseph Smith, Jr., the church was reorganized under the leadership of the founder's son, Joseph Smith III, in 1860. The Church is established in 38 countries including the United States and Canada, with nearly a quarter of a million members. A biennial world conference is held in Independence, Missouri. The current president is W. Grant McMurray.

Headquarters

World Headquarters Complex: P.O. Box 1059, Independence, MO 64051 Tel. (816)833-1000 Fax (816)521-3095

Ontario Regional Ofc.: 390 Speedvale Ave. E., Guelph, ON N1E 1N5

Media Contact, Public Relations Coordinator, Susan Naylor

CANADIAN REGIONS AND DISTRICTS

North Plains & Prairie Provinces Region: Regional Admn., Kenneth Barrows, 84 Hidden Park NW, Calgary, AB T3A 5K5; Alberta District, R.A.(Ryan) Levitt, #325, 51369 Range Rd., Sherwood Park, AB T8C 1H3; Saskatchewan District, Robert G. Klombies, 202 Saskatchewan Crescent W., Saskatoon, SK S7M 0A4

Pacific Northwest Region: Regional Admn., Raymond Peter, P.O. Box 18469, 4820 Morgan, Seattle, WA 98118; British Columbia District, E. Carl Bolger, 410-1005 McKenzie Ave., Victoria, BC V8X 4A9

Ontario Region: Regional Admn., Larry D. Windland, 390 Speedvale Ave. E., Guelph, ON N1E 1N5; Chatham District, David R. Wood, 127 Mount Pleasant Crescent, Wallaceburg, ON N8A 5A3; Grand River District, C. Allen Taylor, R R 2, Orangeville, ON L9W 2Y9; London District, William T. Leney, Jr., 18 Glendon Road, Stratford, ON N5A 5B3; Niagara District, Willis L. Hopkin, 765 Rymal Rd. E., Hamilton, ON L8W 1B6; Northern Ontario District, Douglas G. Bolger, 482 Timmins St., North Bay, ON P1B 4K7; Ottawa District, Marion Smith, 70 Mayburry St., Hull, QC J9A 2E9; Owen Sound District, Robin M. Duff, P.O. Box 52, Owen Sound, ON N1K 5P1; Toronto Metropole, Kerry J. Richards, 74 Parkside Dr., Brampton, ON L6Y 2G9

Periodicals

Saints Herald

The Roman Catholic Church in Canada— please see The Catholic Church in Canada.

Romanian Orthodox Church in America (Canadian Parishes)

The first Romanian Orthodox immigrants in Canada called for Orthodox priests from their native country of Romania. Between 1902 and 1914, they organized the first Romanian parish communities and built Orthodox churches in different cities and farming regions of western Canada (Alberta, Saskatchewan, Manitoba) as well as in the eastern part (Ontario and Quebec).

In 1929, the Romanian Orthodox parishes from Canada joined with those of the United States in a Congress held in Detroit, Michigan, and asked the Holy Synod of the Romanian Orthodox Church of Romania to establish a Romanian Orthodox Missionary Episcopate in America. The first Bishop, Policarp (Morushca), was elected and consecrated by the Holy Synod of the Romanian Orthodox Church and came to the United States in 1935. He established his

headquarters in Detroit with jurisdiction over all the Romanian Orthodox parishes in the United States and Canada.

In 1950, the Romanian Orthodox Church in America (i.e. the Romanian Orthodox Missionary Episcopate in America) was granted administrative autonomy by the Holy Synod of the Romanian Orthodox Church of Romania, and only doctrinal and canonical ties remain with this latter body.

In 1974 the Holy Synod of the Romanian Orthodox Church of Romania recognized and approved the elevation of the Episcopate to the rank of the Romanian Orthodox Archdiocese in America and Canada.

Headquarters

Canadian Office: Descent of the Holy Ghost, Romanian Orthodox Church, 2895 Seminole St., Windsor, ON N8Y 1Y1

Media Contact, Most Rev. Archbishop Victorin, 19959 Riopelle St., Detroit, MI 48203 Tel. (313)893-8390

Officers

Archbishop, Most Rev. Archbishop Victorin, 19959 Riopelle St., Detroit, MI 48203 Tel. (313)893-8390

Vicar, V. Rev. Archim., Dr. Vasile Vasilachi, 45-03 48th Ave., Woodside, Queens, NY 11377 Tel. (718)784-4453

Cultural Councilor, Very Rev. Fr. Nicolae Ciurea, 19 Murray St. W., Hamilton, ON L8L 1B1 Tel. (416)523-8268

Admn. Councilor, V. Rev. Fr. Mircea Panciuk, 11024-165th Ave., Edmonton, AB T5X 1X9

Sec., Rev. Fr. Simion John Catau, 31227 Roan Dr., Warren, MI 48093 Tel. (810)264-1924

The Romanian Orthodox Episcopate of America (Jackson, MI)

This body of Eastern Orthodox Christians of Romanian descent is part of the Autocephalous Orthodox Church in America. For complete description and listing of officers, please see chapter 3, "Religious Bodies in the United States."

Headquarters

2522 Grey Tower Rd., Jackson, MI 49201 Tel. (517)522-4800 Fax (517)522-5907

E-mail: roeasolia@aol.com

Website: www.roea.org

Mailing Address, P.O. Box 309, Grass Lake, MI 49240-0309

Media Contact, Ed./Sec., Rev. Dea. David Oancea, P.O. Box 185, Grass Lake, MI 49240-0185 Tel. (517)522-3656 Fax (517)522-5907

Officers

Ruling Bishop, Rt. Rev. Nathaniel Popp

Deans for the Deanery of Canada, Western Provinces, Very Rev. Daniel Nenson, 2855 Helmsing St., Regina, SK S4V 0W7 Tel.

(306)761-2379; Eastern Provinces, Very Rev. Dumitru Paun, 47 Adelaide S., London, ON N5Z 3K1 Tel. (519)858-4065

Periodicals

Solia—The Herald; Good News- Buna Vestre (in Canada only)

Russian Orthodox Church—please see the Patriarchal Parishes of the Russian Orthodox Church in Canada.

The Salvation Army in Canada

The Salvation Army, an evangelical branch of the Christian Church, is an international movement founded in 1865 in London, England. The ministry of Salvationists, consisting of clergy (officers) and laity, comes from a commitment to Jesus Christ and is revealed in practical service, regardless of race, color, creed, sex or age.

The goals of The Salvation Army are to preach the gospel, disseminate Christian truths, instill Christian values, enrich family life and improve the quality of all life.

To attain these goals, The Salvation Army operates local congregations, provides counseling, supplies basic human needs and undertakes spiritual and moral rehabilitation of any needy people who come within its influence.

A quasi-military system of government was set up in 1878, by General William Booth, founder (1829-1912). Converts from England started Salvation Army work in London, Ontario, in 1882. Two years later, Canada was recognized as a Territorial Command, and since 1933 it has included Bermuda. An act to incorporate the Governing Council of The Salvation Army in Canada received royal assent on May 19, 1909.

Headquarters

2 Overlea Blvd., Toronto, ON M4H 1P4 Tel. (416)425-2111
Media Contact, Major Robert MacKenzie, Tel. (416)425-6153 Fax (416)425-6157
E-mail: bob.mackenzie@sallynet.org
Website: www.sallynet.org

Officers

Territorial Commander, Commissioner Norman Howe
Territorial Pres., Women's Organizations, Commissioner Marian Howe
Chief Sec., Col. Clyde Moore
Sec. for Personnel, Lt. Col. Merv Leach
Bus. Adm. Sec., Lt. Col. Peter Wood
Fin. Sec., Major Susan McMillan
Program Sec., Lt. Col. David Luginbuhl
Community Rel. and Communications Secretary, Major Robert Mac Kenzie
Property Sec., Col. Donald Copple

Periodicals

The War Cry; Faith & Friends; En Avant!; The Young Soldier; The Edge; Catherine; Horizons

Serbian Orthodox Church in the U.S.A. and Canada, Diocese of Canada

The Serbian Orthodox Church is an organic part of the Eastern Orthodox Church. As a local church it received its autocephaly from Constantinople in A.D. 1219. The Patriarchal seat of the church today is in Belgrade, Yugoslavia. In 1921, a Serbian Orthodox Diocese in the United States of America and Canada was organized. In 1963, it was reorganized into three dioceses, and in 1983 a fourth diocese was created for the Canadian part of the church. The Serbian Orthodox Church is in absolute doctrinal unity with all other local Orthodox Churches.

Headquarters

7470 McNiven Rd., RR 3, Campbellville, ON L0P 1B0 Tel. (905)878-0043 Fax (905)878-1909
E-mail: vladika@istocnik.com
Website: www. istocnik.com
Media Contact, Rt. Rev. Georgije

Officers

Serbian Orthodox Bishop of Canada, Rt. Rev. Georgije
Dean of Western Deanery, V. Rev. Mirko Malinovic, 924 12th Ave., Regina, SK S4N 0K7 Tel. (306)352-2917
Dean of Eastern Deanery, V. Rev. Zivorad Subotic, 351 Mellville Ave., Westmount, QC H3Z 2Y7 Tel. + Fax (514)931-6664

Periodicals

Istocnik, Herald of the Serbian Orthodox Church— Canadian Diocese

Seventh-day Adventist Church in Canada

The Seventh-day Adventist Church in Canada is part of the worldwide Seventh-day Adventist Church with headquarters in Washington, D.C. (See "Religious Bodies in the United States" section of this *Yearbook* for a fuller description.) The Seventh-day Adventist Church in Canada was organized in 1901 and reorganized in 1932.

Headquarters

1148 King St., E., Oshawa, ON L1H 1H8 Tel. (905)433-0011 Fax (905)433-0982
Media Contact, Orville Parchment

Officers

Pres., Orville Parchment
Sec., Claude Sabot
Treas., Donald Upson

DEPARTMENTS

Under Treas., Brian Christenson
Asst. Treas., Clareleen Ivany
Computer Services, Brian Ford
Coord. of Ministries, John Howard
Education, Mike Lekic

Public Affairs/Religious Liberty Trust, Karnik Doukmetzian

Periodicals
Canadian Adventist Messenger

Southern Baptists—please see Canadian Convention of Southern Baptists.

Syriac Orthodox Church of Antioch

The Syriac Orthodox Church professes the faith of the first three ecumenical councils of Nicaea, Constantinople and Ephesus and numbers faithful in the Middle East, India, the Americas, Europe and Australia. It traces its origin to the Patriarchate established in Antioch by St. Peter the Apostle and is under the supreme ecclesiastical jurisdiction of His Holiness the Syrian Orthodox Patriarch of Antioch and All the East, now residing in Damascus, Syria.

The Archdiocese of the Syrian Orthodox Church in the U.S. and Canada was formally established in 1957. In 1995, the Archdiocese of North America was divided into three separate Patriarchal Vicariates, including one for Canada. The first Syrian Orthodox faithful came to Canada in the 1890s and formed the first Canadian parish in Sherbrooke, Quebec. Today five official parishes of the Archdiocese exist in Canada—two in Quebec and three in Ontario. There is also an official mission congregation in Calgary, Alberta and Ottawa, Ontario.

Headquarters
Archdiocese of Canada, The New Archdiocesan Centre, 4375 Henri-Bourassa Ouest, St.-Laurent, Quebec H4L 1A5, Canada Tel. (514)334-6993 Fax (514)334-8233

Officers
Archbishop Mor Timotheos Aphrem Aboodi

Ukrainian Orthodox Church of Canada

Toward the end of the 19th century many Ukrainian immigrants settled in Canada. In 1918, a group of these pioneers established the Ukrainian Orthodox Church of Canada (UOCC), today the largest Ukrainian Orthodox Church beyond the borders of Ukraine. In 1990, the UOCC entered into a eucharistic union with the Ecumenical Patriarchate at Constantinople (Istanbul).

Headquarters
Ukrainian Orthodox Church of Canada, Office of the Consistory, 9 St. Johns Ave., Winnipeg, MB R2W 1G8 Tel. (204)586-3093 Fax (204)582-5241
E-mail: consistory@uocc.ca
Website: www. uocc.ca
Media Contacts, Rev. Fr. Andrew Jarmus, 9st. John's Ave., Winnipeg, MB R2W 1G8, Tel. (204)586-3093 Fax (204)582-5241; Ms. M. Zurek, 9 St. Johns Ave., Winnipeg, MB R2W 1G8 Tel. (204)586-3093 Fax (204)582-5241

Officers
Primate, Most Rev. Metropolitan Wasyly Fedak, 9 St. Johns Ave., Winnipeg, MB R2W 1G8 Tel. (204)586-3093 Fax (204)582-5241
Chancellor, Rt. Rev. Dr. Oleg Krawchenko

Periodicals
Visnyk/The Herald/Le Messager (newspaper)
Ridna Nyva (almanac/annual)

Union d'Eglises Baptistes Françaises au Canada

Baptist churches in French Canada first came into being through the labors of two missionaries from Switzerland, Rev. Louis Roussy and Mme. Henriette Feller, who arrived in Canada in 1835. The earliest church was organized in Grande Ligne (now Ste.-Blaise), Quebec in 1838.

By 1900 there were 7 churches in the province of Quebec and 13 French-language Baptist churches in the New England states. The leadership was totally French Canadian.

By 1960, the process of Americanization had caused the disappearance of the French Baptist churches. During the 1960s, Quebec as a society, began rapidly changing in all its facets: education, politics, social values and structures. Mission, evangelism and church growth once again flourished. In 1969, in response to the new conditions, the Grande Ligne Mission passed control of its work to the newly formed Union of French Baptist Churches in Canada, which then included 8 churches. By 1990 the French Canadian Baptist movement had grown to include 25 congregations.

The Union d'Églises Baptistes Françaises au Canada is a member body of the Canadian Baptist Ministries and thus is affiliated with the Baptist World Alliance.

Headquarters
2285 avenue Papineau, Montreal, QC H2K 4J5 Tel. (514)526-6643 Fax (514)526-9269
Media Contact, Gen. Sec., Rev. David Affleck

Officers
Sec. Gen., Rev. Roland Grimard

Periodicals
www.UnionBaptiste.com (Internet)

Union of Spiritual Communities of Christ (Orthodox Doukhobors in Canada)

The Doukhobors are groups of Canadians of Russian origin living in the western provinces of Canada, but their beginnings in Russia are unknown. The name "Doukhobors," or "spirit Wrestlers," was given in derision by the Russian Orthodox clergy in Russia as far back as 1785. Victims of decades of persecution in Russia,

189

about 7,500 Doukhobors arrived in Canada in 1899.

The teaching of the Doukhobors is penetrated with the Gospel spirit of love. Worshiping God in the spirit, they affirm that the outward church and all that is performed in it and concerns it has no importance for them; the church is where two or three are gathered together, united in the name of Christ. Their teaching is founded on tradition, which they call the "Book of Life," because it lives in their memory and hearts. In this book are sacred songs or chants, partly composed independently, partly formed out of the contents of the Bible, and these are committed to memory by each succeeding generation. Doukhobors observe complete pacifism and non-violence.

The Doukhobors were reorganized in 1938 by their leader, Peter P. Verigin, shortly before his death, into the Union of Spiritual Communities of Christ, commonly called Orthodox Doukhobors. It is headed by a democratically elected Executive Committee which executes the will and protects the interests of the people.

At least 99 percent of the Doukhobors are law-abiding, pay taxes, and "do not burn or bomb or parade in the nude" as they say a fanatical offshoot called the "sons of Freedom" does.

Headquarters

USCC Central Office, Box 760, Grand Forks, BC V0H 1H0 Tel. (250)442-8252 Fax (250) 442-3433
Media Contact, John J. Verigin, Sr.

Officers

Hon. Chmn. of the Exec. Comm., John J. Verigin, Sr.
Chpsn., Andrew Evin

Periodicals

ISKRA

United Baptist Convention of the Atlantic Provinces

The United Baptist Convention of the Atlantic Provinces is the largest Baptist Convention in Canada. Through the Canadian Baptist Ministries, it is a member of the Baptist World Alliance.

In 1763 two Baptist churches were organized in Atlantic Canada, one in Sackville, New Brunswick and the other in Wolfville, Nova Scotia. Although both these churches experienced crises and lost continuity, they recovered and stand today as the beginning of organized Baptist work in Canada.

Nine Baptist churches met in Lower Granville, Nova Scotia in 1800 and formed the first Baptist Association in Canada. By 1846 the Maritime Baptist Convention was organized, consisting of 169 churches. Two streams of Baptist life merged in 1905 to form the United Baptist Convention. This is how the term "United Baptist" was derived. Today there are 554 churches within 21 associations across the Convention.

The Convention has two educational institutions: Atlantic Baptist University in Moncton, New Brunswick, a Christian Liberal Arts University, and Acadia Divinity College in Wolfville, Nova Scotia, a Graduate School of Theology. The Convention engages in world mission through Canadian Baptist Ministries, the all-Canada mission agency. In addition to an active program of home mission, evangelism, training, social action and stewardship, the Convention operates ten senior citizen complexes and a Christian bookstore.

Headquarters

1655 Manawagonish Rd., Saint John, NB E2M 3Y2 Tel. (506)635-1922 Fax (506)635-0366
E-mail: ubcap@fundy.net
Media Contact, Interim Dir. of Communications, Dr. Eugene M. Thompson

Officers

Pres., Dr. Robert Wilson
Vice-Pres., Dr. Rick Thomas
Exec. Min., Dr. Harry G. Gardner
Dir. of Admn. & Treas., Daryl MacKenzie
Dir. of Home Missions & Church Planting, Dr. David Cook
Dir. of Evangelism, Dr. Malcolm Beckett
Dir. of Training, Rev. Marilyn McCormick

United Brethren Church in Canada

Founded in 1767 in Lancaster County, Pennsylvania, missionaries came to Canada about 1850. The first class was held in Kitchener in 1855, and the first building was erected in Port Elgin in 1867.

The Church of the United Brethren in Christ had its beginning with Philip William Otterbein and Martin Boehm, who were leaders in the revivalistic movement in Pennsylvania and Maryland during the late 1760s.

Headquarters

302 Lake St., Huntington, IN 46750 Tel. (219)356-2312 Fax (219)356-4730

GENERAL OFFICERS

Pres., Rev. Brian Magnus, 120 Fife Rd., Guelph, ON N1H 6Y2 Tel. (519)836-0180
Treas., Brian Winger, 2233 Hurontario St., Apt. 916, Mississauga, ON L5A 2E9 Tel. (905)275-8140

The United Church of Canada

The United Church of Canada was formed on June 10, 1925, through the union of the Methodist Church, Canada, the Congregational Union of Canada, the Council of Local Union Churches and 70 percent of the Presbyterian Church in Canada. The union culminated years of negotiation between the churches, all of which had integral associations with the development and history of the nation.

In fulfillment of its mandate to be a uniting as well as a United Church, the denomination has been enriched by other unions during its history. The Wesleyan Methodist Church of Bermuda joined in 1930. On January 1, 1968, the Canada Conference of the Evangelical United Brethren became part of The United Church of Canada. At various times, congregations of other Christian communions have also become congregations of the United Church.

The United Church of Canada is a full member of the World Methodist Council, the World Alliance of Reformed Churches (Presbyterian and Congregational), and the Canadian and World Councils of Churches.

The United Church is the largest Protestant denomination in Canada.

NATIONAL OFFICES
The United Church House, 3250 Bloor St. W., Ste. 300, Etobicoke, ON M8X 2Y4 Tel. (416)231-5931 Fax (416)231-3103
Email: info@uccan.org
Website: www.uccan.org
Media Contact, Manager Public Relations & Info. Unit, Mary-Frances Denis

GENERAL COUNCIL
Mod., Marion Pardy
Gen. Sec., K. Virginia Coleman
Human Resources, Sec., Anne Shirley Sutherland
Theology, Faith & Ecumenism, Sec., Rev. S. Peter Wyatt
Archivist, Sharon Larade, 73 Queen's Park Cr., E., Toronto, ON M5C 1K7 Tel. (416)585-4563 Fax (416)585-4584
Email: uccvu.archives@utoronto.ca
Website: www. vicu.utoronto.ca/archives/archives. htm

ADMINISTRATIVE DIVISIONS
Communication: Gen. Sec., Gordon How
Finance: Gen. Sec., Steven Adams
Ministry Personnel & Education: Gen. Sec., Rev. Steven Chambers
Mission in Canada: Gen. Sec., Rev. David Iverson
World Outreach: Gen. Sec., Rev. Christopher Ferguson

CONFERENCE EXECUTIVE SECRETARIES
Alberta and Northwest: Rev. George H. Rodgers, 9911-48 Ave., NW, Edmonton, AB T6E 5V6 Tel. (780)435-3995 Fax (780)438-3317
Email: coffice@anwconf.com
All Native Circle: Speaker, Dianne Cooper (interim), 367 Selkirk Ave., Winnipeg, MB R2W 2N3 Tel. (204)582-5518 Fax (204)582-6649
Email: allnat@mb.aibn.com
Bay of Quinte: Rev. Wendy Bulloch, P.O. Box 700, 67 Mill St., Frankford, ON K0K 2C0 Tel. (613)398-1051 Fax (613)398-8894
Email: bayq.conference@sympatico.ca

British Columbia: Rev. Debra A. Bowman, 4383 Rumble St., Burnaby, BC V5J 2A2 Tel. (604)431-0434 Fax (604)431-0439
Email: bcconf@infoserve.net
Hamilton: Rev. Roslyn A. Campbell, Box 100, Carlisle, ON L0R 1H0 Tel. (905)659-3343 Fax (905)659-7766
Email: office@hamconf.org
London: W. Peter Scott, 359 Windermere Rd., London, ON N6G 2K3 Tel. (519)672-1930 Fax (519)439-2800
Email: lonconf@execulink.com
Manitoba and Northwestern Ontario: Rev. Roger A. Coll, 170 Saint Mary's Rd., Winnipeg, MB R2H 1H9 Tel. (204)233-8911 Fax (204)233-3289
Email: office@confmnwo.mb.ca
Manitou: Rev. Rev. Jim Sinclair, 319 McKenzie Ave., North Bay, ON P1B 7E3 Tel. (705)474-3350 Fax (705)497-3597
Email: manitou@efni.com
Maritime: Rev. Catherine H. Gaw, 32 York St., Sackville, NB E4L 4R4 Tel. (506)536-1334 Fax (506)536-2900
Email: marconf@nbnet.nb,ca
Montreal and Ottawa: Rev. Rev. David C. Estey, 225-50 Ave., Lachine, QC H8T 2T7 Tel. (514)634-7015 Fax (514)634-2489
Email: lachine@istar.ca
Newfoundland and Labrador: Rev. Clarence R. Sellers, 320 Elizabeth Ave., St. John's, NF A1B 1T9 Tel. (709)754-0386 Fax (709)754-8336
Email: newlab@seascape.com
Saskatchewan: Rev. Bruce G. Faurschou (interim), 418 A. McDonald St., Regina, SK S4N 6E1 Tel. (306)721-3311 Fax (306)721-3171
Email: ucskco@sk.sympatico.ca
Toronto: Rev. David W. Allen, 65 Mayall Ave., Downsview, ON M3L 1E7 Tel. (416)241-2677 Fax (416)241-2689
Email: torconf@web.net

Periodicals
Fellowship Magazine; United Church Observer; Mandate; Aujourd'hui Credo

United Pentecostal Church in Canada
This body, which is affiliated with the United Pentecostal Church, International, with headquarters in Hazelwood, Missouri, accepts the Bible standard of full salvation, which is repentance, baptism by immersion in the name of the Lord Jesus Christ for the remission of sins and the baptism of the Holy Ghost, with the initial signs of speaking in tongues as the Spirit gives utterance. Other tenets of faith include the Oneness of God in Christ, holiness, divine healing and the second coming of Jesus Christ.

Headquarters
United Pentecostal Church Intl., 8855 Dunn Rd., Hazelwood, MO 63042 Tel. (314)837-7300 Fax (314)837-4503

Media Contact, Gen. Sec.-Treas., Rev. C. M. Becton

DISTRICT SUPERINTENDENTS

Atlantic: Rev. Harry Lewis, P.O. Box 1046, Perth Andover, NB E0J 1V0

British Columbia: Rev. Paul V. Reynolds, 13447-112th Ave., Surrey, BC V3R 2E7

Canadian Plains: Rev. Johnny King, 615 Northmoon Dr., NW, Calgary, AB T2K 3J6

Central Canadian: Rev. Clifford Heaslip, 4215 Roblin Blvd., Winnipeg, MB R3R 0E8

Newfoundland: Jack Cunningham

Nova Scotia: Superintendent, Rev. John D. Mean, P.O. Box 2183, D.E.P.S., Dartmouth, NS B2W 3Y2

Ontario: Rev. Carl H. Stephenson, 63 Castlegrove Blvd., Don Mills, ON M3A 1L3

Universal Fellowship of Metropolitan Community Churches

The Universal Fellowship of Metropolitan Community Churches is a Christian church which directs a special ministry within, and on behalf of, the gay and lesbian community. Involvement, however, is not exclusively limited to gays and lesbians; U.F.M.C.C. tries to stress its openness to all people and does not call itself a "gay church."

Founded in 1968 in Los Angeles by the Rev. Troy Perry, the U.F.M.C.C. has over 300 member congregations worldwide. Congregations are in Vancouver, Edmonton, Windsor, London, Toronto, Ottawa (2), Guelph, Fredericton, Winnipeg, Halifax, Barrie and Belleville.

Theologically, the Metropolitan Community Churches stand within the mainstream of Christian doctrine, being "ecumenical" or "inter-denominational" in stance (albeit a "denomination" in their own right).

The Metropolitan Community Churches are characterized by their belief that the love of God is a gift, freely offered to all people, regardless of sexual orientation and that no incompatibility exists between human sexuality and the Christian faith.

The Metropolitan Community Churches in Canada were founded in Toronto in 1973 by the Rev. Robert Wolfe.

Headquarters

Media Contact, Marcie Wexler, 33 Holly St., #1117, Toronto, ON M4S 2G8 Tel. (416)487-8429 Fax (416)932-1836

Officers

Eastern Canadian District: Rev. Marcie Wexler, 33 Holly St., #1117, Toronto, ON M4S 2G8 Tel. (416)487-8429

The Wesleyan Church of Canada

This group is the Canadian portion of The Wesleyan Church which consists of the Atlantic and Central Canada districts. The Central Canada District of the former Wesleyan Methodist Church of America was organized at Winchester, Ontario, in 1889 and the Atlantic District was founded in 1888 as the Alliance of the Reformed Baptist Church, which merged with the Wesleyan Methodist Church in July, 1966.

The Wesleyan Methodist Church and the Pilgrim Holiness Church merged in June, 1968, to become The Wesleyan Church. The doctrine is evangelical and Wesleyan Arminian and stresses holiness beliefs. For more details, consult the U.S. listing under The Wesleyan Church.

Headquarters

The Wesleyan Church Intl. Center, P.O. Box 50434, Indianapolis, IN 46250-0434

Media Contact, Dist. Supt., Central Canada, Rev. Donald E. Hodgins, 3 Applewood Dr., Ste. 101, Belleville, ON K8P 4E3 Tel. (613)966-7527 Fax (613)968-6190

DISTRICT SUPERINTENDENTS

Central Canada: Rev. Donald E. Hodgins, 3 Applewood Dr., Ste.101, Belleville, ON K8P 4E3

Email: ccd@on.aibn.com

Atlantic: Rev. Dr. H. C. Wilson, 1600 Main st., Ste. 216, Moncton, NB E1E 1G5

Email: ncwilson@nbnet.nb.ca

Periodicals

Central Canada; The Clarion

Religious Bodies in Canada
Arranged by Families

The following list of religious bodies appearing in the Directory Section of the *Yearbook* shows the "families" or related clusters into which Canadian religious bodies can be grouped. For example, there are many communions that can be grouped under the heading "Baptist" for historical and theological reasons. It should not be assumed, however, that all denominations under one family heading are necessarily consistent in belief or practice. The family clusters tend to represent historical factors more often than theological or practical ones. These family categories provide one of the major pitfalls when compiling church statistics because there is often a tendency to combine the statistics by "families" for analytical and comparative purposes. Such combined totals are deeply flawed, even though they are often used as variables for sociological analysis. The arrangement by families offered here is intended only as a general guide for conceptual organization when viewing the broad sweep of Canadian religious culture.

Religious bodies that can not be categorized under family headings appear alphabetically and are not indented in the following list.

The Anglican Church of Canada
Apostolic Christian Church (Nazarene)
Armenian Evangelical Church
Associated Gospel Churches

Baptist Bodies

Association of Regular Baptist Churches (Canada)
Baptist Convention of Ontario and Quebec
Baptist General Conference of Canada
Baptist Union of Western Canada
Canadian Baptist Ministries
Canadian Convention of Southern Baptists
The Fellowship of Evangelical Baptist Churches in Canada
Free Will Baptists
North American Baptist Conference
Union d'Eglises Baptistes Françaises au Canada
United Baptist Convention of the Atlantic Provinces

Brethren in Christ Church, Canadian Conference
Canadian District of the Moravian Church in America, Northern Province
Canadian Evangelical Christian Churches
Canadian Yearly Meeting of the Religious Society of Friends
The Catholic Church in Canada
Christ Catholic Church International
Christian Brethren (also known as Plymouth Brethren)
Christian and Missionary Alliance in Canada
Church of God (Anderson, Ind.)
Church of the Nazarene in Canada

Churches of Christ—Christian Churches

Christian Church (Disciples of Christ) in Canada
Churches of Christ in Canada

Congregational Christian Churches in Canada

Eastern Orthodox Churches

The Antiochian Orthodox Christian Archdiocese of North America
Greek Orthodox Metropolis of Toronto (Canada)
Orthodox Church in America (Canada Section)
Patriarchal Parishes of the Russian Orthodox Church in Canada
Romanian Orthodox Church in America (Canadian Parishes)
The Romanian Orthodox Episcopate of America (Jackson, MI)
Serbian Orthodox Church in the U.S.A. and Canada, Diocese of Canada
Ukrainian Orthodox Church of Canada

The Evangelical Covenant Church of Canada
Evangelical Free Church of Canada
The Evangelical Missionary Church of Canada
General Church of the New Jerusalem
Jehovah's Witnesses

Latter-Day Saints (Mormons)

The Church of Jesus Christ of Latter-Day Saints in Canada
Reorganized Church of Jesus Christ of Latter Day Saints

Lutheran Bodies

Church of the Lutheran Brethren
The Estonian Evangelical Lutheran Church
Evangelical Lutheran Church in Canada
Lutheran Church—Canada

Mennonite Bodies

Canadian Conference of Mennonite Brethren Churches

193

Church of God in Christ (Mennonite)
Conference of Mennonites in Canada
The Evangelical Mennonite Conference
Evangelical Mennonite Mission Conference
Mennonite Church (Canada)
Old Order Amish Church
Reinland Mennonite Church

Methodist Bodies

British Methodist Episcopal Church of Canada
Free Methodist Church in Canada
Independent Holiness Church
The Wesleyan Church of Canada

The Old Catholic Church of Canada
Open Bible Faith Fellowship of Canada

Oriental Orthodox Churches

Armenian Holy Apostolic Church - Canadian Diocese
The Coptic Orthodox Church in Canada
Syrian Orthodox Church of Antioch

Pentecostal Bodies

The Apostolic Church in Canada
Apostolic Church of Pentecost of Canada Inc.
The Bible Holiness Movement
Church of God (Cleveland, Tenn.)
The Church of God of Prophecy in Canada
Elim Fellowship of Evangelical Churches and Ministers
Foursquare Gospel Church of Canada
Independent Assemblies of God International (Canada)
The Italian Pentecostal Church of Canada
The Pentecostal Assemblies of Canada
Pentecostal Assemblies of Newfoundland
United Pentecostal Church in Canada

Presbyterian Bodies

Presbyterian Church in America (Canadian Section)
Presbyterian Church in Canada

Reformed Bodies

Canadian and American Reformed Churches
Christian Reformed Church in North America
Reformed Church in Canada

The Reformed Episcopal Church of Canada
The Salvation Army in Canada
Seventh-day Adventist Church in Canada
Union of Spiritual Communities of Christ (Orthodox Doukhobors in Canada)
United Brethren Church in Canada
The United Church of Canada
Universal Fellowship of Metropolitan Community Churches

5. The Emerging Electronic Church

Long past are the days when religious bodies posted their first "hello world" World Wide Web page onto the Internet. Churches have kept a respectable pace with changes on the Internet, providing innovative and increasingly informative, user-friendly Web sites.

The percentage of U.S. religious bodies listed in the *Yearbook* with Internet addresses reached 81 percent this year, up from 68 percent last year. The number which have registered their own Internet domain names jumped from 124 to 147.

Recent months have brought a glossary-full of new terms and acronyms related to emerging information dissemination and communication technologies. There are new devices, communication protocols, and networking infrastructures, such as wireless network-connected personal data assistants, cellular telephones with Internet browsing capabilities, ISDN, DSL and cable modems. These emerge at such a rate that no Internet site (including the most sophisticated) can hope to keep up with the implications for web publishing.

With ever more ubiquitous, all-the-time access, people now use the Internet as once they consulted the encyclopedia or utilized a library. Such changes have produced discussion about the future nature of reference publications such as this *Yearbook*.

In many cases, churches and agencies have adopted methods pioneered by commercial sites to their own purposes. In the past year we have seen online donations to religious bodies and agencies become an established fixture. Church-related purchases that were once handled only in person, through the mail, or by phone are increasingly transacted over the Internet. This year saw an explosion of specialized commercially sponsored Internet sites catering to the Christian market.

Religious bodies publish a rising number of digital versions of materials once available only on paper, not only online but also on compact or floppy disk and other digital media. One can acquire or freely access huge amounts of church-related information, news, music, graphic images (including video), disaster reports, speeches, pastoral letters and sermons, historical references, biographical data, program information, bulletin notes, and contact information for staff members of local churches and national agencies. From a relative rarity until recently, email addresses are increasingly available for denominational staff, international mission organizations, teen groups, women's groups and other organizations.

Concern about objectionable Internet material has brought "safe playground" Internet service providers and Internet security software. Sites such as www.FilterReview.com publish evaluations of these filtering technologies.

The Web and email addresses listed here are but the tip of the iceberg. From one you might find links to a variety of additional resources.

—*Marcel A. Welty*

Updated and expanded email and website addresses for entries listed in the *Yearbook* as well as others are provided for *Yearbook* readers at: www.ElectronicChurch.org

Some General Resources

About.com - http://christianity.about.com/religion/christianity

Academic Info - www.academicinfo.net/Christian.html

Adherants - www.adherants.com

All-in-one Christian Index - http://allinone.crossdaily.com

American Religion Data Archive - www.arda.tm

BeliefNet - www.belief.net

Christian Century - www.christiancentury.org

Christianity Today - www.christianitytoday.com

Crosssearch.com - www.crosssearch.com

Ecunet - www.ecunet.org

ForMinistry - www.forministry.com

Goshen. Net - www.goshen.net

Resources for American Christianity - www.resourcingchristianity.org

Virtual Religion Index - www.rci.rutgers.edu/~religion/vri

Internet Addresses of Listed US Religious Bodies

Advent Christian Church—Web: www.adventchristian.org
Email: acpub@adventchristian.org

African Methodist Episcopal Church—Web: www.amecnet.org
Email: Administrator@amecnet.org

African Methodist Episcopal Zion Church—Web: www.amezion.org
Email: info@amezion.org

Albanian Orthodox Archdiocese in America
Web: www.oca.org/OCA/AL/ <http://www.oca.org/OCA/AL/>

Allegheny Wesleyan Methodist Connection (Original Allegheny Conference)
List of Congregations: http://c1web.com/local_info/churches/aw.html
Email: awmc@juno.com

The American Association of Lutheran Churches—Web: www.taalc.org
Email: chuckAALC@aol.com

The American Baptist Association—Web: www.abaptist.org
Email: bssc@abaptist.org

American Baptist Churches in the U.S.A.—Web: www.abc-usa.org
Email: richard.schramm@abc-usa.org

The American Carpatho-Russian Orthodox Greek Catholic Church—Web: www.goarch.org
Email: archdiocese@goarch.org

American Catholic Church—Web: www.geocities.com/WestHollywood/4136/
Email: berzol@apollo3.com

American Evangelical Christian Churches—Web: www.aeccministries.com
Email: alpha@strato.net

American Rescue Workers—Web: www.arwus.com
Email: amerscwk@pcspower.net

The Antiochian Orthodox Christian Archdiocese of North America—Web: www.antiochian.org
Email: FrJoseph@antiochian.org

Apostolic Catholic Assyrian Church of the East, North American Dioceses
Web: www.cired.org/ace.html
Email: ABSoro@aol.com

Apostolic Christian Churches of America—Web: www.apostolicchristian.org
Email: Questions@ApostolicChristian.org

Apostolic Episcopal Church—Web: www.celticsynod.org/aec.htm
Email: HCCAEC@ix.netcom.com

Apostolic Faith Mission of Portland, Oregon—Web: www.apostolicfaith.org

Apostolic Lutheran Church of America—Web: www.apostolic-lutheran.org

Apostolic Orthodox Catholic Church—Website of one parish: www.pe.net/~idyll/para1.htm

Armenian Apostolic Church of America—Web: www.armprelacy.org
Email: prelacy@gis.net

Assemblies of God—Web: www.ag.org/top
Email: info@ag.org

Assemblies of God International Fellowship (Independent/Not affiliated)
Web: www.agifellowship.org
Email: info@agifellowship.org

Associate Reformed Presbyterian Church (General Synod)—Web: www.arpsynod.org
Email: dragondraw@aol.com

The Association of Free Lutheran Congregations—Web: www.aflc.org
Email: hqmail@aflc.org

Baptist Bible Fellowship International—Web: www.bbfi.org
Email: csbc@cherrystreet.org

Baptist General Conference—Web: www.bgc.bethel.edu
Email: gmarsh@baptistgeneral.org

Baptist Missionary Association of America—Web: www.bmaweb.net

Berean Fundamental Church—Web: www.bereanfellowship.org
Email: office@bereanfellowship.org

The Bible Church of Christ, Inc.—Web: www.thebiblechurchofchrist.org
Email: bccbookstore@earthlink.net

Bible Fellowship Church—Web: www.bfc.org
Email: bfc@bfc.org

Bible Way Church of Our Lord Jesus Christ World Wide, Inc.—Web: www.biblewaychurch.org
Email: mr.ed5strings@worldnet.att.net

Brethren in Christ Church—Web: www.bic-church.org
Email: RRoss@BIC-church.org

Brethren Church (Ashland, Ohio)—Web: www.brethrenchurch.org
Email: brethren@brethrenchurch.org

The Catholic Church—Web: www.vatican.va

Christ Catholic Church—Web: christcatholicchurch.freeyellow.com
Email: ergoegosum@aol.com

Christadelphians—Web: www.christadelphia.org
Email: Nzilmer@aol.com

Christian Church (Disciples of Christ) in the United States and Canada—Web: www.disciples.org
Email: cmiller@oc.disciples.org

Christian Church of North America, General Council—Web: www.ccna.org
Email: cnna@nauticom.net

Christian Churches and Churches of Christ—Website (Unofficial): www.cwv.net/christ'n
Email: Jowston@cwv.edu

The Christian Congregation, Inc.—Web: netministries.org/see/churches.exe/ch10619
Email: Revalnas@aol.com

Christian Methodist Episcopal Church—Web: www.c-m-e.org
Email: juanbr4law@aol.com

The Christian and Missionary Alliance—Web: www.gospelcom.net/cmalliance
Email: info@cmalliance.org

Christian Reformed Church in North America—Web: www.crcna.org
Email: btgh@crcna.org

Christian Union—Web: www.christianunion.com
Email: reuhrig@yahoo.com

Church of the Brethren—Web: www.brethren.org
Email: cobweb@brethren.org

Church of Christ—Web: church-of-christ.com

The Church of Christ (Holiness) U.S.A.—Web: www.cochusa.com/main.htm
Email: Everything@cochusa.com

Church of Christ, Scientist—Web: www.tfccs.com
Email: www.tfccs.com/GV/jc/jc.html#form

Church of God (Anderson, Indiana)—Web: www.chog.org
Email: dtaylor@chog.org

The Church Of God In Christ—Web: netministries.org/see/churches/ch00833
Email: EJOHNCOGIC@aol.com

Church of God in Christ, International—Web: www.cogic.org/main.htm
Email: laity@cogic.org

Church of God in Christ, Mennonite—Website (Unofficial): holdeman.cjb.net
Email: webmaster@bibleviews.com

Church of God (Cleveland, Tennessee)—Web: www.churchofgod.cc
Email: www.churchofgod.cc/contact

Church of God by Faith, Inc.—Web: www.cogbf.org
Email: natl-hq@cogbf.org <http://wwwcogbf.org/elders.htm#Matthews>

Church of God General Conference (Oregon, IL and Morrow, GA)—Web: www.abc-coggc.org
Email: info@abc-coggc.org

Church of God, Mountain Assembly, Inc.—Web: www.cgmahdq.org
Email: cgmahdq@jellico.com

Church of God of Prophecy—Web: www.cogop.org
Email: betty@cogop.org

The Church of God (Seventh Day), Denver, Colorado—Web: www.cog7.org
Email: offices@cog7.org

The Church of Illumination—Web: www.soul.org
Email: bevhall@comcat.com

The Church of Jesus Christ of Latter-day Saints—Web: www.lds.org

Church of the Lutheran Brethren of America—Web: www.clba.org
Email: clba@clba.org

Church of the Lutheran Confession—Web: www.clclutheran.org
Email: JohnHLau@juno.com

Church of the Nazarene—Web: www.nazarene.org
Email: www.nazarene.org/cgi-bin/hqadd.cgi

Church of Our Lord Jesus Christ of the Apostolic Faith, Inc.—Web: www.apostolic-faith.org
Email: apostle@apostolic-faith.org

Church of the United Brethren in Christ—Web: www.ub.org
Email: sdennie@ub.org

Churches of Christ in Christian Union—Web: www.bright.net/~cccudoc
Email: devans@bright.net

Churches of God, General Conference—Web: www.cggc.org
Email: director@cggc.org

Congregational Holiness Church—Web: www.ch.church.com
Email: chchurch@bellsouth.net

Conservative Baptist Association of America (CBAmerica)—Web: www.cbamerica.org
Email: cba@cbamerica.org

Conservative Congregational Christian Conference—Web: www.ccccusa.org
Email: CCCC4@juno.com

Conservative Lutheran Association—Web: www.tlcanaheim.com/CLA
Email: PastorPJ@ix.netcom.com

Coptic Orthodox Church—Web: www.coptic.org
Email: Webmaster@coptic.org

Cumberland Presbyterian Church—Web: www.cumberland.org
Email: assembly@cumberland.org

Cumberland Presbyterian Church in America—Web: www.cumberland.org/cpca
Email: mleslie598@aol.com

Elim Fellowship—Web: www.elim.ca
Email: 75551.743@compuserve.com

Episcopal Church—Web: www.ecusa.anglican.org
Email: jrollins@ecusa.anglican.org

The Episcopal Orthodox Church—Web: www.Episcopalorthodox.org
Email: episcopalorthodox1@msn.com

The Estonian Evangelical Lutheran Church—Web: www.eelk.ee
Email: konsistoorium@eelk.ee

The Evangelical Church—Web: quakertownecna.com/conferences.html

The Evangelical Church Alliance—Web: www.ecainternational.org
Email: info@ecainternational.org

The Evangelical Congregational Church—Web: www.eccenter.com/church
Email: eccenter@eccenter.com

The Evangelical Covenant Church—Web: www.covchurch.org
Email: president@covoffice.org

The Evangelical Free Church of America—Web: www.efca.org
Email: president@efca.org

Evangelical Friends International—North American Region
Web: www.evangelical-friends.org/international/efi-na.html
Email: efcer@aol.com

Evangelical Lutheran Church in America—Web: www.elca.org
Email: info@elca.org

Evangelical Lutheran Synod—Web: www.EvLuthSyn.org
Email: gorvick@blc.edu

Evangelical Mennonite Church—Email: emcintlmin@aol.com

Evangelical Methodist Church—Web: www.emchurch.org
Email: headquarters@emchurch.org

Evangelical Presbyterian Church—Web: www.epc.org
Email: EPCHURCH@epc.org

Fellowship of Evangelical Bible Churches—Web: members.aol.com/febcoma
Email: febcoma@aol.com

Fellowship of Fundamental Bible Churches—Web: www.churches-ffbc.org
Email: ecotton@citlink.net

Fellowship of Grace Brethren Churches—Web: www.fgbc.org
Email: fgbc@fgbc.org

Free Methodist Church of North America—Web: www.fmcna.org
Email: info@fmcna.org

Friends General Conference—Web: www.fgcquaker.org
Email: friends@fgcquaker.org

Friends United Meeting—Web: www.fum.org
Email: info@fum.org

Full Gospel Fellowship of Churches and Ministers International—Web: www.fgfcmi.org
Email: FGFCMI@aol.com

General Association of General Baptists—Web: www.generalbaptist.com
Email: rblack@pbmo.net

General Association of Regular Baptist Churches—Web: www.garbc.org
Email: garbc@garbc.org

General Church of the New Jerusalem—Web: www.newchurch.org
Email: svsimpso@newchurch.edu

General Conference of Mennonite Brethren Churches—Web: www.mbconf.org
E-mail: mhein1@fresno.edu

Grace Gospel Fellowship—Web: www.ggfusa.org
Email: info@ggfusa.org

Greek Orthodox Archdiocese of America—Web: www.goarch.org
Email: archdiocese@goarch.org

The Holy Eastern Orthodox Catholic and Apostolic Church in North America, Inc.
Web: www.theocacna.org
Email: theocacna@webtv.net

Holy Ukrainian Autocephalic Orthodox Church in Exile—Web: www.atlantis-bbs.com/uaoc

House of God, Which is the Church of the Living God, the Pillar and Ground of the Truth, Inc.
Web: www.houseofgod.org
Email: info@houseofgod.org

Hungarian Reformed Church in America—Web: www.calvinsynod.org
Email: Bishop@CalvinSynod.org

Hutterian Brethren—Web: www.hutterianbrethren.com
Email: philsjg@juno.com

IFCA International, Inc.—Web: www.ifca.org
Email: office@ifca.org

International Church of the Foursquare Gospel—Web: www.foursquare.org
Email: comm@foursquare.org

International Council of Community Churches—Web: www.akcache.com/community/iccc.html

The International Pentecostal Church of Christ—Web: members.aol.com/hqipcc
Email: hqipcc@aol.com

International Pentecostal Holiness Church—Web: www.iphc.org
Email: webman@iphc.org

Jehovah's Witnesses—Web: www.watchtower.org
Email: http://watch001.securesites.com/contact/submit.htm

The Latvian Evangelical Lutheran Church in America—Email: pulins@flash.net

The Liberal Catholic Church—Province of the United States of America— Web: www.thelcc.org
Email: bshp052497@aol.com

The Lutheran Church—Missouri Synod (LCMS)—Web: www.lcms.org
Email: infocenter@lcms.org

Malankara Orthodox Syrian Church, Diocese of America
Web: www.malankara.org/american.htm
Email: Malankara@malankara.org

Mar Thoma Syrian Church of India—Web: www.marthomachurch.org
Email: webmaster@marthomachurch.org

Mennonite Church—Web: www.mennonites.org
Email: rbyler@juno.com

Mennonite Church, The General Conference—Web: www.southwind.net/~gcmc
Email: gcmc@gcmc.org

The Missionary Church—Web: www.mcusa.org
Email: mcdenomusa@aol.com

Moravian Church in America (Unitas Fratrum)—Web: www.moravian.org
Email: burke@mcnp.org

National Association of Congregational Christian Churches—Web: www.naccc.org
Email: naccc@naccc.org

National Association of Free Will Baptists—Web: www.nafwb.org
Email: webmaster@nafwb.org

National Baptist Convention of America, Inc.—Web: members.aol.com/nbyc1/nbca.html
Email: nbyc1@aol.com

National Missionary Baptist Convention of America—Web: www.natl-missionarybaptist.com

National Organization of the New Apostolic Church of North America—Email: info@nak.org

National Primitive Baptist Convention, Inc.—Web: www.natlprimbaptconv.org

National Spiritualist Association of Churches—Web: www.nsac.org
Email: nsac@nsac.org

Netherlands Reformed Congregations
Website (Unofficial): home.earthlink.net/~vogelaar/nrc/church.html
Email: vogelaar@yahoo.com

North American Baptist Conference—Web: www.nabconference.org
Email: serve@nabconf.org

Open Bible Standard Churches—Web: www. openbible.org
Email: info@openbible.org

The Orthodox Church in America—Web: www.oca.org
Email: jjm@oca.org

The Orthodox Presbyterian Church—Web: www.opc.org
Email: duff.1@opc.org

Patriarchal Parishes of the Russian Orthodox Church in the U.S.A.
Web: www.orthodox.net/directry/index.htm
Email: bmercurius@ruscon.com

Pentecostal Assemblies of the World, Inc.—Web: www.paga.org
Email: Dunemus@aol.com

Pentecostal Church of God—Web: www.pcg.org
Email: pcg@pcg.org

The Pentecostal Free Will Baptist Church, Inc.—Email: pheath@intrstar.net
Web: www.pfwb.org
Email: pamk@interstar.net

Philadelphia Yearly Meeting of the Religious Society of Friends—Web: www.pym.org

Pillar of Fire—Web: www.gospelcom.net/pof
Email: info@zarephath.edu

Polish National Catholic Church of America—Web: www.PNCC.org
Email: ads22244@aol.com

Presbyterian Church in America—Web: www.pcanet.org
Email: info@ac.pca-atl.org

Presbyterian Church (U.S.A.)—Web: www.pcusa.org
Email: presytel@pcusa.org

Primitive Methodist Church in the U.S.A.—Web: www.primitivemethodistchurch.org
Email: pmconf@juno.com <mailto:pmconf@juno.com>

Progressive National Baptist Convention, Inc.—Web: www.pnbc.org
Email: info@pnbc.org

Protestant Reformed Churches in America—Website (Unofficial): www.prca.org
Email: doezema@prca.org

Reformed Church in America—Web: www.rca.org
Email: kbaker@rca.org

Reformed Church in the United States—Web: www.rcus.org
Email: fhw@iname.com

Reformed Episcopal Church—Web: recus.org
Email: wycliffe@jps.net

Reformed Presbyterian Church of North America—Web: www.reformedpresbyterian.org
Email: RPTrustees@aol.com

Religious Society of Friends (Unaffiliated Meetings)—Web: www.quaker.org/fwcc
Email: quaker@simongrant.org

Reorganized Church of Jesus Christ of Latter Day Saints—Web: www.rlds.org
Email: snaylor@rlds.org

The Romanian Orthodox Episcopate of America—Web: www.roea.org
Email: roeasolia@aol.com

The Russian Orthodox Church Outside of Russia—Web: www.synod.com
Email: rocor@rocor.org

The Salvation Army—Web: www.sarmy.org
Email: websa@SalvationArmy.org

Separate Baptists in Christ—Web: www.separatebaptist.org
Email: mail@separatebaptist.org

Serbian Orthodox Church in the U.S.A. and Canada—Web: oea.serbian-church.net
Email: oea@oea.serbian-church.net

Seventh-day Adventist Church—Web: northamerica.adventist.org/mainnew.htm

Seventh Day Baptist General Conference, USA and Canada—Web: www.seventhdaybaptist.org
Email: sdbgen@inwave.com

Southern Baptist Convention—Web: www.sbc.net
Email: bmerrell@sbc.net

Southern Methodist Church—Email: smchq@juno.com

Sovereign Grace Believers—Web: www.searchingtogether.org
Email: jon@searchingtogether.org

The Swedenborgian Church—Web: www.swedenborg.org
Email: manager@swedenborg.org

Syrian (Syriac) Orthodox Church of Antioch—Web: www.syrianorthodoxchurch.org
Email: syrianoc@syrianorthodoxchurch.org

Ukrainian Orthodox Church of the U.S.A.—Web: www.uocofusa.org
Email: uocofusa@aol.com

Unitarian Universalist Association of Congregations—Web: www.uua.org
Email: jhurley@uua.org

United Church of Christ—Web: www.ucc.org
Email: langa @ucc.org

United Holy Church of America, Inc.—Email: books@mohistory.org

The United Methodist Church—Web: www.umc.org
Email: infoserv@umcom.umc.org

United Pentecostal Church International—Web: www.upci.org
Email: upcimain@aol.com

United Zion Church—Web: www.uzrc.org
Email: www.uzrc.org/email

Unity of the Brethren—Web: www.unityofthebrethren.org
Email: BenPolasek@yahoo.com

Universal Fellowship of Metropolitan Community Churches
Email: communications@ufmcchq.com
Web: www.ufmcchq.com

Volunteers of America—Web: www.voa.org
Email: voa@voa.org

The Wesleyan Church—Web: www.wesleyan.org
Email: gensecoff@aol.com

Wisconsin Evangelical Lutheran Synod—Web: www.wels.net
Email: webbin@sab.wels.net

6. Sources of Religion-Related Research
Directory of Selected Research Organizations

The editorial office of the *Yearbook of American & Canadian Churches* receives innumerable requests for data about churches, religious organizations, attendance patterns, and comparative religion concerns. Sometimes we are able to furnish the requested data, but more often we refer the inquirer to other research colleagues in the field. We are always interested in and aided by such requests, and we find ourselves informed by each question.

In response to such inquiries, the "Sources in Religion-Related Research" directory was initiated in the 1999 edition of the *Yearbook*. In addition to asking each organization to provide a brief overall description, each was also asked to indicate any special research foci (i.e. denominational, congregational, interfaith, gender, etc.). Further, each organization was asked to identify the sociological, methodological, or theological approaches that serve to guide their research, and to describe any current or recent research projects. Lastly, we asked for a list of recurrent publications. Below the organizations' responses to these questions are reported as clearly and completely as is possible. Contact information appears just beneath the title of each organization. In most cases, the organizations' websites provide very detailed information about current research projects.

Numerous other research centers in the area of American religious life, each with specific areas of concern, conduct timely and significant research. We hope that readers will find utility in this directory and we invite them to identify additional sources by email: yearbook@ncccusa.org or by Fax: (212) 870-2817.

American Academy of Religion (AAR)

AAR Executive Office
825 Houston Mill Rd., Ste. 300
Atlanta, GA 30329
Tel. (404)727-7920
Email: aar@emory.edu
Website: www.aar-site.org
President: Dr. Lawrence E. Sullivan
Exec. Dir.: Dr. Barbara DeConcini

The AAR is the major learned society and professional association for scholars whose object of study is religion. Its mission—in a world where religion plays so central a role in social, political and economic events, as well as in the lives of communities and individuals' is to meet a critical need for ongoing reflection upon and understanding of religious traditions, issues, questions and values. As a learned society and professional association of teachers and research scholars, the American Academy of Religion has over 8000 members who teach in some 1,500 colleges, universities, seminaries, and schools in North America and abroad. The Academy is dedicated to furthering knowledge of religion and religious institutions in all their forms and manifestations. This is accomplished through Academy-wide and regional conferences and meetings, publications, programs, and membership services. Within a context of free inquiry and critical examination, the Academy welcomes all disciplined reflection on religion—both from within and outside of communities of belief and practice—and seeks to enhance its broad public understanding.

The AAR's annual meeting, over 7,500 scholars gather to share research and collaborate on scholarly projects. The annual meeting sessions are grouped into over 70 program units, each representing an ongoing community of scholars who are collectively engaged in pursuing knowledge about a specific religious tradition or a specific aspect of religion. In addition, the AAR's ten regional organizations sponsor smaller annual meetings that are similar in structure to the Academy-wide meeting. All of the world's major religious traditions, as well as indigenous and historical religions, are explored in the work of AAR members.

Current or Recent Research

Currently, for example, the AAR offers Teaching Workshops for both junior and senior scholars. It is organizing efforts to gather data on the field to facilitate departmental planning and funding. A full explanation of the many current research projects is available on the AAR website, which is listed above.

Periodicals

The *Journal of the American Academy of Religion* is the scholarly periodical of the AAR. In addition, the AAR publishes a semi-annual periodical titled "Spotlight on Teaching" in the society's newsletter, *Religious Studies News*.

American Religion Data Archive (ARDA)

Department of Sociology / Anthropology
Purdue University
1365 Stone Hall
West Lafayette, IN 47907-1476
Tel. (765) 494-0081
Fax (765) 496-1476
Email: archive@sri.soc.purdue.edu
Website: www.TheARDA.com
Director: Dr. Roger Finke

The American Religion Data Archive (ARDA) is an Internet-based data archive that stores and distributes quantitative data sets from the leading studies on American religion—free of charge. Supported by the Lilly Endowment and housed at Purdue University, ARDA strives to *preserve* data files for future use, *prepare* the data files for immediate public use, and make the data files easily *accessible* to all. Data files can be downloaded from the Internet site or they can be analyzed online.

The ARDA includes national surveys on American and Canadian religion, regional surveys, surveys sampling the membership of specific denominations, and surveys of religions professionals. The 1952, 1971, 1980, and 1990 Church and Church Membership surveys for counties and states are also included in the ARDA.

Association of Theological Schools (ATS)

10 Summit Park Dr.
Pittsburgh, PA 15275-1103
Tel. (412) 788-6505
Fax (412) 788-6510
Email: ats@ats.edu
Website: www.ats.edu
Exec. Dir.: Daniel O. Aleshire
Contact: Nancy Merrill, Dir. of Communications and Membership Services

The Association of Theological Schools (ATS) is the accrediting and program agency for graduate theological education in North America. Its 237 member institutions represent the broad spectrum of denominational, ecclesiastical, and theological perspectives evident in North America today, making it the most broad-based religious organization of its kind. The Association comprises Protestant, Roman Catholic, and Orthodox schools of theology, both university-related divinity schools and freestanding seminaries. A full list of members is available on the above website.

The primary purpose of the Association is the improvement of theological schools, which ATS seeks to attain by accrediting schools and by providing programs and service to its membership, such as, among others, a data center of statistical information on the member schools; leadership education for seminary presidents, academic deans, trustees, and development officers; grants for faculty scholarship and research; faculty development programs sponsored by the Faculty Resource Center; student information resources; a program of globalization in theological education; efforts to enhance the participation of under-represented constituencies in theological education; and various publications. In addition, the Association provides a venue for addressing the critical and emerging issues in North American theological education.

Current or Recent Research

The current discussion focuses on identifying the nature, characteristics, and related issues related to the "Public Character of Theological Education." The major activities of the project include convening five study groups to explore the issue from varying ecclesial and institutional contexts; a regranting program to provide the stimulus for schools to experiment with programs to establish a greater civic presence in their communities; and opportunities to focus though and conversation about the public character of theological education broadly among faculties and administrative leaders of ATS schools. The discussion will explore how more rigorous theological thinking about the public issues that face democratic cultures can contribute not only to the intellectual life of the theological school but to the broader society as well.

Periodicals

Fact Book on Theological Education is published annually and provides statistical data on theological education in the U.S. and Canada. Also, the Association publishes a journal, *Theological*

Education bi-annually, a newsletter bimonthly called *Colloquy*, and the formal institutional documents of the Association entitled the *Bulletin*. The Bulletin also contains an ATS directory and a membership list.

Auburn Theological Seminary

3041 Broadway
New York, NY 10027
Tel. (212) 662-4314
Fax (212) 662-4315
Email: mnw@auburn.org
Website: www.auburnsem.org
Director: Dr. Barbara G. Wheeler

Auburn Theological Seminary's mission is to strengthen religious leadership. It carries out its mission through programs of non-degree theological education for clergy and laity; through programs for Presbyterian students enrolled at its partner institution, Union Seminary in New York City; and by conducting research on theological education at its Center for the Study of Theological Education. Auburn was founded in 1818 in Auburn, New York; it is currently located on Union Seminary's campus.

Auburn Seminary is related by covenant agreement with Presbyterian Church (U.S.A.), but most of its programs are ecumenical, and many have a multi-faith focus. The Center for the Study of Theological Education includes rabbinical schools and Protestant and Roman Catholic seminaries and divinity schools in its studies.

Research is conducted using a variety of methods, including survey and ethnographic research, structured interview and documentary research, research reports on surveys and case studies. Reports of findings are frequently published with accompanying information on the history of the issue being studied and with theological commentaries written from a variety of perspectives.

Current or Recent Research

Currently, the Center is completing studies of seminary students, of public perceptions of theological education and church leadership, and of history of religion and urban America. The Center is about to begin a study of seminary trustees and senior administrators.

Periodicals

Auburn Studies, an occasional bulletin in which the Center publishes its research results. Research reports are also available on Auburn's website (listed above).

Barna Research Group, Ltd.

5528 Everglades
Ventura, CA 93003
Tel. (805) 658-8885
Fax (805) 658-7298
Website: www.barna.org
President: George Barna
Contact: David Kinnaman, Vice President

Barna Research Group works with Christian churches and parachurch ministries throughout the nation by providing primary research data related to cultural change, people's lifestyles, values, attitudes, beliefs and religious practices. Its vision is to provide current accurate and reliable information, in bite-sized pieces and at reasonable costs, to ministries who will use the information to make better strategic decisions. They conduct primary research for ministries that commission such research, studying their community, their church or special population. Barna also produces many research-based books, reports, and ministry tools to help churches understand the national context of ministry. Barna Research conducts seminars in many markets across the nation to inform church leaders of its findings, and to train church leaders in the application of that information. The organization works with churches from all Christian denominations.

Barna Research has no special research focus. It conducts projects based upon existing needs in the Church at-large, or for its clients specifically, and analyzes all of its findings in relation to a minimum of three dozen population subgroups involved in the survey interviews. Methodologically, Barna Research uses both qualitative approaches (focus groups, depth interviews) and quantitative approaches (cross-sectional surveys, longitudinal studies, panel research). Data collection methods include telephone surveys, mail surveys, in-person interviews, on-line surveys, self-administered surveys, focus groups.

204

Current or Recent Research

Barna Research conducts more than 50 studies each year, covering a broad range of topics. Some of the recent non-proprietary studies completed are focused on understanding the state of the Church; the habits of highly effective churches; worship efficacy; the unchurched; strategies and techniques for developing lay leaders; understanding effective discipleship processes; pastoral profiles; beliefs and core attitudes of religious donors; Biblical knowledge, and many others.

Periodicals

Barna Research offers a bi-weekly update on current information related to faith matters from its national non-proprietary research. This information is free to those who register for it at the website (listed above).

Center for the Study of Religion and American Culture

Indiana University
Purdue University at Indianapolis
425 University Blvd, Room 341
Indianapolis, IN 46202-5140
Tel. (317) 274-8409
Fax (317) 278-3354
Email: Ccherry@iupui.edu
Website: www.iupui.edu/it/raac
Director: Dr. Conrad Cherry

The Center for the Study of Religion and American Culture is a research and public outreach institute devoted to the promotion of the understanding of the relation between religion and other features of American culture. Research methods are both inter-disciplinary and multi-disciplinary. Established in 1989, the Center is based in the School of Liberal Arts and Indiana University-Purdue University at Indianapolis. Center activities include national conferences and symposia, commissioned books, essays, bibliographies, and research projects, fellowships for younger scholars, data based communication about developments in the field of American religion, a newsletter devoted to the promotion of Center activities, and the semi-annual scholarly periodical, *Religion and American Culture: A Journal of Interpretation.*

Current or Recent Research

The Center is currently conducting research on the "public dimensions of American Religion," and on "Religion in Higher Education."

Periodicals

Religion and American Culture: A Journal of Interpretation. Center books include the series, "The Public Expressions of Religion in America."

empty tomb, inc.

301 North Fourth Street
P.O. Box 2404
Champaign, IL 61825-2404
Tel. (217)356-9519
Fax (217)356-2344
Website: www.emptytomb.org
CEO: John L. Ronsvalle
Exec.Vice-Pres.: Sylvia Ronsvalle

empty tomb, inc. is a Christian research and service organization. On a local level, it coordinates direct services to people in need in cooperation with area congregations. On a national level, it studies church member giving patterns of historically Christian churches, including Roman Catholic, mainline and evangelical Protestant, Anabaptist, Pentecostal, Orthodox, and fundamentalist communions. empty tomb publishes the annual *State of Church Giving* series. Staff also work with a select number of congregations, discovering ways to reverse the negative giving trends indicated by national data, through its project, The National Money for Mission Program.

Current or Recent Research

Current research monitors and analyzes church member giving patters, and is published in *The State of Church Giving* series produced by empty tomb, inc. The description of dynamics affecting current giving patterns is presented in *Behind The Stained Glass Windows: Money Dynamics in The Church* (Grand Rapids, MI: Baker Books, 1996).

Periodicals

The State of Church Giving series is an annual publication. It considers denominational giving data, analysis of giving and membership trends, and other estimates of charitable giving. Each edition has featured a special focus chapter, which discusses giving issues relevant to a broad audience. Selected data tables are posted on the empty tomb website (listed above).

The Hartford Institute for Religion Research of Hartford Seminary

Hartford Seminary
77 Sherman Street
Hartford, CT 06105
Tel. (860)509-9543
Fax (860)509-9559
Email: hirr@hartsem.edu Website: www.hartsem.edu/csrr/

The Hartford Institute for Religion Research of Hartford Seminary was established in 1981, formalizing a research program initiated by the Seminary in 1974. Until recently it was known as The Center for Social and Religious Research. The Institute's work is guided by a disciplined understanding of the interrelationship between (a) the inner life and resources of American religious institutions and (b) the possibilities and limits placed on those institutions by the social and cultural context into which God has called them.

Its twenty-year record of rigorous, policy-relevant research, anticipation of emerging issues, commitment to the creative dissemination of learning, and strong connections to both theological education and the church has earned the Institute an international reputation as an important bridge between the scholarly community and the practice of ministry.

Current or Recent Research

Some of the titles of current projects at the Institute are: "Organizing Religious Work for the 21st Century: Exploring "Denominationalism;" "Cooperative Congregational Studies Project;" "Congregational Consulting Services;" "New England Religion Discussion Society (NERDS);" "Congregational Studies Team." Descriptions of these programs are available on the Institute's website, listed above.

Periodicals

Praxis is Hartford Seminary's magazine, which focuses on the activities and faculty of the Institute.

Institute for Ecumenical and Cultural Research

P.O. Box 6188
Collegeville, MN 56321-6188
Tel. (320) 363-3366
Fax (320) 363-3313
Email: iecr@csbsju.edu
Website: www.csbsju.edu/iecr
Exec. Dir.: Dr. Patrick Henry

The Institute for Ecumenical and Cultural Research brings together well-trained, creative, articulate men and women for careful thought and dialogue in a place of inquiry and prayer. The Resident scholars Program welcomes researchers and their families for either individual semesters or for an entire academic year. Resident scholars work on their own projects but meet once a week for seminars, and have other occasions for conversation. Each scholar presents a public lecture. Ecumenism happens at the Institute as people come to know one another in community. The Institute is an independent corporation, but shares in the Benedictine and academic life of Saint John's Abbey and University, and of nearby Saint Benedict's Monastery and the College of Saint Benedict. In the summer the Institute uses its facilities for invitational consultations on subjects considered by the Board of Directors to be of special ecumenical interest.

In the Resident Scholars Program, the subjects of research are determined by the interests of the applicants who are invited to come by the Admissions Committee. While most of the work tends to be in traditional theological areas, we encourage people in all fields to consider applying, both because ecumenism is of concern across the spectrum of disciplines, and because the term "cultural" in our title extends our reach beyond theology and religious studies. In particular cases, work done here may have a denominational, congregational, or interfaith focus, but the Institute does not prescribe or delimit, in any narrow way, what is appropriate.

Current or Recent Research

Recent summer consultations have had the following titles: "Prayer in the Ecumenical Movement";

"Virtues for an Ecumenical Heart"; "The Price of Disunity"; "Living Faithfully in North America Today." Among subjects dealt with in earlier years are "Orthodoxy at Home in North America"; "Transmitting Tradition to Children and Young People"; "The Nature of Christian Hope"; "Women and the Church"; Jewish and Christian Relatedness to Scripture"; "Confessing Christian Faith in a Pluralistic Society."

Periodicals
Ecumenical People, Programs, Papers is an bi-annual newsletter containing brief sketches of resident scholars, reports on Institute programs, and, in nearly every issue, an "An Occasional Paper" on a subject of ecumenical interest. The newsletter is free.

Institute for the Study of American Evangelicals (ISAE)

Wheaton College
Wheaton, IL 60187
Tel. (630) 752-5437
Fax (630) 752-5916
Email: isae@wheaton.edu
Website: www.wheaton.edu/isae
Director: Dr. Edith Blumhofer

Founded in 1982, the Institute for the Study of American Evangelicals is a center for research and functions as a program of Wheaton College. The purpose of the ISAE is to encourage and support research on evangelical Christianity in the United States and Canada. The institute seeks to help evangelicals develop a mature understanding of their own heritage and to inform others about evangelicals' historical significance and contemporary role. For the most part, the ISAE focuses on historical research, with occasional sociological or economic researchers participating in the projects.

Current or Recent Research
One recent project entitled, "Hymnody in American Protestantism" is a research project focusing on the history of hymnology in American religious life.

Periodicals
Evangelical Studies Bulletin (*ESB*) is designed to aid both the scholar and the layman in his or her education and research of evangelicalism. Issued quarterly, the bulletin contains articles, book reviews, notices, a calendar of events, and bibliographic information on the latest dissertations, articles and books related to the study of evangelicalism.

Institute for the Study of American Religion

P.O. Box 90709
Santa Barbara, CA 93190-0709
Tel. (805)967-7721
Fax (805)961-0141
Website: www.americanreligion.org

The Institute for the Study of American Religion was founded in 1969 in Evanston, Illinois as a religious studies research facility with a particular focus upon the smaller religions of the United States. Those groups which it has concentrated upon have been known under a variety of labels including sect, cult, minority religion, alternative religion, non-conventional religion, spiritual movement, and new religious movement. It quickly extended its attention to Canada developed a worldwide focus in the 1990's. In 1985, the institute moved to its present location in Santa Barbara, California.

Over the years the institute built a large collection of both primary and secondary materials on the religious groups and movements it studied. In 1985 this collection of more than 40,000 volumes and thousands of periodicals and archival materials was deposited to the Davidson Library at the University of California in Santa Barbara. The reference material exists today as the *American Religious Collection* and is open to scholars and the interested public. The institute continues to support the collection with donations of additional materials.

Current or Recent Research
Today the institute has two main foci. It monitors all of the religious denominations, organizations, and movements functioning in North America and regularly publishes reports drawing from that activity in a series of reference books. The most important of these reference books is the *Encyclopedia of American Religions (*Detroit: Gale research, 5th edition, 1996). Among the most called for information is factual data on the many new and more controversial religious movements, which are popularly labeled as "cults." The institute's second focus developed out of its more recent refocusing on the

international scene, provoked by the international life of most of the religious groups which it has studied in previous decades. With support from the Institute of World Spirituality in Chicago, Illinois, the institute launched the International Religions Directory Project in 1996, a massive five year project that aims to create a full directory of religious bodies, interfaith organizations, and other religious groups world-wide. Please see the above website for more information.

J.W. Dawson Institute of Church-State Studies at Baylor University

P.O. Box 97308
Waco, TX 76798-7308
Tel. (254) 710-1510
Fax (254) 710-1571
Email: dere_davis@'.aylor.edu
Website: www.baylor.edu/~Church_State
Director: Dr. Derek Davis

Baylor University established the J.M. Dawson Institute of Church-State Studies in 1957, so named in honor of an outstanding alumnus, an ardent advocate of religious liberty, and a distinguished author of publications on church and state. The Institute is the oldest and most well-established facility of its kind located in a university setting. It is exclusively devoted to research in the broad field of church and state and the advancement of religious liberty around the world.

From its inception in 1957, the stated purpose of the Institute has been to stimulate academic interest and encourage research and publication in the broad area of church-state relations. In carrying out its statement of purpose, the Institute has sought to honor a threefold commitment: to be interfaith, interdisciplinary, and international.

Current or Recent Research

Some current research includes: Government persecution of minority religions in Europe; original intent of Founding Fathers regarding religion and public life; Christian Right views on political activism; conservative versus moderate Baptist views on church-state relations; role of civil religion in America; international treaties and religious liberty.

Periodicals

Journal of Church and State is the only scholarly journal expressly devoted to church-state relations.

The Louisville Institute

1044 Alta Vista Road
Louisville, KY 40205-1798
Tel. (502) 895-3411 ext. 487
Fax (502) 894-2286
Email: info@louisville-institute.org
Website: www.louisville-institute.org
Exec. Dir.: Dr. James W. Lewis

The Louisville Institute is a Lilly Endowment program for the study of American religion based at the Louisville Presbyterian Seminary. As a program of Lilly Endowment, the Louisville Institute builds upon the Endowment's long-standing support of both leadership education and scholarly research on American religion, focusing on American Protestantism, American Catholicism, the historic African-American churches, and the Hispanic religious experience. The distinctive mission of the Louisville Institute is to enrich the religious life of American Christians and to encourage the revitalization of their institutions by bringing together those who lead religious institutions with those who study them, so that the work of each might stimulate and inform the other. The Louisville Institute seeks to fulfil its mission through a program of grantmaking and conferences.

The work of the Louisville Institute focuses on religion in North America, with particular attention to three issues. The first, Christian faith and life, concerns the character and role of the theology and spirituality that are effectively at work in the lives of American Christians. The second, religious institutions, asks how America's religious institutions might respond most constructively in the midst of the bewildering institutional reconfiguration occurring in American society. The third, pastoral leadership, explores various strategies for improving the quality of religious leadership in North America. The various research projects employ a variety of disciplinary perspectives, including but not limited to, theology, history, ethics, and the social sciences. They may also be interdisciplinary in nature.

Current or Recent Research

Please see the Louisville Institute website (listed above) for lists of recent grants made by the Louisville Institute.

208

The Pluralism Project

Harvard University
201 Vanserg Hall
25 Francis Avenue
Cambridge, MA 02138
Tel. (617)496-2481
Fax (617)496-2428
Email: pluralsm@fas.harvard.edu
Website: www.fas.harvard.edu/~pluralsm
Director: Dr. Diana L. Eck
Project Manager: Ellie J. Pierce

The Pluralism Project was developed by Dr. Diana L. Eck at Harvard University to study and document the growing religions diversity of the United States, with a special view to its new immigrant religious communities. The religious landscape of the U.S. has radically changed in the past 30 years; in light of these changes, how Americans of all faiths begin to engage with one another in shaping a positive pluralism is one of the most important questions American society faces in the years ahead. In addressing these phenomena, the Project has three goals: 1) to document some further changes taking place in America's cities and towns by beginning to map their new religious demography with old and new mosques and Islamic centers, Sikh gurdwaras, Hindu and Jain temples, Buddhist temples and meditation centers, Zoroastrian and Taoist religious centers. 2) To begin to study how these religious traditions are changing as they take root in American soil and develop in a new context. How are they beginning to recreate their community life, religious institutions, rites and rituals, and forms of transmission in the cultural environment of the United States? 3) To explore how the United States is changing as we begin to appropriate this new religious diversity in our public life and institutions, and in emerging forms of interfaith relationships.

The Pluralism Project has the most comprehensive archive anywhere of the print materials of America's new immigrant religious communities: newsletters, serial publications, anniversary programs, handbooks, prayer books, calendars, and educational materials. The Project files also include research papers as well as a variety of materials donated directly by centers.

The Pluralism Project On-Line Directory maintains an extensive directory of religious centers in the United States. At present, this directory exists in a sortable database, with listings of nearly 3,000 centers across the U.S.

Current or Recent Research

The Pluralism Project produced a CD-ROM, *On Common Ground: World Religions in America*, to present some of the wide range of work that had emerged from three years of research. A further grant from the Ford Foundation has enabled the Project to extend its research on the American religious landscape.

Princeton Religion Research Center (PRRC)

47 Hulfish Street
P.O. Box 389
Princeton, NJ 08542
Tel. (609) 279-2255
Fax (609) 924-0228
Email: marie_swirsky@gallup.com
Website: www.prrc.com
Exec. Dir.: George Gallup, Jr.
Contact: Marie Swirsky

The Princeton Religion Research Center is a venerable interfaith, non-denominational organization founded by George Gallup, Jr. and Dr. Miriam Murphy in 1977. The PRRC specializes in creative, practical research, utilizing the worldwide Gallup survey facilities. The purpose of the PRRC is to gain a better understanding of the nature and depth of religious commitment, and to explore the factors behind spiritual growth and decline. The research employs qualitative and quantitative Gallup survey research using scientifically-selected samples of people.

Current or Recent Research

The Princeton Religion Research Center, the Gallup Organization, the Gallup Poll, and the Gallup Youth Survey have conducted surveys for more than 100 denominations or religious groups.

Periodicals

Emerging Trends, published since 1979, provides up-to-date Gallup survey information on religion

SOURCES

and society. The six-page monthly keeps readers abreast of national issues facing church and society, as well as the latest findings on religious belief, practice, and knowledge. *Religion in America* is a bi-annual report.

The Public Religion Project

919 North Michigan Ave.
Suite 540
Chicago, IL 60611-1681
Tel. (312)397-6400
Email: prp-info@publicreligionproj.org
Website: www.publicreligionproj.org
Director: Dr. Martin E. Marty

Building on the strength of personal and private expressions of religious faith, the Public Religion Project addresses the issue of public expressions of faith in a diverse civil society. The Chicago-based directors, staff, and advisors of the Project cooperate internationally with the many agencies, academies, and individuals who would bridge the gap between public and private articulations and actions. It is through this cooperation that the Public Religion Project seeks to contribute to the improved quality of life in the republic. The Public Religion Project has no particular ideological bias, and its only agenda is to help assure that the role of religion is given a representative hearing. The Project's leadership listens carefully for expressions by people of profound conviction and institutions that represent the ever-growing variety of religious impulses in America. It seeks to promote that expression in public life. The role of The Public Religion Project is to provide public access to experts; it does not do original research.

Current or Recent Research

The Public Religion Project maintains a comprehensive database of contact information about individuals who can address questions about religion and about the role it plays in public life. The database consists of internationally recognized scholars, experts, spokespersons and authorities who have agreed to be listed as resources. The database serves a great variety of researchers, including academics, politicians, religious leaders, and many others.

Directory of Selected Faith Traditions in America

Compiling a directory of faith groups is an arduous but rewarding task in religiously plural America. In part, because the very self understanding and definition of community varies so greatly from faith group to faith group. In order to present a reasonably parallel and well balanced listing of organizations for each faith, care must be taken not to impose categories or terms from one's own universe of understanding upon other contexts. The very terms, "church," "membership," "denomination, " "hierarchy" which are essential constructs of certain Christian universes of understanding, are rendered meaningless when applied to other faith groups.

Further, it is important to remember that many religious traditions lack a centralized organization which speaks for the whole of the community. Often, this lack of centralization speaks to the existence of several distinct forms or branches of the religion. In some instances, different ethnic groups immigrating to the U.S., bring with them a distinctive form of their religion, which is particular to their culture of origin. In other cases, plural forms of a faith exist resulting from theological, political, or economic differences. Still other faith groups may be more tightly organized, but the religious center which provides guidance in matters of faith and, perhaps, even organizational discipline may not be in the United States. Hence, the organizations before us are not necessarily religious hierarchical organizations, but are often groups assembled for other purposes that are associated with a particular faith group, or subdivision of that faith group. Caution is advised in regarding these entries as one might regard a "church headquarters."

The compilation of any directory relies upon the existence of a some common organizational structure within all the entities listed. Yet, when compiling a directory of faith groups, it cannot be assumed such organizational parallels exist. Oblique ways must be found to adequately represent individual faith groups. The many religious communities in the United States are associated with myriad organizations of all different types. Some of these are primarily places of worship; others are organizations seeking to represent either the religious community as a whole or some particular constituency within it. Others are community centers; some are educational groups; some are organizations particularly for women or youths; and some are political action groups. Still others are peace organizations or relief organizations. That said, a directory of this sort cannot include an exhaustive list of organizations for each faith group nationwide. The omission of any particular organization or branch of any of the major faith groups listed does not reflect a deliberate attempt to homogenize the rich pluralities that exist within faith groups. Instead, the listings which follow are intended to provide the interested reader with a few initial contacts within each religious community.

Despite the above cautions, this directory provides a rich resource for readers and researchers who wish to learn more about other faith groups. The churches listed here consist of organizations of importance within the communities they represent, and serve as excellent introductory points of contact with those communities.

In some cases, these religious communities are in a state of flux; those with access to the Internet will often find it an excellent way to keep contact with changing religious organizations. There is a plethora of information available about nearly all religious traditions on the Internet with varying degrees of accuracy. Some sites provide extensive links to information and to organizations on the web. For an extensive listing of religious search engines, please see Directory 5, "The Electronic Church."

For directory information about national Interfaith organizations in the United States, please see Directory 1, "U.S. Cooperative Organizations". For directory information on local Interfaith organizations, please see Directory 7, "U.S. Regional and Local Ecumenical Bodies".

BAHA'ISM

Baha'ism was founded in Persia during the late 19th century by Mirza Hussein Ali Nuri, also known as Baha'ullah, which means "Glory of God" in Arabic. Baha'i is an outgrowth of an earlier Persian religious movement called Babism, which was initiated by Mirza Ali Muhammad, who was referred to as the "Bab". In 1844, the Bab prophesied that in nineteen years, a divine manifestation of God would appear. Shortly afterward, the Babis endured a massive period of persecution in which the Bab was martyred. In 1863, Baha'ullah, a close follower of the Bab, claimed that he, himself was this divine manifestation of God. Further, he claimed that he was the last in a line of such divine figures, which included Zoroaster, the Buddha, Christ, and Muhammad. Along these lines, Baha'ullah's teachings called for a religious universalism in which moral truths could be gleaned from all faiths. His son, Abd al-Baha, spread his father's teachings to the Western world, insisting on certain social principles such as universal equality of the sexes, or races, and of religious adherence.

The Baha'i National Center of the U.S.A.
536 Sheridan Road
Wilmette, IL 60091
Tel: (708) 869-9039
Website: www.bahai.org

This center can provide information about the Baha'i faith and provide contacts with Baha'i organizations throughout the country and the world. There are over 1,400 Baha'i local spiritual assemblies in the United States. The community is very concerned about issues involving peace, justice, racial unity, economic development, and education (among others) and has available resources on a number of these issues as well as on Baha'i scriptures and theology. The website listed above is the official Baha'i website on the Internet.

BUDDHISM

Buddhism began in northern India between the 6th–5th centuries B.C.E. with the teachings of Siddhartha Gautama, who is called the Buddha, which means "The One Who is Enlightened."

Buddhism grew out of the Hindu tradition of the time, but it rejected certain fundamental philosophical, cosmological, social, hierarchical, and scriptural aspects of that tradition, which set the two deeply apart from each other. Most Buddhists believe that suffering is the central predicament of life, and that desires are the source of this suffering. One need only remove desires and it follows that suffering disappears as well. Buddhism has grown in different directions over the centuries among many different cultures, and its traditions have varied widely. All are usually characterized by an emphasis on meditation and compassion. Buddhism is divided into three major branches: *Theravada*, "the way of the Elders," *Mahayana* "the Great Vehicle," and *Vajrayana*, "the indestructible vehicle" or path of devotion. Buddhism spread through parts of South Asia, the Himalayan region, all over China, Japan, and Korea, and deeply into South East Asia. Although its origins are Indian, Buddhism is almost entirely absent from that country. In the past hundred and fifty years, Buddhism has spread to the Western world. In this religious tradition, with few national bodies and great variation among particular branches and cultural expressions, organization is more localized than in some other faith groups.

American Buddhist Congress
4267 West Third Street
Los Angeles, CA 20020

Tel: 213-386-8139
An association of leaders from a variety of Buddhist traditions in the U.S.

Buddhist Churches of America
1710 Octavia Street
San Francisco, CA 94109
Tel: 415-776-5600
FAX: 415-771-6293
Bishop, Ven. Hakubun Watanabe
     The national body of Japanese Shin tradition was founded in 1899. It provides programmatic resources for local temples around the U.S.

Buddhist Council of the Midwest
2400 Prairie
Evanston, IL 60201
Tel: 847-869-4975
     A regional organization active in coordinating activities among the Buddhist communities in the mid-west.

Buddhist Sangha Council of Southern California
933 South New Hampshire Ave.
Los Angeles, CA 90006
Tel: 213-739-1270
FAX: 213-386-6643
     The umbrella organization of Buddhist communities in Southern California.

Texas Buddhist Council
8727 Radio Road
Houston, TX 77075
Tel: 713-744-1334
     The regional coordinating body for Buddhists in Texas.

The Buddhist Peace Fellowship
P. O. Box 4650
Berkeley, CA 94704
Tel: 510-655-6169
FAX: 510-655-1369
Email: bpf@bpf.org
Director, Alan Senauke
     A national organization through which Buddhists of many traditions work for peace and justice.

HINDUISM

Hinduism has been evolving since roughly 1500 B.C.E. and has its origins in India. Most of the inhabitants of India are still Hindus, but many have emigrated to Europe, North America, East Africa, South and South East Asia. The beliefs and practices of Hinduism vary so deeply and widely throughout India, and are so diffused throughout every aspect of life, that one may describe Hinduism not so much as a tradition, but more accurately as the collection of many traditions, encompassed by the great history and geography of India. Throughout its history, Hinduism has had an enormous propensity for the absorption of new elements into its practices and its understanding of deity. There is no central authority or priestly hierarchy that regulates the evolution of Hinduism, very few traditions are shared by all Hindus; adaptations and evolutions can and do occur, but usually at the regional level. Simultaneously, ancient practices and beliefs persist in some places, where elsewhere, they have been long since replaced or never occurred. Nevertheless, all Hindus believe in the authority of the *Vedas*, the ancient scriptural tradition of India. All accept the *dharma*, or "way," of the four *varnas*, or social classes, which constitute the complex caste system, which is interwoven in the practice of the religion. Further, most Hindus worship Shiva or Vishnu or Devi, in addition to individual devotions to other deities or divine manifestations. Most Hindus are vegetarians.

The International Society for Krishna Consciousness
North American Communications
10310 Oaklyn Drive
Potomac, MD 20854

Tel: 301-299-9707
FAX: 301-299-5025
Email: anuttama.acbsp@com.bbt.se
Communications Director, Anuttama Dasa

Council of Hindu Temples of North America
45-57 Bowne Street
Flushing, NY 11355
Tel: 1-800-99HINDU
   One of a number of Hindu organizations, which connect Hindus in certain regions of the U.S.

American Hindus Against Defamation
8914 Rotherdam Avenue
San Diego, CA 92129
Tel: 619-484-4564
Email: ajay@hindunet.org
Director, Mr. Ajay Shah
   A new organization devoted to defending Hindus from stereotyping and discriminatory or defamatory acts/speech.

ISLAM

   Islam began in 7th century Arabia under the leadership of the Prophet Muhammad, to whom God (*Allah* in Arabic) revealed a collection of verses known as the *Holy Qur'an*. The word *islam* means "making peace through submission" and in the context of religion, it means "submission to the will of God." A person who practices Islam is a Muslim, meaning, "one who is submitting to the will of God." A Muslim follows the teachings of the *Holy Qur'an*, which was presented to human kind by Muhammad, but which is the very word of the one and only God, and is therefore perfect and complete. Integral to the Muslim Tradition are the "Five Pillars of Islam," which are the five obligations each Muslim must uphold. The first of these is the *shahadah*, or profession of faith, which states, "There is no God but God, and Muhammad is his prophet." The second obligation is that a Muslim prays five times each day at prescribed times. Thirdly, a Muslim must pay the *zakat*, which is a form of mandatory almsgiving. Fourth, a Muslim is required to fast from dawn until sunset during the month of *Ramadan*, the ninth month of the Muslim year. And finally, if able, once in his/her lifetime, every Muslim is required to make a pilgrimage called the *Hajj* to the holy city of Mekkah, where the *ka'bah* is housed, a stone structure, built by Abraham and Ishmael. Early in the history of the Islam, the religion split into two distinct branches, known as the Sunni and the Shiah, both of which contain subbranches. Muslims worldwide constitute an enormous community which is rapidly spreading throughout North America as a result of recent immigration as well as conversion.

The Islamic Society of North America (ISNA)
P.O. Box 38
Plainfield, IN 46168
Tel: (317) 839-8157
Website: www.isna.net
Dr. Sayyid M. Syeed, General Secretary
   The Islamic Society of North America grew out of the Muslim Students Association and is one of the oldest national Muslim organizations in the United States. It has a varied program primarily serving the Muslim community, but also seeks to promote friendly relations between Muslims and non-Muslims. It has a speakers' bureau, film loans, library assistance program, and several other services. It has also has a number of publications. Since ISNA is well represented throughout much of the United States, it is a good initial contact. It has been very active in the area of interfaith relations.

The Islamic Circle of North America (ICNA)
166-22 89th Ave.
Jamaica, NY 11432
Tel: (718) 658-1199
Web site: www.icna.org
   The Islamic Circle of North America is a smaller national organization than ISNA, but is involved in many of the same activities. They also have a presence in many different parts of the country and provide a number of resources both to Muslims and non-Muslims. ICNA also has been very active in the world of interfaith relations.

The Muslim American Society
The Ministry of W. Deen Mohammed
P.O. Box 1944
Calumet City, IL 60409

This is the community of Imam W. Deen Mohammed and represents the largest single grouping of orthodox African-American Muslims in the United States. It is important to distinguish this group from the Nation of Islam (Black Muslims). African Americans constitute probably the largest single group of Muslims in the United States. Given the loose structure of the organization, it is often both possible and helpful to make contact with a local mosque in your area.

The American Muslim Council
1212 New York Ave., NW
Washington, DC 20005
Tel: (202) 789-22 62
Web sight: www.amermuslim.org
Dr. Aly R. Abuzaakouk, Executive Director

An organization which exists, in part, to represent the political and social interests of American Muslims and to defend their rights. It often has information about Muslim reaction to national and international events and also publishes informative booklets and brochures which include basic information on Islam and a journalistic style sheet.

JAINISM

Jainism was founded in the 6th century B.C.E. in India by Vardhamana Jnatiputra (also known as Nataputta Mahavira, whom the Jains call Jina, which means "Spiritual Conqueror." Mahavira was a contemporary of the Buddha, and to some extent, Buddhism was an important rival to Jainism at the time. Both grew out of the Hindu tradition but rejected certain of its aspects. Jains honor a number of saints, or prophets from remote history called *tirthankaras*, who had liberated themselves from the bondage of *karma*, and hence from the cycle of reincarnation. Mahavira is the 24th of these *tirthankaras*. Emulating these saints, one may free the soul from the shackles of *karma* and rebirth, by observing the "three jewels" of "right faith," "right knowledge," "and right conduct." There is a strong emphasis in Jainism on peacefulness, moderation, and the refusal to injure animals in any way. There are religious orders, called *yatis*, which observe strict vows. The laity hold a pious respect for the *yatis*. There are two main branches of Jainism, the *Digambara* ("sky-clad" or "naked") and the *vetambara* ("white-clad"). Despite the fact that the Jains constitute a relatively small proportion of the Indian population, they have a great influence on the Hindu community. The essential philosophy of non-violence had a great effect on the teachings of Gandhi in this century.

Federation of Jain Associations in North America
66 Viscount
Williamsville, NY 14221
Tel: 716-688-3030

Siddhachalam/International Mahavira Jain Mission
65 Mud Pond Road
Blairstown, NJ 07285
Tel: 908-362-9793

A residential center for the teaching of the Jain way of life in the United States.

JUDAISM

Judaism is one of the world's oldest religions, encompassing a rich and complex tradition that has evolved over centuries and has given rise to, or influenced, other major world traditions. Numerous expressions of Judaism have always coexisted with one another, as they do today. The central concern shared by all is to live in relation to God and to follow God's will. Jews understand themselves to be in covenant with God, who is the one transcendent God, Creator of the Universe. God revealed the Torah to the people of Israel as his way of life. History brought the Jewish people into contact with many cultures and civilizations, contacts that continuously transformed the nature of their worship, the understanding of God's law, and even their conceptualization of peoplehood. At the time of the second Diaspora, or great migration of Jews throughout the Middle East, North Africa, and Europe at the beginning of the common era, was the rise of the Rabbinical Tradition, with its emphasis on the study of scripture. Today's Judaism has grown out of these roots. In the 19th century, Reform Judaism arose in Europe and the United States as one Jewish response to modernity. Conservative Judaism and Reconstructionism are branches of Jewish practice that first developed in America. Orthodox Judaism also has a number of modern forms.

American Jewish Committee
165 East 56th Street,
New York, NY 10022
Tel: 212-751-4000
FAX: 212-750-0326
Executive Director, David A. Harris
    Founded in 1906, The AJC protects the rights and freedoms of Jews world-wide; combats bigotry and anti-Semitism and promotes democracy and human rights for all. It is an independent community-relations organization, with strong interest in interreligious relations and public-policy advocacy. The AJC publishes the *American Jewish Yearbook*, and *Commentary magazine*.

The Anti-Defamation League of B'nai B'rith
823 United Nations Plaza
New York, NY 10017
Tel: 212-885-7700
FAX: 212-867-0779
Website: www.adl.org
Director, Abraham H. Foxman
    Since 1913, the Anti-Defamation League has been involved in combating and documenting anti-Semitism. It also works to secure fair treatment for all citizens through law, education and community relations.

Jewish Council for Public Affairs
443 Park Avenue South, 11th Floor
New York, NY 10016
Tel: 212-684-6950
FAX: 212-686-1353
Website: www.thejcpa.org
Executive Vice Chairman, Lawrence Rubin
    This national coordinating body for the field of Jewish community relations comprises 13 national and 122 local Jewish communal agencies. Through the Council's work, and in its collaboration with other religious groups, its constituent agencies work on public policy issues, both international and domestic.

Jewish Reconstructionist Federation
7804 Montgomery Ave., Suite 9
Elkins Park, PA 19027
Tel: 212-782-8500
Email: jfrnatl@aol.com
Executive Director, Rabbi Mordechai Liebling
    Fosters the establishment and ongoing life of Reconstructionist congregations and fellowship groups. Publishes *The Reconstructionist* and other materials. Rabbis who relate to this branch of Judaism are often members of the Reconstructionist Rabbinical Association.

Union of American Hebrew Congregations
633 Third Avenue
New York, NY 10017
Tel: 212-650-4000
FAX: 212-650-4169
Website: www.uahc.org
President: Rabbi Eric H. Yoffie
    The central congregational body of Reform Judaism, founded in 1873. It serves approx. 875 affiliated temples and its members through religious, educational, cultural and administrative programs. Sponsors women's, men's and youth organizations. *Reform Judaism* is one of its publications. The Central Conference of American Rabbis is the affiliated rabbinical body.

The Union of Orthodox Jewish Congregations of America
333 Seventh Avenue
New York, NY 10001

215

Tel: 212-563-4000
FAX: 212-564-9058
Website: www.ou.org
Executive Vice-President, Rabbi Raphael Butler
　　The national central body of Orthodox synagogues since 1898, providing kashrut supervision, women's and youth organizations, and a variety of educational, religious and public policy programs and activities. Publishers of *Jewish Action* magazine and other materials. The Rabbinical Council of America is the related organization for Orthodox Rabbis.

The United Synagogue of Conservative Judaism
155 Fifth Avenue
New York, NY 10010-6802
Tel: 212-533-7800
FAX: 212-353-9439
Executive Vice-President, Rabbi Jerome M. Epstein
　　The International organization of 800 congregations, founded in 1913. Provides religious, educational, youth, community and administrative programming. Publishes *United Synagogue Review* and other materials. The Rabbinical Assembly is the association of Conservative Rabbis.

NATIVE AMERICAN TRADITIONAL SPIRITUALITY

　　Native American spirituality is difficult to define or categorize because it varies so greatly across the continent. Further, it is deeply entwined with elements of nature which are associated with different geographical regions. For example, while Plains Indians possess a spiritual relationship with the buffalo, Indigenous Peoples from the Northwest share a similar relationship with salmon. Hence, the character of Native American spirituality is dependent, to some extent, on the surrounding geography and its incumbent ecosystems. Despite this great variety, there are some similarities which allow us to consider the many Native American forms of spirituality together: Contrary to popular belief, Native American peoples are monotheistic; they do not worship the sun or buffalo or salmon, but rather understand that these elements of nature are gifts from the "Great Mystery," and are parts of it. Today, while still working toward religious freedom in the United States, Native Americans are also struggling to protect sacred sites, which they consider to be comparable to "churches." But since these sites are actually part of the land, not man-made structures, many are constantly under attack for the natural resources they contain. Such exploitation of these resources is an offense to the Native American sense of spirituality, which views resources like timber, oil, and gold, as gifts from the Great Mystery. The struggle to protect and respect these sacred sites is a universal and essential part of Native American spirituality.

National Congress of American Indians (NCAI)
1301 Connecticut Ave., NW
Suite 200
Washington, DC 20036
Tel: (202) 466-7767
Fax: (202) 466-7797
Email: jdossett@erols.com
Website: www.ncai.org
Exec. Dir., JoAnn K. Chase
　　The National Congress of American Indians (NCAI), founded in 1944, is the oldest, largest and most representative national Indian organization serving the needs of a broad membership of American Indian and Alaska Native governments. NCAI stresses the need for unity and cooperation among tribal governments and people for the security and protection of treaty and sovereign rights. As the preeminent national Indian organization, NCAI is organized as a representative congress aiming for consensus on national priority issues.
　　The NCAI website contains links for a directory of Indian nations in the continental U.S. and Alaska as well as a directory of tribal governments. There are also links to other Native American websites.

Native American Rights Fund (NARF)
1506 Broadway
Boulder, CO 80302
Tel: (303) 447-8760
Fax: (303) 433-7776

Email: pereira@narf.org
Website: www.narf.org
Exec. Dir., Walter Echohawk

The Native American Rights Fund is the non-profit legal organization devoted to defending and promoting the legal rights of the Indian people. NARF attorneys, most of whom are Native Americans, defend tribes who otherwise cannot bear the financial burden of obtaining justice in the courts of the United States. The NARF mission statement outlines five areas of concentration: 1) Preservation of tribal existence; 2) Protection of tribal natural resources; 3) Promotion of human rights; 4) Accountability of government; 5) Development of Indian law.

SIKHISM

Sikhism was founded by Guru Nanak during the 15th and 16th centuries C.E. in the state of Punjab in northwestern India. Nanak was greatly influenced by the teachings of Kabir, a Muslim who became deeply inspired by Hindu philosophies. Kabir's poems called for a synthesis between Islam and Hinduism. In the footsteps of Kabir's wisdom, Nanak drew upon elements of Bhakti Hinduism and Sufi Islam: He stressed the existence of a universal, single God, who transcends religious distinctions. Union with God is accomplished through meditation and surrender to the divine will. Nanak also called for the belief in reincarnation, karma, and also the cyclical destruction and recreation of the universe. However, he rejected the caste system, the devotion to divine incarnations, priesthood, idol worship, all of which were elements of the Hindu tradition. Nanak was the first of ten *gurus*, or teachers. The fourth guru, built the Golden Temple in Amritsar, the Sikh religious center. The fifth guru compiled the *Adi Granth*, a sort of hymn-book of spiritual authority. All male sikhs are initiated into the religious brotherhood called the *Khalsa*. Members of this order vow never to cut their beard or hair, to wear special pants, to wear an iron bangle as an amulet against evil, to carry a steel dagger, and a comb.

The Sikh Center of Orange County
2514 West Warner Ave.
Santa Ana, CA 92704
Tel: (714) 979-9328
Website: www.sikhcenter.org

The Sikh Center of Orange County describes itself as follows: "Our mission, in following the tradition and teaching of our honorable Guru Nanak, is to provide accurate, reliable and complete religious, social and cultural teachings and understanding of Sikhism and the people who practice it."

7. United States Regional and Local Ecumenical Bodies

One of the many ways Christians and Christian churches relate to one another locally and regionally is through ecumenical bodies. The membership in these ecumenical organizations is diverse. Historically, councils of churches were formed primarily by Protestants, but many local and regional organizations now include Orthodox and Roman Catholics. Many are made up of congregations or judicatory units of churches. Some have a membership base of individuals. Others foster cooperation between ministerial groups, community ministries, coalitions, or church agencies. While "council of churches" is a term still commonly used to describe this form of cooperation, other terms such as "conference of churches," "ecumenical councils," "churches united," and "metropolitan ministries," are coming into use. Ecumenical organizations that are national in scope are listed in Directory 1, "United States Cooperative Organizations."

An increasing number of ecumenical bodies have been exploring ways to strengthen the interreligious aspect of life in the context of religious pluralism in the U.S. today. Some organizations in this listing are fully interfaith agencies primarily through the inclusion of Jewish congregations in their membership. Other organizations nurture partnerships with a broader base of religious groups in their communities, especially in the areas of public policy and interreligious dialogue.

This list does not include all local and regional ecumenical and interfaith organizations in existence today. For information about other groups, contact the Ecumenical Networks Commission of the National Council of Churches of Christ in the U.S.A., 475 Riverside Drive, New York, NY 10115-0050. Tel. (212)870-2228 Fax (212)870-2690.

The terms regional and local are relative, making identification somewhat ambiguous. Regional councils may cover sections of large states or cross-state borders. Local councils may be made up of several counties, towns, or clusters of congregations. The organizations are listed by state. State councils or state-level ecumenical contacts exist in 43 of the 50 states. These state-level or multi-state organizations are marked with an asterisk (*) and are the first organizations listed under each state subheading. The remainder of the organizations are listed alphabetically after the state-level organizations.

ALABAMA

Greater Birmingham Ministries
2304 12th Ave. N, Birmingham, AL 35234-3111
Tel. (205)326-6821 Fax (205)252-8458
Media Contact, Scott Douglas
Exec. Dir., Scott Douglas
Economic Justice, Co-Chpsn.: Helen Holdefer; Karnie Smith
Direct Services, Chpsn., Benjamin Greene
Finance & Fund-Raising, Chpsn., Dick Sales
Pres., Richard Ambrose
Sec., Lois Martin
Treas., Chris Hamlin
Major Activities: Direct Service Ministries (Food, Utilities, Rent and Nutrition Education, Shelter); Alabama Arise (Statewide legislative network focusing on low income issues); Economic Justice Issues (Low Income Housing and Advocacy, Health Care, Community Development, Jobs Creation, Public Transportation); Faith in Community Ministries (Interchurch Forum, Interpreting and Organizing, Bible Study)

Interfaith Mission Service
411-B Holmes Ave. NE, Huntsville, AL 35801
Tel. (256)536-2401 Fax (256)536-2284
Email: ims@hiwaay.net
Exec. Dir., Susan J. Smith

Pres., Richard C. Titus
Major Activities: Foodline & Food Pantry; Local FEMA Committee; Ministry Development; Clergy Luncheon; Workshops; Response to Community Needs; Information and Referral; Interfaith Understanding; Christian Unity; Homeless Needs; School Readiness Screenings

ALASKA

Alaska Christian Conference*
Episcopal Diocese of Alaska, 1205 Denali Way, Fairbanks, AK 99701-4178 Tel. (907)452-3040
Email: MARK_MACDONALD.parti@ecunet.org
Media Contact, Rt. Rev. Mark MacDonald
Pres., Rt. Rev. Mark MacDonald
Vice-Pres., Rev. David I. Blanchett, 1100 Pullman Drive, Wasilla, AK 99654 Tel. (907)352-2517
Sec., Rev. Dianne A. O'Connell, 9851 Basher Avenue, Anchorage, AK 99507-1279 Tel. (907) 261-5053
Treas., Carolyn M. Winters, 2133 Bridgewater Drive, Fairbanks, AK 99709-4101 Tel. (907) 456-8555
Major Activities: Legislative & Social Concerns; Resources and Continuing Education; New Ecumenical Ministries; Communication;

Alcoholism (Education & Prevention); Family Violence (Education & Prevention); Native Issues; Ecumenical/Theological Dialogue; HIV/AIDS Education and Ministry; Criminal Justice

ARIZONA

Arizona Ecumenical Council*
4423 N. 24th St., Ste. 750, Phoenix, AZ 85016 Tel. (602)468-3818 Fax (602)468-3839
Media Contact, Exec. Dir., Dr. Paul Eppinger, Tel. (602)967-6040 Fax (602)468-3839
Exec. Dir., Dr. Paul Eppinger
Pres., Rev. Gail Davis, 4423 N. 24th St. Ste. 700, Phoenix, AZ 85016
Major Activities: Donohoe Ecumenical Forum Series; Political Action Team; Legislative Workshop; Arizona Ecumenical Indian Concerns Committee; Mexican/American Border Issues; ISN-TV; Disaster Relief; Break Violence-Build Community; Truckin" for Kids; "Souper Bowl'; Gun Information and Safety Program

ARKANSAS

Arkansas Interfaith Conference*
P.O. Box 151, Scott, AR 72142 Tel. (501)961-2626
Email: aicark@aol.com
Media Contact, Conf. Exec., Mimi Dortch
Conf. Exec., Mimi Dortch
Pres., Rabbi Eugene Levy, 3700 Rodney Park Ave., Little Rock, AR 72212
Sec., Rev. Thurston Lamb, Bethel AME Church, Little Rock, AR 72202
Treas., Jim Davis, Box 7239, Little Rock, AR 72217
Major Activities: Institutional Ministry; Interfaith Executives' Advisory Council; Interfaith Relations; Church Women United; AIDS Task Force; Our House-Shelter; Legislative Liaison; Ecumenical Choir Camp; Tornado Disaster Relief; Camp for Jonesboro School Children Massacre; Welfare Reform Work; Med Center Chaplaincy

CALIFORNIA

California Council of Churches/ California Church Impact*
2700 L Street, Sacramento, CA 95816 Tel. (916)442-5447 Fax (916)442-3036
Email: cccinfo@calchurches.org
Website: www.calchurches.org
Media Contact, Exec. Dir., Scott D. Anderson
Exec. Dir., Scott D. Anderson
Major Activities: Monitoring State Legislation; California IMPACT Network; Legislative Principles; Food Policy Advocacy; Family Welfare Issues; Health; Church/State Issues; Violence Prevention; Child Care Program/ Capacity Coordinator to Increase Quality Child Care within California for the Working Poor, etc.

Northern California Interreligious Conference*
534 22nd St., Oakland, CA 94612 Tel. (510)433-0822 Fax (510)433-0813
Email: NCIC@igc.org
Media Contact, Pres., Rev. Phil Lawson
Exec. Dir., Charlene Tschirhart
Pres., Rev. Phil Lawson
Vice-Pres.: Nancy Nielsen
Sec., Robert Forsberg
Treas., John Lanehart
Major Activities: Peace with Justice Commission; Knight Initiative (same sex marriage); Interreligious Relationships Commission; Public Policy Advocacy; Same Gender marriage Education Campaign; Welfare Reform

Southern California Ecumenical Council*
54 N. Oakland Ave., Pasadena, CA 91101-2086 Tel. (626)578-6371 Fax (626)578-6358
Email: scec@loop.com
Media Contact, Exec. Dir., Rev. Albert G. Cohen
Exec. Dir., Rev. Albert G. Cohen
Pres., Rev. Donald Smith
Treas., Fr. Arshag Khatchadourian
Sec., Ms. Laura Ramirez
V.P. Faith & Tradition, Rev. Wil Tyrrell, S.A.
V.P. Special Events, Dr. Gwynne Guibord
Member at Large, Rev. Dr. Efstathios Mylonas
Faith and Order Chair, Rev. Dr. Rod Parrott
Past Pres., Rev. Sally Welch
Major Activities: Consultation with the regional religious sector concerning the well being and spiritual vitality of this most diverse and challenging area

The Council of Churches of Santa Clara County
1710 Moorpark Avenue, San Jose, CA 95128 Tel. (408)297-2660 Fax (408)297-2661
Media Contact, Interim Ex. Dir., Rev. R. Richard Roe
Interim Exec. Dir., Rev. R. Richard Roe
Pres., Rev. Dr. Kristin Sundquist
Major Activities: Social Education/Action; Ecumenical and Interfaith Witness; Affordable Housing; Environmental Ministry; Family/ Children; Refugee Immigration Ministry; Interfaith Study Project; Convalescent Hospital Ministries; Gay Ministry

The Ecumenical Council of Pasadena Area Churches
P.O. Box 41125, 444 E. Washington Blvd., Pasadena, CA 91114-8125 Tel. (626)797-2402 Fax (626)797-7353
Email: ecpac@prodigy.net
Exec. Dir., Rev. Frank B. Clark
Major Activities: Christian Education; Community Worship; Community Concerns; Christian

219

Unity; Ethnic Ministries; Hunger; Peace; Food, Clothing Assistance for the Poor; Emergency Shelter

Ecumenical Council of San Diego County

1880 Third Ave., San Diego, CA 92101
Website: http://home.earthlink.net/~searay1/
Exec. Dir., Rev. Glenn S. Allison
Admn., Patricia R. Munley
Pres., George Mitrovich
Treas., Joseph Ramsey
Major Activities: Interfaith Shelter Network/El Nido Transitional Living Program; Emerging Issues; Faith Order & Witness; Worship & Celebration; Ecumenical Tribute Dinner; Advent Prayer Breakfast; AIDS Chaplaincy Program; Third World Opportunities; Seminars and Workshops; Called to Dance Assn.; S.D. Names Project Quilt; Children's Sabbath Workshops and events; Edgemoor Chaplaincy; Stand for Children events; Continuing Education for clergy and laypersons

Fresno Metro Ministry

1055 N. Van Ness, Ste. H, Fresno, CA 93728 Tel. (559)485-1416 Fax (559)485-9109
Email: metromin@qnis.net
Media Contact, Exec. Dir., Rev. Walter P. Parry
Exec. Dir., Rev. Walter P. Parry
Admn. Asst., Linda Jimenez
Pres., Rev. Delman Howard
Major Activities: Hunger Relief Advocacy; Human Relations and Anti-Racism; Health Care Advocacy; Public Education Concerns; Children's Needs; Biblical and Theological Education For Laity; Ecumenical & Interfaith Celebrations & Cooperation; Youth Needs; Community Network Building; Human Services Facilitation; Anti-Poverty Efforts; Hate Crime Prevention and Response

Interfaith Council of Contra Costa County

1543 Sunnyvale Ave., Walnut Creek, CA 94596 Tel. (925)933-6030 Fax (925)952-4554
Chaplains: Rev. Charles Tinsley; Rev. Duane Woida; Rev. Harold Wright; Laurie Maxwell
Pres., Rev. Steve Harms
Treas., Robert Bender
Major Activities: Institutional Chaplaincies, Community Education, Interfaith Cooperation; Social Justice

Interfaith Service Bureau

3720 Folsom Blvd., Sacramento, CA 95816 Tel. (916)456-3815 Fax (916)456-3816
Email: isbdexter@aol.com
Media Contact, Executive Dir., Dexter McNamara
Executive Dir., Dexter McNamara
Pres.: Richard Montgomery

Vice-Pres.: Lloyd Hanson
Major Activities: Religious and Racial Cooperation and Understanding; Welfare Reform Concerns; Refugee Resettlement & Support; Religious Cable Television; Violence Prevention; Graffiti Abatement

Marin Interfaith Council

845 Olive Ave., Suite 110, Novato, CA 94945 Tel. (415)492-1052 Fax (415)492-8907
Email: faiths@peacenet.org
Media Contact, Exec. Dir., Rev. Kevin F. Tripp
Exec. Dir., Rev. Kevin F. Tripp
Major Activities: Interfaith Dialogue; Education; Advocacy; Convening; Interfaith Worship Services & Commemorations

Massachusetts Commission on Christian Unity

845 Olive Ave. Suite 110, Novato, CA 94945 Tel. (415)209-6278 Fax (415)209-6527
Email: faiths@peacenet.org
Media Contact, Exec. Dir., Rev. K. Gordon White
Exec. Sec., Rev. K. Gordon White
Pres., Sr. Katherine Hamilton, O.P.
Major Activities: Faith and Order Dialogue with Church Judicatories; Guidelines & Pastoral Directives for Inter-Church Marriages

Pacific and Asian American Center for Theology and Strategies (PACTS)

Graduate Theological Union, 2400 Ridge Rd., Berkeley, CA 94709 Tel. (510)849-0653
Media Contact, Dir., Deborah Lee
Dir., Deborah Lee
Pres., Ron Nakasone
Major Activities: Collect and Disseminate Resource Materials; Training Conferences; Public Seminars; Women in Ministry; Racial and Ethnic Minority Concerns; Journal and Newsletter; Hawaii & Greater Pacific Programme; Sale of Sadao Watanabe Calendars; Informational Forums on Peace & Social Justice in Asian Pacific American Community and Asia/Pacific Internationally; Forums & Conferences for Seminarians; Asian Pacific Heritage

Pomona Inland Valley Council of Churches

1753 N. Park Ave., Pomona, CA 91768 Tel. (909)622-3806 Fax (909)622-0484
Media Contact, Dir. of Development, Mary Kashmar
Pres., The Rev. Henry Rush
Acting Exec. Dir., The Rev. La Quetta Bush-Simmons
Sec., Ken Coates
Treas., Anne Ashford

Major Activities: Advocacy and Education for Social Justice; Ecumenical Celebrations; Hunger Advocacy; Emergency Food and Shelter Assistance; Farmer's Market; Affordable Housing; Transitional Housing

San Fernando Valley Interfaith Council

10824 Topanga Canyon Blvd., No. 7, Chatsworth, CA 91311 Tel. (818)718-6460 Fax (818)718-0734

Email: sfvic@earthlink.net

Website: www.sfvic.org

Media Contact, Communications Coord., Dyanne Hendrix, ext. 3002

Exec. Dir., Barry Smedberg; Ext. 3011

Pres., Dr. William Huling

Major Activities: Seniors Multi-Purpose Centers; Nutrition & Services; Meals to Homebound; Meals on Wheels; Interfaith Reporter; Interfaith Relations; Social Adult Day Care; Hunger/Homelessness; Volunteer Care-Givers; Clergy Gatherings; Food Pantries and Outreach; Social Concerns; Aging; Hunger; Human Relations; Child Abuse Program; Medical Service; Homeless Program; Disaster Response Preparedness; Immigration Services; Self-Sufficiency Program for Section 8 Families

South Coast Ecumenical Council

3300 Magnolia Ave., Long Beach, CA 90806 Tel. (562)595-0268 Fax (562)490-9920

Email: SCEC2@earthlink.net

Website: www.southcoastecumenical.org

Media Contact, Exec. Dir., Rev. Ginny Wagener

Exec. Dir., Rev. Ginny Wagener

Farmers' Markets, Rev. Dale Whitney

Pres., Fr. Mike Roebert

Centro Shalom, Amelia Nieto

New Communion, David Satchwell

Major Activities: Homeless Support Services; Farmers' Markets; Hunger Projects; Church Athletic Leagues; Community Action; Easter Sunrise Worships; Interreligious Dialogue; Justice Advocacy; Martin Luther King, Jr. Celebration; Violence Prevention; Long Beach Church Women United; Long Beach Interfaith Clergy; Publishing Area Religious Directories; South Bay-Long Beach Million Mom March Chapter

Westside Interfaith Council

P.O. Box 1402, Santa Monica, CA 90406 Tel. (310)394-1518 Fax (310)576-1895

Media Contact, Rev. Janet A. Bregar

Exec. Dir., Rev. Janet A. Bregar

Major Activities: Meals on Wheels; Community Religious Services; Convalescent Hospital Chaplaincy; Homeless Partnership; Hunger & Shelter Coalition

COLORADO

Colorado Council of Churches*

3690 Cherry Creek S. Dr., Denver, CO 80209 Tel. (303)825-4910 Fax (303)744-8605

Email: jryan@americanisp.net

Media Contact, Council Executive, Rev. Dr. James R. Ryan

Pres., Beth Robey Hyde

Staff Assoc, Sandra Boyd

Major Activities: Addressing issues of Christian Unity, Justice, and Environment

Interfaith Council of Boulder

3700 Baseline Rd., Boulder, CO 80303 Tel. (303)494-8094

Media Contact, Pres., Stan Grotegut, 810 Kalma Ave., Boulder, CO 80304 Tel. (303)443-2291

Pres., Stan Grotegut

Major Activities: Interfaith Dialogue and Programs; Thanksgiving Worship Services; Food for the Hungry; Share-A-Gift; Monthly Newsletter

CONNECTICUT

Christian Conference of Connecticut*

60 Lorraine St., Hartford, CT 06105 Tel. (860)236-4281 Fax (860)236-9977

Email: ssidorak@aol.com

Website: www.christconn.org

Media Contact, Exec. Dir., Rev. Stephen J. Sidorak, Jr.

Exec. Dir., Rev. Stephen J. Sidorak, Jr.

Pres., The Most Rev. Daniel A. Cronin

Vice-Pres., The Rev. Erica Wimber Avena

Sec., The Rev. Kevin J. Agee

Treas., Thomas F. Sarubbi

Major Activities: Communications; Institutional Ministries; Conn. Bible Society; Connecticut Ecumenical Council on Addiction; Ecumenical Forum; Faith & Order; Social Concerns; Public Policy; Peace and Justice Convocation; Restorative Justice & Death Penalty; Interreligious Dialogue & Interreligious Action on Economic Justice; Housing and Human Services Ministry

Association of Religious Communities

325 Main St., Danbury, CT 06810 Tel. (203)792-9450 Fax (203)792-9452

Email: arc325@aol.com

Media Contact, Exec. Dir., Samuel E. Deibler, Jr.

Exec. Dir., Samuel E. Deibler, Jr.

Pres., The Rev. Mark Lingle

Major Activities: Refugee Resettlement; Family Counseling; Family Violence Prevention; Affordable Housing

The Capitol Region Conference of Churches

30 Arbor St., Hartford, CT 06106 Tel. (860)236-1295 Fax (860)236-8071

221

Media Contact, Exec. Dir., Rev. Roger W. Floyd
Exec. Dir., Rev. Roger W. Floyd
Pastoral Care & Training, Dir., Rev. Kathleen Davis
Aging Project, Dir., Barbara Malcolm
Community Organizer, Joseph Wasserman
Broadcast Ministry Consultant, Ivor T. Hugh
Pres., Rev. Kenneth Monroe
Major Activities: Organizing for Peace and Justice; Aging; Legislative Action; Cooperative Broadcast Ministry; Ecumenical Cooperation; Interfaith Reconciliation; Chaplaincies; Low-Income Senior Empowerment; Anti-Racism Education

Center City Churches

100 Constitution Plaza, Suite 721, Hartford, CT 06103-1721 Tel. (860)728-3201 Fax (860) 549-8550
Media Contact, Exec. Dir., Paul C. Christie
Exec. Dir., Paul C. Christie
Pres., The Rev. Dr. Jay Terbush
Sec., John Hunt
Treas., Holly Billings
Major Activities: Senior Services; Family Support Center; Energy Bank; Crisis Food Pantry and Intervention; After School Tutoring; Summer Day Camp and Youth Employment; Housing for persons with AIDS; Mental Health Residence; Community Soup Kitchen

Christian Community Action

98 S. Main St., South Norwalk, CT 06854 Tel. (203)899-2487 Fax (203)854-1870
Dir., Jacquelyn P. Miller
Major Activities: Emergency Food Program; Used Furniture; Loans for Emergencies; Loans for Rent, Security

Christian Community Action

168 Davenport Ave., New Haven, CT 06519 Tel. (203)777-7848 Fax (203)777-7923
Email: cca168@aol.com
Media Contact, Exec. Dir., The Rev. Bonita Grubbs
Exec. Dir., The Rev. Bonita Grubbs
Major Activities: Emergency Food Program; Used Furniture & Clothing; Security and Fuel; Emergency Housing for Families; Advocacy; Transitional Housing for Families

Council of Churches of Greater Bridgeport, Inc.

180 Fairfield Ave., Bridgeport, CT 06604 Tel. (203)334-1121 Fax (203)367-8113
Email: ccgb@snet.net
Website: www.ccgb.com
Media Contact, Exec. Dir., Rev. John S. Kidd
Exec. Dir., Rev. John S. Kidd
Pres., Rev. Kevin Agee
Sec., Dorothy Allsop
Treas., Carolyn Jackson

Major Activities: Youth in Crisis; Safe Places; Youth Shelter; Criminal Justice; Nursing Home and Jail Ministries; Local Hunger; Ecumenical Relations, Prayer and Celebration; Covenantal Ministries; Homework Help; Summer Programs; Race Relations/Bridge Building; Good Jobs / First Jobs; Faith Based Community Development Consortium

Council of Churches and Synagogues of Southwestern Connecticut

628 Main St., Stamford, CT 06901 Tel. (203)348-2800 Fax (203)358-0627
Email: council@flvax.ferg.lib.ct.us
Website: www.interfaithcouncil.org
Media Contact, Communications Ofc., Lois Alcosser
Exec. Dir., Jack Penfield, Interim Director
Major Activities: Partnership Against Hunger; The Food Bank of Lower Fairfield County; Friendly Visitors and Friendly Shoppers; Senior Neighborhood Support Services; Christmas in April; Interfaith Programming; Prison Visitation; Friendship House; Help a Neighbor; Operation Fuel; Teaching Place

Greater Waterbury Interfaith Ministries, Inc.

84 Crown St., Waterbury, CT 06704 Tel. (203)756-7831 Fax (203)419-0024
Media Contact, Exec. Dir., Carroll E. Brown
Exec. Dir., Carroll E. Brown
Pres., The Rev. Dr. James G. Bradley
Major Activities: Emergency Food Program; Emergency Fuel Program; Soup Kitchen; Ecumenical Worship; Christmas Toy Sale; Annual Hunger Walk

Manchester Area Conference of Churches

P.O. Box 773, Manchester, CT 06045-0773 Tel. (860)647-8003
Media Contact, Exec. Dir., Denise Cabana
Exec. Dir., Denise Cabana
Dir. of Community Ministries, Joseph Piescik
Dept.of Ministry Development, Dir., Karen Bergin
Pres., Rev. Charles Ericson
Vice-Pres., Theresa Ghabrial
Sec., Jean Richert
Treas., Clive Perrin
Major Activities: Provision of Basic Needs (Food, Fuel, Clothing, Furniture); Emergency Aid Assistance; Emergency Shelter; Soup Kitchen; Reentry Assistance to Sex-Offenders; Pastoral Care in Local Institutions; Interfaith Day Camp; Advocacy for the Poor; Ecumenical Education and Worship

New Britain Area Conference of Churches (NEWBRACC)

830 Corbin Ave., New Britain, CT 06052 Tel. (860)229-3751 Fax (860)223-3445

Media Contact, Exec. Dir., Michael Gorzoch
Exec. Dir., Michael Gorzoch
Pastoral Care/Chaplaincy, Rev. Ron Smith; Rev. Will Baumgartner; Rev. Rod Rinnel
Pres., Alton Brooks
Treas., Joyce Chmura
Major Activities: Worship; Social Concerns; Emergency Food Bank Support; Communications-Mass Media; Hospital; Elderly Programming; Homelessness and Hunger Programs; Telephone Ministry

DISTRICT OF COLUMBIA

The Council of Churches of Greater Washington

5 Thomas Circle N.W., Washington, DC 20005 Tel. (202)722-9240 Fax (202)722-9241
Media Contact, Exec. Dir., The Rev. Rodger Hall Reed, Sr.
Pres., The Rev. Lewis Anthony
Exec. Dir., The Rev. Rodger Hall Reed, Sr.
Program Officer, Daniel M. Thompson
Major Activities: Promotion of Christian Unity/Ecumenical Prayer & Worship; Coordination of Community Ministries; Summer Youth Employment; Summer Camping/Inner City Youth; Supports wide variety of social justice concerns

InterFaith Conference of Metropolitan Washington

1419 V St. NW, Washington, DC 20009 Tel. (202)234-6300 Fax (202)234-6303
Email: ifc@interfaith-metrodc.org
Website: www.interfaith-metrodc.org
Media Contact, Exec. Dir., Rev. Dr. Clark Lobenstine
Exec. Dir., Rev. Dr. Clark Lobenstine
Admn. Sec., Najla Robinson
Pres., Rev. Elizabeth Orens
1st Vice-Pres., Ms. Amrit Kaur
Chpsn., Mr. Jack Serber
Sec., Janice Sadeghian, Ph.D.
Treas., Ms. Frances B. Albers
Major Activities: Interfaith Dialogue; Interfaith Concert; Racial and Ethnic Polarization; Youth Leadership Training; Hunger; Homelessness; Church-State Zoning Issues

FLORIDA

Florida Council of Churches*

924 N. Magnolia Ave., Ste. 304, Orlando, FL 32803 Tel. (407)839-3454 Fax (407)246-0019
Email: fced@aol.com
Website: www.floridachurches.org
Media Contact, Exec. Dir., Rev. Fred Morris
Exec. Dir., Rev. Fred Morris
Associate Dir., H. Basil Nichols,
Project Director, Cherishing the Creation, Russell Gebet
Major Activities: Justice and Peace; Disaster

Response; Legislation & Public Policy; Local Ecumenism; Farmworker Ministry; Cherishing the Creation (Environmental Stewardship)

Christian Service Center for Central Florida, Inc.

808 W. Central Blvd., Orlando, FL 32805-1809 Tel. (407)425-2523 Fax (407)425-9513
Media Contact, Exec. Dir., Robert F. Stuart
Exec. Dir., Robert F. Stuart
Family Emergency Services, Dir., LaVerne Sainten
Alzheimers Respite, Dir., Mary Ellen Ort-Marvin
Fresh Start, Dir., Rev. Haggeo Gautier
Dir. of Mktg., Margaret Ruffier-Farris
Pres., Dr. Charles Horton
Treas., Rick Crandall
Sec., Annie Harris
Major Activities: Provision of Basic Needs (food, clothing, shelter); Emergency Assistance; Noon-time Meals; Sunday Church Services at Walt Disney World; Collection and Distribution of Used Clothing; Shelter & Training for Homeless; Respite for Caregivers of Alzheimers

GEORGIA

Georgia Christian Council*

P.O. Box 7193, Macon, GA 31209-7193 Tel. (478)743-2085 Fax (478)743-2085
Email: lccollins@juno.com
Website: georgiachurches.org
Media Contact, Exec. Dir., Rev. Leland C. Collins
Exec. Dir., Rev. Leland C. Collins
Pres., Rev. Dr. Tom Neal, 2370 Vineville Ave., Macon, GA 31204
Sec., Rev. Scudder Edwards, 6865 Turner Ct., Cumming, GA 30131
Major Activities: Local Ecumenical Support and Resourcing; Legislation; Rural Development; Racial Justice; Networking for Migrant Coalition; Aging Coalition; GA To GA With Love; Medical Care; Prison Chaplaincy; Training for Church Development; Souper Bowl; Disaster Relief; Clustering; Development of Local Ecumenism; Environmental Concerns

Christian Council of Metropolitan Atlanta

465 Boulevard, S.E., Atlanta, GA 30312 Tel. (404)622-2235 Fax (404)627-6626
Email: dojccma@aol.com
Media Contact, Dir. of Development & Communication, Jane Hopson Enniss
Exec. Dir., Rev. Dr. David O. Jenkins
Assoc. Dir., -vacant-
Pres., Rev. Elizabeth Rechter
Major Activities: Refugee Services; Commission on Children and Youth, Supervised Ministry;

223

Homeless; Ecumenical and Interreligious Events; persons with Handicapping Conditions; Women's Concerns; Task Force on Prison Ministry; Quarterly Forums on Ecumenical Issues; Faith and Order Concerns; Interracial & Intercultural Emphasis

IDAHO

The Regional Council for Christian Ministry, Inc.
237 N. Water, Idaho Falls, ID 83403 Tel. (208)524-9935
Exec. Sec., Wendy Schoonmaker
Major Activities: Island Park Ministry; Community Food Bank; Community Observances; Community Information and Referral Service; F.I.S.H.

ILLINOIS

Illinois Conference of Churches*
2211 West Wabash Ave., Springfield, IL 62704 Tel. (217)698-3440 Fax (217)698-3445
Email: ICCDIR@Juno.com
Media Contact, Exec. Dir., Rev. David A. Anderson
Exec. Dir., Rev. David A. Anderson
Assoc. Dir.
Pres., Rev. C. Bruce Naylor Tel. (309)467-2369
Major Activities: Unity and Relationships Commission: Annual Clergy Ecumenical Forum; Triennial Ecumenical Assembly; Church and Society Commission: Public Policy Ecumenical Network; Universal Health Care; Racism; Restorative Justice; Economic Justice

Churches United of the Quad City Area
630 9th St., Rock Island, IL 61201 Tel. (309)786-6494 Fax (309)786-5916
Email: clandon@revealed.net OR awachal@revealed.net
Media Contact, Exec. Dir., Rev. Charles R. Landon, Jr.
Exec. Dir., Rev. Charles R. Landon, Jr.
Program Manager, Anne E. Wachal
Pres., Rev. Ronald Huber
Pres. Elect, Ms. K. Krewer
Treas., Mr. Joseph Lindsay
Major Activities: Jail Ministry; Hunger Projects; Minority Enablement; Criminal Justice; Radio-TV; Peace; Local Church Development

Contact Ministries of Springfield
1100 E. Adams, Springfield, IL 62703 Tel. (217)753-3939 Fax (217)753-8643
Media Contact, Exec. Dir., Ethel Butchek
Exec. Dir., Ethel Butchek
Major Activities: Information; Referral and Advocacy; Ecumenical Coordination; Low Income Housing Referral; Food Pantry

Coordination; Prescription & Travel Emergency; Low Income Budget Counseling; 24 hours on call; Emergency On-site Family Shelter

Evanston Ecumenical Action Council
P.O. Box 1414, Evanston, IL 60204 Tel. (847)475-1150 Fax (847)475-2526
Website: http://members.aol.com/eeachome/eeac.html
Media Contact, Comm. Chpsn., Ken Wylie
Dir. Hospitality Cntr. for the Homeless, Sue Murphy
Co-Pres.: Rev. Ted Miller; Rev. Hardist Lane
Treas., Rev. Charles Hames, Jr.
Admn. Dir., Thomas Sullivan, M.DIV.
Major Activities: Interchurch Communication and Education; Peace and Justice Ministries; Coordinated Social Action; Soup Kitchens; Multi-Purpose Hospitality Center for the Homeless; Worship and Renewal; Racial Reconciliation, Youthwork

Greater Chicago Broadcast Ministries
112 E. Chestnut St., Chicago, IL 60611-2014 Tel. (312)988-9001 Fax (312)988-9004
Media Contact, Exec. Dir., Lydia Talbot
Pres., Bd. of Dir., Eugene H. Winkler
Exec. Dir., Lydia Talbot
Admn. Asst., Margaret Early
Major Activities: Television, Cable, Interfaith/Ecumenical Development; Social/Justice Concerns

The Hyde Park & Kenwood Interfaith Council
5745 S. Blackstone Ave., Chicago, IL 60637 Tel. (773)752-1911 Fax (773)752-2676
Media Contact, Exec. Dir., Lesley M. Radius
Exec. Dir., Lesley M. Radius
Pres., Rev. David Grainger
Sec., Barbara Krell
Major Activities: Interfaith Work; Hunger Projects; Community Development

Oak Park-River Forest Community of Congregations
P.O. Box 3365, Oak Park, IL 60303-3365 Tel. (708)386-8802 Fax (708)386-1399
Website: www.mcs.net/~grossman/comcong.htm
Media Contact, , Patricia C. Koko
Admn. Sec., Patricia C. Koko
Pres., Mr. Leonard Grossman
Treas., Sue Rizzo
Major Activities: Community Affairs; Ecumenical/Interfaith Affairs; Youth Education; FOOD PANTRY; Senior Citizens Worship Services; Interfaith Thanksgiving Services; Good Friday Services; UNICEF Children's Fund Drive; ASSIST (Network); Blood Drive; Literacy Training; CROP/CWS

Hunger Walkathon; Work with Homeless Through PADS (Public Action to Deliver Shelter); Senior Resource Coordinator Program; Diversity Education; Social Justice Workshops

Peoria Friendship House of Christian Service

800 N.E. Madison Ave., Peoria, IL 61603 Tel. (309)671-5200 Fax (309)671-5206
Media Contact, Exec. Dir., Beverly Isom
Pres. of Bd., David Dadds
Major Activities: Children's After-School; Teen Programs; Recreational Leagues; Senior Citizens Activities; Emergency Food/Clothing Distribution; Emergency Payments for Prescriptions, Rent, Utilities; Community Outreach; Economic Development; Neighborhood Empowerment; GED Classes; Family Literacy; Mother's Group; Welfare to Work Programs

INDIANA

The Associated Churches of Fort Wayne & Allen County, Inc.

602 E. Wayne St., Fort Wayne, IN 46802 Tel. (219)422-3528 Fax (219)422-6721
Email: Vernchurch@aol.com
Media Contact, Exec. Dir., Rev. Vernon R. Graham
Exec. Dir., Rev. Vernon R. Graham
Sec., Elaine Williamson
Foodbank: Ellen Graham; John Kaiser; Bob James; Jenny Varecha
Prog. Development, Ellen Graham
WRE Coord., Kathy Rolf
Pres., Rev. Dennis Roberts, 6600 Trier Rd., Ft. Wayne, IN 46815
Treas., Ann Frellick, 170 Curdes Avenue, Ft. Wayne, IN 46805
Major Activities: Weekday Religious Ed.; Church Clusters; Church and Society Commission; Overcoming Racism; A Baby's Closet; Widowed-to-Widowed; CROP; Campus Ministry; Feeding the Babies; Food Bank System; Peace & Justice Commission; Welfare Reform; Endowment Development; Child Care Advocacy; Advocates Inc.; Ecumenical Dialogue; Feeding Children; Vincent House (Homeless); A Learning Journey (Literacy); Reaching Out in Love; The Jail Ministry; Curbing Youth Access to Handguns

Christian Ministries of Delaware County

401 E. Main St., Muncie, IN 47305 Tel. (317)288-0601 Fax (317)282-4522
Media Contact, Exec. Dir., Susan Hughes
Exec. Dir., Susan Hughes
Pres., Sue Klein
Treas., Dr. J. B. Black

Major Activities: Baby Care Program; Youth Ministry at Detention Center; Community Church Festivals; Community Pantry; Community Assistance Fund; CROP Walk; Social Justice; Family Life Education; Combined Clergy; Homeless Shelter (sleeping room only); Clothing and household items available free; workshops for low income clients; homeless people apartments available-short stays only at no cost; provide programs and workshops for pastors and churches in community; work with schools sponsoring programs such as Teen Mom Program; plays about child abuse/conflict resolution

Church Community Services

629 S. 3rd Street, Elkhart, IN 46516-3241 Tel. (219)295-3673
Media Contact, Dir., Trisha Leasor
Exec. Dir., Rosalie J. Day
Major Activities: Advocacy for Low Income persons; Financial Assistance for Emergencies; Food Pantry; Used Furniture; Information and Referral; Clothing Referral; Laundry Voucher; Medication; Transportation Vouchers; Rent Funds; Classes on Cooking; Budget and Money; Credit; Managing a Checking Account

The Church Federation of Greater Indianapolis, Inc.

1100 W. 42nd St., Ste. 345, Indianapolis, IN 46208 Tel. (317)926-5371 Fax (317)926-5373
Email: churches@churchfederationindy.org
Website: www.churchfederationindy.org
Media Contact, Comm. Consultant, Julie Foster
Exec. Dir., Rev. Dr. Angelique Walker-Smith
Pres., Rev. Richard Clough
Treas., R. Wayne Reynolds
Major Activities: "Sacred Spaces" (A Christian Partnership of Neighborhood Action) Reclaiming Our Neighborhoods through Community Formation, Community Resourcing, Community Education, and Communications; The Sanctuary Church Movement; "Loving Our Children": An Educational Partnership Between Church and Public Schools for "at risk" Children; Greater Indianapolis Prayer Network to Stop the Violence; Racial Reconciliation; Clearinghouse Ministry; Ecumenical Project for Reconciliation and Healing; Faith and Fathers Ministry (Family Congregation and Mentoring Program); Benevolence Fund Ministry; TV Broadcasts; Indiana Faith-Based Climate Change Campaign; FaithFest!

Evansville Area Community of Churches, Inc.

414 N.W. Sixth St., Evansville, IN 47708-1332 Tel. (812)425-3524 Fax (812)425-3525
Media Contact, Dir. of Programs & Church Relations, Barbara G. Gaisser

Dir. of Programs/Ofc. Mgr., Barbara G. Gaisser
Exec. Dir., Rev. William F. Bower
Weekday Dir., Linda M. Schenk
Pres., Rev. Steve Lintzench
V. Pres., John Musgrove
Sec., Rev. Shane O'Neill
Treas., Ms. Julia Wood
Major Activities: Christian Education; Community Responsibility & Service; Public Relations; Interpretation; Church Women United; Institutional Ministries; Interfaith Dialogue; Earth Care Ethics; Public Education Support; Disaster Preparedness; Job Loss Networking Support Group; Interfaith TV Program; Women in Ministry Support Group; International Women's Day Celebration Events

Indiana Partners for Christian Unity and Mission

P.O. Box 88790, Indianapolis, IN 46208-0790 Tel. (800)746-2310 Fax (317)927-0957
Email: indunity@aol.com
Website: www.IPCUM.org
Media Contact, James Dougans
Pres., Rev. Robert Kirk
Treas., Rev. Thomas Bridges
Major Activities: Initiating dialogue on issues of social concern by organizing conferences on the death penalty, racism, welfare reform and violence; facilitating communication through an electronic newsletter and web site; promoting the National Day of Prayer and the Week of Prayer for Christian Unity; and advancing Churches Uniting in Christ in Indiana

Interfaith Community Council, Inc.

702 E. Market St., New Albany, IN 47150 Tel. (812)948-9248 Fax (812)948-9249
Email: interfaithcouncil@juno.com
Media Contact, Exec. Dir., Houston Thompson
Exec. Dir., Houston Thompson
Programs/Emergency Assistance, Denise Lochner
RSVP, Dir., Ceil Sperzel
Major Activities: Emergency Assistance; Retired Senior Volunteer Program; New Clothing and Toy Drives; Convalescent Sitter & Mother's Aides; Senior Day College; Emergency Food Distribution; Homeless Prevention; Kids' Café; Youth Employment Scholastic Program

Lafayette Urban Ministry

525 N. 4th St., Lafayette, IN 47901 Tel. (317)423-2691 Fax (317)423-2693
Media Contact, Exec. Dir., Joseph Micon
Exec. Dir., Joseph Micon
Advocate Coord., Rebecca Smith
Public Policy Coord., Harry Brown
Pres., John Wilson
Major Activities: Social Justice Ministries with and among the Poor

United Religious Community of St. Joseph County

2015 Western Ave., Suite 336, South Bend, IN 46629 Tel. (219)282-2397 Fax (219)282-8014
Email: sfisko@sbcsc.k12.in.us
Media Contact, Exec. Dir., Dr. James J. Fisko
Exec. Dir., Dr. James J. Fisko
Pres., Mana Derakhshani
Victim Offender Reconciliation Prog., Victim Impact Panel Coord., Martha Sallows
Volunteer Advocacy Project: Coord., Sara Goetz; Coord., Linda Jung-Zimmerman
Major Activities: Religious Understanding; Interfaith/Ecumenical Education; CROP Walk; Hunger Education; Housing and Homelessness Issues; Clergy Education and Support; Refugee Resettlement; Victim Assistance; Advocacy for the Needy

West Central Neighborhood Ministry, Inc.

1316 Broadway, Fort Wayne, IN 46802-3304 Tel. (219)422-6618 Fax (219)422-9319
Media Contact, Exec. Dir., Andrea S. Thomas
Exec. Dir., Andrea S. Thomas
Ofc. Mgr., J. R. Stopperich
Neighborhood Services Dir., Carol Salge
Senior Citizens Dir., Gayle Mann
Youth Director, Laura Watt
Major Activities: After-school Programs; Teen Drop-In Center; Summer Day Camp; Summer Overnight Camp; Information and Referral Services; Food Pantry; Nutrition Program for Senior Citizens; Senior Citizens Activities; Tutoring; Developmental Services for Families & Senior Citizens; Parent Club

IOWA

Ecumenical Ministries of Iowa (EMI)*

3816-36th St., Ste. 202, Des Moines, IA 50310-4722 Tel. (515)255-5905 Fax (515)255-1421
Email: emofiowa@aol.com
Media Contact, Exec. Dir., Rev. Sarai Schnucker Beck
Exec. Dir., Rev. Sarai Schnucker Beck
Program Cood., Martha E. Hedberg
Major Activities: Facilitating the denominations—cooperative agenda of resourcing local expression of the church; Assess needs & develop responses through Justice and Unity Commissions

Iowa Religious Media Services*

3816 36th St., Des Moines, IA 50310 Tel. (515)277-2920 Fax (515)277-0842
Email: orderirms@aol.com
Website: www.irms.org
Media Contact, Director
Educ. Consultant, Mike Smith
Production Mgr., Dr. Richard Harbart

Major Activities: Media Library for Churches in 7 Denominations in Iowa; Provide Video Production Services for Churches, Non-profit & Educational organizations; will rent media to all churches in the continental U.S. (details on the website)

Churches United, Inc.

1035 3rd Ave., Suite 101, Cedar Rapids, IA 52403 Tel. (319)366-7163
Media Contact, Admn. Sec., Marcey Luxa
Admn. Sec., Marcey Luxa
Pres., Rev. Carroll Brown
Treas., Joseph Luxa, 450 19th St. NW, Cedar Rapids, IA 52405
Major Activities: Communication/resource center for member churches; Community Information and Referral; Community Food Bank; L.E.A.F. (Local Emergency Assistance Fund; Care Center Ministry; Radio/TV Ministry; Ecumenical City-wide Celebrations; CROP/World Hunger; Jail Chaplaincy Ministry

Des Moines Area Religious Council

3816 - 36th St., Des Moines, IA 50310 Tel. (515)277-6969 Fax (515)274-8389
Email: dmreligious@mcleodusa.net
Media Contact, Exec. Dir., Forrest Harms
Exec. Dir., Forrest Harms
Pres., Sharon Baker
Pres. Elect, Bobbretta M. Brewton
Treas., Bill Corwin
Major Activities: Outreach and Nurture; Education; Social Concerns; Mission; Emergency Food Pantry; Ministry to Widowed; Child Care Assistance

KANSAS

Kansas Ecumenical Ministries*

5833 SW 29th St., Topeka, KS 66614-2499 Tel. (785)272-9531 Fax (785)272-9533
Email: kemstaff@cjnetworks.com
Website: kemontheweb.org
Media Contact, Exec. Dir., Dr. Joe M. Hendrixson
Email: joe_hendrixson@ecunet.org
Exec. Dir., Dr. Joe M. Hendrixson
Pres., Rev. Sally Fahrenthold
Vice-Pres., Rev. Winnie Crapson
Sec., Rev. Jane Ireland
Major Activities: State Council of Churches; Legislative Activities; Program Facilitation and Coordination; Education; Mother-to-Mother Program; Rural Concerns; Health Care; Hate group monitoring; Children & Families; AIDS/HIV Programs; Domestic Violence; Faith and Order

Cross-Lines Cooperative Council

736 Shawnee Ave., Kansas City, KS 66105 Tel. (913)281-3388 Fax (913)281-2344
Email: xlines@TFS.net

Media Contact, Dir. of Dev., Bill Scholl
Exec. Dir., Marilynn Rudell
Dir. of Programs, Rev. Robert L. Moore
Major Activities: Emergency Assistance; Family Support Advocacy; Crisis Heating/Plumbing Repair; Thrift Store; Workcamp Experiences; Adult Education (GED and Basic English Literacy Skills); School Supplies; Christmas Store; Institute for Poverty and Empowerment Studies (Education on poverty for the non-poor)

Inter-Faith Ministries—Wichita

829 N. Market, Wichita, KS 67214-3519 Tel. (316)264-9303 Fax (316)264-2233
Email: smuyskens@juno.com
Media Contact, Exec. Dir., Sam Muyskens
Exec. Dir., Rev. Sam Muyskens
Adm. Asst.- Kathy Freed
Inter-Faith Inn (Homeless Shelter), Dir., Sandy Swank
Operation Holiday, Dir., Ashley Davis
Dev./Communications, Dir., -vacant-
Campaign to End Childhood Hunger, Connie Pace
Community Ministry, Cammie Funston
Racial Justice, Coord., Cammie Funston
Major Activities: Communications; Urban Education; Inter-religious Understanding; Community Needs and Issues; Theology and Worship; Hunger; Family Life; Multi-Cultural Concerns

KENTUCKY

Kentucky Council of Churches*

2549 Richmond Road, Suite 302, Lexington, KY 40509 Tel. (859)269-7715 Fax (859)269-1240
Email: kcc@kycouncilofchurches.org
Website: www.kycouncilofchurches.org
Media Contact, Exec. Dir., Nancy Jo Kemper
Exec. Dir., Rev. Nancy Jo Kemper
Pres., The Rev. Dr. C.K. Henry
Kentucky Interchurch Disaster Recovery Program Coodinator., Rev. John Kays
Program Associate for Local Ecumenism, Rev. W. Chris Benham Skidmore
Major Activities: Christian Unity; Public Policy; Justice; Disaster Response; Peace Issues; Anti-Racism; Health Care Issues; Local Ecumenism; Rural Land/Farm Issues; Gambling; Capital Punishment

Eastern Area Community Ministries

P.O. Box 43049, Louisville, KY 40253-0049 Tel. (502)244-6141 Fax (502)254-5141
Email: SueEtn@cs.com
Website: http://ourworld.cs.com/eacministry
Media Contact, Exec. Dir., Rev. Sue Eaton
Exec. Dir., Rev. Sue Eaton
Board Pres., Marcia Lile
Board Sec., Betsy Wilborn
Board Treas., Homer Lacy, Jr.

227

Youth and Family Services, Prog. Dir., Ken Evans

Older Adult Services, Associate Program Dir., Sharon Eckler

Neighborhood Visitor Program, Prog. Dir., Pearl Gillespie

Major Activities: Food Pantry; Clothes Closet; Meals on Wheels; Teen Court; Community Worship Services; Good Start for Kids; Juvenile Court Diversion; Community Development; Transient Fund; Ministerial Association

Fern Creek/Highview United Ministries

7502 Tangelo Dr., Louisvlle, KY 40228 Tel. (502)239-7407 Fax (502)239-7454

Email: FernCreek.Ministries@crnky.org

Media Contact, Exec. Dir., Kay Sanders, 7502 Tangelo Dr., Louisville, KY 40228 Tel. (502)239-7407

Exec. Dir., Kay Sanders

Pres., Katherine Games

Major Activities: Ecumenically supported social service agency providing services to the community, including Emergency Financial Assistance, Food/Clothing, Health Aid Equipment Loans, Information/Referral, Advocacy, Monthly Blood-Pressure Checks; Holiday Programs; Life Skills Training; Mentoring; Case Management; Adult Day-Care Program

Hazard-Perry County Community Ministries, Inc.

P.O. Box 1506, Hazard, KY 41702-1506 Tel. (606)436-0051 Fax (606)436-0071

Media Contact, Gerry Feamster-Roll

Exec. Dir., Gerry Feamster-Roll

Chpsn., Sarah Hughes

V. Chpsn., Susan Duff

Sec., Virginia Campbell

Treas., Margaret Adams

Major Activities: Food Pantry/Crisis Aid Program; Day Care; Summer Day Camp; After-school Program; Christmas Tree; Family Support Center; Adult Day Care; Transitional Housing

Highlands Community Ministries

1140 Cherokee Rd., Louisville, KY 40204 Tel. (502)451-3695

Email: IFADIR@iglou.com

Media Contact, Exec. Dir., Stan Esterle

Exec. Dir., Stan Esterle

Major Activities: Welfare Assistance; Day Care; Counseling with Youth, Parents and Adults; Adult Day Care; Social Services for Elderly; Housing for Elderly and Handicapped; Ecumenical Programs; Community Classes; Activities for Children; Neighborhood and Business organization

Kentuckiana Interfaith Community

1113 South 4th St., Suite 200, Louisville, KY 40203 Tel. (502)587-6265 Fax (502)540-5017

Email: kic@crnky.org

Pres., Annette Turner

Vice-Pres., David L. Kohn

Sec., Geoffrey Ellis

Treas., Arthur Clark

Executive Dir., Reba S. Cobb

Major Activities: Christian/Jewish Ministries in KY, Southern IN; Consensus Advocacy; Interfaith Dialogue; Community Hunger Walk; Racial Justice Forums; Network for Neighborhood-based Ministries; Hunger & Racial Justice Commission; Faith Channel-Cable TV Station, Horizon News Paper; Police/Comm. Relations Task Force; Ecumenical Strategic Planning; Networking with Seminaries & Religious-Affiliated Institutions

Ministries United South Central Louisville (M.U.S.C.L., Inc.)

1207 Hart Avenue, Louisville, KY 42013 Tel. (502)363-9087 Fax (502)363-9087

Media Contact, Ex. Dir., Rev. Antonio (Tony) Aja, M.Div. Tel. (502)363-2383, E-mail: Tony_Aja@pcusa.org

Ex. Dir., Rev. Antonio (Tony) Aja, M.Div.

Airport Relocation Ombudsman, Rev. Phillip Garrett, M.Div. Tel. (502)361-2706; E-mail: philombud@aol.com

Senior Adults Programs, Dir., Mrs. Jeannine Blakeman, BSSW

Emergency Assistance, Dir., Mr. Michael Hundley

Low-Income Coord., Ms. Wanda Irvio

Youth Services, Dir., Rev. Bill Sanders, M.Div.

Volunteers Coord., Mrs. Carol Stemmle

Northern Kentucky Interfaith Commission, Inc.

901 York St., Newport, KY 41072 Tel. (859)581-2237 Fax (859)261-6041

Media Contact, Exec. Dir., Rev. William C. Neuroth

Pres., Ms. Wanda Trinkle

Sec., Ms. Cordelia Koplow

Treas., Ms. Peggy McEntee

Admin. Asst., Pat McDermott

Major Activities: Understanding Faiths; Meeting Spiritual and Human Needs; Enabling Churches to Greater Ministry

Paducah Cooperative Ministry

1359 S. 6th St., Paducah, KY 42003 Tel. (270)442-6795 Fax (270)442-6812

Media Contact, Dir., Heidi Suhrheinrich

Dir., Heidi Suhrheinrich

Chpsn., Rev. Larry Walker

Vice-Chpsn., Rev. Mare Buford

Major Activities: Programs for: Hungry, Elderly, Poor, Homeless, Handicapped, Undereducated

St. Matthews Area Ministries

201 Biltmore Rd., Louisville, KY 40207 Tel. (502)893-0205 Fax (502)893-0206
Media Contact, Exec. Dir., Dan G. Lane
Exec. Dir., Dan G. Lane
Child Care, Dir., Janet Hennessey
Dir. Assoc., Eileen Bartlett
Major Activities: Child Care; Emergency Assistance; Youth Services; Interchurch Worship and Education; Housing Development; Counseling; Information & Referral; Mentor Program; Developmentally Disabled

South East Associated Ministries (SEAM)

6500 Six Mile Ln., Ste.A, Louisville, KY 40218 Tel. (502)499-9350
Media Contact, Mary Beth Helton
Exec. Dir., Mary Beth Helton
Life Skills Center, Dir., Robert Davis
Youth Services, Dir., Bill Jewel
Pres., David Ehresman
Treas., Bill Trusty
Major Activities: Emergency Food, Clothing and Financial Assistance; Life Skills Center (Programs of Prevention and Case Management and Self-Sufficiency Through Education, Empowerment, Support Groups, etc.); Bloodmobile; Ecumenical Education and Worship; Juvenile Court Diversion; TEEN Court; Teen Crime & the Community

South Louisville Community Ministries

Peterson Social Services Center, 204 Seneca Trail, Louisville, KY 40214 Tel. (502)367-6445 Fax (502)361-4668
Email: slcm@crnky.org
Website: www.slcm.org
Media Contact, Exec. Dir., J. Michael Jupin
Bd. Chair., Greg Greenwood
Bd. Vice-Chair., Virginia Woodward
Bd. Treas., Jane Davis
Exec. Dir., Rev. J. Michael Jupin
Major Activities: Food, Clothing & Financial Assistance; Home Delivered Meals; Transportation; Ecumenical Worship; Juvenile Ct. Diversion Program; Affordable Housing; Adult Day Care; Truancy Prevention; Case Management, Prenatal Education

LOUISIANA

Louisiana Interchurch Conference*

660 N. Foster Dr., Ste. A-225, Baton Rouge, LA 70806 Tel. (225)924-0213 Fax (225)927-7860
Email: dan_krutz@ecunet.org
Media Contact, Exec. Dir., Rev. C. Dana Krutz
Exec. Dir., Rev. C. Dana Krutz
Pres., The Most Rev. Michael Jarrell, Bishop
Major Activities: Ministries to Aging; Prison Reform; Liaison with State Agencies; Ecumenical Dialogue; Institutional Chaplains; Racism

Greater Baton Rouge Federation of Churches and Synagogues

P.O. Box 626, Baton Rouge, LA 70821 Tel. (225)925-3414 Fax (225)925-3065
Media Contact, Exec. Dir., Rev. Jeff Day
Exec. Dir., Rev. Jeff Day
Admn. Asst., Marion Zachary
Pres., Bette Lavine
Pres.-Elect, Tom Sylvest
Treas., Randy Trahan
Major Activities: Combating Hunger; Housing (Helpers for Housing); Interfaith Relations; Interfaith Concert; Race Relations

Greater New Orleans Federation of Churches

4640 S. Carrollton Ave, Suite 2B, New Orleans, LA 70119-6077 Tel. (504)488-8788 Fax (504)488-8823
Exec. Dir., Rev. J. Richard Randels
Major Activities: Information and Referral; Food Distribution (FEMA); Forward Together TV Program; Sponsors seminars for pastors (e.g. church growth, clergy taxes,etc.); Police Chaplaincy; Fire Chaplaincy

MAINE

Maine Council of Churches*

15 Pleasant Ave., Portland, ME 04103 Tel. (207)772-1918 Fax (207)772-2947
Email: mecchurches@aol.com
Website: www.mainecouncilofchurches.org
Media Contact, Communications Director, Karen Caouette
Exec. Dir., Thomas C. Ewell
Assoc. Dir., Douglas Cruger
Admin. Asst., Sandra Buzzell
Pres., Rev. Charles Whiston
Sec., ⸺
Treas., Rev. Thomas Merrill
Major Activities: Criminal Justice Reform and Restorative Justice; Legislative Work and Coalition Work in Health, Homelessness, and Children; Advocacy

MARYLAND

Central Maryland Ecumenical Council*

Cathedral House, 4 E. University Pkwy., Baltimore, MD 21218 Tel. (410)467-6194 Fax (410)554-6387
Media Contact, Admn., Martha Young
Pres., Rev. H.J. Siegfried Otto
Major Activities: Interchurch Communications and Collaboration; Information Systems; Ecumenical Relations; Urban Mission and Advocacy; Staff for Judicatory Leadership Council; Commission on Dialogue; Commission on

Church & Society; Commission on Admin. &
Dev.; Ecumenical Choral Concerts; Ecumenical
Worship Services

The Christian Council of Delaware and Maryland's Eastern Shore*

The Lutheran Center, 700 Light St., Baltimore,
·MD 21213 Tel. (410)230-2860 Fax (410)230-
2817
Website: www.DeMdSynod.org
Media Contact, Pres., Bishop Wayne P. Wright,
Diocese of Delaware, 2020 N. Tatnall Street,
Wilmington, DE 19802
Pres., Bishop Wayne P. Wright, Diocese of
Delaware, 2020 N. Tatnall Street, Wilmington,
DE 19802
Moderator, The Rev. Patricia McClurg,
Presbyterian Church (USA), E-62 Omega
Drive, Newark, DE 19713
Major Activities: Exploring Common
Theological, Ecclesiastical and Community
Concerns; Racism; Prisons

Community Ministries of Rockville

114 West Montgomery Ave., Rockville, MD
20850 Tel. (301)762-8682 Fax (301)762-2939
Email: cmr114mr@aol.com
Media Contact, Managing Dir., Agnes Saenz
Exec. Dir. & Comm. Min., Mansfield M. Kaseman
Managing Dir., Agnes Aaenz
Major Activities: Shelter Care; Emergency
Assistance; Elderly Home Care; Affordable
Housing; Political Advocacy; Community
Education; Education to Recent Immigrants

Community Ministry of Montgomery County

114 West Montgomery Ave., Rockville, MD
20850 Tel. (301)762-8682 Fax (301)762-2939
Media Contact, Exec. Dir., Rebecca Wagner
Exec. Dir., Rebecca Wagner
Major Activities: Interfaith Clothing Center;
Emergency Assistance Coalition; The
Advocacy Function; Information and Referral
Services; Friends in Action; The Thanksgiving
Hunger Drive; Thanksgiving in February;
Community Based Shelter

MASSACHUSETTS

Massachusetts Council of Churches*

14 Beacon St., Rm. 416, Boston, MA 02108 Tel.
(617)523-2771 Fax (617)523-1483
Email: council@masscouncilofchurches.org
Website: www.council@masscouncilofchurch-
es.org
Media Contact, Dir., Rev. Diane C. Kessler
Exec. Dir., Rev. Diane C. Kessler
Assoc. Dir., Rev. Jill Wiley
Adjunct Assoc., Rev. Betsy Sowers, Mr. Stanley
Rossier

Pres., Mrs. Mary Alice Stahleker
Vice-Pres., Rev. Canon Edward Rodman
Sec., Eden Grace
Treas., Robert Sarly
Major Activities: Christian Unity; Education and
Evangelism; Defend Social Justice &
Individual Rights; Ecumenical Worship;
Services and Resources for Individuals and
Churches

Attleboro Area Council of Churches, Inc.

505 N. Main St., Attleboro, MA 02703 Tel.
(508)222-2933 Fax (508)222-2933
Media Contact, Interim Executive Director, Rev.
Janet Long
Exec. Dir., Rev. Janet Long
Office Manager- Kathleen Trowbridge
Staff Asst., Emergency Food Program, Lynne F.
Sias
Hosp. Chplns., Rev. Dr. William B. Udall
Pres., Rev. David Hill, 52 Glendale Rd.,
Attleboro, MA 02703
Treas., Ray Larson, 33 Watson Ave., Attleboro,
MA 02703
Major Activities: Hospital Chaplaincy; personal
Growth/Skill Workshops; Ecumenical Worship;
Media Resource Center; Referral Center;
Communications/Publications; Community
Social Action; Food'n Friends Kitchens;
Nursing Home Volunteer Visitation Program;
Lay School of Christian Theology; Clergy
Fellowship/Learning Events

The Cape Cod Council of Churches, Inc.

320 Main St., P.O. Box 758, Hyannis, MA 02601
Tel. (508)775-5073
Media Contact, Exec. Dir., Rev. Susan Royce
Scribner
Exec. Dir., Rev. Susan Royce Scribner
Pres., Mr. Barry Jones-Henry, Sr.
Chaplain, Cape Cod Hospital, Rev. William
Wilcox
Chaplain, Falmouth Hospital, Rev. Allen Page
Chaplain, House of Correction & Jail, Rev.
Thomas Shepherd
Chaplain, Rehabilitation Hospital of the Cape
and Islands, Mrs. Elizabeth Stommel
Service Center & Thrift Shop: P.O. Box 125,
Dennisport, MA 02639 Tel. (508)394-6361
Major Activities: Pastoral Care; Social Concerns;
Religious Education; Emergency Distribution
of Food, Clothing, Furniture; Referral and
Information; Church World Service; Interfaith
Relations; Media Presence; Hospital & Jail
Chaplaincy; Arts & Religion

Cooperative Metropolitan Ministries

474 Centre St., Newton, MA 02158 Tel.
(617)244-3650 Fax (617)244-0569

Email: coopmet@aol.com
Website: cmm.somego.com
Media Contact, Exec. Dir., Claire Kashuck
Exec. Dir., Claire Kashuck
Bd. Pres., Francis Grady
Treas., Karen Gunn
Clk., Alvera Fragen
Major Activities: Low Income; Suburban/Urban Bridges; Racial and Economic Justice

Council of Churches of Greater Springfield

39 Oakland St., Springfield, MA 01108 Tel. (413)733-2149 Fax (413)733-9817
Media Contact, Asst. to Dir., Sr. John Bridgid
Interim Exec. Dir., Rev. Karen L. Rucks
Community Min., Dir.
Pres., The Rev. Dr. David Hunter
Treas., John Pearson, Esq
Major Activities: Advocacy; Emergency Fuel Fund; Peace and Justice Division; Community Ministry; Task Force on Racism; Hospital and Jail Chaplaincies; Pastoral Service; Crisis Counseling; Christian Social Relations; Relief Collections; Ecumenical and Interfaith Relations; Ecumenical Dialogue with Roman Catholic Diocese; Mass Media; Church/Community Projects and Community Dialogues

Greater Lawrence Council of Churches

117A S. Broadway, Lawrence, MA 01843 Tel. (508)686-4012
Email: glcclawrence@juno.com
Media Contact, Exec. Dir., David Edwards
Exec. Dir., David Edwards
Pres., Carol Rabs
Vice-Pres., Rev. Michael Graham
Admn. Asst., Linda Sullivan
Major Activities: Ecumenical Worship; Radio Ministry; Hospital and Nursing Home Chaplaincy; Church Women United; Afterschool Children's Program; Vacation Bible School

Inter-Church Council of Greater New Bedford

412 County St., New Bedford, MA 02740-5096 Tel. (508)993-6242 Fax (508)991-3158
Email: administration@inter-churchcouncil.org
Website: www.inter-churchcouncil.org
Media Contact, Min., Rev. Edward R. Dufresne, Ph.D.
Exec. Min., Rev. Edward R. Dufresne, Ph.D.
Pres., Pamela Pollock
Treas., George Mock
Major Activities: Pastoral Counseling; Spiritual Direction; Chaplaincy; Housing for Elderly; Urban Affairs; Community Spiritual Leadership; Parish Nurse Ministry; Accounting and Spiritual Care for the Developmentally Challenged; Ecumenical and Interfaith Ministries

Worcester County Ecumenical Council

4 Caroline St., Worcester, MA 01604 Tel. (508)757-8385 Fax (508)795-7704
Email: worcecumen@aol.com
Media Contact, Sec., Rev. Steven Alspach
Dir., Rev. Steven Alspach
Pres., Rev. Rrances Langille
Major Activities: Ecumenical worship and dialogue networking congregations together in partnerships of mission, education and spiritual renewal; Clusters of Churches; Ecumenical Worship and Dialogue; Interfaith Activities; Resource Connection for Churches; Group Purchasing Consortium

MICHIGAN

Michigan Ecumenical Forum*

809 Center St., Ste. 5, Lansing, MI 48906 Tel. (517)485-4395 Fax (517)482-8751
Email: ecumenicalforum@aol.com
Media Contact, Coord./Exec. Dir., Candyce Williams
Coord./Exec. Dir., Candyce Williams
Major Activities: Communication and Coordination; Support and Development of Regional Ecumenical Fora; Ecumenical Studies; Fellowship and Celebration; Church and Society Issues; Continuing Education

Bay Area Ecumenical Forum

103 E. Midland St., Bay City, MI 48706 Tel. (517)686-1360
Media Contact, Rev. Karen Banaszak
Major Activities: Ecumenical Worship; Community Issues; Christian Unity; Education; CROP Walk

Berrien County Association of Churches

275 Pipestone, P.O. Box 1042, Benton Harbor, MI 49023-1042 Tel. (616)926-0030
Media Contact, Sec., Mary Ann Hinz
Pres., Rev. Robert Gouwens
Dir., Street Ministry, Rev. James Atterberry
Major Activities: Street Ministry; CROP Walk; Community Issues; Fellowship; Christian Unity; Hospital Chaplaincy Program; Publish Annual County Church Directory and Monthly Newsletter; Resource Guide for Helping Needy; Distribution of Worship Opportunity—Brochure for Tourists

Grand Rapids Area Center for Ecumenism (GRACE)

38 Fulton West, Grand Rapids, MI 49503-2628 Tel. (616)774-2042 Fax (616)774-2883
Email: dbaak@graceoffice.org

231

Website: www.graceoffice.org
Media Contact, Exec. Dir., Rev. David P. Baak
Exec. Dir., Rev. David P. Baak
Prog. Dir., Lisa H. Mitchell
Major Activities: AIDS Care Network (Client Services Education/ Volunteer Services); Hunger Walk; Education/Relationships; (Ecumenical Lecture, Christian Unity Worship/Events, Interfaith Dialogue Conference, Civil Dialogue Series); Affiliates: (ACCESS-All County Churches Emergency Support System, FISH for My People-transportation); Publications (Religious Community Directory, Grace Notes); Racial Justice Institute; Mentoring Partners (Welfare Reform Response)

Greater Flint Council of Churches

310 E. Third St., Suite 600, Flint, MI 48502 Tel. (810)238-3691 Fax (810)238-4463
Media Contact, Mrs. Constance D. Neely
President, Rev. James F. Offrink
Major Activities: Christian Education; Christian Unity; Christian Missions; Nursing Home Visitors; Church in Society; American Bible Society Materials; Interfaith Dialogue; Church Teacher Exchange Sunday; Directory of Area Faiths and Clergy; Thanksgiving & Easter Sunrise Services; CROP Walks

In One Accord

157 Capital Ave., NE, Battle Creek, MI 49017 Tel. (616)966-2500 Fax (616)660-6665
Media Contact, Executive Director, Rev. Ron L. Keller
Pres., Rev. Erick Johnson
Vice-Pres., Haleyon Liew
Exec. Dir., Rev. Ron L. Keller
Secretary: Sally Goss
Major Activities: CROP Walk; Food Closet; Christian Sports; Week of Prayer for Christian Unity; Ecumenical Worship; Health Care Network

The Jackson County Interfaith Council

425 Oakwood, P.O. Box 156, Clarklake, MI 49234-0156 Tel. (517)529-9721
Media Contact, Exec. Dir., Rev. Loyal H. Wiemer
Exec. Dir., Rev. Loyal H. Wiemer
Major Activities: Chaplaincy at Institutions and Senior Citizens Residences; Martin L. King, Jr. Day Celebrations; Ecumenical Council Representation; Radio and TV Programs; Food Pantry; Interreligious Events; Clergy Directory

The Metropolitan Christian Council: Detroit-Windsor

1300 Mutual Building, 28 W. Adams, Detroit, MI 48226 Tel. (313)962-0340 Fax (313)962-9044
Email: councilweb@aol.com

Website: http://users.aol.com/councilweb/index.htm
Media Contact, Rev. Richard Singleton
Exec. Dir., Rev. Richard Singleton
Meals for Shut-ins, Prog. Dir., John Simpson, Mrs. Elaine Kisner, Add. Asst.
Major Activities: Theological and Social Concerns; Ecumenical Worship; Educational Services; Electronic Media; Print Media; Meals for Shut-Ins; Summer Feeding Program

Muskegon County Cooperating Churches

2525 Hall Road, Muskegon, MI 49442-1520 Tel. 231-777-2888 Fax 231-773-4007
Media Contact, Program Coordinator, Delphine Hogston
President, Rev. Tim Vander Haar
Major Activities: Racial Reconciliation, Dialogue, & Healing; Ecumenical Worship; Faith News TV Ministry; CROP Walk; Community Issues; Prison Ministry; Jewish-Christian Dialogue; Tutoring; Senior Issues
SUBSIDIARY ORGANIZATION
Institute for Healing Racism—Muskegon
2525 Hall Road, Muskegon, MI 49442-1520, Tel. 231-777-7883 Fax. 231-773-4007
Media Contact, Gordon Rinard, Dir.
Major Activities: Racial Reconciliation, Dialogue, & Healing

MINNESOTA

Arrowhead Interfaith Council*

230 E. Skyline Pkwy., Duluth, MN 55811 Tel. (218)727-5020 Fax (218)727-5022
Media Contact, Pres., Alan Cutter
Pres., Alan Cutter
Vice-Pres., Amy Berstein
Sec., John H. Kemp
Major Activities: InterFaith Dialogue; Joint Religious Legislative Coalition; Corrections Chaplaincy; Human Justice and Community Concerns; Community Seminars; Children's Concerns

Minnesota Council of Churches*

122 W. Franklin Ave., Rm. 100, Minneapolis, MN 55404 Tel. (612)870-3600 Fax (612)870-3622
Email: mcc@mnchurches.org
Website: www.mnchurches.org
Media Contact, Exec. Dir., Rev. Peg Chemberlin, E-mail: pegchamberlin@mnchurches.org
Officers and Staff
Exec. Dir., Rev. Peg Chemberlin, Pegchemberlin@mn.churches.org
Life & Work, Dir., Robert Hulteen, bobhulteen@mn.churches.org
Unity & Relationships, Dir., Joel Luedtke, refserv@mnchurches.org
Refugee Services, Dir.,
Indian Ministry, Field Organizer, Sandy Berlin
Communications, Dir., Dr. Robert M. Frame, III

Facilities, Dir., Cynthia Darrington-Ottinger
Tri-Council Coordinating Commission: Co-
Dirs., James and Nadine Addington
Research Dir. & Admn. Asst., James Casebolt
Joint Religious Legislative Coalition, Exec.,
Brian A. Rusche
Pres., Bishop Mark Hanson
Renewing the Public Church, Field Organizer,
Karen Roles
Major Activities: Minnesota Church Center;
Local Ecumenism; Life & Work: Rural Life-
Ag Crisis; Racial Reconciliation; Indian
Ministry; Legislative Advocacy; Refugee
Services; Service to Newly Legalized/
Undocumented persons; Unity & Relation-
ships: Sexual Exploitation within the
Religious Community; Chaplaincy; Clergy
Support; Consultation on Church Union;
Ecumenical Study & Dialogue; Jewish-
Christian Relations; Muslim-Christian
Relations; State Fair Ministry; Tri-Council
Coordinating Commission (Minnesota
Churches Anti-Racism Initiative); Active Non-
Violence; No-Interest Small Loan Program

Community Emergency Assistance Program (CEAP)

7231 Brooklyn Blvd., Brooklyn Center, MN
55429 Tel. (612)566-9600 Fax (612)566-9604
Media Contact, Exec. Dir., Tia Henry-Johnson
Exec. Dir., Tia Henry-Johnson
Major Activities: Provision of Basic Needs
(Food, Clothing); Emergency Financial
Assistance for Shelter; Home Delivered
Meals; Chore Services and Homemaking
Assistance; Family Loan Program; Volunteer
Services

Greater Minneapolis Council of Churches

1001 E. Lake St., P.O. Box 7509, Minneapolis,
MN 55407-0509 Tel. (612)721-8687 Fax
(612)722-8669
Email: info@gmcc.org
Website: www.gmcc.org
Media Contact, Dir. of Communications, Darcy
Hanzlik
President and CEO, Rev. Dr. Gary B. Reierson
E-mail: reierson@gmcc.org
Chair, Barbara Koch
Treas., Kent Eklund
Division Indian Work: Sr. Vice President &
Exec. Dir., Mary Ellen Dumas; Assoc. Ex.
Dir., Noya Woodrich
Programs, Vice President., Edward L. Duren, Jr.
Director of Programs, Rev. Bruce Bjork
Minnesota FoodShare, Dir., Rev. Barbara Thell
Handyworks, Dir., Mary Jo Tarasar
Correctional Chaplains: Rev. Susan Allers
Hatlie; Rev. Thomas Van Leer; Rev. Anne
Waters; Imam Charles El-Amin; Susan
Jourdain; Rev. Dennis McKee

Congregations In Community, Dir., Rev. Bruce
Bjork
Discover Learning Centers, Coord., Rev. Janet
Larson
Div. of Indian Work: Director, Youth Services
and Education, Vivinnie Crowe; Director,
Adult Services and Administration, Melanie
Thompson; Finance & Admin., Vice President
and CFO., Dennis Anderson
Institutional Advancement: Vice President., Don
R. Riggs
Urban Immersion Service Retreats, Assoc. Dir.,
Mike Manhard
Metro Paint-A-Thon, Dir., Beth Storey
Discover Support Groups, Coordinator, Paris
Gatlin
Minnesota Churches Anti-Racism Initiative, Dir.,
James and Nadine Addington
Congregations Concerned for Children Child
Advocacy Network, Coord., Norma Bourland
Project Restoration, Coordinator, Pat McDonough
Center for Urban Service, Dir., Rev. Bruce Bjork
Child Care Center Challenge Grant Fund,
President and CEO, Rev. Dr. Gary B. Reierson
Major Activities: Indian Work (Emergency
Assistance, Youth Leadership, self-sufficien-
cy, Jobs Program, Teen Indian Parents
Program, and Family Violence Program);
Minnesota FoodShare; Metro Paint-A-Thon;
Shared Ministries Tutorial Program;
Congregations In Community; Correctional
Chaplaincy Program; HandyWorks; Anti-
racism Initiative; Child Advocacy; Social
Justice Advocacy; Child Care Center Start-up;
Home Renovation; Affordable Housing;
Urban Immersion Service Retreats; Welfare
Reform; Economic Self-Sufficiency; Discover
Support Groups; Job Readiness

The Joint Religious Legislative Coalition

122 W. Franklin Ave., Rm. 315, Minneapolis, MN
55404 Tel. (612)870-3670 Fax (612)870-3671
Email: jrlc@ecunet.org
Website: www.jrlc.org
Media Contact, Exec. Dir., Brian A. Rusche
Exec. Dir., Brian A. Rusche
Research Dir., Dr. James Casebolt
Congregational Organizer, Rev. Becky Myrick
Major Activities: Lobbying at State Legislature;
Researching Social Justice Issues and
Preparing Position Statements; Organizing
Grassroots Citizen's Lobby

Metropolitan Interfaith Council on Affordable Housing (MICAH)

122 W. Franklin Ave., #310, Minneapolis, MN
55404 Tel. (612)871-8980 Fax (612)813-4501
Email: info@micah.org
Website: www.micah.org
Media Contact, Ex. Dir., Joy Sorensen Navarre
Ex. Dir., Joy Sorensen Navarre

233

Assoc. Dir., José Trejo
Congregational Organizer, Jodi Nelson, Jean Pearson, Rev. John Buzza, Gloria Little
Pres., Sue Watlov Phillips
Sec., Rev. Paul Robinson
Vice Pres., Dick Little
Treas., Joseph Holmberg
Pres. Elect, Kristine Gentilini
Major Activities: MICAH is a regional advocacy organization made up of over 100 Catholic, Islamic, Jewish, and Protestant congregations dedicated to ensuring decent, safe, and affordable housing for everyone in our community. Its central organizing motto is, "To think regionally, act locally, and live faithfully." In partnership with its members and other groups, MICAH has created community support for 200 new apartment homes in the past two years. In addition it has preserved over 1,000 structurally sound apartments at risk of demolition.

St. Paul Area Council of Churches

1671 Summit Ave, St. Paul, MN 55105 Tel. (651)646-8805 Fax (651)646-6866
Email: tduke@space.com
Website: www.space.com
Media Contact, Sandy Lucas
Exec. Dir., Rev. Thomas A. Duke
Dir. of Development, Kristi Anderson
Congregations in Community, Bob Walz
Congregations Concerned for Children, Peg Wangensteen
Project Spirit, Rev. Paulette Ajavon
Project Home, Margaret Lovejoy
Dept. of Indian Work, Sheila WhiteEagle
Criminal Justice Care Services, Rev. Kathleen Gatson
Pres. of the Board, Tara Mattessich
Treas., James Verlautz
Sec., Marylyn Deneen
Major Activities: Chaplaincy at Detention and Corrections Authority Institutions; Police Chaplaincy; Education and Advocacy Regarding Children and Poverty; Assistance to Churches Developing Children's Parenting Care Services; Ecumenical Encounters and Activities; Indian Ministries; Leadership in Forming Cooperative Ministries for Children and Youth; After School Tutoring; Assistance to Congregations; Training Programs in Anti-racism; Shelters for homeless

Tri-Council Coordinating Commission

122 W. Franklin, Rm. 100, Minneapolis, MN 55404 Tel. (612)871-0229 Fax (612)870-3622
Email: naja@gmcc.org
Website: www.amcc.org/tcc.html
Media Contact, Co-Dir., Nadine Addington OR Co-Dir., R. James Addington
Co-Dir., R. James Addington
Co-Dir., Nadine Addington

Pres., Rev. Thomas Duke, 1671 Summit Ave., St. Paul, MN 55105
Major Activities: Anti-Racism training and organizational consultation; Institutional anti-racism team development and coaching; training and coaching of anti-racism trainers and organizers (in cooperation with cross roads ministry)

MISSISSIPPI

Mississippi Religious Leadership Conference*

P.O. Box 68123, Jackson, MS 39286-8123 Tel. (601)948-5954 Fax (601)354-3401
Media Contact, Exec. Dir., Rev. Canon Thomas E. Tiller, Jr.
Exec. Dir., Rev. Canon Thomas E. Tiller, Jr.
Chair, Bishop Marshall Meadors
Treas., Rev. Tom Clark
Major Activities: Cooperation among Religious Leaders; Lay/Clergy Retreats; Social Concerns Seminars; Disaster Task Force; Advocacy for Disadvantaged

MISSOURI

Council of Churches of the Ozarks

P.O. Box 3947, Springfield, MO 65808-3947 Tel. (417)862-3586 Fax (417)862-2129
Email: ccozarks@ccozarks.org
Website: www.ccozarks.org
Media Contact, Comm. Dir., Susan Jackson
Exec. Dir., Rev. Jesse Thorton
Dev. Officer, Tammy Mast
Program Dir., Barbara Gardner
Major Activities: Ministerial Alliance; Retired Sr. Volunteer Prog.; Treatment Center for Alcohol and Drug Abuse; Helping Elderly Live More Productively; Daybreak Adult Day Care Services; Ombudsman for Nursing Homes; Homesharing; Family Day Care Homes; USDA Food Program; Youth Ministry; Disaster Aid and Counseling; Homebound Shoppers; Food and Clothing Pantry; Ozarks Food Harvest; Families for Children

Ecumenical Ministries

#2 St. Louis Ave., Fulton, MO 65251 Tel. (573)642-6065
Email: em_fulton@ecunet.org
Website: www.coin.missouri.edu/region/call-away/em.html
Media Contact, Ofc. Mgr., Karen Luebbert
Exec. Dir., Andrea Langton
Pres., William Jessop
Major Activities: Kingdom Hospice; CROP Hunger Walk; Little Brother and Sister; Unity Service; Senior Center Bible Study; County Jail Ministry; Fulton High School Baccalaureate Service, HAVEN House; Missouri Youth Treatment Center Ministry

Interfaith Community Services

200 Cherokee St., P.O. Box 4038, St. Joseph, MO 64504-0038 Tel. (816)238-4511 Fax (816)238-3274

Email: DaveB@PonyExpress.net

Website: www.inter-serv.org

Media Contact, Exec. Dir., David G. Berger

Exec. Dir., David G. Berger

Major Activities: Child Development; Neighborhood Family Services; Group Home for Girls; Retired Senior Volunteer Program; Nutrition Program; Mobile Meals; Southside Youth Program; Church and Community; Housing Development; Homemaker Services to Elderly; Emergency Food, Rent, Utilities; AIDS Assistance; Family Respite; Family and Individual Casework

MONTANA

Montana Association of Churches*

180 24th St. W., Ste. G, Billings, MT 59102 Tel. (406)656-9779 Fax (406)656-2156

Email: montanachurches@earthlink.net

Website: www.montana-churches.org

Media Contact, Exec. Dir., Margaret MacDonald

Exec. Dir., Margaret E. MacDonald

Admn. Asst., Hung Vu

Pres., Rev. Jessica Crist, 401 4th Ave. N., Great Falls, MT 59401-2310

Treas., Rev. Paul Everett, 401 Riverview, Glendive, MT 59330

Sec., Rev. Gretchen Knapp, P.O. Box 794, Hilger, MT 59451

Christian Advocates Network, Betty Whiting

Major Activities: Montana Christian Advocates Network; Christian Unity; Junior Citizen Camp; Public Information; Ministries Development; Social Ministry; Faith Responses to Extremism and Racism through Christian Witness For Humanity; Renewing the Public Church

NEBRASKA

Interchurch Ministries of Nebraska*

215 Centennial Mall S., Rm. 411, Lincoln, NE 68508-1888 Tel. (402)476-3391 Fax (402)476-9310

Email: im50427@navix.net

Media Contact, Exec., Mrs. Marilyn P. Mecham

Pres., The Rev. Dr. Bart Brenner

Treas., Mrs. Shirley Mac Marsh

Exec., Mrs. Marilyn Mecham

Admin. Asst., Sharon K. Kalcik

Major Activities: Interchurch Planning and Development; Comity; Indian Ministry; Rural Church Strategy; United Ministries in Higher Education; Disaster Response; Rural Response Hotline; Health Ministry; Community Organizing Initiative Planning; Peace with Justice

Lincoln Interfaith Council

140 S. 27th St., Ste. B, Lincoln, NE 68510-1301 Tel. (402)474-3017 Fax (402)475-3262

Email: Li92630@navix.net

Website: www.lincolninterfaith.org

Media Contact, Doug Boyd

Exec. Dir., Rev. Dr. Norman E. Leach

Pres., Dr. William Caldwell

Vice-Pres., Mrs. Gail Linderholm

Sec., Barbara Dewey

Treas., Rev. Dr. Clip Higgins, Jr.

Media Specialist, Doug Boyd

Urban Ministries, Rev. Dr. Norman E. Leach

Admn. Asst., Jean Scali

Fiscal Mgr., Jean Scali

Family Outreach Workers:Bich Tang; Tan Pham

Police Community Liaison,Toan Tran

Migrant Child Education Outreach, Marina Wray

Faces of the Middle East, Mohammed Al-Bezerji; Zainab Al-Baaj

Major Activities: Emergency Food Pantries System; MLK, Jr. Observance; Interfaith Passover Seder; Week of Prayer Christian Unity; Center for Spiritual Growth; Festival of Faith & Culture; Holocaust Memorial Observance; Citizens Against Racism & Discrimination; HIV/AIDS Healing Worship Services; Community organization; Anti-Drug & Anti-Alcohol Abuse Projects; Youth Gang & Violence Prevention; Domestic Abuse Prevention; Migrant Child Education; American Citizenship Classes; Survival English for Pre-literate AmerAsians and Elderly Refugees; Ecumenical Deaf Ministry; Multi-Faith & Multi-Cultural Training; Faces of the Middle East Project; Communities Helping Immigrants & Refugees Progress Project; Crop Walk for Hunger; Unicef Drive; New Clergy Orientation; Directory of Clergy, Congregations & Religious Resources; Multi-Faith Planning Calendar Publication; "Faith Report"

NEW HAMPSHIRE

New Hampshire Council of Churches*

316 S. Main St., P.O. Box 1087, Concord, NH 03302-1087 Tel. (603)224-1352 Fax (603)224-9161

Email: churchesnh@aol.com

Media Contact, Exec. Dir., David Lamarre-Vincent, E-mail:davidlv@aol.com

Exec. Dir., David Lamarre-Vincent

Pres., Rev. Janet Smith-Rushton, 19 Norwich St., Concord, NH 03301

Treas., Mr. Alvah Chisholm

Major Activities: Ecumenical Work

NEW JERSEY

New Jersey Council of Churches*

176 W. State St., Trenton, NJ 08608 Tel. (609)396-9546 Fax (609)396-7646

235

Media Contact, Public Policy Dir., Joan Diefenbach, Esq.
Pres., Rev. Jack Johnson
Vice-Pres., -
Sec., Beverly McNally
Treas., Marge Christie
Major Activities: Racial Justice; Children's Issues; Theological Unity; Ethics Public Forums; Advocacy; Economic Justice

Bergen County Council of Churches

58 James Street, Bergenfield, NJ 07621 Tel. (201)384-7505 Fax (201)384-2585
Media Contact, Pres., Rev. Stephen Giordano, Clinton Avenue Reformed Church, Clinton Ave. & James St., Bergenfield, NJ 07621 Tel. (201)384-2454 Fax (201)384-2585
Exec. Sec., Anne Annunziato
Major Activities: Ecumenical and Religious Institute; Brotherhood/Sisterhood Breakfast; Center for Food Action; Homeless Aid; Operation Santa Claus; Aging Services; Boy & Girl Scouts; Easter Dawn Services; Music; Youth; Ecumenical Representation; Support of Chaplains in Jails & Hospitals

Council of Churches of Greater Camden

P.O. Box 1208, Merchantville, NJ 08109 Tel. (856)985-5162
Media Contact, Exec. Sec., Rev. Dr. Samuel A. Jeanes, Braddock Bldg., 205 Tuckerton Road, Medford, NJ 08055 Tel. (609)985-7724
Exec. Sec., Rev. Dr. Samuel A. Jeanes
Pres., Rev. Lawrence L. Dunn
Treas., William G. Mason
Major Activities: Radio & T.V.; Hospital Chaplaincy; United Services; Good Friday Breakfast; Mayors' Prayer Breakfast; Public Affairs; Easter Sunrise Service

Ecclesia

1001 Pennnington Rd., Trenton, NJ 08618-2629 Tel. (609)882-5942
Media Contact, Exec. Dir., Rev. Dr. T.L. Steele
Exec. Dir., Rev. Dr. T.L. Steele
Pres., Rev. Joseph P. Ravenell
Campus Chaplains: Rev. Nancy Schulter; Rev. Joanne B. Bullock
Major Activities: Racial Justice; Children & Youth Ministries; Advocacy; CROP Walk; Ecumenical Worship; Hospital Chaplaincy; Church Women United; Campus Chaplaincy; Congregational Empowerment; Prison Chaplaincy; Substance Abuse Ministry Training

Metropolitan Ecumenical Ministry

525 Orange St., Newark, NJ 07107 Tel. (201)481-6650 Fax (201)481-7883
Media Contact, Pam Smith

Exec. Dir., C. Stephen Jones
Major Activities: Community Advocacy (education, housing, environment); Church Mission Assistance; Community and Clergy Leadership Development; Economic Development; Affordable Housing

Metropolitan Ecumenical Ministry Community Development Corp.

525 Orange St., Newark, NJ 07107 Tel. (201)481-6650 Fax (201)481-7883
Email: memcdc@juno.com
Exec. Dir., Jacqueline Jones
Major Activities: Housing Development; Neighborhood Revitalization; Commercial/Small Business Development; Economic Development; Community Development; Credit Union; Home Ownership Counseling; Credit Repair; Mortgage Approval; Technical Assitance To Congregations

NEW MEXICO

New Mexico Conference of Churches*

124 Hermosa Dr. SE, Albuquerque, NM 87108-2610 Tel. (505)255-1509 Fax (505)256-0071
Email: barbarad@nmchurches.org
Website: www.nmchurches.org
Media Contact, Exec. Sec., Rev. Barbara E Dua
Pres., Rev. Richard Olona
Treas., Ruth Tribeou
Exec. Sec., Rev. Barbara E. Dua
Major Activities: Ecumenical Institute for Ministry; Affordable Housing; Social Justice Coalitions; Spiritual Life & Ministries

Inter-Faith Council of Santa Fe, New Mexico

PO Box 15517, Santa Fe, NM 87506-5517 Tel. (505)438-4782 Fax (505)473-5637
Media Contact, Barbara A. Robinson
Major Activities: Faith Community Assistance Center; providing emergency assistance to the poor; Interfaith Dialogues/Celebrations/Visitations; Peace Projects; Understanding Hispanic Heritage; Newsletter

NEW YORK

New York State Community of Churches, Inc.*

362 State St, Albany, NY 12210-1202 Tel. (518)436-9319 Fax (518)427-6705
Email: nyscoc@aol.com
Website: www.nyscommunityofchurches.org
Media Contact, Mr. Thomas McPheeters
Executive Dir., Ms. Mary Lu Bowen
Pres., The Rev. Dr. Robert White
Corp. Sec., The Rev. Dr. Jon Norton
Treas., Bishop Susan M. Morrison
Convener, Bishop Lee M. Miller

Coordinator of Chaplaincy Services, Ms. Damaris McGuire

Public Policy Advocate, The Rev. Daniel Hahn

Communications Coord: Mr. Thomas McPheeters

Admin. Asst., Sylvenia F. Cochran

Major Activities: Faith & Order; Interfaith Dialogue; State Chaplaincy and Public Policy Advocacy in the following areas: Anti-Racism; Campaign Reform; Criminal Justice System Reform; Disability; Ecomomic/Social Justice; Environmental; Health care; Homelessness/Shelter; Hunger/Food Programs; Immigrant Issues; Public Education; Rural Issues; Substance Abuse; Violence; Women's Issues

Brooklyn Council of Churches

125 Ft. Greene Pl., Brooklyn, NY 11217 Tel. (718)625-5851 Fax 718-522-1231

Media Contact, Dir., Charles Henze

Program Dir., Charles Henze

Pres., Rev. John L. Pratt., Sr.

Treas., Rev. Charles H. Straut , Jr.

Major Activities: Education Workshops; Food Pantries; Welfare Advocacy; Hospital and Nursing Home Chaplaincy; Church Women United; Legislative Concerns

Broome County Council of Churches, Inc.

81 Main St., Binghamton, NY 13905 Tel. (607)724-9130 Fax (607)724-9148

Email: bccouncil@juno.com

Website: www.tier.net/bccc

Media Contact, Assoc. Dir., Jan Aerie

Exec. Dir., William H. Stanton

Assoc. Dir., Jan Aerie

Hospital Chaplains: Betty Pomeroy; Rev. Nadine Ridley

Jail Chaplain, Rev. Philip Singer; Pat Dillon

Aging Ministry Coord., Linda McCalgin

CHOW Prog. Coord., Heidi Kowalchyk

Pres., Rev. Art Suggs

Treas., Rachel Light

Caregiver Program Coord., Rebecca Mebert

Major Activities: Hospital and Jail Chaplains; Youth and Aging Ministries; Broome Bounty (Food Rescue Program); CHOW (Emergency Hunger Program); Faith & Family Values; Ecumenical Worship and Fellowship; Media; Community Affairs; Peace with Justice; Day by Day Marriage Prep Program; Interfaith Coalition; Interfaith Volunteer Caregiver Program

Capital Area Council of Churches, Inc.

646 State St., Albany, NY 12203-3815 Tel. (518)462-5450 Fax (518)462-5450

Media Contact, Admn. Asst.,Kitt Jackson

Exec. Dir., Rev. Dr. Robert C. Lamar

Admn. Asst.,Kitt Jackson

Pres., Harold Howes

Treas.,David Wood

Major Activities: Hospital Chaplaincy; Food Pantries; CROP Walk; Jail and Nursing Home Ministries; Martin Luther King Memorial Service and Scholarship Fund; Emergency Shelter for the Homeless; Campus Ministry; Ecumenical Dialogue; Forums on Social Concerns; Peace and Justice Education; Inter-Faith Programs; Legislative Concerns; Comm. Thanksgiving Day and Good Friday Services; Annual Ecumenical Musical Celebration

CAPITAL Region Ecumenical Organization (CREO)

Box 2199, Scotia, NY 12302 Tel. (518)382-7505 Fax (518)382-7505

Email: TishMurph@aol.com

Media Contact, Coord., Jim Murphy

Coord., Jim Murphy

Major Activities: Promote Cooperation/Coordination Among Member Judicatories and Ecumenical Organizations in the Capital Region in Urban Ministries, Social Action

Chautaugua County Rural Ministry

127 Central Ave., P.O. Box 362, Dunkirk, NY 14048 Tel. (716)366-1787

Media Contact, Exec. Dir., Kathleen Peterson

Exec. Dir., Kathleen Peterson

Major Activities: Chautaugua County Food Bank; Collection/Distribution of Furniture, Clothing, & Appliances; Homeless Services; Advocacy for the Poor; Soup Kitchen; Emergency Food Pantry; Thrift Store

Concerned Ecumenical Ministry to the Upper West Side

286 LaFayette Ave., Buffalo, NY 14213 Tel. (716)882-2442 Fax (716)882-2477

Email: catrg@banet.net

Media Contact, Exec. Dir., The Rev. Catherine Rieley-Goddard

Interim Exec. Dir., The Rev. Catherine Rieley-Goddard

Pres., The Rev. Robert Grimm

Major Activities: Community Center Serving Youth, Young Families, Seniors and the Hungry

Cortland County Council of Churches, Inc.

7 Calvert St., Cortland, NY 13045 Tel. (607)753-1002

Media Contact, Office Mgr., Joy Niswender

Exec. Dir., Rev. Donald M. Wilcox

Major Activities: College Campus Ministry; Hospital Chaplaincy; Nursing Home Ministry; Newspaper Column; Interfaith Relationships; Hunger Relief; CWS; Crop Walk; Leadership Education; Community Issues; Mental Health Chaplaincy; Grief Support; Jail Ministry

Council of Churches of Chemung County, Inc.

330 W. Church St., Elmira, NY 14901 Tel. (607)734-2294

Email: ecumenic@exotrope.net

Media Contact, Exec. Dir., Joan Geldmacher, Tel. (607)734-7622

Exec. Dir., Joan Geldmacher

Pres., Rev. Fred Kelsey, Christ's U.M., (607)734-2293

Major Activities: CWS Collection; CROP Walk; UNICEF; Institut'onal Chaplaincies; Radio, Easter Dawn Service; Communications Network; Produce & Distribute Complete Church Directories; Representation on Community Boards and Agencies; Ecumenical Services; Interfaith Coalition; Taskforce on Children & Families; Compeer; Interfaith Hospitality Center

Council of Churches of the City of New York

475 Riverside Dr., Rm. 720, New York, NY 10115 Tel. (212)367-4222 Fax (212)367-4280

Email: JEHiemstra@aol.com

Media Contact, Exec. Dir., Dr. John E. Hiemstra

Exec. Dir., Dr. John E. Hiemstra

Pres., Rev. Calvin O. Butts

1st Vice-Pres., Friend Carol Holmes

2nd Vice-Pres., Rev. Carolyn Holloway

3rd Vice-Pres., Ven. Michael Kendall

Sec., Rev. N.J. L'Heureux

Treas., Dr. John Blackwell

Major Activities: Radio & TV; Pastoral Care; Protestant Chapel, Kennedy International Airport; Coordination and Strategic Planning; Religious Conferences; Referral & Advocacy; Youth Development; Directory of Churches and Database Available

Dutchess Interfaith Council, Inc.

9 Vassar St., Poughkeepsie, NY 12601 Tel. (914)471-7333

Media Contact, Exec. Dir., Rev. Gail A. Burger

Exec. Dir., Rev. Gail A. Burger

Pres., Rev. Dr. Brian E. McWeeney

Treas., Elizabeth M. DiStefano

Major Activities: CROP Hunger Walk; Interfaith Music Festival; Public Worship Events; Interfaith Dialogue; Christian Unity; Interfaith Youth Evening; Oil Purchase Group; HIV/AIDS Work; Weekly Radio Program; Racial Unity Work

Genesee County Churches United, Inc.

P.O. Box 547, Batavia, NY 14021 Tel. (716)343-6763

Media Contact, Pres., Captain Leonard Boynton, Salvation Army, 529 East Main St., Batavia, NY 14020 Tel. (716)343-6284

Pres., James Woodruff

Exec. Sec., Cheryl Talone

Chaplain, Rev. Peter Miller

Major Activities: Jail Ministry; Food Pantries; Serve Needy Families; Radio Ministry; Pulpit Exchange; Community Thanksgiving; Ecumenical Services at County Fair

Genesee-Orleans Ministry of Concern

Arnold Gregory Memorial Complex, Suite 271 243 South Main St., Albion, NY 14411 Tel. (716)589-9210 Fax (716)589-9617

Media Contact, Exec. Dir., Marian M. Adrian, GNSH

Exec. Dir., Marian M. Adrian, GNSH

Advocates: JoAnn McCowan; Heather Cook

Pres., John W. Cebula, Esq.

Chaplains: Orleans County Jail, Rev. Wilford Moss; Orleans Albion Correctional Facility, Sr. Dolores O'Dowd, GNSH

Major Activities: Advocacy Services for the Disadvantaged, Homeless, Ill, Incarcerated and Victims of Family Violence; Emergency Food, Shelter, Utilities, Medicines

Graymoor Ecumenical & Interreligious Institute

475 Riverside Dr., Rm. 1960, New York, NY 10115-1999 Tel. (212)870-2330 Fax (212) 870-2001

Email: lmnygeii@aol.com

Website: www.atonementfriars.org

Media Contact, Ms. Elizabeth Matos

Major Activities: (See Listing in US Cooperative Directory)

Greater Rochester Community of Churches

2 Riverside St., Rochester, NY 14613-1222 Tel. (716)254-2570 Fax (716)254-6551

Email: grcc@juno.com

Media Contact, Coord., Marie E. Gibson

Major Activities: Ecumenical Worship; Chaplaincy Services; Christian Unity; Beyond Racism Project; Interfaith Cooperation; Community Economic Development; Annual Faith in Action Celebration; Rochester's Religious Community Directory; Religious Information/Resources

InterReligious Council of Central New York

3049 E. Genesee St., Syracuse, NY 13224 Tel. (315)449-3552 Fax (315)449-3103

Email: IRCCNY@aol.com

Media Contact, Dir. for Resource Development, Chrissie Rizzo

Executive Dir., The Rev. Robert E. Hanson

Pres., The Rev. Emily S. Gibson

Bus. Mgr., Joseph Sarno

Director for Resource Development, Chrissie Rizzo

Pastoral Care Prog., Dir., The Rev. Terry Culbertson

Refugee Resettlement Prog., Dir., Nona Stewart

Senior Companion Prog., Dir., Virginia Frey

Long Term Ombudsman Prog., Dir., Linda Kashdin

Covenant Housing Prog., Dir., Kimberlee Dupcak

Southeast Asia Center, Dir., Mai Lan Putnam

Community Wide Dialogue on Racism, Race Relations and Racial Healing, Co-Dirs., Milady Andrews, Morgan and Van Leary-Hammerstedt

InterReligious Council News, Ed., Ed Griffin-Nolan

Major Activities: Pastoral Ministries; Community Ministries; Interreligious and Ecumenical Relations; Diversity Education; Worship; Community Advocacy and Planning

The Long Island Council of Churches

1644 Denton Green, Hempstead, NY 11550 Tel. (516)565-0290

Email: licc@netzero.com

Website: www.ncccusa.org/ecmin/licc

Media Contact, Exec. Dir., Thomas W. Goodhue

Exec. Dir., Rev. Thomas W. Goodhue

Pastoral Care, Dir., Rev. Richard Lehman

Social Services, Dir., Cynthia Morrow, Tel. (516)565-0390

Nassau County Ofc., Social Services Sec., LaToya Walker

Suffolk County Ofc., Food Program & Family Support, Carolyn Gumbs

Major Activities: Pastoral Care in Jails; Emergency Food; Family Support & Advocacy; Advocacy for Domestic and International Peace & Justice; Blood Donor Coordination; Church World Service; Multifaith Education; Clergy/Laity Training; Newsletter; Church Directory; AIDS Interfaith of Long Island

Network of Religious Communities

1272 Delaware Ave., Buffalo, NY 14209-2496 Tel. (716)882-4793 Fax (716)882-3797

Email: ReligiousNet@aol.com

Website: ReligiousNet.org

Media Contact, Co-Exec. Dir., Rev. Dr. G. Stanford Bratton

Co-Exec. Dir. & COO, Rev. Dr. G. Stanford Bratton

Co-Exec. Dir., Rev. Francis X. Mazur

Pres.,Rev. Jeff Carter (Church of God in Christ)

Vice-Pres. For Program, The Rev. Dr. David McKee (General Presbyter, Presbytery of WNY)

Vice-Pres. For Administration, Ms. Marlene Glickman (Dir., American Jewish Committee)

Secretary, Ms. Sheila Nickson (Episcopal Church)

Treasurer, The Rev. Amos Acree (Disciples of Christ)

Chpsn., Interreligious Concerns, Rabbi Michael Feshbach, President Board of Rabbis

Chpsn., Personnel, The Rev. James Croglio (Diocese of Buffalo- Roman Catholic)

Chpsn., Membership, The Rev. Robert Grimm (United Church of Christ)

Chpsn., Riefler Enablement Fund, Mrs. Thelma Lanier (African Methodist Episcopal Church)

Chpsn., Public Issues, Rev. Merle Showers (United Methodist Church)

Chpsn., Religious Leaders Forum, Rev. Paul Litwin (Diocese of Buffalo -Roman Catholic)

Chpsn., Church Women United, Ms. Alma Arnold (United Church of Christ)

STAFF (Other than Executive Directors)

Program Coordinator, Ms. Maureen Gensler

Office Coordinator, Ms. Sally Giordano

Director of Food For All, Patricia Griffin

Nutrition Outreach and Education Coordinator, Ms. Carolyn Williams

Staff Assistant, Mr. Lamont Gist

Major Activities: Regionwide Interreligious Conversation; Hunger Advocacy; Food Distribution; Roll Call Against Racism; Buffalo Coalition for Common Ground; Ecumenical and Interreligious Relations and Celebrations; Radio-TV Broadcast and Production; Church Women United, Lay/Religious Leaders Education; Community Development, Chaplaincy; Yom Hashoah Commemoration Service; AIDS Memorial Service; Police/Community Relations; CROP Walks

The Niagara Council of Churches Inc.

St. Paul UMC, 723 Seventh St., Niagara Falls, NY 14301 Tel. (716)285-7505

Media Contact, Pres., Nessie S. Bloomquist, 7120 Laur Rd., Niagara Falls, NY 14304 Tel. (716)297-0698 Fax (716)298-1193

Exec. Dir., Ruby Babb

Pres., Nessie S. Bloomquist

Treas., Shirley Bathurst

Trustees Chpsn., Rev. Vincent Mattoni, 834 19th St., Niagara Falls, NY 14304

Major Activities: Ecumenical Worship; Bible Study; Christian Ed. & Social Concerns; Church Women United; Evangelism & Mission; Institutional Min. Youth Activities; Hymn Festival; Week of Prayer for Christian Unity; CWS Projects; Audio-Visual Library; UNICEF; Food Pantries and Kitchens; Community Missions, Inc.; Political Refugees; Eco-Justice Task Force; Migrant/Rural Ministries; Interfaith Coalition on Energy

Niagara County Migrant Rural Ministry

6507 Wheeler Rd., Lockport, NY 14094 Tel. (716)434-4405

239

Media Contact, Exec. Dir., Grayce M. Dietz
Chpsn., Lois Farley
Vice-Chpsn., Beverly Farnham
Sec., Anne Eifert
Treas., Rev. Patricia Ludwig
Major Activities: Migrant Farm Worker Program; Assist with Immigration Problems and Application Process for Social Services; Monitor Housing Conditions; Assist Rural Poor; Referrals to Appropriate Service Agencies; Children's Daily Enrichment Program

Queens Federation of Churches

86-17 105th St., Richmond Hill, NY 11418-1597 Tel. (718)847-6764 Fax (718)847-7392
Email: qfc@ecunet.org
Media Contact, Rev. N. J. L'Heureux, Jr.
Exec. Dir., Rev. N. J. L'Heureux, Jr.
York College Chaplain, Rev. Dr. Hortense Merritt
Pres., Rev. Allen D. Maclean
Treas.,Annie Lee Phillips
Major Activities: Emergency Food Service; York College Campus Ministry; Blood Bank; Scouting; Christian Education Workshops; Planning and Strategy; Church Women United; Community Consultations; Seminars for Church Leaders; Directory of Churches and Synagogues; Christian Relations (Prot/RC); Chaplaincies; Public Policy Issues; N.Y.S. Interfaith Commission on Landmarking of Religious Property; Queens Interfaith Hunger Network; "The Nexus of Queens" (tri-weekly newspaper)

Rural Migrant Ministry

P.O. Box 4757, Poughkeepsie, NY 12602 Tel. (914)485-8627 Fax (914)485-1963
Email: rmmyag@aol.com
Media Contact, Exec. Dir., Rev. Richard Witt
Exec. Dir., Rev. Richard Witt
Pres., Melinda Trotti
Major Activities: Serving the Rural Poor and Migrants Through a Ministry of Advocacy & Empowerment; Youth Program; Latino Committee; Organization and Advocacy with and for Rural Poor and Migrant Farm Workers

Schenectady Inner City Ministry

930 Albany St., Schenectady, NY 12307-1514 Tel. (518)374-2683 Fax (518)382-1871
Email: sicm@knick.net
Website: www. crisny.org/not-for-profit/sicm
Media Contact, Marianne Comfort
Urban Agent, Rev. Phillip N. Grigsby
Off. Mgr., Vjuana Anderson
Fiscal Officer, Joan LaMonica
Emergency Food Liaison, Patricia Obrecht
Church/Community Worker, Rev. Jim Murphy
Pres., Starr and Tom DiCiuvcio
Save and Share, Cindy Hofer

Damien Center, Glenn Read
Youth Improvisational Teen Theatre, Laurie Bacheldor
Jobs, Etc., David Coplon
Summer Food
Housing Task Force, Eric Dahl
Major Activities: Food Security; Advocacy; Housing; Neighborhood and Economic Issues; Ecumenical Worship and Fellowship; Community Research; Education in Churches on Faith Responses to Social Concerns; Legislative Advocacy; Food Buying Coop; Homelessness Prevention; CROP Walk; HIV/AIDS Ministry; Teen Theatre; Job Training and Placement Center; Summer Lunch for Youth; Study Circles Initiative on Embracing Diversity; EPRUS/Americorps; Community Crisis Nework; Housing Services and Advocacy

Southeast Ecumenical Ministry

25 Westminster Rd., Rochester, NY 14607 Tel. (716)271-5350 Fax (716)271-8526
Email: sem@frontiernet.net
Media Contact, Laurie Kennedy
Dir., Laurie Kennedy
Pres., Rev. James Widboom
Major Activities: Transportation of Elderly & Disabled; Emergency Food Cupboard; Supplemental Nutrition Program

Staten Island Council of Churches

2187 Victory Blvd., Staten Island, NY 10314 Tel. (718)761-6782
Media Contact, Exec. Sec., Mildred J. Saderholm, 94 Russell St., Staten Island, NY 10308 Tel. (718)761-6782
Pres., Rev. Gard Rowe
Exec. Sec., Mildred J. Saderholm
Major Activities: Support; Christian Education; Pastoral Care; Congregational Concerns; Urban Affairs

Troy Area United Ministries

17 First St., #2, Troy, NY 12180 Tel. (518)274-5920 Fax (518)271-1909
Email: TAUM@crisny.org
Media Contact, Interim Exec. Dir., Arleon L. Kelley
Interim Exec. Dir., Arleon L. Kelley
Pres., Dorcas Rose
Chaplain, R.P.I.
Community Dispute Settlement Program, Dir., Dawn Wallont
Damien Center, Dir., Glenn Read
Furniture Program, Dir., Roger Mahour, Jr.
Major Activities: Community Dispute Settlement (mediation) Program; College Ministry; Nursing Home Ministry; CROP Walk; Homeless and Housing Concerns; Weekend Meals Program at Homeless Shelter; Community Worship Celebrations; Racial

Relations; Furniture Program; Damien Center of Troy Hospitality for persons with HIV/AIDS; Computer Ministries

Wainwright House
260 Stuyvesant Ave., Rye, NY 10580 Tel. (914)967-6080 Fax (914)967-6114
Media Contact, Exec. Dir., Judith W. Milinowski
Exec. Dir., Judith W. Milinowski
Pres., Dr. Robert A. Rothman
Exec. Vice-Pres., Beth Adams Smith
Major Activities: Educational Program and Conference Center; Intellectual, Psychological, Physical and Spiritual Growth; Healing and Health

NORTH CAROLINA

North Carolina Council of Churches*
Methodist Bldg., 1307 Glenwood Ave., Ste. 162, Raleigh, NC 27605-3258 Tel. (919)828-6501 Fax (919)282-9697
Email: nccofc@pagesz.net
Website: www.nccouncilofchurches.org
Media Contact, Exec. Dir., Rev. J. George Reed
Exec. Dir., Rev. J. George Reed
Program Associates,Sr. Evelyn Mattern
Pres., Bridget Johnson, 1208 Hounslow Dr., Greensboro, NC 27410
Treas., Dr. James W. Ferree, 5108 Huntcliff Tr., Winston-Salem, NC 27104
Major Activities: Children and Families; Health Care Justice; Christian Unity; Women's Issues; Legislative Program; Criminal Justice; Farmworker Ministry; Rural Crisis; Racial Justice; Death Penalty; Poverty and Response to Welfare Changes; Climate Change

Asheville-Buncombe Community Christian Ministry (ABCCM)
30 Cumberland Ave., Asheville, NC 28801 Tel. (704)259-5300 Fax (704)259-5923
Media Contact, Exec. Dir., Rev. Scott Rogers, Fax (704)259-5323
Exec. Dir., Rev. Scott Rogers
Pres., Dr. John Grant
Major Activities: Crisis Ministry; Jail/Prison Ministry; Shelter Ministry; Medical Ministry; Home Repair Ministry

Greensboro Urban Ministry
305 West Lee St., Greensboro, NC 27406 Tel. (910)271-5959 Fax (910)271-5920
Email: Guministry@aol.com
Website: www.greensboro.com/gum
Media Contact, Exec. Dir., Rev. Mike Aiken
Exec. Dir., Rev. Mike Aiken
Major Activities: Emergency Financial Assistance; Emergency Housing; Hunger Relief; Inter-Faith and Inter-Racial Understanding; Justice Ministry; Chaplaincy with the Poor

NORTH DAKOTA

North Dakota Conference of Churches
227 W. Broadway, #1, Bismarck, ND 58501 Tel. (701)255-0604 Fax (701)223-6075
Media Contact, Executive Sec., Renee Gopal
Pres., Bishop Andrew Fairfield
Vice Pres., Bishop Michael Coyner
Treas., Christopher Dodson
Secretary, Rev. Arabella Meadows-Rogers
Executive Sec., Renee Gopal
Major Activities: Prison Chaplaincy; Rural Life Ministry; Faith and Order; North Dakota 101; Current Ecumenical Proposals

OHIO

Ohio Council of Churches*
6877 N. High St., Ste. 206, Columbus, OH 43085-2516 Tel. (614)885-9590 Fax (614)885-6097
Email: mail@ohcouncilchs.org
Website: www.ohcouncilchs.org
Exec. Dir., Rev. Rebecca J. Tollefson
Public Policy, Dir., Tom Smith
Ecumenical Issues Dir., Rev. Ronald Botts
Pres., Rev. George Lambert
Vice Pres., Jack Davis
Treas., Sr. Barbara Niehaus
Major Activities: Agricultural Issues; Economic & Social Justice; Ecumenical Relations; Health Care Reform; Public Policy Issues; Theological Dialogue; Racial Relations; Education/Funding; Childcare/Children Issues; Poverty/Welfare; Rural Life/Farm Crisis and Environment

Akron Area Association of Churches
350 S. Portage Path, Akron, OH 44320 Tel. (330)535-3112 Fax (330)374-5041
Email: aaac1@juno.com
Website: www.triple-ac.org
Media Contact, Admin. Asst., Chloe Ann Kriska
Bd. of Trustees, Pres., Rev. Raymond Kovach
Vice-Pres., Rev. J. Wayman Butts
Sec., Dale Kline
Treas., Dr. Stephen Laning
Christian Ed., Dir., Chloe Ann Kriska
Major Activities: Messiah Sing; Interfaith Council; Newsletters; Resource Center; Community Worship; Training of Local Church Leadership; Radio Programs; Clergy and Lay Fellowship Luncheons; Cable TV; Interfaith Caregivers; Neighborhood Development; Community Outreach; Church Interracial Partnerships

Alliance of Churches
470 E. Broadway, Alliance, OH 44601 Tel. (330)821-6648
Media Contact, Dir., Lisa A. Oyster

Dir., Lisa A. Oyster
Pres., Rev. Bud Hoffman
Treas., Betty Rush
Major Activities: Christian Education; Community Relations & Service; Ecumenical Worship; Community Ministry; Peacemaking; Medical Transportation for Anyone Needing It; Emergency Financial Assistance

Churchpeople for Change and Reconciliation

326 W. McKibben, Box 488, Lima, OH 45802 Tel. (419)229-6949
Media Contact, Exec. Dir., Richard Keller
Exec. Dir., Richard Keller
Major Activities: Developing Agencies for Minorities, Poor, Alienated and Despairing; Community Kitchens

Council of Christian Communions of Greater Cincinnati

42 Calhoun St., Cincinnati, OH 45219-1525 Tel. (513)559-3151
Media Contact, Exec. Dir., Joellen W. Grady
Exec. Dir., Joellen W. Grady
Justice Chaplaincy, Assoc. Dir., Rev. Jack Marsh
Educ., Assoc., Lillie D. Bibb
Pres., Rev. Damon Lynch III
Major Activities: Christian Unity & Interfaith Cooperation; Justice Chaplaincies; Police-Clergy Team; Adult and Juvenile Jail Chaplains; Religious Education

Greater Dayton Christian Connections

601 W. Riverview Ave., Dayton, OH 45406 Tel. (513)227-9485 Fax (513)227-9407
Email: gdcc@donet.com
Media Contact, Exec. Dir., James S. Burton
Exec. Dir., James S. Burton
Pres., Rev. Stephen W. Camp
Major Activities: Communications: Service to Churches and Community; Reconciliation Ministry; CROP Walk; Martin Luther King Activities; Workplace Reconnections; Making a Difference

Interchurch Council of Greater Cleveland

2230 Euclid Ave., Cleveland, OH 44115 Tel. (216)621-5925 Fax (216)621-0588
Media Contact, Janice Giering
Exec. Dir., Dr. Dennis N. Paulson, Tel. (216)621-5925
Church & Society, Dir., Rev. Mylion Waite
Communications, Dir., Janice Giering, Karen Drasler
Chmn. of the Assembly, Rev. Jeremiah Pryce
Dir. Of Development, Lynn Paulin
Major Activities: Church and Society; Communications; Hunger; Christian Education; Legislation; Faith and Order; Public Education;

Interchurch News; Tutoring; Parent-Child First Teachers Program; Shelter for Homeless Women and Children; Radio & TV; Interracial Cooperation; Interfaith Cooperation; Adopt-A-School; Women of Hope; Leadership Development; Religious Education; Center for Peace & Reconciliation—Youth and the Courts; Support Services to Local Churches

Mahoning Valley Association of Churches

30 W. Front St., Youngstown, OH 44503 Tel. (330)744-8946 Fax (330)774-0018
Email: mvac@onecom.com
Media Contact, Exec. Dir., Elsie L. Dursi
Exec. Dir., Elsie L. Dursi
Pres., Jack Ritter
Treas., Atty Elaine Greaves
Major Activities: Communications; Christian Education; Ecumenism; Social Action; Advocacy

Metropolitan Area Church Council

760 E. Broad St., Columbus, OH 43205 Tel. (614)461-7103
Media Contact, Exec. Dir., Rev. Burton Cantrell
Exec. Dir., Rev. Burton Cantrell
Chpsn. of Bd., Alvin Hadley
Sec./Treas., Lily Schlichter
Major Activities: Newspaper; Liaison with Community organizations; Assembly; Week of Prayer for Christian Unity; Support for Ministerial Associations and Church Councils; Seminars for Church Leaders; Prayer Groups; CROP Walk; Social Concerns Hearings

Metropolitan Area Religious Coalition of Cincinnati

Ste. 1035, 617 Vine St., Cincinnati, OH 45202-2423 Tel. (513)721-4843 Fax (513)721-4891
Media Contact, Dir., Rev. Duane Holm
Dir., Rev. Duane Holm
Pres., Burton Perlman
Major Activities: Local social policy decisions chosen annually. 1999: Public Education, Welfare Reform.

Pike County Outreach Council

122 E. North St., Waverly, OH 45690-1146 Tel. (614)947-7151
Dir., Judy Dixon
Major Activities: Emergency Service Program; Self Help Groups; Homeless Shelter

Toledo Ecumenical Area Ministries

444 Floyd St., Toledo, OH 43620 Tel. (419)242-7401 Fax (419)242-7404
Media Contact, Admn., Nancy Lee Atkins
Metro-Toledo Churches United, Admn., Nancy Lee Atkins
Toledo Metropolitan Mission, Exec. Dir., Nancy Lee Atkins

Major Activities: Ecumenical Relations; Inter-faith Relations; Food Program; Housing Program; Social Action; Public Education; Health Care; Urban Ministry; Employment; Welfare Rights; Housing; Mental Retardation; Voter Registration/Education; Substance Abuse Treatment; Youth Leadership; Children At-risk; Elimination of Discrimination

Tuscarawas County Council for Church and Community

107 West High, Ste. B, New Philadelphia, OH 44663 Tel. (330)343-6012 Fax (330)343-9845
Media Contact, Barbara E. Lauer
Exec. Dir., Barbara E. Lauer
Pres., Zoe Ann Kelley, 201 E. 12th St., Dover, OH 44622
Treas., James Barnhouse, 120 N. Broadway, New Philadelphia, OH 44663
Major Activities: Human Services; Health; Family Life; Child Abuse; Housing; Educational Programs; Emergency Assistance; Legislative Concerns; Juvenile Prevention Program; Character Formation; Prevention Program for High Risk Children; Bimonthly newsletter The Pilot

West Side Ecumenical Ministry

5209 Detroit Ave, Cleveland, OH 44102 Tel. (216)651-2037 Fax (216)651-4145
Email: Eotero@wsem.org
Website: http://community.cleveland.com/cc/wsem
Media Contact, Community Media Associate, Kami L. Marquardt
Pres., & CEO, Elving F. Otero
Director of Operations, Adam Roth
Major Activities: WSEM is dedicated to serving urban low-income families by providing pro-grams that encourage self-sufficiency. Three food pantries and outreach centers, a job-train-ing program, GED classes, Head Start preschools and school-age child care, crisis intervention, mental health services, youth ser-vices, a theatre education program, and a senior nutrition program.

OKLAHOMA

Oklahoma Conference of Churches*

301 Northwest 36th St., Oklahoma City, OK 73118 Tel. (405)525-2928 Fax (405)525-2636
Email: okconfch@flash.net
Website: www.flash.net/~okconfch
Media Contact, Deborah Canary-Marshall
Exec. Dir., The Rev. Dr. Rita K. Newton
Pres., The Rev. Melvin E. Truiett
Treas. vacant
Major Activities: Christian Unity Issues; Community Building Among Members; Rural Community Care; Ecumenical Decade with Women; Children's Advocacy; Day at the

Legislature; Impact; Criminal Justice; Hunger & Poverty; Legislative Advocacy; Aging

Tulsa Metropolitan Ministry

221 S. Nogales, Tulsa, OK 74127 Tel. (918)582-3147 Fax (918)582-3159
Email: TMM@ionet.com
Website: www. TUMM.org
Media Contact, Operation/Associate Dir., James W. Robinson
Exec. Dir., The Rev. Dr. Stephen V. Cranford
Operations Dir., James Robinson
Pres., Dr. Sandra Rana
Vice-Pres., Rev. Barney McLaughlin
Treas., Kelly Kirby
Major Activities: Religious Understanding; Legislative Issues; Interfaith Dialogue TV Series; Christian Issues; Justice Issues; Against Racism; Disability Awareness; Directory of Metro. Religious Community

OREGON

Ecumenical Ministries of Oregon*

0245 S.W. Bancroft St., Ste. B, Portland, OR 97201 Tel. (503)221-1054 Fax (503)223-7007
Email: emo@emoregon.org
Website: www.emoregon.org
Media Contact, Renee Blakely-Ward, EMO Communications Manager
Exec. Dir., David A. Leslie
Associate Dir., Rick Stoller
Compassionate Care and Education, Dir., Melinda Smith
Finance and Administrative Services, Dir., Gary B. Logsdon
Developments Dir., Teri Ruch
Refugees & Immigration Ministries Division, Dir., Ann Stephani
Russian Oregon Social Services, Yelena Sergeva
Portland International Community School, Ellen Irish
Public Policy Dir., Enid Edwards
Interfaith Network for Earth Concerns, Jenny Holmes
Parent Mentor Program, Sylvia Hart-Landsberg
HIV Day Center, Lowen Berman
Shared Housing, Laura Baumeister
Northeast Emergency Food Program, Jennifer Core
President, Lori Brocker
Communications Manager, Renee Blakely-Ward
Major Activities: Theological Education and Dialogue; Public Policy Advocacy; Community Ministries including "Basic Human Needs" (HIV Day Center, NE Emergency Food, Old Town Clinic, Parent Mentor, Shared Housing); "Refugee and Immigration Ministries" (Portland Inter-national Community School, Russian Oregon Social Services, Sponsors Organized to Assist Refugees); and "Compassionate Care & Education" (Hopewell House Hospice Center).

PENNSYLVANIA

Pennsylvania Conference on Interchurch Cooperation*

P.O. Box 2835, 223 North St., Harrisburg, PA 17105 Tel. (717)238-9613 Fax (717)238-1473
Email: staff@pacatholic.org
Website: www.pacatholic.org/about/pcic.htm
Media Contact, Carolyn Astfalk
Co-Staff: Mr. Robert J. O'Hara, Jr., Rev., Gary Harke
Co-Chpsns.: Bishop Joseph Martino; Bishop Paull Spring.
Major Activities: Theological Consultation; Social Concerns; Public Policy; Conferences and Seminars

The Pennsylvania Council of Churches*

900 S. Arlington Ave., Ste. 100, Harrisburg, PA 17109-5089 Tel. (717)545-4761 Fax (717) 545-4765
Email: pcc@pachurches.org
Website: www.pachurches.org
Media Contact, Exec. Dir., Rev. Gary L. Harke
Exec. Dir., Rev. Gary L. Harke
Public Policy, Dir., Rev. K. Joy Kaufmann
Coord. for Contract Chaplaincy, -vacant-
Coord. for Leisure Ministries, Rev. Robert W. Brown
Coord. For Service Ministries, -vacant-
Pres., Rev. Dr. Lyle J. Weible
Vice-Pres., Rev. Clarice L. Chambers
Sec., Mrs. Nancy S. Ritter
Treas., David B. Hoffman, CPA
Bus. Mgr., Janet A. Gulick
Major Activities: Racial/ethic empowerment; inter-church dialogue; trade association activities; faith and order; seasonal farmworker ministry; trucker/traveler ministry; institutional chaplaincy; public policy advocacy and education; leisure ministry; conferences and continuing education events; disaster response; church education

Allegheny Valley Association of Churches

1333 Freeport Rd., P.O. Box 236, Natrona Heights, PA 15065 Tel. (724)226-0606 Fax (724)226-3197
Email: avac@salsgiver.com
Media Contact, Exec. Dir., Karen Snair
Exec. Dir., Karen Snair
Pres., Rev. Dr. W. James Legge, 232 Tarentum-Culmerville Rd., Tarentum, PA 15084
Treas., Libby Grimm, 312 Butternut Ln., Tarentum, PA 15084
Major Activities: Ecumenical Services; Dial-a-Devotion; Walk for Hunger; Food Bank; Emergency Aid; Cross-on-the-Hill; AVAC Hospitality Network for Homeless Families; AVAC Volunteer Caregivers; Senior Citizen Housing-Pine Ridge Heights Senior Complex, AVAC Chaplaincy Program

Christian Associates of Southwest Pennsylvania

204 37th St., Suite 201, Pittsburgh, PA 15201 Tel. (412)688-9070 Fax (412)688-9091
Email: casp1817@aol.com
Website: www.casp.org
Media Contact, Dir. of Communications, Bruce J. Randolph
Chair of Council, Metropolitan Juson M. Pocyk
Pres., Board of Delegates, Bruce J. Randolph
Television Studio Director, Earl C. Hartman, Jr.
Executive Administrative Asst., Nancy Raymond
Director of Jail Chaplaincy Services, Rev. Ulli Klemm
Protestant Chaplain, Rev. Dallas Brown
Protestant Chaplain- Shuman Youth Detention Center, Rev. Floyd Palmer
Jail Administrative Assistant, Karen Mack
Executive Director, Fr. Gregory C. Wingenbach, Past./Ecum. Th.D.
Director of Communications, Bruce J. Randolph
Cable-TV Coordinator, Earl C. Hartman, Jr.
Jail Chaplaincy Services Director, Rev. Ulli Klemm
Exec. Admin. Assistant, Nancy Raymond
Major Activities: Christian Associates Television (CATV); Christian Associates Radio (the Witness); Media Ministries; Special/ Cooperative/Volunteer Ministries; Jail/Youth-Incarceration Chaplaincies; Church & Community; Social Service Ministries; Theological Dialogue/Religious Education; Racism/Interracial Understanding

Christian Churches United of the Tri-County Area

413 South 19th St., Harrisburg, PA 17106-0750 Tel. (717)230-9550 Fax (717)230-9554
Email: ccuhbg@aol.com
Media Contact, Exec. Dir., Jaqueline P. Rucker
Exec. Dir., Jaqueline P. Rucker
Pres., Ken Wise, Esq.
Treas., James Smeltzer
Vice-Pres., Peter Pennington
Sec., Lenore Cameron, Esq.
HELP & LaCasa Ministries, Dir., Tanya Mitchell-Weston, P.O. Box 60750, Harrisburg, PA 17106-0750 Tel. (717)238-2851 Fax (717) 238-1916
Major Activities: Volunteer Ministries to Prisons; Aging; HELP (Housing, Rent, Food, Medication, Transportation, Home Heating, Clothing); La Casa de Amistad (The House of Friendship) Social Services; AIDS Outreach; Prison Chaplaincy; Lend-A-Hand (Disaster Rebuilding)

Christians United in Beaver County

1098 Third St., Beaver, PA 15009 Tel. (724)774-1446 Fax (724)774-1446

Media Contact, Exec. Sec., Lois L. Smith
Exec. Sec., Lois L. Smith
Chaplains: Rev. Bernard Tench; Erika Bruner; Rev. Anthony Massey; Rev. Frank Churchill; John Pusateri
Pres., Rev. Bernard Tench, 2322 10th Street, Beaver Falls, PA 15010
Treas., Ima Moldovon, 302 Lynn Dr., New Brighton, PA 15066
Major Activities: Christian Education; Evangelism; Social Action; Church Women United; United Church Men; Ecumenism; Hospital, Detention Home and Jail Ministry

East End Cooperative Ministry

250 N. Highland Ave., Pittsburgh, PA 15206 Tel. (412)361-5549 Fax (412)361-0151
Email: eecm@usaor.net
Media Contact, Michele Griffiths, Community Development Director
Exec. Dir., Myrna Zelenitz
Ass. Dir., Rev. Darnell Leonard
Major Activities: Food Pantry; Soup Kitchen; Men's Emergency Shelter; Drop-In Shelter for Homeless; Meals on Wheels; Casework and Supportive Services for Elderly; Information and Referral; Programs for Children and Youth; Bridge Housing Program for Men and PennFree for Women in Recovery and Their Children

Ecumenical Conference of Greater Altoona

1208 - 13th St., P.O. Box 305, Altoona, PA 16603 Tel. (814)942-0512
Email: eilbeck@aol.com
Media Contact, Exec. Dir., Eileen Becker
Exec. Dir., Eileen Becker
Major Activities: Religious Education; Workshops; Ecumenical Activities; Religious Christmas Parade; Campus Ministry; Community Concerns; Peace Forum; Religious Education for Mentally Challenged; Inter-faith Committee; Prison Ministry

Greater Bethlehem Area Council of Churches

1021 Center St., P.O. Box 1245, Bethlehem, PA 18016-1245 Tel. (610)867-8671 Fax (610)866-9223
Exec. Dir., Rev. Dr. Helen Baily Cochrane
Pres., Robert D. Romeril
Treas., Robert Gerst, 900 Wedgewood Rd., Bethlehem, PA 18017
Major Activities: World/local hunger projects; Ecumenical Worship/Cooperation; Prison Ministry Programs; Support for Homeless and Welfare to Work Programs; Emergency Food Pantry; Support for Hospice and Share Care Programs; Regional Grave Bank; Support Summer Youth Camps and Church Sports League

Hanover Area Council of Churches

136 Carlisle St., Hanover, PA 17331-2406 Tel. (717)633-6353 Fax (717)633-1992
Email: cathy@sun-link.com
Website: www. netrax.net/~bouchard/hacc.htm
Exec. Dir., Cathy Ferree
Major Activities: Meals on Wheels; Provide a Lunch Program; Fresh Air Program; Clothing Bank; Hospital Chaplaincy Services; Congregational & Interfaith Relations; Public Ecumenical Programs and Services; State Park Chaplaincy Services & Children's Program; Compeer; Faith at Work; CROP Walk; Stolte Scholarship Fund; Community Needs

Inter-Church Ministries of Erie County

2216 Peach St., Erie, PA 16502 Tel. (814)454-2411
Voucher Program, The Rev. Rommie M. Ross
Pres., Rev. Stephen E. Morse, 3642 W. 26th St., Erie, PA 16506
Treas., Ernest O. Wood, 11471 Scotland Ave., North East, PA 16428
Major Activities: Local Ecumenism; Ministry with Aging; Social Ministry; Continuing Education; North West Pennsylvania Conference of Bishops and Judicatory Execs.; Theological Dialogue; Coats for Kids; Voucher Program for Emergency Assistance

Lancaster County Council of Churches

134 E. King St., Lancaster, PA 17602 Tel. (717)291-2261 Fax (717)291-6403
Media Contact, Executive Dir., Rev. John Smaligo
Pres., Armon Snowden
Prescott House, Dir., John Stoudt
Asst. Admn., Kim Y. Wittel
Child Abuse, Dir., Louise Schiraldi
CONTACT, Dir., Lois Gascho
Service Ministry, Dir., Adela Dohner
Major Activities: Social Ministry; Residential Ministry to Youthful Offenders; CONTACT; Advocacy; Child Abuse Prevention

Lebanon County Christian Ministries

818 Water St., P.O. Box 654, Lebanon, PA 17046 Tel. (717)274-2601
Media Contact, Exec. Dir., Lillian Morales
Exec. Dir., Lillian Morales
Noon Meals Coord., Wenda Dinatale
Major Activities: H.O.P.E. (Helping Our People in Emergencies); Food & Clothing Bank; Free Meal Program; Commodity Distribution Program; Ecumenical Events

Lehigh County Conference of Churches

534 Chew St., Allentown, PA 18102 Tel. (610)433-6421 Fax (610)439-8039

245

Email: lcconfchurch@enter.net
Website: www.enter.net/~lcconfchurch
Media Contact, Exec. Dir., The Rev. Dr. Christine L. Nelson
Assoc. Dir., Marlene Merz
Pres., Mr. Anthony Muir
1st Vice-Pres., Mr. Charles Ehninger
Sec., The Rev. Dr. David Charles Smith
Treas., David Schumacher
Major Activities: Prison Chaplaincy Program; Social Concerns and Action; Clergy Dialogues; Daybreak Drop-In-Center for De-Institutionalized Adults; Ecumenical Soup Kitchen; Housing Advocacy Program; Pathways (Referral to Social Services); Street Contact; Linkage; Guardianship; Community Exchange; Homelessness Prevention; Pharmaceutical Assistance; Campbell Ecumenism/Unity lecture; Clothing Distribution

Metropolitan Christian Council of Philadelphia

1501 Cherry St., Philadelphia, PA 19102-1429 Tel. (215)563-7854 Fax (215)563-6849
Email: geiger@mccp.org
Website: www.mccp.org
Media Contact, Assoc. Communications, Nancy L. Nolde
Exec. Dir., Rev. C. Edward Geiger
Assoc. Communications, Nancy L. Nolde
Office Mgr., Joan G. Shipman
Pres., Rev. Steven B. Laurence
First Vice-Pres., Rev. G. Daniel Jones
Treas., A. Louis Denton, Esq.
Major Activities: Congregational Clusters; Public Policy Advocacy; Communication; Theological Dialogue (Christian & Interfaith); Women's Issues

North Hills Youth Ministry Counseling Center

802 McKnight Park Dr., Pittsburgh, PA 15237 Tel. (412)366-1300
Email: NHYM@SGI.NET
Media Contact, Exec. Dir., Rev. Ronald B. Barnes
Exec. Dir., Ronald B. Barnes
Major Activities: Elementary, Junior and Senior High School Individual and Family Counseling; Elementary Age Youth Early Intervention Counseling; Educational Programming for Churches and Schools; Youth Advocacy; Parent Education; Marital Counseling

Northside Common Ministries

P.O. Box 99861, Pittsburgh, PA 15233 Tel. (412)323-1163 Fax (412)323-1749
Email: NCM@citynet.com
Media Contact, Exec. Dir., Mark Stephen Bibro
Exec. Dir., Mark Stephen Bibro
Pres., vacant

Major Activities: Pleasant Valley Shelter for Homeless Men; Advocacy around Hunger, Housing, Poverty, and Racial Issues; Community Food Pantry and Service Center; Supportive Housing

Northwest Interfaith Movement

6757 Greene St., Philadelphia, PA 19119 Tel. (215)843-5600 Fax (215)843-2755
Media Contact, Exec. Dir., Rev. Richard R. Fernandez
Exec. Dir., Rev. Richard R. Fernandez
Chpsn., Elaine Dushoff
Long Term Care Program, Dir., Donald Carlin
Neighborhood Child Care Resource Prog., Dir., Leslie S. Eslinger
School Age Ministry, Dir., Brenda Rochester
Major Activities: Resources amd Technical Assistance for Child Care Programs; Conflict Mediation and Support for Nursing and Boarding Home Residents; Development of After-School Programs

Project of Easton, Inc.

330 Ferry St., Easton, PA 18042 Tel. (215)258-4361
Pres., Dr. John H. Updegrove
Vice-Pres. Public Relations, Rev. Charles E. Staples
Vice-Pres. Operations, Don Follett
Sec., Rosemary Reese
Treas., Steve Barsony
Exec. Dir., Maryellen Shuman
Major Activities: Food Bank; Adult Literacy Program; English as a Second Language; Children's Programs; Parents as Student Support; CROP Walk; Interfaith Council; Family Literacy; Emergency Assistance; Even Start Family Literacy

Reading Berks Conference of Churches

54 N. 8th St., Reading, PA 19601 Tel. (610)375-6108 Fax (610)375-6205
Email: rdgbrkscc@aol.com
Media Contact, Exec. Dir., Rev. Calvin Kurtz
Exec. Dir., Rev. Calvin Kurtz
Pres., James Elliker
Treas., William Maslo
Major Activities: Institutional Ministry; Social Action; Migrant Ministry; CWS; CROP Walk for Hunger; Emergency Assistance; Prison Chaplaincy; AIDS Hospice Development; Hospital Chaplaincy; Interchurch/Intercultural Services; Children & Youth Ministry

Reading Urban Ministry

134 N. Fifth St., Reading, PA 19601 Tel. (610)374-6917 Fax (610)371-9791
Media Contact, Beth Bitler
Exec. Dir., Beth Bitler
Pres., Edward Robertson

Vice-Pres., Sarah Walters
Sec., Jill Braun
Treas., Karen Good
Major Activities: Youth Ministry Program; Family Action Support Team (Child Abuse Prevention)

South Hills Interfaith Ministries

1900 Sleepy Hollow Rd., Library, PA 15129 Tel. (412)854-9120 Fax (412)854-9123
Media Contact, Exec. Dir., Donald Guinn
Prog. Dir., Susan Simons
Psychological Services, Don Zandier
Family Assistance Coordinator, Sherry Kotz
Business Mgr., Jeff Walley
Volunteer Coordinator, Kristin Snodgrass
Major Activities: Basic Human Needs; Community Organization and Development; Inter-Faith Cooperation; Personal Growth; At-Risk Youth Development; Women in Transition; Elderly Support

United Churches of Lycoming County

202 E. Third St., Williamsport, PA 17701 Tel. (570)322-1110 Fax (570)326-4572
Email: uclc@sunlink.net
Website: www.uclc.org
Media Contact, Exec. Dir., Gwen Nelson Bernstine
Exec. Dir., Gwen Nelson Bernstine
Ofc. Sec., Linda Winter
Pres., Mrs. Mikey Kamienski, 515 Vallamont Dr., Williamsport, PA 17701
Treas., Raymond Fisher, 145 Linden St., S. Williamsport, PA 17701
Shepherd of the Streets, Rev. J. Morris Smith, 130 E. 3rd St., Williamsport, PA 17701
Ecumenism, Dir., vacant
Educ. Ministries, Dir., Rev. Bruce Druckenmiller, 202 E. Third St., Williamsport, PA 17701
Institutional Ministry, Dir., Linda Leonard, 12 E. Water St., Hughesville, PA 17737
Radio-TV, Dir., Rev. Jean Moyer, 513 Spruce Street, Montoursville, PA 17754
Prison Ministry, Dir., Jane Russell, 1200 Almond St., Williamsport, PA 17701
Christian Social Concerns, Dir., Dr. Dan Doyle, 301 South Main St., Muney, PA 17756
Major Activities: Ecumenism; Educational Ministries; Church Women United; Church World Service and CROP; Prison Ministry; Radio-TV; Nursing Homes; Fuel Bank; Food Pantry; Family Life; Shepherd of the Streets Urban Ministry; Peace Concerns; Housing Initiative; Interfaith Dialogue

Wilkinsburg Community Ministry

710 Mulberry St., Pittsburgh, PA 15221 Tel. (412)241-8072 Fax (412)241-8315
Email: wcm@trfn.clpgh.org/wcm
Website: http://trfn.clpgh.org/wcm
Media Contact, Dir., Rev. Vivian Lovingood

Dir., Rev. Vivian Lovingood
Pres. of Bd., Roger Schneider
Major Activities: Hunger Ministry; After School Children's Programs; Summer Reading Camp; Teen-Moms Infant Care; Meals on Wheels; Church Camp Scholarships; Utility Assistance; Clothing/Furniture Assistance; Case Management for Elderly Homebound Persons and Families

Wyoming Valley Council of Churches

70 Lockhart St., Wilkes-Barre, PA 18702 Tel. (570)825-8543
Media Contact, Exec. Dir., Susan Grine Harper
Exec. Dir., Susan Grine Harper
Ofc. Sec., Sandra Karrott
Pres., Dn. Sergei Kapral
Treas., H. Merritt Hughes
Major Activities: Nursing Home Chaplaincy; Martin Luther King, Jr. Fuel Drive in Association with Local Agencies; Hospital Referral Service; Choral Festival of Faith; Migrant Ministry; Ecumenical Pulpit Exchange, Int.; CROP Hunger Walk; Pastoral Care Ministries; Clergy Retreats and Seminars

York County Council of Churches

P.O. Box 1865, York, PA 17405-1865 Tel. (717)854-9504 Fax (717)843-5295
Email: yccc@juno.com
Media Contact, Exec. Dir., Rev. Patrick B. Walker
Pres., Rev. Donald Zobler
Past Pres., Rev. Stephany Sechrist
Exec. Dir., Rev. Patrick B. Walker
Major Activities: Educational Development; Spiritual Growth and Renewal; Worship and Witness; Congregational Resourcing; Outreach and Mission

RHODE ISLAND

The Rhode Island State Council of Churches*

734 Hope St., Providence, RI 02906 Tel. (401)861-1700 Fax (401)331-3080
Email: ricouncil@aol.com
Media Contact, Exec. Min., Rev. James C. Miller
Exec. Min., Rev. James C. Miller
Admn. Asst., Peggy MacNie
Pres., Rev. Carl H. Balark, Jr.
Treas., George Weavill
Major Activities: Urban Ministries; TV; Institutional Chaplaincy; Advocacy/Justice & Service: Legislative Liaison; Faith & Order; Leadership Development; Campus Ministries

SOUTH CAROLINA

South Carolina Christian Action Council, Inc.*

P.O. Drawer 3248, Columbia, SC 29230 Tel. (803)786-7115 Fax (803)786-7116

Email: sc.council@ecunet.org
Media Contact, Exec. Minister, Rev. Brenda Kneece
Exec. Minister, Rev. Brenda Kneece
Pres., Rev. Dr. Richard Dozier
Major Activities: Advocacy and Ecumenism; Continuing Education; Interfaith Dialogue; Citizenship and Public Affairs; Publications; Race Relations; Child Advocacy

United Ministries
606 Pendleton St., Greenville, SC 29601 Tel. (864)232-6463 Fax (864)370-3518
Website: www.united-ministries.org
Media Contact, Exec. Dir., Rev. Beth Templeton
Exec. Dir., Rev. Beth Templeton
Pres., The Rev. David Chandler
Vice-Pres., Dr. Lynne Shackelford
Sec., Don Pilzer
Treas., Robert Clanton
Major Activities: Survival Programs (Emergency Assistance, Place of Hope, a Day Shelter for Homeless, Travelers Aid); Stabilization Program (Transitions); Barrier Removal Programs (Employment Readiness); Magdalene Project (Women in Crisis); Life Skills (Educational Classes, Living Skills)

SOUTH DAKOTA

Association of Christian Churches*
1320 S. Minnesota Ave., Ste. 210, Sioux Falls, SD 57105-0657 Tel. (605)334-1980
Media Contact, Rev. Christian Franklin, First Christian Church, 524 W. 13th St., Sioux Falls, SD 57104-4309 Tel. (605)338-9474
Pres., vacant
Ofc. Mgr., Pat Willard
Major Activities: Ecumenical Forums; Continuing Education for Clergy; Legislative Information; Resourcing Local Ecumenism; Native American Issues; Ecumenical Fields Ministries; Rural Economic Development; Children at Risk

TENNESSEE

Tennessee Association of Churches*
103 Oak St., Ashland City, TN 37015 Tel. (615)792-4631
Ecumenical Admn., vacant
Pres., Rev. Steve Mosley
Treas., Paul Milliken
Major Activities: Faith and Order; Christian Unity; Social Concern Ministries; Governmental Concerns; Governor's Prayer Breakfast

Metropolitan Inter Faith Association (MIFA)
P.O. Box 3130, Memphis, TN 38173-0130 Tel. (901)527-0208 Fax (901)527-3202
Media Contact, Dir., Media Relations, Kim Gaskill

Exec. Dir., Allie Prescott
Major Activities: Emergency Housing; Emergency Services (Rent, Utility, Food, Clothing Assistance); Home-Delivered Meals and Senior Support Services; Youth Services

Volunteer Ministry Center
103 South Gay St., Knoxville, TN 37902 Tel. (423)524-3926 Fax (423)524-7065
Media Contact, Exec. Dir., Angelia Moon
Exec. Dir., Angelia Moon
Pres., David Leech
Vice-Pres., John Moxham
Treas., Doug Thompson
Major Activities: Homeless Program; Food Line; Crisis Referral Program; Subsidized Apartment Program; Counselling Program; Parenting Education for Single Parents

TEXAS

Texas Conference of Churches*
1033 La Posada, Ste. 225, Austin, TX 78752 Tel. (512)451-0991 Fax (512)451-5348
Email: tcc@txconfchurches.org
Website: www.tconfchurches.org
Media Contact, Web Page Services, Liz Yeats
Exec. Dir., Dr. Carol M. Worthing
Office Manager, Caryn Wontos
Pres., Michael Pfeifer
Major Activities: Faith & Order; Related Ecumenism; Christian-Jewish Relations; Church and Society Issues

Austin Metropolitan Ministries
2026 Guadalupe, Ste. 226, Austin, TX 78705 Tel. (512)472-7627 Fax (512)472-5274
Email: amm@ammaustin.org
Website: www.ammaustin.org
Media Contact, Exec. Dir., Susan Wills
Exec. Dir., Patrick Flood
Pres., Rev. James Mayfield
Treas., Camille Miller
Program Director, Carole Hatfield
Admn., Carole Hatfield
Major Activities: Broadcast Ministry; Older Adult Connection; Youth at Risk Mentoring; Interfaith Dialogues; Family Issues; Housing Rehabilitation; Homeless Issues; Hunger Issues; Refugee Resettlement; Racial Reconciliation

Border Association for Refugees from Central America (BARCA), Inc.
P.O. Box 715, Edinburg, TX 78540 Tel. (210)631-7447 Fax (210)687-9266
Media Contact, Exec. Dir., Ninfa Ochoa-Krueger
Exec. Dir, Ninfa Ochoa-Krueger
Refugee Children Services, Dir., Bertha de la Rosa
Major Activities: Food, Shelter, Clothing to Newly Arrived Indigent Immigrants &

Refugees; Medical and Other Emergency Aid; Special Services to Children; Speakers on Refugee and Immigrant Concerns for Church Groups; Orientation, Advocacy and Legal Services for Immigrants and Refugees

Corpus Christi Metro Ministries
1919 Leopard St., P.O. Box 4899, Corpus Christi, TX 78469-4899 Tel. (361)887-0151 Fax (361)887-7900
Email: edseeger@electrotex.com
Media Contact, Exec. Dir., Rev. Edward B. Seeger
Exec. Dir., Rev. Edward B. Seeger
Admn. Dir., Ginger Flewelling-Leeds
Volunteer Dir., Ann Walters
Fin. Coord., Sue McCown
Loaves & Fishes Dir., Ray Gomez
Emergency Services Mgr., Laura Rogers
Employment Dir., Larry Curtis
Health and Human Services, Dir., Ann Walters
Major Activities: Free Cafeteria; Transitional Shelters; Job Readiness; Job Placement; Primary Health Care; Community Service Restitution; Emergency Clothing; Information and Referral; Case Management

East Dallas Cooperative Parish
P.O. Box 720305, Dallas, TX 75372-0305 Tel. (214)823-9149 Fax (214)823-2015
Email: edcp@swbell.net
Media Contact, Larry Cox
Pres., Ford Keith
Sec., Norma Worrall
Major Activities: Emergency Food, Clothing, Job Bank; Medical Clinic; Legal Clinic, Tutorial Education; Home Companion Service; Pre-School Education; Developmental Learning Center; Asian Ministry; Hispanic Ministry; Activity Center for Low Income Older Adults; Pastoral Counseling; English Language Ministry

Greater Dallas Community of Churches
624 N. Good-Latimer #100, Dallas, TX 75204-5818 Tel. (214)824-8680 Fax (214)824-8726
Email: gdcc@churchcommunity.org
Website: www.churchcommunity.org
Media Contact, Exec. Dir., Ray Flachmeier
Exec. Dir., Ray Flachmeier
Assoc. Dirs.: The Rev. Holsey Hickman; John Stoesz
AmeriCorps/Building Blocks Dir., Wendy Hodges-Kent
Development Dir., Mary Sue Foster
Pres., Rev. George Mason, Ph.D.
Treas., Jerry McNabb
Major Activities: Interdenominational, Interfaith and Interracial Understanding and Joint Work; AmeriCorps/Building Blocks (Direct Service to Develop Inner City Children, Youth &

Families); Summer Food & Reading; Hunger; Peacemaking; Public Policy; Social Justice; Faith & Life; Children's Health Outreach; Child Advocacy; Dismantling Racism

Interfaith Ministries for Greater Houston
3217 Montrose Blvd., Houston, TX 77006 Tel. (713)522-3955 Fax (713)520-4663
Media Contact, Exec. Dir., Betty P. Taylor
Exec. Dir., Betty P. Taylor
Pres., Charles R. Erickson
Development, Dir., Sharon Ervine
Assoc. Exec. Dir., Larry Norton
Treas., Fort D. Flowers, Jr.
Sec., Darlene Alexander
Major Activities: Community Concerns: Hunger; Older Adults; Families; Youth; Child Abuse; Refugee Services; Congregational Relations and Development; Social Service Programs: Refugee Services; Hunger Coalition; Youth Victim Witness; Family Connection; Meals on Wheels; Senior Health; RSVP; Foster Grandparents

North Dallas Shared Ministries
2530 Glenda Ln., #500, Dallas, TX 75229 Tel. (214)620-8696 Fax (214)620-0433
Media Contact, Exec. Dir., J. Dwayne Martin
Exec. Dir., J. Dwayne Martin
Pres., ———
Major Activities: Emergency Assistance; Job Counseling; ESL

Northside Inter-Church Agency (NICA)
1600 Circle Park Blvd., Fort Worth, TX 76106-8943 Tel. (817)626-1102 Fax (817)626-9043
Email: nica@startelegram.com
Media Contact, Exec. Dir., Judy Gutierrez
Exec. Dir., Judy Gutierrez
Major Activities: Food; Clothing; Counseling; Information and Referral; Furniture and Household Items; Nutrition Education and Teen Program; Employment Services; Thanksgiving Basket Program; "Last Resort" Christmas Program; Community Networking; Ecumenical Worship Services; Volunteer Training; Newsletter

San Antonio Community of Churches
1101 W. Woodlawn, San Antonio, TX 78201 Tel. (210)733-9159 Fax (210)733-5780
Media Contact, Exec. Dir., Dr. Kenneth Thompson
Exec. Dir., Dr. Kenneth Thompson
Pres., Fr. Jose De La Rosa
Major Activities: Christian Education; Missions; Infant Formula and Medical Prescriptions for Children of Indigent Families; Continuing Education For Clergy and Laity; Media

Resource Center; Social Issues; Aging Concerns; Youth Concerns; Family Concerns; Sponsor annual CROP Walk for Hunger; Peace and Anti-Violence Initiatives

San Antonio Urban Ministries

535 Bandera Rd., San Antonio, TX 78228
Media Contact, Sue Kelly
Exec. Dir., Sue Kelly
Pres., Rev. Leslie Ellison
Major Activities: Homes for Discharged Mental Patients; After School Care for Latch Key Children; Christian Based Community Ministry

Southeast Area Churches (SEARCH)

P.O. Box 51256, Fort Worth, TX 76105 Tel. (817)531-2211
Media Contact, Exec. Dir., Dorothy Anderson-Develrow
Dir., Dorothy Anderson-Develrow
Major Activities: Emergency Assistance; Advocacy; Information and Referral; Community Worship; School Supplies; Direct Aid to Low Income and Elderly

Southside Area Ministries, Inc. (SAM)

305 W. Broadway, Fort Worth, TX 76104 Tel. (817)332-3778 Fax (817)332-3781
Media Contact, Linda Freeto
Exec. Dir., Linda Freeto
Major Activities: Assisting Children for Whom English is a Second Language; Tutoring Grades K-5; Mentoring Grades 6-8; Programs for Senior Citizens

Tarrant Area Community of Churches

P.O. Box 11471, Fort Worth, TX 76110-0471 Tel. (817)534-1790 Fax (817)534-1995
Email: revkm@flash.net
Pres., Regina Taylor
Treas., Don Hoak
Exec. Dir., Dr. Kenneth W. McIntosh
Major Activities: Eldercare Program; Children's Sabbath Sponsorship; Week of Prayer for Christian Unity; CROP Walk for Hunger Relief; Community Issues Forums; Family Pathfinders

United Board of Missions

1701 Bluebonnet Ave., P.O. Box 3856, Port Arthur, TX 77643-3856 Tel. (409)982-9412 Fax (409)985-3668
Media Contact, Admn. Asst., Carolyn Schwarr
Exec. Dir., Clark Moore
Pres., Glenda McCoy
Major Activities: Emergency Assistance (Food and Clothing, Rent and Utility, Medical, Dental, Transportation); Share a Toy at Christmas; Counseling; Back to School Clothing Assistance; Information and Referral; Hearing Aid Bank; Meals on Wheels; Super Pantry; Energy Conservation Programs; Job Bank Assistance to Local Residents Only

VERMONT

Vermont Ecumenical Council and Bible Society*

285 Maple St., Burlington, VT 05401 Tel. (802)864-7723
Email: vecumen@together.net
Media Contact, Admn. Asst., Betsy Wackernagel
Exec. Sec., Mr. Philip C. Kimball
Pres., Most Rev. Kenneth A. Angell
Vice-Pres., Rev. Dr. Lawrence R. Curtis
Treas., Rev. E. Lon Schneider
Major Activities: Christian Unity; Bible Distribution; Social Justice; Committee on Faith and Order; Committee on Peace, Justice and the Integrity of Creation

VIRGINIA

Virginia Council of Churches, Inc.*

1214 W. Graham Rd., Richmond, VA 23220-1409 Tel. (804)321-3300 Fax (804)329-5066
Email: Barton@vcc-net.com
Website: www. vcc-net.org
Media Contact, Gen. Min., Rev. Jonathan Barton
Gen. Min., Rev. Jonathan Barton
Migrant Head Start, Dir., Richard D. Cagan
Refugee Resettlement, Dir., Rev. Richard D. Cline
Weekday Rel. Educ., Coord., Evelyn W. Simmons, P.O. Box 245, Clifton Forge, VA 24422
Campus Ministry Forum, Coord., Rev. Steve Darr, c/o Community College Ministries, 305 Washington St., N.W., Blacksburg, VA 24060-4745
Major Activities: Faith and Order; Network Building & Coordination; Ecumenical Communications; Justice and Legislative Concerns; Educational Development; Rural Concerns; Refugee Resettlement; Migrant Ministries and Migrant Head Start; Disaster Coordination; Infant Mortality Prevention

WASHINGTON

Washington Association of Churches*

419 Occidental Ave. S., Ste. 201, Seattle, WA 98104-2886 Tel. (206)625-9790 Fax (206)625-9791
Email: wac@thewac.org
Website: www.thewac.org
Media Contact, John C. Boonstra, E-mail: boonstra@thewac.org
Exec. Min., Rev. John C. Boonstra
Public Policy Associate, Sara Fleming-Merten, merten@thewac.org

Economic Justice Associate, Michael Ramos, ramos@thewac.org

Admn. Assoc., Bette Schneider, schneider@thewac.org

Racial & Environmental Justice Associate, Shelley Means, means@thewac.org

Major Activities: Faith and Order; Justice Advocacy; Confronting Poverty; Hunger Action; Legislation; Denominational Ecumenical Coordination; Theological Formation; Leadership Development; Refugee Advocacy; Racial Justice Advocacy; International Solidarity; Environmental Justice Advocacy

Associated Ministries of Tacoma-Pierce County

1224 South I St., Tacoma, WA 98405-5021 Tel. (253)383-3056 Fax (253)383-2672

Email: info@associatedministries.org

Website: www. associatedministries.org

Media Contact, Exec. Dir., Rev. David T. Alger

Exec. Dir., Rev. David T. Alger

Deputy Dir., Maureen Fife

Dir. of Mental Health Chaplaincy, Rev. Carole Elizabeth

Dir. of Project Interdependence, Valorie Crout

Dir. of Paint Tacoma/Pierce Beautiful, Sallie Shawl

Dir. Of Development, Tandi Rogers

Dir. of Hilltop Action Coalition, -vacant-

Pres., Rev. Richard Tietjen

Sec., Dorothy Diers

Treas., vacant

Major Activities: County-wide Hunger Walk; Hunger Awareness; Economic Justice; Religious Education; Social Service Program Advocacy; Communication and Networking of Churches; Housing; Paint Tacoma/Pierce Beautiful; Anti-Poverty Resource Center; Mental Health Chaplaincy; Theological Dialogue; Welfare to Work Mentoring; Hilltop Action Coalition; ComPeer

Associated Ministries of Thurston County

P.O. Box 895, Olympia, WA 98507 Tel. (360)357-7224

Email: theamtc@aol.com

Media Contact, Exec. Dir., Cheri Gonyaw

Exec. Dir., Cheri Gonyaw

Pres., George Hinkel

Treas., Bob McCoy

Major Activities: Church Information and Referral; Interfaith Relations; Social and Health Concerns; Community Action; Social Justice

Center for the Prevention of Sexual and Domestic Violence

936 N. 34th St., Ste. 200, Seattle, WA 98103 Tel. (206)634-1903 Fax (206)634-0115

Email: cpsdv@cpsdv.org

Website: www.cpsdv.org

Media Contact, Rev. Dr. Marie M. Fortune

Founder/Senior Analyst, Rev. Dr. Marie M. Fortune

Exec. Dir., Rev. Kathryn J. Johnson

Program Staff, Jean Anton; Rev. Thelma B. Burgonio-Watson; Sandra Barone; Ellen Johanson; Rev. Aubra Love

Finance Director, Marion J. Ward

Major Activities: Prevention and Response Education; Clergy and Lay Training; Video and Print Resources; Bi-national Educational Ministry

Church Council of Greater Seattle

4759 15th Ave. NE, Seattle, WA 98105-4404 Tel. (206)525-1213 Fax (206)525-1218

Email: CCGSea@churchcouncilseattle.org

Website: www.churchcouncilseattle.org

Media Contact, President-Director, Rev. Tom Quigley

Pres./Dir., Rev. Thomas H. Quigley

Associate Dir. for Program & Public Witness, Alice M. Woldt

Associate Dir. for Development & Communications, Meredith E. Brown, CFRE

Emergency Feeding Prog., Dir., Arthur Lee

Friend to Friend, Dir., Marilyn Soderquist

Youth Chaplaincy Program, Rev. Vera Diggins, Rev. Suzanne Seaton, Chaplain

The Sharehouse, Dir., Young Kim

The Homelessness Project, Dir., Nancy Dorman

Mission for Music & Healing, Dir., Susan Gallaher

Sound Youth-AmeriCorps, Dir., Rev. Jeanne Harvey-Duncan

Interfaith Relations, Coord., Rev. Joyce Manson

Academy of Religious Broadcasting, Dir., Rev. J. Graley Taylor

Board Chair, Ed Choe

Board Treas., Steve Faust

Editor, The Source, and website, Leanne Skooglund Hofford

Seattle Youth Garden Works, Dir., Margaret Hauptman

SW King County Mental Health Ministry, Dir., Rev. Richard Lutz

JOY Initiative, Dir., Rev. Vera Diggins

Global Economy Working Group Chair, Margery Prince

St. Petersburg- Seattle Sister Churches Program Chair, Irene Barinoff

Asia Pacific Task Force, Chair Rev. Walt Pulliam

Commission on Racial Justice Chair, Paula Harris-White

Commission on Public Witness Staff, Alice Woldt

Independent Living Programs, Dir., Mindi Uptain

Commission on Children, Youth & Families, Chair, Rev. Steve Baber

Pastors for Peace/Cuba Friendshipment, Chair, Doug Barnes

251

Palestinain Concerns Task Force, Chair, Stan Fowler

Interfaith Network fo Concern for the People of Iraq, Chair, Rev. Randall Mullins

Major Activities: Children; Youth & Families; Hunger Relief; Global Peace and Justice; Housing and Homelessness; Pastoral Care; Services for the Aging; Public Witness; Interfaith and Ecumenical Relations; Publisher of the Source, monthly ecumenical newspaper

The Interfaith Association of Snohomish County

2301 Hoyt, P.O. Box 12824, Everett, WA 98206 Tel. (206)252-6672

Media Contact, Exec. Dir., Pam W. Estes

Exec. Dir., Pam W. Estes

Pres., Evie Stegath

Major Activities: Housing and Shelter; Economic Justice; Hunger; Interfaith Worship and Collaboration

Northwest Harvest/E. M. M.

P.O. Box 12272, Seattle, WA 98102 Tel. (206)625-0755 Fax (206)625-7518

Email: nharvest@blarg.net

Website: www. northwestharvest.org

Media Contact, Comm. Affairs Dir., Ellen Hansen

Exec. Dir., Ruth M. Velozo

Chpsn., Patricia Barcott

Major Activities: Northwest Harvest (Statewide Hunger Response); Cherry Street Food Bank (Community Hunger Response); Northwest Infants Corner (Special Nutritional Products for Infants and Babies)

Spokane Council of Ecumenical Ministries

1620 N. Monroe, Spokane, WA 99205 Tel. (509)329-1410 Fax (509)3291409

Email: scem2000@aol.com

Media Contact, Marylin Ferguson, Admin. Asst.

Interim Co-Directors, Sr. Cathy Beckley & Rev. Ron Greene

Chair, Judy Butler

Vice-Chair, Rev. Jim Burford

Treas., Rev. Mark Randall

Sec., Linda Schearin

Major Activities: Camp PEACE: Multi-Cultural Human Relations- High School Youth Camp; Night Walk Ministry; Fig Tree Newspaper; Dir. of Churches & Community Agencies; Interfaith Thanksgiving Worship; Easter Sunrise Service; Friend to Friend Visitation with Nursing Home Patients; CROP Walk; Eastern Washington Legislative Conference; Inland Northwest Disaster Response; Ecumenical Sunday; Churches Against Racism

WEST VIRGINIA

West Virginia Council of Churches*

1608 Virginia St. E., Charleston, WV 25311 Tel. (304)344-3141 Fax (304)342-1506

Website: www.wvcc.org

Media Contact, Exec. Dir., The Rev. Nathan D. Wilson, E-mail: nathanwilson@wvcc.org

Pres., Dr. William B. Allen, CC (DOC)

Vice-Pres., Bishop S. Clifton Ives, UMC

Sec., The Rev. Peggy Scharff, UMC

Treas., The Very Rev. Frederick P. Annie, RC

Major Activities: Leisure Ministry; Disaster Response; Faith and Order; Family Concerns; Inter-Faith Relations; Peace and Justice; Government Concerns; Support Services Network

Greater Fairmont Council of Churches

P.O. Box 108, Fairmont, WV 26554 Tel. (304)367-0962

Media Contact, President, Rev. Jeremiah Jasper

President, Rev. Jeremiah Jasper

Major Activities: Community Ecumenical Services; Youth and Adult Sports Leagues; CROP Walk Sponsor; Weekly Radio Broadcasts

The Greater Wheeling Council of Churches

1060 Chapline St., 110 Methodist Building, Wheeling, WV 26003 Tel. (304)232-5315

Media Contact, Exec. Dir., Kathy J. Burley

Exec. Dir., Kathy J. Burley

Hospital Notification Sec., Anna Lou Lenz

Pres., Martha J. Morris

Finance Chpn., Rev. Robert P. Johnson/ Doug Clatterbuck

Major Activities: Christian Education; Evangelism; Christian Heritage Week Celebration; Institutional Ministry; Regional Jail Chaplaincy; Church Women United; Volunteer Chaplaincy Care at OVMC Hospital; School of Religion; Hospital Notification; Hymn Sing in the Park; Anti-Gambling Crusade; Pentecost Celebration; Clergy Council; Easter Sunrise Service; Community Seder; Church Secretaries Fellowship; National Day of Prayer Service; Videotape Library/Audiotape Library; Flood Relief Network of the Upper Ohio Valley

WISCONSIN

Wisconsin Council of Churches*

750 Windsor St. Ste. 301, Sun Prairie, WI 53590-2149 Tel. (608)837-3108 Fax (608)837-3038

Email: wcoc@wichurches.org

Website: www.wichurches.org

Media Contact, Comm. Coord., Jeanette Johnson

Exec. Dir., Rev. Jerry Folk

Assoc. Dir., Rev. Gretchen Lord Anderson

Ofc. Mgr., Jeanette Johnson

Millenium Project Coordinator, Melinda Storey

AIDS/HIV Faith in Action Volunteer Coordinator, John Keegan

Pres., Bishop April Ulring Larson

Treas., Dr. Robert Book

Major Activities: Social Witness; Migrant Ministry; Aging; Wisconsin Interfaith IMPACT; Institutional Chaplaincy; Peace and Justice; Faith and Order; Rural Concerns; American Indian Ministries Council; Park Ministry; Women's RoundTable; Wisconsin Housing Partnership; Jesus, Jubilee and the Reign of God Project

Center for Community Concerns

1501 Villa St., Racine, WI 53403 Tel. (414)637-9176 Fax (414)637-9265

Email: ccc1501@miliserv.net

Media Contact, Exec. Dir., Sr. Michelle Olley

Exec. Dir., Sr. Michelle Olley

Skillbank Coord., Eleanor Sorenson

RSVP (Retired Senior Volunteer Program), Chris Udell-Solberg, Cathy Townsend

Volunteer Today (55 and under), Janet LeSuer

Major Activities: Advocacy; Direct Services; Research; Community Consultant; Criminal Justice; Volunteerism; Senior Citizen Services; CROP Walk, Referral

Christian Youth Council

1715-52nd St., Kenosha, WI 53140 Tel. (414)652-9543 Fax (414)652-4461

Media Contact, Exec. Dir., Steven L. Nelson

Exec. Dir., Steven L. Nelson

Sports Dir., Jerry Tappen

Outreach Dir., Linda Osborne

Accountant, Debbie Cutts

Class Director, Jill Cox

Pres. & Chmn. of Board, Lon Knoedler

Gang Prevention Dir., Sam Sauceda

Major Activities: Leisure Time Ministry; Institutional Ministries; Ecumenical Committee; Social Concerns; Outreach Sports(with a Christian Philosophy)

Interfaith Conference of Greater Milwaukee

1442 N. Farwell Ave., Ste. 200, Milwaukee, WI 53202 Tel. (414)276-9050 Fax (414)276-8442

Email: IFCGM@aol.com

Media Contact, Exec. Dir., Jack Murtaugh

Chpsn., Rev. Velma Smith

First Vice-Chair, Archbishop Rembert G. Weakland

Second Vice-Chair, Rev. Charles Graves

Sec., Paula Simon

Treas., Rev. Mary Ann Neevel

Exec. Dir., Jack Murtaugh

Associate Dir., Marcus White

Consultant in Communications, Rev. Robert P. Seater

Major Activities: Economic Issues; Racism; CROP Walk; Public Policy; Suburban and Urban Partnerships; TV Programming; Peace and International Issues Committee; Annual Membership Luncheon; Religion Diversity

Madison Urban Ministry

1127 University Ave., Madison, WI 53715 Tel. (608)256-0906 Fax (608)256-4387

Media Contact, Office Manager, Jennifer Harrington

Exec. Dir., Mary K. Baum

Program Mgr., Judy Collison & Richard Wildermuth

Major Activities: Community Projects; Dialogue/Forums; Social & Economic Justice

WYOMING

Wyoming Church Coalition*

P.O. Box 20812, Cheyenne, WY 82003-7017 Tel. (307)635-4251 Fax (307)778-9060

Email: Dan_Monson@ecunet.org

Media Contact, Rev. Daniel E. Monson, 1032 Melton St., Cheyenne, WY 82009 Tel. (307)635-4251

Dir., Rev. Daniel E. Monson

Assoc. Dir., Mary A. Monson

Chair, Chesie Lee

Penitentiary Chaplain, Rev. Lynn Schumacher, P.O. Box 400, Rawlins, WY 82301

Major Activities: Death Penalty; Empowering the Poor and Oppressed; Peace and Justice; Prison Ministry; Malicious Harassment; Domestic Violence, Public Health Issues; Welfare Reform

253

Index of Select Programs for U.S. Regional and Local Ecumenical Bodies

For many years the *Yearbook of American & Canadian Churches* has published the previous chapter, the "Directory of U.S. Regional and Local Ecumenical Bodies." Each entry of that directory contains a brief description of the diverse programs offered by each agency. However, researchers, pastors, service organizations and theological seminaries often inquire about specific programs and about which agencies carry out such programs. In response we have created this chapter, which indexes the various regional and local ecumenical agencies by twenty-five different program areas. These program areas are the twenty-five that have been the most frequent subjects of inquiry in our office. We have collected this program information directly from these organizations by means of a simple response form. There is an enormous diversity of ministries and missions conducted by these diverse organizations. Most organizations pursue several kinds of programs at once. However, some of these may focus their efforts most especially on only one of their programs; their other programs may be less well developed than their specialty. Consequently, the extent to which any of these ministries is a priority for any particular organization cannot be inferred from this list. For detailed information about the nature and extent of any particular ministry, the reader is urged to contact the organization directly using the directory of "U.S. Regional and Local Ecumenical Bodies," which is found in the pages just prior to this index.

AIDS/HIV Programs

Asheville-Buncombe Community Christian Ministry (ABCCM)—Asheville, NC

Center City Churches—Hartford, CT

Christian Churches United of the Tri-County Area—Harrisburg, PA

Dutchess Interfaith Council, Inc.—Poughkeepsie, NY

East End Cooperative Ministry—Pittsburgh, PA

Ecumenical Ministries—Fulton, MO

Ecumenical Ministries of Oregon—Portland, OR

Grand Rapids Area Center for Ecumenism (GRACE)—Grand Rapids, MI

Graymoor Ecumenical & Interreligious Institute—New York, NY

Greater Chicago Broadcast Ministries—Chicago, IL

Interfaith Community Services—St. Joseph, MO

Kansas Ecumenical Ministries—Topeka, KS

Lincoln Interfaith Council—Lincoln, NE

The Long Island Council of Churches—Hempstead, NY

Marin Interfaith Council—Novato, CA

New Britain Area Conference of Churches (NEWBRACC)—New Britain, CT

New Hampshire Council of Churches—Concord, NH

New Mexico Conference of Churches—Albuquerque, NM

Northern California Interreligious Conference—Oakland, CA

Reading Berks Conference of Churches—Reading, PA

The Rhode Island State Council of Churches—Providence, RI

Schenectady Inner City Ministry—Schenectady, NY

South Carolina Christian Action Council, Inc.—Columbia, SC

Southeast Ecumenical Ministry—Rochester, NY

Toledo Ecumenical Area Ministries—Toledo, OH

Troy Area United Ministries—Troy, NY

Wisconsin Council of Churches—Sun Prairie, WI

York County Council of Churches—York, PA

Anti-Racism Programs

Akron Area Association of Churches—Akron, OH

Arkansas Interfaith Conference—Scott, AR

The Associated Churches of Fort Wayne & Allen County, Inc.—Fort Wayne, IN

Associated Ministries of Tacoma-Pierce County—Tacoma, WA

Association of Christian Churches—Sioux Falls, SD

Association of Religious Communities—Danbury, CT

Austin Metropolitan Ministries—Austin, TX

Bergen County Council of Churches—Bergenfield, NJ

Brooklyn Council of Churches—Brooklyn, NY

Capital Area Council of Churches, Inc.—Albany, NY

The Capitol Region Conference of Churches—Hartford, CT

Christian Associates of Southwest Pennsylvania—Pittsburgh, PA

Christian Conference of Connecticut—Hartford, CT

Christian Council of Metropolitan Atlanta—Atlanta, GA

Church Council of Greater Seattle—Seattle, WA

The Church Federation of Greater Indianapolis, Inc.—Indianapolis, IN

Churches United of the Quad City Area—Rock Island, IL

Cooperative Metropolitan Ministries—Newton, MA

Council of Churches of Chemung County, Inc.—Elmira, NY

Council of Churches of the City of New York—New York, NY

Council of Churches of Greater Bridgeport, Inc.—Bridgeport, CT

Council of Churches of Greater Springfield—Springfield, MA

The Council of Churches of Santa Clara County—San Jose, CA

Council of Churches and Synagogues of Southwestern Connecticut—Stamford, CT

Des Moines Area Religious Council—Des Moines, IA

Dutchess Interfaith Council, Inc.—Poughkeepsie, NY

East End Cooperative Ministry—Pittsburgh, PA

Eastern Area Community Ministries—Louisville, KY

Ecclesia—Trenton, NJ

Ecumenical Conference of Greater Altoona—Altoona, PA

The Ecumenical Council of Pasadena Area Churches—Pasadena, CA

Ecumenical Ministries—Fulton, MO

Ecumenical Ministries of Iowa (EMI)—Des Moines, IA

Ecumenical Ministries of Oregon—Portland, OR

Evanston Ecumenical Action Council—Evanston, IL

Florida Council of Churches—Orlando, FL

Georgia Christian Council—Macon, GA

Grand Rapids Area Center for Ecumenism (GRACE)—Grand Rapids, MI

Greater Chicago Broadcast Ministries—Chicago, IL

Greater Dallas Community of Churches—Dallas, TX

Greater Dayton Christian Connections—Dayton, OH

Greater Flint Council of Churches—Flint, MI

Greater Minneapolis Council of Churches—Minneapolis, MN

Greater Rochester Community of Churches—Rochester, NY

The Greater Wheeling Council of Churches—Wheeling, WV

Greensboro Urban Ministry—Greensboro, NC

Illinois Conference of Churches—Springfield, IL

In One Accord—Battle Creek, MI

Indiana Partners for Christian Unity and Mission—Indianapolis, IN

Inter-Church Council of Greater New Bedford—New Bedford, MA

Inter-Church Ministries of Erie County—Erie, PA

Interfaith Conference of Greater Milwaukee—Milwaukee, WI

Interfaith Council of Contra Costa County—Walnut Creek, CA

Inter-Faith Council of Santa Fe, New Mexico—Santa Fe, NM

Inter-Faith Ministries-Wichita—Wichita, KS

Interfaith Mission Service—Huntsville, AL

Interfaith Service Bureau—Sacramento, CA

InterReligious Council of Central New York—Syracuse, NY

The Joint Religious Legislative Coalition—Minneapolis, MN

Kansas Ecumenical Ministries—Topeka, KS

Kentuckiana Interfaith Community—Louisville, KY

Kentucky Council of Churches—Lexington, KY

Lincoln Interfaith Council—Lincoln, NE

The Long Island Council of Churches—Hempstead, NY

Louisiana Interchurch Conference—Baton Rouge, LA

Madison Urban Ministry—Madison, WI

Mahoning Valley Association of Churches—Youngstown, OH

Marin Interfaith Council—Novato, CA

Massachusetts Council of Churches—Boston, MA

Metropolitan Christian Council of Philadelphia—Philadelphia, PA

The Metropolitan Christian Council: Detroit-Windsor—Detroit, MI

Metropolitan Interfaith Council on Affordable Housing (MICAH)—Minneapolis, MN

Minnesota Council of Churches—Minneapolis, MN

Mississippi Religious Leadership Conference—Jackson, MS

Montana Association of Churches—Billings, MT

Muskegon County Cooperating Churches—Muskegon, MI

Network of Religious Communities—Buffalo, NY

New Britain Area Conference of Churches (NEWBRACC)—New Britain, CT

New Hampshire Council of Churches—Concord, NH

New Mexico Conference of Churches—Albuquerque, NM

New York State Community of Churches, Inc.—Albany, NY

North Carolina Council of Churches—Raleigh, NC

Northern California Interreligious Conference—Oakland, CA

Northern Kentucky Interfaith Commission, Inc.—Newport, KY

Northside Common Ministries—Pittsburgh, PA

255

Christian Education Programs

Staten Island Council of Churches—Staten Island, NY

Tarrant Area Community of Churches—Fort Worth, TX

Toledo Ecumenical Area Ministries—Toledo, OH

United Churches of Lycoming County—Williamsport, PA

Vermont Ecumenical Council and Bible Society—Burlington, VT

Washington Association of Churches—Seattle, WA

West Virginia Council of Churches—Charleston, WV

York County Council of Churches—York, PA

Clothing Distribution Programs

Allegheny Valley Association of Churches—Natrona Heights, PA

Asheville-Buncombe Community Christian Ministry (ABCCM)—Asheville, NC

Christian Churches United of the Tri-County Area—Harrisburg, PA

Community Ministry of Montgomery County—Rockville, MD

Concerned Ecumenical Ministry to the Upper West Side—Buffalo, NY

Cooperative Metropolitan Ministries—Newton, MA

Corpus Christi Metro Ministries—Corpus Christi, TX

Council of Churches of the Ozarks—Springfield, MO

East End Cooperative Ministry—Pittsburgh, PA

Eastern Area Community Ministries—Louisville, KY

Ecumenical Conference of Greater Altoona—Altoona, PA

The Ecumenical Council of Pasadena Area Churches—Pasadena, CA

Evanston Ecumenical Action Council—Evanston, IL

Fern Creek/Highview United Ministries—Louisvlle, KY

Greater Fairmont Council of Churches—Fairmont, WV

Greensboro Urban Ministry—Greensboro, NC

Inter-Church Ministries of Erie County—Erie, PA

Interfaith Community Council, Inc.—New Albany, IN

Interfaith Community Services—St. Joseph, MO

Inter-Faith Ministries-Wichita—Wichita, KS

Lancaster County Council of Churches—Lancaster, PA

Lebanon County Christian Ministries—Lebanon, PA

Lehigh County Conference of Churches—Allentown, PA

The Long Island Council of Churches—Hempstead, NY

Northside Common Ministries—Pittsburgh, PA

Northside Inter-Church Agency (NICA)—Fort Worth, TX

Peoria Friendship House of Christian Service—Peoria, IL

Reading Berks Conference of Churches—Reading, PA

The Rhode Island State Council of Churches—Providence, RI

St. Paul Area Council of Churches—St. Paul, MN

South Coast Ecumenical Council—Long Beach, CA

South East Associated Ministries (SEAM)—Louisville, KY

South Hills Interfaith Ministries—Library, PA

South Louisville Community Ministries—Louisville, KY

Southside Area Ministries, Inc. (SAM)—Fort Worth, TX

West Side Ecumenical Ministry—Cleveland, OH

Wilkinsburg Community Ministry—Pittsburgh, PA

CROP Walks

Allegheny Valley Association of Churches—Natrona Heights, PA

Asheville-Buncombe Community Christian Ministry (ABCCM)—Asheville, NC

The Associated Churches of Fort Wayne & Allen County, Inc.—Fort Wayne, IN

Associated Ministries of Tacoma-Pierce County—Tacoma, WA

Associated Ministries of Thurston County—Olympia, WA

Attleboro Area Council of Churches, Inc.—Attleboro, MA

Austin Metropolitan Ministries—Austin, TX

Bergen County Council of Churches—Bergenfield, NJ

Berrien County Association of Churches—Benton Harbor, MI

Broome County Council of Churches, Inc.—Binghamton, NY

Capital Area Council of Churches, Inc.—Albany, NY

Center for Community Concerns—Racine, WI

Christians United in Beaver County—Beaver, PA

The Church Federation of Greater Indianapolis, Inc.—Indianapolis, IN

Churches United of the Quad City Area—Rock Island, IL

Corpus Christi Metro Ministries—Corpus Christi, TX

Council of Churches of Chemung County, Inc.—Elmira, NY

Council of Churches of the City of New York—New York, NY

Council of Churches of Greater Bridgeport, Inc.—Bridgeport, CT

257

Programs with/for Persons with Disabilities

Inter-Church Council of Greater New Bedford—New Bedford, MA

Interfaith Service Bureau—Sacramento, CA

The Joint Religious Legislative Coalition—Minneapolis, MN

Lincoln Interfaith Council—Lincoln, NE

Massachusetts Council of Churches—Boston, MA

New York State Community of Churches, Inc.—Albany, NY

Reading Berks Conference of Churches—Reading, PA

The Rhode Island State Council of Churches—Providence, RI

Toledo Ecumenical Area Ministries—Toledo, OH

Tulsa Metropolitan Ministry—Tulsa, OK

Domestic Violence Programs

Asheville-Buncombe Community Christian Ministry (ABCCM)—Asheville, NC

Association of Christian Churches—Sioux Falls, SD

Association of Religious Communities—Danbury, CT

Austin Metropolitan Ministries—Austin, TX

Center for the Prevention of Sexual and Domestic Violence—Seattle, WA

The Church Federation of Greater Indianapolis, Inc.—Indianapolis, IN

Churches United of the Quad City Area—Rock Island, IL

Corpus Christi Metro Ministries—Corpus Christi, TX

Eastern Area Community Ministries—Louisville, KY

Ecumenical Ministries of Oregon—Portland, OR

Greater Bethlehem Area Council of Churches—Bethlehem, PA

Greater Chicago Broadcast Ministries—Chicago, IL

Greater Minneapolis Council of Churches—Minneapolis, MN

Indiana Partners for Christian Unity and Mission—Indianapolis, IN

Inter-Church Council of Greater New Bedford—New Bedford, MA

Kansas Ecumenical Ministries—Topeka, KS

Lancaster County Council of Churches—Lancaster, PA

Lincoln Interfaith Council—Lincoln, NE

The Long Island Council of Churches—Hempstead, NY

Madison Urban Ministry—Madison, WI

Peoria Friendship House of Christian Service—Peoria, IL

The Rhode Island State Council of Churches—Providence, RI

St. Paul Area Council of Churches—St. Paul, MN

Toledo Ecumenical Area Ministries—Toledo, OH

West Side Ecumenical Ministry—Cleveland, OH

West Virginia Council of Churches—Charleston, WV

York County Council of Churches—York, PA

Economic/Social Justice Programs

Akron Area Association of Churches—Akron, OH

Arkansas Interfaith Conference—Scott, AR

Asheville-Buncombe Community Christian Ministry (ABCCM)—Asheville, NC

The Associated Churches of Fort Wayne & Allen County, Inc.—Fort Wayne, IN

Associated Ministries of Tacoma-Pierce County—Tacoma, WA

Associated Ministries of Thurston County—Olympia, WA

Association of Christian Churches—Sioux Falls, SD

Association of Religious Communities—Danbury, CT

Berrien County Association of Churches—Benton Harbor, MI

Brooklyn Council of Churches—Brooklyn, NY

Broome County Council of Churches, Inc.—Binghamton, NY

California Council of Churches/California Church Impact—Sacramento, CA

Capital Area Council of Churches, Inc.—Albany, NY

The Capitol Region Conference of Churches—Hartford, CT

Christian Community Action~—New Haven, CT

Christian Conference of Connecticut—Hartford, CT

Christian Council of Metropolitan Atlanta—Atlanta, GA

Church Council of Greater Seattle—Seattle, WA

The Church Federation of Greater Indianapolis, Inc.—Indianapolis, IN

Churches United of the Quad City Area—Rock Island, IL

Community Ministry of Montgomery County—Rockville, MD

Concerned Ecumenical Ministry to the Upper West Side—Buffalo, NY

Cooperative Metropolitan Ministries—Newton, MA

Council of Churches of Chemung County, Inc.—Elmira, NY

Council of Churches of the City of New York—New York, NY

Council of Churches of Greater Bridgeport, Inc.—Bridgeport, CT

Council of Churches of Greater Springfield—Springfield, MA

The Council of Churches of Santa Clara County—San Jose, CA

259

260

South Coast Ecumenical Council—Long Beach, CA

South East Associated Ministries (SEAM)—Louisville, KY

South Louisville Community Ministries—Louisville, KY

Southern California Ecumenical Council—Pasadena, CA

Spokane Council of Ecumenical Ministries—Spokane, WA

Staten Island Council of Churches—Staten Island, NY

Tarrant Area Community of Churches—Fort Worth, TX

Texas Conference of Churches—Austin, TX

Toledo Ecumenical Area Ministries—Toledo, OH

Troy Area United Ministries—Troy, NY

Tulsa Metropolitan Ministry—Tulsa, OK

United Churches of Lycoming County—Williamsport, PA

Vermont Ecumenical Council and Bible Society—Burlington, VT

Virginia Council of Churches, Inc.—Richmond, VA

Washington Association of Churches—Seattle, WA

West Side Ecumenical Ministry—Cleveland, OH

West Virginia Council of Churches—Charleston, WV

Wisconsin Council of Churches—Sun Prairie, WI

Worcester County Ecumenical Council—Worcester, MA

York County Council of Churches—York, PA

Greater Minneapolis Council of Churches—Minneapolis, MN

Greensboro Urban Ministry—Greensboro, NC

Interfaith Community Council, Inc.—New Albany, IN

The Joint Religious Legislative Coalition—Minneapolis, MN

Lehigh County Conference of Churches—Allentown, PA

Lincoln Interfaith Council—Lincoln, NE

Network of Religious Communities—Buffalo, NY

Northern California Interreligious Conference—Oakland, CA

Northside Common Ministries—Pittsburgh, PA

Northside Inter-Church Agency (NICA)—Fort Worth, TX

Peoria Friendship House of Christian Service—Peoria, IL

The Rhode Island State Council of Churches—Providence, RI

Schenectady Inner City Ministry—Schenectady, NY

South East Associated Ministries (SEAM)—Louisville, KY

Toledo Ecumenical Area Ministries—Toledo, OH

United Churches of Lycoming County—Williamsport, PA

United Ministries—Greenville, SC

United Religious Community of St. Joseph County—South Bend, IN

West Side Ecumenical Ministry—Cleveland, OH

York County Council of Churches—York, PA

Employment Assistance Programs

Asheville-Buncombe Community Christian Ministry (ABCCM)—Asheville, NC

The Associated Churches of Fort Wayne & Allen County, Inc.—Fort Wayne, IN

Associated Ministries of Tacoma-Pierce County—Tacoma, WA

Association of Religious Communities—Danbury, CT

Bergen County Council of Churches—Bergenfield, NJ

Corpus Christi Metro Ministries—Corpus Christi, TX

Council of Churches of Greater Bridgeport, Inc.—Bridgeport, CT

East End Cooperative Ministry—Pittsburgh, PA

Evanston Ecumenical Action Council—Evanston, IL

Genesee-Orleans Ministry of Concern—Albion, NY

Grand Rapids Area Center for Ecumenism (GRACE)—Grand Rapids, MI

Greater Chicago Broadcast Ministries—Chicago, IL

Environmental Programs

The Church Federation of Greater Indianapolis, Inc.—Indianapolis, IN

Churches United of the Quad City Area—Rock Island, IL

Council of Churches of Chemung County, Inc.—Elmira, NY

The Council of Churches of Santa Clara County—San Jose, CA

Ecumenical Ministries of Iowa (EMI)—Des Moines, IA

Ecumenical Ministries of Oregon—Portland, OR

Florida Council of Churches—Orlando, FL

Georgia Christian Council—Macon, GA

Greater Chicago Broadcast Ministries—Chicago, IL

Greater Dayton Christian Connections—Dayton, OH

The Greater Wheeling Council of Churches—Wheeling, WV

Inter-Church Council of Greater New Bedford—New Bedford, MA

Interfaith Conference of Greater Milwaukee—Milwaukee, WI

261

Interfaith Mission Service—Huntsville, AL

The Joint Religious Legislative Coalition—Minneapolis, MN

Kansas Ecumenical Ministries—Topeka, KS

Lincoln Interfaith Council—Lincoln, NE

Louisiana Interchurch Conference—Baton Rouge, LA

Mahoning Valley Association of Churches—Youngstown, OH

Maine Council of Churches—Portland, ME

Marin Interfaith Council—Novato, CA

Metropolitan Christian Council of Philadelphia—Philadelphia, PA

The Metropolitan Christian Council: Detroit-Windsor—Detroit, MI

Michigan Ecumenical Forum—Lansing, MI

Mississippi Religious Leadership Conference—Jackson, MS

Montana Association of Churches—Billings, MT

Muskegon County Cooperating Churches—Muskegon, MI

Network of Religious Communities—Buffalo, NY

New Hampshire Council of Churches—Concord, NH

New York State Community of Churches, Inc.—Albany, NY

North Carolina Council of Churches—Raleigh, NC

Northern California Interreligious Conference—Oakland, CA

Ohio Council of Churches—Columbus, OH

The Pennsylvania Council of Churches—Harrisburg, PA

The Rhode Island State Council of Churches—Providence, RI

South Carolina Christian Action Council, Inc.—Columbia, SC

South Coast Ecumenical Council—Long Beach, CA

Southern California Ecumenical Council—Pasadena, CA

Toledo Ecumenical Area Ministries—Toledo, OH

United Churches of Lycoming County—Williamsport, PA

Vermont Ecumenical Council and Bible Society—Burlington, VT

Washington Association of Churches—Seattle, WA

West Virginia Council of Churches—Charleston, WV

Faith and Order Programs

Akron Area Association of Churches—Akron, OH

Allegheny Valley Association of Churches—Natrona Heights, PA

The Associated Churches of Fort Wayne & Allen County, Inc.—Fort Wayne, IN

Associated Ministries of Tacoma-Pierce County—Tacoma, WA

Associated Ministries of Thurston County—Olympia, WA

Association of Christian Churches—Sioux Falls, SD

Broome County Council of Churches, Inc.—Binghamton, NY

Capital Area Council of Churches, Inc.—Albany, NY

The Capitol Region Conference of Churches—Hartford, CT

Christian Conference of Connecticut—Hartford, CT

The Christian Council of Delaware and Maryland's Eastern Shore—Baltimore, MD

Christian Council of Metropolitan Atlanta—Atlanta, GA

The Church Federation of Greater Indianapolis, Inc.—Indianapolis, IN

Churches United of the Quad City Area—Rock Island, IL

Council of Churches of the City of New York—New York, NY

The Council of Churches of Santa Clara County—San Jose, CA

Council of Churches and Synagogues of Southwestern Connecticut—Stamford, CT

East End Cooperative Ministry—Pittsburgh, PA

Eastern Area Community Ministries—Louisville, KY

Ecclesia—Trenton, NJ

The Ecumenical Council of Pasadena Area Churches—Pasadena, CA

Ecumenical Ministries of Iowa (EMI)—Des Moines, IA

Ecumenical Ministries of Oregon—Portland, OR

Florida Council of Churches—Orlando, FL

Georgia Christian Council—Macon, GA

Grand Rapids Area Center for Ecumenism (GRACE)—Grand Rapids, MI

Graymoor Ecumenical & Interreligious Institute—New York, NY

Greater Chicago Broadcast Ministries—Chicago, IL

Greater Dayton Christian Connections—Dayton, OH

Greater New Orleans Federation of Churches—New Orleans, LA

Greater Rochester Community of Churches—Rochester, NY

Greater Waterbury Interfaith Ministries, Inc.—Waterbury, CT

The Greater Wheeling Council of Churches—Wheeling, WV

Illinois Conference of Churches—Springfield, IL

In One Accord—Battle Creek, MI

Indiana Partners for Christian Unity and Mission—Indianapolis, IN

Inter-Church Council of Greater New Bedford—New Bedford, MA

Interchurch Ministries of Nebraska—Lincoln, NE

Interfaith Community Council, Inc.—New Albany, IN

Interfaith Community Services—St. Joseph, MO

Interfaith Council of Contra Costa County—Walnut Creek, CA

Inter-Faith Ministries-Wichita—Wichita, KS

Kansas Ecumenical Ministries—Topeka, KS

Kentucky Council of Churches—Lexington, KY

Lancaster County Council of Churches—Lancaster, PA

Lehigh County Conference of Churches—Allentown, PA

Lincoln Interfaith Council—Lincoln, NE

The Long Island Council of Churches—Hempstead, NY

Louisiana Interchurch Conference—Baton Rouge, LA

Massachusetts Commission on Christian Unity—Novato, CA

Massachusetts Council of Churches—Boston, MA

Metropolitan Christian Council of Philadelphia—Philadelphia, PA

The Metropolitan Christian Council: Detroit-Windsor—Detroit, MI

Michigan Ecumenical Forum—Lansing, MI

Minnesota Council of Churches—Minneapolis, MN

Mississippi Religious Leadership Conference—Jackson, MS

Montana Association of Churches—Billings, MT

Network of Religious Communities—Buffalo, NY

New Hampshire Council of Churches—Concord, NH

New Mexico Conference of Churches—Albuquerque, NM

New York State Community of Churches, Inc—Albany, NY

North Carolina Council of Churches—Raleigh, NC

North Dakota Conference of Churches—Bismarck, ND

Northern California Interreligious Conferenc—Oakland, CA

Northern Kentucky Interfaith Commission, Inc.—Newport, KY

Ohio Council of Churches—Columbus, OH

Oklahoma Conference of Churches—Oklahoma City, OK

The Pennsylvania Council of Churches—Harrisburg, PA

Reading Berks Conference of Churches—Reading, PA

The Rhode Island State Council of Churches—Providence, RI

San Fernando Valley Interfaith Council—Chatsworth, CA

Schenectady Inner City Ministry—Schenectady, NY

South Carolina Christian Action Council, Inc.—Columbia, SC

Southern California Ecumenical Council—Pasadena, CA

Spokane Council of Ecumenical Ministries—Spokane, WA

Texas Conference of Churches—Austin, TX

Vermont Ecumenical Council and Bible Society—Burlington, VT

Virginia Council of Churches, Inc.—Richmond, VA

Washington Association of Churches—Seattle, WA

West Virginia Council of Churches—Charleston, WV

Wisconsin Council of Churches—Sun Prairie, WI

Worcester County Ecumenical Council—Worcester, MA

Healthcare Issues

Arkansas Interfaith Conference—Scott, AR

Asheville-Buncombe Community Christian Ministry (ABCCM)—Asheville, NC

Attleboro Area Council of Churches, Inc.—Attleboro, MA

Bergen County Council of Churches—Bergenfield, NJ

Broome County Council of Churches, Inc.—Binghamton, NY

California Council of Churches/California Church Impact—Sacramento, CA

Churches United of the Quad City Area—Rock Island, IL

Community Ministries of Rockville—Rockville, MD

Corpus Christi Metro Ministries—Corpus Christi, TX

The Council of Churches of Santa Clara County—San Jose, CA

Eastern Area Community Ministries—Louisville, KY

Ecumenical Ministries—Fulton, MO

Ecumenical Ministries of Iowa (EMI)—Des Moines, IA

Ecumenical Ministries of Oregon—Portland, OR

Genesee-Orleans Ministry of Concern—Albion, NY

Greater Chicago Broadcast Ministries—Chicago, IL

Greater Minneapolis Council of Churches—Minneapolis, MN

Greater Rochester Community of Churches—Rochester, NY

Greensboro Urban Ministry—Greensboro, NC

Illinois Conference of Churches—Springfield, IL

In One Accord—Battle Creek, MI

Inter-Church Council of Greater New Bedford—New Bedford, MA

Interchurch Ministries of Nebraska—Lincoln, NE

263

Homelessness/Shelter Programs

264

Metropolitan Interfaith Council on Affordable Housing (MICAH)—Minneapolis, MN

Network of Religious Communities—Buffalo, NY

New Britain Area Conference of Churches (NEWBRACC)—New Britain, CT

New York State Community of Churches, Inc.—Albany, NY

Northern California Interreligious Conference —Oakland, CA

Northern Kentucky Interfaith Commission, Inc.—Newport, KY

Northside Common Ministries—Pittsburgh, PA

Oak Park-River Forest Community of Congregations—Oak Park, IL

Paducah Cooperative Ministry—Paducah, KY

Peoria Friendship House of Christian Service —Peoria, IL

Reading Berks Conference of Churches—Reading, PA

The Rhode Island State Council of Churches —Providence, RI

St. Paul Area Council of Churches—St. Paul, MN

San Fernando Valley Interfaith Council—Chatsworth, CA

Schenectady Inner City Ministry—Schenectady, NY

Staten Island Council of Churches—Staten Island, NY

Tarrant Area Community of Churches—Fort Worth, TX

Toledo Ecumenical Area Ministries—Toledo, OH

Troy Area United Ministries—Troy, NY

United Churches of Lycoming County—Williamsport, PA

United Ministries—Greenville, SC

United Religious Community of St. Joseph County—South Bend, IN

Hunger/Food Programs

Allegheny Valley Association of Churches—Natrona Heights, PA

Arkansas Interfaith Conference—Scott, AR

Asheville-Buncombe Community Christian Ministry (ABCCM)—Asheville, NC

The Associated Churches of Fort Wayne & Allen County, Inc.—Fort Wayne, IN

Associated Ministries of Tacoma-Pierce County—Tacoma, WA

Associated Ministries of Thurston County—Olympia, WA

Association of Christian Churches—Sioux Falls, SD

Attleboro Area Council of Churches, Inc.—Attleboro, MA

Bergen County Council of Churches—Bergenfield, NJ

Brooklyn Council of Churches—Brooklyn, NY

Broome County Council of Churches, Inc.—Binghamton, NY

California Council of Churches/California Church Impact—Sacramento, CA

Capital Area Council of Churches, Inc.—Albany, NY

Center City Churches—Hartford, CT

Christian Churches United of the Tri-County Area—Harrisburg, PA

Christian Community Action—New Haven, CT

Church Council of Greater Seattle—Seattle, WA

The Church Federation of Greater Indianapolis, Inc.—Indianapolis, IN

Churches United of the Quad City Area—Rock Island, IL

Community Ministry of Montgomery County—Rockville, MD

Concerned Ecumenical Ministry to the Upper West Side—Buffalo, NY

Corpus Christi Metro Ministries—Corpus Christi, TX

Council of Churches of Chemung County, Inc.—Elmira, NY

Council of Churches of Greater Bridgeport, Inc.—Bridgeport, CT

Council of Churches of Greater Springfield—Springfield, MA

Council of Churches of the Ozarks—Springfield, MO

The Council of Churches of Santa Clara County—San Jose, CA

Council of Churches and Synagogues of Southwestern Connecticut—Stamford, CT

Des Moines Area Religious Council—Des Moines, IA

East End Cooperative Ministry—Pittsburgh, PA

Eastern Area Community Ministries—Louisville, KY

Ecclesia—Trenton, NJ

Ecumenical Conference of Greater Altoona—Altoona, PA

The Ecumenical Council of Pasadena Area Churches—Pasadena, CA

Ecumenical Ministries of Oregon—Portland, OR

Evanston Ecumenical Action Council—Evanston, IL

Fern Creek/Highview United Ministries—Louisvlle, KY

Genesee County Churches United, Inc.—Batavia, NY

Genesee-Orleans Ministry of Concern—Albion, NY

Grand Rapids Area Center for Ecumenism (GRACE)—Grand Rapids, MI

Greater Bethlehem Area Council of Churches —Bethlehem, PA

Greater Chicago Broadcast Ministries—Chicago, IL

Greater Dallas Community of Churches—Dallas, TX

265

Immigration Issues

Lincoln Interfaith Council—Lincoln, NE

The Long Island Council of Churches—Hempstead, NY

Minnesota Council of Churches—Minneapolis, MN

Mississippi Religious Leadership Conference—Jackson, MS

Network of Religious Communities—Buffalo, NY

New York State Community of Churches, Inc.—Albany, NY

Northside Inter-Church Agency (NICA)—Fort Worth, TX

Ohio Council of Churches—Columbus, OH

The Pennsylvania Council of Churches—Harrisburg, PA

Peoria Friendship House of Christian Service—Peoria, IL

The Rhode Island State Council of Churches—Providence, RI

San Fernando Valley Interfaith Council—Chatsworth, CA

South Coast Ecumenical Council—Long Beach, CA

Southside Area Ministries, Inc. (SAM)—Fort Worth, TX

York County Council of Churches—York, PA

Interfaith Dialogue/Relationships

Akron Area Association of Churches—Akron, OH

Arkansas Interfaith Conference—Scott, AR

The Associated Churches of Fort Wayne & Allen County, Inc.—Fort Wayne, IN

Associated Ministries of Tacoma-Pierce County—Tacoma, WA

Associated Ministries of Thurston County—Olympia, WA

Association of Christian Churches—Sioux Falls, SD

Association of Religious Communities—Danbury, CT

Attleboro Area Council of Churches, Inc.—Attleboro, MA

Austin Metropolitan Ministries—Austin, TX

Bergen County Council of Churches—Bergenfield, NJ

Berrien County Association of Churches—Benton Harbor, MI

Brooklyn Council of Churches—Brooklyn, NY

Broome County Council of Churches, Inc.—Binghamton, NY

Capital Area Council of Churches, Inc.—Albany, NY

Christian Churches United of the Tri-County Area—Harrisburg, PA

Christian Conference of Connecticut—Hartford, CT

The Christian Council of Delaware and Maryland's Eastern Shore—Baltimore, MD

Christian Council of Metropolitan Atlanta—Atlanta, GA

Church Council of Greater Seattle—Seattle, WA

The Church Federation of Greater Indianapolis, Inc.—Indianapolis, IN

Churches United of the Quad City Area—Rock Island, IL

Community Ministries of Rockville—Rockville, MD

Community Ministry of Montgomery County—Rockville, MD

Concerned Ecumenical Ministry to the Upper West Side—Buffalo, NY

Cooperative Metropolitan Ministries—Newton, MA

Council of Churches of Chemung County, Inc.—Elmira, NY

Council of Churches of the City of New York—New York, NY

Council of Churches of Greater Springfield—Springfield, MA

The Council of Churches of Santa Clara County—San Jose, CA

Council of Churches and Synagogues of Southwestern Connecticut—Stamford, CT

Des Moines Area Religious Council—Des Moines, IA

Dutchess Interfaith Council, Inc.—Poughkeepsie, NY

East End Cooperative Ministry—Pittsburgh, PA

Eastern Area Community Ministries—Louisville, KY

Ecclesia—Trenton, NJ

Ecumenical Conference of Greater Altoona—Altoona, PA

The Ecumenical Council of Pasadena Area Churches—Pasadena, CA

Ecumenical Ministries of Oregon—Portland, OR

Evanston Ecumenical Action Council—Evanston, IL

Florida Council of Churches—Orlando, FL

Georgia Christian Council—Macon, GA

Grand Rapids Area Center for Ecumenism (GRACE)—Grand Rapids, MI

Graymoor Ecumenical & Interreligious Institute—New York, NY

Greater Bethlehem Area Council of Churches—Bethlehem, PA

Greater Chicago Broadcast Ministries—Chicago, IL

Greater Dayton Christian Connections—Dayton, OH

Greater Flint Council of Churches—Flint, MI

Greater New Orleans Federation of Churches—New Orleans, LA

Greater Rochester Community of Churches—Rochester, NY

Greater Waterbury Interfaith Ministries, Inc.—Waterbury, CT

Greensboro Urban Ministry—Greensboro, NC

In One Accord—Battle Creek, MI

Inter-Church Council of Greater New Bedford—New Bedford, MA

267

Inter-Church Ministries of Erie County—Erie, PA

Interchurch Ministries of Nebraska—Lincoln, NE

Interfaith Community Council, Inc.—New Albany, IN

Interfaith Community Services—St. Joseph, MO

Interfaith Conference of Greater Milwaukee—Milwaukee, WI

InterFaith Conference of Metropolitan Washington—Washington, DC

Interfaith Council of Contra Costa County—Walnut Creek, CA

Inter-Faith Council of Santa Fe, New Mexico—Santa Fe, NM

Inter-Faith Ministries-Wichita—Wichita, KS

Interfaith Mission Service—Huntsville, AL

Interfaith Service Bureau—Sacramento, CA

InterReligious Council of Central New York—Syracuse, NY

Kentuckiana Interfaith Community—Louisville, KY

Lancaster County Council of Churches—Lancaster, PA

Lehigh County Conference of Churches—Allentown, PA

Lincoln Interfaith Council—Lincoln, NE

The Long Island Council of Churches—Hempstead, NY

Louisiana Interchurch Conference—Baton Rouge, LA

Mahoning Valley Association of Churches—Youngstown, OH

Maine Council of Churches—Portland, ME

Marin Interfaith Council—Novato, CA

Massachusetts Council of Churches—Boston, MA

Metropolitan Christian Council of Philadelphia—Philadelphia, PA

Metropolitan Interfaith Council on Affordable Housing (MICAH)—Minneapolis, MN

Michigan Ecumenical Forum—Lansing, MI

Minnesota Council of Churches—Minneapolis, MN

Mississippi Religious Leadership Conference—Jackson, MS

Montana Association of Churches—Billings, MT

Network of Religious Communities—Buffalo, NY

New Britain Area Conference of Churches (NEWBRACC)—New Britain, CT

New Hampshire Council of Churches—Concord, NH

New Mexico Conference of Churches—Albuquerque, NM

New York State Community of Churches, Inc.—Albany, NY

North Carolina Council of Churches—Raleigh, NC

Northern California Interreligious Conference—Oakland, CA

Northern Kentucky Interfaith Commission, Inc.—Newport, KY

Northside Common Ministries—Pittsburgh, PA

Northwest Interfaith Movement—Philadelphia, PA

Oak Park-River Forest Community of Congregations—Oak Park, IL

Ohio Council of Churches—Columbus, OH

Oklahoma Conference of Churches—Oklahoma City, OK

Pennsylvania Conference on Interchurch Cooperation—Harrisburg, PA

Peoria Friendship House of Christian Service—Peoria, IL

Reading Berks Conference of Churches—Reading, PA

The Rhode Island State Council of Churches—Providence, RI

St. Paul Area Council of Churches—St. Paul, MN

San Fernando Valley Interfaith Council—Chatsworth, CA

South Carolina Christian Action Council, Inc.—Columbia, SC

South Coast Ecumenical Council—Long Beach, CA

South Hills Interfaith Ministries—Library, PA

Southern California Ecumenical Council—Pasadena, CA

Spokane Council of Ecumenical Ministries—Spokane, WA

Staten Island Council of Churches—Staten Island, NY

Texas Conference of Churches—Austin, TX

Toledo Ecumenical Area Ministries—Toledo, OH

Tulsa Metropolitan Ministry—Tulsa, OK

United Religious Community of St. Joseph County—South Bend, IN

Vermont Ecumenical Council and Bible Society—Burlington, VT

Virginia Council of Churches, Inc.—Richmond, VA

Washington Association of Churches—Seattle, WA

West Side Ecumenical Ministry—Cleveland, OH

West Virginia Council of Churches—Charleston, WV

Wisconsin Council of Churches—Sun Prairie, WI

York County Council of Churches—York, PA

Prison Chaplaincy

Asheville-Buncombe Community Christian Ministry (ABCCM)—Asheville, NC

The Associated Churches of Fort Wayne & Allen County, Inc.—Fort Wayne, IN

Association of Christian Churches—Sioux Falls, SD

Bergen County Council of Churches—Bergenfield, NJ

Broome County Council of Churches, Inc.—Binghamton, NY

Capital Area Council of Churches, Inc.—Albany, NY

Christian Associates of Southwest Pennsylvania—Pittsburgh, PA

Christian Churches United of the Tri-County Area—Harrisburg, PA

Christian Conference of Connecticut—Hartford, CT

Christians United in Beaver County—Beaver, PA

Church Council of Greater Seattle—Seattle, WA

The Church Federation of Greater Indianapolis, Inc.—Indianapolis, IN

Churches United of the Quad City Area—Rock Island, IL

Council of Christian Communions of Greater Cincinnati—Cincinnati, OH

Council of Churches of the City of New York—New York, NY

Council of Churches of Greater Springfield—Springfield, MA

Ecclesia—Trenton, NJ

Ecumenical Ministries—Fulton, MO

Genesee County Churches United, Inc.—Batavia, NY

Greater Bethlehem Area Council of Churches—Bethlehem, PA

Greater Chicago Broadcast Ministries—Chicago, IL

Greater Minneapolis Council of Churches—Minneapolis, MN

The Greater Wheeling Council of Churches—Wheeling, WV

Inter-Church Ministries of Erie County—Erie, PA

Interfaith Council of Contra Costa County—Walnut Creek, CA

InterReligious Council of Central New York—Syracuse, NY

Lehigh County Conference of Churches—Allentown, PA

The Long Island Council of Churches—Hempstead, NY

Madison Urban Ministry—Madison, WI

Minnesota Council of Churches—Minneapolis, MN

Montana Association of Churches—Billings, MT

Muskegon County Cooperating Churches—Muskegon, MI

Network of Religious Communities—Buffalo, NY

New Hampshire Council of Churches—Concord, NH

North Dakota Conference of Churches—Bismarck, ND

Northern Kentucky Interfaith Commission, Inc.—Newport, KY

Ohio Council of Churches—Columbus, OH

Reading Berks Conference of Churches—Reading, PA

The Rhode Island State Council of Churches—Providence, RI

St. Paul Area Council of Churches—St. Paul, MN

United Churches of Lycoming County—Williamsport, PA

Vermont Ecumenical Council and Bible Society—Burlington, VT

West Virginia Council of Churches—Charleston, WV

Wisconsin Council of Churches—Sun Prairie, WI

York County Council of Churches—York, PA

Public Education Advocacy

Akron Area Association of Churches—Akron, OH

Arkansas Interfaith Conference—Scott, AR

The Associated Churches of Fort Wayne & Allen County, Inc.—Fort Wayne, IN

Association of Religious Communities—Danbury, CT

Bergen County Council of Churches—Bergenfield, NJ

Berrien County Association of Churches—Benton Harbor, MI

California Council of Churches/California Church Impact—Sacramento, CA

The Capitol Region Conference of Churches—Hartford, CT

Church Council of Greater Seattle—Seattle, WA

The Church Federation of Greater Indianapolis, Inc.—Indianapolis, IN

Community Ministries of Rockville—Rockville, MD

Community Ministry of Montgomery County—Rockville, MD

Council of Churches of the City of New York—New York, NY

The Council of Churches of Santa Clara County—San Jose, CA

East End Cooperative Ministry—Pittsburgh, PA

Ecclesia—Trenton, NJ

Ecumenical Ministries—Fulton, MO

Ecumenical Ministries of Iowa (EMI)—Des Moines, IA

Evanston Ecumenical Action Council—Evanston, IL

Grand Rapids Area Center for Ecumenism (GRACE)—Grand Rapids, MI

Greater Bethlehem Area Council of Churches—Bethlehem, PA

Greater Chicago Broadcast Ministries—Chicago, IL

Greater Fairmont Council of Churches—Fairmont, WV

Greater Waterbury Interfaith Ministries, Inc.—Waterbury, CT

The Greater Wheeling Council of Churches—Wheeling, WV

Refugee Assistance Programs

Rural Issues

Ohio Council of Churches—Columbus, OH

Oklahoma Conference of Churches—Oklahoma City, OK

The Pennsylvania Council of Churches—Harrisburg, PA

Reading Berks Conference of Churches—Reading, PA

The Rhode Island State Council of Churches—Providence, RI

Rural Migrant Ministry—Poughkeepsie, NY

United Churches of Lycoming County—Williamsport, PA

Virginia Council of Churches, Inc.—Richmond, VA

West Virginia Council of Churches—Charleston, WV

Wisconsin Council of Churches—Sun Prairie, WI

Senior Citizen Programs

Allegheny Valley Association of Churches—Natrona Heights, PA

Asheville-Buncombe Community Christian Ministry (ABCCM)—Asheville, NC

The Associated Churches of Fort Wayne & Allen County, Inc.—Fort Wayne, IN

Association of Religious Communities—Danbury, CT

Attleboro Area Council of Churches, Inc.—Attleboro, MA

Austin Metropolitan Ministries—Austin, TX

Bergen County Council of Churches—Bergenfield, NJ

Broome County Council of Churches, Inc.—Binghamton, NY

Capital Area Council of Churches, Inc.—Albany, NY

The Capitol Region Conference of Churches—Hartford, CT

Center for Community Concerns—Racine, WI

Christians United in Beaver County—Beaver, PA

Church Council of Greater Seattle—Seattle, WA

Community Ministries of Rockville—Rockville, MD

Concerned Ecumenical Ministry to the Upper West Side—Buffalo, NY

Council of Churches of the Ozarks—Springfield, MO

Council of Churches and Synagogues of Southwestern Connecticut—Stamford, CT

Eastern Area Community Ministries—Louisville, KY

Fern Creek/Highview United Ministries—Louisvlle, KY

Georgia Christian Council—Macon, GA

Greater Bethlehem Area Council of Churches—Bethlehem, PA

Greater Chicago Broadcast Ministries—Chicago, IL

Greater Minneapolis Council of Churches—Minneapolis, MN

Inter-Church Council of Greater New Bedford—New Bedford, MA

Inter-Church Ministries of Erie County—Erie, PA

Interfaith Community Council, Inc.—New Albany, IN

Interfaith Community Services—St. Joseph, MO

Interfaith Council of Contra Costa County—Walnut Creek, CA

InterReligious Council of Central New York—Syracuse, NY

The Joint Religious Legislative Coalition—Minneapolis, MN

Lincoln Interfaith Council—Lincoln, NE

Louisiana Interchurch Conference—Baton Rouge, LA

Michigan Ecumenical Forum—Lansing, MI

Northside Inter-Church Agency (NICA)—Fort Worth, TX

Northwest Interfaith Movement—Philadelphia, PA

Oak Park-River Forest Community of Congregations—Oak Park, IL

Oklahoma Conference of Churches—Oklahoma City, OK

Paducah Cooperative Ministry—Paducah, KY

Peoria Friendship House of Christian Service—Peoria, IL

The Rhode Island State Council of Churches—Providence, RI

San Fernando Valley Interfaith Council—Chatsworth, CA

South Hills Interfaith Ministries—Library, PA

South Louisville Community Ministries—Louisville, KY

Southeast Ecumenical Ministry—Rochester, NY

Southside Area Ministries, Inc. (SAM)—Fort Worth, TX

Tarrant Area Community of Churches—Fort Worth, TX

Toledo Ecumenical Area Ministries—Toledo, OH

United Churches of Lycoming County—Williamsport, PA

Washington Association of Churches—Seattle, WA

West Central Neighborhood Ministry, Inc.—Fort Wayne, IN

West Side Ecumenical Ministry—Cleveland, OH

Substance Abuse Programs

Asheville-Buncombe Community Christian Ministry (ABCCM)—Asheville, NC

Austin Metropolitan Ministries—Austin, TX

Bergen County Council of Churches—Bergenfield, NJ

Christian Conference of Connecticut—Hartford, CT

Community Ministries of Rockville—Rockville, MD

271

Corpus Christi Metro Ministries—Corpus Christi, TX

Council of Churches of the Ozarks—Springfield, MO

East End Cooperative Ministry—Pittsburgh, PA

Eastern Area Community Ministries—Louisville, KY

Ecumenical Ministries of Oregon—Portland, OR

Evanston Ecumenical Action Council—Evanston, IL

Graymoor Ecumenical & Interreligious Institute—New York, NY

Greater Chicago Broadcast Ministries—Chicago, IL

Greensboro Urban Ministry—Greensboro, NC

The Joint Religious Legislative Coalition—Minneapolis, MN

Lincoln Interfaith Council—Lincoln, NE

Metropolitan Ecumenical Ministry Community Development Corp.—Newark, NJ

New Hampshire Council of Churches—Concord, NH

New York State Community of Churches, Inc.—Albany, NY

Northside Common Ministries—Pittsburgh, PA

The Rhode Island State Council of Churches—Providence, RI

Staten Island Council of Churches—Staten Island, NY

Toledo Ecumenical Area Ministries—Toledo, OH

United Churches of Lycoming County—Williamsport, PA

United Religious Community of St. Joseph County—South Bend, IN

Theology and Worship Programs

Akron Area Association of Churches—Akron, OH

The Associated Churches of Fort Wayne & Allen County, Inc.—Fort Wayne, IN

Associated Ministries of Tacoma-Pierce County—Tacoma, WA

Association of Christian Churches—Sioux Falls, SD

Attleboro Area Council of Churches, Inc.—Attleboro, MA

Bergen County Council of Churches—Bergenfield, NJ

Berrien County Association of Churches—Benton Harbor, MI

Broome County Council of Churches, Inc.—Binghamton, NY

Capital Area Council of Churches, Inc.—Albany, NY

Christian Council of Metropolitan Atlanta—Atlanta, GA

Church Council of Greater Seattle—Seattle, WA

The Church Federation of Greater Indianapolis, Inc.—Indianapolis, IN

Churches United of the Quad City Area—Rock Island, IL

Council of Churches of Greater Springfield—Springfield, MA

The Council of Churches of Santa Clara County—San Jose, CA

Council of Churches and Synagogues of Southwestern Connecticut—Stamford, CT

Ecclesia—Trenton, NJ

Ecumenical Conference of Greater Altoona—Altoona, PA

The Ecumenical Council of Pasadena Area Churches—Pasadena, CA

Ecumenical Ministries—Fulton, MO

Ecumenical Ministries of Iowa (EMI)—Des Moines, IA

Ecumenical Ministries of Oregon—Portland, OR

Georgia Christian Council—Macon, GA

Grand Rapids Area Center for Ecumenism (GRACE)—Grand Rapids, MI

Greater Chicago Broadcast Ministries—Chicago, IL

Greater Dayton Christian Connections—Dayton, OH

Greater Fairmont Council of Churches—Fairmont, WV

Greater New Orleans Federation of Churches—New Orleans, LA

Greater Rochester Community of Churches—Rochester, NY

The Greater Wheeling Council of Churches—Wheeling, WV

Greensboro Urban Ministry—Greensboro, NC

Illinois Conference of Churches—Springfield, IL

In One Accord—Battle Creek, MI

Indiana Partners for Christian Unity and Mission—Indianapolis, IN

Inter-Church Council of Greater New Bedford—New Bedford, MA

Inter-Church Ministries of Erie County—Erie, PA

Interchurch Ministries of Nebraska—Lincoln, NE

Interfaith Mission Service—Huntsville, AL

Kansas Ecumenical Ministries—Topeka, KS

Kentucky Council of Churches—Lexington, KY

Lehigh County Conference of Churches—Allentown, PA

Lincoln Interfaith Council—Lincoln, NE

Marin Interfaith Council—Novato, CA

Massachusetts Council of Churches—Boston, MA

Metropolitan Christian Council of Philadelphia—Philadelphia, PA

The Metropolitan Christian Council: Detroit-Windsor—Detroit, MI

Michigan Ecumenical Forum—Lansing, MI

Montana Association of Churches—Billings, MT

Muskegon County Cooperating Churches—Muskegon, MI

Network of Religious Communities—Buffalo, NY

New Britain Area Conference of Churches (NEWBRACC)—New Britain, CT

North Carolina Council of Churches—Raleigh, NC

Northern Kentucky Interfaith Commission, Inc.—Newport, KY

Northside Common Ministries—Pittsburgh, PA

Northside Inter-Church Agency (NICA)—Fort Worth, TX

Oak Park-River Forest Community of Congregations—Oak Park, IL

Ohio Council of Churches—Columbus, OH

Oklahoma Conference of Churches—Oklahoma City, OK

The Pennsylvania Council of Churches—Harrisburg, PA

The Rhode Island State Council of Churches—Providence, RI

Schenectady Inner City Ministry—Schenectady, NY

South Coast Ecumenical Council—Long Beach, CA

South East Associated Ministries (SEAM)—Louisville, KY

South Louisville Community Ministries—Louisville, KY

Southern California Ecumenical Council—Pasadena, CA

Spokane Council of Ecumenical Ministries—Spokane, WA

Staten Island Council of Churches—Staten Island, NY

Tarrant Area Community of Churches—Fort Worth, TX

Texas Conference of Churches—Austin, TX

Toledo Ecumenical Area Ministries—Toledo, OH

Vermont Ecumenical Council and Bible Society—Burlington, VT

Virginia Council of Churches, Inc.—Richmond, VA

Washington Association of Churches—Seattle, WA

West Virginia Council of Churches—Charleston, WV

Wisconsin Council of Churches—Sun Prairie, WI

Worcester County Ecumenical Council—Worcester, MA

Women's Issues

Asheville-Buncombe Community Christian Ministry (ABCCM)—Asheville, NC

The Associated Churches of Fort Wayne & Allen County, Inc.—Fort Wayne, IN

Bergen County Council of Churches—Bergenfield, NJ

Berrien County Association of Churches—Benton Harbor, MI

Center for the Prevention of Sexual and Domestic Violence—Seattle, WA

Christian Council of Metropolitan Atlanta—Atlanta, GA

Church Council of Greater Seattle—Seattle, WA

Community Ministries of Rockville—Rockville, MD

Concerned Ecumenical Ministry to the Upper West Side—Buffalo, NY

Council of Churches of the City of New York—New York, NY

The Council of Churches of Santa Clara County—San Jose, CA

East End Cooperative Ministry—Pittsburgh, PA

Ecclesia—Trenton, NJ

The Ecumenical Council of Pasadena Area Churches—Pasadena, CA

Georgia Christian Council—Macon, GA

Greater Chicago Broadcast Ministries—Chicago, IL

Greater Minneapolis Council of Churches—Minneapolis, MN

Inter-Church Council of Greater New Bedford—New Bedford, MA

Interchurch Ministries of Nebraska—Lincoln, NE

The Joint Religious Legislative Coalition—Minneapolis, MN

Lincoln Interfaith Council—Lincoln, NE

The Long Island Council of Churches—Hempstead, NY

Metropolitan Christian Council of Philadelphia—Philadelphia, PA

Network of Religious Communities—Buffalo, NY

New Mexico Conference of Churches—Albuquerque, NM

New York State Community of Churches, Inc.—Albany, NY

North Carolina Council of Churches—Raleigh, NC

Oklahoma Conference of Churches—Oklahoma City, OK

Peoria Friendship House of Christian Service—Peoria, IL

The Rhode Island State Council of Churches—Providence, RI

South Coast Ecumenical Council—Long Beach, CA

South Hills Interfaith Ministries—Library, PA

Spokane Council of Ecumenical Ministries—Spokane, WA

United Ministries—Greenville, SC

Virginia Council of Churches, Inc.—Richmond, VA

Washington Association of Churches—Seattle, WA

West Central Neighborhood Ministry, Inc.—Fort Wayne, IN

Wisconsin Council of Churches—Sun Prairie, WI

Youth Activities

Arkansas Interfaith Conference—Scott, AR

Asheville-Buncombe Community Christian Ministry (ABCCM)—Asheville, NC

The Associated Churches of Fort Wayne & Allen County, Inc.—Fort Wayne, IN

Association of Christian Churches—Sioux Falls, SD

Attleboro Area Council of Churches, Inc.—Attleboro, MA

Austin Metropolitan Ministries—Austin, TX

Bergen County Council of Churches—Bergenfield, NJ

Brooklyn Council of Churches—Brooklyn, NY

Broome County Council of Churches, Inc.—Binghamton, NY

Center City Churches—Hartford, CT

Christian Council of Metropolitan Atlanta—Atlanta, GA

Church Council of Greater Seattle—Seattle, WA

The Church Federation of Greater Indianapolis, Inc.—Indianapolis, IN

Concerned Ecumenical Ministry to the Upper West Side—Buffalo, NY

Council of Churches of Greater Bridgeport, Inc.—Bridgeport, CT

The Council of Churches of Santa Clara County—San Jose, CA

East End Cooperative Ministry—Pittsburgh, PA

Eastern Area Community Ministries—Louisville, KY

Ecclesia—Trenton, NJ

Ecumenical Ministries—Fulton, MO

Evanston Ecumenical Action Council—Evanston, IL

Fern Creek/Highview United Ministries—Louisvlle, KY

Genesee-Orleans Ministry of Concern—Albion, NY

Greater Bethlehem Area Council of Churches—Bethlehem, PA

Greater Chicago Broadcast Ministries—Chicago, IL

Greater Fairmont Council of Churches—Fairmont, WV

Greater Minneapolis Council of Churches—Minneapolis, MN

Inter-Church Council of Greater New Bedford—New Bedford, MA

Interfaith Community Council, Inc.—New Albany, IN

Interfaith Community Services—St. Joseph, MO

Lehigh County Conference of Churches—Allentown, PA

Lincoln Interfaith Council—Lincoln, NE

The Long Island Council of Churches—Hempstead, NY

Metropolitan Ecumenical Ministry Community Development Corp.—Newark, NJ

Network of Religious Communities—Buffalo, NY

New Britain Area Conference of Churches (NEWBRACC)—New Britain, CT

Northside Common Ministries—Pittsburgh, PA

Northside Inter-Church Agency (NICA)—Fort Worth, TX

Oak Park-River Forest Community of Congregations—Oak Park, IL

Peoria Friendship House of Christian Service—Peoria, IL

Reading Berks Conference of Churches—Reading, PA

The Rhode Island State Council of Churches—Providence, RI

Rural Migrant Ministry—Poughkeepsie, NY

St. Paul Area Council of Churches—St. Paul, MN

Schenectady Inner City Ministry—Schenectady, NY

South Coast Ecumenical Council—Long Beach, CA

South East Associated Ministries (SEAM)—Louisville, KY

South Hills Interfaith Ministries—Library, PA

South Louisville Community Ministries—Louisville, KY

Southside Area Ministries, Inc. (SAM)—Fort Worth, TX

Spokane Council of Ecumenical Ministries—Spokane, WA

Toledo Ecumenical Area Ministries—Toledo, OH

United Churches of Lycoming County—Williamsport, PA

West Central Neighborhood Ministry, Inc.—Fort Wayne, IN

West Side Ecumenical Ministry—Cleveland, OH

West Virginia Council of Churches—Charleston, WV

8. Canadian Regional and Local Ecumenical Bodies

Most of the Organizations listed below are councils of churches in which churches participate officially, whether at the parish or judicatory level. They operate at the city, metropolitan area, or county level. Parish clusters within urban areas are not included.

Canadian local ecumenical bodies operate without paid staff, with the exception of a few which have part-time staff. In most cases the name and address of the president or chairperson is listed. As these offices change from year to year, some of this information may be out of date by the time the *Yearbook of American and Canadian Churches* is published. Up-to-date information may be secured from the Canadian Council of Churches, 40 St. Clair Ave. E., Ste. 201, Toronto, ON M4T 1M9.

ALBERTA

Calgary Council of Churches
Stephen Kendall, Treas. 1009 - 15 Ave. SW, Calgary, Alberta T3R 0S5

Calgary Inter-Faith Community Association
Rev. V. Hennig, 7515 7th St.SW, Calgary, Alberta T2V 1G1

Calgary Inter-Faith SAWDAP
Mrs. Caroline Brown, #240-15 Ave. SW, Calgary, Alberta T2R 0P7

ATLANTIC PROVINCES

Atlantic Ecumenical Council of Churches
Pres., Rev. John E. Boyd, Box 637, 90 Victoria St., Amherst, Nova Scotia B4H 4B4

Pictou Council of Churches
Rev. D. J. Murphy, Sec., P.O. Box 70, Pictou, Nova Scotia B0K 1H0

BRITISH COLUMBIA

Canadian Ecumenical Action
Coordinator, 1410 West 12th Ave., Vancouver, British Columbia V6H 1M8

Greater Victoria Council of Churches
c/o Rev. Edwin Taylor, St. Alban's Church, 1468 Ryan St. at Balmont, Victoria, British Columbia V8R 2X1

Vancouver Council of Churches
Murray Moerman, 700 Kingsway, Vancouver, British Columbia V5V 3C1 Tel. (604)420-0761

MANITOBA

Association of Christian Churches in Manitoba
The Rev. Ted Chell, President, 484 Maryland St., Winnipeg, Manitoba R3G 1M5 Tel. (204)774-3143 or (204)775-3536

NEW BRUNSWICK

First Miramichi Inter-Church Council
Pres., Ellen Robinson, Doaktown, New Brunswick E0C 1G0

Moncton Area Council of Churches
Rev. Yvon Berrieau, Visitation Ministry, Grande Digue, New Brunswick E0A 1S0

UC Maritime Conference ICIF Com.
The Rev. Leslie Robinson, P.O. Box 174, Chipman, New Brunswick, E0E 1C0 Tel. (506)339-6626
Email: maronf@nbnet.nb.ca

NOVA SCOTIA

Amherst and Area Council of Churches
Mrs. Jean Miller, President, R.R.#3 1065 HWY 204, Amherst, Nova Scotia B4H 3Y1 Tel. (902)667-8107

Atlantic Ecumenical Council of Churches
The Rev. P.A. Sandy MacDonald, 4 Pinehill Road, Dartmouth, Nova Scotia B3A 2E6 Tel.(902)469-4480 or (902)466-6247

Bridgewater Inter-Church Council
Pres., Wilson Jones, 30 Parkdale Ave., Bridgewater, Nova Scotia B4V 1L8

Cornwallis District Inter-Church Council
Pres., Mr. Tom Regan, Centreville, R.R. #2, Kings County, Nova Scotia B0T 1J0

Halifax-Dartmouth Council of Churches
Mrs. Betty Short, 3 Virginia Avenue, Dartmouth, Nova Scotia B2W 2Z4

275

Industrial Cape Breton Council of Churches
Rev. Karen Ralph, 24 Huron Ave., Sydney Mines, Nova Scotia B1S 1V2

Kentville Council of Churches
Rev. Canon S.J.P. Davies, 325-325 Main St., Kentville, Nova Scotia B4N 1C5

Lunenburg Queens BA Association
ØMrs. Nilda Chute, 56 Hillside Dr., R.R.#4, Bridgewater, Nova Scotia B4V 2W3

Mahone Bay Interchurch Council
Patricia Joudrey, R.R. #1., Blockhouse, Nova Scotia B0J1EO

Queens County Association of Churches
Mr. Donald Burns, Box 537, Liverpool, Nova Scotia B0T 1K6

ONTARIO

Burlington Inter-Church Council
Mr. Fred Townsend, 425 Breckenwood, Burlington, Ontario L7L 2J6

Christian Council - Capital Area
Fr. Peter Shonenback, 1247 Kilborn Ave., Ottawa, Ontario K1H 6K9

Christian Leadership Council of Downtown Toronto
Ken Bhagan, Chair, 40 Homewood Ave, #509, Toronto, Ontario M4Y 2K2

Ecumenical Committee
Rev. William B. Kidd, 76 Eastern Ave., Sault Ste. Marie, Ontario P6A 4R2

Glengarry-Prescott-Russell Christian Council
Pres., Rev. G. Labrosse, St. Eugene's, Prescott, Ontario K0B 1PO

Hamilton & District Christian Churches Association
The Rev. Dr. John Johnston, 147 Chedoke Avenue, Hamilton, Ontario L8P 4P2 Tel. (905) 529-6896, [O] (905)528-2730 Fax (509)521-2539

Ignace Council of Churches
Box 5, 205 Pine St., St. Ignace, Ontario P0T 1H0

Inter Church Council of Burlington
Michael Bittle, Box 62120 Burlington Mall R.P.O., Burlington, Ontario L7R 4K2 Tel. (905)526-1523 Fax(509)526-9056

Email: mbittle@istar.ca
Website: http://home.istar.cal/mbittle/eo_schl.htm

Kitchener-Waterloo Council of Churches
Rev. Clarence Hauser, CR, 53 Allen St. E., Waterloo, Ontario N2J 1J3

London Inter-City Faith Team
David Carouthers, Chair, c/o United Church, 711 Colbourne St., London, Ontario N6A 3Z4

Massey Inter-Church Council
The Rev. Hope Jackson, Box 238, Massey, Ontario P0P 1P0 Tel. (705)865-2630

Ottawa Christian Council of the Capital Area
1247 Kilborn Ave., Ottawa, Ontario K1H 6K9

St. Catharines & Dist. Clergy Fellowship
Rev. Victor Munro, 663 Vince4 St., St. Catharines, Ontario L2M 3V8

Spadina-Bloor Interchurch Council
Rev. Frances Combes, Chair, c/o Bathurst St. United Church, 427 Bloor St. W, Toronto, Ontario M5S 1X7

Stratford & District Council of Churches
Rev. Ted Heinze, Chair, 202 Erie St., Stratford, Ontario N5A 2M8

Thorold Inter-Faith Council
1 Dunn St., St. Catharines, Ontario L2T 1P3

Thunder Bay Council of Churches
Rev. Richard Darling, 1800 Moodie St. E., Thunder Bay, Ontario P7E 4Z2

PRINCE EDWARD ISLAND

Atlantic Ecumenical Council
The Rev. Arthur Pendergast, Secretary, Immaculate Conception Church, St. Louis, Prince Edward Island C0B 1Z0 Tel. (902)963-2202 or (902)822-2622

Summerside Christian Council
Ms. A. Kathleen Miller, P.O. Box 1551, Summerside, Prince Edward Island C1N 4K4

QUEBEC

Canadian Centre for Ecumenism/Centre d'oecuménisme
Fr. Emmanuel Lapierre, 2065 Sherbrooke Street West, Montreal, Quebec H3H 1G6 Tel. (514)937-9176 Fax (514)937-2684

Christian Direction
The Rev. Glen Smith, #3602-465 St. Antoine St. W., Montreal, Quebec H2Z 1J1

The Ecumenical Group
c/o Mrs. C. Haten, 1185 Ste. Foy, St. Bruno, Quebec J3V 3C3

Hemmingford Ecumenical Committee
c/o Catherine Priest, Box 300, Hemmingford, Quebec J0L 1H0

Montréal Council of Churches
The Rev. Ralph Watson, 4995 Coronation Avenue, Montréal, Québec H4V 2E1 Tel. (514)484-7196

Mtl. Association for the Blind Foundation
The Rev. Dr. John A. Simms, 7000 Sherbrooke St. W., Montreal, Quebec H4B 1R3 Tel. (514)489-8201

SASKATCHEWAN

Humboldt Clergy Council
Fr. Leo Hinz, OSB, Box 1989, Humboldt, Saskatchewan S0K 2A0

Melville Association of Churches
Attn., Catherine Gaw, Box 878, Melville, Saskatchewan S0A 2P0

Regina Council of Churches
The Rev. Bud Harper, 5 Robinson Crescent, Regina, Saskatchewan S4R 3R1 Tel. (306) 545-3375

Saskatoon Centre for Ecumenism
Nicholas Jesson, 1006 Broadway, Saskatoon, Saskatchewas S7N 1B9 Tel. (306)553-1633 Fax (306)242-8916
Email: sce@sfn.saskatoon.sk.ca

Saskatoon Council of Churches
Dr. Colin Clay, 812 Colony St., Saskatoon, Saskatchewan S7H 0S1

9. Theological Seminaries and Bible Colleges in the United States

The following list includes theological seminaries and departments in colleges and universities in which ministerial training is given. Many denominations have additional programs. The lists of Religious Bodies in the United States (Directory 3) should be consulted for the address of denominational headquarters.

Inclusion in or exclusion from this list implies no judgment about the quality or accreditation of any institution. Those schools that are members (both accredited and affiliated) of the Association of Theological Schools are marked with an asterisk (*). Additional information about enrollment in ATS member schools can be found in the "Trends in Seminary Enrollment" section of chapter III.

Each of the listings include: the institution name, denominational sponsor when appropriate, location, the president or dean of the institution, telephone and fax numbers and email and website addresses when available.

Abilene Christian University (Churches of Christ), Royce Money, Ph.D., President, ACU Station Box 29100, Abilene, TX 79699-9100 Tel. (915)674-2412 Fax (915) 674-2958
Email: moneyr@nicanor.acu.edu
Website: www.acu.edu

Alaska Bible College (Nondenominational), Steven J. Hostetter, President, P.O. Box 289, Glennallen, AK 99588 Tel. (907)822-3201 Fax (907)822-5027
Email: info@akbible.edu
Website: www.akbible.edu

Alliance Theological Seminary* (The Christian and Missionary Alliance), David L. Rambo, President, 350 N. Highland Ave., Nyack, NY 10960-1416 Tel. (914)353-2020 Fax (914) 358-2651

American Baptist College (National Baptist Convention U.S.A., Inc.), Bernard Lafayette, President, 1800 Baptist World Center Dr., Nashville, TN 37207 Tel. (615)262-1369 Fax (615)226-7855

American Baptist Seminary of the West* (American Baptist Churches in the U.S.A.), Dr. Keith A. Russell, President, 2606 Dwight Way, Berkeley, CA 94704-3029 Tel. (510)841-1905 Fax (510)841-2446
Email: krussell@absw.edu
Website: www.absw.edu

Anderson University School of Theology* (Church of God (Anderson, Ind.)), David Sebastian, President, Anderson University, Anderson, IN 46012-3495 Tel. (765)641-4032 Fax (765)641-3005

Andover Newton Theological School* (American Baptist Churches in the U.S.A.; United Church of Christ), Benjamin Griffin, President, 210 Herrick Rd., Newton Centre, MA 02459 Tel. (617)964-1100 Fax (617)965-9756
Email: admissions@ants.edu
Website: www.ants.edu

Appalachian Bible College (Nondenominational), Daniel L. Anderson, President, P.O. Box ABC, Bradley, WV 25818 Tel. (304) 877-6428 or (800)6789 ABC Fax (304)877-5082
Email: abc@appbibco.edu
Website: www.abc.edu

Aquinas Institute of Theology* (The Catholic Church), Charles E. Bouchard, President, 3642 Lindell Blvd., St. Louis, MO 63108 Tel. (314)977-3882 Fax (314)977-7225
Email: aquinas@slu.edu
Website: www.ai.edu

Arizona College of the Bible (Interdenominational), Douglas K. Winn, President, 2045 W. Northern Ave., Phoenix, AZ 85021-5197 Tel. (602)995-2670 Fax (602)864-8183

Arlington Baptist College (Baptist), David Bryant, President, 3001 W. Division, Arlington, TX 76012-3425 Tel. (817)461-8741 Fax (817)274-1138

Asbury Theological Seminary* (Interdenominational), Maxie D. Dunnam, President, 204 N. Lexington Ave., Wilmore, KY 40390-1199 Tel. (606)858-3581
Website: www.ats.wilmore.ky.us

Ashland Theological Seminary* (Brethren Church (Ashland, Ohio), Frederick J. Finks, President, 910 Center St., Ashland, OH 44805 Tel. (419)289-5161 Fax (419)289-5969

Assemblies of God Theological Seminary* (Assemblies of God), Byron D. Klaus, President, 1435 North Glenstone Avenue, Springfield, MO 65802-2131 Tel. (417)268-1000 Fax (417)268-1001
Email: agts@agseminary.edu
Website: www.agts.edu

Associated Mennonite Biblical Seminary* (Mennonite Church; General Conference Mennonite Church), J. Nelson Kraybill, President, 3003 Benham Ave., Elkhart, IN 46517-1999 Tel. (219)295-3726 Fax (219)295-0092

Email: nkraybill@ambs.edu
Website: www.ambs.edu

Athenaeum of Ohio* (The Catholic Church), Robert J. Mooney, President, 6616 Beechmont Ave., Cincinnati, OH 45230-2091 Tel. (513) 231-2223 Fax (513)231-3254

Atlanta Christian College (Christian Churches and Churches of Christ), R. Edwin Groover, President, 2605 Ben Hill Rd., East Point, GA 30344 Tel. (404)761-8861 Fax (404)669-2024 Email: admissions@acc.edu
Website: www.acc.edu

Austin Presbyterian Theological Seminary* (Presbyterian Church (USA)), Robert M. Shelton, President, 100 E. 27th St., Austin, TX 78705-5797 Tel. (512)472-6736 Fax (512) 479-0738
Website: www.austinseminary.edu

Azusa Pacific University* (Interdenominational), Jon R. Wallace, Acting President, 901 E. Alosta, P.O. Box 7000, Azusa, CA 91702 Tel. (626)812-3031 Fax (626)334-5766
Website: www.apu.edu

Bangor Theological Seminary* (United Church of Christ), President Ansley Coe Throckmorton, President, 300 Union St., Bangor, ME 04401 Tel. (207)942-6781 Fax (207)942-4914 Email: jwiebe@bts.edu
Website: www.bts.edu

Baptist Bible College (Baptist Bible Fellowship International), Leland Kennedy, President, 628 E. Kearney, Springfield, MO 65803 Tel. (417)268-6060 Fax (417)268-6694

Baptist Bible College and Seminary (Baptist), Milo Thompson, President, 538 Venard Rd., Clarks Summit, PA 18411 Tel. (570)586-2400 Fax (570)586-1753 Email: bbc@bbc.edu
Website: www.bbc.edu

Baptist Missionary Association Theological Seminary (Baptist Missionary Association of America), Charley Holmes, President, 1530 E. Pine St., Jacksonville, TX 75766 Tel. (903) 586-2501 Fax (903)586-0378 Email: bmaisem@flash.net-
Website: www.geocities.com/Athens/Acropolis/ 3386

Baptist Theological Seminary at Richmond* (Cooperative Baptist Fellowship), Thomas H. Graves, President, 3400 Brook Rd., Richmond, VA 23227 Tel. (804)355-8135 Fax (804)355-8182 Email: btsr@btsr.edu
Website: www.btsr.edu

Barclay College (Interdenominational), Walter E. Moody, President, P.O. Box 288, Haviland, KS 67059 Tel. (316)862-5252 Fax (316)862-5403 Email: barclaycollege@havilandtalco.com

Bay Ridge Christian College (Church of God Anderson, Ind.), Charles Denniston, President, P.O. Box 726, Kendleton, TX 77451 Tel. (409)532-3982 Fax (409)532-4352

Beeson Divinity School of Samford University* (Interdenominational), Timothy George, Dean, President, 800 Lakeshore Dr., Birmingham, AL 35229-2252 Tel. (205)726-2991 Fax (205)726-2260 Email: tfgeorge@samford.edu
Website: http://beeson.samford.edu

Bethany College (Assemblies of God), Tom Duncan, President, 800 Bethany Dr., Scotts Valley, CA 95066 Tel. (408)438-3800 Fax (408)438-4517

Bethany Lutheran Theological Seminary (Evangelical Lutheran Synod), G. R. Schmeling, President, 6 Browns Ct., Mankato, MN 56001 Tel. (507)344-7354 Fax (507)344-7426 Email: gschmeli@blc.edu
Website: http://sem-09.blc.edu/default.html

Bethany Theological Seminary* (Church of the Brethren), Eugene F. Roop, President, 615 National Rd. W., Richmond, IN 47374 Tel. (765)983-1800 Fax (765)983-1840 Email: roopge@earlham.edu
Website: www.brethren.org/bethany

Bethel Seminary* (Baptist General Conference), George K. Brushaber, President, 3949 Bethel Dr., St. Paul, MN 55112 Tel. (651)638-6230 Fax (651)638-6008 Email: webmaster@bethel.edu
Website: www.bethel.edu

Beulah Heights Bible College (The International Pentecostal Church of Christ), Samuel R. Chand, President, 892 Berne St. SE, Atlanta, GA 30316 Tel. (404)627-2681 Fax (404)627-0702 Email: bhbc@beulah.org
Website: www.beulah.org

Bible Church of Christ Theological Institute (Nondenominational), Roy Bryant; Sr., President, 1358 Morris Ave., Bronx, NY 10456-1402 Tel. (718)588-2284 Fax (718) 992-5597
Website: www.thebiblechurchofchrist.org

Biblical Theological Seminary (Interdenominational), David G. Dunbar, President, 200 N. Main St., Hatfield, PA 19440 Tel. (215)368-5000 Fax (215)368-7002

Boise Bible College (Christian Churches and Churches of Christ), Dr. Charles A. Crane, President, 8695 Marigold St., Boise, ID 83714 Tel. (208)376-7731 Fax (208)376-7743 Email: boibible@micron.net
Website: netnow.micron.net/~boibible

279

Boston University (School of Theology)* (The United Methodist Church), Dr. Robert C. Neville, Dean, 745 Commonwealth Ave., Boston, MA 02215 Tel. (617)353-3050 Fax (617)353-3061
Website: www.bu.edu

Brite Divinity School, Texas Christian University (Christian Church (Disciples of Christ)), Leo G. Perdue, President, TCU Box 298130, Ft. Worth, TX 76129 Tel. (817)921-7575 Fax (817)921-7305
Email: L.Perdue@tcu.edu
Website: www.brite.tcu.edu/brite/

Calvary Bible College and Theological Seminary (Independent Fundamental Churches of America), James L. Anderson, President, 15800 Calvary Rd., Kansas City, MO 64147-1341 Tel. (800)326-3960 Fax (816)331-4474

Calvin Theological Seminary* (Christian Reformed Church in North America), President James A. DeJong, President, 3233 Burton St. S.E., Grand Rapids, MI 49546-4387 Tel. (616)957-6036 Fax (616)957-8621
Email: kprg@calvin.edu
Website: www.calvin.edu/seminary

Candler School of Theology, Emory University* (The United Methodist Church), Charles R. Foster, Interim Dean, President, 500 Kilgo Circle N.E., Emory Univ., Atlanta, GA 30322 Tel. (404)727-6324 Fax (404)727-3182
Email: candler@emory.edu
Website: www.emory.edu/candler

Catholic Theological Union at Chicago* (The Catholic Church), Norman Bevan, President, 5401 S. Cornell Ave., Chicago, IL 60615-5698 Tel. (312)324-8000 Fax (312)324-8490

Catholic University of America* (The Catholic Church), Rev. Raymond F. Collins, STD. Dean, President, 113 Caldwell Hall, Cardinal Sta., Washington, DC 20064 Tel. (202)319-5683 Fax (202)319-4967
Email: cua-deansrs@cua.edu
Website: www.cua.edu/www/srs/

Central Baptist College (Baptist Missionary Association of Arkansas), Charles Attebery, President, 1501 College Ave., Conway, AR 72032 Tel. (501)329-6872 Fax (501)329-2941
Email: CaHebery@admin.cbc.edu
Website: www.cbc.edu

Central Baptist Theological Seminary* (Baptist), Thomas E. Clifton, President, 741 N. 31st St., Kansas City, KS 66102-3964 Tel. (913)371-5313 Fax (913)371-8110
Email: central@cbts.edu
Website: www.cbts.edu

Central Baptist Theological Seminary in Indiana (National Baptist Convention USA, Inc.), F. Benjamin Davis, President, 1535 Dr. A. J. Brown Ave. N., Indianapolis, IN 46202 Tel. (317)636-6622

Central Bible College (Assemblies of God), H. Maurice Lednicky, President, 3000 N. Grant Ave., Springfield, MO 65803 Tel. (417)833-2551 Fax (417)833-5141
Email: info@cbcag.edu
Website: www.cbcag.edu

Central Christian College of the Bible (Christian Churches and Churches of Christ), Russell N. James III, President, 911 E. Urbandale Dr., Moberly, MO 65270-1997 Tel. (660)263-3900 Fax (660)263-3936
Email: develop@cccb.edu
Website: www.cccb.edu

Central Indian Bible College (Assemblies of God), Robert Koscak, President, P.O. Box 550, Mobridge, SD 57601 Tel. (605)845-7801 Fax (605)845-7744

Chicago Theological Seminary* (United Church of Christ), Susan Brooks Thistlethwaite, President, 5757 South University Ave., Chicago, IL 60637-1507 Tel. (773)752-5757 Fax (773)752-5925
Email: sthistle@chgosem.edu
Website: www.chgosem.edu

Christ the King Seminary* (The Catholic Church), Richard W. Siepka, President, 711 Knox Rd., P.O. Box 607, East Aurora, NY 14052-0607 Tel. (716)652-8900 Fax (716) 652-8903
Email: rsiepka@pcom.net

Christ the Savior Seminary (The American Carpatho-Russian Orthodox Greek Catholic Church), Nicholas Smisko, President, 225 Chandler Ave., Johnstown, PA 15906 Tel. (814)539-8086 Fax (814)536-4699

Christian Theological Seminary* (Christian Church (Disciples of Christ)), Dr. Edward L. Wheeler, President, 1000 W. 42nd St., Indianapolis, IN 46208 Tel. (317)931-2305 Fax (317)923-1961
Email: ewheeler@cts.edu
Website: www.cts.edu

Church Divinity School of the Pacific* (Episcopal Church), Donn F. Morgan, President, 2451 Ridge Rd., Berkeley, CA 94709 Tel. (510)204-0700 Fax (510)644-0712
Email: rateaver@cdsp.edu

Church of God Theological Seminary* (Church of God (Cleveland, Tenn.)), Cecil B. Knight, President, P.O. Box 3330, Cleveland, TN 37320-3330 Tel. (423)478-1131 Fax (423)478-7711
Email: cogseminary@wingnet.com
Website: www.wingnet.net/~cogseminary

280

Cincinnati Bible College and Seminary (Christian Churches and Churches of Christ), David A. Grubbs, President, 2700 Glenway Ave., Cincinnati, OH 45204-3200 Tel. (513)244-8100 Fax (513)244-8140
Email: info@cincybible.edu
Website: www.cincybible.edu

Circleville Bible College (Churches of Christ in Christian Union), John Conley, President, P.O. Box 458, Circleville, OH 43113 Tel. (614)474-8896 Fax (614)477-7755
Email: cbc@biblecollege.edu
Website: www.biblecollege.edu

Claremont School of Theology* (The United Methodist Church), Philip A. Amerson, President, 1325 N. College Ave., Claremont, CA 91711-3199 Tel. (800)626-7821 Fax (909)626-7062
Email: admissions@cst.edu
Website: www.cst.edu

Clear Creek Baptist Bible College (Southern Baptist Convention), President Bill Whittaker, President, 300 Clear Creek Rd., Pineville, KY 40977 Tel. (606)337-3196 Fax (606)337-2372
Email: ccbbc@ccbbc.edu
Website: www.ccbbc.edu

Colegio Biblico Pentecostal de Puerto Rico (Church of God (Cleveland, Tenn.)), Luz M. Rivera, President, P.O. Box 901, Saint Just, PR 00978 Tel. (787)761-0640 Fax (787)748-9228

Colgate Rochester/Bexley Hall/Crozer Theological Seminary* (American Baptist Churches in the USA, Episcopal Church), G. Thomas Halbrooks, President, 1100 S. Goodman St., Rochester, NY 14620 Tel. (716)271-1320 Fax (716)271-8013
Website: www.crds.edu

Colorado Christian University (Nondenominational), Larry R. Donnithorne, President, 180 S. Garrison St., Lakewood, CO 80226 Tel. (303)202-0100 Fax (303)274-7560
Website: www.ccu.edu

Columbia International University (Multidenominational), Johnny V. Miller, President, P.O. Box 3122, Columbia, SC 29230-3122 Tel. (803)754-4100 Fax (803)786-4209

Columbia Theological Seminary* (Presbyterian Church (USA)), Laura S. Mendenhall, President, 701 Columbia Dr., P.O. Box 520, Decatur, GA 30031 Tel. (404)378-8821 Fax (404)377-9696
Website: www.ctsnet.edu

Concordia Seminary* (The Lutheran Church-Missouri Synod), John F. Johnson, President, 801 De Mun Ave., St. Louis, MO 63105 Tel. (314)505-7000 Fax (314)505-7001

Concordia Theological Seminary* (The Lutheran Church-Missouri Synod), Dean O. Wenthe, President, 6600 N. Clinton St., Ft. Wayne, IN 46825-4996 Tel. (219)452-2100 Fax (219)452-2121
Email: sem_relations@ctsfw.edu
Website: www.ctsfw.edu

Covenant Theological Seminary* (Prebyterian Church in America), Bryan Chapell, President, 12330 Conway Rd., St. Louis, MO 63141-8697 Tel. (314)434-4044 Fax (314)434-4819
Email: admissions@covenantseminary.edu
Website: www.covenantseminary.edu

Cranmer Seminary (The Anglican Orthodox Church; The Anglican Rite Synod in the Americas), The Most Rev. Robert J. Godfrey, Ph.D., President, 2558 Hickory Tree Rd, Winston Salem, NC 27127-9145 Tel. (336)775-9866 Fax (336)775-9867
Email: AOCCRanmer@aol.com
Website: www.divinityschool.org

Criswell Center for Biblical Studies (Southern Baptist Convention), Dr. Richard Wells, President, 4010 Gaston Ave., Dallas, TX 75246 Tel. (214)821-5433 Fax (214)818-1320

Crown College (The Christian and Missionary Alliance), Gary M. Benedict, President, 6425 County Rd. 30, St. Bonifacius, MN 55375-9002 Tel. (952)446-4100 Fax (952)446-4149
Email: crown@crown.edu
Website: www.crown.edu

Cummins Theological Seminary (Reformed Episcopal Church), James C. West, President, 705 S. Main St., Summerville, SC 29483 Tel. (843)873-3451 Fax (843)875-6200
Email: jcw121@aol.com

Dallas Christian College (Christian Churches and Churches of Christ), Dr. John Derry, President, 2700 Christian Pkwy, Dallas, TX 75234 Tel. (972)241-3371 Fax (972)241-8021
Email: dcc@dallas.edu
Website: www.dallas.edu

Dallas Theological Seminary* (Interdenominational), Charles R. Swindoll, President, 3909 Swiss Ave., Dallas, TX 75204 Tel. (214)824-3094 Fax (214)841-3625
Website: www.dts.edu

Denver Seminary* (Conservative Baptist Association of America), Clyde B. McDowell, President, President, Box 10,000, Denver, CO 80250-0100 Tel. (303)761-2482 Fax (303)761-8060
Email: info@densem.edu
Website: www.gospelcom.net/densem/

The Disciples Divinity House of the University of Chicago* (Christian Church (Disciples of Christ)), Dr. Kristine A. Culp, Dean, 1156 E. 57th St., Chicago, IL 60637-1536 Tel. (773)643-4411 Fax (773)643-4413

281

Email: ddh.uchicago.admin@attglobal.net
Website: www.uchicago.edu/aff/ddh

Dominican House of Studies* (The Catholic Church), Thomas McCreesh, O.P., President, 487 Michigan Ave. N.E., Washington, DC 20017-1585 Tel. (202)529-5300 Fax (202) 636-4460
Email: opassistant@aol.com
Website: www.op-dhs.org

Dominican School of Philosophy and Theology* (The Catholic Church), Gregory Rocca, President, 2401 Ridge Rd., Berkeley, CA 94709 Tel. (510)849-2030 Fax (510)849-1372

Dominican Study Center of Bayamon Central University (The Catholic Church), P. Felix Struik, O.P., President, Apartado Postal 1968, Bayamon, PR 00960-1968 Tel. (787)787-1826 Fax (787)798-2712

Drew University (Theological School)* (The United Methodist Church), Leonard I. Sweet, President, 36 Madison Ave., Madison, NJ 07940-4010 Tel. (973)408-3258 Fax (973) 408-3534
Website: www.drew.edu

Duke University (Divinity School)* (The United Methodist Church), Dean L. Gregory Jones, Dean, Box 90968, Durham, NC 27708-0968 Tel. (919)660-3400 Fax (919)660-3473
Email: info@div.duke.edu
Website: divinity.duke.edu

Earlham School of Religion* (Interdenominational-Friends), Dean Andrew P. Grannell, President, 228 College Ave., Richmond, IN 47374 Tel. (800)432-1377 Fax (765)983-1688
Email: woodna@earlham.edu
Website: www.esr.earlham.edu/esr

East Coast Bible College (Church of God (Cleveland, Tenn.)), T. David Sustar, President, 6900 Wilkinson Blvd., Charlotte, NC 28214 Tel. (704)394-2307 Fax (704)393-3689

Eastern Baptist Theological Seminary* (American Baptist Churches in the USA), R. Scott Rodin, President, 6 Lancaster Ave., Wynnewood, PA 19096 Tel. (800)220-3287 Fax (610)649-3834
Website: www.ebts.edu

Eastern Mennonite Seminary* (Mennonite Church), George R. Brunk, President, Eastern Mennonite Seminary, Harrisonburg, VA 22802 Tel. (540)432-4260 Fax (540)432-4444
Email: info@emu.edu
Website: www.emu.edu/units/sem/sem.htm

Eden Theological Seminary* (United Church of Christ), President David M. Greenhaw, President, 475 E. Lockwood Ave., St. Louis, MO 63119 Tel. (314)961-3627 Fax (314)961-9063
Website: www.eden.edu

Emmanuel School of Religion* (Christian Churches and Churches of Christ), C. Robert Wetzel, President, One Walker Dr., Johnson City, TN 37601-9438 Tel. (423)926-1186 Fax (423)926-6198
Email: president@esr.edu
Website: www.esr.edu

Emmaus Bible College (Christian Brethren (also known as Plymouth Brethren)), Daniel H. Smith, President, 2570 Asbury Rd., Dubuque, IA 52001 Tel. (319)588-8000 Fax (319)588-1216
Email: info@emmaus.edu
Website: www.emmaus.edu

Episcopal Divinity School* (Episcopal Church), The Rt. Rev. Steven Charleston, President and Dean, 99 Brattle St., Cambridge, MA 02138-3494 Tel. (617)868-3450 Fax (617)864-5385
Email: fphillips@episdivschool.org
Website: www.episdivschool.org

Episcopal Theological Seminary of the Southwest* (Episcopal Church), Durstan R. McDonald, Dean, P.O. Box 2247, Austin, TX 78768-2247 Tel. (512)472-4133 Fax (512) 472-3098
Website: www.etss.edu

Erskine Theological Seminary* (Associate Reformed Presbyterian Church (General Synod)), John L. Carson, President, Drawer 668, Due West, SC 29639 Tel. (864)379-8885 Fax (864)379-2171
Email: carson@erskine.edu
Website: www.erskine.edu/seminary/

Eugene Bible College (Open Bible Standard Churches, Inc.), Robert L. Whitlow, President, 2155 Bailey Hill Rd., Eugene, OR 97405 Tel. (503)485-1780 Fax (503)343-5801

Evangelical School of Theology* (The Evangelical Congregational Church), Kirby N. Keller, President, 121 S. College St., Myerstown, PA 17067 Tel. (717)866-5775 Fax (717)866-4667
Website: www.evangelical.edu

Faith Baptist Bible College and Theological Seminary (General Association of Regular Baptist Churches), Richard W. Houg, President, 1900 N.W. 4th St., Ankeny, IA 50021-2152 Tel. (515)964-0601 Fax (515) 964-1638
Website: www.faith.edu

Faith Evangelical Lutheran Seminary (Conservative Lutheran Association), R. H. Redal, President, 3504 N. Pearl St., Tacoma, WA 98407 Tel. (206)752-2020 Fax (206)759-1790
Email: fsinfo@faithseminary.edu
Website: www.faithseminary.edu

Florida Christian College (Christian Churches and Churches of Christ), A. Wayne Lowen,

President, 1011 Bill Beck Blvd., Kissimmee, FL 34744 Tel. (407)847-8966 Fax (407)847-3925 Email: fcc@fcc.edu

Franciscan School of Theology (The Catholic Church), William M. Cieslak, President, 1712 Euclid Ave., Berkeley, CA 94709 Tel. (510)848-5232 Fax (510)549-9466

Free Will Baptist Bible College (National Association of Free Will Baptists), Tom Malone, President, 3606 West End Ave., Nashville, TN 37205 Tel. (615)383-1340 Fax (615)269-6028 Email: president@fwbbc.edu Website: www.fwbcc.edu

Fuller Theological Seminary* (Interdenominational), Richard J. Mouw, President, 135 N. Oakland Ave., Pasadena, CA 91182 Tel. (626)584-5200 Fax (626)584-5644 Email: lguernse@fuller.edu Website: www.fuller.edu

Garrett-Evangelical Theological Seminary* (The United Methodist Church), Neal F. Fisher, President, 2121 Sheridan Rd., Evanston, IL 60201 Tel. (847)866-3900 Fax (847)866-3957 Email: seminary@nwu.edu Website: www.garrett.northwestern.edu

The General Theological Seminary* (Episcopal Church), Ward B. Ewing, President, 175 Ninth Ave., New York, NY 10011-4977 Tel. (212)243-5150 Fax (212) 727-3907 Website: www.gts.edu

George Mercer Jr. Memorial School of Theology (Episcopal Church), President, 65 Fourth St., Garden City, NY 11530 Tel. (516)248-4800 Fax (516)248-4883

God's Bible School and College (Nondenominational), Michael Avery, President, 1810 Young St., Cincinnati, OH 45210 Tel. (513)721-7944 Fax (513)721-3971 Email: GBS.po@juno.com Website: www.gbs.edu

Golden Gate Baptist Theological Seminary* (Southern Baptist Convention), William O. Crews, President, 201 Seminary Dr., Mill Valley, CA 94941-3197 Tel. (415)380-1300 Fax (415)380-1302 Email: seminary@ggbts.edu Website: www.ggbts.edu/index.html

Gonzaga University* (The Catholic Church), Fr. Robert Spitzer, S.J., President, Spokane, WA 99258-0001 Tel. (509)328-4220 Fax (509)323-5718 Email: large@gonzaga.edu

Gordon-Conwell Theological Seminary* (Interdenominational), Walter C. Kaiser, Jr., President, 130 Essex St., South Hamilton, MA 01982 Tel. (978)468-7111 Fax (978)468-6691

Email: -info@gcts.edu Website: www.gcts.edu

Grace Bible College (Grace Gospel Fellowship), Bruce Kemper, President, P.O. Box 910, Grand Rapids, MI 49509 Tel. (616)538-2330 Fax (616)538-0599 Email: gbc@gbcol.edu Website: www.gbcol.edu

Grace Theological Seminary (Fellowship of Grace Brethren Churches), Ronald E. Manahan, President, 200 Seminary Dr., Winona Lake, IN 46590-1294 Tel. (219)372-5100 Fax (219)372-5139 Website: www.grace.edu

Grace University (Independent), Neal F. McBride, President, 1311 South 9th St., Omaha, NE 68108 Tel. (402)449-2809 Fax (402)341-9587

Great Lakes Christian College (Christian Churches and Churches of Christ), Larry Carter, President, 6211 W. Willow Hwy., Lansing, MI 48917 Tel. (517)321-0242 Fax (517)321-5902

Greenville College (Free Methodist Church of North America), President Robert E. Smith, President, 315 E. College Ave., P.O. Box 159, Greenville, IL 62246 Tel. (618)664-2800 Fax (618)664-1748 Email: rsmith@Greenville.edu Website: www.greenville.edu

Harding University Graduate School of Religion (Churches of Christ), Bill Flatt, President, 1000 Cherry Rd., Memphis, TN 38117 Tel. (901)761-1352 Fax (901)761-1358

Hartford Seminary* (Interdenominational), Barbara Brown Zikmund, President, 77 Sherman St., Hartford, CT 06105-2260 Tel. (860)509-9502 Fax (860)509-9509 Email: info@hartsem.edu Website: www.hartsem.edu

Harvard Divinity School* (Nondenominational), J. Pryan Hehir, Chair of the Executive Committee, President, 45 Francis Ave., Cambridge, MA 02138 Tel. (617)495-5761 Fax (617)495-9489 Website: www.hds.harvard.edu

Hebrew Union College-Jewish Institute of Religion, NY (Jewish), Sheldon Zimmerman, President, 1 W. 4th St., New York, NY 10012 Tel. (212)674-5300 Fax (212)533-0129 Website: www.huc.edu

Hebrew Union College-Jewish Institute of Religion (Jewish), Sheldon Zimmerman, President, 3077 University Ave., Los Angeles, CA 90007 Tel. (213)749-3424 Fax (213)747-6128 Website: www.huc.edu

283

Hebrew Union College-Jewish Institute of Religion, OH (Jewish), Sheldon Zimmerman, President, 3101 Clifton Ave., Cincinnati, OH 45220 Tel. (513)221-1875 Fax (513)221-4652 Email: rabbiz@cn.huc.edu Website: www.huc.edu

Hobe Sound Bible College (Nondenominational), P. Daniel Stetler, President, P.O. Box 1065, Hobe Sound, FL 33475 Tel. (407)546-5534 Fax (407)545-1421

Holy Cross Greek Orthodox School of Theology* (Greek Orthodox Archdiocese of America), Very Reverend Damaskinos V. Ganas, President, 50 Goddard Ave., Brookline, MA 02445-7495 Tel. (617)731-3500 Fax (617)850-1460 Email: admissions@hchc.edu Website: www.hchc.edu

Holy Trinity Orthodox Seminary (The Russian Orthodox Church Outside of Russia), Archbishop Laurus Skurla, President, P.O. Box 36, Jordanville, NY 13361 Tel. (315)858-0940 Fax (315)858-0505

Hood Theological Seminary* (African Methodist Episcopal Zion Church), Albert J.D. Aymer, President, 800 W. Thomas St., Salisbury, NC 28144 Tel. (704)797-1113 Fax (704)797-1897 Website: www.catawba.edu/html/busint/livingst/html/hood.htm

Hope International University (Christian Churches and Churches of Christ), President E. LeRoy Lawson, President, 2500 E. Nutwood Ave., Fullerton, CA 92831 Tel. (714)879-3901 Fax (714)526-0231 Email: ellawson@hiu.edu Website: www.hiu.edu

Houston Graduate School of Theology* (Friends), Dr. David Robinson, President, 1311 Holman, Ste. 200, Houston, TX 77004-3833 Tel. (713)942-9505 Fax (713)942-9506 Email: hgst@hgst.edu Website: www.hgst.edu

Howard University School of Divinity* (Nondenominational), Clarence G. Newsome, President, 1400 Shepherd St. N.E., Washington, DC 20017 Tel. (202)806-0500 Fax (202)806-0711

Huntington College, Graduate School of Christian Ministries (Church of the United Brethren in Christ), G. Blair Dowden, President, 2303 College Ave., Huntington, IN 46750 Tel. (219)356-6000 Fax (219)358-3700 Email: gscm@huntington.edu Website: www.huntington.edu/academics/gscm

Iliff School of Theology* (The United Methodist Church), David Maldonado, Jr., President, 2201 S. University Blvd., Denver, CO 80210 Tel. (303)744-1287 Fax (303)777-0164 Website: www.iliff.edu

Immaculate Conception Seminary School of Theology* (The Catholic Church), Robert F. Coleman, President, 400 S. Orange Ave., South Orange, NJ 07079 Tel. (201)761-9575 Fax (201)761-9577 Email: theology@shu.edu Website: www.shu.edu

Indiana Wesleyan University (The Wesleyan Church), James Barnes, President, 4201 S. Washington, Marion, IN 46953-4999 Tel. (765)674-6901 Fax (765)677-2499 Email: jbarnes@indwes.edu Website: www.indwes.edu

Interdenominational Theological Center* (Interdenominational), Dr. Robert M. Franklin, President, 700 Martin Luther King, Jr. Dr. S.W., Atlanta, GA 30314-4143 Tel. (404)527-7700 Fax (404)527-7770 Email: info@itc.edu Website: www.itc.edu

International School of Theology* (non-denominational), Donald A. Weaver, President, 7623 East Avenue, Fontana, CA 92336 Tel. 909-770-4000 Fax 909-770-4001 Website: www.leaderu.com/isot

Jesuit School of Theology at Berkeley* (The Catholic Church), T. Howland Sanks, President, 1735 LeRoy Ave., Berkeley, CA 94709 Tel. (510)841-8804 Fax (510)841-8536

Jewish Theological Seminary of America (Jewish), Ismar Schorsch, President, 3080 Broadway, New York, NY 10027-4649 Tel. (212)678-8000 Fax (212)678-8947 Email: webmaster@jtsa.edu Website: www.jtsa.edu

John Wesley College (Interdenominational), Brian C. Donley, President, 2314 N. Centennial St., High Point, NC 27265 Tel. (336)889-2262 Fax (336)889-2261 Email: admissions@johnwesley.edu Website: www.johnwesley.edu

Johnson Bible College (Christian Churches and Churches of Christ), David L. Eubanks, President, 7900 Johnson Dr., Knoxville, TN 37998 Tel. (865)573-4517 Fax (865)251-2336 Email: jbc@jbc.edu Website: www.jbc.edu

Kansas City College and Bible School (Church of God (Holiness), Gayle Woods, President, 7401 Metcalf Ave., Overland Park, KS 66204 Tel. (913)722-0272 Fax (913)722-2135

Kenrick-Glennon Seminary* (The Catholic Church), Rev. Msgr. Dennis Delaney, President, 5200 Glennon Dr., St. Louis, MO 63119 Tel. (314)644-0266 Fax (314)644-3079

Kentucky Christian College (Christian Churches and Churches of Christ), Keith P. Keeran, President, 100 Academic Parkway, Grayson, KY 41143 Tel. (606)474-3246 Fax (606)474-3155
Email: pres@kcc.edu
Website: www.kcc.edu

Kentucky Mountain Bible College (Interdenominational), Philip Speas, President, Box 10, Vancleve, KY 41385 Tel. (606)666-5000 Fax (606)666-7744

La Sierra University (Seventh-day Adventist Church), Lawrence T. Geraty, President, 4700 Pierce St., Riverside, CA 92515-8247 Tel. (909)785-2000 Fax (909)785-2901
Email: pr@lasierra.edu
Website: www.lasierra.edu

Lancaster Bible College (Nondenominational), Gilbert A. Peterson, President, 901 Eden Rd., Lancaster, PA 17601 Tel. (717)569-7071 Fax (717)560-8213
Website: www.lbc.edu

Lancaster Theological Sem. of the United Church of Christ* (United Church of Christ), Peter Schmiechen, President, 555 W. James St., Lancaster, PA 17603-2897 Tel. (717)393-0654 Fax (717)393-0423
Email: dean@lts.org
Website: www.lts.org

Lexington Theological Seminary,* (Christian Church (Disciples of Christ)), Richard L. Harrison, Jr., President, 631 S. Limestone St., Lexington, KY 40508 Tel. (859)252-0361 Fax (859)281-6042
Website: www.lextheo.edu

Liberty Baptist Theological Seminary* (Independent Baptist), A. Pierre Guillermin, President, 1971 University Blvd., Lynchburg, VA 24502-2269 Tel. (804)582-2000 Fax (804)582-2304

L.I.F.E. Bible College (International Church of the Foursquare Gospel), Dick Scott, President, 1100 Covina Blvd., San Dimas, CA 91773 Tel. (909)599-5433 Fax (909)599-6690

Lincoln Christian College and Seminary* (Christian Churches and Churches of Christ), Keith H. Ray, President, 100 Campus View Dr., Lincoln, IL 62656 Tel. (217)732-3168 Fax (217)732-4078
Email: psnyder@lccs.edu
Website: www.lccs.edu

Logos Evangelical Seminary* (Evangelical Formosan Church), Felix Liu, President, 9358 Telstar Ave., El Monte, CA 91731 Tel. (626)571-5110 Fax (626)571-5119
Email: logos@les.edu
Website: www.les.edu

Louisville Presbyterian Theological Seminary* (Presbyterian Church (USA)), John M. Mulder, President, 1044 Alta Vista Rd., Louisville, KY 40205 Tel. (502)895-3411 Fax (502)895-1096
Website: www.lpts.edu

Loyola Univiversity Chicago Institute of Pastoral Studies* (The Catholic Church), Camilla Burns, SND, Ph.D., Director, President, 6525 North Sheridan Rd., Chicago, IL 60626 Tel. (773)508-2320 Fax (773)508-2319
Website: www.luc.edu/depts/ips

Luther Seminary* (Evangelical Lutheran Church in America), David L. Tiede, President, 2481 Como Ave., St. Paul, MN 55108 Tel. (651)641-3456 Fax (651)641-3425
Email: sbooms@luthersem.edu
Website: www.luthersem.edu/

Lutheran Bible Institute in California* (Intersynodical Lutheran), Benjamin Johnson, President, 5321 University Dr., Ste. H, Irvine, CA 92612-2938 Tel. (949)262-9222 Fax (949)262-0283
Email: LBIC@aol.com

Lutheran Brethren Seminary (Church of the Lutheran Brethren of America), Dean Eugene L. Boe, Ph.D., President, 815 W. Vernon, Fergus Falls, MN 56537 Tel. (218)739-3375 Fax (218)739-1259
Email: lbs@clba.org
Website: www.lbs.edu

Lutheran School of Theology at Chicago* (Evangelical Lutheran Church in America), James Kenneth Echols, President, 1100 E. 55th St., Chicago, IL 60615-5199 Tel. (773)256-0700 Fax (773)256-0782
Website: www.lstc.edu

Lutheran Theological Seminary at Gettysburg* (Evangelical Lutheran Church in America), The Rev. Michael L. Cooper-White, President, 61 Seminary Ridge, Gettysburg, PA 17325-1795 Tel. (717)334-6286 Fax (717)334-3469
Email: info@ltsg.edu
Website: www.ltsg.edu

Lutheran Theological Seminary at Philadelphia* (Evangelical Lutheran Church in America), Robert G. Hughes, President, 7301 Germantown Ave., Philadelphia, PA 19119 Tel. (215)248-4616 Fax (215)248-4577
Email: mtairy@ltsp.edu
Website: www.ltsp.edu

Lutheran Theological Southern Seminary* (Evangelical Lutheran Church in America), H. Frederick Reisz, President, 4201 North Main St., Columbia, SC 29203 Tel. (803)786-5150 Fax (803)786-6499
Email: Freisz@ltss.edu
Website: www.ltss.edu

Magnolia Bible College (Churches of Christ), Cecil May, President, P.O. Box 1109, Kosciusko, MS 39090-1620 Tel. (662)289-2896 Fax (601)288-2612

Manhattan Christian College (Christian Churches and Churches of Christ), Kenneth Cable, President, 1415 Anderson Ave., Manhattan, KS 66502 Tel. (785)539-3571 Fax (785)539-0832
Website: www.mccks.edu

McCormick Theological Seminary* (Presbyterian Church (USA)), Cynthia M. Campbell, President, 5555 S. Woodlawn Ave., Chicago, IL 60637 Tel. (773)947-6300 Fax (773)947-0376
Website: www.mccormick.edu

Meadville/Lombard Theological School* (Unitarian Universalist Association), William R. Murry, President, 5701 S. Woodlawn Ave., Chicago, IL 60637 Tel. (773)256-3000 Fax (773)753-1323
Email: bmurry@meadville.edu
Website: www.meadville.edu

Memphis Theological Seminary of the Cumberland Presbyterian Church* (Cumberland Presbyterian Church), Larry A. Blakeburn, President, 168 E. Parkway S at Union, Memphis, TN 38104-4395 Tel. (901)458-8232 Fax (901)452-4051
Email: lblakeburn@mtscampus.edu
Website: www.mtscampus.edu

Mennonite Brethren Biblical Seminary* (General Conference of Mennonite Brethren Churches), President Henry J. Schmidt, President, 4824 E. Butler Ave. (at Chestnut Ave.), Fresno, CA 93727-5097 Tel. (559)251-8628 Fax (559)251-7212
Email: mbseminary@aol.com
Website: www.fresno.edu/MBSeminary

Methodist Theological School in Ohio* (The United Methodist Church), President Norman E. Dewire, President, 3081 Columbus Pike, P.O. Box 8004, Delaware, OH 43015-8004 Tel. (740)363-1146 Fax (740)362-3135
Email: pres@mtso.edu
Website: www.mtso.edu

Mid-America Bible College (The Church of God), Forrest R. Robinson, President, 3500 S.W. 119th St., Oklahoma City, OK 73170 Tel. (405)691-3800 Fax (405)692-3165

Midwestern Baptist Theological Seminary* (Southern Baptist Convention), Michael K. Whitehead, Interim President, 5001 N. Oak Trafficway, Kansas City, MO 64118 Tel. (816)414-3700 Fax (816)414-3799
Website: www.mbts.edu

Minnesota Bible College (Christian Churches and Churches of Christ), Robert W. Cash, President, 920 Mayowood Rd. S.W., Rochester, MN 55902 Tel. (507)288-4563 Fax (507)288-9046
Email: academic@mnbc.edu
Website: www.mnbc.edu

Moody Bible Institute (Interdenominational), Joseph M. Stowell, President, 820 N. La Salle Blvd., Chicago, IL 60610 Tel. (312)329-4000 Fax (312)329-4109

Moravian Theological Seminary* (Moravian Church in America (Unitas Fratrum)), David A. Schattschneider, President, 1200 Main St., Bethlehem, PA 18018 Tel. (610)861-1516 Fax (610)861-1569
Email: seminary@moravian.edu
Website: www.moravianseminary.edu

Moreau Seminary (Congregation of Holy Cross) (The Catholic Church), Rev. Wilson Miscanible, C.S.C., President, Moreau Seminary, Notre Dame, IN 46556 Tel. (219)631-7735 Fax (219)631-9233

Morehouse School of Religion (Interdenominational Baptist), William T. Perkins, President, 645 Beckwith St. S.W., Atlanta, GA 30314 Tel. (404)527-7777 Fax (404)681-1005

Mount Angel Seminary* (The Catholic Church), Lawrence Reilly, President, St. Benedict, OR 97373 Tel. (503)845-3951 Fax (503)845-3126
Website: www.mtangel.edu

Mt. St. Mary's Seminary* (The Catholic Church), Very Rev. Kevin C. Rhoades, Rector, Emmitsburg, MD 21727-7797 Tel. (301)447-5295 Fax (301)447-5636
Email: rhoades@msmary.edu
Website: www.msmary.edu

Mt. St. Mary's Seminary of the West* (The Catholic Church), Gerald R. Haemmerle, President, 6616 Beechmont Ave., Cincinnati, OH 45230 Tel. (513)231-2223 Fax (513)231-3254
Email: jhaemmer@mtsm.org
Website: mtsm.org

Multnomah Bible College and Biblical Seminary* (Interdenominational), Dr. Daniel R. Lockwood, President, 8435 N.E. Glisan St., Portland, OR 97220 Tel. (503)255-0332 Fax (503)254-1268
Website: www.multnomah.edu

Mundelein Seminary of the Univ. of St. Mary-of-the-Lake* (The Catholic Church), John Canary, Rector/President, 1000 E. Maple, Mundelein, IL 60060-1174 Tel. (847)566-6401 Fax (847)566-7330
Email: syopusml@usml.edu
Website: www.vocations.org

Nashotah House (Theological Seminary)* (Episcopal Church), Gary W. Kriss, President, 2777 Mission Rd., Nashotah, WI 53058-9793 Tel. (262)646-6500 Fax (262)646-6504

Email: nashotah@nashotah.edu
Website: www.nashotah.edu

Nazarene Bible College (Church of the Nazarene), Hiram Sanders, President, 1111 Academy Park Loop, Colorado Springs, CO 80910-3717 Tel. (719)596-5110 Fax (719)550-9437
Email: nbc@rmii.com
Website: www.members.aol.com/nazbibleco

Nazarene Theological Seminary* (Church of the Nazarene), A. Gordon Wetmore, President, 1700 E. Meyer Blvd., Kansas City, MO 64131 Tel. (816)333-6254 Fax (816)333-6271

Nebraska Christian College (Christian Churches and Churches of Christ), Ray D. Stites, President, 1800 Syracuse Ave., Norfolk, NE 68701 Tel. (402)379-5000 Fax (402)391-5100

New Brunswick Theological Seminary* (Reformed Church in America), President Norman J. Kansfield, President, 17 Seminary Pl., New Brunswick, NJ 08901-1107 Tel. (732)247-5241 Fax (732)249-5412
Email: prf@nbts.edu
Website: www.nbts.edu

New Orleans Baptist Theological Seminary* (Southern Baptist Convention), Charles S. Kelley, President, 3939 Gentilly Blvd., New Orleans, LA 70126 Tel. (504)282-4455 Fax (504)286-3623
Email: nobts@nobts.edu
Website: www.nobts.edu

N.Y. City Full Gospel Theological Seminary (Full Gospel Assembly), Frank A. Garofalo, President, 6902 11th Ave., Brooklyn, NY 11228 Tel. (908)302-9553 Fax (908)302-9553

New York Theological Seminary* (Non-Denominational), Dr. Ileana Rodriguez-Garcia, Acting President, 5 W. 29th St., 9th Fl., New York, NY 10001 Tel. (212)532-4012 Fax (212)684-0757
Website: www.nyts.edu

North American Baptist Seminary* (North American Baptist Conference), John Binder, Interim President, 1525 S. Grange Ave., Sioux Falls, SD 57105-1526 Tel. (605)336-6588 Fax (605)335-9090
Email: train@nabs.edu
Website: www.nabs.edu

North Central Bible College (Assemblies of God), Gordon L. Anderson, President, 910 Elliot Ave. S., Minneapolis, MN 55404 Tel. (612)332-3491 Fax (612)343-4778

North Park Theological Seminary* (The Evangelical Covenant Church), John E. Phelan, President and Dean, President, 3225 W. Foster Ave., Chicago, IL 60625 Tel. (773)244-6214 Fax (773)244-6244

Email: jphelan@northpark.edu
Website: www.northpark.edu/cs

Northern Baptist Theological Seminary* (American Baptist Churches in the USA), Ian M. Chapman, President, 660 E. Butterfield Rd., Lombard, IL 60148-5698 Tel. (630)620-2100 Fax (630)620-2194
Email: chapman@seminary.edu
Website: www.seminary.edu

Northwest College (Assemblies of God), Don H. Argue, Ed.D., President, 5520 108th Ave. N.E., P.O. Box 579, Kirkland, WA 98083-0579 Tel. (425)822-8266 Fax (425)827-0148
Email: mail@ncag.edu
Website: www.nwcollege.edu

Notre Dame Seminary* (The Catholic Church), Most Rev. Gregory M. Aymond, D.D., President, 2901 S. Carrollton Ave., New Orleans, LA 70118-4391 Tel. (504)866-7426 Fax (504)866-3119

Oak Hills Christian College (Interdenominational), Dr. Thomas J. Bower, President, 1600 Oak Hills Rd. S.W., Bemidji, MN 56601 Tel. (218)751-8670 Fax (218)751-8825

Oblate School of Theology* (The Catholic Church), J. William Morell, President, 285 Oblate Dr., San Antonio, TX 78216-6693 Tel. (210)341-1366 Fax (210)341-4519

Oral Roberts University School of Theology and Missions* (Interdenominational), Jerry Horner, President, 7777 S. Lewis Ave., Tulsa, OK 74171 Tel. (918)495-6096 Fax (918)495-6259
Email: jhorner@oru.edu
Website: www.oru.edu

Ozark Christian College (Christian Churches and Churches of Christ), President Dr. Kenneth D. Idleman, President, 1111 N. Main St., Joplin, MO 64801 Tel. (417)624-2518 Fax (417)624-0090
Email: pres@occ.edu

Pacific Lutheran Theological Seminary* (Evangelical Lutheran Church in America), President Timothy F. Lull, President, 2770 Marin Ave., Berkeley, CA 94708-1597 Tel. (510)524-5264 Fax (510)524-2408
Email: president@plts.edu
Website: www.plts.edu

Pacific School of Religion* (Interdenominational), William McKinney, President, 1798 Scenic Ave., Berkeley, CA 94709 Tel. (510)848-0528 Fax (510)845-8948
Email: comm@psr.edu
Website: www.psr.edu

Payne Theological Seminary* (African Methodist Episcopal Church), Obery M. Hendricks, Jr., Ph.D., President, P.O. Box 474, 1230 Wilberforce-Clifton Rd., Wilberforce,

OH 45384-0474 Tel. (937)376-2946 Fax (937)376-3330
Email: dbalsbau@payne.edu
Website: www.payne-seminary.org

Pepperdine University (Churches of Christ), Rick R. Marrs, Chair of Religion Division, Religion Division, Malibu, CA 90263-4352 Tel. (310)456-4352 Fax (310)317-7271
Email: rmarrs@pepperdine.edu
Website: www.pepperdine.edu/seaver/religion/main.html

Perkins School of Theology (Southern Methodist University)* (The United Methodist Church), Robin W. Lovin, Dean, Kirby Hall, Dallas, TX 75275-0133 Tel. (214)768-2293 Fax (214)768-2966
Email: theoadms@smu.edu
Website: www.smu.edu/~theology

Philadelphia College of Bible (Nondenominational), W. Sherrill Babb, President, 200 Manor Ave., Langhorne, PA 19047-2990 Tel. (215)752-5800 Fax (215)702-4341
Email: president@pcb.edu

Philadelphia Theological Seminary (Reformed Episcopal Church), Wayne A. Headman, President, 7372 Henry Ave., Philadelphia, PA 19128-1401 Tel. (215)483-2480 Fax (215)483-2484
Email: info@ptsorec.edu
Website: www.ptsofrec.edu

Phillips Theological Seminary* (Christian Church (Disciples of Christ)), William Tabbernee, President, 4242 S. Sheridan Rd., Tulsa, OK 74145 Tel. (918)610-8303 Fax (918)610-8404
Email: ptspres@fullnet.net
Website: www.ptsem.org

Piedmont Baptist College (Baptist (Independent)), Howard L. Wilburn, President, 716 Franklin St., Winston-Salem, NC 27101 Tel. (336)725-8344 Fax (336)725-5522
Email: admissions@pbc.edu
Website: www.pbc.edu

Pittsburgh Theological Seminary* (Presbyterian Church (USA)), Carnegie Samuel Calian, President, 616 N. Highland Ave., Pittsburgh, PA 15206 Tel. (412)362-5610 Fax (412)363-3260
Email: calian@pts.edu
Website: www.pts.edu

Point Loma Nazarene College (Church of the Nazarene), President, 3900 Lomaland Dr., San Diego, CA 92106 Tel. (619)849-2200 Fax (619)849-7007
Website: www.ptloma.edu

Pontifical College Josephinum* (The Catholic Church), Brian R. Moore, Acting President, President, 7625 N. High St., Columbus, OH 43235 Tel. (614)885-5585 Fax (614)885-2307
Website: www.pcj.edu

Pope John XXIII National Seminary* (The Catholic Church), Francis D. Kelly, President, 558 South Ave., Weston, MA 02193 Tel. (617)899-5500 Fax (617)899-9057

Practical Bible College (Independent Baptist), Dale E. Linebaugh, President, Box 601, Bible School Park, NY 13737 Tel. (607)729-1581 Fax (607)729-2962
Email: pbc@lakenet.org
Website: www.lakenet.org/~pbc

Princeton Theological Seminary* (Presbyterian Church (USA)), Thomas W. Gillespie, President, P.O. Box 821, Princeton, NJ 08542-0803 Tel. (609)921-8300 Fax (609)924-2973
Email: comm-pub@ptsem.edu
Website: www.ptsem.edu

Protestant Episcopal Theological Seminary in Virginia* (Episcopal Church), Martha J. Horne, Dean, 3737 Seminary Rd., Alexandria, VA 22304 Tel. (703)370-6600 Fax (703)751-0214
Email: mhorne@vts.edu
Website: www.vts.edu

Puget Sound Christian College (Christian Churches and Churches of Christ), R. Allan Dunbar, President, 410 Fourth Ave. N., Edmonds, WA 98020-3171 Tel. (425)775-8686 Fax (425)775-8688
Email: president@pscc.edu
Website: www.pscc.edu

Rabbi Isaac Elchanan Theological Seminary (Jewish), Dr. Norman Lamm, President, 2540 Amsterdam Ave., New York, NY 10033 Tel. (212)960-5344 Fax (212)960-0061
Website: www.yu.edu/riets/

Reconstructionist Rabbinical College (Jewish), David A. Teutsch, President, Church Rd. and Greenwood Ave., Wyncote, PA 19095 Tel. (215)576-0800 Fax (215)576-6143
Email: rrcinfo@rrc.edu

Reformed Bible College (Interdenominational), Nicholas Kroeze, President, 3333 East Beltline N.E., Grand Rapids, MI 49525 Tel. (616)222-3000 Fax (616)222-3045
Email: administration@reformed.edu
Website: www.reformed.edu

Reformed Presbyterian Theological Seminary* (Reformed Presbyterian Church of North America), Jerry F. O'Neill, President, 7418 Penn Ave., Pittsburgh, PA 15208-2594 Tel. (412)731-8690 Fax (412)731-4834
Email: rpseminary@aol.com
Website: www.rpts.edu

Reformed Theological Seminary* (Non-denominational), Dr. Luder G. Whitlock, Jr., President, 5422 Clinton Blvd., Jackson, MS 39209-3099 Tel. (601)923-1600 Fax (601)923-1654

288

Email: rts.jackson@rts.edu
Website: www.rts.edu

Regent University School of Divinity* (Interdenominational), Terry Lindvall, President, 1000 Regent University Dr., Virginia Beach, VA 23464-9801 Tel. (757) 579-4010 Fax (757)579-4037
Email: uinssyn@regent.edu
Website: www.regent.edu

Roanoke Bible College (Christian Churches and Churches of Christ), William A. Griffin, President, 714 N. Poindexter St, Elizabeth City, NC 27909-4054 Tel. (252) 334-2090 or (252)334-2070 Fax (252)334-2071
Email: wag@roanokebible.edu
Website: www.roanokebible.edu

Sacred Heart Major Seminary* (The Catholic Church), Allen H. Vigneron, President, 2701 Chicago Blvd., Detroit, MI 48206 Tel. (313) 883-8500 Fax (313)868-6440

Sacred Heart School of Theology* (The Catholic Church), James D. Brackin, S.C.J., President-Rector, P.O. Box 429, Hales Corners, WI 53130-0429 Tel. (414)425-8300 Fax (414)529-6999
Email: shst@msn.com
Website: www.shst.edu

Saint Bernard's Institute* (The Catholic Church), Patricia A. Schoelles, President, 1100 S. Goodman St., Rochester, NY 14620 Tel. (716)271-3657 Fax (716)271-2045
Email: pschoelles@sbi.edu

St. Charles Borromeo Seminary* (The Catholic Church), Rev. Msgr. Michael F. Burbidge, Rector, 100 East Wynnewood Rd., Wynnewood, PA 19096-3001 Tel. (610)667-3394 Fax (610)667-7635

St. Francis Seminary* (The Catholic Church), Very Rev. Andrew L. Nelson, President, 3257 S. Lake Dr., St. Francis, WI 53235 Tel. (414)747-6400 Fax (414)747-6442
Email: anelson1@sfs.edu
Website: www.sfs.edu

St. John's Seminary* (The Catholic Church), Timothy Moran, President, 127 Lake St., Brighton, MA 02135 Tel. (617)254-2610 Fax (617)787-2336

St. John's Seminary College* (The Catholic Church), Msgr. Edward Wm. Clark, President, 5118 Seminary Rd., Camarillo, CA 93012-2599 Tel. (805)482-2755 Fax (805)987-5097

St. John's University, School of Theology Seminary* (The Catholic Church), William J. Cahoy, Dean, Box 7288, Collegeville, MN 56321-7288 Tel. (320)363-2100 Fax (320)363-3145
Website: www.csbsju.sot

St. Joseph's Seminary* (The Catholic Church), Edwin F. O'Brien, President, 201 Seminary Ave., (Dunwoodie) Yonkers, NY 10704 Tel. (914)968-6200 Fax (914)968-7912

St. Louis Christian College (Christian Churches and Churches of Christ), Kenneth L. Beck, President, 1360 Grandview Dr., Florissant, MO 63033 Tel. (314)837-6777 Fax (314)837-8291

St. Mary Seminary and Graduate School of Theology* (The Catholic Church), Donald B. Cozzens, President, 28700 Euclid Ave., Wickliffe, OH 44092 Tel. (216)943-7600 Fax (216)943-7577

St. Mary's Seminary* (The Catholic Church), Rev. Msgr. Chester L. Borski, Rector, 9845 Memorial Dr., Houston, TX 77024-3498 Tel. (713)686-4345 Fax (713)681-7550

St. Mary's Seminary and University* (The Catholic Church), Robert F. Leavitt, President, 5400 Roland Ave., Baltimore, MD 21210 Tel. (410)323-3200 Fax (410)323-3554

St. Meinrad School of Theology* (The Catholic Church), Mark O'Keefe, President, St. Meinrad, IN 47577 Tel. (812)357-6611 Fax (812)357-6964

St. Patrick's Seminary* (The Catholic Church), Gerald D. Coleman, President, 320 Middlefield Rd., Menlo Park, CA 94025 Tel. (415)325-5621 Fax (415)322-0997

Saint Paul School of Theology* (The United Methodist Church), Lovett H. Weems, Jr., President, 5123 Truman Rd., Kansas City, MO 64127-2499 Tel. (816)483-9600 Fax (816) 483-9605
Email: spst@spst.edu
Website: www.spst.edu

St. Paul Seminary School of Divinity* (The Catholic Church), Phillip J. Rask, President, 2260 Summit Ave., St. Paul, MN 55105 Tel. (612)962-5050 Fax (612)962-5790

St. Tikhon's Orthodox Theological Seminary (The Orthodox Church in America), Archbishop Herman, Rector, Box 130, St. Tikhon's Rd., South Canaan, PA 18459-0121 Tel. (570)937-4411 Fax (570)937-3100
Email: stots@stots.edu (Admin.)
stotsfac@stots.edu (Faculty)
library@stots.edu (Library)
Website: www.stots.edu and
www.oca.org/OCA/ pim/oca-stostots.html

St. Vincent de Paul Regional Seminary* (The Catholic Church), Pablo A. Navarro, President, 10701 S. Military Trail, Boynton Beach, FL 33436-4899 Tel. (561)732-4424 Fax (561)737-2205

St. Vincent Seminary* (The Catholic Church), Very Rev. Thomas Acklin, O.S.B., President,

289

300 Fraser Purchase Rd., Latrobe, PA 15650-2690 Tel. (724)537-4592 Fax (724)532-5052

St. Vladimir's Orthodox Theological Seminary* (The Orthodox Church in America), His Beatitude Metropolitan Theodosius, Dean, 575 Scarsdale Rd., Crestwood, NY 10707-1699 Tel. (914)961-8313 Fax (914)961-4507 Email: info@svots.edu
Website: www.svots.edu

San Francisco Theological Seminary* (Presbyterian Church (USA)), President, 2 Kensington Rd., San Anselmo, CA 94960 Tel. (415)258-6500 Fax (415)258-1608
Email: sftsinfo@sfts.edu
Website: www.sfts.edu

San Jose Christian College (Christian Churches and Churches of Christ), Bryce L. Jessup, President, 790 S. 12th St., P.O. Box 1090, San Jose, CA 95108 Tel. (408)293-9058 Fax (408)293-7352

Savonarola Theological Seminary (Polish National Catholic Church of America), Most Rev. John F. Swantek, Rector, 1031 Cedar Ave., Scranton, PA 18505 Tel. (570)343-0100

Seabury-Western Theological Seminary* (Episcopal Church), James B. Lemler, Dean, 2122 Sheridan Rd., Evanston, IL 60201-2976 Tel. (847)328-9300 Fax (847)328-9624
Email: swts@nwu.edu
Website: www.swts.nwu.edu

Seattle University School of Theology and Ministry* (The Roman Catholic Church and 10 Mainline Protestant Denominations and Associations), Rev. Patrick Howell, S.J., Interim Dean, 900 Broadway, Seattle, WA 98122 Tel. (206)296-5330 Fax (206)296-5329 Email: jrdavis@seattleu.edu
Website: www.seattleu.edu

Seminario Evangelico de Puerto Rico* (Interdenominational), Samuel Pagán, President, 776 Ponce de León Ave., San Juan, PR 00925 Tel. (787)763-6700 Fax (787)751-0847
Email: drspagan@icepr.com / jvaldes@tld.net
Website: netministries.org/see/charmin/CM01399

Seminary of the East (Conservative Baptist) (Conservative Baptist Association of America), Philip J. Baur, President, 1605 N. Limekiln Pike, Dresher, PA 19025 Tel. (215)641-4801 Fax (215)641-4804

Seminary of the Immaculate Conception* (The Catholic Church), Vincent F. Fullam, President, 440 West Neck Rd., Huntington, NY 11743 Tel. (516)423-0483 Fax (516)423-2346

Seventh-day Adventist Theological Seminary* (Seventh-day Adventist Church), John K. McVay, Dean, Andrews University, Berrien Springs, MI 49104-1500 Tel. (616)471-3537 Fax (616)471-6202
Email: seminary@andrews.edu
Website: www.andrews.edu/sem

Seventh Day Baptist School of Ministry (Seventh Day Baptist General Conference), Gabriel Bejjani, Dean of School of Ministry, 3120 Kennedy Rd., P.O. Box 1678, Janesville, WI 53547 Tel. (608)752-5055 Fax (608)752-7711
Email: sdbgen@inwave.com

Shaw Divinity School (Baptist), Talbert O. Shaw, President, P.O. Box 2090, Raleigh, NC 27602 Tel. (919)832-1701 Fax (919)832-6082

Simpson College (The Christian and Missionary Alliance), James M. Grant, President, 2211 College View Dr., Redding, CA 96003 Tel. (916)224-5600 Fax (916)224-5608

Southeastern Baptist College (Baptist Missionary Association of America), Jentry W. Bond, President, 4229 Highway 15N, Laurel, MS 39440 Tel. (601)426-6346 Fax (601)426-6346

Southeastern Baptist Theological Seminary* (Southern Baptist Convention), President Paige Patterson, President, 150-A North White Street, P.O. Box 1889, Wake Forest, NC 27588-1889 Tel. (919)556-3101 Fax (919)556-0998
Website: www.sebts.edu

Southeastern Bible College (Interdenominational), John D. Talley, President, 3001 Highway 280 E., Birmingham, AL 35243 Tel. (205)969-0880 Fax (205)970-9207
Email: 102064.406@compuserve.com
Website: www.sebc.edu

Southeastern College of the Assemblies of God (Assemblies of God), James L. Hennesy, President, 1000 Longfellow Blvd., Lakeland, FL 33801 Tel. (941)667-5000 Fax (941)667-5200

Southern Baptist Theological Seminary* (Southern Baptist Convention), R. Albert Mohler, Jr., President, 2825 Lexington Rd., Louisville, KY 40280 Tel. (502)897-4121 Fax (502)899-1770
Email: presoffice@sbts.edu
Website: www.sbts.edu

Southern Christian University (Churches of Christ), President Dr. Rex A. Turner, Jr., President, 1200 Taylor Rd., Montgomery, AL 36117-3553 Tel. (334)387-3877 Fax (334)387-3878
Email: southernchristian@southernchristian.edu
Website: www.southernchristian.edu

Southern Wesleyan University (The Wesleyan Church), President David J. Spittal, President, 907 Wesleyan Dr., P.O. Box 1020, Central, SC

29630-1020 Tel. (864)644-5000 Fax (864) 644-5900
Email: dspittal@swu.edu
Website: www.swu.edu

Southwestern Assemblies of God University (Assemblies of God), Delmer R. Guynes, President, 1200 Sycamore St., Waxahachie, TX 75165 Tel. (972)937-4010 Fax (972)923-0488

Southwestern Baptist Theological Seminary* (Southern Baptist Convention), Kenneth S. Hemphill, President, P.O. Box 22000, Fort Worth, TX 76122 Tel. (817)923-1921 Fax (817)923-0610
Website: www.swbts.edu

Southwestern College (Conservative Baptist Association of America), Brent D. Garrison, President, 2625 E. Cactus Rd., Phoenix, AZ 85032 Tel. (602)992-6101 Fax (602)404-2159

SS. Cyril and Methodius Seminary* (The Catholic Church), Francis B. Koper, Rector, 3535 Indian Trail, Orchard Lake, MI 48324-1623 Tel. (248)683-0311 Fax (248)738-6735
Email: 103244.3555@compuserve.com OR deansoff@sscms.edu
Website: www.metronet.lib.mi.us/aml.html (Library)
www.sscms.edu/deansoff (Seminary)

Starr King School for the Ministry* (Unitarian Universalist Association), Rebecca Parker, President, 2441 LeConte Ave., Berkeley, CA 94709 Tel. (510)845-6232 Fax (510)845-6273

Swedenborg School of Religion (The Swedenborgian Church), Dr. Mary Kay Klein, President, 48 Sargent St., Newton, MA 02458 Tel. (617)244-0504 Fax (617)558-0357
Email: maryk59988@aol.com

Talbot School of Theology* (Nondenominational), Dennis H. Dirks, President, 13800 Biola Ave., La Mirada, CA 90639-0001 Tel. (562)903-4816 Fax (562) 903-4759
Email: biola.edu/biola/talbot/
Website: www.talbot.edu

Temple Baptist Seminary (Independent Baptist), Barkev Trachian, President, 1815 Union Ave., Chattanooga, TN 37404 Tel. (423)493-4221 Fax (423)493-4471

Theological School of the Protestant Reformed Churches (Protestant Reformed Churches in America), Robert D. Decker, President, 4949 Ivanrest Ave., Grandville, MI 49418 Tel. (616)531-1490 Fax (616)531-3033
Email: decker@prca.org

Toccoa Falls College (The Christian and Missionary Alliance), Paul L. Alford, President, P.O. Box 800777, Toccoa Falls, GA 30598 Tel. (706)886-6831 Fax (706)282-6005
Email: president@toccoafalls.edu
Website: www.toccoafalls.edu

Trevecca Nazarene University (Church of the Nazarene), Millard Reed, President, 333 Murfreesboro Rd., Nashville, TN 37210-2877 Tel. (615)248-1200 Fax (615)248-7728
Website: www.trevecca.edu

Trinity Bible College (Assemblies of God), Howard Young, President, 50 S. 6th Ave., Ellendale, ND 58436 Tel. (701)349-3621 Fax (701)349-5443

Trinity College of Florida (Nondenominational), Paul L. Alford, President, 2430 Welbilt Blvd., New Port Richey, FL 34655-4401 Tel. (727)376-6911 Fax (727)376-0781
Email: trinity@gte.net
Website: www.trinitycollege.edu

Trinity Episcopal School for Ministry* (Episcopal Church), The Very Rev. Peter C. Moore, Dean and President, President, 311 Eleventh St., Ambridge, PA 15003 Tel. (412)266-3838 Fax (412)266-4617
Email: tinalockett@tesm.edu
Website: www.episcopalian.org

Trinity International University* (The Evangelical Free Church of America), Gregory L. Waybright, President, 2065 Half Day Rd., Deerfield, IL 60015 Tel. (847)945-8800 Fax (847)317-8090
Email: tedsadm@tiu.edu
Website: www.tiu.edu

Trinity Lutheran College (Interdenominational/Lutheran), John M. Stamm, President, 4221 - 228th Ave. S.E., Issaquah, WA 98029-9299 Tel. (425)392-0400 Fax (425)392-0404
Email: info@tlc.edu
Website: www.tlc.edu

Trinity Lutheran Seminary* (Evangelical Lutheran Church in America), Dennis A. Anderson, President, 2199 E. Main St., Columbus, OH 43209-2334 Tel. (614)235-4136 Fax (614)238-0263
Email: webmaster@trinity.capital.edu
Website: www.trinity.capital.edu

Union Theological Seminary* (Interdenominational), Joseph C. Hough, President, 3041 Broadway, New York, NY 10027 Tel. (212)662-7100 Fax (212)280-1416

Union Theological Seminary and Presbyterian School of Christian Education (Union-PSCE)* (Presbyterian Church (USA)), Louis B. Weeks, President, 3401 Brook Rd., Richmond, VA 23227 Tel. (804)355-0671 Fax (804)355-3919
Website: www.union-psce.edu

United Theological Seminary* (The United Methodist Church), Rev. Dr. G. Edwin Zeiders, President, 1810 Harvard Blvd., Dayton, OH 45406-4599 Tel. (937)278-5817 Fax (937)278-1218

291

Email: utsadmis@united.edu
Website: www.united.edu

United Theological Seminary of the Twin Cities* (United Church of Christ), Wilson Yates, President, 3000 Fifth St. N.W., New Brighton, MN 55112 Tel. (651)633-4311 Fax (651)633-4315
Email: general@unitedseminary-mn.org
Website: www.unitedseminary-mn.org

University of Chicago (Divinity School)* (Interdenominational), Richard Rosengarten, Dean, 1025 E. 58th St., Chicago, IL 60637 Tel. (773)702-8221 Fax (773)702-6048
Website: www2.uchicago.edu/divinity

University of Dubuque Theological Seminary* (Presbyterian Church (USA)), Jeffrey Bullock, President, 2000 University Ave., Dubuque, IA 52001 Tel. (319)589-3223 Fax (319)589-3682

University of Notre Dame, Dept. of Theology* (The Catholic Church), John C. Cavadini, Department Chair, Notre Dame, IN 46556 Tel. (219)631-7811 Fax (219)631-4268

University of St. Thomas School of Theology (The Catholic Church), Louis T. Brusatti, President, 9845 Memorial Dr., Houston, TX 77024 Tel. (713)686-4345 Fax (713)683-8673

University of the South School of Theology* (Episcopal Church), Guy Fitch Lytle, Dean, President, 335 Tennessee Ave., Sewanee, TN 37383-0001 Tel. (931)598-1288 Fax (931)598-1412
Email: glytle@seraph1.sewanee.edu
Website: www.sewanee.edu

Valley Forge Christian College (Assemblies of God), Earl Baldwin, President, 1401 Charlestown Rd., Phoenixville, PA 19460 Tel. (610)935-0450 Fax (610)935-9353

Vanderbilt University Divinity School* (Interdenominational), James Hudnut-Beumler, Dean, Nashville, TN 37240 Tel. (615)322-2776 Fax (615)343-9957
Website: www.vanderbilt.edu

Vennard College (Interdenominational), W. Edward Rickman, President, Box 29, University Park, IA 52595 Tel. (641)673-8391 Fax (641)673-8365
Email: vennard@vennard.edu
Website: www.vennard.edu

Virginia Union University (School of Theology)* (American Baptist Churches in the USA, National Baptist Convention, USA, Inc., Progressive National Baptist Convention, Inc., Lott Carey), John W. Kinney, Dean, 1500 N. Lombardy St., Richmond, VA 23220 Tel. (804)257-5715 Fax (804)342-3911

Walla Walla College (School of Theology) (Seventh-day Adventist Church), Ernest

Bursey, Dean, 204 S. College Ave., College Place, WA 99324-1198 Tel. (509)527-2194 Fax (509)527-2253
Email: burser@wwc.edu
Website: www.wwc.edu

Wartburg Theological Seminary* (Evangelical Lutheran Church in America), Duane H, Larson, President, 333 Wartburg Pl., Dubuque, LA 52004-5004 Tel. (319)589-0200 Fax (319)589-0333
Email: mailbox@wartburgseminary.edu

Washington Bible College/Capital Bible Seminary (Nondenominational), Homer Heater, President, 6511 Princess Garden Pkwy., Lanham, MD 20706 Tel. (301)552-1400 Fax (301)552-2775

Washington Theological Consortium (Non-denominational), John W. Crossin, Exec. Dir., President, 487 Michigan Ave. N.E., Washington, DC 20017 Tel. (202)832-2675 Fax (202)526-0818
Email: wtconsort@aol.com
Website: www.washtheocon.org

Washington Theological Union* (The Catholic Church), Daniel McLellan, O.F.M., President, 6896 Laurel St. N.W., Washington, DC 20012 Tel. (202)726-8800 Fax (202)726-1716
Email: mclellan@wtu.edu
Website: www.wtu.edu

Wesley Biblical Seminary* (Interdenominational), Robert R. Lawrence, President, P.O. Box 9938, Jackson, MS 39286-0938 Tel. (601)957-1314 Fax (601)957-1314

Wesley Theological Seminary* (The United Methodist Church), G. Douglass Lewis, President, 4500 Massachusetts Ave. N.W., Washington, DC 20016-5690 Tel. (800)882-4987 Fax (202)885-8600
Email: admiss@clark.net
Website: www.WesleySem.org

Western Evangelical Seminary* (Interdenominational), Ed Stevens, President, 12753 S.W. 68th Ave., Portland, OR 97223 Tel. (503)538-8383 Fax (503)598-4338

Western Seminary (Conservative Baptist Association of America), Ronald E. Hawkins, President, 5511 S.E. Hawthorne Blvd., Portland, OR 97215 Tel. (503)233-8561 Fax (503)239-4216

Western Theological Seminary* (Reformed Church in America), Dennis N. Voskuil, President, 101 E. 13th St., Holland, MI 49423 Tel. (616)392-8555 Fax (616)392-7717
Website: www.westernsem.org

Westminster Theological Seminary* (Non-denominational), Samuel T. Logan, President, Chestnut Hill, P.O. Box 27009, Philadelphia, PA 19118 Tel. (215)887-5511 Fax (215)887-3459

Email: slogan@wts.edu
Website: www.wts.edu

Westminster Theological Seminary in California* (Nondenominational), W. Robert Godfrey, President, 1725 Bear Valley Pkwy, Escondido, CA 92027-4128 Tel. (760)480-8474 Fax (760)480-0252
Website: www.wtscal.edu

Weston Jesuit School of Theology* (The Catholic Church), Robert Manning, President, 3 Phillips Pl., Cambridge, MA 02138 Tel. (617)492-1960 Fax (617)492-5833
Email: Admissionsinfo@wjst.edu

William Tyndale College (Interdenominational), James C. McHann, President, 35700 W. Twelve Mile Rd., Farmington Hills, MI 48331 Tel. (248)553-7200 Fax (248)553-5963
Website: www.williamtyndale.edu

Winebrenner Theological Seminary* (Churches of God, General Conference), David E. Draper, President, 701 E. Melrose Ave., P.O. Box 478, Findlay, OH 45839 Tel. (419)422-4824 Fax (419)422-3999
Email: wts@winebrenner.edu
Website: www.winebrenner.edu

Wisconsin Lutheran Seminary (Wisconsin Evangelical Lutheran Synod), David J. Valleskey, President, 11831 N. Seminary Dr., 65W, Mequon, WI 53092 Tel. (262)242-8100 Fax (262)242-8110
Website: www.wls.wels.net

Yale University Divinity School* Richard J. Wood, President, 409 Prospect St., New Haven, CT 06511 Tel. (203)432-5303 Fax (203)432-5356
Email: ydsadmsn@yale.edu
Website: www.yale.edu/divinity

10. Theological Seminaries and Bible Colleges in Canada

The following list includes theological seminaries and departments in colleges and universities in which ministerial training is provided. Many denominations have additional programs. Consult Directory 4, "Religious Bodies in Canada" for headquarters information for these denominations. The list has been developed from direct correspondence with the institutions. Inclusion in or exclusion from this list implies no judgment about the quality or accreditation of any institution. Those schools that are members (both accredited and affiliated) of the Association of Theological Schools are marked with an asterisk (*). Each of the listings include: the institution name, denominational sponsor when appropriate, location, the president or dean, telephone and fax numbers when known and email and website addresses when available.

Acadia Divinity University* (United Baptist Convention of the Atlantic Provinces), Lee M. McDonald, Principal, Acadia University, Wolfville, NS B0P 1X0 Tel. (902)585-2210 Fax (902)542-7527
Email: adcinfo@acadiau.ca
Website: http://ace.acadiau.ca/divcol

Alberta Bible College (Christian Churches and Churches of Christ in Canada), Ronald A. Fraser, President, 635 Northmount Dr. N.W., Calgary, AB T2K 3J6 Tel. (403)282-2994 Fax (403)282-3084
Email: abbible@cadvision.com
Website: www.abc-ca.org

Associated Canadian Theological Schools of Trinity Western University* (Baptist General Conference of Canada, Evangelical Free Church of Canada, The Fellowship of Evangelical Baptist Churches in Canada, Christian and Missionary Alliance, Canadian Conference of Mennonite Brethren Churches), Guy S. Saffold, Coordinator, 7600 Glover Rd., Langley, BC V2Y 1Y1 Tel. (604)513-2044 Fax (604)513-2045
Email: acts@twu.ca
Website: www.acts.twu.ca

Atlantic School of Theology* (Interdenominational), Gordon Mac Dermid, President, 640 Francklyn St., Halifax, NS B3H 3B5 Tel. (902)423-6801 Fax (902)492-4048

Baptist Leadership Training School (Canadian Baptist Ministries), Hugh Fraser, President, 4330 16th St. S.W., Calgary, AB T2T 4H9 Tel. (403)243-3770 Fax (403)287-1930
Email: blts@imag.net
Website: www.yet.ca

Bethany Bible College-Canada (The Wesleyan Church), Dr. David S. Medders, President, 26 Western St., Sussex, NB E4E 1E6 Tel. (506)432-4400 Fax (506)432-4425
Website: www.bethany.ca.edu

Bethany Bible Institute (Canadian Conference of Mennonite Brethren Churches of SK; Canadian Conference of Mennonite Brethren Churches of AB; Evangelical Mennonite Mission Conference of SK), Rick Schellenberg, President, Box 160, Hepburn, SK S0K 1Z0 Tel. (306)947-2175 Fax (306)947-4229
Email: bethany@sk.sympatico.ca
Website: www.bethany.sk.ca

Briercrest Biblical Seminary* (Interdenominational), President, Enrollment Services, Briercrest Family of Schools 510 College Dr., Caronport, SK S0H 0S0 Tel. (800)667-5199 Fax (306)756-3366
Website: www.briercrest.ca

Briercrest Family of Schools (Bible College & Seminary)* (Transdenominational), Dr. Paul Magnus, President, Enrollment Services, Briercrest family of schools 510 College Dr., Caronport, SK S0H 0S0 Tel. (800)667-5199 Fax (306)756-3366
Email: enrollment@briercrest.ca
Website: www.briercrest.ca

Canadian Bible College (Christian and Missionary Alliance in Canada), Dr. George Durance, President, 4400-4th Ave., Regina, SK S4T 0H8 Tel. (306)545-1515 Fax (306)545-0210
Email: gdurance@cbccts.sk.ca
Website: www.cbccts.sk.ca

Canadian Lutheran Bible Institute (Lutheran), Norman C. Miller, President, 4837 52A St., Camrose, AB T4V 1W5 Tel. (780)672-4454 Fax (780)672-4455
Email: clbi@clbi.edu

Canadian Nazarene College (Church of the Nazarene Canada), Riley Coulter, President, 610, 833 4th Ave. SW, Calgary, AB T2P 3T5 Tel. (403)571-2550 Fax (403)571-2556
Email: cncoff@cnaz.ab.ca
Website: www.cnaz.ab.ca

Canadian Theological Seminary* (Christian and Missionary Alliance in Canada), Dr. George Durance, President, 4400 4th Ave., Regina, SK S4T 0H8 Tel. (306)545-1515 Fax (306)545-0210
Email: gdurance@cbccts.sk.ca
Website: www.cbccts.sk.ca

Central Pentecostal College, University of Saskatchewan (The Pentecostal Assemblies of Canada), D. Munk, President, 1303 Jackson Ave., Saskatoon, SK S7H 2M9 Tel. (306)374-6655 Fax (306)373-6968
Email: admissions@cpcsk.org
Website: www.cpssk.org

Centre for Christian Studies (The Anglican Church of Canada, The United Church of Canada), Caryn Douglas, Principal, 60 Maryland, Winnipeg, MB R3G 1K7 Tel. (204)783-4490 Fax (204)786-3012
Email: centre@escape.ca
Website: www.escape.ca/~centre

Church Army College of Evangelism (The Anglican Church of Canada), Roy E. Dickson, President, 397 Brunswick Ave., Toronto, ON M5R 2Z2 Tel. (416)924-9279 Fax (416)924-2931

College Biblique Québec (The Pentecostal Assemblies of Canada), William Raccah, President, 740 Lebourgneuf, Ste. 100, Ancienne Lorette, QC G2J 1E2 Tel. (418)622-7552 Fax (418)622-1470

Collége Dominicain de Philosophie et de Théologie (The Roman Catholic Church in Canada), Michel Gourgues, President, 96 Avenue Empress, Ottawa, ON K1R 7G3 Tel. (613)233-5696 Fax (613)233-6064

College of Emmanuel and St. Chad (The Anglican Church of Canada), William Niels Christensen, President, 1337 College Dr., Saskatoon, SK S7N 0W6 Tel. (306)975-3753 Fax (306)934-2683
Email: christen@duke.usask.ca

Columbia Bible College (Mennonite), Walter Unger, President, 2940 Clearbrook Rd., Abbotsford, BC V2T 2Z8 Tel. (604)853-3358 Fax (604)853-3063
Email: info@columbiabc.edu
Website: www.columbiabc.edu

Concord College at Canadian Mennonite University (Mennonite Brethren Churches), John H. Unger, President, 500 Shaftesbury Blvd., Winnipeg, MB R3P 2N2 Tel. (204)669-6583 Fax (204)663-2468
Email: info@cmu.ca
Website: www.cmu.ca

Concordia Lutheran Seminary* (Lutheran Church-Canada), L. Dean Hempelmann, President, 7040 Ada Blvd., Edmonton, AB T5B 4E3 Tel. (780)474-1468 Fax (780)479-3067
Email: gstresma@spartan.ac.brocku.ca

Concordia Lutheran Theological Seminary* (Lutheran Church-Canada), Jonathan Grothe, President, 470 Glenridge Ave., St. Catharines, ON L2T 4C3 Tel. (905)688-2362 Fax (905)688-9744

Covenant Bible College (The Evangelical Covenant Church of Canada), Campuses: CANADA: 630 Westchester Rd., Strathmore, AB T1P 1H8 Tel. (403)934-6200 Fax (403)934-6220
Email: covbibco@cadvision.com
Website: www.covenantbiblecollege.ab.ca
COLORADO: 675 Southwood Ln., Windsor, CO 80550 Tel. (970)686-6977 Fax (970)686-6977
Email: 103354.2431@compuserve.com

Eastern Pentecostal Bible College (The Pentecostal Assemblies of Canada), Carl F. Verge, President, 780 Argyle St., Peterborough, ON K9H 5T2 Tel. (705)748-9111 Fax (705)748-3931

Edmonton Baptist Seminary* (North American Baptist Conference), Dr. Marvin Dewey, President, 11525-23 Ave., Edmonton, AB T6J 4T3 Tel. (780)431-5200 Fax (780)436-9416
Email: mdewey@nabcebs.ab.ca
Website: www.nabcebs.ab.ca

Emmanuel Bible College (The Evangelical Missionary Church of Canada), Thomas E. Dow, President, 100 Fergus Ave., Kitchener, ON N2A 2H2 Tel. (519)894-8900 Fax (519)894-5331
Email: dmin@ebcollege.on.ca
Website: www.ebcollege.on.ca

Emmanuel College* (The United Church of Canada), Roger C. Hutchinson, Principal, 75 Queens Park Crescent, Toronto, ON M5S 1K7 Tel. (416)585-4539 Fax (416)585-4516
Email: ec.office@utoronto.ca
Website: http://vicu.utoronto.ca

Faculté De Théologie Évangélique (Union d'Eglises Baptistes Françaises au Canada), Amar Djaballah, President, 2285 Avenue Papineau, Montréal, QC H2K 4J5 Tel. (514)526-2003 Fax (514)526-6887

Faith Alive Bible College (Nondenominational), David Pierce, President, 637 University Dr., Saskatoon, SK S7N 0H8 Tel. (306)652-2230 Fax (306)665-1125
Email: faithalive@dlcwest.com

Full Gospel Bible Institute (Apostolic Church of Pentecost of Canada Inc.), Rev. Lauren E. Miller, President, Box 579, Eston, SK S0L 1A0 Tel. (306)962-3621 Fax (306)962-3810
Email: fgbi.eston@sk.sympatico.ca
Website: fgbi.sk.ca

Gardner College, A Centre for Christian Studies (Church of God (Anderson, Ind.)), John Alan Howard, President, 4704 55th St., Camrose, AB T4V 2B6 Tel. (780)672-0171 Fax (780)672-6888
Email: gardnerc@cable-lynx.net
Website: http://cable-lynx/~gardnerc

Grand Seminaire de Montréal* (The Roman Catholic Church in Canada), Louis-Paul Gauvreau, President, 2065 Sherbrook Ouest, Montréal, QC H3H 1G6 Tel. (514)935-1169 Fax (514)935-5497
Email: Information Generale: infor@gsdm.qc.ca OR Bibliotheque: biblio@gsdm.qc.ca
Website: www.gsdm.qc.ca

Great Lakes Bible College (Churches of Christ in Canada), Dr. Geoffrey Ellis, Principal, 62 Hickory St. W., Waterloo, ON N2L 3J4 Tel. (519)884-4310 Fax (519)884-4412
Email: learn@glbc.on.ca
Website: www.glbc.on.ca

Heritage Baptist College and Heritage Theological Seminary* (The Fellowship of Evangelical Baptist Churches in Canada), Marvin Brubacher, President, 175 Holiday Inn Dr., Cambridge, ON N3C 3T2 Tel. (519)651-2869 Fax (519)651-2870
Email: admin@heritage-theo.edu
Website: www.heritage-theo.edu

Huron College* (The Anglican Church of Canada), Dr. David Bevan, Principal, 1349 Western Rd., London, ON N6G 1H3 Tel. (519)438-7224 Fax (519)438-3938

Institut Biblique Beree (The Pentecostal Assemblies of Canada), André L. Gagnon, President, 1711 Henri-Bourassa Est, Montréal, QC H2C 1J5 Tel. (514)385-4238 Fax (514)385-4238

Ecole de Theologie Evangelique de Montreal (Canadian Conference of Mennonite Brethren Churches), Eric Wingender, President, 1775, boul Édouard-Laurin, Ville Saint-Laurent, QC H4L 2B9 Tel. (514)331-0878 Fax (514)331-0879
Email: iblinstitute@proxyma.net

Institute for Christian Studies (Nondenominational), Harry Fernhout, President, 229 College St., Suite 200, Toronto, ON M5T 1R4 Tel. (416)979-2331 or 1 (888)326-5347 Fax (416)979-2332
Email: email@icscanada.edu
Website: www.icscanada.edu

International Bible College (Church of God (Cleveland, Tenn.), Alex Allan, President, 401 Trinity La., Moose Jaw, SK S6H 0E3 Tel. (306)692-4041 Fax (306)692-7968

Joint Board of Theological Colleges* (Interdenominational), Dr. John Simons, President, 3473 University St., MontrÇal, QC H3A 2A8 Tel. (514)849-8511 Fax (514)849-4113
Email: dio@colba.net
Website: www.mcgill.ca/religion/jbtc.htm

Key-Way-Tin Bible Institute (Nondenominational), Dir. Dave Petkau, President, Box 540,

Lac La Biche, AB T0A 2C0 Tel. (780)623-4565 Fax (780)623-1788
Email: kbi@telusplanet.net

Knox College* (The Presbyterian Church in Canada), J. Dorcas Gordon, President, 59 St. George St., Toronto, ON M5S 2E6 Tel. (416)978-4500 Fax (416)971-2133
Email: knox.college@utoronto.ca
Website: www.utoronto.ca/knox

Living Faith Bible College (Fellowship of Christian Assembies (Canada)), Cliff A. Stalwick, President, Box 100, Caroline, AB T0M 0M0 Tel. (403)722-2225 Fax (403)722-2459
Email: office@lfbc.net
Website: www.lfbc.net

Lutheran Theological Seminary* (Evangelical Lutheran Church in Canada), Faith Rohrbough, President, 114 Seminary Crescent, Saskatoon, SK S7N 0X3 Tel. (306)966-7850 Fax (306)966-7852
Email: rohrb@duke.usask.ca
Website: www.usask.ca/stu/luther

Maritime Christian College (Christian Churches and Churches of Christ in Canada), Fred C. Osborne, President, 503 University Ave., Charlottetown, PE C1A 7Z4 Tel. (902)628-8887 Fax (902)892-3959
Email: registrar@maritimechristiancollege.pe.ca
Website: www.maritimechristiancollege.pe.ca

McGill University Faculty of Religious Studies* (Interdenominational), Donna R. Runnalls, President, 3520 University St., Montréal, QC H3A 2A7 Tel. (514)398-4121 Fax (514)398-6665

McMaster Divinity College* (Baptist), Principal/Dean, McMaster Divinity College, Hamilton, ON L8S 4K1 Tel. (905)525-9140 Ext 24401 Fax (905)577-4782
Email: divinity@mcmaster.ca
Website: www.mcmaster.ca/divinity

Millar College of the Bible (Interdenominational), A. Brian Atmore, President, Box 25, Pambrun, SK S0N 1W0 Tel. (306)582-2033 Fax (306)582-2027

Montreal Diocesan Theological College* (The Anglican Church of Canada), The Rev. Dr. Jon Simons, Principal, 3473 University St., Montreal, QC H3A 2A8 Tel. (514)849-3004 Fax (514)849-4113
Email: diocoll@netrover.com
Website: www.montreal.anglican.org/mdtc

Mount Carmel Bible School (Christian Brethren (also known as Plymouth Brethren)), Gordon King, President, 4725 106 Ave., Edmonton, AB T6A 1E7 Tel. (780)465-3015 Toll-free 1(800) 561-6443 Fax (780)466-2485
Email: carmel@worldgate.com

National Native Bible College (Elim Fellowship of Evangelical Churches and

Ministers), Donovan Jacobs, College Director, Box 478, Deseronto, ON K0K 1X0 Tel. (613)396-2311 Fax (613)396-2314

Newman Theological College* (The Roman Catholic Church in Canada), Kevin J. Carr, President, 15611 St. Albert Trail, Edmonton, AB T6V 1H3 Tel. (780)447-2993 Fax (780)447-2685
Email: ntc.webmaster@newman.edu
Website: www.newman.edu

Nipawin Bible Institute (Interdenominational), Mark Leppington, President, Box 1986, Nipawin, SK S0E 1E0 Tel. (306)862-5095 Fax (306)862-3651
Email: nbi@sk.sympatico.ca
Website: www.nipawinbibleinstitute.sk.ca

Northwest Baptist Theological College and Seminary (The Fellowship of Evangelical Baptist Churches in Canada), Dr. Larry Perkins, Interim President, 7600 Glover Rd., Langley, BC V2Y 1Y1 Tel. (604)888-7592 Fax (604)888-8511
Email: College: nbs@twu.ca OR Seminary-NBS: acts@twu.ca
Website: www.nbseminary.com

Northwest Bible College (The Pentecostal Assemblies of Canada), G. Johnson, President, 11617-106 Ave., Edmonton, AB T5H 0S1 Tel. (780)452-0808 Fax (780)452-5803
Email: info@nwbc.ab.ca
Website: www.nwbc.ab.ca

Ontario Christian Seminary (Christian Churches and Churches of Christ in Canada), James R. Cormode, President, P.O. Box 324, Stn. D 260 High Park Ave., Toronto, ON M6P 3J9 Tel. (416)769-7115 Fax (416)769-7047

Pacific Life Bible College (Foursquare), Rob Buzza, President, 15100 66 A Ave., Surrey, BC V3S 2A6 Tel. (604)597-9082 Fax (604)597-9090
Email: paclife@pacificlife.edu
Website: www.pacificlife.edu

Parole de Vie Bethel/Word of Life Bethel (Nondenominational), Ken Beach, President, 1175 Chemin Woodward, Lennoxville, QC J1M 2A2 Tel. (819)823-8435 Fax (819)823-2468
Email: quebec@canada.wol.org
Website: www.wol.org

Peace River Bible Institute (Interdenominational), Reuben Kvill, President, Box 99, Sexsmith, AB T0H 3C0 Tel. (780)568-3962 Fax (780)568-4431
Email: prbi@telusplanet.net
Website: www.prbi.edu

Prairie Graduate School* (Interdenominational), Rick Down, President, 2540 5 Ave. NW, Calgary, AB T2N 0T5 Tel. (403)777-0150 Fax (403)270-2336

The Presbyterian College, Montreal* (Presbyterian Church in Canada), John Vissers, Principal, 3495 University St., Montreal, QC H3A 2A8 Tel. (514)288-5256 Fax (514)288-8072

Providence College and Theological Seminary* (Interdenominational), Larry J. McKinney, President, General Delivery, Otterburne, MB R0A 1G0 Tel. (204)433-7488 Fax (204)433-7158
Email: info@providence.mb.ca
Website: www.providence.mb.ca

Queens College* (The Anglican Church of Canada), Boyd Morgan, President, 210 Prince Phillip Dr., St. Johns, NF A1B 3R6 Tel. (709)753-0116 Fax (709)753-1214
Email: queens@morgan.ucs.mun.ca
Website: www.mun.ca/queens

Queen's Theological College* (The United Church of Canada), Hallett E. Llewellyn, President, Queen's Theological College, Kingston, ON K7L 3N6 Tel. (613)545-2110 Fax (613)545-6879
Email: theology@post.queensu.ca
Website: http://info.queensu.ca/theology/qtchome.html

Reformed Episcopal Theological College (Reformed Episcopal Church of Canada), Rt. Rev. Michael Fedechko, President, 320 Armstrong St., Box 2532, New Liskeard, ON P0J 1P0 Tel. (705)647-4565 Fax (705)647-4565
Email: fed@nt.net
Website: www.recorg.us

Regent College* (Interdenominational), Walter C. Wright, President, 5800 University Blvd., Vancouver, BC V6T 2E4 Tel. (800)663-8664 Fax (604)224-3097
Email: regentcollege@compuserve.com
Website: www.regent-college.edu

Regis College* (The Roman Catholic Church in Canada), John Allan Loftus, S.J, President, 15 St. Mary St., Toronto, ON M4Y 2R5 Tel. (416)922-5474 Fax (416)922-2898
Email: regis.registrar@utoronto.ca
Website: www.utoronto.ca/regis

Rocky Mountain College: Centre for Biblical Studies (The Evangelical Missionary Church of Canada), Gordon Dirks, President, 4039 Brentwood Rd. NW, Calgary, AB T2L 1L1 Tel. (403)284-5100 Fax (403)220-9567
Email: admin@rockyme.edu
Website: www.rockyme.edu

St. Andrew's Theological College* (The United Church of Canada), Dr. Christopher Lind, President, 1121 College Dr., Saskatoon, SK S7N 0W3 Tel. (306)966-8970 Fax (306)966-8981
Website: www.usask.ca/stul

297

St. Augustine's Seminary of Toronto* (The Roman Catholic Church in Canada), John A. Boissonneau, President, 2661 Kingston Rd., Scarborough, ON M1M 1M3 Tel. (416)261-7207 Fax (416)261-2529
Website: www. canxsys.com/staugust.htm

St. John's College, Univ. of Manitoba, Faculty of Theology (The Anglican Church of Canada), B. Hudson McLean, President, 92 Dysart Rd., Winnipeg, MB R3T 2M5 Tel. (204)474-6852 Fax (204)261-1215

Saint Paul University, Faculty of Theology (The Roman Catholic Church), David B. Perrin, Ph.D., Dean, 223 Main St., Ottawa, ON K1S 1C4 Tel. (613)236-1393 x. 2246 Fax (613)751-4016
Email: fquesnal@ustpaul.uottawa.ca
Website: www.ustpaul.ca

St. Peter's Seminary* (The Roman Catholic Church in Canada), Thomas C. Collins, President, 1040 Waterloo St., London, ON N6A 3Y1 Tel. (519)432-1824 Fax (519)432-0964

St. Stephen's College, Grad. & Continuing Theological Educucation* (The United Church of Canada), Dr. Christopher Lind, President, 8810 112th St., Edmonton, AB T6G 2J6 Tel. (780)439-7311 Fax (780)433-8875
Email: clind@ualberta.ca
Website: www.ualberta.ca/st.stephens

Salvation Army College for Officer Training (The Salvation Army in Canada), Wayne N. Pritchett, Principal, 2130 Bayview Ave., North York, ON M4N 3K6 Tel. (416)481-6131 Fax (416)481-6810; (416)481-2895 (Library)

The Salvation Army William and Catherine Booth College (The Salvation Army in Canada), Dr. Jonathan S. Raymond, President, 447 Webb Pl., Winnipeg, MB R3B 2P2 Tel. (204)947-6701 Fax (204)942-3856
Email: wcbc@sallynet.org
Website: www.wcbc-sa.edu

Steinbach Bible College (Mennonite), Stan Plett, President, Box 1420, Steinbach, MB R0A 2A0 Tel. (204)326-6451 Fax (204)326-6908
Email: pr@sbcollege.mb.ca
Website: www.sbcollege.mb.ca

Theological College of the Canadian Reformed Churches (Canadian and American Reformed Churches), N. H. Gootjes, President, 110 West 27th St., Hamilton, ON L9C 5A1 Tel. (416)575-3688 Fax (416)575-0799

Toronto Baptist Seminary and Bible College (Nondenominational), Andrew M. Fountain, Principal, 130 Gerrard St., E., Toronto, ON M5A 3T4 Tel. (416)925-3263 Fax (416)925-8305

Email: tbs@tbs.edu
Website: www.tbs.edu

Toronto School of Theology* (Interdenominational), W. David Neelands, Director, 47 Queens Park Crescent E., Toronto, ON M5S 2C3 Tel. (416)978-4039 Fax (416)978-7821
Email: registrar.tst@utoronto.ca
Website: www.utoronto.ca/tst

Trinity College, Faculty of Divinity* (The Anglican Church of Canada), D. Wiebe, Dean, 6 Hoskin Ave., Toronto, ON M5S 1H8 Tel. (416)978-2133 Fax (416)978-4949
Email: divinity@trinity.utoronto.ca
Website: www.trinity.utoronto.ca/divinity

Tyndale College & Seminary* (Trans-denominational), Dr. Brian C. Stiller, President, 25 Ballyconnor Ct., Toronto, ON M2M 4B3 Tel. (416)226-6380 Fax (416)226-6746
Email: info@tyndale-canada.edu
Website: www.tyndale-canada.edu

United Theological College/Le Séminaire Uni* (The United Church of Canada), Rev. Philip Joudrey, President, 3521 rue Université, Montréal, QC H3A 2A9 Tel. (514)849-2042 Fax (514)849-8634
Email: infoutc@colba.net
Website: www.colba.net/~utc/

Université Laval, Faculté de théologie et de sciences religieuses (The Roman Catholic Church in Canada), Marc Pelchat, President, Cité Universitaire, Ste-Foy, QC G1K 7P4 Tel. (418)656-2131 Fax (418)656-3273
Email: ftsr@ftsr.ulaval.ca
Website: www.ulaval.ca

Université de Montréal, Faculté de théologie (The Roman Catholic Church in Canada), Jean-Marc Charron, President, C. P. 6128 Succ. Centre Ville, Montréal, QC H3C 3J7 Tel. (514)343-7160 Fax (514)343-5738
Email: theologie@ere.umontreal.ca
Website: www.theo.umontreal.ca

Université de Sherbrooke, Faculté de theologié (The Roman Catholic Church in Canada), Jean-François Malherbe, President, 2500 boul. Université, Sherbrooke, QC J1K 2R1 Tel. (819)821-7600 Fax (819)821-7677

University of St. Michael's College, Faculty of Theology* (The Roman Catholic Church in Canada), Dean Brian F. Hogan, President, 81 St. Mary St., Toronto, ON M5S 1J4 Tel. (416)926-7140 Fax (416)926-7294
Website: www.utoronto.ca/stmikes/index.html

The University of Winnipeg, Faculty of Theology* (Multi-denominational and the United Church of Canada), Gordon MacDermid, Dean, 515 Portage Ave., Winnipeg, MB R3B 2E9 Tel. (204)786-9390 Fax (204)772-2584

Email: theology@uwinnipeg.ca
Website: www.uwinnipeg.ca/academic/theology

Vancouver School of Theology* (Interdenominational), Rev. Dr. W. J. Phillips, President, 6000 Iona Dr., Vancouver, BC V6T 1L4 Tel. (604)822-9031 Fax (604)822-9212
Email: vstinfo@vst.edu
Website: www.vst.edu

Waterloo Lutheran Seminary* (Evangelical Lutheran Church in Canada), Richard C. Crossman, President, 75 University Ave. W., Waterloo, ON N2L 3C5 Tel. (519)884-1970 Fax (519)725-2434
Website: www.wlu.ca/~wwwsem/

Western Christian College (Churches of Christ in Canada), John McMillan, President, Box 5000, 220 Whitmore Ave. W., Dauphin, MB R7N 2V5 Tel. (204)638-8801 Fax (204)638-7054
Email: jmcmilla@mbnet.mb.ca
Website: http://wcc.pein.org

Western Pentecostal Bible College (The Pentecostal Assemblies of Canada), James G. Richards, President, Box 1700, Abbotsford, BC V2S 7E7 Tel. (604)853-7491 Fax (604)853-8951
Email: wpbcr@uniserve.com

Winkler Bible Institute (Canadian Conference of Mennonite Brethren Churches), Paul Kroeker, President, 121 7 St. S., Winkler, MB R6W 2N4 Tel. (204)325-4242 Fax (204)325-9028

Wycliffe College* (The Anglican Church of Canada), Rev. Dr. George R. Sumner, Jr., President, 5 Hoskin Ave., Toronto, ON M5S 1H7 Tel. (416)946-3535 Fax (416)946-3545
Email: wycliffe.college@utoronto.ca
Website: www.chass.utoronto.ca/wycliffe

11. Religious Periodicals in the United States

This list focuses on publications of the organizations listed in Directory 3, "Religious Bodies in the United States," however there are also some independent publications listed. The list does not include all publications prepared by religious bodies, and not all the publications listed here are necessarily the official publication of a particular church. Regional publications and newsletters are not included. A more extensive list of religious periodicals published in the United States can be found in *Gale Directory of Publications and Broadcast Media*, (Gale Research, Inc., P.O. Box 33477, Detroit MI 48232-5477).

Each entry in this directory contains: the title of the periodical, frequency of publication, religious affiliation, editor's name, address, telephone and fax number and e-mail and website addresses when available. The frequency of publication, which appears in parenthesis after the name of the publication is represented by a "W." for weekly; "M." for monthly; "Q." for quarterly.

21st Century Christian, (M.) Churches of Christ, M. Norvel Young and Prentice A. Meador, Jr., Box 40304, Nashville, TN 37204 Tel. (800)331-5991 Fax (615)385-5915

The A.M.E. Christian Recorder, (bi-W.) African Methodist Episcopal Church, Ricky Spain, 500 8th Ave., S., Suite 213 Nashville, TN 37203 Tel. (615)256-8548 Fax (615)244-1833

A.M.E. Church Review, (Q.) African Methodist Episcopal Church, Paulette Coleman, PhD., 500 Eighth Ave., S., Ste.211, Nashville, TN 37203-4181 Tel. (615)256-7020 Fax (615) 256-7092
Email: AMERVW@aol.com

Action, (10/Y.) Churches of Christ, Dr. R. H. Tex Williams, P.O. Box 2169, Cedar Park, TX 78630-2169 Tel. (512)345-8191 Fax (512) 345-6634
Email: wbschool@bga.com
Website: www.wbschool.org

Adra Today, (Q.) Seventh-day Adventist Church, Beth Schaefer, 12501 Old Columbia Pike, Silver Spring, MD 20904-6600 Tel. (301)680-6355 Fax (301)680-6370
Email: 74617.2105@compuserve.com
Website: www.adra.org

Adult Lessons Quarterly, (Q.) Nondenominational, Braille and cassette tape only, Darcy Quigley, J. Milton Society for the Blind, 475 Riverside Dr., Rm. 455, New York, NY 10115-0455 Tel. (212)870-3335 Fax (212)870-3229
Email: order@jmsblind.org
Website: www.jmsblind.org

The Adult Quarterly, (Q.) Associate Reformed Presbyterian Church (General Synod), Mr. W. H. F. Kuykendall PhD., P.O. Box 575, Due West, SC 29639 Tel. (864)379-2284
Email: wkuykend@erskine.edu

Advent Christian News, (M.) Advent Christian Church, Rev. Keith D. Wheaton, P.O. Box 23152, Charlotte, NC 28227 Tel. (704)545-6161 Fax (704)573-0712
Email: Mayerpub@aol.com

The Advent Christian Witness, (M.) Advent Christian Church, Rev. Keith D. Wheaton, P.O. Box 23152, Charlotte, NC 28227 Tel. (704)545-6161 Fax (704)573-0712
Email: Mayerpub@aol.com

Adventist Review, (W.) Seventh-day Adventist Church, W. G. Johnsson, 12501 Old Columbia Pike, Silver Spring, MD 20904-6600 Tel. (301)680-6560 Fax (301)680-6638
Email: 74617,15.compuserve.com
Website: www.adventistreview.com

The Advocate, (10/Y.) Episcopal, Kay Collier-Slone, Ph.D., PO Box 610, Lexington, KY 40588-0610 Tel. (606)252-6527 Fax (606) 231-9077
Email: diolex@aol.com

Again Magazine, (Q.) The Antiochian Orthodox Christian Archdiocese of North America, R. Thomas Zell, P.O. Box 76, Ben Lomond, CA 95005-0076 Tel. (831)336-5118 Fax (831) 336-8882
Email: marketing@conciliarpress.com
Website: www.conciliarpress.com

Agenda, (10/Y.) Church of the Brethren, Howard Royer and Walt Wiltschek, 1451 Dundee Ave., Elgin, IL 60120-1676 Tel. (847)742-5100
Email: hroyer-gb@brethren.org or wwiltschek-gb@brethren.org
Website: www.brethren.org

Alive Now, (6/Y.) The United Methodist Church, George Graham, P.O. Box 34004, Nashville, TN 37203-0004 Tel. (615)340-7218
Email: alivenow@upperroom.org
Website: www.upperroom.org/alivenow/

The Allegheny Wesleyan Methodist, (M.) Allegheny Wesleyan Methodist Connection (Original Allegheny Conference), Michael

Marshall, P.O. Box 357, Salem, OH 44460 Tel. (330)337-9376 Fax (330)337-9700 Email: awmc@juno.com

Alliance Life, (M.) The Christian and Missionary Alliance, Stephen P. Adams, P.O. Box 35000, Colorado Springs, CO 80935 Tel. (719)599-5999 Fax (719)599-8234 Email: alife@cmalliance.org Website: www.alliancelife.org

American Baptist In Mission, (6/Y.) American Baptist Churches in the USA, Richard W. Schramm, P.O. Box 851, Valley Forge, PA 19482-0851 Tel. (610)768-2077 Fax (610)768-2320 Email: richard.schramm@abc-usa.org Website: www.abc-usa.org

American Baptist Quarterly, (Q.) American Baptist Churches in the USA, Dr. Robert E. Johnson, P.O. Box 851, Valley Forge, PA 19482-0851 Tel. (610)768-2269 Fax (610)768-2266 Email: naomi.reynolds@abc-usa.org Website: www.abc-usa/abhs

American Bible Society Record, (6/Y.) Nondenominational, Peter Feuerherd, 1865 Broadway, New York, NY 10023-7505 Tel. (212)408-1419 Fax (212)408-1456 Email: absrecord@americanbible.org Website: www.americanbible.org

El Aposento Alto, (6/Y.) The United Methodist Church, Carmen Gaud, P.O. Box 340004, Nashville, TN 37203-0004 Tel. (615)340-7253 Fax (615)340-7267 Email: ElAposentoAlto@upperroom.org Website: www.upperroom.org

The Armenian Church, (M.) Diocese of the Armenian Church of America, Michael A. Zeytoonian, 630 Second Avenue, New York, NY 10016 Tel. (212)686-0710 Fax (212)779-3558

The Associate Reformed Presbyterian, (M.) Associate Reformed Presbyterian Church (General Synod), Mr. Ben Johnston, One Cleveland St., Greenville, SC 29601 Tel. (864)232-8297 Fax (864)271-3729 Email: arpmaged@arpsynod.org Website: www.arpsynod.org

At Ease, (bi-M.) Assemblies of God, Charles W. Marvin, 1445 Boonville Ave., Springfield, MO 65802 Tel. (417)862-2781 Fax (417)863-7276 Email: chaplaincy@ag.org Website: http://chaplaincy.ag.org

Attack, A Magazine for Christian Men, (Q.) National Association for Free Will Baptists, James E. Vallance, P.O. Box 5002, Antioch, TN 37011-5002 Tel. (615)731-4950 Fax (615)731-0771

The Banner of Truth, (M.) Netherlands Reformed Congregations, J. den Hoed, 824 18th Ave. S., Rock Valley, IA 51247 Tel. (712)476-2442

The Banner, (26/Y.) Christian Reformed Church in North America, John A. Suk, 2850 Kalamazoo Ave., S.E., Grand Rapids, MI 49560 Tel. (616)224-0732 Fax (616)224-0834 Email: editorial@thebanner.org Website: www.thebanner.org

The Baptist Bible Tribune, (M.) Baptist Bible Fellowship International, Mike Randall, P.O. Box 309, Springfield, MO 65801-0309 Tel. (417)831-3996 Fax (417)831-1470 Email: editors@tribune.org Website: www.tribune.org

Baptist Bulletin, (M.) General Association of Regular Baptist Churches, David M. Gower, 1300 N. Meacham Rd., Schaumburg, IL 60173-4806 Tel. (847)843-1600 Fax (847)843-3757 Email: baptistbulletin@garbc.org Website: www.garbc.org

Baptist History and Heritage, (3/Y.) Southern Baptist Historical Society, Merrill M. Hawkins, Jr., Carson-Newman College, P.O. Box 71919 Jefferson City, TN 37760 Tel. (865)471-3246 Fax (865)471-3502 Email: hawkins@cncacc.cn.edu

Baptist Peacemaker, (Q.) Baptist, Katie Cook, 4800 Wedgewood Dr., Charlotte, NC 28210 Tel. (704)521-6051 Fax (704)521-6053 Email: bpfna@bpfna.org Website: www.bpfna.org

Baptist Progress, (Q.) Progresive National Baptist Convention, Inc., Archie Logan, 601 50th St. NE, Washington, DC 20019 Tel. (202)396-0558 Fax (202)398-4998

Baptist Witness, (M.) Primitive Baptists, Lasserre Bradley, Jr., Box 17037, Cincinnati, OH 45217 Tel. (513)821-7289 Fax (513)821-7303 Website: www.BaptistBibleHour.org

The Bible Advocate, (10/Y.) The Church of God (Seventh Day), Denver, Colo., Calvin Burrell, PO Box 33677, Denver, CO 80233 Tel. (303)452-7973 Fax (303)452-0657 Email: bibleadvocate@cog7.org Website: www.cog7.org/BA

The Brethren Evangelist, (M.) Brethren Church (Ashland, Ohio), Rev. Richard C. Winfield, 524 College Ave., Ashland, OH 44805 Tel. (419)289-1708 Fax (419)281-0450 Email: brethren@brethrenchurch.org

Brethren Journal, (10/Y.) Unity of Brethren, Rev. Milton Maly, 6703 FM 2502, Brenham, TX 77833-9803 Tel. (409)830-8762

The Bridegroom's Messenger, (bi-M.) The International Pentecostal Church of Christ, Janice Boyce, 121 W. Hunters Trail, Elizabeth City, NC 27909 Tel. (919)338-3003 Fax (919)338-3003

Builder, (M.) Mennonite Church and General Conference Mennonite Church, David R. Hiebert, 616 Walnut Ave., Scottdale, PA 15683 Tel. (724)887-3363 Fax (707)897-3788 Email: Hiebert@mph.org Website: www.mph.org/builder/

The Burning Bush, (Q.) The Metropolitan Church Association, Inc. (Wesleyan), Rev. E. L. Adams, The Metropolitan Church Assoc., 323 Broad St. Lake Geneva, WI 53147 Tel. (414)248-6786

The Calvary Messenger, (M.) Beachy Amish Mennonite Churches, David Sommers, Rt. 2, Box 187-A, Abbeville, SC 29620 Tel. (814) 662-2483

Campus Life, (9/Y.) Nondenominational, Christopher Lutes, 465 Gunderson Dr., Carol Stream, IL 60188 Tel. (630)260-6200 Fax (630)260-0114 Email: clmag@campuslife.net Website: www.campuslife.net

Capsule, (M.) General Association of General Baptists, Jack Eberhardt, 100 Stinson Dr., Poplar Bluff, MO 63901 Tel. (573)785-7746 Fax (573)785-0564

Caring, (6/Y.) Assemblies of God, Owen Wilkie, Gospel Publishing House, 1445 Boonville Ave. Springfield, MO 65802 Tel. (417)862-2781 Fax (417)862-4832 Email: benevolences@ag.org

Cathedral Age, (Q.) Interdenominational, Craig W. Stapert, Mass & Wisconsin Ave. NW, Washington, DC 20016-5098 Tel. (202)537-5681 Fax (202)364-6600 Email: cathedral_age@cathedral.org Website: www.cathedral.org/cathedral

Catholic Chronicle, (bi-W.) The Catholic Church, Patricia Lynn Morrison, PO Box 1866, Toledo, OH 43603-1866 Tel. (419)885-6397 Fax (419)885-6398 Email: catholicchronicle@earthlink.com

Catholic Digest, (M.) The Catholic Church, Richard Reece, 2115 Summit Avenue, St. Paul, MN 55105-1081 Tel. (612)962-6725 Fax (612)962-6755 Email: Cdigest@stthomas.edu Website: www.CatholicDigest.or

Catholic Herald, (W.) The Catholic Church, Ethel M. Gintoft, 3501 S. Lake Dr., St. Francis, WI 53235-0913 Tel. (414)769-3468 Email: chn@execpc.com Website: www.execpc.com/~chn

Catholic Light, (bi-W.) The Catholic Church, Jerome M. Zufelt, 300 Wyoming Ave., Scranton, PA 18503 Tel. (570)346-8915 Fax (570)346-8917 Email: jzufeltcatholiclight@worldnet.att.net

The Catholic New World, (W.) The Catholic Church, Thomas H. Sheridan, 1144 W. Jackson Blvd., Chicago, IL 60607 Tel. (312)243-1300 Fax (312)243-1526 Email: Neworld201@aol.com Website: catholicnewworld.com

The Catholic Peace Voice, (Q.) The Catholic Church, Dave Robinson, 532 W. 8th Street, Erie, PA 16502 Tel. (814)453-4955 Fax (814)452-4784

The Catholic Review, (W.) The Catholic Church, Daniel L. Medinger, P.O. Box 777, Baltimore, MD 21203 Tel. (410)625-8477 Fax (410)332-1069 Email: dmedinger@aol.com

Catholic Standard and Times, (W.) The Catholic Church, Rev Paul S. Quinter, 222 N. 17th St., Philadelphia, PA 19103 Tel. (215) 587-3660 Fax (215)587-3979

The Catholic Transcript, (W.) The Catholic Church, Christopher M. Tiano, 785 Asylum Ave., Hartford, CT 06105-2886 Tel. (203)527-1175 Fax (203)947-6397

Catholic Universe Bulletin, (bi-W.) The Catholic Church, Dennis Sadowski, 1027 Superior Ave., N.E., Cleveland, OH 44114-2556 Tel. (216)696-6525 Fax (216)696-6519

Catholic Worker, (7/Y.) The Catholic Church, Brian Harte, 36 E. First St., New York, NY 10003 Tel. (212)777-9617

Cela Biedrs, (10/Y.) The Latvian Evangelical Lutheran Church in America, Velta Pelcis, 5808 W. Carmen Ave., Milwaukee, WI 53218-2051 Tel. (414)463-6613

Celebration: An Ecumenical Worship Resource, (M.) Interdenominational, Patrick Marrin, P.O. Box 419493, Kansas City, MO 64141-6493 Tel. (816)531-0538 Fax (816)968-2280 Email: patmarrin@aol.com Website: www.ncrpub.com

The Challenge, (Q.) The Bible Church of Christ, Inc., A.M. Jones, 1358 Morris Ave., Bronx, NY 10456 Tel. (718)588-2284 Fax (718)992-5597 Website: www.thebiblechurchofchrist.org

Charisma, (M.) Nondenominational, J. Lee Grady, 600 Rinehart Rd., Lake Mary, FL 32746 Tel. (407)333-0600 Fax (407)333-7133 Email: grady@strang.com Website: www.charismamag.com

302

Childlife, (Q.) Nondenominational, Terry Madison, PO Box 9716, Federal Way, WA 98063-9716 Tel. (206)815-2300 Fax (206) 815-3445
Email: tmadison@aol.com

The Children's Friend, (Q.) Seventh-day Adventist Church, Jerry Stevens, P.O. Box 6097, Lincoln, NE 68506 Tel. (402)488-0981 Fax (402)488-7582
Email: CRSnet@compuserve.com
Website: www.ChristianRecord.org

Christadelphian Advocate, (M.) Christadelphians, Edward W. Farrar, 4 Mountain Park Ave., Hamilton, ON L9A 1A2 Tel. (905)383-1817 Fax (905)383-2705

Christadelphian Tidings, (M.) Christadelphians, Donald H. Styles, 42076 Hartford Dr., Canton, MI 48187 Tel. (313)844-2426 Fax (313)844-8304

Christadelphian Watchman, (M.) Christadelphians, George Booker, 2500 Berwyn Cir., Austin, TX 78745 Tel. (512)447-8882

The Christian Baptist, (M.) Primitive Baptists, Elder S. T. Tolley, P.O. Box 68, Atwood, TN 38220 Tel. (901)662-7417
Email: cbl@aeneas.net

Christian Bible Teacher, (M.) Churches of Christ, J. J. Turner, Box 1060, Abilene, TX 79604 Tel. (915)677-6262 Fax (915)677-1511

The Christian Century, (36/Y.) Nondenominational, John Buchanan, 104 South Michigan Ave., Chicago, IL 60603 Tel. (312)263-7510 Fax (312)263-7540
Email: main@christiancentury.org
Website: www.christiancentury.org

The Christian Chronicle, (M.) Churches of Christ, Bailey McBride, Box 11000, Oklahoma City, OK 73136-1100 Tel. (405) 425-5070 Fax (405)425-5076

The Christian Community, (5/Y.) International Council of Community Churches, Rev. Michael E. Livingston, 21116 Washington Pkwy., Frankfort, IL 60423 Tel. (815)464-5690 Fax (815)464-5692
Email: ICCC60423@aol.com

Christian Education Counselor, (bi-M.) Assemblies of God, Sylvia Lee, Sunday School Promotion and Training, 1445 Boonville Ave., Springfield, MO 65802-1894 Tel. (417)862-2781 Fax (417)862-0503
Email: salee@publish.ag.org
Website: www.we-build-people.org/cec

The Christian Endeavor World, (Q.) Nondenominational, David G. Jackson, P.O. Box 820, 3575 Valley Rd. Liberty Corner, NJ 07938-0820 Tel. (908)604-9440 Fax (908) 604-6075

The Christian Index, (M.) Christian Methodist Episcopal Church, Rev. Lawrence L Reddick III, P.O. Box 665, Memphis, TN 38101-0665 Tel. (901)345-1173

Christian Leader, (M.) U.S. Conference of Mennonite Brethren Churches, Don Ratzlaff, Box V, Hillsboro, KS 67063 Tel. (316)947-5543 Fax (316)947-3266

Christian Living, (8/Y.) Mennonite Church, Levi Miller, 616 Walnut Ave., Scottdale, PA 15683 Tel. (724)887-8500 Fax (724)887-3111
Email: cl@mph.org
Website: www.mph.org/cl/

Christian Monthly, (M.) Apostolic Lutheran Church of America, Linda Mattson, Christian Monthly, P.O. Box 220 Yamhill, OR 97148 Tel. (503)662-5909
Email: christianM@Apostolic-Lutheran.org
Website: www.Apostolic-Lutheran.org

Christian Outlook, (M.) Pentecostal Assemblies of the World, Inc., Johnna E. Hampton, 3939 Meadows Dr., Indianapolis, IN 46205 Tel. (317)547-9541 Fax (317)543-0512

The Christian Reader, (bi-M.) Nondenominational, Bonne Steffer, 465 Gunderson Dr., Carol Stream, IL 60188 Tel. (630)260-6200 Fax (630)260-0114

Christian Record, (Q.) Seventh-day Adventist Church, Jerry Stevens, P.O. Box 6097, Lincoln, NE 68506 Tel. (402)488-0981 Fax (402)488-7582
Email: CRSnet@compuserve.com
Website: www.ChristianRecord.org

The Christian Science Journal (M.) Church of Christ, Scientist, William E. Moody, One Norway St., Boston, MA 02115 Tel. (617)450-2000 Fax (617)450-2707
Email: moodyw@csps.com
Website: www.csjournal.com

The Christian Science Monitor, (D.&W.) Church of Christ, Scientist, David T. Cook, One Norway St., Boston, MA 02115 Tel. (617)450-2000 Fax (617)450-7575
Website: www.csmonitor.com

Christian Science Quarterly Weekly Bible Lessons, (Q.) Church of Christ, Scientist, Carol Humphry, Circulation Marketing Manager, One Norway St., C-40, Boston, MA 02115 Tel. (617)450-2000 Fax (617)450-7575
Email: service@csps.com
Website: www.biblelesson.com

Christian Science Sentinel, (W.) Church of Christ, Scientist, William E. Moody, One Norway St., Boston, MA 02115-3112 Tel. (617)450-2000 Fax (617)450-2707
Email: moodyw@csps.com
Website: www.cssentinel.com

US PERIODICALS

303

Christian Social Action, (bi-M.) The United Methodist Church, Rev. Erik Alsgaard, 100 Maryland Ave. NE, Washington, DC 20002 Tel. 202/488-5621 Fax 202/488-1617 Email: EAlsgaard@umc-gbcs.org Website: www.umc-gbcs.org

Christian Standard, (W.) Christian Churches and Churches of Christ, Sam E. Stone, 8121 Hamilton Ave., Cincinnati, OH 45231 Tel. 513/931-4050 Fax 513/931-0950 Email: christianstd@standardpub.com Website: www.standardpub.com

Christian Woman, (bi-M.) Churches of Christ, Sandra Humphrey, Box 150, Nashville, TN 37202 Tel. (615)254-8781 Fax (615)254-7411

Christianity & The Arts, (Q.) Nondenominational, Marci Whitney-Schenck, P.O. Box 118088, Chicago, IL 60611 Tel. (312)642-8606 Fax (312)266-7719 Email: chrnarts@aol.com

The Church Advocate, (Q.) Churches of God, General Conference, Mac Cordell, P.O. Box 926, 700 E. Melrose Ave. Findlay, OH 45839 Tel. (419)424-1961 Fax (419)424-3433 Email: communications@cggc.org Website: www.cggc.org

Church of God Evangel, (M.) Church of God (Cleveland, Tenn.), Bill George, P.O. Box 2250, Cleveland, TN 37320 Tel. (423)478-7592 Fax (423)478-7616 Email: bill_george@pathwaypress.org Website: www.pathwaypress.org

Church of God Missions, (bi-M.) Church of God (Anderson, Ind.), J. David Reames, Box 2337, Anderson, IN 46018-2337 Tel. (765)648-2128 Fax (765)642-4279 Email: mbchogvp@aol.com

Church of God Progress Journal, (bi-M.) Church of God General Conference (Oregon, Ill. & Morrow, GA), David Krogh, Box 100,000, Morrow, GA 30260 Tel. (404)362-0052 Fax (404)362-9307 Email: info@abc-coggc.org Website: www.abc-coggc.org

The Church Herald, (11/Y.) Reformed Church in America, Christina Van Eyl, 4500 60th St., SE, Grand Rapids, MI 49512 Tel. (616)698-7071 Fax (616)698-6606 Email: evaneyl@rca.org

Church History: Studies in Christianity and Culture, (Q.) Scholarly, Elizabeth A. Clark, Grant Wacker, Hans J. Hillerbrand, and Richard P. Heitzenrater, The Divinity School, Duke University, Box 90975 Durham, NC 27708-0975 Tel. (919)660-3470 Fax (919-660-3473 Email: church-history@duke.edu Website: www.churchhistory.org

The Church Messenger, (bi-M.) , James S. Dutko, 280 Clinton St., Binghamton, NY 13905

Church School Herald, (Q.) African Methodist Episcopal Zion Church, Ms. Mary A. Love, P.O. Box 32305, Charlotte, NC 28232-2305 Tel. (704)332-9873 Fax (704)333-1769

Church & Society Magazine, (bi-M.) Presbyterian Church (U.S.A.), Kathy Lancaster, 100 Witherspoon St., Louisville, KY 40202-1396 Tel. (502)569-5810 Fax (502) 569-8116 Email: kathyl@ctr.pcusa.org Website: horeb.pcusa.org/churchsociety

Church and State, (M.) Independent, Joseph L. Conn, 1816 Jefferson Pl. N.W., Washington, DC 20036 Tel. (202)466-2587

Church and State, (M.) Independent journal of religion and politics, Joseph L. Conn, 1816 Jefferson Place NW, Washington, DC 20036 Tel. (202)466-2587 Email: conn@aol.com Website: www.netplexgroup.com/

The Churchman's Human Quest, Nondenominational, Edna Ruth Johnson, 1074 23rd Ave. N., St. Petersburg, FL 33704 Tel. (813)894-0097

Churchwoman, (Q.) Interdenominational, Rev. Martha M. Cruz, Editor and Elizabeth Young, Managing Editor, 475 Riverside Dr., New York, NY 10115 Tel. (212)870-2347 Fax (212)870-2338 Email: mmcruz@churchwomen.org Website: www.churchwomen.org

Circuit Rider, (6/Y.) The United Methodist Church, Jill S. Reddig, 201 Eighth Ave. S, Nashville, TN 37202 Tel. 615/749-6358 Fax 615/749-6512 Email: jreddig@umpublishing.org Website: www.umph.org/resources/publications

Clarion Herald, (bi-W.) The Catholic Church, Peter P. Finney, Jr., P. O. Box 53247, 1000 Howard Ave. Suite 400 New Orleans, LA 70153 Tel. (504)596-3035 Fax (504)596-3020

The Clergy Journal, (10/Y.) Nondenominational, Sharilyn A. Figueroa, Managing Editor & Clyde J. Steckel, Executive Editor, 6160 Carmen Avenue E, Inver Grove Heights, MN 55076-4422 Tel. (800)328-0200 Fax (651)457-4617 Email: fig@logostaff.com

Club Connection, (Q.) Assemblies of God, Kerry Clarensau, 1445 Boonville Ave., Springfield, MO 65802-1894 Tel. (417)862-2781 Fax (417)862-0503 Email: clubconnection@ag.org Website: www.ag.org/missionettes

Co-Laborer, (bi-M.) National Association of Free Will Baptists, Suzanne Franks, Women Nationally Active for Christ, P.O. Box 5002 Antioch, TN 37011-5002 Tel. (615)731-6812 Fax (615)731-0771
Email: colaborer@nafwb.org

Collegiate Quarterly, (Q.) Seventh-day Adventist Church, Gary B. Swanson, 12501 Old Columbia Pike, Silver Spring, MD 20904 Tel. (301)680-6160 Fax (301)680-6155

Columbia, (M.) The Catholic Church, Tim S. Hickey, One Columbus Plaza, New Haven, CT 06510 Tel. (203)772-2130 Fax (203)777-0114 Email: thickey@kofc-supreme.com
Website: www.kofc.org

The Commission, (10/Y.) International Mission Board, Southern Baptist Convention, Mary Jane Welch, Box 6767, Richmond, VA 23230-0767 Tel. (804)219-1327 Fax (804)219-1410 Email: commission@imb.org
Website: www.imb.org/commission

Common Lot, (4/Y.) United Church of Christ, Martha J. Hunter, 700 Prospect Ave., Cleveland, OH 44115 Tel. (216)736-2150 Fax (216)736-2156

Commonweal, (bi-W.) The Catholic Church, Margaret O'Brien Steinfels, 475 Riverside Drive, Rm 405, New York, NY 10115 Tel. (212)662-4200 Fax (212)662-4183

Communique, (M.) National Baptist Convention of America, Inc., Robert Jeffrey, 1320 Pierre Avenue, Shreveport, LA 71103 Tel. (318)221-3701 Fax (318)222-7512

The Congregationalist, (5/Y.) National Association Congregational Christian Churches, Joseph B. Polhemus, 1105 Briarwood Rd., Mansfield, OH 44907 Tel. (419) 756-5526 Fax (419)756-5526
Email: jbpedit@aol.com
Website: www.congregationalist.org

Conqueror, (bi-M.) United Pentecostal Church International, John F. Sills, 8855 Dunn Rd., Hazelwood, MO 63042 Tel. (314)837-7300 Fax (314)837-4503
Email: GYouth8855@aol.com

Contact, (M.) National Association of Free Will Baptists, Jack Williams, P.O. Box 5002, Antioch, TN 37011-5002 Tel. (615)731-6812 Fax (615)731-0771

Context, (22/Y.) Nondenominational, Martin Marty, 205 W. Monroe St., Chicago, IL 60606-5013 Tel. (312)236-7782 Fax (312)236-8207 Email: editors@uscatholic.org
Website: www.contextonline.org

Cornerstone Connections, (Q.) Seventh-day Adventist Church, Gary B. Swanson, 12501 Old Columbia Pike, Silver Spring, MD 20904 Tel. (301)680-6160 Fax (301)680-6155

Courage in the Struggle for Justice and Peace, (Q.) United Church of Christ, Sandy Sorensen, 110 Maryland Ave., Ste. 207, NE, Washington, DC 20002 Tel. (202)543-1517 Fax (202)543-5994

The Covenant Companion, (M.) Evangelical Covenant Church, Jane K. Swanson-Nystrom, 5101 N. Francisco Ave., Chicago, IL 60625 Tel. (773)906-3326 Fax (773)784-4366 Email: companion@covoffice.org
Website: www.covchurch.org/cov/companion

Covenant Home Altar, (Q.) Evangelical Covenant Church, Donald L. Meyer, 5101 N. Francisco Ave., Chicago, IL 60625 Tel. (773)784-3000 Fax (773)784-4366 Email: covcom@compuserve.com

Covenant Quarterly, (Q.) Evangelical Covenant Church, Wayne C. Weld, 3225 W. Foster Ave., Chicago, IL 60625-4895 Tel. (773)244-6230 Fax (773)244-6244 Email: WeldDone@aol.com

The Covenanter Witness, (11/Y.) Reformed Presbyterian Church of North America, Drew Gordon and Lynne Gordon, 7408 Penn Ave., Pittsburgh, PA 15208 Tel. (412)241-0436 Fax (412)731-8861
Email: cwmailbag@aol.com
Website: www.psalms40.com

Credinta—The Faith, (Q.) The Romanian Orthodox Church in America, V. Rev. Archim. Dr. Vasile Vasilac, 45-03 48th Ave., Woodside, Queens, NY 11377 Tel. (313)893-8390

Credo, (M.) The Antiochian Orthodox Christian Archdiocese of North, Charles Dinkler, P.O. Box 84, Stanton, NJ 08885-0084 Tel. (908) 236-7890

The Criterion, (W.) The Catholic Church, John F. Fink, P. O. Box 1717, 1400 N. Meridian Indianapolis, IN 46206 Tel. (317)236-1570

Cross Walk, (W.) Church of the Nazarene, Jim Hampton, Word Action Publishing, 6401 The Paseo Kansas City, MO 64131 Tel. (816)333-7000 Fax (816)333-4315
Email: crosswalk@nazarene.org
Website: www.nazarene.org

The Cumberland Flag, (M.) Cumberland Presbyterian Church in America, Rev. Robert Stanley Wood, 226 Church St., Huntsville, AL 35801 Tel. (205)536-7481 Fax (205)536-7482

The Cumberland Presbyterian, (15/Y.) Cumberland Presbyterian Church in America, M. Jacqueline De Berry Warren, 1978 Union Ave., Memphis, TN 38104 Tel. (901)276-4572 Fax (901)272-3913

Currents in Theology and Mission, (6/Y.) Evangelical Lutheran Church in America, Ralph W. Klein, 1100 E. 55th St., Chicago, IL 60615 Tel. (773)256-0695 Fax (773)256-0782

US PERIODICALS

305

Email: currents@lstc.edu
Website: www.lstc.edu/about/cu

Decision, (11/Y.) Nondenominational, Kersten Beckstrom, 1300 Harmon Pl., Minneapolis, MN 55403 Tel. (612)338-0500 Fax (612)335-1299 Email: decision@bgea.org Website: www.decisionmag.org

The Disciple, (10/Y.) Christian Church (Disciples of Christ), Patricia R. Case, 6219 N Guilford, Suite B Indianapolis, IN 46220 Tel. 317-253-1600 Fax 317-253-1460 Email: The Disciple@disciples.org Website: www.thedisciple.com

Discovery, (Q.) Nondenominational, Braille Only, for Youth, Darcy Quigley, J. Milton Society for the Blind, 475 Riverside Drive, Rm 455 New York, NY 10115-0455 Tel. (212)870-3335 Fax (212)870-3229 Email: order@jmsblind.org Website: www.jmsblind.org

Doors and Windows, (Q.) The Evangelical Congregational Church, Brad Waldman, 100 W. Park Ave, Myerstown, PA 17067

Ecu-Link, (Q.) Interdenominational, Sarah Vilankulu, 475 Riverside Drive, Rm 850, New York, NY 10115-0050 Tel. (212)870-2227 Fax (212)870-2030 Email: sarah@ncccusa.org

Ecumenical Trends, (M.) Nondenominational, Kevin McMorrow, SA, Greymoor Ecumenical & Interreligious Institute, PO Box 300 Garrison, NY 10524 Tel. (845)424-3671 Fax (845)424-2163

Eleventh Hour Messenger, (bi-M.) Wesleyan Holiness Association of Churches, John Brewer, R R 2 Box 9, Winchester, IN 47394 Tel. (317)584-3199

Elim Herald, (Q.) Elim Fellowship, Bernard J. Evans, 1703 Dalton Road, P.O. Box 57A Lima, NY 14485 Tel. (716)582-2790 Fax (716)624-1229 Email: 75551.743@compuserve.com

EMC Today, (Q.) Evangelical Mennonite Church, Donald W. Roth, 1420 Kerrway Ct., Fort Wayne, IN 46805 Tel. (219)423-3649 Fax (219)420-1905

Emphasis on Faith and Living, (bi-M.) The Missionary Church, Rev. Robert Ransom, PO Box 9127, Ft. Wayne, IN 46899 Tel. (219)747-2027 Fax (219)747-5331 Email: RLRansom@aol.com Website: www.mcusa.org

Enrichment: A Journal for Pentecostal Ministry, (Q.) Assemblies of God, Wayde I. Goodall, 1445 Boonville Ave., Springfield, MO 65802 Tel. (417)862-2781 Fax (417)862-0416

Email: Wgoodall@ag.org
Website: www.enrichmentjournal.ag.org

The Ensign, (M.) The Church of Jesus Christ Latter-day Saints, Jay M. Todd, Managing Editor, 50 E North Temple Street, 24th Fl, Salt Lake City, UT 84150 Tel. (801)240-2950 Fax (801)240-5732

Epiphany Journal, (Q.) Interdenominational, Nun Macaria, 1516 N. Delaware, Indianapolis, IN 46202 Tel. (317)926-7468

Episcopal Life, (M.) The Episcopal Church, Jerrold Hames, 815 Second Ave., New York, NY 10017-4503 Tel. (800)334-7626 Fax (212) 949-8059 Email: jerry.hames@ecunet.org Website: www.ecusa.anglican.org/episcopal-life

The Evangel, (6/Y.) American Association of Lutheran Churches, The, Charles D. Eidum, 10800 Lyndale Ave. S., #210, Minneapolis, MN 55420-5614 Tel. (612)884-7784 Fax (612)884-7894 Email: ChuckAALC@aol.com Website: www.taalc.org

The Evangel, (Q.) The Evangelical Church Alliance, Derick Miller, 205 W. Broadway, Bradley, IL 60915 Tel. (815)937-0720 Fax (815)937-0001 Email: eca@keynet.net Website: www.keynet.net/~eca

The Evangelical Advocate, (M.) Churches of Christ in Christian Union, Ralph Hux, P.O. Box 30, Circleville, OH 43113 Tel. (740)474-8856 Fax (740)477-7766 Email: cccudoc@bright.net Website: www.bright.net/~cccudoc

Evangelical Beacon, (7/Y.) The Evangelical Free Church of America, Ms. Carol Madison, 901 East 78th St., Minneapolis, MN 55420-1300 Tel. (612)854-1300 Fax (612)853-8488

Evangelical Challenge, (Q.) The Evangelical Church, John F. Sills, 7733 West River Road, Minneapolis, MN 55444 Tel. (612)561-0886 Fax (612)561-0774

Evangelical Visitor, (6/Y.) Brethren in Christ Church, Ronald C. Ross, P.O. Box 166, Nappanee, IN 46550 Tel. (219)773-3164 Fax (219)773-5934

Evangelism USA, (M.) International Pentecostal Holiness Church, Dr. Ronald W. Carpenter, Sr., P.O. Box 12609, Oklahoma City, OK 73157 Tel. (405)787-7110 Fax (405)789-3957 Email: JDL@iphc.org Website: www.iphc.org/evusa/ev

The Evangelist, (W.) The Catholic Church, James Breig, 40 N. Main Ave., Albany, NY 12203 Tel. (518)453-6688 Fax (518)453-8448

306

Email: evannews@global2000.net

Website: www.evangelist.org

Explorations, (4/Y.) Nondenominational, Irvin J. Borowsky, 321 Chestnut Street, 4th Floor, Philadelphia, PA 19106-2779 Tel. (215)925-2800 Fax (215)925-3800

Extension, (M.) The Catholic Church, Bradley Collins, 150 S. Wacker Drive, 20th Floor Chicago, IL 60606 Tel. (312)236-7240 Fax (312)236-5276

Email: magazine@catholic-extension.org

Website: www.catholic-extension.org

Faith & Fellowship, (M.) Church of the Lutheran Brethren of America, Brent Juliot, P.O. Box 655, Fergus Falls, MN 56538 Tel. 218/736-7357 Fax 218/736-2200

Email: juliot@clba.org

Website: www.clba.org

Faith-Life, (bi-M.) Lutheran, Pastor Marcus Albrecht, 2107 N. Alexander St., Appleton, WI 54911 Tel. 920/733-1839 Fax 920/733-4834

Email: malbrecht@milwpc.com

Faith and Truth, (M.) Pentecostal Fire-Baptized Holiness Church, Edgar Vollratlt, 593 Harris-Lord Rd., Commerce, GA 30529 Tel. (706) 335-5796

Fellowship, (6/Y.) Interfaith, Richard Deats, P.O. Box 271, Nyack, NY 10960-0271 Tel. (845)358-4601 Fax (845)358-1179

Email: fellowship@forusa.org

Website: www.forusa.org/~

Fellowship Focus, (bi-M.) Fellowship of Evangelical Bible Churches, Robert L. Frey, 5800 S. 14th St., Omaha, NE 68107 Tel. (402) 731-4780 Fax (402)731-1173

Email: febcoma@aol.com

Website: http://members.aol.com/febcoma

The Fellowship Magazine, (6/Y.) Assemblies of God International Fellowship (Independent), Rev. T. A. Lanes, 5284 Eastgate Mall, San Diego, CA 92121 Tel. (858)677-9701 Fax (858)677-0038

Email: TheodoreaLanes@compuserve.com

Website: www.agifellowship.org

Fellowship News, (M.) Bible Fellowship Church, Carol Snyder, 3000 Fellowship Drive, Whitehall, PA 18052-3343 Tel. 717-337-3408 Fax 215-536-2120

Email: ccsnyder@supernet.com

Website: www.bfc.org

Fellowship Tidings, (Q.) Full Gospel Fellowship of Churches and Ministers Intern, Chester P. Jenkins, 1000 N. Beltline Road, Irving, TX 75061 Tel. (214)339-1200

Email: FGFCMI@aol.com

Website: www.fgfcmi.org

Firm Foundation, (M.) Churches of Christ, H. A. Dobbs, P.O. Box 690192, Houston, TX 77269-0192 Tel. (713)469-3102 Fax (713) 469-7115

Email: HAD@onramp.net

First Things: A Monthly Journal of Religion & Public Life, (M.) Interdenominational, Richard J. Neuhaus, 156 Fifth Ave., Ste. 400, New York, NY 10010 Tel. (212)627-1985 Fax (212)627-2184

Website: www.firstthings.com

The Flaming Sword, (M.) Bible Holiness Church, Susan Davolt, 10th St. & College Ave., Independence, KS 67301 Tel. (316)331-2580 Fax (316)331-2580

For the Poor, (bi-M.) Primitive Baptists, W. H. Cayce, PO Box 38, Thornton, AR 71766 Tel. (501)352-3694

Foresee, (bi-M.) Conservative Congregational Christian Conference, Walter F. Smith, 7582 Currell Blvd., #108, St. Paul, MN 55125 Tel. (651)739-1474 Fax (651)739-0750

Email: cccc4@juno.com

Website: www.ccccusa.org

Forum Letter, (M.) Independent, Intra-Lutheran (companion publication to the quarterly, Lutheran Forum), Pastor Russell E. Saltzman, Ruskin Heights Lutheran Church, 10801 Ruskin Way Kansas City, MO 64134 Tel. (816)761-6815

Email: Saltzman@Integritynetwork.net

Forward, (Q.) United Pentecostal Church International, Rev. J. L. Hall, 8855 Dunn Rd., Hazelwood, MO 63042 Tel. (314)837-7300 Fax (314)837-4503

Forward in Christ /Northwestern Lutheran, (M.) Wisconsin Evangelical Lutheran Synod, Gary Baumler, 2929 N. Mayfair Rd., Milwaukee, WI 53222 Tel. (414)256-3210 Fax (414)256-3899

Email: nl@sab.wels.net

Foursquare World Advance, (6/Y.) International Church of the Foursquare Gospel, Rev. Ron Williams, PO Box 26902, 1910 W. Sunset Blvd., Ste 2 Los Angeles, CA 90026-0176 Tel. (213)989-4220 Fax (213)989-4544

Email: COMM@foursquare.org

Website: www.foursquare.org

Free Methodist World Mission People, (4/Y.) Free Methodist Church of North America, Paula Innes, Magazine Editor, P.O. Box 535002, Indianapolis, IN 46253-5002 Tel. (317)244-3660 Fax (317)241-1248

Email: fmcPeople@aol.com

Website: www.fmcna.org/fmwm

Free Will Baptist Gem, (M.) National Association of Free Will Baptists, Nathan Ruble, P.O. Box 991, Lebanon, MO 65536 Tel. (417)532-6537

The Free Will Baptist, (M.) Original Free Will Baptist Church, Tracy A McCoy, P.O. Box 159, 811 N. Lee Street Ayden, NC 28513 Tel. (919)746-6128 Fax (919)746-9248

Free Will Bible College Bulletin, (6/Y.) National Association of Free Will Baptists, Bert Tippett, 3606 West End Ave., Nashville, TN 37205 Tel. (615)383-1340 Fax (615)269-6028 Email: bert@fwbbc.edu Website: www.fwbbc.edu

Friend Magazine, (M.) The Church of Jesus Christ of Latter-day Saints, Vivian Paulsen, 50 E South Temple Street, 23rd Fl, Salt Lake City, UT 84150 Tel. (801)240-2210 Fax (801)240-5997

Friends Bulletin, (10/Y.) Religious Society of Friends, Anthony Manousos, 5238 Andalucia Court, Whittier, CA 90601 Tel. (562)699-5670 Fax (562)692-2472 Email: friendsbul@aol.com Website: www.quaker.org/fb and www.quaker.org/western

Friends Journal, (M.) Friends General Conference, Vinton Deming, 1501 Cherry Street, Philadelphia, PA 19102-1497 Tel. (215)241-7277 Fax (215)568-1377 Email: FriendsJnl@aol.com

The Friends Voice, (4/Y.) Evangelical Friends International - North America Regio, Becky Towne, 2748 E. Pikes Peak Ave, Colorado Springs, CO 80909 Tel. (719)632-5721 Fax (719)636-2194 Email: mcrcs@codenet.net Website: evangelical-friends.org

Front Line, Conservative Baptist Association of America, Al Russell, P.O. Box 66, Wheaton, IL 60189 Tel. (630)260-3800 Fax (630)653-5387 Email: chaplruss@aol.com

Full Gospel Ministries Outreach Report, (Q.) Full Gospel Assemblies International, Simeon Strauser, P.O. Box 1230, Coatsville, PA 19320 Tel. (610)857-2357 Fax (610)857-3109

The Gem, (W.) Churches of God, General Conference, Mac Cordell, P.O. Box 926, Findlay, OH 45839 Tel. (419)424-1961 Fax (419)424-3433 Email: communications@cggc.org Website: www.cggc.org

General Baptist Messenger, (M.) General Association of General Baptists, Samuel S. Ramdial, 400 Stinson Dr., Poplar Bluff, MO 63901 Tel. (573)686-9051 Fax (573)686-5198

The Gleaner, (M.) Baptist Missionary Association of America, F. Donald Collins, Po Box 193920, Little Rock, AR 72219-3920 Tel. (501)455-4977 Fax (501)455-3636 Email: BMAAM@aol.com

Global Partners, (Q.) Baptist Bible Fellowship International, Loran McAlister, P.O. Box 191, Springfield, MO 65801 Tel. (417)862-5001 Fax (417)865-0794

God's Field, (bi-W.) Polish National Catholic Church of America, Very Rev. William Chromey (English) and Rt. Rev. Casimir Grotnik (Polish), 1006 Pittston Ave., Scranton, PA 18505 Tel. (570)346-9131 Fax (570)346-2188

Gospel Advocate, (M.) Churches of Christ, Neil W. Anderson, Box 150, Nashville, TN 37202 Tel. (615)254-8781 Fax (615)254-7411 Email: info@gospeladvocate.com Website: www.gospeladvocate.com

Gospel Herald, (W.) Mennonite Church, J. Lorne Peachey, 616 Walnut Ave, Scottdale, PA 15683 Tel. (412)887-8500 Fax (412)887-3111

The Gospel Herald, (M.) Church of God, Mountain Assembly, Inc., Bob Vance, P.O. Box 157, Jellico, TN 37762 Tel. (423)784-8260 Fax (423)784-3258 Email: cgmahdq@jellico.com Website: www.cgmahdq.org

The Gospel Light, (Q.) The Bible Church of Christ, Inc., Carol Crenshaw, 1358 Morris Ave., Bronx, NY 10456 Tel. (718)588-2284 Fax (718)992-5597 Website: www.thebiblechurchofchrist.org

The Gospel Messenger, (M.) Congregational Holiness Church, Inc., Cullen L. Hicks, Congregational Holiness Church, 3888 Fayetteville Highway Griffin, GA 30223 Tel. (770-228-4833 Fax (770-228-1177) Email: CHChurch@bellsouth.net Website: www.CHChurch.com

The Gospel News, (M.) The Church of Jesus Christ (Bickertonites), Donald Ross, 201 Royalbrooke Dr., Venetia, PA 15367 Tel. (412)348-6828 Fax (412)348-0919

The Gospel Truth, (M.) Church of the Living God, W.E. Crumes, 430 Forest Avenue, Cincinnati, OH 45229 Tel. (513)569-5660 Fax (513)569-5661

Grow Magazine, (4/Y.) Church of the Nazarene, Neil B. Wiseman, 6401 The Paseo, Kansas City, MO 64131 Tel. (816)333-7000 Fax (816)361-5202

Guide, (W.) Seventh-day Adventist Church, Randy Fishell, 55 W. Oak Ridge Dr., Hagerstown, MD 21740 Tel. (301)393-4038 Fax (301)393-4055 Email: guide@rhpa.org Website: www.guidemagazine.org

The Handmaiden, (Q.) The Antiochian Orthodox Christian Archdiocese of North America, Mary Armstrong, P.O. Box 76, Ben

Lomond, CA 95005-0076 Tel. (831)336-5118 Fax (831)336-8882 Email: marketing@conciliarpress.com

The Happy Harvester, (M.) Church of God of Prophecy, Diane Pace, P.O. Box 2910, Cleveland, TN 37320-2910 Tel. (423)559-5435 Fax (423)559-5444 Email: JoDiPace@wingnet.net

HeartBeat, (M.) The Evangelical Church, John F. Sills, 7733 West River Road, Minneapolis, MN 55444 Tel. (612)561-8404 Fax (612)561-2899

Heartbeat, (bi-M.) National Association of Free Will Baptists, Don Robirds, Foreign Missions Office, P.O. Box 5002 Antioch, TN 37011-5002 Tel. (615)731-6812 Fax (615)731-5345 Email: Heartbeat@NAFWB.org

Helping Hand, (bi-M.) International Pentecostal Holiness Church, Mrs. Doris Moore, P.O. Box 12609, Oklahoma City, OK 73157 Tel. (405)787-7110 Fax (405)789-3957

The Herald of Christian Science, (M.) Church of Christ, Scientist, William E. Moody, One Norway St., Boston, MA 02115 Tel. (617)450-2000 Fax (617)450-2707 Email: moodyw@csps.com Website: www.csherald.com

Heritage, (Q.) Assemblies of God, Wayne E. Warner, 1445 Boonville Ave., Springfield, MO 65802 Tel. (417)862-1447 Fax (417)862-6203 Email: wwarner@ag.org

High Adventure, (Q.) Assemblies of God, Marshall Bruner, Gospel Publishing House, 1445 Boonville Ave. Springfield, MO 65802-1894 Tel. (417)862-2781 Fax (417)862-0416

Higher Way, (bi-M.) Apostolic Faith Mission of Portland, Oregon, Darrel D. Lee, 6615 S.E. 52nd Ave., Portland, OR 97206 Tel. (503)777-1741 Fax (503)777-1743 Email: kbarrett@apostolicfaith.org Website: www.apostolicfaith.org

Holiness Digest, (Q.) Nondenominational, Marlin Hotle, 263 Buffalo Road, Clinton, TN 37716 Tel. (423)457-5978 Fax (423)463-7280

Holiness Today, (M.) Church of the Nazarene, R. Franklin Cook, 6401 The Paseo, Kansas City, MO 64131 Tel. (816)333-7000 Fax (816)333-1748 Email: HolinessToday@nazarene.org Website: www.nazarene.org

The Holiness Union, (M.) United Holy Church of America, Inc., Dr. Joseph T. Durham, 13102 Morningside La., Silver Spring, MD 20904 Tel. (301)989-9093 Fax (301)989-9020

Homelife, (6/Y.) United Pentecostal Church International, Scott Graham, 8855 Dunn Rd., Hazelwood, MO 63042 Tel. (314)837-7300 Fax (314)837-4503

Email: gyouth8855@ol.com Website: www.upci.org/youth

Homiletic and Pastoral Review, (M.) The Catholic Church, Kenneth Baker, 10 Audrey Pl., Fairfield, NJ 7004 Tel. (201)882-8700

Horizons, (7/Y.) Presbyterian Church (U.S.A.), Marie T. Cross, Presbyterian Women, 100 Witherspoon St. Louisville, KY 40202-1396 Tel. (502)569-5367 Fax (502)569-8085 Email: MarieC@ctr.pcusa.org Website: www/pcusa.org/horizons

Horizons, (M.) Christian Churches and Churches of Christ, Reggie Hundley, Box 13111, Knoxville, TN 37920-0111 Tel. 800/655-8524 Fax 865-573-5950 Email: msa@missionservices.org Website: www.missionservices.org

Insight, (W.) Seventh-day Adventist Church, Lori Peckham, 55 W. Oak Ridge Dr., Hagerstown, MD 21740 Tel. (301)393-4038 Fax (301)393-4055 Email: insight@rhpa.org Website: www.insightmagazine.org

Insight, (Q.) Advent Christian Church, Dawn Rutan, P.O. Box 23152, Charlotte, NC 28227 Tel. (704)545-6161 Fax (704)573-0712 Email: ACPub@adventchristian.org Website: www.adventchristian.org

Interlit, (6/Y.) Nondenominational magazine on Christian publishing worldwide, Kim A. Pettit, 4050 Lee Vance View Drive, Colorado Springs, CO 80918 Tel. (719)536-0100 Fax (719)536-3266 Email: ccmintl@ccmi.org Website: www.ccmi.org

International Bulletin of Missionary Research, (Q.) Nondenominational, Jonathan J. Bonk, 490 Prospect St., New Haven, CT 06511-2196 Tel. (203)624-6672 Fax (203)865-2857 Email: ibmr@OMSC.org Website: www.omsc.org

Interpretation, (Q.) Presbyterian Church (U.S.A.), John T. Carroll and William P. Brown, 3401 Brook Rd., Richmond, VA 23227 Tel. (804)278-4296 Fax (804)278-4208 Email: email@interpretation.org Website: www.interpretation.org

el Interprete, (6/Y.) The United Methodist Church, Martha E. Rovira Raber, P.O. Box 320, Nashville, TN 37202-0320 Tel. (615)742-5115 Fax (615)742-5460 Email: elinterprete@umcom.umc.org Website: www.interpretermagazine.org

Interpreter, (8/Y.) The United Methodist Church, M. Garlinda Burton, P.O. Box 320, Nashville, TN 37202-0320 Tel. 615/742-5107 Fax 615/742-5460

309

Email: gburton@umcom.umc.org
Website: www.interpretermagazine.org

IssacharFile, (M.) International Pentecostal Holiness Church, Shirley Spencer, P.O. Box 12609, Oklahoma City, OK 73157 Tel. (405)787-7110 Fax (405)789-3957

John Milton Magazine, (Q.) Nondenominational, Large Print, Darcy Quigley, J. Milton Society for the Blind, 475 Riverside Drive, Rm 455 New York, NY 10115-0455 Tel. (212)870-3335 Fax (212)870-3229
Email: order@jmsblind.org
Website: www.jmsblind.org

John Three Sixteen, (Q.) Bible Holiness Church, Mary Cunningham, 10th St. & College Ave., Independence, KS 67301 Tel. (316)331-2580 Fax (316)331-2580

Journal of the American Academy of Religion, (Q.) Nondenominational, Glenn Yocum, Whittier College, PO Box 634 Whittier, CA 90608-0634 Tel. (562)907-4200 Fax (562)907-4910
Email: gyocum@whittier.edu
Website: www.aarweb.org

Journal of Adventist Education, (5/Y.) Seventh-day Adventist Church, Beverly Rumble, 12501 Old Columbia Pike, Silver Spring, MD 20904-6600 Tel. (301)680-5075 Fax (301)622-9627
Email: 74617.1231@compuserve.com

Journal of Christian Education, (Q.) African Methodist Episcopal Church, Kenneth H. Hill, 500 Eighth Ave., S., Nashville, TN 37203 Tel. (615)242-1420 Fax (615)726-1866
Email: ameced@edge.net
Website: www.ameced.com

Journal of Ecumenical Studies, (Q.) Interdenominational, Leonard Swidler, Temple Univ. (022-38), 1114 West Berks St. Philadelphia, PA 19122-6090 Tel. (215)204-7714 Fax (215)204-4569
Email: dialogue@vm.temple.edu

The Journal of Pastoral Care, (Q.) Nondenominational, Orlo Strunk Jr., 1068 Harbor Dr., SW, Calabash, NC 28467 Tel. (910)579-5084 Fax (910)579-5084
Email: OrloS@aol.com

Journal of Presbyterian History: Studies in Reformed History and Culture, (Q.) Presbyterian Church (U.S.A.), Charles H. Moorhead, 425 Lombard St., Philadelphia, PA 19147 Tel. (215)627-1852 Fax (215)627-0509

Journal From the Radical Reformation, (Q.) Church of God General Conference (Morrow, GA), Kent Ross and Anthony Buzzard, Sr. Editors, Box 100,000, Morrow, GA 30260-7000 Tel. (404)362-0052 Fax (404)362-9307
Email: kross@abc-coggc.org
Website: www.abc-coggc.org

Journal of Theology, (4/Y.) Church of the Lutheran Confession, Prof. Paul Schaller, Immanuel Lutheran College, 501 Grover Rd. Eau Claire, WI 54701-7199 Tel. (715)832-9936 Fax (715)836-6634
Email: schallers@usa.net
Website: www.primenet.com/~clcpub/clc/clc.html

The Joyful Noiseletter, (10/Y.) Interdenominational, Cal Samra, P.O. Box 895, Portage, MI 49081-0895 Tel. (616)324-0990 Fax (616)324-3984
Email: joyfulnz@aol.com
Website: www._joyful_noiseletter.com

Keeping in Touch, (M.) Universal Fellowship of Metropolitan Community Churches, Ravi Verma, 8704 Santa Monica Blvd, 2nd Fl., West Hollywood, CA 90069-4548 Tel. (310)360-8640 Fax (310)360-8680
Email: UFMCCHQ@aol.com
Website: www.ufmcc.com

Kindred Minds, (Q.) Sovereign Grace Baptists, Larry Scouten, P.O. Box 10, Wellsburg, NY 14894 Tel. (607)734-6985

The Lantern, (bi-M.) National Baptist Convention of America, Inc., Robert Jeffrey, 1320 Pierre Avenue, Shreveport, LA 71103 Tel. (318)221-3701 Fax (318)222-7512

Leadership: A Practical Journal for Church Leaders, (Q.) Nondenominational, Marshall Shelley, 465 Gundersen Dr., Carol Stream, IL 60188 Tel. (630)260-6200 Fax (630)260-0114
Email: LeaderJ@aol.com
Website: www.Leadershipjournal.net

Liahona, (varies by language) The Church of Jesus Christ of Latter-day Saints (42 language editions), Marvin K. Gardner, 50 East North Temple St., Salt Lake City, UT 84150-3223 Tel. 801/240-2490 Fax 801/240-4225
Email: CUR-Liahona-IMag@ldschurch.org
Website: www.lds.org

Liberty, (bi-M.) Seventh-day Adventist Church, Clifford R. Goldstein, 12501 Old Columbia Pike, Silver Spring, MD 20904 Tel. (301)680-6691 Fax (301)680-6695

Lifeglow, (Q.) Seventh-day Adventist Church, Large Print, Gaylena Gibson, P.O. Box 6097, Lincoln, NE 68506 Tel. (402)488-0981 Fax (402)488-7582

Light and Life Magazine, (bi-M.) , Douglas M. Newton, P.O. Box 535002, Indianapolis, IN 46253-5002 Tel. 317/244-3660
Email: llmeditor@fmcna.org

Liguorian, (M.) The Catholic Church, Allen J. Weinert, C.SS.R., 1 Liguori Dr., Liguori, MO 63057 Tel. (636)464-2500 Fax (636)464-8449
Email: 104626.1547@compuserve.com
Website: www.liguori.org

US PERIODICALS

Listen, (M.) Seventh-day Adventist Church, Lincoln E. Steed, 55 W. Oak Ridge Dr., Haggerstown, MD 21740 Tel. (301)791-7000 Fax (301)790-9734

Living Orthodoxy, (bi-M.) The Russian Orthodox Church Outside of Russia, Fr. Gregory Williams, 1180 Orthodox Way, Liberty, TN 37095 Tel. (615)536-5239 Fax (615)536-5945
Email: info@kronstadt.org
Website: www.kronstadt.org

The Lookout, (W.) Christian Churches and Churches of Christ, David Faust, 8121 Hamilton Ave., Cincinnati, OH 45231 Tel. (513)931-4050 Fax (513)931-0950
Email: lookout@standardpub.com
Website: www.standardpub.com

The Lutheran, (M.) Evangelical Lutheran Church in America, Rev. David L. Miller, 8765 W. Higgins Rd., Chicago, IL 60631-4183 Tel. (773)380-2540 Fax (773)380-2751
Email: lutheran@elca.org
Website: www.thelutheran.org

The Lutheran Ambassador, (16/Y.) The Association of Free Lutheran Congregations, Craig Johnson, 86286 Pine Grove Rd., Eugene, OR 97402 Tel. (541)687-8643 Fax (541)683-8496
Email: cjohnson@efn.org

The Lutheran Educator, (Q.) Wisconsin Evangelical Lutheran Synod, Prof. John R. Isch, Martin Luther College, 1995 Luther Ct. New Ulm, MN 56073 Tel. (507)354-8221 Fax (507)354-8225
Email: lutheraneducator@mlc-wels.edu

Lutheran Forum, (Q.) Interdenominational Lutheran, Ronald B. Bagnall, 207 Hillcrest Ave., Trenton, NJ 8618 Tel. (856)696-0417

The Lutheran Layman, (M.) The Lutheran Church—Missouri Synod, Gerald Perschbacher, 2185 Hampton Ave., St. Louis, MO 63139-2904 Tel. (314)951-4100 Fax (314)951-4295

Lutheran Parent, (bi-M.) Wisconsin Evangelical Lutheran Synod, Kenneth J. Kremer, 1250 N. 113th Street, Milwaukee, WI 53226-3284 Tel. (414)475-6600 Fax (414) 475-7684

Lutheran Parent's Wellspring, (bi-M.) Wisconsin Evangelical Lutheran Synod, Kenneth J. Kremer, 1250 N. 113th Street, Milwaukee, WI 53226-3284 Tel. (414)475-6600 Fax (414)475-7684

Lutheran Partners, (6/Y.) Evangelical Lutheran Church in America, Carl E. Linder, 8765 W. Higgins Rd., Chicago, IL 60631-4195 Tel. (773)380-2875 Fax (773)380-2829
Email: lutheran_partners@ecunet.org or lpart-mag@elca.org
Website: www.elca.org/dm/lp

Lutheran Sentinel, (M.) Evangelical Lutheran Synod, Theodore Gullixson, 1451 Pearl Pl., Escondido, CA 92027 Tel. (619)745-0583 Fax (619)743-4440

The Lutheran Spokesman, (M.) Church of the Lutheran Confession, Rev. Paul Fleischer, 710 4th Ave., SW, Sleepy Eye, MN 56085 Tel. (507)794-7793 Fax (507)794-5410
Email: pgflei@prairie.lakes.com
Website: www.primenet.com/~mpkelly/clc/spokesman.html

Lutheran Synod Quarterly, (Q.) Evangelical Lutheran Synod, G.R. Schmeling, Bethany Lutheran Theological Seminary, 6 Browns Ct. Mankato, MN 56001 Tel. (507)344-7855 Fax (507)344-7426
Email: elsynod@blc.edu
Website: www.blts.edu

The Lutheran Witness, (M.) The Lutheran Church—Missouri Synod, Rev. David Mahsman, 1333 S. Kirkwood Road, St. Louis, MO 63122-7295 Tel. (314)965-9000 Fax (314)965-3396
Email: lutheran.witness@lcms.org

Lutheran Woman Today, (10/Y.) Evangelical Lutheran Church in America, Nancy J. Stelling, 8765 W. Higgins Rd., Chicago, IL 60631-4101 Tel. (773)380-2732 Fax (773) 380-2419
Email: lwt@elca.org
Website: www.elca.org/wo/lwthome.html

Lyceum Spotlight, (10/Y.) National Spiritualist Association of Churches, Rev. Cosie Allen, 1418 Hall St., Grand Rapids, MI 49506 Tel. (616)241-2761 Fax (616)241-4703
Email: cosie@grgig.net

Magyar Egyhaz, (Q.) Hungarian Reformed Church in America, Stephen Szabo, 464 Forrest Ave., Paramus, NJ 7652 Tel. (201)262-2338 Fax (914)359-2313

Maranatha, (Q.) Advent Christian Church, Dawn Rutan, P.O. Box 23152, Charlotte, NC 28227 Tel. (704)545-6161 Fax (704)573-0712
Email: acpub@adventchristian.org
Website: www.adventchristian.org

Marriage Partnership, (Q.) Nondenominational, Ron R. Lee, 465 Gundersen Dr., Carol Stream, IL 60188 Tel. (630)260-6200 Fax (630)260-0114
Email: Mpedit@aol.com
Website: www.christianity.net/

Maryknoll, (11/Y.) The Catholic Church, Joseph R. Veneroso, Maryknoll Fathers and Brothers, PO Box 308 Maryknoll, NY 10545-0308 Tel. (914)941-7590 Fax (914)945-0670
Email: maryknollmag@igc.apc.org

Mature Years, (Q.) The United Methodist Church, Marvin W. Cropsey, 201 Eighth Ave. S, Nashville, TN 37202 Tel. (615)749-6292

Fax (615)749-6512
Email: mcropsey@umpublishing.org

Mennonite Historical Bulletin, (Q.) Mennonite Church, John E. Sharp, 1700 South Main St., Goshen, IN 46526 Tel. (219)535-7477 Fax (219)535-7756
Email: johnes@goshen.edu
Website: www.Goshen.edu/mcarchives

Mennonite Quarterly Review, (Q.) Mennonite Church, John D. Roth, 1700 S. Main St., Goshen, IN 46526 Tel. (219)535-7433 Fax (219)535-7438
Email: MQR@goshen.edu
Website: www.goshen.edu/mgr

The Mennonite, (48/Y.) General Conference Mennonite Church and the Mennonite Church, Everett Thomas, 722 Main St., P.O. Box 347, Newton, KS 67114-0347 Tel. (316)283-5100 Fax (316)283-0454
Email: TheMennonite@gcmc.org
Website: www.mph.org/themennonite

Message, (bi-M.) Seventh-day Adventist Church, Dr. Ron C. Smith, 55 West Oak Ridge Dr., Hagerstown, MD 21740 Tel. (301)393-4099 Fax (301)393-4103
Email: message@rhpa.org
Website: MESSAGEMAGAZINE.org

Message of the Open Bible, (bi-M.) Open Bible Standard Churches, Inc., Andrea Johnson, 2020 Bell Ave., Des Moines, IA 50315-1096 Tel. (515)288-6761 Fax (515)288-2510
Email: message@openbible.org
Website: www.openbible.org

Messenger, (11/Y.) Church of the Brethren, Fletcher Farrar, 1451 Dundee Ave., Elgin, IL 60120 Tel. (847)742-5100 Fax (847)742-1407
Email: wmcfadden_gb@brethren.org

Messenger of Truth, (bi-W.) Church of God in Christ (Mennonite), Gladwin Koehn, P.O. Box 230, Moundridge, KS 67107 Tel. (316)345-2532 Fax (316)345-2582

The Messenger, (M.) The Swedenborgian Church, Patte LeVan, PO Box 985, Julian, CA 92036 Tel. (760)765-2915 Fax (760)765-0218
Email: messenger@jinet.com

The Messenger, (M.) The (Original) Church of God, Inc., Wayne Jolley and William Dale, PO Box 3086, Chattanooga, TN 37404-0086 Tel. (800)827-9234

The Messenger, (M.) Pentecostal Free Will Baptist Church, Inc., George Thomas, P.O. Box 1568, Dunn, NC 28335 Tel. (910)892-4161 Fax (910)892-6876

Methodist History, (Q.) The United Methodist Church, Charles Yrigoyen Jr., P.O. Box 127, Madison, NJ 07940 Tel. (973)408-3189 Fax (973)408-3909

Email: cyrigoyen@gcah.org
Website: www.gcah.org

Mid-Stream: The Ecumenical Movement Today, (Q.) Christian Church (Disciples of Christ), Robert K. Welsh, P.O. Box 1986, Indianapolis, IN 46206-1986 Tel. (317)713-2586 Fax (317)713-2588
Email: rwelsh@ccu.disciples.org
Website: www.disciples.org/ccu

Ministry, (M.) Seventh-day Adventist Church, Willmore D. Eva, 12501 Old Columbia Pike, Silver Spring, MD 20904 Tel. (301)680-6510 Fax (301)680-6502
Email: 74532.2425@compuserve.com

Mission Grams, (bi-M.) Free Will Baptists, National Association of, Ida Lewis, Home Missions Office, P.O. Box 5002 Antioch, TN 37011-5002 Tel. (615)731-6812 Fax (615) 731-7655
Email: ida@nafwb.org

Mission Herald, (bi-M.) National Baptist Convention, U.S.A., Inc., William J. Harvey, 701 S. 19th Street, Philadelphia, PA 19146 Tel. (215)735-9853 Fax (215)735-1721

Mission, Adult, and Youth Children's Editions, (Q.) Seventh-day Adventist Church, Charlotte Ishkanian, 12501 Old Columbia Pike, Silver Spring, MD 20904 Tel. (301)680-6167 Fax (301)680-6155
Email: 74532.2435@compuserve.com

The Missionary Magazine, (9/Y.) , Bertha O. Fordham, 800 Risley Ave., Pleasantville, NJ 08232-4250

The Missionary Messenger, (M.) Christian Methodist Episcopal Church, Doris F. Boyd, 213 Viking Dr., W., Cordova, TN 38108-7263 Tel. 901-757-1103 Fax 901-751-2104
Email: dboyd@pschem.com

The Missionary Messenger, (6/Y.) Cumberland Presbyterian Church, Carol Penn, 1978 Union Ave., Memphis, TN 38104 Tel. (901)276-4572 Fax (901)276-4578
Email: messenger@cumberland.org

Missionary Seer, (M.) African Methodist Episcopal Zion Church, Rev. Kermit J. DeGraffenreidt, 475 Riverside Dr., Rm. 1935, New York, NY 10115 Tel. (212)870-2952 Fax (212)870-2808

The Missionary Signal, (bi-M.) Churches of God, General Conference, Kathy Rodabaugh, P.O. Box 926, Findlay, OH 45839 Tel. (419)424-1961 Fax (419)424-3433

MissionsUSA, (bi-M.) Southern Baptist Convention, Wayne Grinstead, 4200 North Point Pkwy., Alphretta, GA 30202-4174 Tel. (770)410-6251 Fax (770)410-6006

Monday Morning, (21/Y.) Presbyterian Church (U.S.A.), Houston Hodges, 100 Witherspoon St., Louisville, KY 40202 Tel. (502)569-5502 Fax (502)569-8073 Email: H2@pcusa.org

Moody Magazine, (6/Y.) Nondenominational, Bruce Anderson, 820 N. LaSalle Blvd., Chicago, IL 60610 Tel. (312)329-2164 Fax (312)329-2149 Email: moodyltrs@moody.edu Website: www.moody.edu/moodyma

The Moravian, (10/Y.) Moravian Church in America (Unitas Fratrum), Ms. Roxann Miller, 1021 Center St., P.O. Box 1245, Bethlehem, PA 18016 Tel. (610)867-0594 Fax (610)866-9223

The Mother Church, (M.) Western Diocese of the Armenian Church of North America, Rev. Fr. Sipan Mekhsian, 3325 N. Glenoaks Blvd., Burbank, CA 91504 Tel. (818)558-7474 Fax (818)558-6333 Email: armenianchwd@earthlink.net Website: www.armenianchurchwd.com

My Soul Sings: A Magazine of Inspirational/ Gospel Music, (Q.) Nondenominational, Irene C. Franklin, President and Publisher, P.O. Box 16181, St. Louis, MO 63105 Tel. (888)862-0179 Fax (888)862-0179 Email: Irene@postnet.com Website: www.mysoulsings.com

NAE Washington Insight, (M.) Interdenominational, Rev. Richard Cizik, 450 E. Gundersen Dr., Carol Stream, IL 60188 Tel. (630)665-0500 Fax (630)665-8575 Email: oga@nae.net Website: www.nae.net

National Baptist Union Review, (M.) Nondenominational, Willie Paul, 6717 Centennial Blvd., Nashville, TN 37209-1000 Tel. (615) 350-8000 Fax (615)350-9018

National Catholic Reporter, (44/Y.) The Catholic Church, Tom Roberts, P.O. Box 419281, Kansas City, MO 64141 Tel. (816) 531-0538 Fax (816)968-2280 Email: editor@natcath.org Website: www.natcath.org

The National Christian Reporter, (W.) Nondenominational, John A. Lovelace, P.O. Box 222198, Dallas, TX 75222 Tel. (214)630-6495 Fax (214)630-0079 Email: 76113.662@compuserve.com

The National Spiritualist Summit, (M.) National Spiritualist Association of Churches, Rev. Sandra Pfortmiller, 3521 W. Topeka Dr., Glendale, AZ 85308-2325 Tel. (623)581-6686 Fax (623)581-5544 Email: G2s2pfont@aol.com

New Church Life, (M.) General Church of the New Jerusalem, Rev. Donald L. Rose, Box 277, Bryn Athyn, PA 19009 Tel. (215)947-6225 Fax (215)938-1871 Email: DonRocBACS-GC.org Website: www.newchurch.org

The New Era, (M.) The Church of Jesus Christ of Latter-day Saints, Larry Hiller, 50 E. North Temple St., Salt Lake City, UT 84150 Tel. (801)240-2951 Fax (801)240-2270 Email: rmromney@chq.byu.edu

New Horizons in the Orthodox Presbyterian Church, (11/Y.) The Orthodox Presbyterian Church, Thomas E. Tyson, 607 N. Easton Rd., Bldg. E, P.O. Box P Willow Grove, PA 19090-0920 Tel. (215)830-0900 Fax (215)830-0350 Email: tomtyson@aol.com Website: www.opc.org/

New Oxford Review, (11/Y.) The Catholic Church, Dale Vree, 1069 Kains Ave., Berkeley, CA 94706 Tel. (510)526-5374 Fax (510)526-3492

New World Outlook, (bi-M.) Mission Magazine of The United Methodist Church, Alma Graham, 475 Riverside Dr., Rm. 1476, New York, NY 10115 Tel. (212)870-3765 Fax (212)870-3654 Email: NWO@gbgm-umc.org Website: http://gbgm-umc.org/nwo/

The News, (Q.) The Anglican Orthodox Church, The Rev. Roger Jessup, Anglican Orthodox Church, P.O. Box 128 Statesville, NC 28687-0128 Tel. (704)873-8365 Fax (704)873-5359 Email: aocusa@energyunited.net

Newscope, (W.) The United Methodist Church, Victoria A. Rebeck, P.O. Box 801, Nashville, TN 37202 Tel. (615)749-6320 Fax (615)749-6061 Email: vrebeck@umpublishing.org Website: www.umph.org

The North American Catholic, (M.) North American Old Catholic Church, Theodore J. Remalt, 4200 N. Kedvale Ave., Chicago, IL 60641 Tel. (312)685-0461 Fax (312)286-5783

The North American Challenge, (M.) Home Missions Division of The United Pentecostal Church International, Joseph Fiorino, 8855 Dunn Rd., Hazelwood, MO 63042-2299 Tel. (314)837-7300 Fax (314)837-5632

NRB Magazine, (10/Y.) Nondenominational, Christine Pryor, National Religious Broadcasters, 7839 Ashton Ave Manassas, VA 20109-2883 Tel. (703)330-7000 Fax (703) 330-6996 Email: cpryor@nrb.org Website: www.nrb.org

Nuestra Parroquia, (M.) The Catholic Church, Carmen Aguinaco, 205 W. Monroe St.,

313

Chicago, IL 60606-5013 Tel. (312)236-7782 Fax (312)236-8207
Email: USCath@aol.com

On Course, (Q.) Assemblies of God, Melinda Booze, 1445 Boonville Ave., Springfield, MO 65802-1894 Tel. (417)862-2781 Fax (417)866-1146
Email: oncourse@ag.org
Website: oncourse.ag.org

On the Line, (M.) Mennonite Church, Mary C. Meyer, 616 Walnut Ave., Scottdale, PA 15683 Tel. (724)887-8500 Fax (724-887-3111
Email: otl@mph.org
Website: www.mph.org/otl

One Church, (bi-M.) Patriarchal Parishes of the Russian Orthodox Church in the U.S.A., Bishop Mercurius, 15 E. 97th St., New York, NY 10029 Tel. (212)831-6294 Fax (212)427-5003
Email: bmercurius@ruscon.com

Open Hands, (Q.) Interdenominational, Chris Glaser, 3801 N. Keeler Ave., Chicago, IL 60641-3007 Tel. (773)736-5526 Fax (773)736-5475
Email: openhands@rcp.org
Website: www.rcp.org/openhands/index.html

Orthodox America, (8/Y.) The Russian Orthodox Church Outside of Russia, Mary Mansur, P.O. Box 383, Richfield Springs, NY 13439-0383 Tel. (315)858-1518
Email: niko@telenet.net
Website: www.roca.org/oa

The Orthodox Church, (M.) The Orthodox Church in America, Leonid Kishkovsky, P.O. Box 675, Syosset, NY 11791 Tel. (516)922-0550 Fax (516)922-0954
Email: info@oca.org

Orthodox Family, (Q.) The Russian Orthodox Church Outside of Russia, George Johnson and Deborah Johnson, P.O. Box 45, Beltsville, MD 20705 Tel. (301)890-3552
Email: 1lew@cais.com
Website: www.roca.org/orthodox

Orthodox Life, (bi-M.) The Russian Orthodox Church Outside of Russia, Fr. Luke, Holy Trinity Monastery, P.O Box 36 Jordanville, NY 13361-0036 Tel. (315)858-0940 Fax (315)858-0505
Email: 72204.1465@compuserve.com

The Orthodox Observer, (M.) Greek Orthodox Archdiocese of America, Stavros H. Papagermanos, 8 E. 79th St., New York, NY 10021 Tel. (212)570-3555 Fax (212)774-0239
Email: observer@goarch.org
Website: www.goarch.org/goa/observer

Orthodox Russia (English translation of Pravoslavnaya Rus), (24/Y.) The Russian Orthodox Church Outside of Russia,

Archbishop Laurus, Holy Trinity Monastery, P.O. Box 36 Jordanville, NY 13361-0036 Tel. (315)858-0940 Fax (315)858-0505
Email: orthrus@telenet.net

Orthodox Voices, (4/Y.) The Russian Orthodox Church Outside of Russia, Thomas Webb and Ellen Webb, P.O. Box 23644, Lexington, KY 40523 Tel. (606)271-3877

The Other Side, (bi-M.) Interdenominational, Dee Dee Risher and Douglas Davidson, 300 W. Apsley St., Philadelphia, PA 19144-4221 Tel. (215)849-2178 Fax (215)849-3755
Email: editors@theotherside.org
Website: www.theotherside.org

Our Daily Bread, (M.) The Swedenborgian Church, Lee Woofenden, P.O. Box 396, Bridgewater, MA 02324 Tel. (508)946-1767 Fax (508)946-1757
Email: odb@swedenborg.org
Website: www.swedenborg.org/odb/odb.html

Our Little Friend, (W.) Seventh-day Adventist Church, Aileen Andres Sox, P.O. Box 5353, Nampa, ID 83653-5353 Tel. (208)465-2500 Fax (208)465-2531

Our Sunday Visitor, (W.) The Catholic Church, David Scott, 200 Noll Plaza, Huntington, IN 46750 Tel. (219)356-8400 Fax (219)356-8472
Email: 76440.3571@compuserve.com

Outreach, (10/Y.) Armenian Apostolic Church of America, Iris Papazian, 138 E. 39th St., New York, NY 10016 Tel. (212)689-7810 Fax (212)689-7168

Pastoral Life, (M.) The Catholic Church, Matthew Roehrig, Box 595, Canfield, OH 44406-0595 Tel. (330)533-5503 Fax (330)553-1076
Email: paultheapostle@msn.com
Website: www.albahouse.org

The Path of Orthodoxy (Serbian), (M.) Serbian Orthodox Church in the U.S.A. and Canada, V. Rev. Nedeljko Lunich, 300 Striker Ave., Joliet, IL 60436 Tel. (815)741-1023 Fax (815)741-1023
Email: dinara2@aol.com

Pentecostal Evangel, (W.) Assemblies of God, Hal Donaldson, Gospel Publishing House, 1445 Boonville Ave. Springfield, MO 65802-1894 Tel. (417)862-2781 Fax (417)862-0416
Email: pevangel@ag.org
Website: pe.ag.org

Pentecostal Evangel, Missions World Edition, (M.) Assemblies of God, Randy Hurst, Editor; John Maempa, General Editor, Gospel Publishing House, 1445 Boonville Ave. Springfield, MO 65802 Tel. (417)862-2781 Fax (417)862-0085
Email: jmaempa@publish.ag.org

The Pentecostal Herald, (M.) United Pentecostal Church International, Rev. J. L. Hall, 8855 Dunn Rd., Hazelwood, MO 63042 Tel. (314)837-7300 Fax (314)837-4503

Pentecostal Leader, (Q.) The International Pentecostal Church of Christ, Clyde M. Hughes, P.O. Box 439, London, OH 43140 Tel. (740)852-4722 Fax (740)852-0348 Email: hqipcc@aol.com

The Pentecostal Messenger, (M.) Pentecostal Church of God (Joplin, MO), John Mallinak, P.O. Box 850, Joplin, MO 64802 Tel. (417)624-7050 Fax (417)624-7102 Email: johnm@pcg.org Website: www.pcg.org

The People's Mouthpiece, (Q.) Apostolic Overcoming Holy Church of God, Inc., Juanita R. Arrigton, Ph.D., 1120 North 24th St., Birmingham, AL 35234 Tel. (205)324-2202

Perspectives, (10/Y.) Reformed Church in America, Evelyn Diephouse, P.O. Box 470, Ada, MI 49301-0470 Tel. (616)241-2053 Fax (616)241-2064 Email: perspectives_@hotmail.com

Perspectives on Science and Christian Faith, (Q.) Nondenominational, Roman J. Miller, 4956 Singers Glen Rd., Harrisonburg, VA 22802 Tel. (540)867-0854 Email: millerrj@rica.net Website: http://asa.calvin.edu

The Pillar Monthly, (12/Y.) , Donald J. Wolfram and Mark Tomlin, PO Box 9045, Zarephath, NJ 08890 Tel. (908)356-0561

The Pilot, (W.) The Catholic Church, Peter V. Conley, 141 Tremont St., Boston, MA 02111 Tel. (617)482-4316 Fax (617)482-5647 Email: pilotpub@concentric.net Website: www.rcab.org

Pockets, (11/Y.) The United Methodist Church, Janet R. Knight, P.O. Box 189, Nashville, TN 37202 Tel. (615)340-7333 Fax (615)340-7767 Email: pockets@upperroom.org Website: www.upperroom.org/pockets

Polka, (Q.) Polish National Catholic Church of America, Cecelia Lallo, 1127 Frieda St., Dickson City, PA 18519-1304 Tel. (570)489-4364 Fax (570)346-2188

Pravoslavnaya Rus (Russian), (24/Y.) The Russian Orthodox Church Outside of Russia, Archbishop Laurus, Holy Trinity Monastery, P.O. Box 36 Jordanville, NY 13361-0036 Tel. (315)858-0940 Fax (315)858-0505 Email: orthrus@telenet.net

Pravoslavnaya Zhisn (Monthly Supplement to Pravoslavnaya Rus), (M.) The Russian Orthodox Church Outside of Russia, Archbishop Laurus, Holy Trinity Monastery, P.O. Box 36 Jordanville, NY 13361-0036 Tel. (315)858-0940 Fax (315)858-0505 Email: Orthrus@telenet.net

Praying, (bi-M.) Spirituality for Everyday Living, Rich Heffern, P.O. Box 419335, 115 E. Armour Blvd. Kansas City, MO 64141 Tel. (816)968-2258 Fax (816)968-2280

Preacher's Magazine, (bi-M.) Church of the Nazarene, Randal Denney, 10814 E. Broadway, Spokane, WA 99206 Tel. (509)226-3464 Fax (509)926-8740

The Preacher, (Q.) Baptist Bible Fellowship International, Mike Randall, P.O. Box 309 HSJ, Springfield, MO 65801 Tel. (417)831-3996 Fax (417)831-1470

Presbyterian News Service "News Briefs", (W.) Presbyterian Church (U.S.A.), Jerry L. VanMarter, 100 Witherspoon St., Rm. 5418 Louisville, KY 40202 Tel. (502)569-5493 Fax (502)569-8073 Email: jerryv@ctr.pcusa.org

Presbyterian Outlook, (43/Y.) Presbyterian Church (U.S.A.), Robert H. Bullock Jr., Box 85623, Richmond, VA 23285-5623 Tel. (804)359-8442 Fax (804)353-6369 Email: outlook.parti@pcusa.org Website: www.pres-outlook.com

Presbyterians Today, (10/Y.) Presbyterian Church (U.S.A.), Eva Stimson, 100 Witherspoon St., Louisville, KY 40202-1396 Tel. (502)569-5637 Fax (502)569-8632 Email: today@pcusa.org Website: www.pcusa.org/today

Primary Treasure, (W.) Seventh-day Adventist Church, Aileen Andres Sox, P.O. Box 5353, Nampa, ID 83653-5353 Tel. (208)465-2500 Fax (208)465-2531

The Primitive Baptist, (bi-M.) Primitive Baptists, W. H. Cayce, PO Box 38, Thornton, AR 71766 Tel. (501)352-3694

Priority, (M.) The Missionary Church, Rev. Robert Ransom, P.O. Box 9127, Ft. Wayne, IN 46899 Tel. (219)747-2027 Fax (219)747-5331 Email: mcdenomusa@aol.com Website: mcusa.org

Providence Visitor, (W.) The Catholic Church, Michael Brown, 184 Broad St., Providence, RI 02903 Tel. (401)272-1010 Fax (401)421-8418 Email: 102344.3235@compuserve.com

Purpose, (W.) Mennonite Church USA, James E. Horsch, 616 Walnut Ave., Scottdale, PA 15683 Tel. (412)887-8500 Fax (412)887-3111 Email: horsch@mph.org Website: www.mph.org

Pursuit, (Q.) The Evangelical Free Church of America, Carol Madison, 901 East 78th St.,

315

Minneapolis, MN 55420-1300 Tel. (612)853-1763 Fax (612)853-8488

Qala min M'Dinkha (Voice from the East), (Q.) Apostolic Catholic Assyrian Church of the East, North A, Shlemon Hesequial, Diocesan Offices, 7201 N. Ashland Chicago, IL 60626 Tel. (773)465-4777 Fax (773)465-0776

Quaker Life, (10/Y.) Friends United Meeting, Patricia Edwards-Konic, 101 Quaker Hill Dr., Richmond, IN 47374-1980 Tel. (765)962-7573 Fax (765)966-1293
Email: QuakerLife@fum.org
Website: www.fum.org

Quarterly Review, (Q.) The United Methodist Church, Hendrik R. Pieterse, Box 340007, Nashville, TN 37203-0007 Tel. (615)340-7334 Fax (615)340-7048
Email: hpieterse@gbhem.org
Website: www.quarterlyreview.org

Quarterly Review, A.M.E. Zion, (Q.) African Methodist Episcopal Zion Church, Rev. James D. Armstrong, P.O. Box 33247, Charlotte, NC 28231 Tel. (704)334-0728 Fax (704)333-1769

Reflections, (bi-M.) United Pentecostal Church International, Melissa Anderson, 8855 Dunn Rd., Hazelwood, MO 63402 Tel. (918)370-2659 Fax (918)371-6320

Reformation Today, (bi-M.) Sovereign Grace Baptists, Erroll Hulse, c/o Tom Lutz, 3743 Nichol Ave. Anderson, IN 46011-3008 Tel. (317)644-0994 Fax (317)644-0994

Reformed Herald, (M.) Reformed Church in the United States, David Dawn, 1000 Evergreen Way, Rock Springs, WY 82901-4104 Tel. (307)362-5107

Reformed Worship, (Q.) Christian Reformed Chuch in North America, Emily R. Brink, 2850 Kalamazoo Ave. SE, Grand Rapids, MI 49560-0001 Tel. (616)224-0785 Fax (616)224-0834
Email: info@reformedworship.org
Website: www.reformedworship.org

Rejoice!, (Q.) Mennonite & Mennonite Brethren Church, Philip Wiebe, 1218 Franklin St. NW, Salem, OR 97304 Tel. (503)585-4458 Fax (503)585-4458

Rejoice!, (Q.) Mennonite Church, Phil Wiebe, Rose Mary Stutzman, 616 Walnut Ave., Scottdale, PA 15683 Tel. (724)887-8500 Fax (724)887-3111
Email: rstutz@mph.org

Report From The Capital, (24/yr) Baptist Joint Committee, Larry Chesser, 200 Maryland Ave. NE, Washington, DC 20002-5797 Tel. (202)544-4226 Fax (202)544-2094
Email: Larry_Chesser@bjcpa.org
Website: www.bjcpa.org

Reporter, (M.) The Lutheran Church—Missouri Synod, David Mahsman, 1333 S. Kirkwood Rd., St. Louis, MO 63122-7295 Tel. (314)965-9000 Fax (314)965-3396
Email: REPORTER@lcms.org
Website: www.lcms.org

The Rescue Herald, (Q.) American Rescue Workers, Col. Robert N. Coles, National Field Office, 1209 Hamilton Blvd. Hagerstown, MD 21742 Tel. (301)797-0061 Fax (301)797-1480

Response, (M.) The United Methodist Church, Dana Jones, 475 Riverside Dr., Room 1356, New York, NY 10115 Tel. (212)870-3755 Fax (212)870-3940

The Restitution Herald, (bi-M.) Church of God General Conference (Oregon, Ill. & Morrow, Jeffery Fletcher, Box 100,000, Morrow, GA 30260-7000 Tel. (504)543-0290 Fax (404)362-9307

Restoration Herald, (M.) Christian Churches and Churches of Christ, H. Lee Mason, 5664 Cheviot Rd., Cincinnati, OH 45247-7071 Tel. (513)385-0461 Fax (513) 385-0660
Email: thecra@aol.com
Website: www.thecra.org

Restoration Quarterly, (Q.) Churches of Christ, James W. Thompson, Box 28227, Abilene, TX 79699-8227 Tel. (915)674-3781 Fax (915)674-3776
Email: rq@bible.acu.edu
Website: www.rq.acu.edu

Restoration Witness, (bi-M.) Reorganized Church of Jesus Christ of Latter Day Saints, Richard A. Brown, Herald Publishing House, P.O. Box 390 Independence, MO 64051-0390 Tel. (816)521-3043 Fax (816)521-3043
Email: rbrown@rlds.org

Review for Religious, (bi-M.) The Catholic Church, David L. Fleming, S.J., 3601 Lindell Blvd., St. Louis, MO 63108 Tel. (314)977-7363 Fax (314)977-7362
Email: foppema@slu.edu

Review of Religious Research, (4/Y.) Nondenominational, Dr. Darren E. Sherkat & Dr. Christopher Ellison, Co-editors, Sociology Department, University of Texas-Austin Austin, TX 78712 Tel. (512)471-1122 Fax (512)471-1748
Email: cellison@jeeves.la.utexas.edu

Rocky Mountain Christian, (M.) Churches of Christ, Ron L. Carter, P.O. Box 26620, Colorado Springs, CO 80936 Tel. (719)598-4197 Fax (719)528-1549
Email: 76102.2461@compuserve.com

Sabbath Recorder, (M.) Seventh Day Baptist General Conference, USA and Canada, Rev. Kevin J. Butler, 3120 Kennedy Rd., P.O. Box

1678 Janesville, WI 53547 Tel. (608)752-5055 Fax (608)752-7711
Email: sdbmedia@inwave.com
Website: www.seventhdaybaptist.org

Sabbath School Leadership, (M.) Seventh-day Adventist Church, Faith Crumbly, Review and Herald Publishing Assoc., 55 W. Oak Ridge Dr. Hagerstown, MD 21740 Tel. (301)393-4095 Fax (301)393-4055
Email: mharris@rhpa.org
Website: www.rhpa.org

Saint Anthony Messenger, (M.) The Catholic Church, Jack Wintz, O.F.M., 1615 Republic St., Cincinnati, OH 45210 Tel. (513)241-5616 Fax (513)241-0399
Email: StAnthony@AmericanCatholic.org
Website: www.americancatholic.org

Saint Willibrord Journal, (Q.) Christ Catholic Church, The Rev. MonsignorCharles E. Harrison, P.O. Box 271751, Houston, TX 77277-1751 Tel. (713)515-8206 Fax (713) 622-5311
Website: www.christcatholic.org

Saints Herald, (M.) Reorganized Church of Jesus Christ of Latter Day Saints, Linda L. Booth, P.O. Box 1059, Independence, MO 64051 Tel. (816)833-1000 Fax (816)521-3043

SBC Life, (10/Y.) Southern Baptist Convention, Bill Merrell, 901 Commerce St., Nashville, TN 37203 Tel. (615)244-2355 Fax (615)782-8684
Email: jrevell@sbc.net
Website: sbc.net

The Schwenkfeldian, (Q.) The Schwenkfelder Church, Andrew C. Anders, 105 Seminary Street, Pennsburg, PA 18073 Tel. (215)244-2355

SCROLL- Computer Resources for Church and Family, (6/Y.) Nondenominational, Marshall N. Surratt, 304C Crossfield Drive, P.O. Box 603 Versailles, KY 40383-0603 Tel. (606)873-0550 Fax (606)879-0121
Email: scroll@deerhaven.com
Website: wwww.deerhaven.com/

Searching Together, (Q.) Sovereign Grace Believers, Jon Zens, Box 548, St. Croix Falls, WI 54024 Tel. (651)465-6516 Fax (651)465-5101
Email: jon@searchingtogether.org
Website: www.searchingtogether.org

Secret Chamber, (Q.) African Methodist Episcopal Church, George L. Champion, Sr., 5728 Major Blvd., Orlando, FL 82819 Tel. (407)352-8797 Fax (407)352-6097

The Secret Place, (Q.) American Baptist Churches in the USA, Kathleen Hayes, Senior Editor, P.O. Box 851, Valley Forge, PA 19482-0851 Tel. (610)768-2240 Fax (610)768-2441

Seeds for the Parish, (bi-M.) Evangelical Lutheran Church in America, Kate Elliott, 8765 W. Higgins Rd., Chicago, IL 60631-4101 Tel. (773)380-2949 Fax (773)380-1465
Email: kelliott@elca.org

Sharing, (Q.) Interdenominational Anabaptist, Judy Martin Godshalk, P.O. Box 438, Goshen, IN 46527 Tel. (219)533-9511 Fax (219)533-5264

Shiloh's Messenger of Wisdom, (M.) Israelite House of David, William Robertson, P.O. Box 1067, Benton Harbor, MI 49023

The Shining Light, (bi-M.) Church of God (Anderson, Ind), Wilfred Jordan, Box 1235, Anderson, IN 46015 Tel. (317)644-1593

Signs of the Times, (M.) Seventh-day Adventist Church, Marvin Moore, P.O. Box 5353, Nampa, ID 83653-5353 Tel. (208)465-2577 Fax (208)465-2531

The Silver Lining, (M.) Apostolic Christian Churches of America, Bruce Leman, R.R. 2, Box 50 Roanoke, IL 61561-9625 Tel. (309) 923-7777 Fax (309)923-7359

Social Questions Bulletin, (bi-M.) The United Methodist Church, Rev. Kathryn J. Johnson, 212 East Capitol St., NE, Washington, DC 20003 Tel. (202)546-8806 Fax (202)546-6811
Email: mfsa@olg.com
Website: www.olg.com/mfsa

Sojourners, (6/Y.) Nondenominational, Jim Wallis, 2401 15th St. NW, Washington, DC 20009 Tel. (202)328-8842 Fax (202)328-8757
Email: sojourners@sojourners.com
Website: www.sojourners.com

Solia - The Herald, (M.) The Romanian Orthodox Episcopate of America, Rev. Deacon David Oancea, P.O. Box 185, Grass Lake, MI 49240-0185 Tel. (517)522-3656 Fax (517)522-5907
Email: roeasolia@aol.com
Website: www.roea.org

The Southern Methodist, (bi-M.) Southern Methodist Church, Thomas M. Owens, Sr., P.O. Box 39, Orangeburg, SC 29116-0039 Tel. (803)534-9853 Fax (803)535-3881
Email: smchq@juno.com

Spectrum, (bi-M.) Conservative Baptist Association of America (CBAmerica), Ed Mitchell and Sylvia Allen, 1501 W. Mineral Ave., Suite B Littleton, CO 80120 Tel. (720)283-3030 Fax (720)283-3333
Email: CBA@CBAmerica.org
Website: www.CBAmerica.org

Spirit, (Q.) Volunteers of America, Arthur Smith and Denis N. Baker, 1321 Louisiana Ave., New Orleans, LA 70115 Tel. (504)897-1731

317

The Spiritual Sword, (Q.) Churches of Christ, Alan E. Highers, 1511 Getwell Rd., Memphis, TN 38111 Tel. (901)743-0464 Fax (901)743-2197
Email: getwellcc@aol.com

The Standard Bearer, (21/Y.) Protestant Reformed Churches in America, David J. Engelsma, 4949 Ivanrest Ave., Grandville, MI 49418 Tel. (616)531-1490 Fax (616)531-3033
Email: engelsma@prca.org

The Standard, (M.) Baptist General Conference, Gary D. Marsh, 2002 S. Arlington Heights Rd., Arlington Heights, IL 60005 Tel. (847)228-0200 Fax (847)228-5376
Email: GMBGCSTD@aol.com

Star of Zion, (bi-W.) African Methodist Episcopal Zion Church, Dr. Morgan W. Tann, P.O. Box 31005, Charlotte, NC 28231 Tel. (704)377-4329 Fax (704)377-2809
Email: star0zion@juno.com

Stewardship USA, (Q.) Nondenominational, Raymond Barnett Knudsen II, 4818 Quarton Rd., Bloomfield Hills, MI 48302 Tel. (248) 737-0895 Fax (248)737-0895

Story Friends, (M.) Mennonite Church, Rose Mary Stutzman, 616 Walnut Ave., Scottdale, PA 15683 Tel. (724)887-8500 Fax (724)887-3111
Email: rstutz@mph.org
Website: www.mph.org

The Student, (M.) Seventh-day Adventist Church, Jerry Stevens, P.O. Box 6097, Lincoln, NE 68506 Tel. (402)488-0981 Fax (402)488-7582
Email: CRSnet@compuserve.com
Website: www.ChristianRecord.org

Sunday, (Q.) Interdenominational, Jack P. Lowndes, 2930 Flowers Rd., S., #16, Atlanta, GA 30341-5532 Tel. (770)936-5376 Fax (770) 452-6582

The Tablet, (W.) The Catholic Church, Ed Wilkinson, 653 Hicks St., Brooklyn, NY 11231 Tel. (718)858-3838 Fax (718)858-2112

Teacher Touch, (Q.) Nondenominational, Marlene LeFever, 4050 Lee Vance View, Colorado Springs, CO 80918 Tel. (800)708-5550 Fax (719)535-3202
Email: lefeverm@cookministries.org
Website: www.cookministries.org

Theology Digest, (Q.) The Catholic Church, 3634 Lindell Blvd., St. Louis, MO 63108-3395 Tel. (314)977-3410 Fax (314)977-247

Theology Today, (Q.) Nondenominational, Patrick D. Miller, P.O. Box 29, Princeton, NJ 08542 Tel. (609)497-7714 Fax (609)497-7870

These Days, (bi-M.) Interdenominational, Kay Snodgrass, 100 Witherspoon St., Louisville,

KY 40202-1396 Tel. (502)569-5080 Fax (502)569-5113
Website: www.pcusa.org/ppc/

The Tidings, (W.) The Catholic Church, Tod M. Tamberg, 3424 Wilshire Blvd., Los Angeles, CA 90010 Tel. (213)637-7360 Fax (213)637-6360
Website: www.the-tidings.com

Timbrel: The Publication of Mennonite Women, (6/Y.) Mennonite Church and General Conference Mennonite Churc, Cathleen Hockman-Wert, 828 Washington St., Apt. 3B Huntingdon, PA 16652 Tel. (814)641-5259
Email: timbrel@vicon.net

Today's Christian Woman, (6/Y.) Nondenominational, Jane Johnson Struck, 465 Gundersen Dr., Carol Stream, IL 60188 Tel. (630)260-6200 Fax (630)260-0114
Email: TCWedit@aol.com
Website: www.christianity.net/

Tomorrow Magazine, (Q.) American Baptist Churches in the USA, Sara E. Hopkins, 475 Riverside Dr., Room 1700, New York, NY 10115-0049 Tel. (800)986-6222 Fax (800)986-6782

The Tover of St. Cassian, (2/Y.) Apostolic Episcopal Church- Province of the East, Rt. Rev. Francis C. Spataro DD, Order of Corporate Reunion- US Council/ Society of St. Cassian, 80-46 234th Street Jamaica, NY 11427 Tel. (718)740-4134 Fax (718)599-5260
Email: vilatte@aol.com
Website: http://VGUSA.InJesus.com

Truth, (bi-M.) Grace Gospel Fellowship, Roger G. Anderson and Sherry Macy, 2125 Martindale SW, Grand Rapids, MI 49509 Tel. (616)247-1999 Fax (616)241-2542
Email: ggfpres@aol.com

Truth Magazine, (bi-W.) Churches of Christ, Mike Willis, Box 9670, Bowling Green, KY 42102 Tel. (800)428-0121

U.S. Catholic, (M.) The Catholic Church, Rev. Mark J. Brummel, 205 W. Monroe St., Chicago, IL 60606 Tel. (312)236-7782 Fax (312)236-8207
Email: editors@uscatholic.org
Website: www.uscatholic.org

Ubique, (Q.) The Liberal Catholic Church— Province of the United Sta, Rt. Rev. Joseph Tisch, P.O. Box 1117, Melbourne, FL 32902 Tel. (407)254-0499

Ukrainian Orthodox Herald, Ukrainian Orthodox Church of the USA, Rev. Dr. Anthony Ugolnik, P.O. Box 774, Allentown, PA 18105

United Church News, (10/Y.) United Church of Christ, W. Evan Golder, 700 Prospect Ave.,

Cleveland, OH 44115 Tel. (216)736-2218 Fax (216)736-2223
Email: goldere@ucc.org
Website: www.ucc.org

UMR Communications, Inc., Independent, Protestant organization which publishes: The United Methodist Reporter (W.); The United Methodist Reporter (bi-W.); The National Christian Reporter (W.); Good Works Online (daily Internet); Reporter Interactive (daily Internet), Cynthia B. Astle, P.O. Box 660275, Dallas, TX 75266-0275 Tel. (214)630-6495 Fax (214)630-0079
Email: united_methodist_reporter@compuserve. com
Website: www.umr.org

The Upper Room, (6/Y.) The United Methodist Church, Janice Grana, P.O. Box 189, Nashville, TN 37202 Tel. (615)340-7200 Fax (615)340-7006

Vibrant Life, (bi-M.) Seventh-day Adventist Church, Larry Becker, 55 W. Oak Ridge Dr., Hagerstown, MD 21740 Tel. (301)393-4019 Fax (301)393-4055
Email: vibrantlife@rhpa.org
Website: www.vibrantlife.com

Victory (Youth Magazine), (M.) Church of God of Prophecy, Dewayne Hamby, P.O. Box 2910, Cleveland, TN 37320-2910 Tel. (423)559-5207 Fax (423)559-5202
Email: CGPYOUTH@aol.com
Website: www.cogop.org

The Vindicator, (M.) Old German Baptist Brethren, Steve L. Bayer, 6952 N. Montgomery Co. Line Rd., Englewood, OH 45322-9748 Tel. (937)884-7531 Fax (937) 884-7531

Vista, (bi-M.) Christian Church of North America, General Council, Eric Towse, 1294 Rutledge Rd., Transfer, PA 16154 Tel. (412)962-3501 Fax (412)962-1766
Email: ccna@nauticom.net
Website: www.ccna.org

Voice!, (Q.) General Association of General Baptists, Rev. Ron Byrd, 100 Stinson Dr., Poplar Bluff, MO 63901 Tel. (573)785-7746 Fax (573)785-0564
Email: gbnm@pbmo.net
Website: www.generalbaptist.com

The Voice, (6/Y.) IFCA International, Inc., Les Lofquist, P.O. Box 810, Grandville, MI 49468-0810 Tel. (616)531-1840 Fax (616) 531-1814
Email: Voice@ifca.org

The Voice, (Q.) The Bible Church of Christ, Inc., Montrose Bushrod, 1358 Morris Ave., Bronx, NY 10456 Tel. (718)588-2284 Fax (718)992-5597
Website: www.thebiblechurchofchrist.org

The War Cry, (bi-W.) The Salvation Army, Marlene Chase, 615 Slaters Lane, Alexandria, VA 22313 Tel. (703)684-5500 Fax (703)684-5539
Email: warcry@usn.salvationarmy.org
Website: http://publications.salvationarmyusa. org

Weavings: A Journal of the Christian Spiritual Life, (6/Y.) The United Methodist Church, John S. Mogabgab, P.O. Box 189, Nashville, TN 37202 Tel. (615)340-7254 Fax (615)340-7267
Email: weavings@upperroom.org
Website: www.upperroom.org

The Wesleyan Advocate, (11/Y.) The Wesleyan Church, Norman G. Wilson, P.O. Box 50434, Indianapolis, ID 46250-0434 Tel. (317)570-5204 Fax (317)570-5260

Wesleyan Woman, (Q.) The Wesleyan Church, Martha Blackburn, P.O. Box 50434, Indianapolis, IN 46250 Tel. (317)570-5164 Fax (317)570-5254
Email: wwi@wesleyan.org
Website: www.wesleyan.org

Wesleyan World, (Q.) The Wesleyan Church, Wayne Derr, P.O. Box 50434, Indianapolis, IN 46250 Tel. (317)570-5172 Fax (317)570-5256
Email: wwm@iquest.net

The White Wing Messenger, (bi-W.) Church of God of Prophecy, Virginia E. Chatham, P.O. Box 3000, Cleveland, TN 37320-3000 Tel. (423)559-5413 Fax (423)559-5444
Email: jenny@wingnet.net
Website: www.cogop.org

Whole Truth, (M.) The Church of God in Christ, Larry Britton, P.O. Box 2017, Memphis, TN 38101 Tel. (901)578-3841 Fax (901)57-6807

Wineskins, (bi-M.) Churches of Christ, Mike Cope and Rubel Shelly, Box 129004, Nashville, TN 37212-9004 Tel. (615)373-5004 Fax (615)373-5006
Email: wineskins@edge.net

The Winner, (9/Y.) Nondenominational, Lincoln Sterd, The Health Connection, P.O. Box 859 Hagerstown, MD 21741 Tel. (301)790-9735 Fax (301)790-9734

Wisconsin Lutheran Quarterly, (Q.) Wisconsin Evangelical Lutheran Synod, John F. Brug, 11831 N. Seminary Dr., Mequon, WI 53092 Tel. (262)242-8813 Fax (262)242-8110
Email: wl@wlqindex.htm
Website: www.wls.wels.net/publications

With: The Magazine for Radical Christian Youth, (6/Y.) Interdenominational, Carol Duerksen, P.O. Box 347, Newton, KS 67114 Tel. (316)283-5100 Fax (316)283-0454
Email: deliag@gcmc.org

319

The Witness, (10/Y.) Nondenominational, Julie A. Wortman, 7000 Michigan Ave., Detroit, MI 48210 Tel. (313)841-1967 Fax (313)841-1956 Email: office@thewitness.org Website: www.thewitness.org

Woman to Woman, (M.) General Association of General Baptists, Sandra Trivitt, 100 Stinson Dr., Poplar Bluff, MO 63901 Tel. (573)785-7746 Fax (573)785-0564 Email: strivitt@pbmo.net

The Woman's Pulpit, (Q.) Nondenominational, LaVonne Althouse, 5227 Castor Ave., Philadelphia, PA 19124-1742 Tel. (215)743-4528

Woman's Touch, (bi-M.) Assemblies of God, Lillian Sparks, 1445 Boonville Ave., Springfield, MO 65802-1894 Tel. (417)862-2781 Fax (417)862-0503 Email: womanstouch@ag.org Website: www.ag.org/womanstouch

Women's Missionary Magazine, (9/Y.) African Methodist Episcopal Church, Dr. Bettye J. Allen, 1901 E. 169th Pl., South Holland, IL 60473 Tel. (708)895-0703 Fax (708)895-0706

Word and Work, (11/Y.) Churches of Christ, Alex V. Wilson, 2518 Portland Ave., Louisville, KY 40212 Tel. (502)897-2831

The Word, (10/Y.) The Antiochian Orthodox Christian Archdiocese of North America, V. Rev. John Abdalah, 1777 Quigg Dr., Pittsburgh, PA 15241-2071 Tel. (412)681-2988 Fax (412)831-5554 Email: frjpa@aol.com Website: www.heinz.cmv.edu/~klo

The Worker, (Q.) Progressive National Baptist Convention, Inc., Mattie A Robinson, 601 50th St. NE, Washington, DC 20019 Tel. (202)398-5343 Fax (202)398-4998 Website: www.pnbc.org

World Harvest Today, (Q.) United Pentecostal Church International, J. S. Leaman, 8855 Dunn Rd., Hazelwood, MO 63042 Tel. (314) 837-7300 Fax (314)837-2387

World Parish: International Organ of the World Methodist Council, (s-M.) Inter-denominational Methodist (Christian World Communion of Methodist and WMC-Related Churches), Joe Hale, P.O. Box 518, Lake Junaluska, NC 28745 Tel. (828)456-9432 Fax (828)456-9433 Email: wmc6@juno.com

World Vision, (bi-M.) Open Bible Standard Churches, Inc., Paul V. Canfield, 2020 Bell Ave., Des Moines, IA 50315-1096 Tel. (515)288-6761 Fax (515)288-2510 Email: missions@openbible.org Website: www.openbible.org

World Vision Today, (bi-M.) Nondenominational, P.O. Box 9716, Federal Way, WA 98063-9716 Tel. (206)815-2300 Fax (206) 815-3445 Email: tmadison@aol.com

Worldorama, (M.) Pentecostal Holiness Church, International, Donald Duncan, P.O. Box 12609, Oklahoma City, OK 73157 Tel. (405)787-7110 Fax (405)787-7729 Email: jds@iphc.org

Worship, (6/Y.) The Catholic Church, R. Kevin Seasoltz, St. John's Abbey, Collegeville, MN 56321 Tel. (320)363-3883 Fax (320)363-3145 Email: kseasoltz@csbsju.edu Website: www.sja.org/worship

Worship Arts, (6/Y.) Nondenominational, David A Wiltse, P.O. Box 6247, Grand Rapids, MI 49516-6247 Tel. (616)459-4503 Fax (616) 459-1051 Email: graphics@iserv.net

Young & Alive, (Q.) Seventh-day Adventist Church, Braille and Large Print, Gaylena Gibson, P.O. Box 6097, Lincoln, NE 68506 Tel. (402)488-0981 Fax (402)488-7582

Youth Ministry Accent, (Q.) Seventh-day Adventist Church, David S.F. Wong, 12501 Old Columbia Pike, Silver Spring, MD 20904-6600 Tel. (301)680-6180 Fax (301)680-6155 Email: 74532.1426@compuserve.com

Zion's Advocate, (M.) Church of Christ, Mike McGhee, P.O. Box 472, Independence, MO 64051-0472 Tel. (816)796-6255

Zion's Herald, (M.) United Zion Church, Ms. Kathy Long, 5095 School Creek Lane, Annville, PA 17003 Tel. (717)867-1201

12. Religious Periodicals in Canada

The religious periodicals below constitute a basic core of important journals and periodicals circulated in Canada. The list does not include all publications prepared by religious bodies, and not all the publications listed here are necessarily the official publication of a particular church. Each entry gives: the title of the periodical, frequency of publication, religious affiliation, editor's name, address, telephone and fax number and email and website addresses when available. The frequency of publication, which appears in parenthesis after the name of the publication, is represented by a "W." for weekly; "M." for monthly; "Q." for quarterly.

Again, (Q.) The Antiochian Orthodox Christian Archdiocese of North America, R. Thomas Zell, Conciliar Press, P.O. Box 76 Ben Lomond, CA 95005-0076 Tel. (800)967-7377 Fax (831)336-8882
Email: conciliar@got.net
Website: www.conciliarpress.com

Anglican Journal, (10/Y.) The Anglican Church of Canada, David Harris, 600 Jarvis St., Toronto, ON M4Y 2J6 Tel. (416)924-9199 x. 306 Fax (416)921-4452
Email: editor@national.anglican.ca
Website: www.anglicanjournal.com

The Anglican, (10/Y.) The Anglican Church of Canada, Stuart Mann, 135 Adelaide St. E., Toronto, ON M5C 1L8 Tel. (416)363-6021 Fax (416)363-7678

Armenian Evangelical Church, (Q.) Armenian Evangelical Church, Yessayi Sarmazian, 2600 14th Avenue, Markham, ON L3R 3X1 Tel. (905)305-8144 Fax (905)305-8125

Aujourd'hui Credo, (10/Y.) The United Church of Canada, David Fines, 1332 Victoria, Greenfield Park, QC J4V 1L8 Tel. (450)446-7733 Fax (450)466-2664
Email: copermit@sympatico.ca
Website: www.egliseunie.org

The Banner, (bi-W.) Christian Reformed Church in North America, John A. Suk, 2850 Kalamazoo Ave. SE, Grand Rapids, MI 49560 Tel. (616)224-0732 Fax (616)224-0834
Email: editorial@thebanner.org
Website: www.thebanner.org

The Baptist Horizon, (M.) Canadian Convention of Southern Baptists, Nancy McGough, P.O. Box 300, Cochrane, AB T0L 0W0 Tel. (403)932-5688 Fax (403)932-4937
Email: office@ccsb.ca

B.C. Fellowship Baptist, (Q.) The Fellowship of Evangelical Baptist Churches in BC and Yukon, Bruce Christensen, Box 800, Langley, BC V3A 8C9 Tel. (604)888-3616 Fax (604)888-3601

BGC Conference Corner, (4/Y.) Baptist General Conference of Canada, Abe Funk, 4306 97th St. NW, Edmonton, AB T6E 5R9 Tel. (780)438-9127 Fax (780)435-2478

Email: bgcc@bgc.ca
Website: www.bgc.ca

Blackboard Bulletin, (10/Y.) Old Order Amish Church, Old Order Amish Church, Rt. 4 Aylmer, ON N5H 2R3

Die Botschaft, (W.) Old Order Amish Church, James Weaver, Brookshire Publishing, Inc., 200 Hazel St. Lancaster, PA 17603 Tel. (717)392-1321 Fax (717)392-2078

The Budget, (W.) Old Order Amish Church, George R. Smith, P.O. Box 249, Sugarcreek, OH 44681 Tel. (330)852-4634 Fax (330)852-4421

Cahiers de Spiritualite Ignatienne, (Q.) The Roman Catholic Church in Canada, Rene Champagne, Centre de Spiritualite Manrse, 2370 Rue Nicolas-Pinel Ste-Foy, QC G1V 4L6 Tel. (418)653-6353 Fax (418)653-1208

Canada Lutheran, (10/Y.) Evangelical Lutheran Church in Canada, Kenn Ward, 302-393 Portage Avenue, Winnipeg, MB R3B 3H6 Tel. (204)984-9150 Fax (204)984-9185
Email: communications@lutheranchurch-canada.ca
Website: www.elcic.ca/clweb

Canada Update, (Q.) The Church of God of Prophecy in Canada, Adrian L. Varlack, P. O. Box 457, Brampton, ON L6V 2L4 Tel. (905)843-2379 Fax (905)843-3990

Canadian Adventist Messenger, (12/Y.) Seventh-day Adventist Church in Canada, Carolyn Willis, 1148 King St. E., Oshawa, ON L1H 1H8 Tel. (905)433-0011 Fax (905)433-0982
Email: cwillis@sdacc.org
Website: www.sdacc.org

The Canadian Baptist, (10/Y.) Baptist Convention of Ontario and Quebec, Larry Matthews, 195 The West Mall, Ste.414, Etobicoke, ON M9C 5K1 Tel. (416)622-8600 Fax (416)622-0780
Email: thecb@baptist.ca

Canadian Disciple, (4/Y.) Christian Church (Disciples of Christ) in Canada, Stanley Litke, 255 Midvalley Dr. SE, Calgary, AB T2X 1K8 Tel. (403)256-3280 Fax (403)254-6178
Email: litkes@cia.com

321

The Canadian Friend, (bi-M.) Canadian Yearly Meeting of the Religious Society of Friends, Anne Marie Zilliacus, 218 Third Ave., Ottawa, ON K1S 2K3 Tel. (613)567-8628 Fax (613) 567-1078
Email: zilli@cyberus.ca

The Canadian Lutheran, (9/Y.) Lutheran Church—Canada, Ian Adnams, 3074 Portage Ave., Winnipeg, MB R3K 0Y2 Tel. (204)895-3433 Fax (204)897-4319
Email: communications@luthernchurch-canada.ca
Website: www.lutheranchurch-canada.ca

Canadian Mennonite, (bi-W.) Mennonite Church Canada, Ron Rempel, Suite C5, 490 Dutton Dr. Waterloo, ON N2L 6H7 Tel. (519)884-3810 Fax (519)884-3331
Email: editor@canadianmennonite.org
Website: www.canadianmennonite.org

Canadian Orthodox Messenger, (Q.) Orthodox Church in America (Canada Section), Nun Sophia (Zion), P.O. Box 179, Spencerville, ON K0E 1X0 Tel. (613)925-0645 Fax (613) 925-1521
Email: sophia@recorder.ca

The Catalyst, (6/Y.) Nondenominational, Murray MacAdam, Citizens for Public Justice, 229 College St. #311 Toronto, ON M5T 1R4 Tel. (416)979-2443 Fax (416)979-2458
Email: cpj@web.net
Website: www.cpj.ca

The Catholic Register, (W.) The Roman Catholic Church in Canada, Joseph Sinasac, 1155 Yonge St., Ste. 401, Toronto, ON M4Y 1W2 Tel. (416)934-3410 Fax (416)934-3409
Email: editor@catholicregister.org
Website: www.catholicregister.org

The Catholic Times (Montreal), (10/Y.) The Roman Catholic Church in Canada, Eric Durocher, 2005 St. Marc St., Montreal, QC H3H 2G8 Tel. (514)937-2301 Fax (514)937-3051

Channels, (Q.) Presbyterian Church in Canada, J. H. (Hans) Kouwenberg, 5800 University Blvd., Vancouver, BC V6T 2E4 Tel. (604)224-3245 Fax (604)224-3097

Chinese Herald, (Q.) Canadian Conference of Mennonite Brethren Churches, Keynes Kan, 2622 St. Johns St., Port Moody, BC V3H 2B6 Tel. (604)939-8281 Fax (604)939-8201

The Christian Contender, (M.) Mennonite Church (Canada), James Baer, Box 584, McBride, BC V0J 2E0 Tel. (604)569-3302 Fax (604)569-0020

Christian Courier, (bi-W.) Nondenominational, Harry der Nederlanden, 261 Martindale Rd., Unit 4, St. Catharines, ON L2W 1A1 Tel. (905)682-8311 Fax (905)682-8313
Email: cceditor@aol.com

Church of God Beacon, (Q.) Church of God (Cleveland, Tenn.), Canute Blake, P.O. Box 2036, Brampton Commercial Service Center Brampton, ON L6T 3T0 Tel. (905)793-2213 Fax (905)793-2213

Clarion: The Canadian Reformed Magazine, (bi-W.) Canadian and American Reformed Churches, J. Visscher, One Beghin Ave., Winnipeg, MB R2J 3X5 Tel. (204)663-9000 Fax (204)663-9202
Email: clarion@premier.mb.ca
Website: premier.mb.ca/clarion.html

CLBI-Cross Roads, (bi-M.) Lutheran, Felicitas Ackermann, 4837-52A St., Camrose, AB T4V 1W5 Tel. (780)672-4454 Fax (780)672-4455
Email: clbipbad@cable-lynx.net

College News & Updates, (6/Y.) Church of God (Anderson, Ind.), John Alan Howard, 4704 56th St, Camrose, AB T4V 2C4 Tel. (780)672-2465 Fax (780)672-6888
Email: garnderc@cable-lynx.net
Website: http://cable-lynx/~gardnerc

Communications Bi Monthly, (6/Y.) Congregational Christian Churches in Canada, Don Bernard, 5 Townsville Ct., Brantford, ON N3S 7H8 Tel. (519)751-0421 Fax (519)751-0852
Email: ccccnews@bfree.on.ca

The Communicator, (3/Y.) The Roman Catholic Church in Canada, P. Giroux, P.O. Box 142, Tantallon, NS B0J 3J0 Tel. (902) 826-7236 Fax (902)826-7236

Companion Magazine, (10/Y.) The Roman Catholic Church in Canada, Friar Philip Kelly, OFM Con., Conventual Franciscan Centre, 695 Coxwell Ave., Suite 600 Toronto, ON M4C 5R6 Tel. (416)690-5611 Fax (416)690-3320
Email: companion@franciscan.on.ca
Website: www.franciscan.on.ca

Connexions, (4/Y.) Interdenominational, Ulli Diemer, P.O. Box 158, Stn. D, Toronto, ON M6P 3J8 Tel. (416)537-3949
Email: connexions@sources.com
Website: www.connexions.org

The Covenant Messenger, (5/Y.) The Evangelical Covenant Church of Canada, 2791 Pembina Hwy., Winnipeg, MB R3T 2H5 Tel. (204)269-3437 Fax (204)269-3584
Email: messengr@escape.ca

Crux, (Q.) Nondenominational, Donald Lewis, Regent College, 5800 University Blvd. Vancouver, BC V6T 2E4 Tel. (604)224-3245 Fax (604)224-3097

Diakonia-A Magazine of Office-Bearers, (4/Y.) Canadian and American Reformed Churches, J. Visscher, Brookside Publishing, 3911 Mt. Lehman Rd. Abbotsford, BC V4X 2M9 Tel. (604)856-4127 Fax (604)856-6724

The Diary, (M.) Old Order Amish Church, Don Carpenter, P.O. Box 98, Gordonville, PA 17529 Tel. (717)768-7262 Fax (717)768-7261

Discover the Bible, (W.) The Roman Catholic Church in Canada, Guy Lajoie, P.O. Box 2400, London, ON N6A 4G3 Tel. (519)439-7211 Fax (519)439-0207

Ecumenism/Oecumenisme, (Q.) Interdenominational, 2065 Sherbrooke St. W, Montreal, QC H3H 1G6 Tel. (514)937-9176 Fax (514)937-4986
Email: ccocce@total.net
Website: www.total.net/~ccocce

The Edge (Christian Youth Magazine), (10/Y.) The Salvation Army in Canada, Captain Brenda Smith, 2 Overlea Blvd., Toronto, ON M4H 1P4 Tel. (416)422-6114 Fax (416)422-6120
Email: edge@sallynet.org
Website: www.salvationarmy.ca

Eesti Kirik, (Q.) The Estonian Evangelical Lutheran Church, Rev. U. Petersoo, 383 Jarvis St., Toronto, ON M5B 2C7 Tel. (416)925-5465 Fax (416)925-5688
Email: udo.petersoo@eelk.ee
Website: www.eelk.ee/evr/

L'Eglise Canadienne, (11/Y.) The Roman Catholic Church in Canada, Madame Rolande Parrot, C.P. 990, Ville Mont-Royal, QC H3P 3M8 Tel. (514)278-3020 x. 228 Fax (514)278-3030
Email: cmilette@novalis-inc.com
Website: www.novalis.ca

EMMC Recorder, (M.) Evangelical Mennonite Mission Conference, Jack Heppner, Box 52059 Niakwa P.O., Winnipeg, MB R2M 5P9 Tel. (204)253-7929 Fax (204)256-7384
Email: emmc@mb.sympatico.ca
Website: www.sbcollege.mb.ca/emmc/

En Avant!, (24/Y.) The Salvation Army in Canada, Betty Lessard, 2050 Rue Stanley, bureau 602, Montreal, QB H3A 3G3 Tel. (514)288-2848 Fax (514)849-7600

The Ensign, (M.) The Church of Jesus Christ of Latter-day Saints, Jay M. Todd, 50 E. North Temple St., 24th Floor Salt Lake City, UT 84150 Tel. (801)240-2950 Fax (801)240-5732
Email: toddjm@ldschurch.org

Esprit, (Q.) Evangelical Lutheran Church in Canada (Evangelical Lutheran Women), Gayle Johannesson, 302-393 Portage Avenue, Winnipeg, MB R3B 3H6 Tel. (204)984-9160 Fax (204)984-9162
Email: esprit@elcic.ca
Website: www.elw.ca

Evangel: The Good News of Jesus Christ, (4/Y.) Canadian and American Reformed Churches, D. Moes, 21804 52nd Ave.,

Langley, BC V3A 4R1 Tel. (604)576-2124 Fax (604)576-2101
Email: visscher@eznet.ca

The Evangelical Baptist, (5/Y.) The Fellowship of Evangelical Baptist Churches in Canada, Terry D. Cuthbert, 679 Southgate Dr., Guelph, ON N1G 4S2 Tel. (519)821-4830 Fax (519)821-9829
Email: president@fellowship.ca
Website: www.fellowship.ca

Expression, (bi-Y.) Canadian Conference of Mennonite Brethren Churches, Dorothy Siebert, 225 Riverton Ave., Winnipeg, MB R2L 0N1 Tel. (204)667-9576 Fax (204)669-6079
Email: fln@mbcom.com
Website: www.mbcom.com

Faith and Fellowship, (M.) Church of the Lutheran Brethren, Brent Juliot, P.O. Box 655, Fergus Falls, MN 56538 Tel. (218)736-7357 Fax (218)736-2200
Email: ffpress@clba.org
Website: www.clba.org/ffmag.htm

Faith & Friends, (M.) The Salvation Army in Canada, Geoff Moulton, 2 Overlea Blvd., Toronto, ON M4H 1P4 Tel. (416)422-6110 Fax (416)422-6120
Email: faithandfriends@sallynet.org
Website: http://faithandfriends.sallynet.org

Faith Today, (bi-M.) Evangelical Fellowship of Canada (a cooperative organization), Larry Matthews, M.I.P. Box 3745, Markham, ON L3R 0Y4 Tel. (905)479-5885 Fax (905)479-4742
Email: ft@efc-canada.com
Website: www.efc-canada.com

Family Life, (11/Y.) Old Order Amish Church, Joseph Stoll and David Luthy, Old Order Amish Church, Rt. 4 Aylmer, ON N5H 2R3

Fellowship Magazine, (4/Y.) The United Church of Canada, Gail Reid, Box 237, Barrie, ON L4M 4T3 Tel. (705)737-0114 or (800)678-2607 Fax (705)726-7160
Email: felmag@planeteer.com
Website: http://wwwebcity.com/fellowshipmug

Foi & Vie, (M.) The Salvation Army in Canada, Marie-Michele Roy, 2050 rue Stanley, Bureau 301 Montreal, QC H3A 3G3 Tel. 514-288-2848 Fax 514-288-4657
Email: foivie@sallynet.org
Website: enavant@sallynet.org

The Free Methodist Herald, (bi-M.) Free Methodist Church in Canada, Donna Elford, 3719-44 St. SW, Calgary, AB T3E 3S1 Tel. (403)246-6838 Fax (403)686-3787
Email: fmccan@inforamp.net

Glad Tidings, (6/Y.) Presbyterian Church in Canada, L. June Stevenson, Women's

Missionary Society, 50 Wynford Dr. North York, ON M3C 1J7 Tel. (800)619-7301 Fax (416)441-2825
Email: jstevenson@presbyterian.ca

Global Village Voice, (Q.) The Roman Catholic Church in Canada, Jack J. Panozzo, 420-10 Saint Mary St., Toronto, ON M4Y 1P9 Tel. (416)922-1592 Fax (416)922-0957

Good Tidings, (10/Y.) The Pentecostal Assemblies of Newfoundland, Rev. A.Earl Batstone, 57 Thorburn Rd., P.O. Box 8895, Sta. A, St. John's, NF A1B 3T2 Tel. (709)753-6314 Fax (709)753-4945
Email: paon@paon.nf.ca
Website: www.paon.nf.ca

The Gospel Contact, (4/Y.) Church of God (Anderson, Ind.), Editorial Committee, 4717 56th St., Camrose, AB T4V 2C4 Tel. (780)672-0772 Fax (780)672-6888
Email: wcdncog@cable-lynx.net
Website: www.cable-lynx.net/~wcdncog

Gospel Herald, (M.) Churches of Christ in Canada, Wayne Turner and Eugene C. Perry, 4904 King St., Beamsville, ON L0R 1B6 Tel. (905)563-7503 Fax (905)563-7503
Email: points@gospelherald.org OR editorial@gospelherald.org
Website: www.gospelherald.org

The Gospel Standard, (M.) Nondenominational, Perry F. Rockwood, Box 1660, Halifax, NS B3J 3A1 Tel. (902)423-5540

Gospel Tidings, (M.) Independent Holiness Church, R. E. Votary, 1564 John Quinn Rd., Greely, ON K4P 1J9 Tel. (613)821-2237 Fax (613)821-4663
Email: rvotary@hotmail.com
Website: www.holiness.ca

The Grape Vine, (12/Y.) Reformed Episcopal Church in Canada, Lynne Ellis, 626 Blanshard Street, Victoria, BC V8W 3G6 Tel. (250)383-8915 Fax (250)383-8916
Email: cool@islandnet.com
Website: www.churchofourlord.org

Hallelujah!, (bi-M.) The Bible Holiness Movement, Wesley H. Wakefield, Box 223, Postal Stn. A, Vancouver, BC V6C 2M3 Tel. (250)492-3376

Handmaiden, (Q.) The Antiochian Orthodox Christian Archdiocese of North America, Mary Armstrong and Virginia Nieuwsma, Conciliar Press, P.O. Box 76 Ben Lomond, CA 95005-0076 Tel. (800)967-7377 Fax (831)336-8882
Email: marketing@conciliarpress.com
Website: conciliarpress.com

Herold der Wahrheit, (M.) Old Order Amish Church, Cephas Kauffman, 1829 110th St., Kalona, IA 52247

In Holy Array, (9/Y.) Canadian and American Reformed Churches, N. Gunnink, Canadian Ref. Young Peoples' Societies, 17655-48 Ave. Surrey, BC V4P 1M5 Tel. (604)574-6227

Horizons, (bi-M.) The Salvation Army in Canada, Frederich Ash, 2 Overlea Blvd., Toronto, ON M4H 1P4 Tel. (416)425-6118 Fax (416)422-6120
Email: horizons@sallynet.org

IdeaBank, (Q.) Canadian Conference of Mennonite Brethren Churches, Sharon Johnson, Christian Ed. Office, 3-169 Riverton Ave. Winnipeg, MB R2L 2E5 Tel. (204)669-6575 Fax (204)654-1865
Email: cem@mbconf.ca
Website: www.mbconf.ca

InfoMission, (11/Y.) Canadian Baptist Ministries, Donna Lee Pancorvo, 7185 Millcreek Dr., Mississauga, ON L5N 5R4 Tel. (905)821-3533 Fax (905)826-3441
Email: dlpancorvo@cbmin.org
Website: www.cbmin.org

Insight-Insound-In Touch, (6/Y. (Insight); 6/Y. (In Sound); 4/Y. (In Touch) Interdenominational. Insight (large print newspaper); In Sound (audio magazine); In Touch (braille newspaper), Rebekah Chevalier, Graham Down, John Milton Society for the Blind in Canada, 40 St. Clair Ave. E., Ste. 202 Toronto, ON M4T 1M9 Tel. (416)960-3953 Fax (416-960-3570
Email: jmscan@netcom.ca

Intercom, (bi-M.) The Fellowship of Evangelical Baptist Churches in Canada, Terry D. Cuthbert, 679 Southgate Dr., Guelph, ON N1G 4S2 Tel. (519)821-4830 Fax (519)821-9829
Email: president@fellowship.ca
Website: www.fellowship.ca

ISKRA, (20/Y.) Union of Spiritual Communities of Christ (Orthodox Doukhobors in Canada), Dmitri E. (Jim) Popoff, Box 760, Grand Forks, BC V0H 1H0 Tel. (604)442-8252 Fax (604)442-3433
Email: iskra@sunshinecable.com

Istocnik, (4/Y.) Serbian Orthodox Church in the U.S.A. and Canada, Diocese of Canada, Very Rev. VasilijeTomic, 7470 McNiven Rd., RR 3, Campbellville, ON L0P 1B0 Tel. (905)878-0043 Fax (905)878-1909
Email: vladika@istocnik.com
Website: www.istocnik.com

Le Lien, (11/Y.) Canadian Conference of Mennonite Brethren Churches, Annie Brosseau, 1775 Edouard-Laurin, St. Laurent, QC H4L 2B9 Tel. (514)331-0878 Fax (514)331-0879
Email: LeLien@total.net
Website: www.mbconf.ca/comm/lelien

Liturgie, Foi et Culture (Bulletin Natl. de Liturgie), (4/Y.) The Roman Catholic Church in Canada, Service des Editions de la CECC, Office national de liturgie, 3530 rue Adam Montreal, QC H1W 1Y8 Tel. (514)522-4930 Fax (514)522-1557
Email: onl@videotron.ca
Website: www.cccb.ca

Mandate, (4/Y.) The United Church of Canada, Rebekah Chevalier, Div. of Communication, 3250 Bloor St W., Ste. 300 Etobicoke, ON M8X 2Y4 Tel. (416)231-5931 Fax (416)232-6004
Email: rchevali@uccan.org
Website: www.uccan.org/mandate

The Mantle, (M.) Independent Assemblies of God International (Canada), Philip Rassmussen, P.O. Box 2130, Laguna Hills, CA 92654-9901 Tel. (514)522-4930 Fax (514)522-1557

Marketplace, The: A Magazine for Christians in Business, (bi-M.) Interdenominational Mennonite, Wally Kroeker, 302-280 Smith St., Winnipeg, MB R3C 1K2 Tel. (204)956-6430 Fax (204)942-4001
Website: www.meda.org

Mennonite Brethren Herald, (bi-W.) Canadian Conference of Mennonite Brethren Churches, Jim Coggins, 3-169 Riverton Ave., Winnipeg, MB R2L 2E5 Tel. (204)669-6575 Fax (204) 654-1865
Email: mbherald@mbconf.ca
Website: www.mbherald.com

Mennonite Historian, (Q.) Canadian Conference of Mennonite Brethren Churches, Conference of Mennonites in Canada, Abe Dueck and Ken Reddig, Ctr. for Menn. Brethren Studies, 169 Riverton Ave. Winnipeg, MB R2L 2E5 Tel. (204)669-6575 Fax (204)654-1865
Email: adueck@mbconf.ca
Website: http://mbconf.ca/mbstudies/

Die Mennonitische Post, (bi-M.) Interdenominational Mennonite, Abe Warkentin, Box 1120, 383 Main St. Steinbach, MB R0A 2A0 Tel. (204)326-6790 Fax (204)326-6302

Mennonitische Rundschau, (M.) Canadian Conference of Mennonite Brethren Churches, Brigitte Penner; Marianne Dulder, 3-169 Riverton Ave., Winnipeg, MB R2L 2E5 Tel. (204)669-6575 Fax (204)654-1865
Email: MR@mbconf.ca

Messenger (of the Sacred Heart), (M.) The Roman Catholic Church in Canada, F. J. Power, Apostleship of Prayer, 661 Greenwood Ave. Toronto, ON M4J 4B3 Tel. (416)466-1195

Messenger of Truth, (bi-W.) Church of God in Christ (Mennonite), Gladwin Koehn, P.O. Box 230, Moundridge, KS 67107 Tel. (316)345-2532 Fax (316)345-2582

The Messenger, (22/Y.) The Evangelical Mennonite Conference, Terry Smith, Box 1268, Steinbach, MB R0A 2A0 Tel. (204)326-6401 Fax (204)326-1613
Email: emcmessenger@mts.net
Website: www.sbcollege.mb.ca/emc

The Messenger, (Q.) The Reformed Episcopal Church of Canada, Rt. Rev. Michael Fedechko, 320 Armstrong St., New Liskeard, ON P0J 1P0 Tel. (705)647-4565 Fax (705)647-5429
Email: fed@nt.net

The Messenger, (bi-M.) Church of God (Anderson, Ind.), C. Paul Kilburn, 65 Albacore Cres., Scarborough, ON M2H 2L2 Tel. (416) 431-9800
Email: dc581@torfree.net

Missions Today, (bi-M.) Roman Catholic, Patricia McKinnon, Society for the Propagation of the Faith, 3329 Danforth Ave. Scarborough, ON M1L 4T3 Tel. (416)699-7077 or 800-897-8865 Fax (416)699-9019
Email: missions@eda.net
Website: www.eda.net/~missions

The Monitor, (M.) The Roman Catholic Church in Canada, Larry Dohey, P.O. Box 986, St. John's, NF A1C 5M3 Tel. (709)739-6553 Fax (709)739-6458
Email: 1dohey@seascape.com
Website: www.delweb.com/rcec/monitor.htm

Multiply, (4/Y.) Presbyterian Church in America (Canadian Section), Fred Marsh, 1852 Century Pl., Ste. 205, Atlanta, GA 30345 Tel. (404)320-3330 Fax (404)982-9108

N.A.B. Today, (6/Y.) North American Baptist Conference, Marilyn Schaer, 1 S. 210 Summit Ave., Oakbrook Terrace, IL 60181 Tel. (630)495-2000 Fax (630)495-3301
Email: NABtoday@nabconf.org
Website: NABConference.org

National Bulletin on Liturgy, (4/Y.) The Roman Catholic Church in Canada, Margaret Bick, 90 Parent Ave., Ottawa, ON K1N 7B1 Tel. (613)241-9461 x. 276 Fax (613)241-8117
Email: liturgy@cccb.ca
Website: www.cccb.ca

The New Freeman, (W.) The Roman Catholic Church in Canada, Bill Donovan, One Bayard Dr., Saint John, NB E2L 3L5 Tel. (506)653-6806 Fax (506)653-6818

News of Québec, Christian Brethren (also known as Plymouth Brethren), Richard E. Strout, P.O. Box 1054, Sherbrooke, QC J1H 5L3 Tel. (819)820-1693 Fax (819)821-9287

Orthodox Way, (M.) Greek Orthodox Metropolis of Toronto (Canada), Orthodox Way Commit-tee, 86 Overlea Blvd., 4th Floor Toronto, ON M4H 1C6 Tel. (416)429-5757 Fax (416)429-4588
Website: www.gocanada.org

Passport, (Q.) Interdenominational, Lois Penner, Briercrest Family of Schools, 510 College Dr. Caronport, SK S0H 0S0 Tel. (306)756-3200 Fax (306)756-3366
Website: www.briercrest.ca

Pentecostal Testimony, (M.) The Pentecostal Assemblies of Canada, Richard P. Hiebert, 6745 Century Ave., Mississauga, ON L5N 6P7 Tel. (905)542-7400 Fax (905)542-7313
Email: testimony@PAOC.org

PMC: The Practice of Ministry in Canada, (4-5/Y.) Interdenominational, Jim Taylor, 10162 Newene Rd., Winfield, BC V4V 1R2 Tel. (604)766-2778 Fax (604)766-2736
Email: jimt@silk.net
Website: www.interword.com/pmc

Pourastan, (bi-M.) Armenian Holy Apostolic Church - Canadian Diocese, N. Ouzounian, 615 Stuart Ave., Outremont, QC H2V 3H2 Tel. (514)279-3066 Fax (514)276-9960
Email: ararat@videotron.ca
Website: www.sourpkrikor.org

Prairie Messenger, (W.) The Roman Catholic Church in Canada, Andrew M. Britz, O.S.B., Box 190, Muenster, SK S0K 2Y0 Tel. (306)682-1772 Fax (306)682-5285
Email: pm.editor@stpeters.sk.ca
Website: www.stpeters.sk.ca/prairie_messenger

The Presbyterian Message, (10/Y.) Presbyterian Church in Canada, Janice Carter, Kouchibouguac, NB E0A 2A0 Tel. (506)876-4379
Email: mjcarter@nb.sympatico.ca

Presbyterian Record, (11/Y.) The Presbyterian Church in Canada, John Congram, 50 Wynford Dr., Toronto, ON M3C 1J7 Tel. (416)441-1111 Fax (416)441-2825
Email: pcrecord@presbyterian.ca
Website: www.presbyterian.ca/record

Presence, (8/Y.) The Roman Catholic Church in Canada, Jean-Claude Breton, Presence Magazine Inc., 2715 chemin de la Cote St. Catherine Montreal, QC H3T 1B6 Tel. (514) 739-9797 Fax (514)739-1664
Email: presence@presencemag.qc.cq
Website: www.dominicains.ca

The Pulse, (4/Y.) Evangelical Free Church of Canada, Rick Penner, EFCC Box 56109, Valley Ctr. P.O., Langley, BC V3A 8B3 Tel. (604)888-8668 Fax (604)888-3108
Email: efcc@twu.ca

Quaker Concern, (Q.) Canadian Yearly Meeting of the Religious Society of Friends, Jane Orion Smith, 60 Lowther Ave., Toronto, ON M5R 1C7 Tel. (416)920-5213 Fax (416)920-5214
Email: cfsc@web.ca
Website: www.web.net/~cfsc

Reformed Perspective: A Magazine for the Christian Family, (M.) Canadian and American Reformed Churches, Jon Dykstra, 13820-106 A Avenue, Edmonton, AB T5N 1C9 Tel. (780)452-3978
Email: editor@reformedperspective.ca
Website: www.reformedperspective.ca

Relations, (10/Y.) The Roman Catholic Church in Canada, Carolyn Sharp, 25 Jarry Ouest, Montreal, QC H2P 1S6 Tel. (514)387-2541 Fax (514)387-0206
Email: relations@cjf.qc.ca

RESCUE, (bi-M.) Association of Gospel Rescue Missions, Philip Rydman, 1045 Swift, N. Kansas City, MO 64116 Tel. (816)471-8020 Fax (816)471-3718
Email: iugm@iugm.org
Website: www.iugm.org

Resource: The National Leadership Magazine, (5/Y.) The Pentecostal Assemblies of Canada, Michael P. Horban, 6745 Century Ave., Mississauga, ON L5N 6P7 Tel. (905) 542-7400 Fax (905)542-7313
Email: mhorban@paoc.org

Revival Fellowship News, (Q.) Interdenominational, Harold Lutzer, Canadian Revival Fellowship, Box 584 Regina, SK S4P 3A3 Tel. (306)522-3685 Fax (306)522-3686
Email: crf@dlewest.com
Website: www.revivalfellowship.com

Rupert's Land News, (10/Y.) The Anglican Church of Canada, J. D. Caird/ M.A. Jackson, Anglican Centre, 935 Nesbitt Bay Winnipeg, MB R3J 3R1 Tel. (204)453-6130 / (204)284-2097 Fax (204)452-3915

Saints Herald, (M.) Community of Christ, Linda Booth, The Herald Publishing House, P.O. Box 1770 Independence, MO 64055-0770 Tel. (816)252-5010 Fax (816)252-3976
Email: comdiv@rlds.org
Website: www.rlds.org

Catherine, (10/Y.) The Salvation Army in Canada, Linda Bradbury, 2 Overlea Blvd., Toronto, ON M4H 1P4 Tel. (416)422-6113 Fax (416)422-6120

Scarboro Missions, (9/Y.) The Roman Catholic Church in Canada, G. Curry, S.F.M., 2685 Kingston Rd., Scarborough, ON M1M 1M4 Tel. (416)261-7135 Fax (416)261-0820
Email: sfmmag@web.net

Servant Magazine, (4/Y.) Interdenominational, Phil Callaway, Prairie Bible Institute, Box 4000 Three Hills, AB T0M 2N0 Tel. (403)443-5511 Fax (403)443-5540
Website: www.pbi.ab.ca

The Shantyman, (bi-M.) Nondenominational, Arthur C. Dixon, 2476 Argentia Rd., Ste. 213, Mississauga, ON L5N 6M1 Tel. (905)821-6310 Fax (905)821-6311
Email: shanty@pathcom.com

Sister Triangle, (Q.) churches of Christ, Marge Roberts, P.O. 948, Dauphin, MB R7N 3J5 Tel. (204)638-8156 Fax (204)638-6640
Email: amrobert@mb.sympatico.ca

Solia - The Herald, (M.) The Romanian Orthodox Episcopate of America (Jackson, MI), Rev. Deacon David Oancea, P.O. Box 185, Grass Lake, MI 49240-0185 Tel. (517)522-3656 Fax (517)522-5907
Email: ROEASOLIA@aol.com
Website: www.roea.org

SR: Studies in Religion: Sciences religieuses, (Q.) Nondenominational, Willi Braun, University of Alberta, 347 Arts Bldg Edmonton, AB T6H 2E6 Tel. (780)492-2879
Email: willi.braun@ualberta.ca

St. Luke Magazine, (M.) Christ Catholic Church International, Donald W. Mullan, 5165 Palmer Ave., Niagara Falls, ON L2E 6S8 Tel. (905)354-2329 Fax (905)354-9934
Email: dmullan1@home.com
Website: www3.sympatico.ca/dwmullan

Topic, (M.) The Anglican Church of Canada, Lorie Chortyk, 580-401 W. Georgia St., Vancouver, BC V6B 5A1 Tel. (604)684-6306 Fax (604)684-7017
Email: loriec@synod.nw.anglican.ca

Le Trait d'Union, (4-5/Y.) Union d'Eglises Baptistes Francaises au Canada, Fritz Obas, 2285 Ave. Papineau, Montreal, QC H2K 4J5 Tel. (514)526-6643 Fax (514)526-9269

United Church Observer, (M.) The United Church of Canada, Muriel Duncan, 478 Huron St., Toronto, ON M5R 2R3 Tel. (416)960-8500 Fax (416)960-8477
Email: general@ucobserver.org
Website: www.ucobserver.org

La Vie Chretienne (French), (M.) Presbyterian Church in Canada, Jean Porret, PO Box 272, Suzz. Rosemont, Montreal, QC H1X 3B8 Tel. (514)737-4168

La Vie des Communautes religieuses, (5/Y.) The Roman Catholic Church in Canada, Monique Theriault, s.m.j.m., 251 St-Jean-Baptiste, Nicolet, QC J3T 1X9 Tel. (819)293-8736 Fax (819)293-2419

Vie Liturgique, (8/Y.) The Roman Catholic Church in Canada, Novalis, 6255 Rue Hutchison, Bureau 103 Montreal, QC H2V 4C7 Tel. (800)668-3020 Fax (514)278-3030
Email: info@novalis-inc.com

VIP Communique, Foursquare Gospel Church of Canada, Timothy Peterson, 8459-160th St., Ste. 100, Surrey, BC V3S 3T9 Tel. (604)543-8414 Fax (604)543-8417
Email: fgcc@canada.com

Visnyk: The Herald, (M.) Ukrainian Orthodox Church of Canada, Ihor Kutash and Marusia Tarnawecka Zurek, 9 St. John's Ave., Winnipeg, MB R2W 1G8 Tel. (204)586-3093 Fax (204)582-5241

Voce Evangelica/Evangel Voice, (Q.) The Italian Pentecostal Church of Canada, Rev. Daniel Costanza, 140 Woodbridge Ave., Suite 400 Woodbridge, ON L4L 4K9 Tel. (905)850-1578 Fax (905)850-1578
Email: bethel@idirect.com
Website: www.the-ipcc.org

The War Cry, (M.) The Salvation Army in Canada, Sharon Stinka, 2 Overlea Blvd., Toronto, ON M4H 1P4 Tel. (416)425-2111 Fax (416)422-6120
Email: warcry@sallynet.org
Website: http://sallynet.org

Word Alive, (Q.) Nondenominational, Dwayne Janke, Wycliffe Bible Translators of Canada Inc., 4316 10 St. NE Calgary, AB T2E 6K3 Tel. (403)250-5411 Fax (403)250-2623
Email: dwayne_janke@wycliffe.ca
Website: www.wycliffe.ca

The Word, (10/Y.) The Antiochian Orthodox Christian Archdiocese of North America, John P. Abdalah, 1777 Quigg Dr., Pittsburgh, PA 15241-2071 Tel. 412-831-7388 Fax 412-831-5554
Email: wordmag@aol.com
Website: antiochian.org

World:Journal of Unitarian Universalist Association, (bi-M.) Unitarian, Tom Stites, 25 Beacon St., Boston, MA 02108 Tel. (617)742-2100 Fax (617)367-3237
Email: worldmag@uua.org
Website: www.uua.org

Young Companion, (11/Y.) Old Order Amish Church, Joseph Stoll and Christian Stoll, Old Order Amish Church, Rt. 4 Aylmer, ON N5H 2R3

The Young Soldier, (24/Y.) The Salvation Army in Canada, Sharon Stinka, 2 Overlea Blvd., Toronto, ON M4H 1P4 Tel. (416)422-6114 Fax (416)422-6120

13. Church Archives and Historical Records Collections

American and Canadian history is interwoven with the social and cultural experience of religious life and thought. Most repositories of primary research materials in North America will include some documentation on religion and church communities. This directory is not intended to replace standard bibliographic guides to those resources. The intent is to give a new researcher entry to major archival holdings of religious collections and to programs of national scope. In the interest of space, no attempt has been made to list the specific contents of the archives or to include the numerous specialized research libraries of North America. The repositories listed herein are able to re-direct inquirers to significant regional and local church archives, and specialized collections such as those of religious orders, educational and charitable organizations, and personal papers. This directory has been thoroughly re-edited to include updated entries and contact information.

Repositories marked with an asterisk (*) are designated by their denomination as the official archives. The reference departments at these archives will assist researchers in locating primary material of geographic or subject focus.

Mark J. Duffy, C.A.

UNITED STATES

Adventist

Aurora University, Charles B. Phillips Library, 347 S. Gladstone, Aurora, IL 60506, Volunteer Curator: David T. Arthur, Tel. (630) 844-5437, Fax (630) 844-3848, E-mail: jhuggins@aurora.edu

Adventual archival materials on the Millerite/Early Adventist movement (1830-1860); also denominational archives relating to Advent Christian Church, Life and Advent Union, and to a lesser extent, Evangelical Adventists and Age-to-Come Adventists.

Adventist Heritage Center, James White Library, Andrews University, Berrien Springs, MI 49104, Curator: Jim Ford, Tel. (616) 471-3274, Fax (616) 471-6166, E-mail: ahc@andrews.edu, Website: http://www.andrews. edu/library/collections/departments/ahc.html

Large collection of Seventh-day Adventist material.

Department of Archives and Special Collections/ Ellen G. White Estate Branch Office, Loma Linda University Library, Loma Linda, CA 92350, Chairman/Director: Elder Merlin D. Burt, Tel. (909) 824-4942, Fax (909) 824-4188, E-mail: whiteest.llu.edu, Website: http://www.llu.edu/llu/library.heritage

Photographs, sound and video recordings, personal papers, and library pertaining to the Seventh-day Adventist Church.

Ellen G. White Estate, Inc., 12501 Old Columbia Pike, Silver Spring, MD 20904, Archivist: Tim Poirier, Tel. (301) 680-6540, Fax (301) 680-6559, Website: http://www.whiteestate.org

Records include letters and manuscripts (1840s to 1915), pamphlets and publications, and the White papers.

*General Conference of Seventh-day Adventists: Archives and Statistics, 12501 Old Columbia Pike, Silver Spring, MD 20904-6600, Director: Bert Haloviak, Tel. (301) 680-5022, Fax (301) 680-5038, E-mail: HaloviakB@GC.Adventist.org, Website: http://www.adventist.org

Repository of the records created at the world administrative center of the Seventh-day Adventist Church and includes the period from the 1860s to the present.

Assemblies of God

*Flower Pentecostal Heritage Center, 1445 Boonville Ave., Springfield, MO 65802, Director: Wayne Warner, Tel. (417) 862-1447x4400, Fax (417) 862-6203, E-mail: archives@ag.org

Official repository for materials related to the Assemblies of God, as well as materials related to the early Pentecostal movement in general.

Baptist

American Baptist-Samuel Colgate Historical Library, 1106 S Goodman St., Rochester, NY 14620-2532, Director: Stuart W. Campbell, Tel. (716) 473-1740, Fax (716) 473-1740 [Call first], E-mail: abhs@crds.edu, Website: http://www.crds.edu/abhs/default.htm

Manuscript holdings include collections of Baptist ministers, missionaries, and scholars, and some records of Baptist churches, associations, and national and international bodies.

*American Baptist Archives Center, P.O. Box 851, Valley Forge, PA 19482-0851, Executive Director: Deborah Bingham VanBroekhoven, Tel. (610) 768-2374, Fax (610) 768-2266, E-mail: dbvanfro@abc-usa.org, Website: http://www.abc-usa.org/abhs

Repository for the non-current records of the national boards and administrative organizations of American Baptist churches in the

USA. Collections include mission files, publications, correspondence, official minutes and annual reports.

Andover Newton Theological School, Franklin Trask Library, 159 Herrick Rd., Newton Centre, MA 02159, Associate Director: Diana Yount, Tel. (617) 964-1100x252, Fax (617) 965-9756, E-mail: dyount@ants.edu, Website: http://www.ants.edu

The collections document Baptist, Congregational and United Church history, including personal papers relating to national denominational work and foreign missions, with emphasis on New England Church history.

Primitive Baptist Library of Carthage, Illinois, 416 Main St., Carthage, IL 62321, Director of Library: Elder Robert Webb, Tel. (217) 357-3723, Fax (217) 357-3723, E-mail: bwebb9@juno.com, Website: http://www. carthage.lib.il.us/community/churches/primbap/pbl.html

Collects the records of congregations and associations.

*Seventh-day Baptist Historical Society, 3120 Kennedy Rd., P.O. Box 1678, Janesville, WI 53547, Historian: Rev. Don A. Sanford, Tel. (608) 752-5055, Fax (608) 752-7711, E-mail: sdbhist@inwave.com, Website: http://www.seventhdaybaptist.org

Serves as a depository for records of Seventh-day Baptists, Sabbath and Sabbath-keeping Baptists since the mid-seventeenth century.

*Southern Baptists Historical Library & Archives, 901 Commerce St., Suite 400, Nashville, TN 37203-3630, Director and Archivist: Bill Sumners, Tel. (615) 244-0344, Fax (615) 782-4821, E-mail: bsumners@edge.net, Website: http://www.sbhla.org

Central depository of the Southern Baptist Convention. Materials include official records of denominational agencies; personal papers of denominational leaders; records of related Baptist organizations; and annual proceedings of national and regional bodies.

Brethren in Christ

*Brethren in Christ Historical Library and Archives, One College Avenue, P. O. Box 3002, Grantham, PA 17027, Director: Dori I. Steckbeck, Tel. 717) 691-6048, Fax (717) 691-6042, E-mail: archives@messiah.edu

Records of general church boards and agencies, regional conferences, congregations and organizations; also includes personal papers of church members.

Church of the Brethren

*Brethren Historical Library and Archives, 1451 Dundee Ave., Elgin IL 60120, Librarian/Archivist: Kenneth M. Shaffer, Jr., Tel. (847) 742-5100, Fax (847) 742-6103, E-mail: kshaffer_gb@brethren.org, Website: http://www.brethren.org/genbd/bhla

Archival materials dating from the 19th Century relating to the cultural, socio-economic, theological, genealogical, and institutional history of the Church of the Brethren.

Churches of God, General Conference

*Winebrenner Theological Seminary, 701 East Melrose Ave., Findlay, OH 45804, Director of Library Services: Kimball Winters, Tel. (419) 422-4824, Fax (419) 422-3999, E-mail: wts@winebrenner.edu, Website: http://www.winebrenner.edu

Archival materials of the Churches of God, General Conference including local conference journals.

Churches of Christ

Center for Restoration Studies, Abilene Christian University, 760 Library Court, P.O. Box 29208, Abilene, TX 79699, Archivist: Erma Jean Loveland, Tel. (915) 674-2538, Fax (915) 674-2202, E-mail: lovelande@acu.edu, Website: http://www.bible.acu.edu/crs

Archival materials connected with the Stone-Campbell Movement. The chief focus is on the Church of Christ in the twentieth century.

Emmanuel School of Religion Library, One Walker Drive, Johnson City, TN 37601-9438, Director: Thomas E. Stokes, Tel. (423) 926-1186, Fax (423) 926-6198, E-mail: library@esr.edu, Website: http://www.esr.edu

Materials related to the Stone-Campbell/Restoration Movement tradition. Collection includes items from the Christian Church and Churches of Christ, the a capella Churches of Christ, and the Christian Church (Disciples of Christ).

Disciples of Christ

Christian Theological Seminary Library, 1000 W. 42nd St., P.O. Box 88267, Indianapolis, IN 46208, Archives Manager: Don Haymes, Tel. (317) 931-2368, Fax (317) 928-1961, E-mail: dhames@cts.edu, Website: http://www.cts.edu

Archival materials dealing with the Disciples of Christ and related movements.

*Disciples of Christ Historical Society, 1101 19th Ave. South, Nashville, TN 37212, Director of Library and Archives: David McWhirter, Tel. (615) 327-1444, Fax (615) 327-1445, E-mail: dishistsoc@aol.com, Website: http://www.users.aol.com/dishistsoc.index.html

Collects documents of the Stone-Campbell Movement.

Episcopal

*Archives of the Episcopal Church, P.O. Box 2247, Austin, TX 78768-2247, Archivist: Mark J. Duffy, Tel. (512) 472-6816, Fax (512) 480-0437, E-mail: Research@EpiscopalArchives.org, Website: http://www.EpiscopalArchives.org

Repository for the official records of the national Church, its corporate bodies and affiliated agencies, personal papers, and some diocesan archives. Contact the Archives for reference to diocesan and parochial church records.

General Theological Seminary, Saint Mark's Library, 175 Ninth Ave., New York, NY 10011, Consulting Director of Special Collections: Isaac Gewirtz, Tel. (212) 243-5150, Fax (212) 924-6304, E-mail: gewirtz @gts.edu, Website: http://www.gts.edu

Manuscript collections of eighteenth through twentieth century Episcopal bishops and organizations, and proceedings of Church bodies.

Evangelical Congregation Church

*Archives of the Evangelical Congregational Church, Evangelical School of Theology, Rostad Library, 121 S. College St., Myerstown, PA 17067, Archivist: Terry M. Heisey, Tel. (717) 866-5775, Fax (717) 866-4667, E-mail: theisey@evangelical.edu, Website: http://www.evangelical.edu

Repository of records of the administrative units of the denomination, affiliated organizations, and closed churches. Also collected are records of local congregations and materials related to the United Evangelical Church and the Evangelical Association.

Evangelical and Reformed

*Evangelical and Reformed Historical Society, Lancaster Theological Seminary, 555 W. James St., Lancaster, PA 17603, Archivist: Richard R. Berg, Tel. (717) 290-8711, E-mail: ehrs@lts.edu

Manuscripts and transcriptions of early German Reformed Church and pastoral records and minutes of synods and classes, as well as records of the Evangelical and Reformed Church (1934-1957).

Friends

Friends' Historical Library of Swarthmore, Swarthmore College, 500 College Ave., Swarthmore, PA 19081-1399, Acting Curator: Patricia C. O'Donnell, Tel. (610) 328-8496, E-mail: friends@swarthmore.edu, Website: http://www.swarthmore.edu/library/friends

Official depository for the records of the Philadelphia, Baltimore, and New York Yearly Meetings. Comprehensive collection of originals and copies of other Quaker meeting archives.

The Quaker Collection, Haverford College, Haverford, PA 19041-1392, Quaker Bibliographer: Elizabeth Potts-Brown, Tel. (610) 896-1161, Fax (610) 896-1102, E-mail: ebrown@haverford.edu, Website: http://www. haverford.edu/library/sc

Repository for material relating to the Society of Friends, especially to the segment known from 1827 to the mid-20th century as "Orthodox."

Interdenominational

American Bible Society Library, 1865 Broadway, New York, NY 10023-9980, Director: Mary F. Cordato, Tel. (212) 408-1495, Fax (212) 408-1526, E-mail: mcordato@americanbible.org, Website: http://www. americanbible.org

Billy Graham Center Archives, Wheaton College, 500 College Ave., Wheaton, Il 60187-5593, Director of Archives: Robert Shuster , Tel. (630) 752-5910, Fax (630) 752-5916, E-mail: bgcarc@wheaton.edu, Website: http:// www.wheaton.edu/bgc/archives.archhp1.html

Graduate Theological Union Archives, 2400 Ridge Road, Berkeley, CA 94709, Archivist: Lucinda Glenn Rand, Tel. (510) 649-2507, Fax (510) 649-2508, E-mail: LGlenn@gtu.edu, Website: http://www.gtu.edu/library/archives. html

Holy Spirit Research Center, Oral Roberts University (LRC 5E 02), 7777 S. Lewis, Tulsa OK 74171, Director: Mark E. Roberts, Tel. (918) 495-6898, Fax (918) 495-6662, E-mail: hsrc@oru.edu, Website: http://www.oru.edu/ university/library/holyspirit

Pentecostal and Charismatic records.

National Council of Churches of Christ Archives, Department of History and Records Management Services, Presbyterian Church (USA), 425 Lombard St., Philadelphia, PA 19147-1516, Manager: Marjorie N. Sly, Tel. (215) 627-1852, Fax (215) 627-0509, E-mail: preshist@shrsys.hslc.org, Website: http:// www.libertynet.org/pacscl/phs/

Schomburg Center for Research in Black Culture, 515 Malcolm X Blvd., New York, NY 10037, Manuscripts, Archives, and Rare Books Division: Tel. (212) 491-2200, Fax (212) 491-6760, Email: marbref@nypl.org, Website: http://www.nypl.org

Union Theological Seminary, Burke Library, 3041 Broadway, New York, NY 10027, Archivist and Head of Special Collections: Claire McCurdy, Tel. (212) 280-1502, Fax (212) 280-1456, E-mail: awt@uts.columbia. edu, Website: http://www.uts.columbia.edu

University of Chicago, Regenstein Library, 1100 E 57th St., Chicago, IL 60537-1502, Curtis Bochanyin , Tel. (312) 702-8740

Yale Divinity School Library, 409 Prospect St., New Haven, CT 06511, Research Services Librarian: Martha Smalley, Tel. (203) 432-6374, Fax (203) 432-3906, E-mail: divinity.library@yale.edu, Website: http:// www.Library.yale.edu/div

Jewish

American Jewish Historical Society (2 locations):

Center for Jewish History, 15 W. 16th St., New York, NY 10011 and 2 Thornton Rd., Waltham, MA 02453, Director: Michael Feldberg, Tel. (212) 294-6162 (NY); (781) 891-8110 (MA), Fax (212) 294-6161 (NY); (781) 899-9208 (MA), E-mail: ajhs@ajhs.org, Website: http://www.ajhs.org

Friedman Memorial Library, 2 Thornton Rd., Waltham, MA 02453, Tel. (781) 891-8110, Fax (781) 899-9208, E-mail: mfeldberg@ajhs..cjh.org,

Archival repositories of the Jewish people in America, including significant religious contributions to American life.

Jacob Rader Marcus Center of the American Jewish Archives, 3101 Clifton Ave., Cincinnati, OH 45220, Chief Archivist: Kevin Proffitt, Tel. (513) 221-1875, Fax (513) 221-7812, E-mail: aja@cn.huc.edu, Website: http://www.huc.edu/aja

Materials documenting the Jewish experience in the Western Hemisphere with emphasis on the Reform movement. Included in the collection are congregational and organizational records, personal papers of rabbis and secular leaders, and genealogical materials.

Latter-day Saints

*Archives, Church of Jesus Christ of the Latter-day Saints, 50 E. North Temple, Salt Lake City, UT 84150-3800, Archives Director: Steven R. Sorensen, Tel. (801) 240-2272, Fax (801) 240-1845

Repository of official records of church departments, missions, congregations, and associated organizations. Includes personal papers of church leaders and members.

Family History Library, 35 North West Temple, Salt Lake City, UT 84150, Tel. (801) 240-2331, Fax (801) 240-5551, E-mail: fhl@ldschurch.org

Primarily microfilmed vital, church, probate, land, census, and military records including local church registers.

Lutheran

*Archives of the Evangelical Lutheran Church in America, 8765 West Higgins Rd., Chicago, IL 50531-4198, Archivist: Elisabeth Wittman, Tel. (773) 380-2818, Fax (773) 380-2977, E-mail: archives@elca.org, Website: http://www.elca.org

Official repository for the church-wide offices of the denomination and its predecessors. For further information on synod and regional archives, contact the Chicago archives or check the ELCA World Wide Web site. For ELCA college and seminary archives, contact those institutions directly, or consult the ELCA Archives.

*Concordia Historical Institute, Dept. of Archives and History, Lutheran Church-Missouri Synod, 801 De Mun Ave., St. Louis, MO 63105-3199, Director: Rev. Daniel Preus, Tel. (314) 505-7900, Fax (314) 505-7901, E-mail: chi@chi.lcms.org, Website: http://chi.lcms.org

Official repository of The Lutheran Church-Missouri Synod. Collects synodical and congregational records, personal papers and records of Lutheran agencies.

Mennonite

*Archives of the Mennonite Church, 1700 South Main, Goshen, IN 46526, Director: John E. Sharp, Tel. (219) 535-7477, Fax (219) 535-7293, E-mail: johnes@goshen.edu, Website: http://www.goshen.edu/mcarchives

Repository of the official organizational records of the Mennonite Church and personal papers of leaders and members.

*Center for Mennonite Brethren Studies, 1717 S. Chestnut, Fresno, CA 93702, Archivist: Kevin Enns-Rempel, Tel. (559) 453-2225, Fax (559) 453-2124, E-mail: kennsrem@fresno.edu, Website: http://www.fresno.edu/affiliation/cmbs

Official repository for the General Conference of Mennonite Brethren churches.

*Mennonite Library and Archives, Bethel College, 300 East 27th Street, North Newton, KS 67117-0531, Archivist: John Thiesen, Tel. (316) 284-5304, Fax (316) 284-5843, E-mail: mla@bethelks.edu, Website: http://www.bethelks.edu/services/mla

Official repository for the General Conference Mennonite Church and several other organizations related to the General Conference.

Methodist

B. L. Fisher Library, Asbury Theological Seminary, 204 N. Lexington Ave., Wilmore, KY 40390, Archivist and Special Collections Librarian: Bill Kostlevy, Tel. (606) 858-3581, Fax (606) 858-2350, E-mail: bill_kostlevy@asburyseminary.edu

Documents the Holiness Movement and evangelical currents in the United Methodist Church. Holdings include records of related associations, camp meetings, personal papers, and periodicals.

Center for Evangelical United Brethren Heritage, United Theological Seminary, 1810 Harvard Blvd., Dayton, OH 45406-4599, Director: James D. Nelson, Tel. (937) 278-5817x214, Fax (937) 275-5701, E-mail: jnelson@united.edu, Website: http://www.united.edu/eubcenter

Documents predecessor and cognate church bodies of the United Methodist Church including the Evangelical Association, United Brethren in Christ, United Evangelical, Evangelical, Evangelical United Brethren, Evangelical Congregational, and Evangelical of North America.

*Heritage Hall at Livingstone College, 701 W. Monroe St., Salisbury, NC 28144, Director: Phyllis H. Galloway, Tel. (704) 638-5664

Records of the African Methodist Episcopal Zion Church.

*General Commission on Archives and History, The United Methodist Church, P. O. Box 127, Madison, NJ 07940, Archivist/Records Administrator: L. Dale Patterson, Tel. (973) 408-3189, Fax (973) 408-3909, E-mail: gcah@gcah.org, Website: http://www.gcah.org

Collects administrative and episcopal records, and personal papers of missionaries and leaders. Holds limited genealogical information on ordained ministers. Will direct researchers to local and regional collections of congregational records and information on United Methodism and its predecessors.

*Office of the Historiographer of the African Methodist Episcopal Church, P.O. Box 301, Williamstown, MA 02167, Historiographer: Dennis C. Dickerson, Tel. (413) 597-2484, Fax (413) 597-3673, E-mail: dennis.c.dickerson@williams.edu

General and annual conference minutes; reports of various departments such as missions and publications; and congregational histories and other local materials. The materials are housed in the office of the historiographer and other designated locations.

Moravian

The Moravian Archives, 41 W. Locust St., Bethlehem, PA 18018-2757, Archivist: Vernon H. Nelson, Tel. (610) 866-3255, Fax (610) 866-9210

Records of the Northern Province of the Moravian Church in America, including affiliated provinces in the Eastern West Indies, Nicaragua, Honduras, Labrador, and Alaska.

Moravian Archives, Southern Province, 4 East Bank St., Winston-Salem, NC 27101, Archivist: C. Daniel Crews, Tel. (336) 722-1742, E-mail: dcrews@mcsp.org, Website: http://www.moravianarchives.org

Repository of the records of the Moravian Church, Southern Province, its congregations, and its members.

Nazarene

*Nazarene Archives, Church of the Nazarene, 6401 The Paseo, Kansas City, MO 64131, Archives Manager: Stan Ingersol, Tel. (816) 333-7000x2437, Fax (816) 361-4983, E-mail: singersol@nazarene.org, Website: http://www.nazarene.org/hoo/archives.html

Focus is on denominational archives, including those of leaders, agencies, and study commissions. The Archives also collects materials on districts, congregations, church-related colleges and seminaries around the world.

Pentecostal

David du Plessis Archives, Fuller Theological Seminary, 135 North Oakland, Pasadena, CA 91182, Archivist: Kate McGin, Tel. (626) 584-5311, Fax (626) 584-5644, E-mail: archive@fuller.edu, Website: http://www.fuller.edu/archive

Collects material related to the Pentecostal and Charismatic movements; also includes material related o the Old Fashioned Revival Hour broadcast.

*International Pentecostal Holiness Church Archives and Research Center, P. O. Box 12609, Oklahoma City, OK 73157, Director: Harold D. Hunter, Tel. (405) 787-7110, Fax (405) 789-3957, E-mail: archives@iphc.org, Website: http://www.pctii.org/arc/archives.html

Official repository for records and publications produced by the international headquarters, conferences, and influential leaders.

*Hal Bernard Dixon Jr. Pentecostal Research Center, 260 11th St. NE, Cleveland, TN 37311, Director: David G. Roebuck, Tel. (423) 614-8576, Fax (423) 614-8555, E-mail: dixon_research@leeuniversity.edu, Website: http://www.leeuniversity.edu/library/dixon

Official repository of the Church of God (Cleveland, TN). Also collects other Pentecostal and Charismatic materials.

United Pentecostal Church International Historical Center, 8855 Dunn Rd., Hazelwood, MO 63042, Chair, Historical Committee: Rev. J. L. Hall, Tel. (314) 837-7300, Fax (314) 837-4503, E-mail: main@upci.org, Website: http://www.upci.org

Collects a variety of Pentecostal archives, primarily the United Pentecostal (Oneness) Branch.

Polish National Catholic

*Polish National Catholic Church Commission on History and Archives, 1031 Cedar Ave., Scranton, PA 18505, Chair: Joseph Wieczerzak, Tel. (717) 343-0100

Documents pertaining to the Church's national office, parishes, Prime Bishop, leaders, and organizations.

Presbyterian

*Historical Foundation of the Cumberland Presbyterian Church and the Cumberland Presbyterian Church in America, 1978 Union Ave., Memphis, TN 38104, Archivist: Susan Knight Gore, Tel. (901) 276-8602, Fax (901) 272-3913, E-mail: skg@cumberland.org, Website: http://www.cumberland.org/hfcpc

*Presbyterian Historical Society Presbyterian Church (USA)(2 offices):

Headquarters, 425 Lombard St., Philadelphia, PA 19147-1516, Manager: Marjorie N. Sly, Tel. (215) 627-1852, Fax (215) 627-0509, E-mail: reference@history.

pcusa.org, Website: http://www.history.pcusa. org

Southern Regional Office, P. O. Box 849, Montreat, NC 28757, Deputy Director: Michelle A. Francis, Tel. (828) 669-7061, Fax (828) 669-5369, E-mail: pcusadoh@montreat.edu

Collects the official records of the Church's national offices and agencies, synods, presbyteries, and some congregations. The Society also houses records of the Church's predecessor denominations, personal papers of prominent Presbyterians, and records of ecumenical organizations. The Southern Regional Office holds central and local records of the predecessor Presbyterian Church in the US.

Princeton Theological Seminary Libraries, Library Place and Mercer Street, P. O. Box 111, Princeton, NJ 08542-0803, Librarian for Archives and Special Collections: William O. Harris, Tel. (609) 497-7950, Fax (609) 497-1826, E-mail: william.harris@ptsem.edu, Website: http://www.ptsem.edu/grow/library/index.htm

Documents the history of American Presbyterianism, including an extensive collection of congregational histories and missionary reports.

Reformed

Evangelical and Reformed Historical Society, Lancaster Theological Seminary, 555 W. James St., Lancaster, PA 17603, Archivist: Richard R. Berg, Tel. (717) 290-8711, E-mail: ehrs@lts.org

Materials on the early German Reformed Church and pastoral records and minutes of synods and classes, as well as records of the Evangelical and Reformed Church (1934-1957).

*Heritage House, Calvin College, 3201 Burton St. S.E., Grand Rapids, MI 49546, Curator of Archives: Richard H. Harms, Tel. (616) 957-6313, Fax (616) 957-6470, E-mail: rharms@calvin.edu, Website: http://www. calvin.edu

Repository of the official records of the Christian Reformed Church in North America, including classes, congregations, and denominational agencies and committees.

*Reformed Church Archives, 21 Seminary Place, New Brunswick, NJ 08901-1159, Archivist: Russell Gasero, Tel. (732) 246-1779, Fax (732) 249-5412, E-mail: rgasero@aol.com, Website: http://www.rca.org

Official repository for denominational records including congregations, classes, synods, missions, and national offices.

Roman Catholic

Catholic University of America (Mullen Library), 5 Mullen, Washington, DC 20064, Archivist: Timothy Meagher, Tel. (202) 319-5065, Fax (202) 319-6554, E-mail: meagher@cua.edu

Marquette University, Department of Special Collections and Archives, P. O. Box 3141, Milwaukee, WI 93201-3141, Department Head: Charles Elston, Tel. (414) 288-7256, Fax (414) 288-6709, E-mail: charles.elston@marquette.edu, Website: http://www.marquette.edu/library/collections/archives/index.html

Collection strengths are in the areas of Catholic social action, American missions and missionaries, and other work with Native Americans and African Americans.

University of Notre Dame Archives, 607 Hesburgh Library, Notre Dame, IN 46556, Curator of Manuscripts: William Kevin Cawley, Tel. (219) 631-6448, Fax (219) 631-7980, E-mail: archives.1@nd.edu, Website: http://www.nd.edu/~archives

Papers of bishops and prominent Catholics and records of Catholic organizations. Includes parish histories, but few parish records.

U.S. Catholic Documentary Heritage Project, For holdings information on various dioceses and religious orders, consult: http://www.uschs.com.

Salvation Army

*Salvation Army Archives and Research Center, 615 Slaters Lane, Alexandria, VA 22313, Archivist: Susan Mitchem, Tel. (703) 684-5500, Fax (703) 299-5552, E-mail: archives@usa.salvationarmy.org, Website: http://www.salvationarmy.org

Holds the documents of Salvation Army history, personalities, and events in the United States from 1880.

Swedenborgian

*Bryn Athyn College of the New Church, Swedenborg Library, 2875 College Drive, P. O. Box 740, Bryn Athyn, PA 19009-1740, Carroll C. Odhner, Tel. (215) 938-2547, Fax (215) 938-2637, E-mail: ccodhner@new-church.edu, Website: http://www.newchurch.edu/college/facilities/swedlib.html

Unitarian Universalist Association

*Andover-Harvard Theological Library, Harvard Divinity School, 45 Francis Ave., Cambridge, MA 02138, Curator: Frances O'Donnell, Tel. (617) 496-5153, Fax (617) 496-4111, E-mail: frances_odonnell@harvard.edu, Website: http://www.hds.harvard.edu/library/index.html

Institutional archives of the Unitarian Universalist Association (including some congregational records) and the Unitarian Universalist Service Committee. The library also houses numerous personal manuscript collections of Unitarian ministers and church leaders.

Unitarian and Universalist

Meadville/Lombard Theological School Library, 5701 S. Woodlawn Ave., Chicago, IL 60637, Director: Neil W. Gerdes, Tel. (773) 256-3000, Fax (773) 256-3008, E-mail: ngerdes@meadville.edu, Website: http://www.meadville.edu

Repository for materials relating to Unitarian Universalism in particular and liberal religion in general. Includes personal papers and church records from many UU churches in the Midwestern USA.

United Church of Christ

Andover Newton Theological School, Franklin Trask Library, 159 Herrick Rd., Newton Centre, MA 02159, Associate Director for Special Collections: Diana Yount, Tel. (617) 964-1100x252, Fax (617) 965-9756, E-mail: dyount@ants.edu, Website: http://www.ants.edu

Collections document Baptists, Congregational, and UCC history. Some personal papers relating to national denominational work and foreign missionary activity; majority of collections relate to New England history.

Archives of the Evangelical Synod of North America, Eden Theological Seminary, Luhr Library, 475 E. Lockwood Ave., Webster Groves, MO 63119-3192, Archivist: Clifton W. Kerr, Tel. (314) 918-2515, E-mail: ckerr@eden.edu

Archival records include organization records, personal papers and immigration records.

Congregational Library, 14 Beacon St., Boston, MA 02108, Archivist: Jessica Steytler, Tel. (617) 523-0470, Fax (617) 523-0491, E-mail: jsteytler@14beacon.org, Website: http://www.14beacon.org

Documentation on the Congregational, Congregational Christian, Christian, and United Church of Christ throughout the world, including local church records, associations, charitable organizations, and papers of clergy, missionaries and others.

Elon College Library, P. O. Box 187, Elon College, NC 27244, Archivist/Technical Services Librarian: Connie L. Keller, Tel. (336) 278-6578, Fax (336) 278-6638, E-mail: keller@elon.edu

Collection of membership records and other archival material on the predecessor churches of the UCC: Christian Church and the Southern Conference of the Christian Church; also maintains records of churches that no longer exist.

*United Church of Christ Archives, 700 Prospect Ave., Cleveland, OH 44115, Archivist: Ng. George Hing, Tel. (216) 736-3285, Fax (216) 736-2120, E-mail: hingg@ucc.org

Records created in the national setting of the Church since its founding in 1957, including the General Synod, Executive Council, officers, instrumentalities, and bodies created by and/or related to the General Synod.

Standard Guides to Church Archives

William Henry Allison, *Inventory of Unpublished Material for American Religious History in Protestant Church Archives and other Depositories*, (Washington, DC, Carnegie Institution of Washington, 1910) 254 pp.

John Graves Barrow, *A Bibliography of Bibliographies in Religion*, (Ann Arbor, Mich., 1955), pp. 185-198

Edmund L. Binsfield, "Church Archives in the United States and Canada: A Bibliography," in *American Archivist*, V.21, No. 3 (July 1958) pp. 311-332, 219 entries.

Nelson R. Burr, "sources for the Study of American Church History in the Library of Congress," 1953. 13 pp. Reprinted from *Church History*, Vol. XXII, No. 3 (Sept. 1953).

Canadian Archival Resources on the Internet: University of Saskatchewan Archives, Web Site maintained by Cheryl Avery and Steve Billington at http://www.usask.ca/archives/menu.html

Mable Deutrick, "supplement to Church Archives in the United States and Canada, a Bibliography," (Washington, DC, 1964).

Donald L. DeWitt, "Articles Describing Archives & Manuscript Collections in the United States: An Annotated Bibliography," in Bibliographies & Indexes in Library & Information Science, V.11 (1997) p.480.

Andrea Hinding, ed., *Women's History Sources: A guide to Archives and Manuscript Collections in the U.S.*, (New York, Bowker, 1979) 2 vols.

Kay Kirkham, *A Survey of American Church Records, for the Period Before The Civil War, East of the Mississippi River*, (Salt Lake City, 1959-60) 2 vols. Includes the depositories and bibliographies.

Peter G. Mode, *Source Book and Bibliographical Guide for American Church History*, (Menasha, Wisc., George Banta Publishing Co., 1921) 735 pp.

Martha Lund Smalley, "Archives and Manuscript Collections in Theological Libraries," in *The American Theological Library Association*, ed. By M. Graham, (1996), pp. 122-130.

Society of American Archivists, *American Archivist, 1936/37 (continuing). Has articles* on church records and depositories. Website: www.archivists.org

A.R. Suelflow, *A Preliminary Guide to Church Records Repositories*, (Society of American Archivists, Church Archives Committee, 1969) Lists more than 500 historical-archival depositories with denominational and religious history in America.

Evangeline Thomas, *Women's Religious History Sources: A Guide to Repositories in the United States*, (New York, Bowker, 1983).

U.S. National Historical Publications and Records Commission, *Directory of Archives and Manuscript Repositories in the United States*, (Washington, D.C., 1988).

United States, Library of Congress, Division of Manuscripts, *Manuscripts in Public and Private Collections in the United States*, (Washington, DC, 1924).

U.S. Library of Congress, Washington, DC: The *National Union Catalog of Manuscript Collections*, Serially published from 1959 to 1993 (1959-1993).Contains many entries for collections of church archives. Researchers may consult the cumulative paper indexes or use the NUCMC home page to access the RLIN database of archives and manuscripts collections at http://lcweb.loc.gov/coll/nucmc/nucmc.html

Jean M. White, *Address List of Church Archives and Libraries*, (Glendale, AZ, J.M. White, 1993).

CANADA

Anglican

*General Synod Archives, 600 Jarvis St. Toronto, ON M4Y 2J6, Archivist: Terry Thompson, Tel. (416) 924-9199 x 279, Fax (416) 968-7983, E-mail: archives@national. anglican.ca, Website: http://www.anglican.ca

Collects the permanent records of the General Synod, its committees, and its employees. The Archives has a national scope, and provides referral services on local Church records.

Baptist

*Atlantic Baptist Historical Collection of the Acadia University Archives, Vaughan Memorial Library, Wolfville, NS BOP 1XO, Archivist: Patricia Townsend, Tel. (902) 585-1412, Fax (902) 585-1748, E-mail: patricia. cadiau.ca, Website: http://www. cadiau.ca/vaughan/archives

Records of associations and churches of the United Baptist Convention of the Atlantic Provinces; also personal papers of pastors and missionaries.

Canadian Baptist Archives, McMaster Divinity College, Hamilton, ON L8S 4K1, Director: Dr. Kenneth R. Morgan, Tel. (905) 525-9140, ext. 23511, Fax (905) 577-4782, E-mail: morgankr@mcmaster.ca, Website: http://www. mcmaster.ca/divinity/archives.html

Friends

Canadian Yearly Meeting Archives, Pickering College, 16945 Bayview Avenue, New Market, ON L3Y 4X2, Yearly Meeting Archivist: Jane Zavitz-Bond, Tel. (905) 895-1700, Fax (905) 895-9076

Holds the extant records for Quakers in Canada beginning with Adolphus in 1798 to the present, including the records of the Canadian Friends Service Committee.

Interdenominational

Canadian Council of Churches Archives, on deposit in National Archives of Canada, 395 Wellington, Ottawa,ON K1A 0N3, Tel. Research Services Division: (613) 992-3884; Geneological assistance: (613) 996-7458, Fax (613) 995-6274, E-mail: reference@archives. ca, Website: http://www.archives.ca

National Archives of Canada, 395 Wellington, Ottawa, ON K1A 0N3, : , Tel. Research Services Division: (613) 992-3884; Geneological assistance: (613) 996-7458, E-mail: reference @archives.ca, Website: http://www. archives.ca

Records of interdenominational and ecumenical organizations, missionary societies, denominational churches, parish registers, and papers of prominent clergy.

Jewish

Canadian Jewish Congress National Archives, 1590 Avenue Docteur Penfield, Montreal, Que. H3G 1C5, Director of Archives: Janice Rosen, Tel. (514) 931-7531, Fax (514) 931-0548, E-mail: archives@cjc.ca, Website: http://www.cjc.ca/archives.htm

Collects documentation on all aspects of social, political, and cultural history of the Jewish presence in Quebec and Canada.

Lutheran

*Archives of the Evangelical Lutheran Church in Canada, 302-393 Portage Ave., Winnepeg, MB R3B 3H6, National Secretary/Archivist: Robert H. Granke, Tel. (204) 984-9150, Fax (204) 984-9185, E-mail: rhgranke@elcic.ca, Website: http://www.elcic.org

Official repository for the ELCIC and its predecessor bodies, the Evangelical Lutheran Church of Canada and the Evangelical Lutheran Church of America-Canada Section.

Lutheran Historical Institute, 7100 Ada Blvd., Edmonton, Alberta T5B 4E4, Archivist: Karen Baron, Tel. (403) 474-8156, Fax (403) 477-9829, E-mail: abclcc@connect.ab.ca

Mennonite

*Centre for Mennonite Brethren Studies, 1-169 Riverton Ave., Winnepeg, MB R2L 2E5, Director: Dr. Abe Dueck, Tel. (204) 669-6575, Fax (204) 654-1865, E-mail: adueck@mbconf.ca

Institutional records of the boards and agencies of the Mennonite Brethren Church in Canada with some holdings pertaining to other parts of North America; also personal papers of leaders.

*Mennonite Heritage Centre, 600 Shaftesbury Blvd., Winnipeg, MB R3P OM4, Director: Alf Redekopp, Tel. (204) 888-6781, Fax (204) 831-5675, E-mail: aredekopp@mennonitechurch.ca, Website: http://www.mennonitechurch.ca/heritage/mhc.html

Institutional records and personal papers of leaders within the Mennonite Community. Holdings include the records of the Conference, various Church boards, and agencies.

Pentecostal

*Pentecostal Assemblies of Canada, 2450 Milltower Court, Mississauga, ON L5N 6P7, Director of Archives: James D. Craig, Tel. (905) 542-7400, Fax (905) 542-7313, E-mail: archives@paoc.org, Website: http://www.paoc.org

Repository of archival records created by the Pentecostal Assemblies of Canada.

Presbyterian

*Presbyterian Church in Canada Archives and Records, 50 Wynford Drive, North York, ON M3C 1J7, Archivist/Records Administrator: Kim M. Arnold, Tel. (416) 441-1111x310, Fax (416) 441-2825, E-mail: karnold@presbyterian.ca, Website: http://www.presbyterian.ca

Records of the Presbyterian Church in Canada, its officials, ministers, congregations and organizations.

Roman Catholic

Research Centre for the Religious History of Canada, St. Paul University, 223 Main St., Ottawa, ON K1S 1C4, Director: Michel Bergeron, Tel. (613) 236-1393, ext. 2306, Fax (613) 782-3001, E-mail: crh-rc-rhc@ustpauluottowa.ca

Holds guides to many Canadian Catholic archives.

Salvation Army

George Scott Railton Heritage Centre, 2130 Bayview Ave., Toronto, ON M4N 3K6, Director: Major Ira Barrow, Tel. (416) 481-4441, Fax (416) 481-6096, E-mail: Ira.Barrow@sallynet.org

Records include publications and comprehensive financial, personnel, social welfare, and immigration records.

United Church of Canada

*United Church of Canada Central Archives, Victoria University, 73 Queens Park Crescent, Toronto, ON M5S 1K7, Chief Archivist: Sharon Larade, Tel. (416) 585-4563, E-mail: uccvu.archives@utoronto.ca, Website: http://www.vicu.utoronto.ca/archives/archives.htm

Records of the United Church and its antecedent denominations and local and regional records of the Church in Ontario. Call or view the web page for information on other regional archives.

III

STATISTICAL SECTION

Guide to Statistical Tables

Since there are no questions regarding religion in the United States Census, the *Yearbook of American & Canadian Churches* is as near an "official" record of denominational statistics as is available.

Because the data represent the most complete annual compilation of church statistics, there is a temptation to expect more than is reasonable. These tables provide the answers to very simple and straightforward questions. Officials in church bodies were asked: "How many members does your organization have?" "How many clergy?" and "How much money does your organization spend?" Each respondent interprets the questions according to the policies of the organization.

Caution should, therefore, be exercised when comparing statistics across denominational lines, comparing statistics from one year to another and adding together statistics from different denominations.

Some particular methodological issues and therefore cautions in interpretation include the following considerations:

1. Definitions of membership, clergy, and other important characteristics differ from religious body to religious body. In this section, full or confirmed membership refers to those with full communicant status. Inclusive membership refers to those who are full communicants or confirmed members plus other members baptized, non-confirmed or non-communicant. Each church determines the age at which a young person is considered a member. Churches also vary in their approaches to statistics. For some, very careful counts are made of members. Other groups only make estimates.

2. Each year the data are collected with the same questions. While most denominations have consistent reporting practices from one year to the next, any change in practices is not noted in the tables. Church mergers and splits can also influence the statistics when they are compared over a number of years. Churches have different reporting schedules and some do not report on a regular basis.

3. The two problems listed above make adding figures from different denominations problematic. However, an additional complication is that individuals who attend two different churches may be included more than once. For example, a person who attends the Church of God in Christ Wednesday evening and an AME service on Sunday morning will likely be included in both counts.

Table 1. Membership Statistics in Canada

Religious Body	Year Reporting	Number of Churches Reporting	Full Communicant or Confirmed Members	Inclusive Membership	Number of Pastors Serving Parishes	Total Number of Clergy	Number of Sunday or Sabbath Schools	Total Enrollment
The Anglican Church of Canada	1996	2,957	739,699	739,699	1,622	3,368	1,827	66,756
Antiochian Orthodox Christian Archdiocese of North America	1996	215	350,000	350,000	400	445	200	
Apostolic Christian Church (Nazarene)	1985	14		830	49	49		
The Apostolic Church in Canada	1999	17	1,200	1,600	17	21	17	350
Apostolic Church of Pentecost of Canada, Inc.	1999	153	16,000	16,000	313	453		
Armenian Holy Apostolic Church—Canadian Diocese	1999	15	80,000	80,000	10	51	6	530
Associated Gospel Churches	1999		10,076	10,076	123	254		
Association of Regular Baptist Churches (Canada)	1994	12			8	11		
Baptist Convention of Ontario and Quebec	1997	386	32,000	57,800	408	734		
Baptist General Conference of Canada	1999	92	7,045	7,045	95	143		4,079
Baptist Union of Western Canada	2000	155	20,427	20,427	279	530		
The Bible Holiness Movement	1999	18	527	863	14	16	20	
Brethren in Christ Church, Canadian Conference	1998	40	3,387	3,387	19	43		1,673

Table 1. Membership Statistics in Canada (continued)

Religious Body	Year Reporting	Number of Churches Reporting	Full Communicant or Confirmed Members	Inclusive Membership	Number of Pastors Serving Parishes	Total Number of Clergy	Number of Sunday or Sabbath Schools	Total Enrollment
Canadian and American Reformed Churches	1999	49	8,150	15,213	44	61		
Canadian Baptist Ministries	1996	1,133	129,055	129,055				
Canadian Conference of Mennonite Brethren Churches	1999	214	33,214	33,214	366			22,150
Canadian Convention of Southern Baptists	1999	152	9,626	9,626	120	131	133	7,620
Canadian District of the Moravian Church in America, Northern Province	1999	9	1,199	1,667	6	10	9	511
Canadian Evangelical Christian Churches	1999	30	10,000	10,000	40	100	40	3,500
Canadian Yearly Meeting of the Religious Society of Friends	1995	22	1,125	1,893			30	
Christian Brethren (also known as Plymouth Brethren)	1999	600		50,000		250	550	
Christian Church (Disciples of Christ) in Canada	1997	30	2,053	3,285	22	46	15	291
Christian and Missionary Alliance in Canada	1995	376	31,719	87,197	1,054	1,211	376	36,860
Christian Reformed Church in North America	1999	237	48,766	80,557	207	312		
Church of God (Anderson, Ind.)	1998	47	3,777	3,777	64	97	43	1,994

Table 1. Membership Statistics in Canada (continued)

Religious Body	Year Reporting	Number of Churches Reporting	Full Communicant or Confirmed Members	Inclusive Membership	Number of Pastors Serving Parishes	Total Number of Clergy	Number of Sunday or Sabbath Schools	Total Enrollment
Church of God (Cleveland, Tenn.)	1999	130	10,914	10,914	106	128	120	9,376
Church of God in Christ (Mennonite)	1999	46	4,132	4,132	156	156	47	
Church of God of Prophecy in Canada	1995	40	3,107	3,107	98	100	37	
The Church of Jesus Christ of Latter-day Saints in Canada	1998	433	151,000	151,000			433	
Church of the Lutheran Brethren	1999	10	383	587	10	11	10	513
Church of the Nazarene Canada	1998	166	12,042	12,042	130	275	149	15,035
Churches of Christ in Canada	1997	140	8,000	8,000				
Congregational Christian Churches in Canada	1997	96	4,302	4,302		230		
The Coptic Orthodox Church in Canada	1992	12			20		17	
The Estonian Evangelical Lutheran Church	1997	11	5,089	5,089	10	13	3	106
The Evangelical Covenant Church of Canada	1997	22	1,290	1,290	15	25	21	1,763
Evangelical Free Church of Canada	1999	147	6,504	24,054		147	147	
Evangelical Lutheran Church in Canada	1999	631	138,857	193,915	406	856	389	15,257
The Evangelical Mennonite Conference	1999	53	7,000	7,000		220		

Table 1. Membership Statistics in Canada (continued)

Religious Body	Year Reporting	Number of Churches Reporting	Full Communicant or Confirmed Members	Inclusive Membership	Number of Pastors Serving Parishes	Total Number of Clergy	Number of Sunday or Sabbath Schools	Total Enrollment
Evangelical Mennonite Mission Conference	1997	44	4,633	4,633	75	201		
The Evangelical Missionary Church of Canada	1993	145	9,923	12,217	172	367	125	7,475
The Fellowship of Evangelical Baptist Churches in Canada	1995	506	72,288					
Foursquare Gospel Church of Canada	1996	54	3,063	3,063	66	103		1,258
Free Methodist Church in Canada	1998	128	6,444	11,396	145	245		
Free Will Baptists	1998	10	347		3	4	8	
Greek Orthodox Metropolis of Toronto (Canada)	1997	76	350,000	350,000	58	71	76	
Independent Assemblies of God International (Canada)	1997	214			265	508		
Independent Holiness Church	1994	5		150	4	10	4	118
Jehovah's Witnesses	1998	1,383	113,136	184,787				
Lutheran Church—Canada	1994	329	58,316	79,844	251	373	291	13,259
Mennonite Church (Canada)	1996	117	8,172	8,172	177	291	173	21,827
North American Baptist Conference	1999	124	17,531	17,531	125	210	124	

Table 1. Membership Statistics in Canada (continued)

Religious Body	Year Reporting	Number of Churches Reporting	Full Communicant or Confirmed Members	Inclusive Membership	Number of Pastors Serving Parishes	Total Number of Clergy	Number of Sunday or Sabbath Schools	Total Enrollment
The Old Catholic Church of Canada	2000	4	30	100	4	5		
Old Order Amish Church	1999	22						
Open Bible Faith Fellowship of Canada	1999	68			142	189	68	3,500
Orthodox Church in America (Canada Section)	1993	606	1,000,000	1,000,000	740		502	
Patriarchal Parishes of the Russian Orthodox Church in Canada	1997	23	800	1,500	3	4	3	34
The Pentecostal Assemblies of Canada	1995	1,100		218,782	1,758	1,758	753	65,928
Pentecostal Assemblies of Newfoundland	1997	140	14,715	29,361	189	301	121	10,272
Presbyterian Church in America (Canadian Section)	1997	16	701	1,140	20	27		457
Presbyterian Church in Canada	1999	1,100	134,683	200,738		1,256		28,120
Reformed Church in Canada	1999	44	4,091	6,609	34	71		1,838
The Reformed Episcopal Church of Canada	2000	7	260	355	9	11	2	16
Reinland Mennonite Church	1995	6	877	1,816	10	13	5	347
Reorganized Church of Jesus Christ of Latter Day Saints	1995	75	11,264	11,264	1,020	1,020		

Table 1. Membership Statistics in Canada (*continued*)

Religious Body	Year Reporting	Number of Churches Reporting	Full Communicant or Confirmed Members	Inclusive Membership	Number of Pastors Serving Parishes	Total Number of Clergy	Number of Sunday or Sabbath Schools	Total Enrollment
The Roman Catholic Church in Canada	1997	5,716	12,498,605	12,498,605		10,760		
The Romanian Orthodox Episcopate of America (Jackson, MI)	1997	19	900		13	14	12	
The Salvation Army in Canada	1998	376	27,920	80,180	638	1,959	346	
Serbian Orthodox Church in the U.S.A. and Canada, Diocese of Canada	1998	23	6,000	230,000	24	27	14	1,876
Seventh-day Adventist Church in Canada	1999	324	48,900	48,900	162	279	394	31,596
Syrian Orthodox Church of Antioch	1995	5	2,500	2,500	3	4		
Ukranian Orthodox Church of Canada	1988	258		120,000	75	91		
Union d'Eglises Baptistes Françaises au Canada	1999	27	1,264	1,294	32	39	27	760
United Baptist Convention of the Atlantic Provinces	1998	553	62,784	62,784	281	496	312	
United Brethren Church in Canada	1992	9	835	835	5	12	9	447
The United Church of Canada	1999	3,764	668,579	1,589,886	1,949	4,160	2,989	76,751
United Pentecostal Church in Canada	1997	199				340		

343

Table 1. Membership Statistics in Canada (continued)

Religious Body	Year Reporting	Number of Churches Reporting	Full Communicant or Confirmed Members	Inclusive Membership	Number of Pastors Serving Parishes	Total Number of Clergy	Number of Sunday or Sabbath Schools	Total Enrollment
Universal Fellowship of Metropolitan Community Churches	1992	12	50	1,500	8	9	1	36
The Wesleyan Church of Canada	1999	75	5,698	5,992	121	188	75	3,336
TOTALS		**26,839**	**17,055,894**	**18,960,572**	**15,093**	**36,377**	**11,073**	**457,615**

Table 2. Membership Statistics in the United States

Religious Body	Year Reporting	Number of Churches Reporting	Full Communicant or Confirmed Members	Inclusive Membership	Number of Pastors Serving Parishes	Total Number of Clergy	Number of Sunday or Sabbath Schools	Total Enrollment
Advent Christian Church	1999	302	16,482	25,702	285	409	298	15,300
African Methodist Episcopal Church*	1999	6,200	2,500,000	2,500,000		8,000	8,000	
African Methodist Episcopal Zion Church*	1999	3,125	1,060,256	1,276,662	2,731	3,002	1,699	69,460
Albanian Orthodox Diocese of America	2000	2	2,203	2,203		2	2	56
Allegheny Wesleyan Methodist Connection (Original Allegheny Conference)	1998	117	1,812	1,961	86	189	117	5,893
The Alliance of Baptists in the U.S.A.*	1999	130	64,000	64,000				
The American Association of Lutheran Churches	1999	101	14,095	18,252	91	141	83	3,612
The American Baptist Association	1998	1,760		275,000	1,740	1,760		
American Baptist Churches in the USA*	1999	5,775	1,454,388	1,454,388	4,895	9,049		187,820
The American Carpatho-Russian Orthodox Greek Catholic Church	1999	80	13,120	13,120	88	105	76	
American Catholic Church	1997	100		25,000	80	100		
American Rescue Workers	1999	15	2,500	2,500	35	35	8	285
Antiochian Orthodox Christian Archdiocese of North America*	1999	227	65,000	65,000	290	343	203	18,800
Apostolic Christian Church (Nazarene)	1993	63	3,723	3,723	217	234	55	

Table 2. Membership Statistics in the United States (*continued*)

Religious Body	Year Reporting	Number of Churches Reporting	Full Communicant or Confirmed Members	Inclusive Membership	Number of Pastors Serving Parishes	Total Number of Clergy	Number of Sunday or Sabbath Schools	Total Enrollment
Apostolic Christian Churches of America	1999	91	12,800	12,800	300	387	88	6,824
Apostolic Episcopal Church	2000	300	14,000	14,000	300	316	50	1,150
Apostolic Faith Mission Church of God	1999	19	8,301	10,651	36	48	20	3,960
Apostolic Faith Mission of Portland, Oregon	1994	54	4,500	4,500	60	85	54	
Apostolic Lutheran Church of America	2000	58			68	69		
Apostolic Orthodox Catholic Church	2000	21		1,400	20	26	15	
Apostolic Overcoming Holy Church of God, Inc.	2000	129	10,714	10,714	396	416	396	
Armenian Apostolic Church of America	1999	36	360,000	360,000	35	47	25	1,470
Armenian Apostolic Church, Diocese of America*	1991	72	14,000	414,000	49	70		
Assemblies of God	1999	12,055	1,492,196	2,574,531	18,159	32,304	11,390	1,393,176
Associated Reformed Presbyterian Church (General Synod)	1998	244	34,642	40,113	194	325	206	17,078
The Association of Free Lutheran Congregations	1999	241	25,060	32,984	138	213	221	7,166
Baptist Bible Fellowship International	1997	4,500	1,200,000	1,200,000		7,500	4,500	
Baptist General Conference	1999	880	142,871	142,871				
Baptist Missionary Association of America	1999	1,334	234,732	234,732	1,525	3,055	1,300	88,921

Table 2. Membership Statistics in the United States *(continued)*

Religious Body	Year Reporting	Number of Churches Reporting	Full Communicant or Confirmed Members	Inclusive Membership	Number of Pastors Serving Parishes	Total Number of Clergy	Number of Sunday or Sabbath Schools	Total Enrollment
Beachy Amish Mennonite Churches	1997	114	7,853	7,853	381	381		
Berean Fundamental Church	1997	51		8,000				
The Bible Church of Christ, Inc.	1993	6	4,150	6,850	11	52	6	5,896
Bible Fellowship Church	1998	56	7,169	7,169	58	112	56	12,771
Brethren in Christ Church	1999	252	20,010	20,010	140	343		
Brethren Church (Ashland, Ohio)	1999	118	13,227	13,227	84	180	107	
The Catholic Church	1999	19,627	62,391,484	62,391,484		46,603		
Christ Catholic Church	1996	7	1,205	2,728	7	8	2	23
Christ Community Church (Evangelical-Protestant)	1999	3	895	1,687	4	7	1	521
Christian Brethren (also known as Plymouth Brethren)	1997	1,150		100,000		500	1,000	
Christian Church (Disciples of Christ) in the United States and Canada*	1999	3,765	535,893	831,125	3,307	6,073	3,503	228,380
Christian Church of North America, General Council	1999	96	7,200	7,200	100	157	96	
Christian Churches and Churches of Christ	1988	5,579		1,071,616	5,525			
The Christian Congregation, Inc.	1999	1,438	118,209	118,209	1,436	1,437	1,294	39,069
Christian Methodist Episcopal Church*	1999	3,069	784,114	784,114	2,058	2,378	2,103	
The Christian and Missionary Alliance	1999	1,973	164,196	347,973	1,493	2,370	1,643	154,223

Table 2. Membership Statistics in the United States (continued)

Religious Body	Year Reporting	Number of Churches Reporting	Full Communicant or Confirmed Members	Inclusive Membership	Number of Pastors Serving Parishes	Total Number of Clergy	Number of Sunday or Sabbath Schools	Total Enrollment
Christian Reformed Church in North America	1999	732	136,831	198,400	675	1,168		
Church of the Brethren*	1997	1,095	141,400	141,400	827	1,945	858	43,577
The Church of Christ (Holiness) U.S.A.	1998	167	10,383	10,383	199	207	162	7,357
Church of Christ, Scientist	1998	2,200						
Church of God (Anderson, Indiana)	1998	2,353	234,311	234,311	3,034	5,468		115,946
The Church of God in Christ	1991	15,300	5,499,875	5,499,875	28,988	33,593		
Church of God in Christ, Mennonite	1999	102	12,144	12,144	439	439	102	
Church of God (Cleveland, Tennessee)	1999	6,328	870,039	870,039	3,352	6,143	5,596	335,760
Church of God by Faith, Inc.	1991	145	6,819	8,235	155	170		
Church of God General Conference (Oregon, IL and Morrow, GA)	1999	92	4,083	5,308	63	78	65	2,244
The Church of God, Mountain Assembly, Inc.	1994	118	6,140	6,140				
Church of God of Prophecy	1999	1,862	75,112	75,112	2,000	2,042	1,725	55,524
The Church of God (Seventh Day), Denver, Colorado	1999	185	8,000	11,000	76	122	185	
The Church of Illumination	1996	3	300	1,200	8	15	2	216
The Church of Jesus Christ (Bickertonites)	1989	63		2,707	183	262		
The Church of Jesus Christ of Latter-day Saints	1999	11,315	4,593,136	5,113,409	33,945	37,818	11,315	3,979,167

Table 2. Membership Statistics in the United States *(continued)*

Religious Body	Year Reporting	Number of Churches Reporting	Full Communicant or Confirmed Members	Inclusive Membership	Number of Pastors Serving Parishes	Total Number of Clergy	Number of Sunday or Sabbath Schools	Total Enrollment
Church of the Living God (Motto: Christian Workers for Fellowship)	1985	170		4,200	170			
Church of the Lutheran Brethren of America	1999	115	8,229	13,920	136	230	105	9,182
Church of the Lutheran Confession	1999	72	6,475	8,631	59	86	71	1,345
Church of the Nazarene	1998	5,101	623,028	627,054	4,598	9,998	4,822	798,141
Church of Our Lord Jesus Christ of the Apostolic Faith, Inc.		500						
Church of the United Brethren in Christ	1997	228	23,585	23,585	315	449	228	12,837
Churches of Christ	1999	15,000	1,500,000	1,500,000	14,500	16,350	12,500	1,600,000
Churches of Christ in Christian Union	2000	216	10,104	10,104	208	601		10,050
Churches of God, General Conference	1999	340	32,045	32,045	239	443	340	15,629
Congregational Holiness Church	1993	190		2,468			190	
Conservative Baptist Association of America (CBAmerica)	1998	1,200	200,000	200,000				
Conservative Congregational Christian Conference	1999	242	40,414	40,414	273	545	223	13,263
Conservative Lutheran Association	1999	5	841	1,313	7	23	4	165
Coptic Orthodox Church*	1992	85	180,000	180,000	65	68	85	

Table 2. Membership Statistics in the United States (continued)

Religious Body	Year Reporting	Number of Churches Reporting	Full Communicant or Confirmed Members	Inclusive Membership	Number of Pastors Serving Parishes	Total Number of Clergy	Number of Sunday or Sabbath Schools	Total Enrollment
Cumberland Presbyterian Church	1999	775	86,049	86,049	535	842	685	37,407
Cumberland Presbyterian Church in America	1996	152	15,142	15,142	141	156	152	9,465
Elim Fellowship	1999	98			655	845		
Episcopal Church*	1998	7,390	1,765,562	2,317,794				
The Estonian Evangelical Lutheran Church	1997	21	3,508	3,508	10	12		
The Evangelical Church	1998	132	12,369	12,369	152	250	125	9,030
The Evangelical Congregational Church	1999	143	22,349	22,349	107	183	137	
The Evangelical Covenant Church	1999	636	98,526	98,526	607	1,177	577	93,136
The Evangelical Free Church of America	1995	1,224	124,499	242,619	1,936	2,436		
Evangelical Friends International—North American Region	1995	288	36,760	36,760			90	7,226
Evangelical Lutheran Church in America*	1999	10,851	3,825,228	5,149,668	9,542	17,611	8,872	940,335
Evangelical Lutheran Synod	1999	139	16,734	2,203	100	177	124	3,357
Evangelical Mennonite Church	2000	33	4,929	4,929	29	68	33	4,081

Table 2. Membership Statistics in the United States (continued)

Religious Body	Year Reporting	Number of Churches Reporting	Full Communicant or Confirmed Members	Inclusive Membership	Number of Pastors Serving Parishes	Total Number of Clergy	Number of Sunday or Sabbath Schools	Total Enrollment
Evangelical Methodist Church	1997	123	8,615	8,615	105	215	120	6,547
Evangelical Presbyterian Church	1999	197	59,369	63,447	240	424	148	34,572
Fellowship of Evangelical Bible Churches	1990	16	1,880	1,880	14	28	16	1,370
Fellowship of Fundamental Bible Churches	1999	22	1,125	1,125	29	46	22	1,036
Fellowship of Grace Brethren Churches	1997	260	30,371	30,371		564		
Free Methodist Church of North America	1999	971	60,499	70,556		1,869	860	89,352
Friends General Conference	1999	620	32,000	32,000	6	7	400	
Friends United Meeting*	1999	479	33,908	33,908	288	288	409	
Full Gospel Assemblies International	1998	286	31,128	52,500	508		286	
Full Gospel Fellowship of Churches and Ministers International	2000	896	325,000	325,000	2,070	2,424	896	364,000
Fundamental Methodist Church, Inc.	1993	12	682	787	17	22	12	454
General Assembly of the Korean Presbyterian Church in America*	2000	310	35,802	50,221	450	568		
General Association of General Baptists	1998	719	67,314	67,314	780	921	719	34,163

Table 2. Membership Statistics in the United States *(continued)*

Religious Body	Year Reporting	Number of Churches Reporting	Full Communicant or Confirmed Members	Inclusive Membership	Number of Pastors Serving Parishes	Total Number of Clergy	Number of Sunday or Sabbath Schools	Total Enrollment
General Association of Regular Baptist Churches	1999	1,398	92,129	92,129				
General Church of the New Jerusalem	2000	34	3,060	5,553	28	58		
General Conference of Mennonite Brethren Churches	1996	368	50,915	82,130	590			34,668
Grace Gospel Fellowship	1992	128		60,000	160	196	128	
Greek Orthodox Archdiocese of America*	1998	523		1,954,500	596	806	500	
The Holy Eastern Orthodox Catholic and Apostolic Church in North America, Inc.	1998	19	4,300	4,300	10	12		
Hungarian Reformed Church in America*	1998	27		6,000	27	30		
Hutterian Brethren	1997	428	36,000	42,800	500	575	50	8,900
IFCA International, Inc.	1999	659	61,655	61,655			659	57,768
International Church of the Foursquare Gospel	1999	1,836	233,412	253,412	4,802	7,202		
International Council of Community Churches*	1999	180	200,000	200,000	198	296		
The International Pentecostal Church of Christ	1999	69	2,420	5,572	65	161	61	2,573
International Pentecostal Holiness Church	1999	1,771	185,431	185,431	1,609	2,574		93,360
Jehovah's Witnesses	1999	11,257	990,340	990,340				

Table 2. Membership Statistics in the United States *(continued)*

Religious Body	Year Reporting	Number of Churches Reporting	Full Communicant or Confirmed Members	Inclusive Membership	Number of Pastors Serving Parishes	Total Number of Clergy	Number of Sunday or Sabbath Schools	Total Enrollment
The Latvian Evangelical Lutheran Church in America	1999	71	13,431	15,012	52	69	20	
The Liberal Catholic Church—Province of the U.S.A.	2000	27	6,500	6,500	57	57		
The Lutheran Church—Missouri Synod	1999	6,220	1,945,846	2,582,440	5,210	8,365	5,645	561,045
Mar Thoma Syrian Church of India*	1997	65	30,000	30,000	33	38	50	3,950
Mennonite Church	1999	935	92,002	92,002		2,967	916	43,719
Mennonite Church, The General Conference	1999	295	35,759	35,759	271	541	295	13,174
The Missionary Church	1999	354	30,019	46,015	596	845	320	31,412
Moravian Church in America (Northern Province)*	1999	93	20,400	26,103	89	177	90	6,082
National Association of Congregational Christian Churches	1999	426	65,502	65,502	506	669		
National Association of Free Will Baptists	1999	2,476	216,711	216,711	2,800	2,900	2,476	127,277
National Baptist Convention of America, Inc.*	1987	2,500		3,500,000	8,000			
National Missionary Baptist Convention of America*	1992			2,500,000				

Table 2. Membership Statistics in the United States (*continued*)

Religious Body	Year Reporting	Number of Churches Reporting	Full Communicant or Confirmed Members	Inclusive Membership	Number of Pastors Serving Parishes	Total Number of Clergy	Number of Sunday or Sabbath Schools	Total Enrollment
National Organization of the New Apostolic Church of North America	1999	385	36,254	36,254	1,880	1,880	254	2,429
National Spiritualist Association of Churches	1999	136	3,000	3,000	87	87	46	1,221
Netherlands Reformed Congregations	1999	24	4,315	9,047	9	12	20	
North American Baptist Conference	1999	271	45,738	45,738	319	447	271	
Old German Baptist Brethren	1999	55	6,050	6,050	254	254		
Old Order Amish Church	1993	898	80,820	80,820	3,592	3,617	55	
Open Bible Standard Churches, Inc.	1999	357		35,700	477	1,061		
The Orthodox Church in America*	1999	710	1,000,000	1,000,000	735	796	481	
The Orthodox Presbyterian Church	1999	204	17,327	25,302		397	341	12,516
Patriarchal Parishes of the Russian Orthodox Church in the U.S.A.*	1985	38		9,780	37	45		
Pentecostal Assemblies of the World, Inc.	1998	1,750	1,500,000	1,500,000	4,500	4,500		
Pentecostal Church of God	1999	1,237	46,800	105,200		1,796		
Pentecostal Fire-Baptized Holiness Church	1996	27	223	223		28	25	400

Table 2. Membership Statistics in the United States (continued)

Religious Body	Year Reporting	Number of Churches Members	Full Communicant or Confirmed	Inclusive Membership Parishes	Number of Pastors Serving	Total Number of Clergy	Number of Sunday or Sabbath Schools	Total Enrollment
The Pentecostal Free Will Baptist Church, Inc.	1998	150	28,000	28,000	175	280	160	
Polish National Catholic Church of America*	1960	162						
Presbyterian Church in America	1999	1,206	236,361	299,055		2,873		121,325
Presbyterian Church (U.S.A.)*	1999	11,216	2,560,201	3,561,184	9,292	20,988	9,398	1,082,456
Primitive Advent Christian Church	1993	10	345	345	11	11	10	292
Primitive Methodist Church in the U.S.A.	1999	77	4,607	6,031	70	112	77	3,197
Progressive National Baptist Convention, Inc.*	1995	2,000	2,500,000	2,500,000				
Protestant Reformed Churches in America	1999	27	3,788	6,730	26	41	23	
Reformed Church in America*	1999	901	178,246	293,147	880	1,874		
Reformed Church in the United States	1998	40	3,201	4,257	34	42	37	869
Reformed Episcopal Church	1998	125	6,400	6,400	150	185		
Reformed Mennonite Church	2000	10	289	308	19	20		
Reformed Presbyterian Church of North America	1997	86	4,363	6,105	70	137	78	3,373
Religious Society of Friends (Conservative)	1994	1,200		104,000				

Table 2. Membership Statistics in the United States (continued)

Religious Body	Year Reporting	Number of Churches Reporting	Full Communicant or Confirmed Members	Inclusive Membership	Number of Pastors Serving Parishes	Total Number of Clergy	Number of Sunday or Sabbath Schools	Total Enrollment
Reorganized Church of Jesus Christ of Latter Day Saints	1999	1,236	137,038	137,065		20,370		
The Romanian Orthodox Episcopate of America	1990	56	6,606	25,000	37	81	30	1,800
The Russian Orthodox Church Outside of Russia	1994	177			319	319		
The Salvation Army	1999	1,410	124,922	472,871	3,072	5,415	1,410	108,139
The Schwenkfelder Church	1995	5	2,524	2,524	8	9	5	701
Separate Baptists in Christ	1992	100	8,000	8,000	95	140	100	
Serbian Orthodox Church in the U.S.A. and Canada*	1986	68		67,000	60	82		
Seventh-day Adventist Church	1999	4,421	861,860	861,860	2,501	5,116	4,666	469,136
Seventh Day Baptist General Conference, USA and Canada	1995	80	4,800		46	74		
Southern Baptist Convention	1999	41,099	15,851,756	15,851,756	76,680	100,387	39,683	8,147,457
Southern Methodist Church	1999	117	7,686	7,686	82	114	115	3,987
Sovereign Grace Believers	1998	300	3,000	3,000	400	400	300	
The Swedenborgian Church*	2000	44	2,104	2,104	28	44		

Table 2. Membership Statistics in the United States *(continued)*

Religious Body	Year Reporting	Number of Churches Reporting	Full Communicant or Confirmed Members	Inclusive Membership	Number of Pastors Serving Parishes	Total Number of Clergy	Number of Sunday or Sabbath Schools	Total Enrollment
Syrian (Syriac) Orthodox Church of Antioch*	1999	22	32,500	32,500	18	24	17	1,380
True Orthodox Church of Greece (Synod of Metropolitan Cyprian), American Exarchate	1993	9	1,095	1,095	18	19		
Ukranian Orthodox Church of the U.S.A.*	1986	27		5,000	36	37		
Unitarian Universalist Association of Congregations	1999			216,931		1,400		61,482
United Christian Church	1998	11	328	328	6	11	9	523
United Church of Christ*	1999	5,961	1,401,682	1,401,682	4,264	10,302	3,137	342,560
The United Methodist Church*	1999	35,609	8,377,662	8,377,662	24,998	43,872	33,027	3,626,134
United Pentecostal Church International	1995	3,790			7,903			
United Zion Church	1998	13	883	883	13	23	11	818
Unity of the Brethren	1998	27	2,548	3,218	25	39	24	1,442
Universal Fellowship of Metropolitan Community Churches	1998	300		44,000	324	372		
The Wesleyan Church	1999	1,594	112,615	121,356	1,946	3,172	1,594	354,494
Wisconsin Evangelical Lutheran Synod	1999	1,239	315,628	722,754	1,230	1,760		44,130
Totals		**320,827**	**133,567,039**	**151,161,906**	**332,182**	**541,830**	**198,492**	**26,273,977**

*National Council of Churches of Christ in the U.S.A. member communion

Table 3. Membership Statistics for the National Council of the Churches of Christ in the U.S.A.

Religious Body	Year Reporting	Number of Churches Reporting	Inclusive Membership	Number of Pastors Serving Parishes
African Methodist Episcopal Church	1999	6,200	2,500,000	
African Methodist Episcopal Zion Church	1999	3,125	1,276,662	2,731
The Alliance of Baptists in the U.S.A.	1999	130	64,000	
American Baptist Churches in the U.S.A.	1999	5,775	1,454,388	4,895
The Antiochian Orthodox Christian Archdiocese of North America	1999	227	65,000	290
Armenian Apostolic Church, Diocese of America	1991	72	414,000	49
Christian Church (Disciples of Christ) in the United States and Canada	1999	3,765	831,125	3,307
Christian Methodist Episcopal Church	1999	3,069	784,114	2,058
Church of the Brethren	1997	1,095	141,400	827
Coptic Orthodox Church	1992	85	180,000	65
Episcopal Church	1998	7,390	2,317,794	
Evangelical Lutheran Church in America	1999	10,851	5,149,668	9,542
Friends United Meeting	1999	479	33,908	288
General Assembly of the Korean Presbyterian Church in America	2000	310	50,221	450
Greek Orthodox Archdiocese of America	1998	523	1,954,500	596
Hungarian Reformed Church in America	1998	27	6,000	27
International Council of Community Churches	1999	180	200,000	198
Mar Thoma Syrian Church of India	1997	65	30,000	33
Moravian Church in America (Northern Province)	1999	93	26,103	89

Table 3. Membership Statistics for the National Council of the Churches of Christ in the U.S.A. *(continued)*

Religious Body	Year Reporting	Number of Churches Reporting	Inclusive Membership	Number of Pastors Serving Parishes
National Baptist Convention of America, Inc.	1987	2,500	3,500,000	8,000
National Missionary Baptist Convention of America	1992		2,500,000	
The Orthodox Church in America	1999	710	1,000,000	735
Patriarchal Parishes of the Russian Orthodox Church in the U.S.A.	1985	38	9,780	37
Polish National Catholic Church of America	1960	162		
Presbyterian Church (U.S.A.)	1999	11,216	3,561,184	9,292
Progressive National Baptist Convention, Inc.	1995	2,000	2,500,000	
Reformed Church in America	1999	901	293,147	880
Serbian Orthodox Church in the U.S.A. and Canada	1986	68	67,000	60
The Swedenborgian Church	2000	44	2,104	28
Syrian (Syriac) Orthodox Church of Antioch	1999	22	32,500	18
Ukranian Orthodox Church of the U.S.A.	1986	27	5,000	36
United Church of Christ	1999	5,961	1,401,682	4,264
The United Methodist Church	1999	35,609	8,377,662	24,998

Table 4. Selected Statistics of Church

Religious Body	Year	Full or Confirmed Members	Inclusive Members	TOTAL CONTRIBUTIONS		
				Total Contributions	Per Capita Full or Confirmed Members	Per Capita Inclusive Members
The Antiochian Orthodox Christian Archdiocese of North America	1996	350,000	350,000	$3,475,000	$9.93	$9.93
The Apostolic Church in Canada	1999	1,200	1,600	$1,184,700	$987.25	$740.44
Armenian Holy Apostolic Church—Canadian Diocese	1999	80,000	80,000	$618,300	$7.73	$7.73
Baptist Union of Western Canada	1999	20,427	20,427	$5,107,654	$250.04	$250.04
The Bible Holiness Movement	1999	527	863	$256,834	$487.35	$297.61
Brethren in Christ Church, Canadian Conference	1998	3,387	3,387	$5,283,709	$1,560.00	$1,560.00
Canadian District of the Moravian Church in America, Northern Province	1999	1,199	1,667	$1,210,214	$1,009.35	$725.98
Christian Church (Disciples of Christ) in Canada	1997	2,053	3,285	$1,353,560	$659.31	$412.04
Church of God (Anderson Ind.)	1998	3,777	3,777	$630,769	$167.00	$167.00
Church of God (Cleveland, Tenn.)	1999	10,914	10,914	$3,950,557	$361.97	$361.97
Church of the Lutheran Brethren	1999	383	587	$595,181	$1,554.00	$1,013.94
Church of the Nazarene in Canada	1998	12,042	12,042	$8,773,477	$728.57	$728.57
The Evangelical Covenant Church of Canada	1997	1,290	1,290	$7,690,321	$5,961.49	$5,961.49
Evangelical Lutheran Church in Canada	1999	138,857	193,915	$59,407,907	$427.84	$306.36
Foursquare Gospel Church of Canada	1996	3,063	3,063	$4,376,923	$1,428.97	$1,428.97
Free Methodist Church in Canada	1996	6,444	11,396	$3,177,707	$493.13	$278.84
Lutheran Church—Canada	1994	58,316	79,844	$26,046,000	$446.64	$326.21
Mennonite Church (Canada)	1996	8,172	8,172	$12,924,965	$1,581.62	$1,581.62
North American Baptist Conference	1999	17,531	17,531	$32,127,723	$1,832.62	$1,832.62
Pentecostal Assemblies of Newfoundland	1997	14,715	29,361	$3,143,197	$213.60	$107.05
Presbyterian Church in America (Canadian Section)	1997	701	1,140	$1,708,607	$2,437.39	$1,498.78
Presbyterian Church in Canada	1997	134,683	200,738	$85,326,113	$633.53	$425.06
Reformed Church in Canada	1999	4,091	6,609	$4,825,600	$1,179.56	$730.16
The Reformed Episcopal Church of Canada	2000	260	355	$252,000	$969.23	$709.86
Seventh-day Adventist in Canada	1999	48,900	48,900	$44,060,626	$901.04	$901.04
Union d'Eglises Baptistes Françaises au Canada	1999	1,264	1,294	$1,106,209	$875.17	$854.88
The United Church of Canada	1999	668,549	1,589,886	$301,471,981	$450.93	$189.62
The Wesleyan Church of Canada	1997	5,698	5,992	$10,193,278	$1,788.92	$1,701.15

Finances—Canadian Churches

CONGREGATIONAL FINANCES			BENEVOLENCES			
Total Congregational Contributions	Per Capita Full or Confirmed Members	Per Capita Inclusive Members	Total Benevolences	Per Capita Full or Confirmed Members	Per Capita Inclusive Members	Benevolences as a Percentage of Total Giving
$1,385,000	$3.96	$3.96	$2,090,000	$5.97	$5.97	60%
$1,069,200	$891.00	$668.25	$115,500	$96.25	$72.19	10%
$297,800	$3.72	$3.72	$320,500	$4.01	$4.01	52%
$562,511	$27.54	$27.54	$4,545,143	$222.51	$222.51	89%
$31,685	$60.12	$36.71	$225,149	$427.23	$260.89	88%
$4,597,458	$1,357.38	$1,357.38	$686,251	$202.61	$202.61	13%
$1,131,659	$943.84	$678.86	$78,555	$65.52	$47.12	6%
$1,237,213	$602.64	$376.62	$116.347	$56.67	$35.42	9%
$265,698	$70.35	$70.35	$365,071	$96.66	$96.66	58%
$3,669,948	$336.26	$336.26	$280,609	$25.71	$25.71	7%
$460,140	$1,201.41	$783.88	$135,041	$352.59	$230.05	23%
$7,095,713	$589.25	$589.25	$1,677,764	$139.33	$139.33	19%
$2,096,979	$1,625.57	$1,625.57	$5,593,342	$4,335.92	$4,335.92	73%
$51,905,651	$373.81	$267.67	$7,502,256	$54.03	$38.69	13%
$4,248,451	$1,387.02	$1,387.02	$128,472	$41.94	$41.94	3%
$925,703	$143.65	$81.23	$2,252,004	$349.47	$197.61	71%
$21,405,000	$367.05	$268.09	$4,641,000	$79.58	$58.13	18%
$9,310,612	$1,139.33	$1,139.33	$3,614,353	$442.28	$442.28	28%
$26,901,766	$1,534.53	$1,534.53	$5,225,957	$298.10	$298.10	16%
$1,835,046	$124.71	$62.50	$1,308,151	$88.90	$44.55	42%
$1,486,362	$2,120.35	$1,303.83	$222,245	$317.04	$194.95	13%
$73,507,501	$545.78	$366.19	$11,818,612	$87.75	$58.88	14%
$4,050,601	$990.12	$612.89	$775,999	$189.68	$117.42	16%
$124,500	$478.85	$350.70	$127,500	$490.38	$359.15	$51%
$15,012,717	$307.01	$307.01	$29,047,909	$594.03	$594.03	66%
$750,000	$593.35	$579.60	$356,209	$281.81	$275.28	32%
$257,096,100	$384.56	$161.71	$44,375,881	$66.38	$27.91	15%
$8,755,161	$1,536.53	$1,461.14	$1,438,117	$252.39	$240.01	14%

361

Table 5. Selected Statistics of Church

Religious Body	Year	Full or Confirmed Members	Inclusive Members	TOTAL CONTRIBUTIONS Total Contributions	Per Capita Full or Confirmed Members	Per Capita Inclusive Members
African Methodist Episcopal Zion Church*	1999	1,060,256	1,276,662	$85,561,368	$80.70	$67.02
Albanian Orthodox Diocese of America	1996	2,203	2,203	$171,900	$78.03	$78.03
Allegheny Wesleyan Methodist Connection (Original Allegheny Conference)	1999	1,812	1,961	$5,326,739	$2,939.70	$2,716.34
American Baptist Churches in the U.S.A.*	1999	1,454,388	1,454,388	$373,551,252	$256.84	$256.84
Apostolic Faith Mission Church of God	1999	8,301	10,651	$994,000	$119.74	$93.32
Associate Reformed Presbyterian Church (General Synod)	1998	34,642	40,113	$36,210,103	$1,045.27	$902.70
Baptist Missionary Association of America	1998	234,732	234,732	$70,087,434	$298.58	$298.58
Bible Fellowship Church	1998	7,169	7,169	$12,220,021	$1,704.56	$1,704.56
Brethren in Christ Church	1999	20,010	20,010	$28,568,117	$1,427.69	$1,427.69
Christ Community Church (Evangelical-Protestant)	1999	895	1,687	$1,165,360	$1,302.08	$690.79
Christian Church (Disciples of Christ) in the United States and Canada*	1999	535,893	831,125	$458,378,693	$855.35	$551.52
The Christian and Missionary Alliance	1999	164,196	347,973	$261,867,726	$1,594.85	$752.55
Church of the Brethren*	1997	141,400	141,400	$77,644,344	$549.11	$549.11
The Church of Christ (Holiness) U.S.A.	1998	10,383	10,383	$8,200,657	$789.82	$789.82
Church of God (Anderson, Ind.)	1997	234,311	234,311	$223,492,670	$953.83	$953.83
Church of God General Conference (Oregon, IL and Morrow, GA.)	1999	4,083	5,308	$3,860,665	$945.55	$727.33
Church of the Lutheran Brethren of America	1999	8,229	13,920	$12,284,566	$1,492.84	$882.51
Church of the Lutheran Confession	1999	6,475	8,631	$4,958,343	$765.77	$574.48
Church of the Nazarene	1998	623,028	627,054	$565,702,637	$907.99	$902.16
Church of the United Brethren in Christ	1997	23,585	23,585	$27,184,899	$1,152.64	$1,152.64
Churches of Christ	1997	1,500,000	1,500,000	$1,445,000,000	$963.33	$963.33
Churches of God, General Conference	1999	32,045	32,045	$23,987,489	$748.56	$748.56
Conservative Congregational Christian Conference	1999	40,414	40,414	$37,096,674	$917.92	$917.92
Cumberland Presbyterian Church	1999	86,049	86,049	$43,707,210	$507.93	$507.93
Cumberland Presbyterian Church in America	1996	15,142	15,142	$40,408,524	$2,668.64	$2,668.64
Episcopal Church*	1998	1,765,562	2,317,794	$1,977,012,320	$1,119.76	$852.97

Finances—United States Churches

CONGREGATIONAL FINANCES			BENEVOLENCES			
Total Congregation Contributions	Per Capita Full or Confirmed Members	Per Capita Inclusive Members	Total Benevolences	Per Capita Full or Confirmed Members	Per Capita Inclusive Members	Benevolences as a Percentage
$82,340,065	$77.66	$64.50	$3,221,303	$3.04	$2.52	4%
$164,600	$74.72	$74.72	$7,300	$3.31	$3.31	4%
$4,258,815	$2,350.34	$2,171.76	$1,067,924	$589.36	$544.58	20%
$314,876,092	$216.50	$216.50	$58,675,160	$40.34	$40.34	16%
$420,000	$50.60	$39.43	$574,000	$69.15	$53.89	58%
$28,831,982	$832.28	$718.77	$7,378,121	$212.98	$183.93	20%
$57,481,427	$244.88	$244.88	$12,606,007	$53.70	$53.70	18%
$9,752,170	$1,360.33	$1,360.33	$2,467,851	$344.24	$344.24	20%
22,654,566	$1,132.16	$1,132.16	$5,913,551	$295.53	$295.53	21%
$977,681	$1,092.38	$579.54	$187,679	$209.70	$111.25	16%
$410,583,119	$766.17	$494.01	$47,795,574	$89.19	$57.51	10%
$222,911,542	$1,357.59	$640.60	$38,956,184	$237.25	$111.95	15%
$60,923,817	$430.86	$430.86	$16,720,527	$118.25	$118.25	22%
$7,806,279	$751.83	$751.83	$394,378	$37.98	$37.98	5%
$194,438,623	$829.83	$829.83	$29,054,047	$124.00	$124.00	13%
$3,357,300	$822.26	$632.50	$503,365	$123.28	$94.83	13%
$10,363,380	$1,259.37	$744.50	$1,921,186	$233.47	$138.02	16%
$4,252,615	$656.77	$492.71	$705,728	$108.99	$81.77	14%
$460,776,715	$739.58	$734.83	$104,925,922	$168.41	$167.33	19%
$23,770,417	$1,007.86	$1,007.86	$3,414,482	$144.77	$144.77	13%
$1,414,000,000	$942.67	$942.67	$31,000,000	$20.67	$20.67	2%
$19,597,034	$611.55	$611.55	$4,390,455	$137.01	$137.01	18%
$31,165,218	$771.15	$771.15	$5,931,456	$146.77	$146.77	16%
$36,656,534	$426.00	$426.00	$6,236,485	$72.48	$72.48	14%
$34,921,064	$2,306.24	$2,306.24	$5,487,460	$362.40	$362.40	14%
$1,709,830,976	$968.43	$737.70	$267,181,344	$151.33	$115.27	14%

Table 5. Selected Statistics of Church

Religious Body	Year	Full or Confirmed Members	Inclusive Members	TOTAL CONTRIBUTIONS		
				Total Contributions	Per Capita Full or Confirmed Members	Per Capita Inclusive Members
The Evangelical Church	1998	12,369	12,369	$14,556,445	$1,176.85	$1,176.85
The Evangelical Congregational Church	1999	22,349	22,349	$20,162,660	$902.17	$902.17
The Evangelical Covenant Church	1998	98,526	98,526	$160,958,308	$1,633.66	$1,633.66
Evangelical Lutheran Church in America	1999	3,825,228	5,149,668	$2,193,597,874	$573.46	$425.97
Evangelical Lutheran Synod	1999	16,734	2,203	$11,192,869	$668.87	$5,080.74
Evangelical Mennonite Church	2000	4,929	4,929	$12,368,306	$2,509.29	$2,509.29
Fellowship of Evangelical Bible Churches	1999	1,880	1,880	$2,465,596	$1,311.49	$1,311.49
Free Methodist Church of North America	1999	60,499	70,556	$99,552,963	$1,645.53	$1,410.98
General Association of General Baptists	1998	67,314	67,314	$35,134,293	$521.95	$521.95
General Conference of Mennonite Brethren Churches	1996	50,915	82,130	$65,851,481	$1,293.36	$801.80
The Holy Eastern Orthodox Catholic and Apostolic Church in North America, Inc.	1998	4,300	4,300	$113,775	$26.46	$26.46
The International Pentecostal Church of Christ	1999	2,420	5,572	$6,245,068	$2,580.61	$1,120.79
The Latvian Evangelical Lutheran Church in America	1999	13,431	15,012	$2,834,000	$211.00	$188.78
The Lutheran Church—Missouri Synod (LCMS)	1999	1,945,846	2,582,440	$1,109,927,685	$570.41	$429.80
Mennonite Church	1999	92,002	92,002	$102,248,913	$1,111.38	$1,111.38
Mennonite Church, The General Conference	1999	35,759	35,759	$22,702,777	$634.88	$634.88
The Missionary Church	2000	30,019	46,015	$58,737,761	$1,956.69	$1,276.49
Moravian Church in America (Northern Province)*	1999	20,400	26,103	$12,377,521	$606.74	$474.18
National Association of Free Will Baptists	1999	216,711	216,711	$91,038,553	$420.09	$420.09
North American Baptist Conference	1999	45,738	45,738	$56,262,995	$1,230.11	$1,230.11
Open Bible Standard Churches	1999		35,700	$4,980,382		$139.51
The Orthodox Presbyterian Church	1999	17,327	25,302	$29,799,245	$1,719.82	$1,177.74
Presbyterian Church (U.S.A.)*	1999	2,560,201	3,561,184	$2,711,029,296	$1,058.92	$761.27
Primitive Methodist Church in the U.S.A.	1999	4,607	6,031	$4,733,757	$1,027.51	$784.90
Reformed Church in America*	1999	178,246	293,147	$229,763,954	$1,289.03	$783.78
Reformed Church in the United States	1998	3,201	4,257	$3,657,850	$1,142.72	$859.26
Reformed Presbyterian Church of North America	1997	4,363	6,105	$6,446,899	$1,477.63	$1,056.00

Finances—United States Churches (*continued*)

CONGREGATIONAL FINANCES			BENEVOLENCES			
Total Congregation Contributions	Per Capita Full or Confirmed Members	Per Capita Inclusive Members	Total Benevolences	Per Capita Full or Confirmed Members	Per Capita Inclusive Members	Benevolences as a Percentage
11,891,562	$961.40	$961.40	$2,664,883	$215.45	$215.45	18%
$16,574,783	$741.63	$741.63	$3,587,877	$160.54	$160.54	18%
$140,823,872	$1,429.31	$1,429.31	$20,134,436	$204.36	$204.36	13%
$1,972,950,623	$515.77	$383.12	$220,647,251	$57.68	$42.85	10%
$10,062,900	$601.34	$4,567.82	$1,129,969	$67.53	$512.92	10%
$10,388,702	$2,107.67	$2,107.67	$1,979,604	$401.62	$401.62	16%
$1,984,300	$1,055.48	$1,055.48	$481,296	$256.01	$256.01	20%
$86,906,899	$1,436.50	$1,231.74	$12,646,064	$209.03	$179.23	13%
$32,541,289	$483.43	$483.43	$2,593,004	$38.52	$38.52	7%
$50,832,814	$998.39	$618.93	$15,018,667	$294.98	$182.86	23%
$110,275	$25.65	$25.65	$3,500	$0.81	$0.81	3%
$3,059,829	$1,264.39	$549.14	$3,185,239	$1,316.21	$571.65	51%
$2,353,000	$175.19	$156.74	$481,000	$35.81	$32.04	17%
$986,295,136	$506.87	$381.92	$123,632,549	$63.54	$47.87	11%
$75,796,469	$823.86	$823.86	$26,452,444	$287.52	$287.52	26%
$18,388,432	$514.23	$514.23	$4,314,345	$120.65	$120.65	19%
$49,351,430	$1,644.01	$1,072.51	$9,386,331	$312.68	$203.98	16%
$11,527,684	$565.08	$441.62	$849,837	$41.66	$32.56	7%
$72,181,403	$333.08	$333.08	$18,857,150	$87.02	$87.02	21%
$47,207,867	$1,032.14	$1,032.14	$9,055,128	$197.98	$197.98	16%
$1,564,287		$43.82	$3,416,095		$95.69	69%
$24,878,935	$1,435.85	$983.28	$4,920,310	$283.97	$194.46	17%
$2,326,583,688	$908.75	$653.32	$384,445,608	$150.16	$107.95	14%
$4,072,620	$884.01	$675.28	$661,137	$143.51	$109.62	14%
$194,710,130	$1,092.37	$664.21	$36,894,123	$206.98	$125.86	16%
$3,008,116	$939.74	$706.63	$649,734	$202.98	$152.63	18%
$5,792,856	$1,327.72	$948.87	$654,043	$149.91	$107.13	10%

Table 5. Selected Statistics of Church

Religious Body	Year	Full or Confirmed Members	Inclusive Members	Total Contributions	Per Capita Full or Confirmed Members	Per Capita Inclusive Members
				TOTAL CONTRIBUTIONS		
Reorganized Church of Jesus Christ of Latter Day Saints	1997	137,038	137,065	$30,691,085	$223.96	$223.92
Seventh-day Adventist Church	1999	861,860	861,860	$931,166,537	$1,080.42	$1,080.42
Southern Baptist Cᵣnvention	1998	15,729,356	15,729,356	$7,452,098,393	$473.77	$473.77
United Church of Christ*	1999	1,401,682	1,401,682	$777,195,512	$554.47	$554.47
The United Methodist Church*	1999	8,377,662	8,377,662	$4,523,284,851	$539.92	$539.92
Unity of the Brethren	1998	2,548	3,218	$165,184	$64.83	$51.33
Universal Fellowship of Metropolitan Community Churches	1998		44,000	$1,570,860		$35.70
The Wesleyan Church	1999	112,615	121,356	$164,869,426	$1,464.01	$1,358.56
Wisconsin Evangelical Lutheran Synod	1999	315,628	722,754	$223,183,803	$707.11	$308.80

*National Council of the Churches of Christ in the U.S.A. member communion

Summary Statitistics

Nation	Number Reporting	Full or Confirmed Members	Inclusive Members	Total Contributions	Per Capita Full or Confirmed Members	Per Capita Inclusive Members
				TOTAL CONTRIBUTIONS		
United States	62	44,288,906	49,196,965	$26,997,610,588	$609.58	$548.77
Canada	28	1,598,443	2,688,035	$630,279,112	$394.31	$234.48

Finances—United States Churches (*continued*)

CONGREGATIONAL FINANCES			BENEVOLENCES			
Total Congregation Contributions	Per Capita Full or Confirmed Members	Per Capita Inclusive Members	Total Benevolences	Per Capita Full or Confirmed Members	Per Capita Inclusive Members	Benevolences as a Percentage
15,921,761	$116.19	$116.16	$14,769,324	$107.78	$107.75	48%
$301,221,572	$349.50	$349.50	$629,944,965	$730.91	$730.91	68%
$6,498,607,390	$413.15	$413.15	$953,491,003	$60.62	$60.62	13%
$700,645,114	$499.86	$499.86	$76,550,398	$54.61	$54.61	10%
$3,639,161,294	$434.39	$434.39	$884,123,557	$105.53	$105.53	20%
$51,465	$20.20	$15.99	$113,719	$44.63	$35.34	69%
$1,415,000		$32.16	$155,860		$3.54	10%
$137,064,166	$1,217.10	$1,129.44	$27,805,260	$246.91	$229.12	17%
$178,509,021	$565.57	$246.98	$44,674,782	$141.54	$61.81	20%

of Church Finances

CONGREGATIONAL FINANCES			BENEVOLENCES			
Total Congregational Contributions	Per Capita Full or Confirmed Members	Per Capita Inclusive Members	Total Belevolences	Per Capita Full or Confirmed Members	Per Capita Inclusive Members	Benevolences as a Percentage of Total Contributions
$22,801,548,715	$514.84	$463.47	$4,197,087,981	$94.77	$85.31	16%
$501,216,175	$313.57	$186.46	$129,063,937	$80.74	$48.01	20%

Trends in Seminary Enrollment

Data Provided by The Association of Theological Schools (ATS) in the United States and Canada

Table 1: ATS total student enrollment figures include the number of individuals enrolled in degree programs as well as persons enrolled in non-degree programs of study. Growth in total enrollment is a function of both increased enrollment in the seminaries and the increased number of member schools in the Association. Over the past five years, the total head count enrollment increased 9.23 percent, and the full-time equivalent (FTE) enrollment increased 4.05 percent.

Table 1 Number of Member Schools from 1988 to 1999

Year	Number of Schools	Total Enrollment	Canada Head Count	FTE	United States Head Count	FTE	By Membership Accredited	Non-Accredited
1988	207	55,746	3,995	2,679	51,751	34,827	51,863	4,063
1989	205	56,178	4,142	2,668	52,036	35,013	52,949	3,229
1990	211	59,003	4,053	2,636	54,950	37,590	54,052	4,951
1991	211	59,897	4,648	2,631	55,249	36,456	55,028	4,869
1992	220	63,484	4,897	2,999	58,587	39,554	57,784	5,700
1993	219	63,429	5,040	3,150	58,389	39,506	57,823	5,606
1994	226	65,089	5,241	3,212	59,848	40,293	60,490	4,599
1995	224	64,480	5,203	3,267	59,277	39,834	59,813	4,667
1996	233	65,637	5,568	3,304	60,069	40,111	60,527	5,110
1997	229	65,361	5,544	3,225	59,817	40,022	61,498	3,863
1998	237	68,875	5,847	3,683	63,028	40,994	64,412	4,463
1999	237	70,432	6,010	3,224	64,422	41,528	65,674	4,758

Table 2: ATS computes enrollment both by the total number of individual students (Head Count) and the equivalent of full-time students (FTE). If all students were enrolled full-time, the Head Count number and the full-time equivalency number would be the same. The FTE is calculated by dividing the total number of credits required for the degree by the number of semesters prescribed for degree duration to determine the average academic load. The total of credit hours taken by all students in a given degree program in a semester is then divided by the average academic load. During the last five years, full-time equivalent enrollment as a percentage of head count enrollment has decreased slightly, which indicates an increase in the number of part-time students.

Table 2 Head County and FTE for all Member Schools 1988 to 1999

Year	Head Count	% Change	FTE	% Change	FTE % of Head Count
1988	55,746	-0.04	37,506	-2.15	67.3%
1989	56,178	0.77	37,681	0.47	67.1%
1990	59,003	5.03	40,226	6.75	68.2%
1991	59,897	1.52	39,087	-2.83	65.3%
1992	63,484	5.99	42,553	8.87	67.0%
1993	63,429	0.09	42,656	0.24	67.2%
1994	65,089	2.62	43,505	1.99	66.8%
1995	64,480	-0.94	43,101	-0.93	66.8%
1996	65,637	1.79	43,414	0.73	66.1%
1997	65,361	-0.42	43,247	-0.38	66.2%
1998	68,937	5.47	44,540	2.99	64.6%
1999	70,432	2.17	44,845	0.68	63.7%

Table 3: ATS member schools offer a variety of degree programs, as reflected in Table 3. Table 3 displays enrollment by categories of degree programs. The Master of Divinity (M.Div.) degree is the normative degree to prepare persons for ordained ministry and for general pastoral and religious leadership responsibilities in congregations. Enrollment in the M.Div. degree has increased 8.52 percent from 1995 to 1999. The largest increase (by percentage) in student head count enrollment, over the same five-year period, has been in the Master of Pastoral Studies degree program (32.0 percent) within the Basic Ministerial Leadership (Non-M.Div.) category. This is followed by an increase (within the same degree category) of 28.9 percent in the Master of Arts in a variety of specialized ministry areas. Enrollment in Advanced Theological Research programs has increased over the past five years, largely due to rising enrollment in Ph.D./Th.D. programs, up 9.05 percent since 1995, and an increase in the number of institutions within the Association that grant these advanced degrees.

Table 3 Total Enrollment By Degree Categories 1988 to 1999
(Categories based on new accrediting standards—adopted in 1996)

Year	Basic Ministerial Leadership (M.Div.)	(Non-M.Div.)	General Theological Studies	Advanced Ministerial Leadership	Advanced Theological Research	Others
1988	26,581	5,131	5,423	6,511	4,203	7,897
1989	25,954	5,080	5,485	7,004	4,186	8,469
1990	25,615	5,284	6,144	7,417	5,046	9,497
1991	25,710	5,805	6,105	7,598	5,044	9,635
1992	26,956	5,812	6,872	7,961	5,036	10,847
1993	27,264	6,536	7,131	8,302	5,157	9,039
1994	27,240	6,891	7,229	7,841	5,330	10,558
1995	27,497	6,964	7,211	8,233	5,302	9,273
1996	28,035	7,474	7,157	8,315	5,499	9,157
1997	28,283	7,463	7,095	8,195	5,391	8,934
1998	29,263	8,066	7,601	8,658	5,712	9,637
1999	29,842	8,361	7,862	8,743	5,396	10,228

Table 4: In 1999, women constituted 34.16 percent of the total enrollment in all ATS schools. When ATS first began gathering enrollment data by gender in 1972, women represented 10.2 percent of enrollment. Only once in the past 25 years has the number of women students decreased from one year to the next, that being in 1993, with a 0.65 percent decrease. In 1999, women constituted 30.5 percent of the total enrollment in the Master of Divinity degree program.

Table 4 Women Student Head Count Enrollment 1988 to 1999

Year	Number of Students	% Annual Increase	% of Total Enrollment
1988	16,326	0.00	29.29%
1989	16,525	1.20	29.42%
1990	17,498	5.56	29.66%
1991	18,188	3.79	30.37%
1992	19,856	8.40	31.28%
1993	19,727	-0.65	31.10%
1994	20,564	4.07	31.59%
1995	20,795	1.12	32.25%
1996	21,495	3.37	32.75%
1997	21,622	0.59	33.08%
1998	23,192	7.26	33.64%
1999	24,057	3.73	34.16%

Tables 5, 6, 7: Enrollment of North American racial/ethnic minority students in ATS schools has grown from 6.3 percent of total enrollment in 1977 to 20.25 percent in 1999. Over the past five years (1995 to 1999), the number of African American students increased by 20.3 percent; Hispanic students by 24.2 percent; and Pacific/Asian American students by 29.2 percent. Tables 5, 6, and 7 show the number of African American, Hispanic and Pacific/Asian American students enrolled by year. White enrollment experienced the smallest increase (4.2 percent) over the five years. The percentage of racial/ethnic minority students in ATS schools continues to be smaller than the percentage of racial/ethnic minority persons in the North American population as a whole.

Table 5 African American Student Head Count Enrollment 1988 to 1999

Year	Number of Students	% Annual Increase	% of Total Enrollment
1988	3,660	8.72	6.57%
1989	3,925	6.75	6.99%
1990	4,265	7.97	7.23%
1991	4,658	8.44	7.78%
1992	5,558	16.19	8.75%
1993	5,223	-6.41	8.23%
1994	5,526	5.48	8.49%
1995	5,698	3.11	8.84%
1996	5,550	-2.60	8.45%
1997	5,802	4.54	8.87%
1998	6,328	9.07	9.19%
1999	6,854	8.31	9.73%

Table 6 Hispanic Student Head Count Enrollment 1988 to 1999

Year	Number of Students	% Annual Increase	% of Total Enrollment
1988	1,415	1.13	2.54%
1989	1,485	4.71	2.64%
1990	1,912	22.33	3.24%
1991	1,626	-17.59	2.71%
1992	1,689	3.73	2.66%
1993	1,790	5.64	2.82%
1994	1,799	0.50	2.76%
1995	1,817	1.00	2.82%
1996	1,785	-1.76	2.72%
1997	1,915	7.28	2.93%
1998	2,176	13.63	3.16%
1999	2,256	3.68	3.20%

Table 7 Pacific/Asian American Student Head Count Enrollment 1988 to 1999

Year	Number of Students	% Annual Increase	% of Total Enrollment
1988	1,963	13.75	3.52%
1989	2,062	4.80	3.67%
1990	2,437	15.39	4.13%
1991	2,649	8.00	4.42%
1992	3,142	15.69	4.95%
1993	3,631	13.47	5.72%
1994	3,876	6.32	5.95%
1995	4,245	9.52	6.58%
1996	4,492	5.82	6.84%
1997	4,545	1.18	6.95%
1998	4,992	8.95	7.25%
1999	4,932	-1.20	7.00%

IV

A CALENDAR FOR CHURCH USE

2001–2004

This Calendar presents for a four-year period the major days of religious observances for Christians, Jews, Baha'is, and Muslims; and, within the Christian community, major dates observed by Roman Catholic, Eastern and Oriental Orthodox, Episcopal, and Lutheran churches. Within each of these communions many other days of observance, such as saints' days, exist, but only those regarded as major are listed. Dates of interest to many Protestant communions are also included.

In the Orthodox dates, immovable observances are listed in accordance with the Gregorian calendar. Movable dates (those depending on the date of Easter) often will differ from Western days, since the date of Easter (Pascha) in the Orthodox communions does not always correlate with the date for Easter of the Western churches. For Orthodox churches that use the old Julian calendar, observances are held thirteen days later than listed here.

For Jews and Muslims, who follow differing lunar calendars, the dates of major observances are translated into Gregorian dates. Since the actual beginning of a new month in the Islamic calendar is determined by the appearance of the new moon, the corresponding dates given here on the Gregorian calendar may vary slightly. Following the lunar calendar, Muslim dates fall roughly eleven days earlier each year on the Gregorian calendar.

(Note: "RC" stands for Roman Catholic, "O" for Orthodox, "E" for Episcopal, "L" for Lutheran, "ECU" for Ecumenical).

Event	2001	2002	2003	2004
New Year's Day (RC-Solemnity of Mary; O-Circumcision of Jesus Christ; E-Feast of Holy Name; L-Naming of Jesus)	Jan 01	Jan 01	Jan 01	Jan 01
Epiphany (Christian)	Jan 06	Jan 06	Jan 06	Jan 06
Armenian Christmas (O)	Jan 06	Jan 06	Jan 06	Jan 06
Feast Day of St. John the Baptist (Armenian O)	Jan 13	Jan 13	Jan 13	Jan 13
First Sunday After Epiphany (Feast of the Baptism of Our Lord) (Christian)	Jan 14	Jan 13	Jan 12	Jan 11
Week of Prayer for Christian Unity (ECU)	Jan 18	Jan 18	Jan 18	Jan 18
Theophany (Oriental O)	Jan 19	Jan 19	Jan 19	Jan 19
Ecumenical Sunday (ECU)	Jan 21	Jan 20	Jan 19	Jan 18
Week of Prayer for Christian Unity, Canada (ECU)	Jan 22	Jan 21	Jan 20	Jan 19
Presentation of Jesus in the Temple (Candlemas; Purification of the Virgin Mary; O—The Meeting of Our Lord and Savior Jesus Christ) (Christian)	Feb 02	Feb 02	Feb 02	Feb 02
Tu B'Shevat (Jewish)	Feb 08	Jan 28	Feb 18	Feb 07
Brotherhood Week (Interfaith)	Feb 18	Feb 17	Feb 16	Feb 15
Great Lent (First Day of Lent) (O)	Feb 26	Feb 18	Mar 10	Mar 01
Ash Wednesday (Western Churches)	Feb 28	Feb 13	Mar 05	Feb 25
World Day of Prayer (ECU)	Mar 02	Mar 01	Mar 07	Mar 05
Baha'i Fasting Season begins (19 days) (Baha'i)	Mar 02	Mar 02	Mar 02	Mar 02
Waqf al Arafah (Eve of Eid al-Adha) (Muslim)	Mar 04	Feb 21	Feb 10	Jan 31
Eid al-Adha (Festival of Sacrifice at time of Pilgrimage to Mecca) (Muslim)	Mar 05	Feb 22	Feb 11	Feb 01
Joseph, Husband of Mary (RC, E, L)	Mar 19	Mar 19	Mar 19	Mar 19
Purim (Jewish)	Mar 21	Mar 09	Mar 07	Mar 05
Feast of Naw-Ruz (Baha'i New Year) (Baha'i)	Mar 21	Mar 21	Mar 21	Mar 21

371

Event	2001	2002	2003	2004
The Annunciation (Christian)	Mar 25	Mar 25	Mar 25	Mar 25
Muharram Begins (First Day of the Month of Muharram; Muslim New Year) (Muslim)	Mar 26	Mar 15	Mar 05	Feb 22
Ashura' (Martyrdom of Imam Hussein) (Muslim [Shi'a])	Apr 04	Mar 24	Mar 14	Mar 02
Palm Sunday (O)	Apr 08	Apr 28	Apr 20	Apr 04
Holy Week (O)	Apr 08	Apr 28	Apr 20	Apr 04
Passover (Pesach) [8 days] (Jewish)	Apr 08	Mar 28	Apr 17	Apr 06
Holy Week (Western Churches)	Apr 08	Mar 22	Apr 14	Apr 04
Holy Thursday (O)	Apr 12	May 02	Apr 24	Apr 08
Holy Thursday (Western Churches)	Apr 12	Mar 28	Apr 17	Apr 08
Good Friday (Friday of the Passion of Our Lord) (Western Churches)	Apr 13	Mar 29	Apr 18	Apr 09
Holy Friday (Good Friday; Burial of Jesus Christ) (O)	Apr 13	May 03	Apr 25	Apr 09
Pascha (Orthodox Easter) (O)	Apr 15	May 05	Apr 27	Apr 11
Easter (Western Churches)	Apr 15	Mar 31	Apr 20	Apr 11
Yom Hashoah (Jewish)	Apr 20	Apr 09	Apr 29	Apr 18
Feast of Ridvan (Declaration of Baha'u'llah) (12 days) (Baha'i)	Apr 21	Apr 21	Apr 21	Apr 21
Yom Haatzmaut (Jewish)	Apr 26	Apr 17	May 07	Apr 26
National Day of Prayer (ECU)	May 03	May 02	May 01	May 06
May Fellowship Day (ECU)	May 04	May 03	May 02	May 07
Lag B'Omer (Jewish)	May 11	Apr 30	May 20	May 09
Rural Life Sunday (ECU)	May 13	May 12	May 11	May 09
Declaration of the Bab (Baha'i)	May 23	May 23	May 23	May 23
Ascension Thursday (Western Churches)	May 24	May 09	May 29	May 20
Ascension Day (O)	May 24	Jun 13	Jun 05	May 20
Shavuout (Pentecost) (2 days) (Jewish)	May 28	May 17	Jun 06	May 26
Ascension of Baha'u'llah (Baha'i)	May 29	May 29	May 29	May 29
Visitation of the Blessed Virgin Mary (RC, E, L)	May 31	May 31	May 31	May 31
Pentecost (Whitsunday) (Western Churches)	Jun 03	May 19	Jun 08	May 30
Pentecost (O)	Jun 03	Jun 23	Jun 15	May 30
Mawlid an-Nabi (Anniversary of the Prophet Muhammed's Birthday) (Muslim)	Jun 04	May 24	May 14	Jul 02
Martyrdom of the Bab (Baha'i)	Jun 09	Jun 09	Jun 09	Jun 09
Holy Trinity (RC, E, L)	Jun 10	May 26	Jun 15	Jun 06
Corpus Christi (RC)	Jun 17	Jun 02	Jun 22	Jun 13
Sacred Heart of Jesus (RC)	Jun 22	Jun 07	Jun 27	Jun 18
Nativity of St. John the Baptist (RC, E, L)	Jun 24	Jun 24	Jun 24	Jun 24
Saint Peter and Saint Paul, Apostles of Christ (O)	Jun 29	Jun 29	Jun 29	Jun 29
Feast Day of the Twelve Apostles of Christ (O)	Jun 30	Jun 30	Jun 30	Jun 30
Tisha B'Av (Jewish)	Jul 29	Jul 18	Aug 07	Jul 27
Transfiguration of the Lord (RC, O, E)	Aug 06	Aug 06	Aug 06	Aug 06
Assumption of the Blessed Virgin Mary (E-Feast of the Blessed Virgin Mary; O-Falling Asleep) (Domition of the Blessed Virgin) (RC, O, E)	Aug 15	Aug 15	Aug 15	Aug 15
The Birth of the Blessed Virgin (RC, O)	Sep 08	Sep 08	Sep 08	Sep 08
Holy Cross Day (RC-Triumph of the Cross; (O-Adoration of the Holy Cross) (Christian)	Sep 14	Sep 14	Sep 14	Sep 14
Rosh Hashanah (New Year) (2 days) (Jewish)	Sep 18	Sep 07	Sep 27	Sep 16
Yom Kippur (Day of Atonement) (Jewish)	Sep 27	Sep 16	Oct 06	Sep 25
Michaelmas (St. Michael and All Angels) (Christian)	Sep 29	Sep 29	Sep 29	Sep 29
Sukkot (Tabernacles) (7 days) (Jewish)	Oct 02	Sep 21	Oct 11	Sep 30
World Communion Sunday (ECU)	Oct 07	Oct 06	Oct 05	Oct 03
Thanksgiving Day (Canada) (National)	Oct 08	Oct 14	Oct 13	Oct 11
Sh'mini Atzeret (Solemn Assembly) (Jewish)	Oct 09	Sep 28	Oct 18	Oct 7
Simchat Torah (Rejoicing of the Law) (Jewish)	Oct 10	Sep 29	Oct 19	Oct 08
Laity Sunday (ECU)	Oct 14	Oct 13	Oct 12	Oct 10
Laylat al Miraj (Ascent of the Prophet) (Muslim)	Oct 15	Oct 04	Sep 24	Sep 12

Event	2001	2002	2003	2004
Birth of the Bab (Baha'i)	Oct 20	Oct 20	Oct 20	Oct 20
Reformation Sunday (L)	Oct 28	Oct 27	Oct 26	Oct 31
Reformation Day (L)	Oct 31	Oct 31	Oct 31	Oct. 31
World Community Day (ECU)	Nov 01	Nov 07	Nov 06	Nov 04
All Saints Day (RC, E, L)	Nov 01	Nov 01	Nov 01	Nov 01
Laylat al Bara'a (Muslim)	Nov 02	Oct 22	Oct 12	Sep 30
Birth of Baha'u'llah (Baha'i)	Nov 12	Nov 12	Nov 12	Nov 12
Ramadan Begins (First day of the month of Ramadan) (Muslim)	Nov 17	Nov 06	Oct 27	Oct 15
Bible Sunday (ECU)	Nov 18	Nov 17	Nov 16	Nov 21
National Bible Week (ECU)	Nov 18	Nov 17	Nov 16	Nov 21
Thanksgiving Sunday (U.S.) (Christian)	Nov 18	Nov 17	Nov 16	Nov 21
Presentation of the Blessed Virgin Mary in the Temple (Presentation of the Theotokos) (O)	Nov 21	Nov 21	Nov 21	Nov 21
Thanksgiving Day (U.S.) (National)	Nov 22	Nov 28	Nov 27	Nov 25
Last Sunday After Pentecost (L-Feast of Christ the King) (RC, L)	Nov 25	Nov 24	Nov 23	Nov 21
The Day of the Covenant (Baha'i)	Nov 26	Nov 26	Nov 26	Nov 26
Ascension of 'Abdu'l-Baha (Baha'i)	Nov 28	Nov 28	Nov 28	Nov 28
Feast Day of St. Andrew the Apostle (RC, O, E, L)	Nov 30	Nov 30	Nov 30	Nov 30
First Sunday of Advent (Advent Sunday) (Christian)	Dec 02	Dec 01	Nov 30	Nov 28
Immaculate Conception of the Blessed Virgin May (RC)	Dec 08	Dec 08	Dec 08	Dec 08
Hanukkah (Chanukah, Festival of Lights) (8 days) (Jewish)	Dec 10	Nov 30	Dec 20	Dec 08
Laylat al Qadr (Night of Destiny, Revelation of the Holy Qur'an) (Muslim)	Dec 13	Dec 02	Nov 22	Nov 10
Eid al- Fitr (Festival of the End of Ramadan; First day of the month of Shawwal) (Muslim)	Dec 17	Dec 06	Nov 26	Nov 14
Fourth Sunday of Advent (Christmas Sunday) (Christian)	Dec 23	Dec 22	Dec 21	Dec 19
Christmas (Christian Except Armenian)	Dec 25	Dec 25	Dec 25	Dec 25

V
INDEXES
Organizations

INDEX

379

381

INDEX

Individuals

INDEX

385

INDEX

386

INDEX

387

388

INDEX

391

393

396

398

INDEX

404

INDEX

405

407

INDEX

409

410

411